The Law of Actionable Misrepresentation

SPENCER BOWER AND TURNER

The Law of Actionable Misrepresentation

STATED IN THE FORM OF A CODE, FOLLOWED BY A COMMENTARY
AND APPENDICES

The Original Text by

GEORGE SPENCER BOWER

*Sometime one of His Majesty's Counsel, and a Master of the Bench of the
Inner Temple*

The Third Edition by

THE RIGHT HONOURABLE

SIR ALEXANDER KINGCOME TURNER

K.B.E., M.A., LL.B. (N.Z.); (HON.) LL.D. (AUCKLAND)

President of the Court of Appeal of New Zealand

Quam illa aurea: UT INTER BONOS BENE AGIER OPORTET ET SINE FRAUDATIONE;
sed qui sint boni, et quid sit bene agi, magna quaestio est

— CIC. DE OFF. III. 17.

Quid detur tibi aut quid adponatur tibi ad linguam dolosam

— Ps. CXX. 3.

LONDON

BUTTERWORTHS

1974

ENGLAND: BUTTERWORTH & CO. (PUBLISHERS) LTD.
LONDON: 88 KINGSWAY, WC2B 6AB

AUSTRALIA: BUTTERWORTHS PTY. LTD.
SYDNEY: 586 PACIFIC HIGHWAY, CHATSWOOD, NSW 2067
MELBOURNE: 343 LITTLE COLLINS STREET, 3000
BRISBANE: 240 QUEEN STREET, 4000

CANADA: BUTTERWORTH & CO. (CANADA) LTD.
TORONTO: 14 CURITY AVENUE, 374

NEW ZEALAND: BUTTERWORTHS OF NEW ZEALAND LTD.
WELLINGTON: 26/28 WARING TAYLOR STREET, 1

SOUTH AFRICA: BUTTERWORTH & CO. (SOUTH AFRICA) (PTY.) LTD.
DURBAN: 152/154 GALE STREET

First edition by George Spencer Bower   1911
Second edition by George Spencer Bower   1927
Third edition by Sir Alexander Kingcome Turner   1974

ISBN: 0 406 38190 9

Made and printed in Great Britain by
William Clowes & Sons, Limited, London, Beccles and Colchester

Preface to the Third Edition

Mr Spencer Bower's *Law of Actionable Misrepresentation*, the first edition of which appeared in 1911, is one of a series of treatises from his pen, written during the years 1908–1927, so remarkable as to establish themselves immediately on publication as classics of legal exposition. Unlike the *Law of Estoppel by Representation* (1923) and the *Principles of Res Judicata* (1924), the *Law of Actionable Misrepresentation* was re-issued during the lifetime of the original author in a revised form; the second edition appeared in 1927, only shortly before his death. During the forty-five years which has since elapsed there has been no further re-publication, though the work has been long out of print. The text has during that time become first, obsolescent, and more lately, almost dangerously unreliable; the impact upon the common law rules of the Misrepresentation Act 1967 has been the last blow. Encouraged by the reception which has been given to new editions of the two other works mentioned above, I have now ventured upon a third edition of *Actionable Misrepresentation*, in the hope that I may be able to administer to this book resuscitative treatment such as to give it a well-deserved further lease of useful life.

In taking this third edition in hand I have carefully conserved the arrangement and treatment of the subject as it was presented in the original text. The conception of a summarised Code at the beginning of the work, in which an attempt is made to state the cardinal principles shortly and without embroidery before proceeding to any detailed discussion of them, is one which might not have commended itself to me, had I been embarking on an entirely original treatment of the subject; but this is the way in which Mr Spencer Bower chose to present his treatise, and I have thought it right not to change it. To do so would have been to produce a different book. The order in which the chapters are arranged is the same in this work as in the second edition. True, the numbers of the chapters do not correspond throughout; I have broken several of them into halves, where this has seemed advantageous, and there are two entirely new chapters on topics which have emerged as of importance only since Mr Spencer Bower's death—the *Hedley Byrne* action for negligent misrepresentation, and the action in damages for innocent misrepresentation given by the Act of 1967.

In bringing the work up to date I found it quite impossible, after the lapse of forty-five years, to be satisfied with the kind of renovation which might have followed from adding the new authorities to the footnotes and making minimal alterations to the text above them. Some re-writing was necessary on nearly every page. I have tried to indicate as clearly as possible, however, in the places in which any major alteration has been made in the original author's development of the subject, just what that alteration is, and why it has been made. Where the reader is confronted with my own views, in substitution for those originally expressed by Mr Spencer Bower, it should be reasonably apparent to him that this is indeed the position. Examples of the topics where drastic re-writing has been found necessary are (of course) to be found in all the passages in which fraud, with its attendant action for damages, is contrasted with innocent misrepresentation, which at the time of the last edition gave rise to no such action, and in the account of the defence of *non est factum*, which since the decision of the House of Lords in *Saunders* v. *Anglia Building Society* has had to be revised completely. The disappearance of the rule in *Seddon* v. *North-East Salt Co.*, [1905] 1 Ch. 326, first seriously eroded by the cases, and finally extinguished by statute, provides another instance; and the evolution of new rules governing the liability of corporations in fraud for corporate acts carried out partly by one agent and partly by another, following upon the decision of ATKINSON J. in *Anglo-Scottish Beet Sugar Corporation, Ltd.* v. *Spalding U.D.C.*, [1937] 2 K.B. 607, and the subsequent decision of the Court of Appeal in *Armstrong* v. *Strain*, [1952] 1 K.B. 232 affords yet another.

There have been places in this book, as in the *Estoppel by Representation* and the *Res Judicata*, where I have deliberately left passages as they came from the pen of the original author, with the vehemence of which I would perhaps hardly have brought myself fully to concur as a contemporary co-author; but these are part of the stuff of Mr Spencer Bower's writing, and I have left them as they stood, remembering the flavour of them as I first read them years ago. The reader may find examples of these in the treatment of delay *per se* as a possible defence to an action for rescission (Chapter XIV, paras. 308 *et seq.*) and in the passage dealing with the liability of promoters for a misleading prospectus (Chapter XVI, para. 336).

During the near half-century which has elapsed since the second edition was printed, it has not been anyone's responsibility to collect the comments upon it which are often so valuable in directing an editor's attention to slips and errors in the text as printed. There must consequently be many errors which have escaped me in my self-imposed task; but I have tried to consider the work page by page, and even sentence by sentence.

In preparing this third edition I have had to consider the cost of publishing in a more expensive world than that in which the original author lived. Some of the passages in the text, of lesser importance to the practising lawyer, have had to be dropped. It has been impossible for reasons of expense to reproduce in this work, for instance, the discourse in the original Appendix A upon the distinction between legal and moral fraud, to which the original author added his "criticism of the existing law of misrepresentation". Appendix B in the second edition has likewise had to be omitted—twenty pages on "a comparison between the English juridical and ethical treatment of misrepresentation and fraud". It caused me something of a pang to jettison the sixteen pages of superb scholarship in which, in Appendix C in earlier editions, Mr Spencer Bower expounded the Roman law of misrepresentation to his readers, and compared it with modern doctrines; but considerations of economy had to decide their fate. I have added, in more modern Appendices, the text of the masterly report of the Law Reform Committee presided over by Lord Jenkins, which led up to the passing of the Misrepresentation Act 1967, and of some of the more important statutory provisions pertaining to the law of misrepresentation. I hope that the result may be a textbook, containing not too many errors, which may be of use in day-to-day practice.

As in the *Estoppel by Representation* and the *Res Judicata* I have added some Australian and New Zealand authorities. I have again omitted the Canadian decisions, not because of lack of respect for the courts of that jurisdiction, but simply because my knowledge of the Canadian cases is not sufficient to enable me to deal with these safely.

I express my grateful thanks to my wife, who has put up with a good deal while I have been writing this text, and to my Judge's Associate, Mrs Winifred Everitt, whose faithful and accurate transcription has been an important part of its preparation.

The law is stated, I hope, as at June 30th, 1973.

A. K. TURNER

Court of Appeal of New Zealand,
WELLINGTON

June 1973

Extract from the Preface to the First Edition

It has been insisted by a courtly writer of the eighteenth century that a preface to a book is, in all cases, a seemly concession to the ceremonial conventions and amenities, if not to the decencies, of literature. "A preface," he observes, "is part of the habit of a book, and no author can appear full dressed without it."

The convention referred to can no longer claim the universal allegiance it enjoyed in the days of Queen Anne; but it is still true to say that a preface is expected from any work which aspires to deal with a scientific or serious subject. An explanation of this demand, conceived in a spirit of sardonic gloom and somewhat overdone modesty, is given by the late Sir Leslie Stephen, when introducing to the world his *Science of Ethics*: "a preface is generally the most interesting, and not seldom the only interesting, part of the book. It is useful to the hasty critic who wishes to avoid the trouble of reading at all, and to the more serious student who wishes to have the clue to the author's speculations put into his hands at the earliest possible period." This deliverance sounds a rather harsh note, and seems gratuitously churlish to the prospective critic. The author who was accustomed to describe the *lector benevolus* as " that beast, the general reader," did not do so in a preface.

A more graceful justification of the custom is to be found in the preface to the *Examen* of Roger North, who there reflects that "it is some ease to a Reader to be advertised, first, of the design the writer proposes, and next, of the Methods he hath chosen to obtain it."

Adopting, then, this last and most simple and genial formula, and with the view to the "ease" of the reader, let me say at once that "the design the writer proposes" in this work is, as its title indicates, a statement of the law relating to misrepresentation, in so far as it is the subject of civil proceedings, whether at common law, or by statute. For a more detailed explanation of what "actionable misrepresentation" includes, and what it excludes, I refer the "hasty critic" to the short Introductory Chapter of the Commentary, in the hope that his "haste" will not prevent him trespassing for a matter of some three pages beyond the confines of the exiguous territory assigned to him by the cynical humour of Sir Leslie Stephen.

The "methods chosen to obtain this design"—reverting again to Roger North's prescription—are these. First, the law is stated in the form of a Code. Then follows a Commentary, the first twelve Chapters of which are intended to justify and illustrate, step by step, and in the same order of treatment, the several propositions of the Code which precedes it. Marginal references to the respective Chapters and Sections of the Commentary are set opposite the successive Articles of the Code.

The plan adopted differs from that of my work on Actionable Defamation, in which the Commentary was contained in footnotes to the Code, and thus made continuous with it. There are inconveniences in the "continuous" system, which some readers have kindly pointed out to me. There may be others in the present method; but it seemed at least worth while to give it a trial.

The last three Chapters of the Commentary deal with matters which find no place in the Code, *viz.* Statutory Proceedings (Ch. XIII), Misrepresentation to Courts or to the State or to the public (Ch. XIV), Jurisdiction and Procedure (Ch. XV).[1]

My original intention was to comprise in one treatise not only Misrepresentation, but Non-disclosure and Estoppel as well, since the two latter topics in some of their aspects are, with Misrepresentation, joint tenants of large tracts of English jurisprudence. But this joint tenancy was soon found to be severed as regards so many important topics that the attempt became hopelessly distracting. I was in fact aspiring to write three books at once. It requires more skill in literary equitation than I can claim to drive, troika-fashion, three horses abreast, one trotting and the others galloping. In more homely phrase, I found that I had bitten off more than I could chew. Non-disclosure, therefore, except in so far as it constitutes a form of misrepresentation, and Estoppel, except in so far as its principles feed the law of misrepresentation with illustrations and analogies, have been thrown overboard for present purposes, perhaps to be picked up again and dealt with separately, if fates are kind—*habent sua fata libelli*—on some future occasion. A single Horatius can only hope to overcome three Curiatii singly.

It will be noticed that the rights of shareholders and others against

---

[1] These three chapters correspond to Chapters XVI, XVII and XVIII in the present edition.

companies and their directors, officers and agents, in respect of misrepresentation in prospectuses, and otherwise, constitute the subject-
matter of very considerable portions of the book. Particular attention
has been paid to these matters, for their importance obviously demands it.
Not only are company transactions by far the most prolific in examples
of the working of the principles of misrepresentation law, but they have
received the special attention of the legislature, and of the courts interpreting the legislature, in regard to rectification of the register, variation
of the list of contributories and the like, on the ground of misrepresentation, and also as to liquidation, which has so vital a bearing on the rights
of shareholders in respect of misstatements whereby they are induced to
take shares. All these matters are treated separately in their proper
places. But by far the most important matter in this connection, and
the one which has accordingly been subjected to the most detailed
examination, is the statutory law as to untrue statements in prospectuses
which was introduced by the Directors' Liability Act, 1890, and is now
incorporated in the Companies (Consolidation) Act, 1908.[1] This topic
is minutely dealt with in Ch. XIII, Sect. 1.[2]

The statutory provisions affecting the employment of puffers at
auction sales are the subject of similarly detailed treatment in Sect. 2 of
the same Chapter, whilst Sect. 3 briefly, but, it is hoped, completely,
deals with other enactments relating to misrepresentation.

Chapter XIV[3] is devoted to certain causes of action not now deemed
in the strictest sense actions for misrepresentation, but which involve
most of its elements, being based on misrepresentation, though that
misrepresentation is not alleged to have been made to the person suing.
This subject involves consideration of the remedies of a party litigant
against whom a judgment has been given, or of an individual prejudiced
by the grant to another of a charter or patent or privilege, where such
judgment or grant has been procured by deceit practised upon the courts
or the State. It also includes "passing off" cases, which indeed did once
undoubtedly belong, and even in modern times have been regarded by
high authorities (such as MELLISH, L.J., and VAUGHAN WILLIAMS, L.J.—
see § 417) as belonging, to the class of "actions of deceit" properly so
called.

The vital questions in the consideration of any title of the law are,
first, the nature of the *alleganda et probanda*; next, the question on whom
the burden of such allegation and proof rests in the first instance, and

---

[1] Now sections 43 *et seq.* of the Companies Act 1948.
[2] The topic is dealt with in Chapter XVI of the third edition.
[3] See Chapter XVII of the third edition.

when and under what conditions it may be shifted; and, thirdly, the question which of the matters in dispute are matters of law, and which are matters of fact. Accordingly, in the case of every species of remedy or relief based on misrepresentation I have endeavoured to state definitely and separately what I conceive the law to be as to (1) the constituent elements of the cause of action or ground of defence; (2) the burden of allegation and proof; and (3) the questions of law and fact; but not until after having first considered and defined successively, in Chapters II–VIII, the various constitutive concepts in this branch of the law (representation, misrepresentation, fraud, innocence, inducement, materiality, alteration of position, damage, and parties to the representation).

G. SPENCER BOWER

2, Hare Court, Temple
October 1911

Memoir

George Spencer Bower was born on October 12th, 1854, the son of
George Bower of St Neots. He died on September 4th, 1928, aged 73
years. He was a scholar of Winchester and New College, retaining all his
life an intense Wykehamical patriotism. His record at Oxford was a
distinguished one, including first classes in both the Classical Schools, the
Gaisford Greek Prose and the Chancellor's English Essay; and classical
literature never ceased to be the interest nearest to his heart.

He was called to the Bar by the Inner Temple in 1880, and acquired an
extensive and miscellaneous junior practice. Like many of his profession
he enjoyed the society of actors, being a friend of some of the most
notable theatrical personalities of the day, including Sir Henry Irving and
Sir Charles Wyndham, whose daughter he married in 1885. He took
silk in 1903, and, although his practice within the Bar was never very
extensive, it included such famous cases as that which ended with the
"Osborne Judgment" of the House of Lords in 1909. Spencer Bower
was one of the two leading counsel for the successful appellant, Osborne.
He was made a Bencher of his Inn in 1912, an honour that he greatly
appreciated and of which he took full advantage. He thoroughly enjoyed
the social life of the Benchers, among whom he was the acknowledged
arbiter on points of classical scholarship.

His name is remembered by lawyers—and will long continue so to be
remembered—for the series of textbooks which he published between
the years 1907 and 1927, all on some aspect of the law as to representations
of fact. These books, besides remaining classic authorities on the subjects
with which they deal, have a special charm in the great wealth of literary
illustration (largely drawn from his beloved classical authors) with which
Spencer Bower delighted to illustrate his work. It was said of him that a
quotation from Horace might set him off on a veritable flood-tide of
reminiscences of great advocates and judges; a point of law reported from
the Courts might give him occasion to quote a hundred lines of Shakespeare, Homer, or Sophocles (he could actually recite the whole of the

Oedipus Tyrannus).   It was as a scholar of the old type, knowing the
ancient authors through and through by constant daily intercourse, that
he himself said that he would best like to be remembered; and those who
read this book may add this thought to the regard in which they continue
to hold him, half a century after his death, still as a contemporary
expositor of the living law.

Contents

Table of Cases

In the following Table references are given where applicable to the English and Empire Digest where a digest of the case will be found.

PAGE

Higgins v. Pitt (1849), 4 Exch. 312; 18 L.J. Ex. 488; 15 L.T.O.S. 139; 26 Digest (Repl.) 256 394

Higgins v. Samels (1862), 2 John. & H. 460; 7 L.T. 240; 35 Digest (Repl.) 45: 140, 146, 216

Higgons v. Burton (1857), 26 L.J. Ex. 342; 29 L.T.O.S. 165; 5 W.R. 683; 35 Digest (Repl.) 87 76

Hill v. Balls (1857), 2 H. & N. 299; 27 L.J. Ex. 45; 3 Jur. N.S. 592; 5 W.R. 740; 2 Digest (Repl.) 404 . . . . 75, 134, 209

Hill v. Gray (1816), 1 Stark. 434; 35 Digest (Repl.) 50 . . . 150, 153, 257

Hill v. Thompson (1818), 8 Taunt. 375; 2 Moore C.P. 424; 1 Web. Pat. Cas. 239; 1 Carp. Pat. Cas. 381; 36 Digest (Repl.) 647 . . . . . 383, 384

Hilo Manufacturing Co., Ltd. v. Williamson (1911), 28 T.L.R. 164, C.A.; 9 Digest (Repl.) 262 . . . . 40, 332

Hilton v. Eckersley (1855), 6 E. & B. 47; 24 L.J.Q.B. 353; 25 L.T.O.S. 214; 20 J.P. 4; 1 Jur. N.S. 874; 3 C.L.R. 1415; affirmed (1856), 6 E. & B. 66; 25 L.J.Q.B. 199; 26 L.T.O.S. 314; 20 J.P. 196; 2 Jur. N.S. 587; 4 W.R. 326; 12 Digest (Reissue) 296. 331

Hindle v. Brown (1908), 98 L.T. 791; 3 Digest (Repl.) 41 . . . 181

Hip Foong Hong v. H. Neotia & Co., [1918] A.C. 888; 87 L.J.P.C. 144; 119 L.T. 588, P.C.; 51 Digest (Repl.) 741 . . . . 375, 378

Hirschfield v. London, Brighton and South Coast Rail. Co. (1876), 2 Q.B.D. 1; [1874–80] All E.R. Rep. 1191; 46 L.J.Q.B. 94; 35 L.T. 473; 35 Digest (Repl.) 12 . . . . 64, 160, 330, 331

Hirst v. West Riding Union Banking Co., [1901] 2 K.B. 560; [1900–3] All E.R. Rep. 782; 70 L.J.K.B. 828; 85 L.T. 3; 49 W.R. 715; 17 T.L.R. 629; 45 Sol. Jo. 614, C.A.; 26 Digest (Repl.) 33 . . . . . . 226, 227, 228

Hoare v. Bremridge (1872), 8 Ch. App. 22; 42 L.J. Ch. 1; 27 L.T. 593; 21 W.R. 43, C.A.; 20 Digest (Repl.) 305 277

Holland v. Manchester and Liverpool District Banking Co., Ltd. (1909), 25 T.L.R. 386; 14 Com. Cas. 241; 3 Digest (Repl.) 243 85

Holliday v. Lockwood, [1917] 2 Ch. 47; [1916–17] All E.R. Rep. 232; 86 L.J. Ch. 556; 117 L.T. 265; 61 Sol. Jo. 525; 35 Digest (Repl.) 77 . . 144, 273, 331, 334

Holmes v. Jones (1907), 4 C.L.R. 1692; 35 Digest (Repl.) 63   209, 214, 216, 217, 220, 231, 232

Home Counties and General Life Assurance Co., *Re*, Woollaston's Case (1859), 4 De G. & J. 437; 28 L.J. Ch. 721; 33 L.T.O.S. 294; 5 Jur. N.S. 853; 7 W.R. 645; 9 Digest (Repl.) 258 270

Hoole v. Speak, [1904] 2 Ch. 732; 73 L.J. Ch. 719; 91 L.T. 183; 20 T.L.R. 649; 11 Mans. 421; 9 Digest (Repl.) 110 . . . . . . 173, 181, 346

Hop and Malt Exchange and Warehouse Co., *Re*, *Ex parte* Briggs (1866), L.R. 1 Eq. 483; 35 Beav. 273; 35 L.J. Ch. 320; 14 L.T. 39; 12 Jur. N.S. 322; 9 Digest (Repl.) 95 . 307

Hornal v. Neuberger Products, Ltd., [1956] 3 All E.R. 970; [1957] 1 Q.B. 247; [1956] 3 W.L.R. 1034; 100 Sol. Jo. 915, C.A.; 35 Digest (Repl.) 40 . . 210, 211

Horncastle v. Moat (1824), 1 C. & P. 166; 35 Digest (Repl.) 30 . . 209

Horsfall v. Thomas (1862), 1 H. & C. 90; 2 F. & F. 785; 31 L.J. Ex. 322; 6 L.T. 462; 8 Jur. N.S. 721; 10 W.R. 650; 35 Digest (Repl.) 27 . . 73, 104, 114, 134

Hough v. Guardian Fire and Life Assurance Co. (1902), 18 T.L.R. 273; 29 Digest (Repl.) 76 . . . . 59, 61

Houldsworth v. City of Glasgow Bank (1880), 5 App. Cas. 317; 42 L.T. 194; 28 W.R. 677, H.L.; 9 Digest (Repl.) 256 180

Howarth v. Pioneer Life Assurance Co., Ltd. (1912), 107 L.T. 155; [1911–13] All E.R. Rep. 587; 29 Digest (Repl.) 80 . . . . . . 61, 214, 393

Howatson v. Webb, [1907] 1 Ch. 537; 76 L.J. Ch. 346; 97 L.T. 730; affirmed, [1908] 1 Ch. 1; 77 L.J. Ch. 32; 97 L.T. 730; 52 Sol. Jo. 11, C.A.; 17 Digest (Repl.) 247 . . . . 65, 265, 273

Howden v. Haigh (1840), 11 Ad. & El. 1033; 3 Per. & Dav. 661; 9 L.J.Q.B. 198; 4 Jur. 821; 5 Digest (Repl.) 1220 394

Howell v. Dering, [1915] 1 K.B. 54; 84 L.J.K.B. 198; 111 L.T. 790; 58 Sol. Jo. 669, C.A.; 51 Digest (Repl.) 726 . . . . . . 355, 359

PAGE

PAGE

Table of Statutes

References in this Table to "*Statutes*" are to Halsbury's Statutes of England (Third Edition) showing the volume and page at which the annotated text of the Act will be found. Page references printed in bold type indicate where the Act is set out in part or in full.

The Code

The Code

(The marginal references are to the Chapters and Paragraphs of the Commentary which follows the Code.)

PART I: REPRESENTATION

Article 1   *What constitutes a representation*

A representation is a statement made by, or on behalf of, one person Ch. II paras. 10 et seq. (hereinafter called "the representor") to, or with the intention that it shall come to the notice of, another person (hereinafter called "the representee"), which relates, by way of affirmation, denial, description, or otherwise, to a matter of fact. A "matter of fact" means either an existing fact or thing, or a past event.

Note: This article reproduces *verbatim* Article 1 of Mr Spencer Bower's Code.

Article 2   *Statements of intention, etc.*

A statement of the representor's, or of a third person's, intention, Ch. II paras. 14 et seq. readiness, or capacity to do or abstain from doing anything, or of his expectation as to a matter *in futuro*, is a representation of the then existence of such intention, readiness, capacity, or expectation; but any statement as to a matter *in futuro* which was intended or expressed by the parties to constitute, or which can only be construed as constituting, a promise, is not a representation.

Note: This article reproduces *verbatim* Article 2 of Mr Spencer Bower's Code.

Article 3   *Statements of opinion, etc.*

A statement of the representor's, or of a third person's, opinion, be- Ch. II paras. 29 et seq. lief, or information, as such, is a statement of the fact that the representor, or such third person, entertains such opinion or belief, or is in possession of such information, as the case may be, and in that sense, and to that extent, but not further or otherwise, is a representation. A statement, as matter of fact, of that which is actually matter of opinion, belief, or information, and also a statement as matter of opinion, belief, or information, of that which is actually matter of fact, is wholly a representation.

Note: This article reproduces *verbatim* Article 3 of Mr Spencer Bower's Code.

Article 4 *Statements of law*

Ch. II
paras. 36 *et
seq.*

(1) A statement of fact accompanied by, or involving, an inference or proposition of law, where such inference or proposition is not distinct or severable from the statement of fact, is wholly and for all purposes a representation.

(2) A statement of a rule, principle, or proposition of the general law, or a statement of the legal effect of facts which form the subject of another and a distinct and severable statement, or which are within the common knowledge of the parties, is a representation in the same sense and to the same extent as in Article 3 mentioned with reference to statements of opinion, but not further or otherwise.

Note: This article reproduces *verbatim* Article 4 of Mr Spencer Bower's Code.

Article 5 *Statements as to documents*

Ch. II
paras. 43 *et
seq.*;
Ch. XIII
paras. 242–
243

A statement as to the existence of a document, or as to its contents, effect, object, or purpose, or as to its nature, character, class or description, is a representation.

Note: The wording of this article has not been significantly altered from the text of Mr Spencer Bower's Article 5, but the particular form in which he set it out in the second edition of this work has been abandoned. The reason is to be found in the abolition of distinctions formerly held important in the application of the rules as to the plea of *non est factum*, brought about by the decision of the House of Lords in *Saunders* v. *Anglia Building Society*, [1971] A.C. 1004, H.L. This case is to be found fully discussed in Chapter XIII, paras. 242–243, *post*.

Article 6 *Statements in the nature of general commendation, puffing, exaggeration etc.*

Ch. II
paras. 49 *et
seq.*

Mere general vaunting, puffing, or commendation of the merits or value of any person or thing, or mere exaggeration, unaccompanied by any particular or definite statement, is not a representation.

Note: This article reproduces *verbatim* Article 6 of Mr Spencer Bower's Code.

Article 7 *How a representation may be made*

Ch. III

A representation may be made in express terms, or may be implied, as hereinafter stated.

Note: This Article reproduces *verbatim* Article 7 of Mr Spencer Bower's Code.

Article 8   *Express and implied representations*

   (1) An express representation is a representation which is made either Ch. III

   (*a*) in writing, or by equivalent permanent signs; or paras. 53 *et*

   (*b*) orally, or by gestures or other transitory signs. *seq.*

   (2) An implied representation is a representation which is implied, Ch. III
either paras. 55 *et*

                                               seq.

   (*a*) from an express statement or statements, as in Articles 2, 3 and 4
mentioned, or in accordance with the Rules of Construction contained in Article 12; or

   (*b*) from acts and conduct.

Note: This Article reproduced *verbatim* Article 8 of Mr Spencer Bower's Code.

Article 9   *Continuing representations*

   In any case where there is an interval between the representation and Ch. IV
the alteration of position induced thereby, the representor is at liberty to paras. 73 *et*
withdraw or modify the representation at any time during such interval. *seq.*
Unless so withdrawn or modified, and, if modified, subject only to the
modification, the representation is deemed to be repeated at each successive moment during the whole of such interval, and is hereinafter
called "a continuing representation".

Note: This article reproduces *verbatim* Article 9 of Mr Spencer Bower's Code.

PART II: MISREPRESENTATION

Article 10   *What constitutes misrepresentation*

   A misrepresentation is a representation which, when made, or, in the Ch. IV
case of a continuing representation, when acted upon by the representee, paras. 66–75
was false.

Note: This article reproduces *verbatim* Article 10 of Mr Spencer Bower's Code.

Article 11   *What constitutes falsity*

   A representation is false when there is a substantial discrepancy be- Ch. IV
tween it and any material fact which it expressly or impliedly purports to paras. 66–75
state. A discrepancy is substantial when it would be deemed material by
any normal representee in the circumstances of the individual case.

Note: This article reproduces *verbatim* Article 11 of Mr Spencer Bower's Code.

Article 12 *Canons of construction*

The following are rules for the determination of the falsity or truth of any representation:

Rule 1.—The meaning of any representation is that which was thereby conveyed to the mind of the representee, and, in the absence of special circumstances, the meaning deemed to have been conveyed is the natural and ordinary meaning (hereinafter called "the primary sense") of the words or other signs used: provided that it is competent to either party to allege, in which case the burden is on such party of proving, special circumstances in virtue of which the representee in fact understood the representation in a sense other than the primary sense (hereinafter called a "secondary sense"). Where the representation is susceptible of more than one primary sense, the burden is on the representee of alleging and proving in which of such possible senses he understood it, and that in that sense it was false: provided nevertheless, that where there is other and independent evidence that the representor used ambiguous language or other signs for the express purpose of misleading, the burden is on the representor of proving that the representee in fact understood it in some one of such possible senses in which it was true.

Rule 2.—Where a representation, by reason of the omission therefrom of all reference to qualifying conditions, subject to which alone it would be true, or by reason of the representor's suppression of facts which in the circumstances of the individual case it was his duty to disclose, is rendered a partial, fragmentary, incomplete, or misleading representation of the entirety of the facts to which it relates, it is deemed false, notwithstanding that the statement, or each of the statements, if more than one, made by the representor may be, when taken by itself, literally accurate. Except as aforesaid, silence or reticence is not a misrepresentation.

Rule 3.—In the case of a representation which is compounded of several connected statements, or contained in several connected documents, the question to be determined is whether, in the primary, or in any alleged and proved secondary, sense (as the case may be) of the entirety of such statements or documents, in their bearing upon and relation to one another, such representation is false or true, and not whether any particular one of such statements or documents is false or true, unless it is complete and intelligible in itself, and neither incorporates by reference, nor purports to qualify, any other of such statements or documents.

Margin notes:

Ch. IV para. 76

Ch. IV paras. 77–81

Ch. IV paras. 82–90

Ch. IV paras. 91–92

Rule 4.—The question whether the representation in any case is or is not _{Ch. IV} capable of any primary, or (as the case may be) secondary, meaning ^{para. 93} alleged is a question of law. Further, the question of the primary sense of any representation the terms of which are wholly in writing or undisputed is a question of law. All other questions as to the meaning conveyed to the representee by any representation are questions of fact.

Note: This article reproduces *verbatim* Article 12 of Mr Spencer Bower's Code.

PART III: MISREPRESENTATION IN RELATION TO THE MIND OF THE REPRESENTOR

Article 13 *What constitutes fraud in misrepresentation*

A fraudulent misrepresentation is a misrepresentation which, when Ch. V made, or in the case of a continuing representation, when acted upon by paras. 96 et seq. the representee, the representor did not in fact honestly believe to be true.

Note: This article reproduces *verbatim* Article 13 of Mr Spencer Bower's Code.

Article 14 *Motive of representor irrelevant*

Fraud necessarily involves an intention on the part of the representor Ch. V that he shall act in the way in which he does eventually act; but it is not para. 99; Ch. VI necessary to prove any intention on his part further and other than this, para. 117 and certainly the motive of the representor in making his representation is immaterial.

Note: In the 2nd Edition of this work this article was written thus: "For the above purpose, it is immaterial whether the representor, in making the misrepresentation, had or had not any intention to deceive, defraud, or injure the representee or any other person, or to benefit himself or any other person, or what, if any, was his motive for making the same." It is conceived by the editor of the present edition that the reworded statement removes a certain obscurity in the earlier text.

Article 15 *What constitutes innocence in misrepresentation*

An innocent misrepresentation is a misrepresentation which, when Ch. V made, or, in the case of a continuing representation, when acted upon by paras. 105 et seq. the representee, the representor did in fact honestly believe to be true.

Note: This article reproduces *verbatim* Article 15 of Mr Spencer Bower's Code.

Article 16   *Unreasonableness or negligence not fraud*

Ch. V
paras. 107 *et
seq.*
An innocent misrepresentation is not rendered fraudulent by the mere fact that the belief of the representor was unreasonable, or was based upon inadequate materials, information, or inquiry, or arose from negligence, forgetfulness, inadvertence, or incompetence.

Note: This article reproduces *verbatim* Article 16 of Mr Spencer Bower's Code.

PART IV: MISREPRESENTATION IN ITS EFFECT ON THE REPRESENTEE

Article 17   *Inducement*

Ch. VI
paras. 114–
123
The representee is deemed to have been induced to alter his position by the representation if he was, and was intended by the representor to be, influenced in so doing by his belief in the truth thereof. Provided that—

(i) If inducement be proved as a fact, it is not necessary to show that the representation was the sole inducement, or that, but for his belief in the truth thereof, the representee would not have altered his position in the manner alleged:

(ii) In the case of a number of connected representations, or a representation compounded of a number of statements, it is sufficient to prove that the representee was induced to alter his position by his belief in the truth of such representations or statements in their entirety, and it is not necessary to prove that he was separately induced by any particular one or more of them:

(iii) It is sufficient to prove that the representee relied upon some one or more of several representations or statements not so connected as aforesaid:

(iv) Where the representation relied upon is not reasonably capable of more than one primary sense, it is necessary and sufficient to prove that the representee was induced by it in that sense. Where the representation is so capable, the representee must specify the sense in which he alleges that he understood it, and prove that he was induced by it, in that sense, to alter his position. It is nevertheless competent to the representee to allege and prove that the representor intended him to, and that he did, assign a secondary sense to the representation, and that he was induced by it, in that sense, to alter his position.

Note: This article reproduces *verbatim* Article 17 of Mr Spencer Bower's Code.

Article 18 *Materiality*

A material representation is a representation the tendency, or the natural and probable effect, of which, either in the ordinary course of events, or in special circumstances of the case known to the representor, was to induce the representee to alter his position in the manner alleged. Ch. VI paras. 124–131

Note: This article reproduces *verbatim* Article 18 of Mr Spencer Bower's Code.

Article 19 *Questions of fact and law in relation to inducement and materiality*

(1) It is a question of law whether there is any evidence of the alleged inducement, and also whether the proved or admitted representation is capable of being considered material, or of a sense in which it can be so considered. Subject to the above, all questions in relation to inducement and materiality are questions of fact. Ch. VI paras. 132 *et seq.*

(2) Inducement and materiality are separate and distinct facts, and must be proved independently: provided that inducement may be inferred, as a fact, from proved materiality of a sufficiently obvious character to justify such an inference: but it cannot be so inferred as a conclusion of law.

Note: This article reproduces *verbatim* Article 19 of Mr Spencer Bower's Code.

Article 20 *Alteration of position*

A representee is deemed to have altered his position on the faith of a representation when he was induced by his belief in the truth thereof to become a party to any contract or transaction either with the representor or with a third person, or to do, or abstain from doing, any act of whatsoever nature which he was not compelled by law to do, or abstain from doing. "Transaction" herein means and includes any act done, or relationship established, between two persons, which is of a binding or irrevocable nature, though it may not of itself amount in law to a contract. Ch. VII paras. 138–139

Note: This article reproduces *verbatim* Article 20 of Mr Spencer Bower's Code.

Article 21 *Damage*

A representee is deemed to have sustained damage by reason of his belief in the truth of a representation—(i) when any alteration of position induced thereby has, either in the ordinary course of events, or as a consequence actually foreseen and intended by the representor, resulted in loss to the representee of money, or money's worth, or in any Ch. VII paras. 141 *et seq.*

temporal detriment, or physical injury; or (ii) when, without having so altered his position, the representee has in fact suffered personal and physical injury in consequence of such belief.

Note: The author of the 3rd edition has amended the text of this article by altering "the consequence" to "a consequence" in line 4.

PART V: PARTIES TO THE REPRESENTATION

Article 22   *The representor*

Ch. VIII
I. *Representor*. "Representor" means and includes—
(a) Any person who actually and personally made the representation; provided that, where several persons concurred or combined in making it, all such persons are deemed joint representors, and, in the case of a fraudulent misrepresentation, joint and several representors:
(b) Any person, whether principal or partner of the actual representor, by whose express or implied authority the representation was made.
(c) A principal is liable for representations made by a sub-agent (i.e. the appointee of an agent) if, but not unless, it was in the ordinary course of business, or was contemplated, or was necessary in the circumstances of the case, that the immediate agent should delegate any of the duties of his agency, and the sub-agent, when making the representation, was acting within the scope of any duty so delegated; provided that a co-agent of any agent who made the representation is not, merely as such, deemed a representor.

A body corporate or politic may be a representor.

II. Where rescission is claimed, or where the representation is set up as an answer to a claim on a contract induced thereby, the accountability of a principal for a representation made by his agent or sub-agent will depend upon the application of the ordinary principles of the law of agency.

III. Where damages are claimed, whether for fraud or for innocent misrepresentation, the state of mind of the person making the representation is relevant, and the following rules apply:
(1) Where the same person both (a) himself actually made the representation and (b) had the necessary state of mind (i.e., (i) in the case of fraud had no honest belief in its truth, and (ii) in the case of innocent misrepresentation, is unable to prove reasonable belief) then the liability of any *other* person for the misrepresentation will depend upon the ordinary principles of the law of agency.

(2) Fraud will not be held proved against a representor who did not himself make the representation unless he is shown himself to have participated in the fraudulence of the representation in accordance with the following rules:

(*a*) Where the representation is actually made by one person, and the necessary absence of honest belief in its truth is proved only in some other person[1] whom it is sought to make liable for fraud as the principal of the actual representor,

   (i) if the principal has actually authorised or ratified the making of the representation, he is liable for fraud,

   (ii) in other cases he is not liable for fraud unless he has been guilty of some conduct identifying himself with the making of the representation sufficient to convict him of the fraud.[2]

(*b*) Where the servant or agent of a common master or principal makes a representation honestly believing in its truth, and another servant or agent of the same master has the knowledge which, if the knowledge of the representor, would have made his representation fraudulent, then their common master or principal will not be liable in fraud unless the circumstances are such that the actual representor must be held to have made the representation without genuine belief in its truth.

Note: This Article has been rewritten to take account of the restatement of the law originally put forward by ATKINSON J. in *Anglo-Scottish Beet Sugar Corporation, Ltd.* v. *Spalding Urban District Council*[3] and later approved and adopted by the Court of Appeal in *Armstrong* v. *Strain*.[4]

Article 23   *The representee*

A "representee" means and includes:

Ch. IX

(i) Any person to whom the representation was actually and personally made:

(ii) Any principal, or partner, of such person:

(iii) Any other person to whom the representor intended that the

---

[1] This rule deals with the case where the agent makes the representation, and the principal knows the truth. The converse case—where the principal makes the representation, the agent knowing the truth, is not considered, because it makes no sense unless agent may be an agent simply for the purpose of knowing the truth. Where the principal makes a representation, his liability for fraud must depend simply upon whether *he* has an honest belief in the truth of what is represented, or no.

[2] Such conduct may be found, e.g. in employing the agent with the intention that he shall make the representation innocently, in ignorance of the true facts.

[3] [1937] 2 K.B. 607.

[4] [1952] 1 K.B. 232, C.A.

representation should be, and to whom in fact it was, transmitted or communicated:

(iv) In the case of a representation made or addressed to the public or a class,—any member of the public, or of such class, to whose notice it came, and who acted upon it.

Note: This article reproduces *verbatim* Article 23 of Mr Spencer Bower's Code.

PART VI: WHEN MISREPRESENTATION IS ACTIONABLE

Article 24   *When subject of action for damages: fraudulent misrepresentation*

Ch. X   Fraudulent misrepresentation will support an action for damages, in accordance with the provisions of Part VII.

Note: This article reproduces *verbatim* Article 24 of Mr Spencer Bower's Code.

Article 25   *When subject of action for damages: innocent misrepresentation*

Ch. XII   Innocent misrepresentation by which a representee is induced to enter into a contract may, since the passing of the Misrepresentation Act 1967, also support an action for damages, as set out in that Act.

Notes: (*a*) This article is new; when Mr Spencer Bower wrote his text an innocent misrepresentation could not support an action for damages. His Article 27, which stated this proposition, is not reproduced in the Code of this edition.
(*b*) Section 2 of the Misrepresentation Act 1967 is to be found in Article 30, below.
(*c*) Nothing is said here of the so-called action for damages for innocent misrepresentation founded upon the decision of the House of Lords in *Hedley Byrne & Co. Ltd.* v. *Heller & Partners, Ltd.*, [1964] A.C. 465, H.L., which is made the subject of Chapter XIX of this work. This action, as is pointed out in that chapter, is not, strictly speaking, an action for misrepresentation at all, but one in negligence. It consequently does not find a place in this Code, but is mentioned here for the sake of completeness.

Article 26   *When subject of proceedings for rescission, or ground of defence*

Ch. X   Where the representee's alteration of position consisted in becoming party to a contract or transaction with the representor, the misrepresentation, whether fraudulent or innocent, may be the subject of proceedings for rescission, and a ground of affirmative defence to any action to enforce such contract or transaction, pursuant to the provisions of Parts VIII, and IX, respectively.

In the case of innocent misrepresentation, the right to rescind is not unqualified, for the Court is invested by section 2 (2) of the Misrepresentation Act 1967 with a discretion enabling it, if such a course is deemed just, to declare the contract subsisting, and in such a case, to award such damages as may be just in lieu of rescission.

Note: The last sub-paragraph has been added in this text to Mr Spencer Bower's original Article 25.

Article 27 *To what proceedings statutory misrepresentation is amenable*

Where misrepresentation is the subject of any statute or enactment, it is actionable under the conditions, and amenable to the several proceedings, mentioned in such statute or enactment, and not otherwise.

Notes: 1. This article reproduces *verbatim* Article 26 of Mr Spencer Bower's Code.
2. Article 27 of Mr Spencer Bower's Code has been omitted from this text; see note (*a*) to Article 25, above.

PART VII: ACTION FOR DAMAGES FOR MISREPRESENTATION

Article 28 *Action for damages for fraud*

An action may be maintained for damages for fraudulent misrepresenta- Ch. XI tion upon the following conditions: It is necessary and sufficient, in order to establish the plaintiff's right to relief in any such action, to allege, with such particulars as are reasonably adequate to the requirements of the individual case, and having alleged, to prove (except in so far as any allegation may be expressly or impliedly admitted at or before the trial) each and every of the following matters:

(i) That the alleged representation was in fact made, and was a representation within the meaning of Part I:

(ii) That the defendant was the representor within the meaning of Article 22, or is otherwise liable for the representation within the meaning of Article 34:

(iii) That the plaintiff was the representee within the meaning of Article 23, or is otherwise entitled to sue in respect of the representation within the meaning of Article 34:

(iv) Inducement and materiality, within the meaning of Articles 17, and 18, respectively:

(v) Falsity of the representation at the material date, within the meaning of Articles 10, 11, and 12:

(vi) That the representation was fraudulent at the material date, within the meaning of Articles 13 and 14:

(vii) Alteration of position, and resultant damage, or physical and personal injury, within the meaning of Articles 20 and 21.

Note: This is Mr Spencer Bower's Article 28. In the first line the word "fraudulent" has been inserted in his original text, this article being thus restricted, in the text which appears above, to the action for *fraudulent* misrepresentation. A new Article (Article 30) lists the requirements of the new action for damages for innocent misrepresentation.

Article 29 *Affirmative defences to an action for fraud*

It is competent to the defendant in any action founded on fraudulent misrepresentation, with or without a denial of all or any of the plaintiff's allegations, to set up any one or more of the affirmative defences available to a defendant in any action for tort, and also any one or more of the affirmative defences special to actions for damages for fraudulent misrepresentation: provided that the burden is on such defendant of alleging, with such particulars as are reasonably adequate to the requirements of the individual case, and, having so alleged, of proving, all such matters as are necessary to establish the defence or defences so set up. Such special affirmative defences are as follow:

(i) That, at the date of the representation, or before altering his position on the faith thereof, the plaintiff had acquired exact and complete knowledge of the truth in relation to the facts alleged to have been misrepresented: provided that proof that the plaintiff had the means of acquiring such knowledge does not of itself constitute any defence:

(ii) In any case in which the plaintiff's alteration of position consisted in becoming a party to a contract or transaction with the defendant, —that the plaintiff had, before action, avoided such contract or transaction; but not merely that he was in a position to avoid it:

(iii) In any case in which the representation was as to the credit of a third person,—that the representation was not in writing, or, if in writing, was not personally signed by the representor, within the meaning of s. 6 of the Statute of Frauds Amendment Act 1828.

Note: In this article as it appeared in Mr Spencer Bower's second edition, an additional available special affirmative defence was included, *viz.*:

"That the plaintiff had expressly, or (by his acts and conduct) impliedly, agreed to waive all inquiry into the subject-matter of the representation, and to dispense with, or not to rely upon, any information, or facilities for investigation, given or offered by the defendant; or had expressly agreed to take any property purchased from the defendant with all faults, or at his own risk, or with such title thereto as the defendant could give, or on the basis of an express refusal by the defendant to give any warranty: provided, nevertheless, that none of the foregoing facts constitute any defence in any case where it is shown that the representor had fraudulently concealed any such fault, risk, or defect of title, by active devices or positive means: provided also that any stipulation between the parties that the representor shall not be liable for fraudulent misrepresentation is a nullity:"

It is doubted by the author of this edition how far the courts would have supported the text of this paragraph in its original form, even at the time of publication of the second edition of this work; but whatever may have been the position then, it is conceived that since the passing of the Misrepresentation Act 1967 it has been unlikely that a plea of waiver or acceptance will in any circumstances be accepted as an answer to a charge of fraud that has been substantiated by the evidence. Section 3 of that Act provides:

> "If any agreement (whether made before or after the commencement of this Act) contains a provision which would exclude or restrict—
>> (a) any liability to which a party to a contract may be subject by reason of any misrepresentation made by him before the contract was made; or
>> (b) any remedy available to another party to the contract by reason of such a misrepresentation;
> that provision shall be of no effect except to the extent (if any) that, in any proceedings arising out of the contract, the court or arbitrator may allow reliance on it as being fair and reasonable in the circumstances of the case."

In para. 194, *post*, it is suggested that this defence will no longer lie.

Article 30   *Action for damages for innocent misrepresentation*

By s. 2 of the Misrepresentation Act 1967 it is provided: Ch. XII

(i) Where a person has entered into a contract after a misrepresentation has been made to him by another party thereto and as a result thereof he has suffered loss, then, if the person making the misrepresentation would be liable to damages in respect thereof had the misrepresentation been made fraudulently, that person shall be so liable notwithstanding that the misrepresentation was not made fraudulently, unless he proves that he had reasonable ground to believe and did believe up to the time the contract was made that the facts represented were true.

(ii) Where a person has entered into a contract after a misrepresentation has been made to him otherwise than fraudulently, and he would be entitled, by reason of the misrepresentation, to rescind the contract, then, if it is claimed, in any proceedings arising out of the contract, that the contract ought to be or has been rescinded the court or arbitrator may declare the contract subsisting and award damages in lieu of rescission, if of opinion that it would be equitable to do so, having regard to the nature of the misrepresentation and the loss that would be caused by it if the contract were upheld, as well as to the loss that rescission would cause to the other party.

(iii) Damages may be awarded against a person under subsection (ii) of this section whether or not he is liable to damages under subsection (i) thereof, but where he is so liable any award under the said subsection (ii) shall be taken into account in assessing his liability under the said subsection (i).

Notes: 1. This article is new, and reproduces the text of s. 2 of the 1967 Act.

2. The provision does not apply to any misrepresentation made before the coming into operation of that Act (March 23rd 1967).

3. The remedy in damages for innocent misrepresentation is confined to the case where the alteration in the representee's position consists in his having "entered into a contract".

Article 31   *Affirmative defences to actions for damages for innocent misrepresentation*

Ch. XII   As in the case of an action for damages for fraudulent misrepresentation it is competent for the defendant in any action for damages for innocent misrepresentation to set up any one or more of the affirmative defences available to a defendant in any action for tort. He may also set up in such an action any one or more of the affirmative defences special to actions for damages for fraudulent misrepresentation which have been enumerated in Article 29 above; provided that the burden is on such defendant of alleging, with such particulars as are reasonably adequate to the requirements of the individual case, and, having so alleged, of proving, all such matters as are necessary to establish the defence or defence so set up.

Beside the special defences available in actions for damages for fraudulent misrepresentation, which are equally available in actions for damages for innocent misrepresentation, an additional affirmative defence is also available in the case of actions based on innocent misrepresentation, but subject as appears in the next paragraph hereof.

It may be pleaded as a defence to an action for damages for innocent misrepresentation that the plaintiff had expressly, or (by his acts and conduct) impliedly, agreed to waive all inquiry into the subject-matter of the representation, and to dispense with, or not to rely upon, any information, or facilities for investigation, given or offered by the defendant; or had expressly agreed to take any property purchased from the defendant with all faults, or at his own risk, or with such title thereto as the defendant could give, or on the basis of an express refusal by the defendant to give any warranty: provided, nevertheless, that none of the foregoing facts constitute any defence in any case where it is shown that the representor had fraudulently concealed any such fault, risk, or defect of title, by active devices or positive means: provided also that any stipulation between the parties that the representor shall not be liable for fraudulent misrepresentation is a nullity.

But the availability of this special defence is limited by the provisions of s. 3 of the Act which provides:

"If any agreement (whether made before or after the commencement of this Act) contains a provision which would exclude or restrict—

(*a*) any liability to which a party to a contract may be subject by reason of any misrepresentation made by him before the contract was made; or

(*b*) any remedy available to another party to the contract by reason of such a misrepresentation;

that provision shall be of no effect except to the extent (if any) that, in any proceedings arising out of the contract, the court or arbitrator may allow reliance on it as being fair and reasonable in the circumstances of the case.''

Note: This Article is new; in Mr Spencer Bower's Code there were no actions for damages for innocent misrepresentation.

Article 32   *Nature and quantum of relief: damages for fraudulent misrepresentation*

A plaintiff who succeeds in an action for damages for *fraudulent* Ch. XI misrepresentation, is entitled to recover, as such damages, the then present money value of the whole of the net loss, damage, or injury which has resulted, or will result, within the meaning of Article 21, from his having altered his position, in the manner alleged and proved, on the faith of the fraudulent misrepresentation.   The following are rules for the ascertainment and computation of such damages:

(i) Where the plaintiff's alteration of position consisted in becoming a party to any contract or transaction with the defendant, or with a third person, the sum recoverable as damages is the amount of the excess (if any) of all moneys paid or payable, and the money value (if any) of all property transferred or transferable, by the plaintiff under the contract or transaction, over and above the total of all moneys (if any), and the money value (if any) of all property, received or receivable by him thereunder: provided that the money value of property received or receivable by the plaintiff means the real value which such property had, in the proved circumstances of the case, immediately after the conclusion of such contract or transaction:

(ii) Where the plaintiff's alteration of position consisted in the bestowal of time, services, or labour, the sum recoverable is the money value thereof on a fair estimate in all the circumstances of the case:

(iii) Where the plaintiff's alteration of position consisted in the incurring of any liability which has not been discharged at the date of the trial, the sum recoverable is the estimated then present money value thereof:

(iv) Where the plaintiff's alteration of position consisted in the doing of or abstaining from some act, in consequence of which he has sustained physical and personal injury, or where he has sustained such injury in consequence of his belief in the truth of the representation, without having altered his position as abovementioned, the sum recoverable is that which would be recoverable if the plaintiff were suing for damages for personal injuries caused by negligence.

Note: This Article repeats Mr Spencer Bower's Article 30.

Article 33   *Nature and quantum of relief: damages for innocent misrepresentation*

Chs. XII:
App. D

(1) A plaintiff who succeeds in an action for damages for innocent misrepresentation, pursuant to s. 2 (1) of the Misrepresentation Act 1967, who has entered into a contract on the faith of the representation and has thereby suffered loss, is entitled to recover damages on the same principles as are set out in Article 32 (i) above.

(2) Damages may be awarded in its discretion by the court, in lieu of rescission, to a plaintiff who has claimed rescission for innocent misrepresentation. It is provided by s. 2 (3) of the Misrepresentation Act 1967 that the court may so exercise its discretion, awarding damages in lieu of rescission, whether or not there is a liability pursuant to para. (1) above. But where there is such a liability any award made under this sub-article must be taken into account in assessing damages under para. (1) above.

Note: This article is new.

Article 34   *Questions of law and fact*

Ch. XI &
XII

In any action for damages for fraudulent or for innocent misrepresentation, the following are questions of law:

(i) Whether the alleged, or proved, representation is a representation in law, within the meaning of Articles 1–6;

(ii) Whether the alleged, or proved, representation is capable of the meaning assigned to it by either party;

(iii) Whether the alleged, or proved, representation is capable of being deemed material, within the meaning of Article 18;

(iv) Whether, in the case of an affirmative defence of the kind maintained in Article 29 (iii), the alleged, or proved, representation relates to the credit of a third person, or to any of the other matters referred to in s. 6 of the Statute of Frauds Amendment Act 1828;

(v) Whether the damages claimed are recoverable in law, and all questions as to the proper measure of damages;

(vi) Generally, in the case of any of the necessary allegations on the part of the plaintiff, or of the defendant, as stated in Articles 28 and

29 respectively, whether there is any evidence thereof, or whether, *prima facie* evidence of any such allegation having been adduced, there is any evidence to the contrary thereof.

Except as aforesaid, all disputed questions are questions of fact.

Note: This article reproduces almost *verbatim* Article 31 of Mr Spencer Bower's Code.

Article 35 *Parties to actions for damages*

(1) Any representee, within the meaning of Article 23, or any person Chs. VIII & who, in virtue of the rules of common law or any statutory provision re- IX lating to parties to actions of tort in general, is entitled to stand in the place of such representee, in case of his death, disability, incapacity, or otherwise, may maintain an action or counterclaim for damages for mis-representation; and any representor, within the meaning of Article 22, or any person who, in accordance with any such rule or statutory provi-sion, is required to stand in the place of such representor, in case of his death, disability, incapacity, or otherwise, is liable to be sued in such action, or proceeded against by such counterclaim. In the foregoing Articles of this Part, the expression "plaintiff" includes a party so counterclaiming, and, where the action or counterclaim is brought, not by the representee, but by some person in right of him or his estate, it means such representee only: and the expression "defendant" in like manner includes a party resisting such counterclaim, and where the ac-tion or counterclaim is brought, not against the representor, but against a person required to stand in his place, it means such representor only.

(2) A bare right to sue for damages for fraudulent or innocent mis-representation is not assignable *inter vivos*.

(3) An action or counterclaim against a corporation or firm for damages in respect of any fraudulent misrepresentation, whereby the plaintiff alleges that he was induced to become a member thereof, is not maintainable whilst the plaintiff remains such member.

Note: This article reproduces, with one modification, Article 32 of Mr Spencer Bower's Code. The text has been altered to include actions for damages for innocent misrepresentation.

PART VIII: PROCEEDINGS FOR RESCISSION OR ANALOGOUS RELIEF

Article 36 *Nature and limits of the right to avoid a contract or transaction induced by misrepresentation*

(1) Subject as appears in para. (2) hereof, below, where a representee Ch. XIII has been induced to enter into a contract or transaction with the repre-

sentor by any misrepresentation on the part of such representor, the contract or transaction, whether the representee has, or has not, sustained, or is, or is not, likely to sustain, damage by reason of his having entered into it, and whether the misrepresentation was fraudulent or innocent, is voidable at the option of the representee, on discovery of the truth of the facts misrepresented, but remains valid and binding unless and until he elects to repudiate it (not having previously in words, or by acts and conduct, elected to affirm it), and gives notice of such repudiation to the representor. On such notice being given, if the representor refuses to accept or recognise the repudiation, or to treat the contract or transaction as at an end, the representee is entitled to enforce his avoidance thereof by any of the proceedings in Articles 38–41 mentioned, subject to the conditions stated in Article 37; provided that, without resort to any such proceedings, he is entitled to resume physical possession of any property delivered under the contract or transaction, if and when he becomes in a position to do so without violating the rights of any third person. The avoidance must be of the entire contract or transaction; provided that the representee is entitled to avoid a particular term or part thereof, without avoiding the residue, or to avoid it as against one of the parties thereto, without affecting the rights or liabilities thereunder of any other party, if, but not unless, such term or part is wholly distinct and severable from such residue, or if, but not unless, the party against whom it is sought to avoid the contract or transaction is a party severally liable thereunder.

(2) By s. 2 (2) of the Misrepresentation Act 1967 it is provided that where the representee's claim to rescind is founded upon an *innocent* misrepresentation only, the court, if it is of opinion that it would be equitable so to do, may (notwithstanding that apart from this provision the misrepresentation would give rise to a right to rescind) declare that the contract susbsists and award damages in lieu of rescission.

Note: The text of this Article follows that of Mr Spencer Bower's Article 33, but para. (2) has been added in this edition to include a note of the discretion now conferred upon the court by s. 2 (2) of the Misrepresentation Act 1967, to declare the contract subsisting, and award damages in lieu of rescission.

Article 37   *What must be alleged and proved by the representee in any proceedings for rescission or analogous relief*

Ch. XIII
paras. 228–
243

In any of the proceedings mentioned in the next Article for the purpose of obtaining a judicial rescission or avoidance of any contract or transaction induced by misrepresentation, or for analogous relief, it is necessary and sufficient, in order to establish the plaintiff's right to such relief, to allege, with such particulars as are reasonably adequate to the requirements of the individual case, and (except so far as any allegation may be expressly or impliedly admitted at or before the trial) to prove, each and every of the following matters:—

(i) That the alleged representation was in fact made, and was a representation within the meaning of Part I;

(ii) That the defendant was the representor within the meaning of Article 22, or is otherwise liable for the representation within the meaning of Article 44 (2);

(iii) That the plaintiff was the representee within the meaning of Article 23, or is otherwise entitled to maintain the proceedings, within the meaning of Article 44 (1);

(iv) That the plaintiff in fact entered into the contract or transaction sought to be rescinded, and that he was induced to do so, within the meaning of Article 17, by the alleged representation, being a material one, within the meaning of Article 18;

(v) Falsity of the representation at the material date, within the meaning of Articles 10, 11, and 12;

(vi) That the alleged contract or transaction is in law subsisting and binding, and is still voidable at the plaintiff's instance, or by the court: that is to say, that it was concluded, and, having been concluded, has never been put an end to by mutual consent, forfeiture, or otherwise, provided however that if a contract or transaction has been induced by a misrepresentation as to the identity of the person with whom it purports to have been entered into or by a misrepresentation as to the effect of what was signed, inducing the signatory to sign a document fundamentally different from what was represented, it is not voidable, but void;

(vii) That the alleged contract or transaction was one which in law created and affected contractual rights and liabilities only.

Notes: 1. This Article follows, but with some modification, Mr Spencer Bower's Article 34. Following the so-called rule in *Seddon* v. *North Eastern Salt Co.*, [1905] 1 Ch. 326, Mr Spencer Bower's text made the remedy of rescission unavailable in the case of executed contracts. This exception to the liability to rescission has been abolished by s. 1 of the Misrepresentation Act 1967.

2. The text of the concluding part of the Article has been amended. That of Mr Spencer Bower followed the rule as to the plea of *non est factum* as it was generally understood up to the decision of the House of Lords in *Saunders* v. *Anglia Building Society*, [1970] 3 All E.R. 961, H.L. The rule as stated above follows the judgments in the Lords in that case.

Article 38   *Action for rescission*

On allegation of the several matters set forth in Article 37, the representee (subject, however, in the case of an innocent misrepresentation, Ch. XIII paras. 249–262.

to the discretion to declare the contract subsisting and award damages in lieu, conferred upon the court by s. 2 (2) of the Misrepresentation Act 1967) may maintain an action for the rescission of the contract or transaction, wherein he is entitled to claim, and, on proof of such matters, to obtain, the following remedies, or such of them as may be appropriate to the circumstances of the particular case:

(i) A declaration that the contract or transaction is void, and that it is to be treated as having been void since his repudiation thereof;

(ii) An order for rescission or annulment of the contract or transaction *ab initio*, in its entirety or, under the conditions mentioned in Article 36, but not otherwise, partially; provided that, in a proper case, any instrument purporting to contain or record the contract or transaction may be set aside in one character, or for one purpose, and allowed to stand in another character, or for another purpose: provided also that the mere fact that the contract sought to be rescinded was a contract for the purchase of property sold under the direction of the court in any cause or matter in no way affects the title of the representee to rescission: but in that case his remedy is not by action, but by application to the court directing the sale in such cause or matter;

(iii) An order for the cancellation, or delivering up to be cancelled, of any instrument or document purporting to contain or record the contract or transaction, where there is an appreciable danger that, if allowed to remain in the defendant's possession, it may, though judicially declared void, be negotiated (if negotiable), or used thereafter for the purpose of harassing the plaintiff by frivolous and vexatious proceedings, or so as otherwise injuriously to affect the plaintiff's title or rights;

(iv) Where the contract sought to be rescinded was a contract to take shares in a company, within the meaning of the Companies Act 1948, —an order for the rectification of the register of members;

(v) An order for the repayment to the plaintiff (with interest, in the absence of special circumstances) of all moneys, and the retransfer to him of all property, received by the defendant under the contract or transaction, together with all rents, profits, dividends, and benefits received in respect of such property (less the cost of any permanent improvements thereto in the case of real property), as against the like repayment and retransfer by the plaintiff to the defendant of all moneys and property (if any) received by the plaintiff thereunder, and payment of all rents, profits, dividends, and benefits received by him in respect of such property;

(vi) Where necessary, an indemnity against any liability of the plaintiff to third persons under the contract or transaction;

(vii) Where necessary, an injunction restraining the defendant from dealing or parting with any property the subject of the contract or transaction;

(viii) Payment, by way of indemnity, of the amount of any expenses or liabilities incurred by the plaintiff in relation to the property the subject of the contract or transaction, and pursuant thereto, during the period when he was in possession of the property;

(ix) Generally, all such directions for inquiries, accounts, or otherwise, as may be necessary for the purpose of effecting a restoration of the *status quo*, and mutual restitution *in specie* of all moneys, property, and benefits acquired by the parties under the contract or transaction.

Note: This Article substantially reproduces Mr Spencer Bower's Article 35, but with an amendment to provide for the effect of s. 2 (2) of the Misrepresentation Act 1967.

Article 39   *Action for money had and received*

Where the representee has paid money to the representor pursuant to the contract or transaction, and has received from him no money or money's worth thereunder, he is entitled to recover what he has so paid in an action for money had and received, on proof of the matters set forth in Article 37. Ch. XIII paras. 263–266

Note: This Article reproduces without substantial modification Mr Spencer Bower's Article 36.

Article 40   *Statutory proceedings for rectification of the register of members of a company*

Where the representee alleges that he was induced by the misrepresentation of a company, within the meaning of the Companies Act 1948, to agree to become a shareholder therein, or where the representee is such a company, and alleges that it was induced by the misrepresentation of a shareholder to accept and register another person as the transferee of his shares, it is competent to the representee, in either of such cases, to apply to the court for rectification of the register of members of the company as provided by s. 116 of the statute. Ch. XIII para. 267

Note: This Article substantially reproduces Mr Spencer Bower's Article 37.

Article 41   *Proceedings for variation of the list of contributories of a company in liquidation*

In any such case as that mentioned in the last Article, if the company is in liquidation, the application must be made in the winding up of such company, pursuant to s. 257 of the Companies Act 1948, to vary the list of contributories by striking out the applicant's name therefrom, on which application the court has jurisdiction also to rectify the register of members. No contributory is entitled to an order on such application except subject to the conditions stated in the proviso to Article 42 (v).

Note: This article reproduces Mr Spencer Bower's Article 38, the only modification being to the statutory references.

Article 42   *Affirmative defences to proceedings for rescission*

It is competent to the defendant in any proceedings for rescission, with or without a denial of all or any of the plaintiff's allegations, to set up any one or more of the affirmative defences available to a defendant in any action of contract, and also any one or more of the affirmative defences special to proceedings for the rescission of contracts and transactions on the ground of misrepresentation: provided that the burden is on such defendant of alleging, with particulars reasonably adequate to the requirements of the individual case, and, having so alleged, of proving, all such matters as are necessary to establish the defence or defences so set up. Such special defences are as follow:

(i) The affirmative defence set forth in Article 29 (i) subject to the proviso therein stated;

(ii) In the case of any contract of purchase and sale,—that the plaintiff had expressly agreed to accept compensation in lieu of rescission in respect of any misrepresentation as to the property the subject of such contract: provided that such agreement constitutes no defence in any case where it is proved that the misrepresentation was fraudulent, or that it was a misrepresentation of the entire substance and nature of the property, or where the compensation does not admit of pecuniary assessment;

(iii) That by express agreement, or impliedly by acts and conduct, or by inaction, the plaintiff, with full and precise knowledge of all the material facts, had elected to affirm, and adhere to, the contract or transaction sought to be rescinded;

(iv) That it has become physically, commercially, or legally impossible to restore the parties to the position in which they were before the contract or transaction was entered into, or impossible to do so without injustice to innocent third parties who have acquired rights thereunder for value, or without injustice to the defendant;

(v) Where the defendant is a company within the meaning of the Companies Act 1948, and the contract sought to be rescinded is a contract to become a member thereof—that the company is in liquidation, whether voluntary, compulsory, or under the supervision of the court: provided that it is competent to the plaintiff to displace such *prima facie* defence by proof that before the commencement of such liquidation he had not only given the company notice of his repudiation of the contract, but had effectively avoided the same by a binding agreement for that purpose with the company, or had commenced proceedings against the company for rescission thereof, or had agreed with the company to be bound by the result of a test action or proceeding against the company on the part of some other person for the like purpose, and based on the same misrepresentation; or that, before the commencement of the liquidation, the contract had been in fact determined by forfeiture of his shares, or otherwise, or that it was void *ab initio*, and not merely voidable, or had never been a concluded contract at all;

(vi) In the case of a claim for rescission for *innocent* misrepresentation the discretion of the court may be invoked to declare the contract subsisting;

(vii) To the extent (if any) that the court may allow reliance upon it, an agreement between the parties, the effect of which is to deprive the plaintiff of his claim to rescission, may be pleaded as a defence.

Notes: 1. This article corresponds with Mr Spencer Bower's Article 39, but there are some important modifications. In the first place, the defence (included by Mr Spencer Bower) of "taking with all faults" is now excluded as an absolute defence, and reincluded at the end of the list as No. (vii) as one available only so far as the court may allow, in accordance with s. 3 of the Misrepresentation Act 1967.

2. It is also to be noticed that in the case of a claim for innocent misrepresentation, the court now has a discretion, pursuant to s. 2 of the Misrepresentation Act 1967, to declare the contract susbsisting and to award damages in lieu of rescission, if of opinion that it would be equitable so to do. This seems to open the door to the possibility that delay *simpliciter* may ultimately be held available as a defence to claims for rescission for innocent misrepresentation, such delay being put forward in support of a plea for the exercise of the court's discretion (see para. 313 of the text, *post*).

Article 43 *Questions of law and fact*

In any proceedings for rescission, the following are questions of law: Ch. XIII para. 270

(i) Whether the alleged, or proved, representation is a representation in law, within the meaning of Articles 1–6;

(ii) Whether the alleged, or proved, representation is capable of the meaning assigned to it by either party;

(iii) Whether the alleged, or proved, representation is capable of being deemed material, within the meaning of Article 18;

(iv) Whether, in the proved or admitted circumstances of the case, it is, or is not, legally possible to restore the parties to their former position;

(v) Whether the contract or transaction is voidable, or void; and whether it was ever a concluded contract, or had been lawfully determined;

(vi) Generally, in the case of any of the necessary allegations on the part of the plaintiff, or of the defendant,—whether there is any evidence thereof, or whether, *prima facie* evidence of any such allegation having been adduced, there is any evidence to the contrary thereof.

Except as aforesaid, all disputed questions are questions of fact.

Note: This article reproduces *verbatim* Mr Spencer Bower's Article 40.

Article 44 *Parties to the proceedings*

Ch. XIII
paras. 271–
281

(1) The persons entitled to institute any of the proceedings in this Part mentioned, are the following:

(*a*) Any representee within the meaning of Article 23;

(*b*) Any person who, in virtue of the rules of common law or any statutory provision relating to parties to actions of contract in general, is entitled to stand in the place of such representee, in case of his death, disability, incapacity, or otherwise;

(*c*) Any person who, by assignment or devolution, has acquired property to which the contract or transaction relates, and who is accordingly deemed to have at the same time acquired such equities to avoid or rescind the same as his predecessor in title had: provided, nevertheless, that a bare right to rescind is not assignable.

Any person entitled to sue, or to make an application to the court, for any of the remedies in this Part mentioned, may also counter-claim or make a cross-application therefor. In the foregoing Articles of this Part, the expression "plaintiff" includes a person so counter-claiming, applying, or making such cross-application. Where such action, counter-claim, application, or cross-application is brought, set up, or made, not by the representee, but by some person in right of him or his estate, the said expression is intended to apply to such representee only.

(2) The persons against whom any of the proceedings in this Part mentioned may be instituted are the following:

(*a*) Any representor, within the meaning of Article 22;

(*b*) Any person who, in accordance with the rules of common law or any statutory provision relating to parties to actions of contract in general, is required to stand in the place of such representor, in case of his death, disability, incapacity, or otherwise;

(*c*) Any assignee of a chose in action from a representor who acquired the same under the contract or transaction sought to be rescinded;

(*d*) Any assignee of property in possession from a representor who acquired the same under the contract or transaction, if, but not unless, the property was assigned after the representee had avoided such contract or transaction, or if such assignee took the property otherwise than for value, or with notice of any circumstances rendering the contract or transaction voidable, or in bad faith.

The expression "defendant", in the foregoing Articles of this Part, includes a person resisting any such counter-claim, application, or cross-application as aforesaid. Where the proceeding is brought, not against the representor, but against a person defending in right of him or his estate, the said expression is intended to apply to such representor only.

Note: This article reproduces *verbatim* Mr Spencer Bower's Article 41.

PART IX: RELIEF BY WAY OF DEFENCE TO AN ACTION OR PROCEEDING TO ENFORCE THE CONTRACT OR TRANSACTION

Article 45 *When misrepresentation may be set up as a defence*

Where any action, or other proceeding of whatsoever kind, is insti- Ch. XV tuted by one of the parties to a contract for the purpose of enforcing the same, whether specifically or otherwise directly, or for the recovery of damages for the breach thereof, or for an injunction, or otherwise for the purpose of indirectly enforcing the same, it is competent to the party against whom the proceeding is instituted to set up as a defence or answer thereto, with or without any cross-claim for rescission, that he was induced to enter into the contract by the misrepresentation of the party seeking to enforce it.

Note: This article reproduces *verbatim* Article 42 in Mr Spencer Bower's Code.

Article 46   *What must be proved to establish the defence or to defeat it*

The defence or answer is established by allegation and proof of all matters required to establish a right to rescission, as stated in Article 37, and of the further fact that, on discovering the truth, the representee repudiated the contract, and has never since recognised it as valid, or taken any benefit thereunder: provided that, where the action is for specific performance, the representee is required to establish only such of the said matters as may be sufficient, in all the circumstances of the particular case, to satisfy the court, in its discretion, that the special remedy is not appropriate, and to refuse accordingly to grant it, either absolutely, or except upon terms.   It is competent to the representor to resist such defence or answer by allegation of any of the matters stated in Article 42, and, on proof of the same, the defence or answer is invalidated.   Article 43 (as to questions of law and fact), and Article 44 (as to parties), in respect of proceedings for rescission, apply *mutatis mutandis* to the defences and answers in this Part referred to, with the following variation in the case of Article 44, *viz.* that, where the defence or answer is set up against an action or other proceeding instituted by an indorsee or transferee of a negotiable instrument, it is sufficient in the first instance to allege and prove that such negotiable instrument was obtained from the person setting up the defence or answer by the misrepresentation of some person through whom the plaintiff claims, whereupon the burden of proof is shifted, and it is incumbent on the plaintiff, in order to invalidate the defence or answer, to establish affirmatively that he acquired title to the instrument for value, without notice, and in good faith.

Note: This Article reproduces *verbatim* Article 43 of Mr Spencer Bower's Code.

The Commentary

CHAPTER I

Introductory

Scope of the treatise

1   This Commentary, and the Code which it is designed to justify and illustrate, are concerned with misrepresentation only so far as it conduces to acts, or abstention from action, on the part of the person to whom it is addressed,[1] whereby his position is altered, and only so far as it confers upon that person a right to civil remedy and relief.   So much, indeed, appears from the title itself, which indicates substantially which of the topics, more or less connected with statements made by one person to another, are excluded from, and which on the other hand fall within, the scope of this treatise.

Excluded topics

2   A representation, and a promise, are mutually exclusive of, and antithetical to, one another.   In the case of a statement which has formed the inducement to another's alteration of position, there is no question of any contractual engagement having been violated: whereas in the case of a contract, or a term or condition of a contract, or a warranty, the sole question is, breach or no breach, and the application of the terms "false" or "true", to such breach or observations, is inapposite.[2]

There may be cases, of course, in which the same matter is made first the subject of a representation, and then, separately, the subject of a

---

[1] But the anomalous cases of persons suffering damage from misrepresentations addressed to *others*, or to the public at large, though perhaps strictly outside the scope of this work, are nevertheless given some consideration in Chapters XVII and XIX, *post*.

[2] The distinction between a representation and a warranty is adverted to in paras. 20 *et seq.*, *post*.   In Chapter II, para. 22, an allusion is made to the assimilation to one another of "veritas" and "constantia" in Roman jurisprudence, and Veracity and Good Faith in modern systems of ethics.

promise, being incorporated into the ultimate contract as a condition or warranty. These will be noticed in the next chapter.[1]

Misrepresentation and mistake

3   "Misrepresentation" as treated in this work also excludes "mistake", which imports a self-induced misapprehension, either on the part of each of the parties to a transaction, or on the part of one of them, but in neither case resulting from any misrepresentation. Every misrepresentation does, no doubt, induce "mistake" in the literal sense of the word: but a "mistake" so induced brings the case within the legal definition of "misrepresentation", and not within the quite different and distinct juridical conception of "mistake".

Misrepresentation and non-disclosure

4   *Ex vi termini*, "misrepresentation" has no concern with cases of non-disclosure, *as such*, that is, with cases of the *mere* violation of a duty, imposed by the policy of the law on parties standing in certain relations to one another, to observe the utmost good faith by (in particular) disclosure of all known material facts.[2]   But, where non-disclosure takes the form of such concealment, omission, or suppression of facts as renders false a representation already made, and which the revelation of these facts is required to make true, it amounts in law to misrepresentation and falls accordingly within the limits of this work.[3]

Estoppel: criminal responsibility

5   There are several legal consequences of misrepresentation besides liability to civil proceedings at the suit of the person to whom the misrepresentation was made. Estoppel by representation is one[4]; criminal responsibility, where the misrepresentation is a false pretence, is another.

---

[1] See para. 24, in the next chapter.

[2] The relations referred to are those of insurance, suretyship, trustee and *cestui que trust*, guardian and ward, solicitor and client, medical practitioner and patient, spiritual adviser and penitent, principal and agent, promoter and company, and various others, where *uberrima fides*, or at least *bona fides*, in the matter of disclosure is peremptorily required, as a duty quite independent of the duty not to mislead by suppression or concealment of facts qualifying those which have already been the subject of a representation. All such cases belong to a separate chapter of law (Non-Disclosure).

[3] In Chapter IV it will be seen how the tendency to include cases of non-disclosure in the class of implied misrepresentation has grown.

[4] Estoppel is a rule of evidence, not a cause of action. The same facts which establish the estoppel may of course be ground for an action of misrepresentation; but this is only an accident. Estoppel, as such, merely removes a barrier in the way of, or interposes an obstacle to, a cause of action, or ground of defence, which would otherwise fail or succeed in the respective cases. See, in this regard, the authors' *Law of Estoppel by Representation* (2nd Edn.) at pp. 6–11.

But, since neither of these constitutes or confers, as such, a *cause of action*, neither of them comes within the scope of *actionable* misrepresentation.

Topics included

6 On the other hand, the subject as treated in this work comprehends innocent as well as fraudulent, and implied as well as express, representation.[1]

In the earlier editions of this work the subject of negligent misrepresentation received no significant treatment, for it was not until the decision of the House of Lords in *Hedley Byrne & Co., Ltd.* v. *Heller & Partners, Ltd.*[2] that it was laid down that at least in some circumstances a misrepresentation negligently, but not fraudulently, made might give rise to an action in damages. In this edition an attempt is made to deal comprehensively with claims based on negligent misrepresentations.[3]

Those causes of action, or grounds of defence, in respect of misrepresentation which are established by statute are the subject of special treatment apart from, and in addition to, those which are established by the common law.[4]

Misrepresentations addressed to persons other than the plaintiff

7 There are certain causes of action, and affirmative defences, founded on misrepresentation and deceit addressed to and practised upon persons other than the party setting up the claim or plea, but resulting in injury, either to that party, or to the public at large. These are not, in the strictest sense, cases of misrepresentation; but have sufficient elements in common with it to justify inclusion in this Commentary, and separate treatment in the proper place.[5]

Principles summarised

8 The propositions underlying the law of actionable misrepresentations may be stated, broadly and summarily, as follow: I—Any false representation made by one person to another, with the object and result of inducing him to enter into a contract or transaction with the representor, or otherwise to alter his position to his prejudice, may be the subject of a claim for damages at the instance of the latter person.[6] Alternatively

---

[1] As to innocent and fraudulent misrepresentation, see Chapter V. As to express and implied representation, see Chapter III.

[2] [1963] 2 All E.R. 575; [1964] A.C. 465, H.L.

[3] In Chapter XIX.

[4] See Chapter XVI.

[5] See Chapters XVII and XIX.

[6] For the special defences available in an action for innocent misrepresentation, see Chapter XII.

it may be made the subject of civil proceedings for the purpose of avoiding the contract or transaction; if the representation is fraudulent the right to rescission will be absolute, but if it is innocent, rescission will be in the discretion of the court. II—Where the representation was negligently made, an action in damages will lie in cases in which the principle in *Hedley Byrne & Co., Ltd.* v. *Heller & Partners, Ltd.*[1] is applicable.

Leading conceptions

9 It will be apparent from the above summary statement that the following are the leading conceptions, and constituent elements, in the jurisprudence of the subject, which it is accordingly proposed to analyse and discuss in the following (which is conceived to be their logical) order:

(i) Representation[2]:
(ii) Misrepresentation—Falsity[3]:
(iii) Fraudulent and Innocent Misrepresentation[4]:
(iv) Inducement and Materiality[5]:
(v) Alteration of Position and Damage[6]:

After which it will be possible and necessary to consider:

(vi) The Parties to the Misrepresentation[7]:
(vii) Relief and Remedies[8]:
(viii) Statutory Proceedings[9]:
(ix) The kinds of misrepresentation referred to in para. 7, *supra*[10]:
(x) Pleadings and Practice.[11]

A chapter will be inserted to deal with the effect of the Misrepresentation Act 1967[12]; and a concluding chapter[13] on the law as to misrepresentations negligently made will deal with the position which has developed since the decision of the House of Lords in *Hedley Byrne & Co., Ltd.* v. *Heller & Partners, Ltd.*[14] Appendices contain a short historical

---

[1] [1963] 2 All E.R. 575; [1964] A.C. 465, H.L.
[2] See Chapters II and III.
[3] See Chapter IV.
[4] See Chapter V.
[5] See Chapter VI.
[6] See Chapter VII.
[7] See Chapters VIII and IX.
[8] See Chapter X (When Misrepresentation is Actionable), XI and XII (Action for Damages), XIII and XIV (Proceedings for Rescission), and XV (Misrepresentation as a Defence).
[9] See Chapter XVI.
[10] See Chapter XVII and XIX.
[11] See Chapter XVIII.
[12] Chapter XII.
[13] Chapter XIX.
[14] [1963] 2 All E.R. 575; [1964] A.C. 465, H.L.

account of the development of the action in deceit; a reprint of the Jenkins Report on the law of misrepresentation furnished to the Lord Chancellor in 1962; and a reprint of the principal statutory provisions referred to in this work, including a reprint of the whole of the Misrepresentation Act 1967.

CHAPTER II

Representation

Introductory

10 Nothing can be a *misrepresentation* which was never, in law, a representation at all. It is essential, therefore, in the first place, to form a clear conception of what it is that the law pronounces to be a representation. Not all statements are representations. Some clearly contain all the necessary elements: others, as clearly, fall short of the requirements of the law; but there is a third class—an important one—of statements *ancipitis sensus*, the designation of which is doubtful and difficult, and which, according to the aspect in which it is proper to regard them, may be placed in the one category or the other, such as expressions of intention, opinion, and the like.[1]

The constituent elements of representation

11 The definition of "representation" is set out in Article 1 of the Code, which is as follows:

> "A representation is a statement made by, or on behalf of, one person (hereinafter called 'the representor') to, or with the intention that it shall come to the notice of, another person (hereinafter called 'the representee'), which relates, by way of affirmation, denial, description, or otherwise, to a matter of fact. A 'matter of fact' means either an existing fact or thing, or a past event."

The above definition specifies two distinguishing marks of a "representation": (i) communication between two (or more) persons, and (ii) relation to a fact, present or past.

Communication between two persons

12 It takes two to make a representation, just as it takes two to make a contract. That which is still either *in scrinio* or *in gremio* is innocuous.

---

[1] See paras. 14 *et seq.*, *post*.

A statement made in the course of a soliloquy which is overheard, or contained in a diary, or private document, which is overlooked, or surreptitiously read, is not made to the person so overhearing, overlooking, or reading, or to any one, and is, therefore, no representation.[1] "Lying at large" will not do. There must be two parties, a "representor" and a "representee",[2] who must be distinct from one another, in substance as well as in name and form.[3] A man can no more lie to himself, except in the highly metaphorical sense of the philosopher or the theologian, then he can defame himself,[4] or assault himself.

Relation to matter of fact

13 It is commonly said that, in order to constitute a representation a statement must be one of "existing fact". In so far as this form of expression serves to distinguish and exclude from the definition all statements *de futuro*, and to include in it all such as do not in any way relate to the future, it is intelligible enough; but, except in this broad sense, it is not adequate, or strictly accurate; for, in the first place a past event is not an existing fact, and yet a statement as to a past event is undoubtedly a representation; and, secondly, a statement wholly denying a fact is not literally a statement of fact, and yet it is certainly a representation. It must always be remembered, moreover, that it requires very little ingenuity to put a statement as to a past event in a form which will render it a statement of an existing condition of things, and even less to transform a negative into an affirmative statement. In any case, it is now well settled that any statement which purports to affirm, deny, describe, or which otherwise relates to, any existing fact, circumstance, or thing, or any

---

[1] The reader is referred to the cases cited in support of the corresponding text in the authors' *Law of Estoppel by Representation* (2nd Edn.) p. 28.

[2] The term "representee" is novel; it is, moreover, unscientifically framed, and uncouth, but not more so than the terms (long since in established use), "mortgagee", "vendee", "pledgee", "bailee", "obligee", "addressee", "referee", "sendee" (used by the Court of Queen's Bench in relation to a telegram at p. 714 of *Playford* v. *United Kingdom Telegraph Co., Ltd.* (1869), L.R. 4 Q.B. 706), "optionee" (*per* RICH J. in *Sun Newspapers, Ltd.* v. *Federal Commissioner of Taxation* (1938), 61 C.L.R. 337, 342); "advisee" (used by Lord DIPLOCK in *Mutual Life and Citizens' Assurance Co., Ltd.* v. *Evatt*, [1971] A.C. 793, P.C.) and "promisee"; and the enormous convenience of such a term in avoiding reduplication of language, and involution of sentences, will be appreciated by any one who has had occasion, in a book, essay, judgment, or opinion, to deal in any detail with the principles of misrepresentation. This, and the respectability and antiquity of the family of abbreviated words with which it has associated itself, must be the excuse for its introduction.

[3] See *Re Ambrose Lake Tin and Copper Mining Co.* (1880), 14 Ch.D. 390, C.A., where, as BRETT L.J. at pp. 396–397 observes, the people claiming to be deceived were practically the same as those who were alleged to have practised the deceit, and the action was an absurdity and "a farce".

[4] This aspect of defamation is dealt with by Mr Spencer Bower in his *Law of Actionable Defamation*, Appendix IV.

past event, amounts in law to a representation. So far, all is plain. The difficulties arise when the definition is applied to the expressions of mental states and other matters which form the subject of the remainder of this chapter.

Statements of intention, or otherwise relating to the future

14   Article 2 of the Code is framed as follows:

"A statement of the representor's, or of a third person's, intention, readiness, or capacity to do or abstain from doing anything, or of his expectation as to a matter *in futuro*, is a representation of the then existence of such intention, readiness, capacity, or expectation; but any statement as to a matter *in futuro* which was intended or expressed by the parties to constitute, or which can be construed only as constituting, a promise, is not a representation."

This proposition involves the consideration of (1) statements of the representor's own intention, (2) statements which can be regarded only as promises on the part of the representor, (3) statements of a third person's intention, and (4) other statements *de futuro*.

Statements of the representor's own intention

15   In early times it was frequently said that statements by a man as to his own intention, or generally as to his own mental state, are not statements of fact, and therefore not representations.[1] It is now recognised, however, that, in this unqualified form, the proposition is quite incorrect. "The state of a man's mind", according to BOWEN L.J.,

"is as much a fact as the state of his digestion. It is true that it is very difficult to prove what the state of a man's mind at a particular time is, but, if it can be substantiated, it is as much fact as anything else. A misstatement of the state of a man's mind is a misrepresentation of fact".[2]

And, in a later case, the same high authority expresses himself to the same effect:

"A man may tell a lie about the state of his own mind, just as much as he can tell a lie about the state of the weather, or the state of his own digestion",

though "the inquiry", as he again observes, may be "a difficult and complicated one".[3]

---

1 See for instance *per* Lord ELLENBOROUGH C.J. in *Vernon* v. *Keys* (1810), 12 East 632; *per* Lord CRANWORTH L.C. in *Jorden* v. *Money* (1854), 5 H.L.Cas. 185 at pp. 214–216; *per* COZENS-HARDY J. in *Re Fickus, Farina* v. *Fickus*, [1900] 1 Ch. 331, at p. 331, and *per* Lord ATKINSON, albeit *obiter*, and unsupported by anything in the other judgments, in *Cavalier* v. *Pope*, [1906] A.C. 428, H.L. at p. 432.

2 *Edgington* v. *Fitzmaurice* (1885), 29 Ch.D. 459, C.A. at p. 483.

3 *Angus* v. *Clifford*, [1891], 2 Ch. 449, C.A. at p. 470. *Cp.* WILLS J. at p. 360 of *R.* v. *Gordon* (1889), 23 Q.B.D. 354, Div.Ct.

16 The difficulty in proving the falsity of the fact stated, to which BOWEN L.J. alluded as set out in the preceding paragraph, does not make the statement any the less one of fact: nor does the difficulty (a much more serious one) of proving inducement, which, as will be seen hereafter, is an essential ingredient in any cause of action or defence founded on misrepresentation. Nobody doubts the futility of establishing that a statement was representation, if it is impossible to show that the representation was false: but the representee is in an equally hopeless position if, after having surmounted this obstacle, he cannot prove that he was induced by the representation, in the only sense in which it was or could have been a false representation, to act as he did to his injury.

The mere fact, moreover, that the intention was not fulfilled is in itself no proof of its non-existence at the date of the representation,[1] though it may perhaps, in certain cases, tend, with other circumstances, to raise such an inference[2]; but what the representee is generally found, in the last resort, to complain of, is the *non-execution* of the intention, which is tantamount to an acknowledgment that what induced him to alter his position was his belief that the intention would ripen into accomplishment, in other words his reliance upon the statement as a promise, and not as a representation. His belief that the representor had a then present intention to act according to his statement would, in the ordinary run of cases, have had no effect on his mind, unless he had also believed that performance would follow.

17 Some cases may here be noticed, in which courts have shown some inclination to interpret as statements of fact expressions capable of being regarded alternatively as promises. The following statements have been held or assumed to constitute representations: statements, implied from the act of ordering goods, of a then present intention of paying for them[3];

---

[1] *Hemingway* v. *Hamilton* (1838), 4 M. & W. 115; *Benham* v. *United Guarantee and Life Assurance Co.* (1852), 7 Exch. 744 (*per* POLLOCK C.B. at pp. 752, 753); *Jorden* v. *Money* (*ubi sup.*); *Bold* v. *Hutchinson* (1855), 5 De G.M. & G. 558 (*per* Lord CRANWORTH L.C. at p. 565); *Beattie* v. *Lord Ebury* (1872), 7 Ch.App. 777 (*per* MELLISH L.J. delivering the judgment of the Lords Justices, at p. 804). A subsequent change of purpose, whether the purpose was announced to another or not, does not even argue inconstancy or inconsistency, according to Cicero ("*nemo doctus unquam mutationem consilii inconstantiam dixit esse*", *Epist. ad Att.* xvi, 7); much less does it prove insincerity in the announcement of it. Benedict's "when I said I would die a bachelor, I did not think I should live till I were married" was an avowal of an original purpose, the abandonment of which could have harmed nobody.

[2] *Clydesdale Bank* v. *J. and G. Paton*, [1896] A.C. 381, H.L., *per* Lord HALSBURY L.C. at pp. 386–388, and Lord HERSCHELL at p. 395.

[3] *Earl of Bristol* v. *Wilsmore* (1823), 1 B. & C. 514; *Load* v. *Green* (1846), 15 M. & W. 216, Exch. Ch.; *White* v. *Garden* (1851), 10 C.B. 919; *Clough* v. *London and North Western Rail. Co.* (1871), L.R. 7 Exch. 26, Exch. Ch.; *Re Shackleton, Ex parte Whittaker* (1875), 10 Ch. App. 446

statements that the representor was prepared to lend money, or hand over
moneys[1]; statements as to the objects to which subscriptions to an issue
of shares or debentures of a company were intended to be applied[2]; a
statement of the use which the representor intended to make of demised
premises[3]; a statement that the representor had power to stop a sale of
certain goods under an execution, and would stop it[4]; a statement that
the representor was bound not to build on certain land[5]; a statement by
a vendor of his intention to complete a road on the land for vehicles and
(impliedly) for the use and enjoyment of the purchaser[6]; a statement
that a company intended to commence operations with a certain number
of steamships of a certain type[7]; a statement that a company was minded
to take a third of a certain insurance risk[8]; and statements that the applicant for, or the holder of, a policy of life insurance would, in certain
events, become entitled to a policy, or to a free policy, or to the status
and rights of a validly assured person.[9]   The above illustrations and

---

(per MELLISH L.J. at pp. 449, 450: "I think that Shackleton, when he went for the goods, must
be taken to have made an implied representation that he intended to pay for them, and if it were
clearly made out that *at that time* he did not intend to pay for them, I should consider that a case
of fraudulent misrepresentation was shown"); *Re Eastgate, Ex parte Ward*, [1905] 1 K.B. 465
(per BIGHAM J. at pp. 466, 467).

[1] *Barwick* v. *English Joint Stock Bank* (1867), L.R. 2 Exch. 259, Exch. Ch. (*per cur.* at pp. 264,
265); *Ramshire* v. *Bolton* (1869), L.R. 8 Eq. 294; *Blake* v. *Albion Life Assurance Society* (1878),
4 C.P.D. 94; *Babcock* v. *Lawson* (1880), 5 Q.B.D. 284, C.A.

[2] *Re Deposit and General Life Assurance Co., Ex parte Ayre* (1858), 27 L.J. Ch. 579; *Edgington* v.
Fitzmaurice (1885), 29 Ch.D. 459, C.A. (*per* COTTON L.J. at pp. 479, 480, and BOWEN L.J.
at pp. 482, 483); *Aaron's Reefs, Ltd.* v. *Twiss*, [1896] A.C. 273, H.L. (*per* Lord HALSBURY L.C.
at pp. 283–285, and Lord WATSON at p. 286).

[3] *Feret* v. *Hill* (1854), 15 C.B. 207, where, however, on other grounds the party setting up
the representation failed.

[4] *Cooper* v. *Joel* (1859), 1 De G.F. & J. 240 (Lord CAMPBELL L.C.).

[5] *Piggott* v. *Stratton* (1859), 1 De G.F. & J. 33.

[6] *Dendy* v. *Cary* (1863), 9 Jur. N.S. 845.

[7] *Hallows* v. *Fernie* (1868), 3 Ch.App. 467.

[8] *Traill* v. *Baring* (1864), 4 De G.J. & Sm. 318.

[9] *Levy* v. *Scottish Employers' Insurance Co.* (1901), 17 T.L.R. 229, Div. Ct.; *Kettlewell* v.
Refuge Assurance Co., Ltd., [1908] 1 K.B. 545, C.A. (*per* Lord ALVERSTONE C.J. at p. 550 and
GORELL BARNES P. at p. 551). This decision was affirmed by the House of Lords *sub nom.*,
Refuge Assurance Co., Ltd. v. *Kettlewell*, [1909] A.C. 243. On this occasion the tribunal of ulti-
mate resort contented itself with discharging the function of silent registration: "Lord
LOREBURN L.C.", we are told on p. 245, "without giving any reasons, moved that the appeal
be dismissed. The EARL OF HALSBURY, and Lords ASHBOURNE, MACNAGHTEN, and JAMES OF
HEREFORD silently concurred". *Cf. Hilo Manufacturing Co., Ltd.* v. *Williamson* (1912), 28
T.L.R. 164, C.A. *Curtis* v. *Bottomley* (1911), *Times*, 1st August, C.A., may be regarded as an
illustration of this species of representation: for the defendant's fraud was there distinctly
put by both MOULTON L.J. and BUCKLEY L.J. as a misrepresentation, or as a false profession
of a disposition, intention, and capacity to help the deceased to recover the losses sustained by
him in supporting the defendant's financial schemes and projects.

others[1] amply justify the view entertained by BOWEN L.J., as above stated.[2]

Criminal misrepresentation

18 In previous editions of this work[3] it was suggested at this point that a parallel might be perceived between the civil decisions on representations of intention, and corresponding criminal cases.[4] The relevance of the cases there cited was diminished, if indeed the decisions were not positively overruled, by the later decision of the Court of Criminal Appeal in *R. v. Dent*.[5] There it was laid down that a statement of intention about future conduct, whether or not a statement of existing fact, cannot amount to a false pretence in criminal law. This decision has now in turn been abrogated by statute,[6] and the law since 1968 has been that a deception as to the present intention of the representee or of any other person will support a conviction. In view of this statutory proposition which now governs criminal liability, no further attempt will be made in this work to draw any useful parallel between the decisions on representations as to intention in civil and criminal cases.

Statements which are promises only

19 Contrasted with, and distinguishable (though often with difficulty) from, the class of case which we have been considering, is the type of statement which is shown (by evidence or argument) to have been intended by the representor, and accepted by the representee, as a promise, if anything, and as a promise *only*, or which, whatever the parties meant and intended at the time, can only be construed as such on any fair principle of interpretation. In all such cases, the words amount either to a

---

[1] Other instances cited in earlier editions are: Colt v. *Woollaston* (1723), 2 P.Wms. 154; *Biddle and Loyd* v. *Levy* (1815), 1 Stark 20; *Beaumont* v. *Dukes* (1822), Jac. 422; *Benham* v. *United Guarantee and Life Assurance Co.* (1852), 7 Exch. 744; *Evans* v. *Edmonds* (1853), 13 C.B. 777.

[2] See para. 15, *ante*. The now celebrated dictum of BOWEN L.J. was cited again, and adopted with approval, in the Court of Appeal in *Brown* v. *Raphael*, [1958] Ch. 636 *per* Lord EVERSHED M.R. at p. 642.

[3] E.g. 2nd Edn., para. 18.

[4] The cases cited in previous editions included: *R.* v. *Hazelton* (1874), L.R. 2 C.C.R. 134; *R.* v. *Cooper* (1877), 2 Q.B.D. 510; *R.* v. *Carpenter* (1911), 22 Cox C.C. 618, at p. 624; *R.* v. *Giles* (1865), 34 L.J. M.C. 50; *R.* v. *Gordon* (1889), 23 Q.B.D. 354; *R.* v. *Jones*, [1898] 1 Q.B. 119; *R.* v. *Bancroft* (1909), 26 T.L.R. 10. To these may be added one reported since the second edition of this work—*R.* v. *Lord Kylsant*, [1932] 1 K.B. 442, C.C.A. *Cf.* in New Zealand, *Root* v. *Badley*, [1960] N.Z.L.R. 756, at p. 758.

[5] [1955] 2 All E.R. 806; [1955] 2 Q.B. 590, C.C.A. In *Australia, cf. Greene* v. *R.* (1949), 79 C.L.R. 353 (H. Ct. of Aus.).

[6] Theft Act 1968, s. 15. A parallel provision, not exactly to the same effect, may be found in the *New Zealand* Crimes Act 1961, s. 245.

promise, or to nothing at all which entails any legal liability. If a promise is made out, then, as in any other case of contract, if it is legally binding upon the promisor the only questions are whether it has been performed or broken, and, in the latter event, whether there is any obstacle by statute or at common law to its enforcement. To such issues the question of the promisor's intention, or statement of intention, at the time of making the promise, is just as irrelevant as (conversely) the question of fulfilment or non-fulfilment of a declared intention is to an issue of misrepresentation of such intention.

20   There is a clear psychological distinction between a statement of a present intention to act in a certain manner, and an undertaking or engagement so to act. A representation means, as the etymology of the word imports, a presentment over again—a reproduction, repetition, or reflection, in words or equivalent signs, of a fact or thing which has already occurred, or already exists, *in rerum natura*. A promise, on the other hand, obviously does not represent anything. It is not a portrait, or transcript, of any fact or thing. A promise, or proposal, or offer, puts forward ("promittere", "proponere", "proferre", "offerre") something *sur le tapis*, or *in medium*, which was not there before, for consideration or acceptance. It deals with a *faciendum*, not a *factum*. In either case, there must be a correspondence between word and action, if the representation is to be true, or the promise is to be kept. But the duty of the representor is "to suit the word to the action"; of the promisor, to "suit the action to the word".

21   In the province of ethics, indeed, and in the earlier stages of our own and other systems of jurisprudence, where ethical and legal principles were scarcely distinguishable, the responsibility attaching to a false declaration of intention is considered much the same as that attaching to a breach of a promise. In the view of moralists, and primitive jurisprudence, veracity and good faith occupy practically the same ground, or, at least, "thin partitions do their realms divide". Truth and Justice are treated as conterminous, in such phrases as the "true and just in all my dealings" of the Church Catechism, in Cicero's definition of "justitia", "fides", and "veritas",[1] and in several passages of the Digest.[2] A modern writer on ethics experiences a difficulty in distinguishing between the characteristic qualities of the two duties. He says:

---

[1] "*Fundamentum justitiae est fides, id est dictorum conventorumque constantia et veritas*" De Off. I.9.
[2] The concept of misrepresentation in Roman Law was the subject of an essay by Mr Spencer Bower, printed as Appendix C to the 2nd edition, but omitted in this.

"We fulfil the obligations of Veracity and Good Faith alike by effecting a correspondence between words and facts—in the one case by making fact correspond with statement, and in the other by making statement correspond with fact".[1]

Representation distinguished from warranty

22   The important difference between the legal consequences and incidents of misrepresentation, and those of breach of contract or warranty, which flow from the above distinction in principle would seem to be obvious, but for the fact that the courts have found it necessary from time to time, since at least the year 1778, to insist and enlarge upon this theme, and to point out that neither falsity, nor fraud, nor inducement, nor materiality, all of which are vital elements in any proceedings founded on misrepresentation, has the slightest relevance to any issue in an action for breach of warranty or contract.[2]   He who promises or warrants, undertakes for exact and literal performance of that which he promises or warrants: but he who makes a statement, inducing another to contract or otherwise alter his position, undertakes only for the absence of any untruth which misleads, that is, for the absence of any *substantial* untruth of sufficient materiality to be capable of inducing, and which does in fact induce.   All these matters are made of absolutely no importance by the parties themselves in the case of a contract or warranty, the very object of which is to make it impossible for either of them to raise any such question thereafter.[3]   Consequently not only is it the law, as will be seen immediately, that he who sues on a promise, as if it were a

---

[1] Sidgwick's *Methods of Ethics*, p. 279.

[2] See *Pawson* v. *Watson* (1778), 2 Cowp. 785, *per* Lord MANSFIELD C.J. at pp. 788–790.   Some *dicta* of Lord DENNING M.R. in *Dick Bentley Productions, Ltd.* v. *Harold Smith (Motors), Ltd.*, [1965] 2 All E.R. 65, C.A. to the contrary must be noticed.   At p. 67 he said:

". . . it seems to me that if a representation is made in the course of dealings for a contract for the very purpose of inducing the other party to act on it, and it actually induces him to act on it by entering into the contract, there is *prima facie* ground for inferring that the representation was intended as a warranty.   Suffice it that the representation was intended to be acted on and was in fact acted on.   But the maker of the representation can rebut this inference if he can show that it really was an innocent misrepresentation, in that he was in fact innocent of fault in making it, and that it would not be reasonable in the circumstances for him to be bound by it."

But it is here respectfully suggested that this reasoning finds no support in authority, and that the true *ratio decidendi* of that case may be found in more orthodox reasoning on the facts proved before the trial judge.   The case is not reported in the official reports.

[3] See *Thomson* v. *Weems* (1884), 9 App. Cas. 671, H.L., *per* Lord BLACKBURN at pp. 683, 684, and Lord WATSON at p. 689, as applied to life insurance; s. 33 (3), as contrasted with s. 20 (4), of the Marine Insurance Act, 1906 (6 Edw. 7, c. 41), as regards marine insurance; *Dawsons, Ltd.* v. *Bonnin*, [1922] 2 A.C. 413, H.L., in relation to fire insurance.   *Cf.* note 2, p. 131, *post*, where the above, and other insurance cases are cited on the point under discussion.

representation, must fail; but it is equally true that he who sues on a representation, as if it were a promise or warranty, cannot succeed either.[1]

23 The distinction between a representation and a warranty may be of crucial importance.[2] As Lord MOULTON said in his famous judgment in *Heilbut, Symons & Co.* v. *Buckleton*[3]:

> "It is, my Lords, of the greatest importance, in my opinion, that this House should maintain in its full integrity the principle that a person is not liable in damages for an innocent misrepresentation, no matter in what way or under what form the attack is made."[4]

And in a more recent judgment, in which the authorities are to be found very conveniently collected, DENNING L.J.[5] has said:

> "The crucial question is: Was it a binding promise or only an innocent misrepresentation? The technical distinction between a 'condition' and a 'warranty' is quite immaterial in this case, because it is far too late for the buyer to reject the car. He can, at best, only claim damages. The material distinction here is between a statement which is a term of the contract and a statement which is only an innocent misrepresentation. The distinction is best expressed by the ruling of HOLT C.J., 'Was it intended as a warranty or not?', using the word 'warranty' there in its ordinary English meaning: because it gives the exact shade of meaning that is required. It is something to which a man must be taken to bind himself."

Representation repeated as a promise

24 Though a representation is to be regarded as something entirely different from a promise, its substance may be repeated (as has already been stated in the introductory chapter) in the form of a promise. The

---

[1] On this latter ground the plaintiff was non-suited by Lord ELLENBOROUGH C.J. in *Thompson* v. *Bond* (1807), 1 Camp. 4, and *Read* v. *Hutchinson* (1813), 3 Camp. 352. In *Heilbut, Symons & Co.* v. *Buckleton*, [1913] A.C. 30, H.L. (see para. 23 *infra*.) the plaintiff alleged misrepresentation, and alternatively warranty; the jury negatived misrepresentation, and the House of Lords, reversing the courts below, held that there was no evidence of a warranty.

[2] Less so now than before the passing of the Misrepresentation Act 1967. Since that Act it has become possible in proper cases to seek damages for innocent misrepresentation, whereas previously this remedy was not available. It is to be remembered, however, that the measure of damages may be different, and at least to this extent the distinction remains one of importance.

[3] *Heilbut, Symons & Co.* v. *Buckleton*, [1913] A.C. 30, H.L. at p. 51. Lord HOLT C.J.'s test in *Crosse* v. *Gardner* (1688), Carth. 90, 90 E.R. 656 and in *Medina* v. *Stoughton* (1700), 1 Salk. 210, 91 E.R. 188 is "an affirmation at the time of the sale is a warranty, provided it appear on evidence to be so intended"—see *per* BULLER J. in *Pasley* v. *Freeman* (1789), 3 Term Rep. 51, 57, 100 E.R. 450, 453.

[4] But see now s. 2 of the Misrepresentation Act 1967: *post*, Chapter XII.

[5] *Oscar Chess Ltd.* v. *Williams*, [1957] 1 All E.R. 325, C.A. at p. 328. *Cf. Routledge* v. *McKay*, [1954] 1 All E.R. 855, C.A. *per* Sir R. EVERSHED M.R. at p. 859. In *Dick Bentley Productions, Ltd.* v. *Harold Smith (Motors) Ltd.*, [1965] 2 All E.R. 65, C.A., Lord DENNING M.R. in an extempore judgment took matters rather further, holding that the test might be the "innocence of fault" of the representor; the judgment was not reported in the official Reports.

result then is that the same matter has become first the subject-matter of a representation, then separately, that of a promise, by virtue of its having been adverted to by the representor on two quite separate occasions.

It has been supposed, and indeed was clearly the law between 1936 and 1967, that where this happens the earlier representation merges in the subsequent contract of the parties; and that, if shown to be a misrepresentation, it will not in such a case give rise to a right in the representee to rescind for misrepresentation, he being left only with such rights as may be available to him under his contract.[1]   This state of affairs has been altered by s. 1 of the Misrepresentation Act 1967.[2]

Statement of a third person's intention

25   If a statement by a person of his own intention may be a representation, so *a fortiori* may a statement by him of a third person's intention, which obviously lends itself more readily to this construction, and less naturally assumes the aspect of a contractual obligation.[3]   If I say something as to my own proposals or purposes, or as to what I am contemplating for the future, it is far more plausible to construe my language in a promissory sense than when I am asserting the intentions of another person, over whose actions I may have, and may be understood by the representee to have, no control whatever.   In that event, if I am to be supposed to assume any liability at all as a promisor, it can only be a secondary, not a primary, liability; and neither law nor mercantile usage is prone to fix a man with the responsibilities of a surety, unless his declarations are plain and clear to this effect, and (so far as regards the law) unless they comply with certain ceremonial conditions.[4]

26   Accordingly a statement as to a third person's intention or purpose has nearly always been held to be a statement of fact, *viz.* the fact of the present existence of that intention or purpose in the mind of the third person, and therefore a representation,[5] and not a guarantee, even where

---

[1] See *Pennsylvania Shipping Co.* v. *Compagnie Nationale de Navigation,* [1936] 2 All E.R. 1167 (BRANSON J.); *Leaf* v. *International Galleries,* [1950] 1 All E.R. 693; [1950] 2 K.B. 86, C.A.

[2] See Appendix C.

[3] So WILLS J. appears to have thought in *R.* v. *Gordon* (1889), 23 Q.B.D. 354. See his judgment at p. 360.

[4] Required by the Statute of Frauds, s. 4.

[5] *Hamar* v. *Alexander* (1806), 2 Bos. & P. N.R. 241, with which compare the other "credit" cases cited in note 1 on p. 209, *post*; *Viscount Clermont* v. *Tasburgh* (1819), 1 Jac. & W. 112 (statement that certain interested parties were agreeable to a proposed exchange of lands); *Barley* v. *Walford* (1846), 9 Q.B. 197 (a statement that the persons entitled to a certain registered design intended to proceed against the plaintiff for infringement); *Beck* v. *Kantorowicz* (1857), 3 Kay. & J. 230 (statement that the vendors of certain property would not consent to

such words as "I durst be bound to pay for him", or "we do not hesitate to guarantee", accompany the assertion.[1]

Other expressions "de futuro".   (Expectation, hope, etc.)

27   When the alleged representor uses merely the general and indefinite language of hope and sanguine anticipation of the future, his expressions are not construed as statements of fact in any sense, or to any extent[2]; but if he expresses his own, or another's expectation of the happening of a definite event at a definite future date, or within definable limits, his statement is a representation, in the same way, and to the same extent, as any statement of his own, or another's, intention; that is to say, he is understood in law to assert the fact that the expectation is at the

---

take less than a certain sum); *Re Hull and London Life Assurance Co., Gibson's Case, Kemp's Case, Hudson's Case* (1858), 2 De G. & J. 275 (a statement that two persons would execute a deed of settlement); *Towle* v. *National Guardian Assurance Co.* (1861), 30 L.J. Ch. 900 (statement that the employer of a certain person would check his accounts weekly: *per* KNIGHT-BRUCE L.J. at pp. 910, 911, and TURNER L.J. at pp. 914, 915); *Hallows* v. *Fernie* (1868), 3 Ch.App. 467 (where, amongst others, there was a statement in the prospectus that two named persons had consented to become directors, which Lord CHELMSFORD L.C. agreeing with PAGE-WOOD V.-C., treated as a statement of fact, but one which was not proved to have been false by the mere fact that after allotment these persons retired from the directorate). Some of the expressions in the judgments of Sir James MANSFIELD C.J. and of Lord ELLENBOROUGH C.J. in *Vernon* v. *Keys* (1810), 12 East, 632, Exch. Ch. (see p. 637), and in that of PLUMER M.R. in *Beaumont* v. *Dukes* (1822), Jac. 422; 23 E.R. 110 (at p. 424: "the subject of the representation was not a future project contemplated by a third person. If that had been the case . . . it would only be holding out a hope as to the future conduct of a third person not under his control; and it would be the fault of the bidder, if he relied on so loose and vague a report"), which, if literally understood, and taken apart from the subject-matter and context, would seem to imply that the statement of a third person's intention can never be actionable, are clearly at variance with the later authorities, and cannot be relied upon as law.

[1] In *Hamar* v. *Alexander* (1806), 2 Bos. & P. N.R. 241 the defendant had assured the plaintiff orally that "Christopher Leo is a good man, and may be trusted to any amount and I durst be bound to pay for him", and the plaintiff relied upon the latter expression as amounting to a guarantee, which of course would have been unenforceable as such by reason of the Statute of Frauds. Lord MANSFIELD C.J. however, assuming it to be capable of being so construed, held that (the plaintiff not having relied on it at the time as a guarantee) it must be regarded as a mere phrase intended to add force and weight to the previous lie direct (*cp.* such popular forms of expressions as "I will go bail that, etc.," or "I warrant that, etc.," or "I will be bound that, etc.''); but Lord MANSFIELD might very well have gone much further, since obviously the words were not capable of being interpreted as a promise to assume a secondary liability, then and there, but only as a statement by the defendant that, if called upon, which he never was, he would not object to bind himself by such an engagement. In *Gerhard* v. *Bates* (1853), 2 E. & B. 476, where the directors of the company had stated in the prospectus that they "did not hesitate to guarantee a minimum dividend of 33 per cent.," COLERIDGE J. observed, at p. 482, "surely a man when he says 'I do not hesitate to guarantee' means to say, 'I represent.'"

[2] *Beaumont* v. *Dukes* (1822), Jac. 422, *per* PLUMER M.R. at p. 424 ("holding out a hope", "loose and vague report"); *Bellairs* v. *Tucker* (1884), 13 Q.B.D. 562, Div. Ct., where the expressions used in the prospectus as to anticipated profits of the company were held not to be representations, *per* DENMAN J. at pp. 572–574; *Bentley & Co., Ltd.* v. *Black* (1893), 9 T.L.R. 580, C.A. (*per* Lord ESHER M.R.).

time entertained by himself, or by the third person, but not the fact that the expectation is to be realised.[1]

28   There are instances of statements as to the future which, even though clearly expressed in the future tense, may import an existing state of things.   Thus, a statement, by one who had insured another against being drawn for the militia under the provisions of a certain Act of Parliament, that "all billetings under the Act would cease" on a certain day, was treated as a representation, being presumably considered a statement of fact as to the existing procedure established by a statute then in force[2]; statements that a certain mine would yield so much, and that a dividend of 33 per cent. was so confidently anticipated that the directors "did not hesitate to guarantee it", were held to be statements of the present state and capacity of the mine, and of the present flourishing condition of the company, respectively[3]; and, in a third case, JESSEL M.R. was of opinion that a statement to the effect that certain costs *would be paid* out of a sum described as applicable for that purpose was not a statement as to the future, but as to the present, *viz.* that these costs *were payable* out of the designated fund.[4] In *New Zealand*, the vendor of land on the distant side of a harbour represented to a prospective purchaser that a contract for a ferry boat *had been entered into*, and that the boat *would be plying within three months*.   It was argued that the latter representation could not be used as the foundation, or even as part of the foundation, of an action in fraud.   But the New Zealand Court of Appeal held that the two statements should be read together as constituting a representation of fact.[5]

---

[1] *Willes* v. *Glover* (1804), 1 Bos. & P. N.R. 14 (statement of a shipper that he "expects the captain to sail tomorrow", which, said Sir James MANSFIELD C.J. at p. 16, "imports that he who writes knows the ship to be in such a condition as to give a just expectation of her sailing at that time"); *Re Metropolitan Coal Consumers' Association, Karberg's case*, [1892] 3 Ch. 1, C.A., where LINDLEY L.J. says, at p. 11, that a statement of expectation is a statement of fact that the party does actually expect as stated; *A. W. Gamage, Ltd.* v. *Charlesworth*, 1910 S.C. 257 (statement of pecuniary "expectations").   On the other hand, in *Barber* v. *Fletcher* (1779), 1 Doug. K.B. 305, where the statement was—"the ship is expected to leave the coast of Africa in November or December", Lord MANSFIELD C.J. described it as "*only* an expectation", meaning presumably that it was not a representation; but he was probably also referring to the vagueness and generality of the words used, which did not impute the expectation to any person in particular.

[2] *Duffell* v. *Wilson* (1808), 1 Camp. 401.

[3] *Gerhard* v. *Bates* (1853), 2 E. & B. 476.

[4] *Mathias* v. *Yetts* (1882), 46 L.T. 497, C.A., at p. 503. *Cf.* the cases cited in note 6 to para. 40, *post*.

[5] *Smith* v. *MacKenzie* (1881), 1 N.Z.L.R. 1, C.A. *Cf.* in the same jurisdiction, *Klingenstein* v. *Walters* (1885), 3 N.Z.L.R. 18, C.A.

Statements of opinion, belief, or information

29   When it is pronounced (as it frequently is even now, and *ex cathedra*) that statements of opinion are not statements of fact, the proposition, in its absolute and literal sense, is quite incorrect and misleading. "It is often fallaciously assumed", observes BOWEN L.J., "that the statement of an opinion cannot involve the statement of a fact".[1]   As in the case of statements of intention, a statement of opinion, belief, information, or other condition of mind, whether of the representor or of a third person, *does* involve at least one statement of fact, *viz.* that the representor or other person did entertain the alleged opinion or belief, or was possessed of the alleged information, at the date of the representation.[2]   It is *not*, however, a statement of the subject-matter as a fact, if the statement *purports to be* no more than a statement of opinion, belief, or information.   On the other hand, if a man chooses to express in the form of a statement of fact that which he merely believes as opinion, or as information, the statement is for all purposes a representation.   And again, if what he states is fact, his statement is not the less a representation because he cloaks it in the language of opinion, belief, or information, or in language susceptible of being so construed by an ingenious metaphysician or philologist.   The above rules of law, which are embodied in Article 3 of the Code, may now be considered separately in relation to the four species of statement to which they apply, *viz*: (1) statements of a man's own opinion, etc; (2) statements of a third person's opinion, etc.; (3) statements of opinion, etc., as fact; and (4) statements of fact as opinion, etc.

Representations as to the representor's own opinion, belief, or information

30   The principles enunciated above with reference to statements of a man's own intention[3] apply equally, *mutatis mutandis*, to statements of a man's own opinion, belief, or information.   In this, as in that, class of statement, the mere subsequent occurrence of events which are in disaccord with, in the sense of failing to realize or justify, the declared intention or opinion or other mental condition or attitude, does not falsify

---

[1] *Smith* v. *Land and House Property Corporation* (1884), 28 Ch.D. 7 C.A. at p. 15.   This dictum of BOWEN L.J. was cited and adopted by the Court of Appeal in *Brown* v. *Raphael*, [1958] Ch. 636 *per* Lord EVERSHED M.R. at p. 642; *cf. per* ROMER L.J. at p. 649.   In *New Zealand*, see *Root* v. *Badley*, [1960] N.Z.L.R. 756 (McGREGOR J.).

[2] See the observations of BOWEN L.J. which are of quite general application, and refer to any state of a man's mind, at p. 483 of *Edgington* v. *Fitzmaurice* (1885), 29 Ch. D. 459, C.A., and at p. 470 of *Angus* v. *Clifford*, [1891] 2 Ch. 449, C.A.   These are cited in the text to notes 3 and 2 to para. 15, *ante*.

[3] See paras. 15, 16, *ante*.

the statement; but disproof of the existence of the declared condition of the mind does falsify the statement, because this was the fact, and the only fact, which it impliedly asserted.   Thus an expression of opinion on the part of the directors of a railway company that there was no probability of a rival line being constructed, was treated by the House of Lords as a statement of the fact that they entertained such an opinion, but of no other fact, and the mere circumstance that a rival line was afterwards constructed, did not make the statement a misrepresentation, because there had never been a representation at all as to what would actually happen in the future; whilst, on the other hand, there was no proof of the falsity of the statement in the only respect in which it was a representation, that is to say, no proof that the directors did not believe what they said they believed.[1]   Similarly, the Privy Council considered a bank's valuation of a security to be a statement of the fact that the bank had *bona fide* formed the opinion which it had expressed as to its value, and not a statement of the correctness of such valuation: and, the only fact as to which the statement was in law a representation not having been negatived, there was held to have been no misrepresentation.[2]   On the other hand, where a solicitor had both formed an opinion of his own, and had taken another opinion, to the effect that a certain person's interest under a will was absolute, and had concealed both the one and the other from the party to whom he was under a duty of disclosure, thereby leaving him under the impression that his interest was contingent only, he was held liable for such concealment[3]; *a fortiori*, if he had stated as his own, or as the third person's, opinion, that the party's interest under the will was contingent only, he would have been liable for misrepresentation, because he would have falsely stated, not that the interest was contingent, but that he, or the third person, believed it to be.   In reference to contracts of marine insurance, the rule is neatly and succinctly stated in s. 20 (5) of the Marine Insurance Act 1906.[4]   Similarly, as regards information, a book purporting to be a "journal of bores", and handed as such to railway contractors, was held to involve a representation that it was a faithful

---

[1] *New Brunswick and Canada Railway and Land Co.* v. *Conybeare* (1862), 9 H.L. Cas. 711.

[2] *Melbourne Banking Corporation* v. *Brougham* (1882), 7 App. Cas. 307, P.C., at pp. 319, 320. Cp. *Bisset* v. *Wilkinson*, [1927] A.C. 177, P.C., a similar decision by the Judicial Committee as to a statement that certain land, the subject of the sale, had "a carrying capacity" of so many sheep.

[3] *Luddy's Trustee* v. *Peard* (1886), 33 Ch.D. 500.

[4] "A representation as to a matter of . . . belief is true, if it be made in good faith."

record of information supplied by those who had actually put down the
bores, and no more.[1]

31   The obstacles which beset the path of the representee in cases of
statements of intention, and which have already been adverted to, are not
present to the same extent in the case of statements of opinion.   There is
no doubt the same difficulty of proving another man's state of mind, to
which BOWEN L.J. more than once alludes,[2] but the further difficulty of
credibly asserting, when it comes to the question of inducement, that the
representee relied upon the personality of the representor is not present
here to the same extent as it is there.[3]   It is quite natural, particularly
where the opinion or belief is as to a matter involving scientific, mercantile, artistic, or professional knowledge, experience, or skill, or where
the information is said to be that of a person expert in collecting it, to
trust to the name and reputation of the individual; indeed, a layman can
trust to nothing else.   In most cases of this description, the representee
can truthfully affirm that he relied not so much upon the correctness of the
opinion, as to which there was no representation, but on the fact that such
and such a well-known authority in the branch of knowledge or business
in question *did actually hold the opinion expressed*, as to which there was a
representation.   *Cuique in sua arte credendum.*   "I was told", he might
fairly say, "that Mr X., an eminent patent lawyer, man of science, literary
or art critic, valuer, accountant, financier, stockbroker, or expert in trade,
whose name was well-known to me, was of such and such an opinion as to
the merits and value of an invention, picture, drama, book, business,
enterprise, security, or estate.   I should not have entered into the contract or transaction which I did enter into, if I had known that this particular individual did not in fact entertain the alleged opinion.   To tell me
that I am damaged only by the opinion turning out to be wrong, is not to
the purpose; because, if I had known that the opinion did not carry with
it the authority of the name on which alone, in my ignorance, I did or
could rely, I should not have touched the concern at all, or have been
drawn into a position in which the incorrectness of the opinion could
have had any effect upon my interest."   In the case, however, of statements of intention, it is far more unlikely that the representee trusted to

---

[1] *Boyd and Forrest* v. *Glasgow and South Western Rail. Co.*, 1911 S.C. 33, at p. 73.   This decision was overruled, *sub nom. Glasgow and South Western Rail. Co.* v. *Boyd and Forrest*, No. 1,
[1913] A.C. 404, H.L., but not on any ground affecting the subject of the present discussion.
(The litigation subsequently proceeded (1914 S.C. 472 and [1915] A.C. 526 on the ground
of innocent misrepresentation only.)

[2] See notes 2 and 3 on p. 38, *ante*.

[3] See para. 16, *ante*.

the personality of the representor, rather than to the promissory aspect of his statement, in proportion as the individual skill and eminence of the specialist is a rarer quality than common honesty. The above observations of course do not apply to a case where the person professing the opinion is, and is known to be, as inexpert as the representee. There both parties are on equal terms, and no importance is attached to the fact that either of them has such and such views, or to the views themselves.[1] So, where the representor, in stating his opinion, gives the facts on which he bases it, again the parties are on the same footing.[2]

Statement of a third person's opinion, belief, or information, as such

32 The rules applying to statements as to the representor's own opinion, belief, or information, are equally applicable to statements of a third person's similar condition of mind. Thus, a statement as to the belief of the owners of a vessel with respect to her safety, in a marine insurance case,[3] or a description of the effect of counsel's opinion,[4] or a statement of a medical diagnosis,[5] or a version in a prospectus of a report or valuation of an expert,[6] are all statements of fact to the extent above indicated, but not further or otherwise.

Representations as to matters of information or opinion

33 If a man, having a genuine opinion on any matter,[7] chooses, nevertheless, to state it as a fact, or, having information, expresses the subject of it, in Beatrice's phrase, "better than reportingly", he must take all the risks, and abide by all the consequences, attending a representation pure and simple. And where a man states as a positive fact that which is merely

---

[1] "In a case where the facts are equally well known to both parties, what one of them says to the other is frequently nothing but an expression of opinion. The statement of such an opinion is in a sense a statement of fact, about the condition of the man's own mind, but only of an irrelevant fact, for it is of no consequence what the opinion is": Bowen L.J. at p. 15 of *Smith* v. *Land and House Property Corporation* (1884), 28 Ch.D. 7, C.A. In *New Zealand*, *Root* v. *Badley*, [1960] N.Z.L.R. 756, at p. 758.

[2] *Legge* v. *Croker* (1811), 1 Ball & B. 506, *per* Lord Manners, L.C. (Ir.), at pp. 515, 516.

[3] *Rickards* v. *Murdock* (1830), 10 B. & C. 527 (a case of non-disclosure of a letter stating the belief, or implying the doubt, in question: but, obviously, a decision that the existence of the belief, or doubt, was a *fact* which ought to have been disclosed is a decision that any statement concerning it would have been a statement of fact, and therefore a representation).

[4] *Leonard* v. *Leonard* (1812), 2 Ball & B. 171; *Luddy's Trustee* v. *Peard* (1886), 33 Ch.D. 500; and *Re Roberts, Roberts* v. *Roberts*, [1905] 1 Ch. 704, C.A.

[5] *Stewart* v. *Great Western Rail. Co.* (1865), 2 De G.J. & Sm. 319.

[6] *Re Mount Morgan (West) Gold Mine, Ltd., Ex parte West* (1887), 56 L.T. 622, *per* Kay J. at p. 624.

[7] The cases where a man states as fact that about which he has *no* opinion at all are dealt with in Chapter V, para. 97, *post*. These are even more obviously statements of fact.

the outcome of an imperfect recollection, he makes a representation that the fact is so: and, if it is not so, it is no defence that he has forgotten something.[1]   Again, a statement as to the value of property, or the nature of its tenure, may be made in such a form, and in such circumstances, as to warrant its being construed as an assertion, and not as a mere inference or estimate.[2]   So, where the defendant, in a case of representation as to a person's credit, took upon himself to assert, in answer to a question expressly directed to the very point, that what he had previously communicated was the fact, and that he was speaking of his own knowledge, and not from mere hearsay, Lord KENYON C.J. was of opinion that the statement should be treated as a representation for all purposes and in every sense.[3] Similarly, where an insurance company, having been misinformed as to the facts relating to the birth and parentage of a certain person, passed on this information to the government when purchasing an annuity, but *as fact*, and not as information,[4] and when a professional "water-finder" stated, apparently as a fact, but certainly not in the form of an opinion, that water could be found at a certain depth,[5] the same construction was adopted. And in *New Zealand* where, again in answer to a question directed to the very point, a surgeon informed a patient that there was no substantial danger in a contemplated surgical procedure, taking insufficient care in so stating, the trial judge held this to be a representation of fact, and was upheld by the New Zealand Court of Appeal.[6]

So in one of the most recent decisions a report by a banker as to the credit of a customer in the words "respectably constituted company considered good for its ordinary business engagements" was dealt with by the Lords almost without argument to the contrary as a representation of fact as to creditworthiness,[7] and more recently still CAIRNS J. without hesitation held the words "he is a good account and a good payer" to be a representation of fact which in the circumstances would support an action for damages for negligence.[8]

---

[1] *Brownlie* v. *Campbell* (1880), 5 App. Cas. 925, H.L., at pp. 936, 945, and 953.

[2] As in *Haygarth* v. *Wearing* (1871), L.R. 12 Eq. 320 (*per* WICKENS V.-C. at pp. 327, 328); *Hart* v. *Swaine* (1877), 7 Ch.D. 42 (*per* FRY J. at p. 46).

[3] *Haycraft* v. *Creasy* (1801), 2 East 92, at pp. 102–104.   *Aliter* in *New Zealand* in *National Bank of New Zealand* v. *Macintosh* (1881), 3 N.Z.L.R. 217, C.A., where an alleged misrepresentation as to creditworthiness was held an expression of opinion only.   The decision appears to have rested on the exact words of the representation as proved.

[4] *A.-G.* v. *Ray* (1874), 9 Ch.App. 397, *per* JAMES L.J. at p. 405.

[5] *Pritty* v. *Child* (1902), 71 L.J. K.B. 512, Div. Ct., *per* Lord ALVERSTONE C.J. at p. 513, and DARLING J. at p. 514.

[6] *Smith* v. *Auckland Hospital Board*, [1965] N.Z.L.R. 191, C.A.

[7] *Hedley Byrne & Co., Ltd.* v. *Heller & Partners, Ltd.*, [1964] A.C. 465, H.L., at p. 468.

[8] *W. B. Anderson & Sons Ltd.*, v. *Rhodes (Liverpool), Ltd.*, [1967] 2 All E.R. 850, at p. 856.

On the other hand, if the representor does no more than express his opinion, or state as information received such information as he has, he makes no representation except to the extent already stated. So, where a seller of a cargo of coffee stated to the purchaser that *it had been invoiced to him* as of first shipping quality, it was held that he did not thereby represent that it was of that quality, and Lord ABINGER C.B. refused to ask the jury the question whether he had or had not so represented[1]; and where a prospectus had adopted what had been stated to the directors by the vendor, but professed to give the information *only as information*, there was held to have been no representation that the information given corresponded with the actual facts, and therefore no misrepresentation merely because it did not.[2]

It will be seen from the examples given in the text how important it may be in any given case to ascertain and prove satisfactorily the exact actual text of any express representation of this kind, wherever it is possible to do so.[3]

Matters of fact represented as opinion or as information

34 Just as something strictly to be regarded as a matter of *opinion* or of *information* can be made the subject of a representation of fact if the representor chooses so to express his representation, so a representation as to a matter strictly to be regarded as a matter of *fact* does not lose its quality because of being stated either in the form of an opinion, or in a form which is susceptible of being so construed. In the former type of case, the proposition is of course self-evident: a statement that at such a time and place something gross and palpable to the senses, and not merely "probal to thinking", happened, is a statement of fact, however much it may be entrenched behind, or prefaced by, expressions of opinion. Examples, however, of the latter kind of case, where the construction is not so obvious, are not wanting. A statement, for instance, as to the credit, character, or reputation of another, relates to a matter of fact, however plausibly it may be suggested afterwards, when responsibility is sought to be affixed to the statement, that the language used must be taken to have pointed to mere belief, judgment, or inference, though not expressly

---

[1] *Moens* v. *Heyworth* (1842), 10 M. & W. 147.

[2] *Craig* v. *Phillips* (1876), 3 Ch.D. 722. Contrast *Re Reese River Silver Mining Co., Smith's Case* (1867), 2 Ch.App. 604, *per* Lord CAIRNS L.J. at p. 615.

[3] This cautionary rule is exemplified in a number of the cases cited in footnotes to this paragraph; reference may particularly be made to *Moens* v. *Heyworth* (1842), 10 M. & W. 147; *Re Reese River Silver Mining Co., Smith's Case* (1867), 2 Ch.App. 604, and (in *New Zealand*) *National Bank of New Zealand* v. *Macintosh* (1881), 3 N.Z.L.R. 217, C.A.; *Smith* v. *Auckland Hospital Board*, [1965] N.Z.L.R. 191, C.A.

assuming that guise; or that "whether" the person in question "deserved credit, depended on the opinion of many, for credit consists in the good opinion of many".[1] It is strange that GROSE J. who is responsible for the above observation, did not realise, as Lord KENYON C.J. did in directing a jury eleven years later,[2] that though an opinion is an opinion, the existence of that opinion, still more the existence of many opinions, the joint effect of which is to confer, or deny, reputation or "credit", is a fact. As has been well said in a case where a statement as to the character and habits of an assured was vainly argued to be one of opinion merely,

> "there are facts innumerable which can only be ascertained by the test of opinion, but they are not the less facts in a legal, whatever they may be in a metaphysical, sense".[3]

In another case[4] the defendant, having stated, as his opinion and valuation, that a life policy was worth so much, though he knew that in fact the person whose life was insured was at the point of death, was not heard to say that the statement was one of opinion, or (to put it as the Court of Appeal did in the case next cited), the expression of opinion here was considered to be of such a character as to involve the assertion of facts, known to him, which justified the opinion. So, where the statement was that a certain person was "a most desirable tenant", it was vainly argued (inter alia) in the Court of Appeal that this was a mere expression of opinion,[5] BOWEN L.J. observing that

> "if the facts are not equally known to both sides, then a statement of opinion by one who knows the facts best involves very often a statement of a material fact, for he impliedly states that he knows facts which justify his opinion"[6];

---

[1] *Pasley* v. *Freeman* (1789), 3 Term Rep. 51, the famous leading case on representation as to a third person's credit. The dissentient judgment of GROSE J. which contains the dictum cited, is at pp. 52–56. *Cf.* other "credit" cases cited in notes 7 and 8 to para. 33, *supra*, and in note 1 on p. 209, *post*. Of course where the representation as to credit takes the form of an inference from facts stated or documents referred to, the inference is pure opinion, and the basis of that opinion is pure fact, as in the case of the banker's report in *Parsons* v. *Barclay & Co. Ltd.* (1910), 103 L.T. 196, C.A. And see the cases cited in notes 7 and 8 to para. 33, *supra*.

[2] In *Foulkes* v. *Sellway* (1800), 3 Esp. 236.

[3] *Per* Lord WATSON, at p. 690 of *Thomson* v. *Weems* (1884), 9 App. Cas. 671, H.L.

[4] *Jones* v. *Keene* (1841), 2 Mood & R. 348.

[5] *Smith* v. *Land and House Property Corporation* (1884), 28 Ch.D. 7, C.A.

[6] *Smith* v. *Land and House Property Corporation* (1884), 28 Ch.D. 7, C.A., at p. 15. The dictum of BOWEN L.J. was recalled, and followed, by the Court of Appeal of our own day in *Brown* v. *Raphael*, [1958] Ch. 636, Lord EVERSHED M.R. adding (at p. 642) the following gloss upon it—"I observe two things; first, that the Lord Justice is not laying down a universal rule. His language is: 'A statement of opinion . . . involves *very often* a statement of a material fact.' Second, he observes that for that possibility to arise one party must know the facts better than the other. Observe that he is not saying that one party must know *all* the facts; it suffices for the application of the principle if it appears that between the two parties one is better equipped with information or the means of information than the other." This case is discussed in more detail in para. 35 of the text. In *New Zealand*, *Root* v. *Badley*, [1960] N.Z.L.R. 756, at p. 758.

to which FRY L.J. adds, in the course of his judgment:

> "it seems to me that the vendors, by describing [the person in question] as such, stated in substance that they knew no fact which showed him not to be a desirable tenant".[1]

35 A more modern application of these principles is to be found in *Brown v. Raphael*.[2] One of the lots to be offered at an auction was the reversion of a trust fund after the death of the life tenant. The particulars contained the words:

> "The Trustee is the Public Trustee. Estate duty will be payable on the death of the annuitant, who is believed to have no aggregable estate."

The plaintiff was the successful bidder at the auction. He ascertained before completion of the purchase that the life tenant was possessed of estate which ultimately increased the duty which would become payable on her death out of the fund. It was proved that the advertisement had been drafted by a solicitor's clerk who had included the words "no aggregable estate" without comprehension of their meaning, or of their importance to a would-be purchaser. In these circumstances the representation in the advertisement was held to be a representation of fact, Lord EVERSHED M.R. observing:

> "It is very often said, and truly said, that each case must depend on its own facts; and I apprehend that the real question for the court is to say, on the basis of the facts and the context of this case, whether this is an instance in which the representation that the vendor has reasonable grounds for his belief ought to be imported. Counsel argued that to hold, as the Judge did, affirmatively on that point was to lay down the principle that wherever it is stated that one party entertains a particular belief, then it must follow that there is a representation that he has grounds reasonably supporting his belief. But I lay down no such general proposition. The question here is whether in this case, and in the context of these particulars concerning lot 11, such a representation of reasonable grounds to support the belief ought to emerge; and, as the judge held, I think that in this case the answer is in the affirmative."

In support of this conclusion Lord EVERSHED listed the following points: (1) the actual value of the property would be substantially decreased by the fact that the life tenant had aggregable estate; (2) a well known and respectable firm of solicitors was named in the particulars as acting in the estate; this could fairly lead to the inference that the vendor had been competently advised as to the position; (3) the vendor was in a position

---

[1] *Smith v. Land and House Property Corporation (supra)* at p. 17. *Cf. Ferguson v. Wilson* 1904, 6 F. (Ct. of Sess.) 779, at p. 783 (statement of profits of a business held not to be a mere speculative forecast or estimate).

[2] [1958] Ch. 636, C.A.

to know, or at least to find out from her the true position; (4) a person contemplating bidding at auction, on the other hand, would find it very difficult, and probably impossible, to ascertain the facts for himself.

Misrepresentations of law

36 Article 4 of the Code is thus stated[1]:

(1) A statement of fact accompanied by, or involving, an inference or proposition of law, where such inference or proposition is not distinct or severable from the statement of fact, is wholly and for all purposes a representation.

(2) A statement of a rule, principle, or proposition of the general law, or a statement of the legal effect of facts which form the subject of another and a distinct and severable statement, or which are within the common knowledge of the parties, is a representation in the same sense and to the same extent as in Article 3 mentioned with reference to statements of opinion, but not further or otherwise.

Distinction between questions of law and questions of fact

37 The distinction between questions of law and questions of fact has so thoroughly permeated the fabric of our jurisprudence by reason of the separation of the judicial functions assigned to judge and jury respectively,[2] that there has always been a tendency to draw a sharp contrast between law and fact in reference to every single topic to which those terms can be applied. It must have been owing to this tendency that judges and jurists have so persistently marked off statements of law from statements of fact, in dealing with the principles of misrepresentation, as if they were two separate and self-contained species of statements, standing to one another in a relation of opposition and mutual exclusion. And it is by way of concession to this inveterate habit that statements of law are here dealt with separately. Yet, if the matter be considered closely, it is plain that, for purposes of the doctrine of misrepresentation, a statement of law is only a subspecies of the species just discussed, and that any such statement constitutes a representation in precisely the same sense, to the same extent, and for the same reasons, as any other statement of

---

1 See p. 4, *ante*.

2 The procedural foundation for the distinction is rapidly disappearing with the decline of the jury as a tribunal in civil proceedings. *Cessante ratione, cessat lex ipsa*; there being less reason for the distinction when the judge is judge of fact as well as of law, the pendulum may swing in the opposite direction, and the courts may now begin to incline to treat as questions of fact, for the purpose of the law of misrepresentation, what would have been regarded by a former generation more strictly as questions of law.

opinion.[1] That is to say, it is not a statement of the fact of the law being thus, or thus, and is not falsified by the law turning out to be other than as stated[2]: but it is an implied statement by the representor of the fact that the opinion expressed as to the law is actually entertained by him, or by the person to whom it is attributed, and to that extent is a representation. He who expresses his views on law to another is in exactly the same position as one who expresses his views on any other question of science, art, or business, and the inquiry as to whether, and to what extent, his statement is a representation is governed by the same considerations.

38 Further, the same difficulties in the way of the representee's assertion that he relied upon the personality of the individual to whom the opinion is attributed, rather than upon the correctness of this opinion,[3] are encountered when the opinion is one of law, as when it relates to any other matter, but to a much greater degree, if, as Bowen L.J. thought,

> "where there is a representation made as to a mere matter of law, it is, in nineteen cases out of twenty, made by a person who does not know the law better than the person to whom it is made, and at whose risk it is taken and acted on".[4]

39 Nice questions, however, arise very frequently, as to whether the form of expression used makes the statement one of law wholly, or one of fact wholly, or involves several separate statements, some one or more being of pure fact, and the other or others an inference or inferences of pure law. The rules applicable to these several classes of case are stated and distinguished in Article 4 of the Code.[5] Two main types of statement are there indicated: (1) statements of fact, involving and inextricably intermingled with inferences of law, or statements of the existence of a particular document or thing which is alleged to confer a legal right or impose a legal liability; and (2) statements of abstract propositions of law, or of legal inferences from facts separately stated or within the common

---

[1] So regarded, its consequences may, however, be less than those which attend upon misrepresentations of a more obviously factual nature; for a misrepresentation of law, amounting to a misrepresentation of no more than the representor's opinion as to the law, can hardly give rise to an estoppel of any material benefit to the representee. See, for instance, *London County Territorial and Auxiliary Forces Association, Ltd.* v. *Nichols*, [1949] 1 K.B. 35, C.A. *per* Scott L.J. at p. 50; *Kai Nam* v. *Ma Kam Chan*, [1956] 1 All E.R. 783; [1956] A.C. 358. This topic is more fully treated in the authors' *Law of Estoppel by Representation* (2nd Edn.) pp. 36–40.

[2] Thus a statement that a certain right of way had been extinguished was not shewn to be a misrepresentation by the mere fact that the representor was afterwards convicted of a nuisance: *Legge* v. *Croker* (1811), 1 Ball & B. 506, *per* Lord Manners, L.C. (Ir.), at p. 515.

[3] See para. 31, *ante.*

[4] *West London Commercial Bank* v. *Kitson* (1884), 13 Q.B.D. 360, C.A., at p. 362.

[5] See para. 36, *ante.*

knowledge of the parties. The former are statements of fact, and wholly representations; the latter are statements of law, and not therefore representations, except in so far as they involve statements of the fact that the person alleged to entertain the legal opinion does actually entertain it. Of these in their order.

Statements of mixed and indivisible law and fact

40 These are the commoner type of so-called statements of law. And naturally so, because, as pointed out, and illustrated with a variety of common instances, by JESSEL M.R.,[1] it is extremely difficult to make any statement in a matter of business which does not involve some inference or proposition of law. Such statements, however, are not merely by this circumstance rendered statements of law, if law and fact are inseparably interwoven as the compound substructure of the statement, or if the statement is susceptible of being construed either as one of fact, or as one of law, and, owing to the representor's remissness or fraud in hiding his meaning under ambiguous or ambidextrous phraseology, it is impossible to say with certainty which is the proper construction, whereupon every intendment is made *contra proferentem*, and the statement is deemed one of fact. Thus, where an auctioneer on the sale of a public house by auction stated that it was a "free" house, and that there had been a recent decision of Lord ELLENBOROUGH C.J. that "tying" clauses in leases of such property were invalid—an admittedly incorrect statement—the auctioneer might have been regarded as having said, either that Lord ELLENBOROUGH had so ruled (which would be fact), or that the inference which he drew from a perusal of his judgment was that he so held (which would be law). The statement was treated as one of fact.[2] An attorney told the trustees of a marriage settlement that they could safely advance money to his client, who was, in fact, an infant. This statement could fairly be construed either as a statement of fact that his client was not an infant, or as a statement of law that such trustees could safely advance money to an infant. PLUMER V.-C. dealt with it as a statement of fact.[3] Similarly, a statement that the representee took no interest under a certain will, though his heir possibly might do so,[4] a statement as to the powers of companies under

---

[1] At pp. 702, 703 of *Eaglesfield* v. *Marquis of Londonderry* (1875), 4 Ch.D. 693, C.A. In *Australia*, see *per* STARKE J. in *Life Insurance Co. of Australia, Ltd.* v. *Phillips* (1925), 36 C.L.R. 60 (High Ct. of Aus.) at p. 87.

[2] *Jones* v. *Edney* (1812), 3 Camp. 285.

[3] *Cory* v. *Gertcken* (1816), 2 Madd. 40.

[4] *Reynell* v. *Sprye: Sprye* v. *Reynell* (1852), 1 De G.M. & G. 660. *Cf.* a similar statement in *Murray* v. *Palmer* (1805), 2 Sch. & Lef. 472, at p. 485.

private Acts of Parliament,[1] and (in *New Zealand*) a statement that War Regulations did not apply to certain premises so as to prevent the rent being raised[2] have all been regarded as statements of fact. The same has been held of a statement as to a title or interest to or in a particular estate by virtue of certain deeds and circumstances,[3] and statements (express or implied from conduct) as to the regularity and safety of, or absence of objection to, a particular expedition,[4] or voyage.[5] Again, statements by insurance companies as to the validity of their policies in certain events, or on compliance with certain conditions, though they might very well be deemed propositions of general insurance law, can also be, and they accordingly have been (wherever it was possible), construed as statements of the fact of the existing regulations or practice of the company.[6] And as to a misrepresentation by a respondent bank "that the plaintiffs' shares were still bound to the Bank, with the necessary inference . . . that the shares were already lost" their Lordships of the Judicial Committee observed that

> "it (did) not seem to admit of doubt that such a representation made as to the plaintiffs' private rights and depending upon transactions in bankruptcy . . . was a representation of fact",

---

[1] *West London Commercial Bank* v. *Kitson* (1884), 13 Q.B.D. 360, *per* Brett M.R. at p. 362, Bowen L.J. at p. 363 (who says that such a statement in no way differs from a statement "that I have a particular bound copy of Johnson's Dictionary"), and Fry L.J. at p. 363. In *Derry* v. *Peek* (1889), 14 App. Cas. 337, the H.L. did not differ from the C.A. in so far as the latter treated the statement in the prospectus regarding the statutory powers of the company as a statement of fact.

[2] *Oudaille* v. *Lawson*, [1922] N.Z.L.R. 259.

[3] *Cooper* v. *Phibbs* (1867), L.R. 2 H.L. 149. This was a case of "mistake", but the same principles apply to both classes of case, as regards the question of what is fact, and what law. Moreover, it appears from the judgment of Lord Cranworth L.C. at p. 164, that there was a misrepresentation too, though an innocent one. Lord Westbury, at p. 170, says that "a private right of ownership is a matter of fact; it may be the result also of matter of law". *Cp. Earl Beauchamp* v. *Winn* (1873), L.R. 6 H.L. 223 *per* Lord Chelmsford L.C. at p. 234.

[4] *Burrows* v. *Rhodes*, [1899] 1 Q.B. 816, Div. Ct.

[5] *Mitchell, Cotts & Co.* v. *Steel Brothers & Co., Ltd.*, [1916] 2 K.B. 610.

[6] *British Workman's and General Assurance Co., Ltd.* v. *Cunliffe* (1902), 18 T.L.R. 425, Div. Ct., *per* Lord Alverstone C.J. at p. 425, and Channell J. at p. 426, who appear to have so treated the statement; but the C.A., who affirmed the decision (1902), 18 T.L.R. 502, seem to have regarded it rather as a fraudulent representation of the general law, and on this ground alone can the decision be supported. It does appear from the judgments in the Court of Appeal, however, that the court regarded the case as a special one. See, also, *Hough* v. *Guardian Fire and Life Assurance Co.* (1902), 18 T.L.R. 273; *Evanson* v. *Crooks* (1912), 106 L.T. 264; *Hughes* v. *Liverpool Victoria Legal Friendly Society*, [1916] 2 K.B. 482, C.A.; *Byrne* v. *Rudd* (1920), 2 I.R. 12. Compare and contrast the cases cited in note 7 on p. 61, *post. Cf.* the representation of mixed law and fact made by defendant to plaintiff in *Siveyer* v. *Allison*, [1935] 2 K.B. 403, that he was entitled in law to a decree of nullity of his existing marriage, and was therefore free in law to marry.

notwithstanding that the legal position must have depended substantially on the position at law.[1]

In *Re Mahmoud and Ispahani*[2] the Court of Appeal had before it a claim by a vendor against a purchaser for damages for breach of contract to accept goods. The claim was resisted on the ground of the illegality of the contract, in that the necessary licence to deal in the goods had not been obtained. This defence was upheld by the court; but both BANKES L.J.[3] and SCRUTTON L.J.,[4] noting that the findings of fact of the arbitrator included one that the purchaser had fraudulently represented to the vendor that he had obtained a legally valid licence in due form, reserved the point (which did not arise on the pleadings) that the plaintiff might conceivably have succeeded on an action for fraud based upon such a misrepresentation, notwithstanding that the performance of the contract would have been in fact illegal.[5] In *New South Wales* a contractor who had done, without a permit having been obtained, work which a statute forbade in the absence of a permit, and whose claim for remuneration under his contract had been defeated by a plea of illegality, successfully recovered damages (though the amount recovered in damages was necessarily less) on a claim that the defendant had fraudulently misrepresented that the agreement could legally be entered into, in that he had in fact actually obtained a permit.[6]

Statements of inference of law from given or known facts

41 In contrast to the above is the class of case where the facts either (a) being separately stated or (b) being known to the parties, the representor cannot be thought to make any representation as to them, and his representation must be taken as no more than his opinion as to the legal incidents of those facts, and the proper legal inference to be drawn from them. In such cases, the matter asserted is only matter of opinion on law, and what has been said is no more than a representation of the fact that the person to whom the opinion is attributed actually holds it. It is generally

---

1 *MacKenzie* v. *Royal Bank of Canada*, [1934] A.C. 468, P.C. at pp. 475–476.

2 [1921] 2 K.B. 716, C.A. *Cf. per* GREAVES-LORD J. in *Siveyer* v. *Allison*, [1935] 2 K.B. 403, 406.

3 [1921] 2 K.B. 716, C.A., at p. 726.

4 At p. 730.

5 At p. 720.

6 *Hatcher* v. *White* (1953), 53 S.R.N.S.W. 285; see *per* STREET C.J. at pp. 288–289. The decision of the Full Court of New South Wales on appeal was a majority one; STREET C.J. and HERRON J. held for the plaintiff, OWEN J. dissenting in a deliberate and vigorous judgment in which he recalled and examined *Burrows* v. *Rhodes*, [1899] 1 Q.B. 816.

a very nice question as to which class the particular statement belongs[1]: but the line has to be drawn in accordance with the above principles, as laid down by Lord WESTBURY[2] and afterwards by JESSEL M.R.[3] Accordingly, the following have been held to be statements of law, and, as such, not statements of the correctness of the legal proposition put forward, or such as to render the representor answerable for it, if it turns out otherwise: an inference of the extinction of an ancient right of way, coupled with facts from which the representor drew the inference[4]; a statement by the secretary of a company, all the relevant facts and documents being known to both parties, that the company had, or would shortly have, in virtue of those facts and documents, power to issue debentures[5]; a statement by a company, assuming it to have been made (which was not proved), that it had power to overdraw, the facts and documents again being common to both parties[6]; and a statement on behalf of an insurance company that a policy on the life of the representee's mother, who had no insurable interest, would be a valid insurance.[7]

Fraudulent misstatements of law

42 It has been held, or recognised, however, in several of the authorities, that if the law is *fraudulently* misstated, the representor will be liable for misrepresentation[8]; which is only another way of saying that a state-

---

[1] Once again the importance of ascertaining and proving as satisfactorily as possible the precise text of the representation may be emphasised.

[2] In *Cooper* v. *Phibbs* (1867), L.R. 2 H.L. 149.

[3] In *Eaglesfield* v. *Marquis of Londonderry* (1876), 4 Ch.D. 693, C.A.

[4] *Legge* v. *Croker* (1811), 1 Ball & B. 506, at pp. 515, 516.

[5] *Rashdall* v. *Ford* (1866), L.R. 2 Eq. 750 (*per* WOOD V.-C. at p. 754.)

[6] *Beattie* v. *Lord Ebury* (1872), 7 Ch.App. 777 (*per* MELLISH L.J. at p. 800).

[7] *Harse* v. *Pearl Life Assurance Co.*, [1904] 1 K.B. 558, C.A. *Cp. Phillips* v. *Royal London Mutual Insurance Co.* (1911), 105 L.T. 136, Div. Ct.; *Howarth* v. *Pioneer Life Assurance Co. Ltd.* (1912), 107 L.T. 155, Div. Ct.; *Tofts* v. *Pearl Life Assurance Co. Ltd.*, [1915] 1 K.B. 189, C.A. In these cases, there were similar statements of abstract law (insurance law), unlike the statements in *Hough* v. *Guardian Fire and Life Assurance Co.* (1902), 18 T.L.R. 273, *Kettlewell* v. *Refuge Assurance Co., Ltd.*, [1908] 1 K.B. 545, C.A., and *Evanson* v. *Crooks* (1912), 106 L.T. 264.

[8] *Coulson* v. *Allison* (1860), 2 De G.F. & J. 521, where the representor having stated to his deceased wife's sister, with whom he contemplated marriage, that such marriage might be valid, well knowing that, according to then existing law, it could not possibly be so, and having by such representation of the law procured a settlement from her, the deed of settlement was cancelled (*per* Lord CAMPBELL L.C. at p. 525); *West London Commercial Bank* v. *Kitson* (1884), 13 Q.B.D. 360, C.A. (*per* BOWEN L.J. at pp. 362, 363: "I am not prepared to say, and I doubt whether, if a man wilfully misrepresented the law, he would be allowed in equity to retain any benefit he got by such misrepresentation"—a proposition worded with needless caution, for it cannot be supposed that, if a statement of law is a representation to the extent indicated for one purpose, it is not so for all, or that the application of the rule is confined to equity, or to proceedings for rescission); *Harse* v. *Pearl Life Assurance Co. ubi sup., per* COLLINS M.R. at p. 563, and ROMER L.J. at p. 566; *British Workman's and General Assurance Co., Ltd.* v. *Cunliffe* (1902), 18 T.L.R. 502, C.A.; *Tofts* v. *Pearl Life Assurance Co., Ltd., supra.* In *New Zealand, Oudaille* v. *Lawson* (1922), 41 N.Z.L.R. 259 (SIM J.). *Cf.* in *New South Wales, Hatcher* v. *White* (1953), 53 S.R.N.S.W. 285.

ment of law implies a representation of fact that the person professing to expound it believes it to be as stated.

Statements as to documents

43 Article 5 of the Code provides:

A statement as to the existence of a document, or as to its contents, effect, object, or purpose, or as to its nature, character, class or description, is a representation.[1]

44 In many departments of the law, particularly those concerned with the rules of evidence[2] or of practice[3] it has been found necessary to draw a sharp line of demarcation between documents and facts, or, rather, between facts proved by documents, and facts proved otherwise. For this reason it has been thought advisable to deal with statements relating to documents as if they constituted a special class of statement. But, in truth, this is not the case, if "matter of fact" is correctly defined (see Article 1 of the Code) as "an existing fact or thing, or past event". A document is a thing. Its existence or non-existence is a fact. Its actual contents, in the sense of the words, figures, or other permanent signs, contained in or appearing upon it, constitute fact. Its purport, office, object, or purpose is fact. Still more clearly, its nature, character, class, or description is fact. All these facts may be the subject of statement and misstatement, description and misdescription. The four classes of statement above referred to are enumerated separately in Article 5 of the Code, and all of them are expressed to be representations. It will be mentioned hereafter that there was formerly an important difference between the consequences of misrepresentations of the first three types referred to in Article 5, and those which may attend upon a misrepresentation of the fourth type[4]; but for the purposes of the topic now under discussion there is no significance in this distinction, which has in fact now been dis-

---

[1] See p. 4, *ante*. The decision of the House of Lords in *Saunders* v. *Anglia Building Society*, [1970] 3 All E.R. 961; [1971] A.C. 1004, H.L. (as to which see paras. 243 *et seq.*, Chapter XIII, *post*) has rendered the classification set forth in this Article obsolete, as is observed in the text of para. 48, *infra*. It has been thought unnecessary, however, to alter the writing of the text of earlier editions significantly at this point.

[2] e.g., the rules as to the construction of a document being for the court, the rule as to a document "speaking for itself", the rules as to primary and secondary evidence, etc., etc.

[3] e.g., discovery of documents, as contrasted with discovery of facts (by interrogatories), etc., etc.

[4] See paras. 243 *et seq.*, *post*; but see in this regard para. 48 *infra* as to the effect of *Saunders* v. *Anglia Building Society*, [1970] 3 All E.R. 961, [1971] A.C. 1004, H.L.

countenanced in a recent decision in the Lords.[1]   Statements of all four kinds are alike representations, whatever difference may exist in the respective legal consequences of their falsity.

Statements as to the existence of a document

45   From the earliest times, there has never been any doubt but that the existence of a document, of whatever kind, is a matter of fact.   The judges, in answer to one of the questions addressed to them by the House of Lords on the consideration of Fox's Libel Bill, declared that

> "whether there exists such a letter [the question related to threatening letters] is doubtless matter of fact. . . . It is also matter of fact whether an Act of Parliament, public or private, exists.   And the same may be said of every other writing, from records of the highest nature down to any scrap of paper whereon words are written".[2]

Where the document happens to be a statute, it has been argued that any statement relating to it must necessarily be a statement of law, but BOWEN L.J. effectually disposed of this erroneous view.   He said:

> "Suppose I were to say that I have a private Act of Parliament which gives me powers to do so and so.   Is not that an assertion that I have such an Act of Parliament?   It appears to me to be as much a representation of a matter of fact as if I had said I have a particular bound copy of Dr Johnson's Dictionary."[3]

Statements as to the actual contents of a document

46   Equally, of course, a statement as to the wording, or the contents (in this sense), of a document, is a statement of fact; and a misdescription, or a misreading, or a mistranslation of such contents to the representee is a misstatement of fact.   Thus the following were held to have been misrepresentations, which of course implied that they were deemed representations—a misreading of a writing of release as a mere acquittance for arrears of rent[4]; a misreading of a lease for one year as a lease for twenty-one years[5]; a statement that a deed of compromise corresponded with

---

[1] *Saunders* v. *Anglia Building Society*, [1970] 3 All E.R. 961; [1971] A.C. 1004, H.L.   For an examination of this decision see paras. 243 *et seq*, Chapter XIII, *post*.

[2] These Questions, which were intended to elicit the then state of judicial opinion as to the proper functions of judge and jury respectively in cases of criminal defamation, were presented on the 27th April, 1792, and Lord ABINGER C.B. laid the Answers thereto of the judges on the table of the House on the 11th May, 1792.   The Question referred to in the text was the fifth on the list.   See *Parl. Hist.*, vol. 29, col. 1366.

[3] *West* London Commercial Bank v. *Kitson* (1884), 13 Q.B.D. 360, C.A., at p. 363.

[4] *Thoroughgood* v. *Cole* (1584), 2 Co Rep. 9a.

[5] *Anon.* (1684), Skin. 159.

the draft settled by counsel[1]; misdescriptions of the contents of a draft
lease,[2] of the figures on a negotiable instrument,[3] of the provisions of a
will,[4] of the contents of an Act of Parliament,[5] and of the conditions of an
engineering contract[6]; a mistranslation to an Indian native of an English
proclamation of sale[7]; and an incomplete reading of a letter,[8] or of conditions of sale.[9]

Statements as to effect and purport of a document

47   Statements as to the general effect, import, or object, of a document, or of any provision or clause thereof, stand on the same footing as
statements purporting to record or report the actual language used; the
only difference being that the one assumes to be a transcript, and the
other a summary, or version, or analysis, of the contents of the document.
Instances of statements of this character which have been held to be
representations, and, on proof of falsity, misrepresentations, are: a
description of the effect of a release of claims for personal injuries[10]; a
statement of the purport of contracts for the remuneration of directors[11];
a summary or version of a government official's report on a mining district[12]; a statement of the import of a letter offering property for sale[13];
a statement that a certain parcel of land was not the subject of a previous
conveyance[14]; a version of the effect of certain contracts and orders for
patented articles[15]; a statement as to the tenor of counsel's opinion[16];

---

1 *Beadles* v. *Burch* (1839), 10 Sim. 332.
2 *Clapham* v. *Shillito* (1844), 7 Beav. 146.
3 *Billage* v. *Southee* (1852), 9 Hare, 534; 21 L.J. Ch. 472. The statement, however, was not
proved here to have been made.
4 *Reynell* v. *Sprye, Sprye* v. *Reynell* (1852), 1 De G.M. & G. 660.
5 *West London Commercial Bank* v. *Kitson* (1884), 13 Q.B.D. 360, C.A.; *Derry* v. *Peek* (1889),
14 App. Cas. 337.
6 *Moss & Co., Ltd.* v. *Swansea Corporation* (1910), 74 J.P. 351.
7 *Mahomed Kala Mea* v. *A. V. Harperink* (1908), 25 T.L.R. 180, P.C. The like effect of mistranslation in conveying a false imputation of fact for purpose of defamation is dealt with by Mr.
Spencer Bower in the *Law of Actionable Defamation*, App. VI, Sect. 7.
8 *Rickards* v. *Murdock* (1830), 10 B. & C. 527.
9 *Clements* v. *Conroy*, [1911] 2 I.R. 500, *per* Lord O'BRIEN C.J. (Ir.) at p. 507.
10 *Stewart* v. *Great Western Rail. Co.* (1865), 2 De G.J. & Sm. 319; *Lee* v. *Lancashire and
Yorkshire Rail. Co.* (1871), 6 Ch.App. 527; *Hirschfield* v. *London, Brighton and South Coast Rail.
Co.* (1876), 2 Q.B.D. 1.
11 *Arkwright* v. *Newbold* (1881), 17 Ch.D. 301, C.A.
12 *Re Mount Morgan (West) Gold Mine, Ltd., Ex parte West* (1887), 56 L.T. 622 (described by
KAY J. at p. 624, as a "travesty of" the official's "report"). *Cf.* the observations of JAMES L.J.
at p. 318 of *Arkwright* v. *Newbold* (*ubi supra*).
13 *Stewart* v. *Kennedy, No. 2* (1890), 15 App.Cas. 108, H.L.
14 *Onward Building Society* v. *Smithson*, [1893] 1 Ch. 1, C.A.
15 *Components Tube Co., Ltd.* v. *Naylor*, [1900] 2 I.R. 1.
16 *Leonard* v. *Leonard* (1812), 2 Ball & B. 171; *Luddy's Trustee* v. *Peard* (1886), 33 Ch.D. 500;
Re Roberts, Roberts v. *Roberts*, [1905] 1 Ch. 704, C.A.

and a description of the purport of a public announcement of a sale by direction of the court.[1]

Statements as to the character, nature, class, or description of a document

48   Like the class of statements referred to in the preceding paragraph, statements as to the character or nature of a document are statements of fact, and indeed they are statements of fact which may in some circumstances be of crucial importance.   As will later be seen,[2] such statements were until 1970 held to be *sui generis*, such as to enable those signing deeds or other instruments upon the faith of them to set up the plea of *non est factum*, and consequently to disclaim all liability thereunder.[3] Since the decision of the House of Lords in *Saunders (Executrix of Gallie)* v. *Anglia Building Society*,[4] however, the availability of the plea of *non est factum* no longer depends on whether the representation was made as to the *nature or character* of the document, as distinct from its *effect or purport*; and the distinction formerly made between representations as to character or nature on the one hand and representations as to effect, purport, or contents, on the other, is consequently no longer of importance.

Exaggeration, puffing, etc.

49   Article 6 of the Code[5] states the principle as follows:

> "Mere general vaunting, puffing, or commendation of the merits or value of any person or thing, or mere exaggeration, unaccompanied by any particular or definite statement, is not a representation."

Simplex commendatio non nocet, or (as otherwise expressed) *non obligat*. Self-praise is no recommendation, and, for that reason, is no representation either, because nobody trusts to it as such.   In mere general laudation of a man's own wares, or inventions, or projects, if the party confines himself to puffery and pushing, and does not condescend to particulars, there is no statement of any issuable fact, and nothing is put forward

---

[1] *Mahomed Kala Mea* v. *A. V. Harperink* (1908), 25 T.L.R. 180 P.C., where a statement of this kind was made, in addition to the mistranslation above referred to.

[2] See Chapter XIII, paras. 242 *et seq.*, *post*.

[3] Mr Spencer Bower, in the earlier editions of this work, cited *inter alia Thoroughgood* v. *Cole* (1584), 2 Co. Rep. 9a; *Foster* v. *Mackinnon* (1869), L.R. 4 C.P. 704; *Hunter* v. *Walters* (1871), 7 Ch.App. 75; *King* v. *Smith*, [1900] 2 Ch. 425; *Howatson* v. *Webb*, [1908] 1 Ch. 1, C.A.; *Carlisle and Cumberland Banking Co.* v. *Bragg*, [1911] 1 K.B. 489, C.A. in support of his text as it then stood.   These decisions must now be read in the light of the decision of the House of Lords in *Saunders* v. *Anglia Building Society*, [1970] 3 All E.R. 961; [1971] A.C. 1004, H.L., by which *Howatson* v. *Webb* was disapproved and *Carlisle and Cumberland Banking Co.* v. *Bragg* positively overruled.

[4] [1970] 3 All E.R. 961; [1971] A.C. 1004, H.L.

[5] See p. 4, *ante*.

which can be supposed to mislead or influence any rational being. The vauntings, or sanguine anticipations, of the advertiser, the prospectus-monger, or the inventor, can deceive nobody. Indiscriminate commendation in the law of misrepresentation is as distinguishable from a statement of fact as, in the law of slander, indiscriminate abuse is from the imputation of a crime.[1] Exaggeration of this description is not taken by the community *au pied de la lettre*, but only for what it is worth, and what it is. Thus, vague indefinite or loose expressions such as that a leasehold property was "*nearly* equal to freehold",[2] or that certain land was "uncommonly rich water meadow-land",[3] "warm protestations of" a person's "power and influence", and "coloured expressions" of certain appointments being "in his gift",[4] "exaggeration of the prisoner's prosperity", in a criminal case of false pretences,[5] and a description of farms as "fertile and improvable", and such as might be *considerably* improved at a *moderate* cost,[6] were all held to be too general and indefinite to amount to representations. With regard to prospectuses in particular, it was recognised in the House of Lords that "some high colouring and even exaggeration is to be expected" in such documents,[7] though, in the particular case, it was held that the directors had exceeded the limits of legitimate allurement. So, where "the glowing and exaggerated colours" of another prospectus,[8] and the sanguine expectations expressed in a third,[9] and the "puffery" of a fourth,[10] were "unmixed with baser matter", in the shape of false statements of fact, they were held not to be representations.

50 Where, however, the exaggeration or puffery, instead of being based on facts separately stated (in which case the two things stand on their own footings) is punctuated by detail, or quantified by figures, it assumes the aspect, and renders the representor liable to the consequences, of a

---

1 This is dealt with in Mr Spencer Bower's *Code of Actionable Defamation* Article 12, notes (b) (c) and (d). The same distinction is drawn between mere innocent vaunting and actionable "disparagement of property" in Article 61 (2), and note (c) thereto, of the same work.

2 *Fenton* v. *Browne* (1807), 14 Ves. 144.

3 *Scott* v. *Hanson* (1829), 1 Russ. & M. 128.

4 *Neeley* v. *Lock* (1838), 8 C. & P. 527.

5 *R.* v. *Watson* (1857), 4 Jur. N.S. 14.

6 *Dimmock* v. *Hallett* (1866), 2 Ch. App. 21.

7 *Central Rail. Co. of Venezuela* v. *Kisch* (1867), L.R. 2 H.L. 99, 113.

8 *Jennings* v. *Broughton* (1854), 5 De G.M. & G. 126, *per* ROMILLY M.R. who was affirmed by the L.JJ.

9 *Cargill* v. *Bower* (1878), 10 Ch.D. 502.

10 *McKeown* v. *Boudard-Peveril Gear Co.* (1896), 65 L.J. Ch. 735, C.A., *per* LINDLEY L.J. and LOPES L.J. at p. 736.

simple statement of fact.[1] If I say that my pills are "worth a guinea a box" (though this again is, in a sense, a statement of fact), no one could possibly understand the expression as referring to anything but my confident opinion of the intrinsic merits of the pills, or a "guinea" as more than a mere laudatory phrase. But if I say that my "bile beans" contain a new ingredient discovered by such and such an explorer in such and such a tropical country,[2] or that my "carbolic smoke ball" is a prophylactic against catching a cold, if used so many times,[3] I am stating facts, and cannot escape liability, if the facts are false, by urging that they were embedded in a mass of encomiastic generalities. If a statement is made of a fact such as that A.B. is dead, it may be open to the subject of the statement to protest, in the modest spirit of Mark Twain on a memorable occasion, "that the report is much exaggerated", but it certainly does not lie in the mouth of the maker of the statement to say so. An auctioneer is entitled to say that a desirable residential estate is "buried under rose leaves, or drowned in the songs of nightingales",[4] but if he deserts the pathless realm of generalities for the high road and *terra firma* of fact, it is no longer a case of the "loose opinion" or "puffery" of an "auctioneer or vendor".[5] The same judge who decided that "rich watered meadow-land" was not a representation, as regards the mere assertion of richness, held nevertheless that it was a statement of the fact that the land was water

---

[1] So, in *New Zealand*, in *Easterbrook* v. *Hopkins*, [1918] N.Z.L.R. 428 C.A., the New Zealand Court of Appeal held statements (a) that the business was a valuable one and a little goldmine, (b) that the business was one of the best in the town, and (c) that the goodwill was worth £265, taken together, to amount to representations inducing the purchase of the business.

[2] *Bile Bean Manufacturing Co.* v. *Davidson* 1906, 8 F. (Ct. of Sess.) 1181, where it was held that, in actions for misrepresentation, though "mere puffing will not do", and "exaggeration, however gross, of the merits and virtues of a remedy will not do" (Lord STORMONTH-DARLING at p. 1200), and phrases such as "incomparable", "unique", "worth a guinea a box", come to nothing, yet it is a totally different matter where there is proof, as there was in that case, of "statements of alleged facts, carefully elaborated, and intended to be accepted as facts" (*per* the Lord Justice-Clerk at p. 1197).

[3] *Carlill* v. *Carbolic Smoke Ball Co.*, [1893] 1 Q.B. 256, C.A. This was a case of contract, but the observations of LINDLEY L.J. at p. 261, and A. L. SMITH L.J. at p. 273, to the effect that the advertisement was not a mere puff, but an offer, which on acceptance, would become a contract, are distinctly germane to the present question, because it is obvious that, if a statement that a man will give £100 to any one who catches a cold after having used the remedy so many times, is not a mere puff, a statement that the remedy has the preventive effect invariably, or almost invariably, would still less be so. If the one is an offer, the other is certainly a representation.

[4] These "absurd puffs" are nothing but "flourishes which in practice mislead nobody; which no purchaser ever acts upon": *Magennis* v. *Fallon* (1828), 2 Mol. 561 at p. 587.

[5] *Beaumont* v. *Dukes* (1822), Jac. 422; 23 R.R. 110 (*per* PLUMER M.R. at p. 426; *Scott* v. *Hanson* (1826), 1 Sim. 13, *per* LEACH V.-C. at p. 15, whose opinion was, on this point, affirmed by Lord ELDON L.C. (1 Russ. & M. 128). Cp. *Sibbald* v. *Hill* (1814), 2 Dow 263, H.L., where Lord ELDON L.C. at p. 266, held that a statement that the representor had effected insurances on certain whalers at no more than 8 per cent. was a definite assertion, and not a mere profusion of "verba jactantia", such as is usual in chaffering.

meadow-land.[1]   And in the same case in which it was held that the description of farms as "fertile" and "improvable at a moderate cost" was not a statement of fact, it was held that a description of their occupation and tenancy was.[2]

51   Conversely, a purchaser's mere general belittling and deprecation is no more a representation than a vendor's mere vague and exaggerated appreciation.   In such a case as has been said,

> "a stranger bargaining for himself . . . might say, Your house is not a good one; he might say it was valueless. . . .   Such has been the course of business for at least 3000 years; 'It is naught, it is naught, saith the buyer, but when he is gone his way, then he boasteth' ".[3]

---

1 *Scott* v. *Hanson* (*supra*), where Lord ELDON L.C. (1 Russ. & M. 131) reversed LEACH V.-C. as to two out of the fourteen acres in dispute, on the ground stated in the text, affirming him as to the other twelve acres, as stated in the preceding note.

2 *Dimmock* v. *Hallett* (1866), 2 Ch. App. 21.

3 *McPherson* v. *Watt* (1877), 3 App. Cas. 254, H.L.   Lord BLACKBURN's citation is from Prov. xx. 14.

CHAPTER III

How a Representation
May be Made

Introductory

52 The modes and forms of representation are infinite. Any physical symbol which reproduces or assumes to reproduce a fact, presents or assumes to present it over again, and is, therefore, literally, as it is substantially, a representation. These symbols, as stated in Articles 7 and 8 of the Code, may be either express or implied. When express, they consist either of writing or analogous permanent signs, or of speech or other transitory signs. When implied, the implication may arise from the conjoint effect of several express statements, or from all that is said coupled with all that is left unsaid; or it may arise from acts and conduct, or (in a limited class of case) even from silence and inaction.

Express representations

53 Besides words and figures expressed in writing or print, or by analogous processes, a representation may be made by the use of any other permanent symbols or means, such as plans and drawings,[1]

---

1 In *Beaumont* v. *Dukes* (1822), Jac. 422, a plan was used to add force to a verbal representation. In *Denny* v. *Hancock* (1870), 6 Ch. App. 1, a plan played a very important part. It was a question whether certain trees and shrubs had been represented as passing on the sale of land. The vendor relied on this plan as correcting the falsity of his representation in words, and as negativing deceit. It was held, on the contrary, to have been part of it (*per* JAMES L.J. at pp. 11, 12, and MELLISH L.J. at pp. 13, 14). A similar view was taken of the plan which accompanied the particulars of sale in *Dykes* v. *Blake* (1838), 4 Bing. N.C. 463 (*per* TINDAL C.J. at pp. 475, 476). *Re Arnold, Arnold* v. *Arnold* (1880), 14 Ch.D. 270, C.A., was a case in which it was held by BAGGALLAY L.J. at p. 282, and BRAMWELL L.J. at p. 284, that it was impossible to exclude the plan from the particulars of sale in determining whether there had been a misrepresentation or not. In *Pearson* (*S.*) & *Son, Ltd.* v. *Dublin Corporation*, [1907] A.C. 351, H.L., the representation complained of, as to the existence and position of a certain wall, was contained in, *inter alia*, plans and drawings prepared by the defendant's engineer. On the other hand, in *Eastwood* v. *Ashton*, [1914] 1 Ch. 68, C.A., plans were considered to be a mere *falsa dem-*

maps,[1] pictures and photographs,[2] or any like scientific or artistic transcript of thought.

54   Similarly, it is not only the spoken word which conveys a statement of fact.   "A nod, or a wink, or a shake of the head, or a smile"[3] may equally well serve the purpose.   The very meaning of "innuendo" is a nod.   Gestures and demeanour are, under some circumstances, as efficacious to convey a deceptive representation, as, in cases of slander, to insinuate a defamatory imputation.   In this way looks and gestures may subsidise language; they may also stand altogether in the place of words, or even contradict them, and the representor may by the use of such means convey a statement as clearly as another may convey a menace, and, as Lord REDESDALE said of such a person,

> "prevail without using a single word of threat, like the beggar in Gil Blas who, with his gun at his shoulder, extorted money from the traveller without uttering a word".[4]

Whenever there is such a discrepancy, it is safe to say that, in nine cases out of ten, the representation is made in a more real sense by manner, glance, and gesture than it is by voice; but it is sufficient, for present purposes, to note that the one is as much a medium of representation as the other.

In *Curtis* v. *Chemical Cleaning and Dyeing Co.*[5] a "receipt" was handed to a customer to sign, the shop assistant saying that the company did not accept liability for beads and sequins.   Actually the document contained a clause purporting to give a general exemption from *all* liability.   In disallowing the exemption, the members of the Court of Appeal were all

---

onstratio. *Cf.* in *Australia, Dabbs* v. *Seaman* (1925), 36 C.L.R. 538 (High Court of Australia), an estoppel case in which a plan showing a strip of land as marked "20 ft. lane" was held a representation such as to estop the owner. In *New Zealand* see *Burns* v. *Dilworth Trust Board*, [1925] N.Z.L.R. 488, at pp. 503–4.

[1] *Re Mount Morgan (West) Gold Mine, Ltd., Ex parte West* (1887), 56 L.T. 622, where the company in vain relied upon a map accompanying the prospectus as revealing the truth, and so neutralising the express and implied false statements therein.

[2] *Newman* v. *Pinto* (1887), 57 L.T. 31, C.A. (pictures and emblematic designs on the lids of cigar-boxes for the purpose of representing cigars imported from Germany as "Havana cigars"); *Slingsby* v. *Bradford Patent Truck and Trolley Co.*, [1906] W.N. 51, C.A. (picture of buildings, described as "a photograph, not a sketch", to the negative or printing-block of which the plaintiff's name had been added by hand, though it did not appear on the actual buildings, or in the photograph).

[3] *Walters* v. *Morgan* (1861), 3 De G.F. & J. 718 (*per* Lord CAMPBELL L.C. at p. 724), a case cited for the above proposition by CHITTY J. at p. 209 of *Turner* v. *Green*, [1895] 2 Ch. 205. *Cf.* Jeremy Taylor, *Ductor Dubitantium*, Book III, Ch. II, Rule 5, Para. 43: "a man may look a lie, and a nod a lie, and smile a lie".

[4] At p. 668 of *Webb* v. *Rorke* (1806), 2 Sch. & Lef. 661. The incident referred to by Lord REDESDALE, then L.C. of Ireland, is to be found in Ch. II of *Gil Blas*.

[5] [1951] 1 K.B. 805.

of opinion that the words and conduct of the shop assistant constituted a misrepresentation. DENNING L.J. said[1]:

> "In my opinion any behaviour, by words or conduct, is sufficient to be a misrepresentation if it is such as to mislead the other party . . ."

and again[2]:

> "In those circumstances the conduct of the cleaners might well be such that it conveyed the impression that the document contained no conditions, or, at any rate, no condition exempting them from their common law liability . . ."

Representations implied from acts or conduct

55   The types of representation which are implied from direct and express representations (such as implied statements of an existing intention, opinion, or belief), or from absolute representations coupled with silence as to matters which it was the duty of the representor not to suppress, are discussed elsewhere.[3]   In the present place it is proposed to consider the other class of implied representation—that which is inferred from acts and conduct—a class which, in the growing complexity of modern life, assumes ever-increasing proportions and importance.

56   To take the simplest illustrations, "a man may act a lie", says Paley[4] "as by pointing his finger in a wrong direction, when a traveller inquires of him the road, or when a tradesman shuts up his windows to induce his creditors to believe he is abroad; for, to all moral purposes, and therefore as to veracity, speech and action are the same".   Indeed, conduct in many cases is a more real expression of thought than language, just as circumstantial evidence is sometimes more valuable and cogent than direct evidence.

57   Apart from the above simple cases, where the inference is plain and palpable, there are a variety of others where it is a somewhat more complicated or subtle process to extract the representation from the acts

---

[1] At p. 808.

[2] At p. 809.

[3] See, as to the former class, paras. 16, 30 and 37 *ante*, and, as to the latter, Chapter IV, paras. 82 *et seq.*, *post.*

[4] *Principles of Moral and Political Philosophy*, Book III, Pt. I, Ch. XV (*cf.* Book III, Pt. I, Ch. V, on "tacit promises" by acts and conduct). In *Barley* v. *Walford* (1846), 9 Q.B. 197, Lord DENMAN C.J. at p. 208, speaks of the absurdity of supposing that a man, "having a conspicuous clock too slow", could be liable to any one who went by it. No doubt this would be ridiculous; but the act of pointing to a clock, known to the pointer to be too slow or too fast, might well be a misrepresentation of the kind mentioned by Paley.

and conduct. In the succeeding paragraphs of this section a rough classification of these is attempted.

58   In cases of delivery of property under a contract of sale, or otherwise, the following implications of a representation may be made.   On the one hand, the purchaser of goods, by the mere act of ordering them, is understood to represent that he then has the intention of paying for them.[1] On the other hand the person assuming to sell or let property impliedly represents that the property exists, and that he has the power to sell or let it, as the case may be, and, in the case of an agreement to sell, that it is unincumbered[2]; he who delivers or issues to another instruments of title, or securities, or business documents, impliedly represents that they are genuine[3]; and the seller of an article presenting a certain appearance to the senses of the purchaser, impliedly represents that the article *est quod videtur*—is in fact what *ex facie* it purports to be—for, when this is not so, and falsehood's "goodly outside" is manufactured by a concealment of defects, there is a misrepresentation; and this there could not be unless there were an implied representation in the first instance of the kind indicated.   Thus selling sea-damaged pimento by samples from bulk, which showed no damage (this being only apparent on unpacking), and sending out the advertisements of the sale too late to enable any purchaser to inspect and so discover the defect, was held to be a misrepresentation of the pimento as sound[4]; on the sale of a patented invention for baking bread without the use of spirit or ferment, the conducting of a

---

[1] See the cases cited in note 3 to para. 17, *ante*.

[2] *Colt* v. *Woollaston* (1723), 2 P.Wms. 154; *Wilbraham* v. *Livesey* (1854), 18 Beav. 206 (*per* ROMILLY M.R. at p. 209: "a contract to grant an ordinary lease is virtually a representation that the party can grant such a lease"); *Ungley* v. *Ungley* (1871), 5 Ch.D. 887, C.A. (*per* JESSEL M.R., at p. 891: "it is quite clear that, if you once prove that a man has made an agreement to sell a house, it must be taken that he means to get it free from incumbrances, without his saying so. So, if a man agrees to settle a house in consideration of marriage, it must be taken to mean free from incumbrances"); *Richardson* v. *Silvester* (1873), L.R. 9 Q.B. 34 (advertising a farm to let held a representation that the party has a farm to let); *Ajello* v. *Worsley*, [1898] 1 Ch. 274 (advertisement of piano held to involve a representation that party had pianos in stock).

[3] *Edinburgh United Breweries* v. *Molleson*, [1894] A.C. 96, H.L. (handing over of books, which one of the appellants was entitled to have examined by an accountant as a condition of sale of a business, deemed an implied representation that they were genuine, *per* Lord HERSCHELL L.C., at p. 111); *Marnham* v. *Weaver* (1899), 80 L.T. 412, where the putting forward as security of fictitious leases by the party to himself under an alias was held an implied misrepresentation of their genuineness; *Boyd and Forrest* v. *Glasgow and South Western Rail. Co.*, 1911 S.C. 33 (where the putting forward of a "journal of bores" was held an implied representation of its genuineness as a record of bores actually taken). So, in *Scholefield* v. *Templer* (1859), 4 De G. & J. 429, where a debtor and his surety proposed to execute a transfer of a mortgage, Lord CAMPBELL L.C. held this to be a representation that there *was* such a mortgage.

[4] *Jones* v. *Bowden* (1813), 4 Taunt. 847.

demonstration or experiment which appeared to satisfy the description, but in which spirit and a special ferment had been secretly introduced, was treated as one of the means by which an implied misrepresentation of the nature of the invention had been made[1]; and the "false packing" of goods, or the covering up of a defect in a cannon by artifice,[2] have been treated as acts and conduct amounting to misrepresentation.[3] So clearly, indeed, is any such device deemed a representation that not even an express term in the contract to take the property with all faults, or at all risks, will countervail it, if false and (as in all such cases must follow) fraudulent.[4] Conversely, an intending buyer who conceals and depreciates the value of the property which he is desirous of purchasing by "fraudulent manoeuvres", is as guilty of implied misrepresentation as the intending seller who, by the like manoeuvres, conceals and minimises faults and defects in the property to be sold.[5] The mere handing to a customer of an article of a certain substance and quality, without saying a word, is a representation that it is of that substance or quality.[6] Lastly, the common device of "rigging the market", or (more euphemistically) "making a market", by procuring persons to pretend to buy and sell in the market at fictitious prices, is clearly an implied misrepresentation, and a fraudulent one.[7]

---

[1] *Lovell* v. *Hicks* (1836), 2 Y. & C. (Ex.) 46, *per* ALDERSON B. at p. 55 ("every experiment became of itself a fraudulent misrepresentation"), and at p. 57 ("fallacious experiments which were so many laborious frauds").

[2] *Ormrod* v. *Huth* (1845), 14 M. & W. 651, and *Horsfall* v. *Thomas* (1862), 1 H. & C. 90. In the first case the defendant escaped because he was not proved to have had anything to do with the "false packing", and, in the second, because the covering up of the defect in the cannon was not proved to have deceived the purchaser; but in neither case was it doubted that acts and conduct of the character in question constitute implied representation.

[3] *Cf*, the devices of "salting" mines, and "faking" furniture, whether for the purpose of making old present the appearance of new, or new that of antique—the latter perhaps a particularly flourishing industry at the present time. See case cited in note 2 on p. 78, *post*. False weights and measures, etc. are also "silent asserters".

[4] See Chapter XI, paras. 194–5, *post*.

[5] *Perens* v. *Johnson* (1857), 3 Sm. & G. 419 (removing gear, and withdrawing iron, from a colliery, and rendering access thereto impossible, treated as misrepresentations of inferior value by an intending purchaser); *Walsham* v. *Stainton* (1863), 1 De G.J. & Sm. 678, where a buyer of shares manipulated accounts of dealings in them for this purpose (*per* TURNER L.J. at pp. 689, 690).

[6] 17 Halsbury's Laws of England (3rd Edn.) 487.

[7] In *National Exchange Co. of Glasgow* v. *Drew* (1855), 2 Macq. H.L. 103, the company lent shareholders money with which to buy further shares, assuring them that they would not be called upon for any further contribution until the stock could be sold at a profit. The defence to the action (which was to recover the money so advanced) was that the above acts and conduct amounted to an implied misrepresentation of the then flourishing state of the company, and (*per* Lord BROUGHAM in the course of the argument) that a *turpis causa* was shown, viz. an attempt by the company to do that which was equivalent to "rigging the market". This defence prevailed. In *Scott* v. *Brown, Doering, McNab & Co.*, [1892] 2 Q.B. 724, C.A., the parties were shown to have conspired to create fictitious prices for shares in a company by procuring

59 Another class of representation by conduct comprises cases in which an act or transaction may be lawfully or unlawfully carried out, and where (since the law presumes against illegality) the mere doing of the act or entering into the transaction is equivalent to a representation that all those circumstances and conditions exist but for which the act or transaction would be unlawful. Thus the act of delivering an article of food to a customer, at his request, the delivery of which article in an adulterated state would be a statutory offence, is, of itself, a representation that it is unadulterated[1]; the mere paying of addresses to a lady with a view to matrimony may, even in a criminal case, be deemed tantamount to a representation or pretence that the person so acting is unmarried[2]; the mere act of going through the ceremony of marriage is a representation of the representor's legal capacity to marry[3]; the mere act of sending an animal to a repository or market or place for public sale may raise the inference of a representation that, so far as the party knows, the animal is not suffering from any contagious or infectious disease which would make the act unlawful, or a violation of any statute for the time being in force[4]; shipment of goods on a voyage may amount to a

---

imaginary bargains to be made and quoted as real in the Stock Exchange. This was misrepresentation by conduct, said the C.A., and, further, an indictable conspiracy, as in *R.* v. *De Berenger* (1814), 3 M. & S. 67, cited in Chapter VIII, *post*. "I see no distinction", observed LOPES L.J. (see p. 730), "between rumours (as in this case) and false and fictitious *acts*". "Test it this way", added A. L. SMITH L.J. at p. 734,—"suppose a purchaser induced to purchase shares . . . by means of a fictitious premium created by them" (sc. the parties to the action) "solely for the purpose of inducing such purchaser to buy, could he, or not, have successfully sued either or both for a false and fraudulent misrepresentation? I say that he could." In this connection a somewhat similar description of case, *Lindsay Petroleum Co.* v. *Hurd* (1874), L.R. 5 P.C. 221, may be noted. There a scheme was devised whereby communications were to pass between a person posing as absolute owner of property and another person making him sham offers at fictitious prices, and this was held to be an implied fraudulent misrepresentation (see p. 243.)

[1] *Fitzpatrick* v. *Kelly* (1873), L.R. 8 Q.B. 337, at pp. 341, 342, 343.

[2] *R.* v. *Copeland* (1842), Car. & M. 516, *per* Lord DENMAN C.J.

[3] *Meluish* v. *Milton* (1876), 3 Ch.D. 27, C.A. (*per* MELLISH L.J. at p. 35, who there added that "every day when they were living together, she"—the representor—"must be taken as continuously representing to him that she was his lawful wife").

[4] *Bodger* v. *Nicholls* (1873), 28 L.T. 441, where BLACKBURN J. says, at p. 449: "I entertain no doubt, but it is not necessary to decide the point, that the defendant by taking the cow to a public market to be sold, though he does not warrant her to be sound, yet thereby furnishes evidence of a representation that, so far as his knowledge goes, the animal is not suffering from any infectious disease. To say otherwise would be to run counter to the common sense of mankind." In *Ward* v. *Hobbs* (1878), 4 App. Cas. 13, H.L., the House of Lords did not differ from this very strong pronouncement, which was cited and much relied upon in argument. There pigs, suffering from typhoid fever, had been sent to a market, contrary to the provisions of a statute: but the seller who so sent them expressly refused to warrant their soundness, and on that ground escaped. It was not necessary, therefore, to consider whether the seller's act was a "representation by conduct", which Lord CAIRNS L.C. evidently thought it might be, though he added (at p. 22): "I desire, so far as I am concerned, to hold myself unpledged, if such a case had to be considered". Therefore the opinion, or (if it be a dictum) the very strong

representation by the shipper to the shipowner that the shipment is subject to no risk or danger, physical,[1] or legal[2]; in company transactions, the declaration of a dividend may amount to a statement that the dividend has not been paid out of capital, which would be illegal; and the issue of fully paid shares is, similarly, an implied representation that cash has been paid for them, in any case where there has been no filed contract.[3]   On the other hand, the mere entering into a contract is not a representation that the contractor has no principal, because it is not unlawful to contract for an undisclosed principal[4]; nor is the mere act of trading a representation that the trader is of full age, because it is not unlawful for an infant to trade[5]; nor is the mere advertisement of an article, with the description "trade mark" appended, an implied representation that the party has registered the trade mark, for it is not illegal to have and use one which is unregistered.[6]

60   Where a person, in entering into a transaction, conducts himself as if he bore a certain character or *persona* he is deemed to represent that he actually fills that character or *persona*.   Thus a party, by sending bought and sold notes to the other party, and guaranteeing the performance of the contract, impliedly states that he has a principal,[7] and all

---

dictum, of BLACKBURN, J. remains unaffected, and it would seem to be quite sound.   Of course in any case where there is no statute prohibiting the act in question, no implication of a representation arises. In *Hill* v. *Balls* (1857), 2 H. & N. 299, there was no clear allegation that the glandered horse had been sent *to a public place* (which was all that the statute prohibited), and no representation of its soundness was implied from the mere act of selling it at a repository, which, for aught that appeared, might have been a private place.

[1] *Brass* v. *Maitland* (1856), 26 L.J. Q.B. 49 (*per* CROMPTON J. at p. 57).

[2] *Mitchell, Cotts & Co.* v. *Steel Brothers & Co., Ltd.*, [1916] 2 K.B. 610 (*per* ATKIN J. at p. 614).

[3] In *Jackson* v. *Turquand* (1869), L.R. 4 H.L. 305, the question whether a declaration of a dividend and bonus (which it would be illegal to pay out of capital) amounts to a representation by conduct, was discussed by Lord HATHERLEY L.C., at pp. 308, 309, and Lord WESTBURY at p. 315, but not decided, because the conclusion of the House that there had at any rate been no dishonesty in any representation which might have been made, rendered it unnecessary to do so; but in a previous case in the House of Lords, *Burnes* v. *Pennell* (1849), 2 H.L. Cas. 497, Lord CAMPBELL, at pp. 524, 525, and Lord BROUGHAM at p. 531, express, in the strongest possible language, confident opinions that such payment is an implied declaration to the world by acts and deeds that "the company has made profits which justify such a dividend". The case as to the issue of fully paid shares (a case of representation for the purpose of estoppel) is *Bloomenthal* v. *Ford*, [1897] A.C. 156, H.L. (*per* Lord HALSBURY L.C. at pp. 163, 164, and Lord HERSCHELL at p. 169).   *Cf. R.* v. *Lord Kylsant*, [1932] 1 K.B. 442, at pp. 448–449.

[4] *Nelthorpe* v. *Holgate* (1844), 1 Coll. 203 (*per* KNIGHT-BRUCE V.-C. at p. 220).

[5] *Re Jones, Ex parte Jones* (1881), 18 Ch.D. 109, C.A., *per* JESSEL M.R. in the argument, at p. 115 ("a boy selling oranges in the street does not represent himself to be of full age"), and in his judgment at p. 121, and LUSH L.J. at p. 125.   *Cf.* the observations of KNIGHT-BRUCE V.-C. at pp. 116, 117 of *Stikeman* v. *Dawson* (1847), 1 De G. & Sm. 90, and those of GROVE J. at pp. 528, 529 of *Miller* v. *Blankley* (1878), 38 L.T. 527.

[6] *Sen Sen Co.* v. *Britten*, [1899] 1 Ch. 692, *per* STIRLING J.

[7] *Wilson* v. *Short* (1847), 6 Hare, 366.   *Cf. Waddell* v. *Blockey* (1879), 4 Q.B.D. 678.

the cases of implied warranty of authority from assuming to act as if such authority existed may also be, and in some instances have been, put as cases of implied representation.[1] Nearly all the non-disclosure cases also, though usually considered not to fall within the province of representation, strictly so called, may be, and have been, treated as implied statements that the transaction which the party purports to have entered into is, so far as he knows, of the normal and usual type, and that he has withheld nothing which, if revealed, would show it to be otherwise.[2]

61 Personation by "make believe", a device as old as Jacob and Esau, is of course as much a representation as an assumption of an alias by direct statement. The appearance of a man at a shop in the cap and gown of a member of a university is, by itself, a representation that he is such a member.[3] So the giving of a business card of a firm is a representation that the person so acting is a member or representative of that firm, even if no words are used.[4] A man who had been agent for another, but had ceased to be so, by continuing to do business with those who had known him as such agent, without more, was held to have impliedly represented himself to be still acting in that capacity.[5] Conversely, a man who is in fact agent or partner or confederate of another may, by conduct, represent himself to be entirely independent of him,[6] or, by granting leases to himself under another name, may represent that there is a person who bears that name, and is distinct from himself.[7]

---

[1] See paras. 182–3, Chapter X, *post.*

[2] See paras. 82 *et seq.*, Chapter IV, *post.*

[3] *R.* v. *Barnard* (1837), 7 C. & P. 784, where BOLLAND B. in summing up said: "If nothing had passed in words, I should have laid down that the fact of the prisoner's appearing in cap and gown would have been pregnant evidence from which a jury should infer that he pretended he was a member of the university, and, if so, would have been a sufficient false pretence to satisfy the statute".

[4] *Hardman* v. *Booth* (1863), 1 H. & C. 803; *cf.* the personation by acts and conduct in *Cundy* v. *Lindsay* (1878), 3 App. Cas. 459, cited in note 4, to para. 88, *post.*

[5] *Higgons* v. *Burton* (1857), 26 L.J. Ex. 342.

[6] *Moens* v. *Heyworth* (1842), 10 M. & W. 147, where it was held that it was for the jury to say whether a party, by the act of exhibiting an invoice stating goods to be of first shipping quality, had or had not impliedly represented that the shippers so stating were independent persons, and not mere agents or partners (*per* Lord ABINGER C.B. at p. 156, PARKE B. at p. 156, who speaks of a representation "by words or acts", and ALDERSON B. at pp. 156–158; *Blake* v. *Albion Life Assurance Society* (1878), 4 C.P.D. 94, where an agent and confederate of the defendant company by conduct assumed and pretended to be another person having no connection with it.

[7] *Marnham* v. *Weaver* (1899), 80 L.T. 412. *Cf.* in *New Zealand, Fawcett* v. *Star Car Sales Ltd.,* [1960] N.Z.L.R. 406 C.A. in which the agent of the owner of a car, acting within her authority, sold the car, but in doing so represented to the purchaser that she was herself the person whose name appeared on the certificate of ownership.

62   Where it is necessary to make periodically repeated representations in order to maintain a deception once practised, and to keep the
victim in his original state of delusion and false security, such representations are frequently made by acts and conduct alone; as, for instance, by
regularly transmitting to the party entitled the exact amount which would
represent interest payable under a mortgage, as if the mortgage had been
effected according to the instructions of, and with the moneys deposited
by, the other party,[1] or by producing, without handing over, the title
deeds of the property supposed to have been mortgaged[2]; which acts are,
of course, so many implied representations that the moneys deposited
have been invested as required.

63   Further, the practice of employing puffers at auction sales,[3] the
various modes of "passing off" goods, by "dressing" and "making up",[4]
and the "invitation" and "trap" cases,[5] all of which are dealt with elsewhere in their appropriate places, may be treated as species of representation by conduct.

64   Other illustrations of a miscellaneous and unclassifiable character
are the following.   A man, in order to induce a lady to marry him,
procures his brother to give him a note for a large sum of money as the
pretended balance of account due to him.   The production of this note
was held an implied representation to the lady of possession of property
to the amount of the note.[6]   A man procures another to become the
apparent owner of a farm: he may thereby represent him to be a person
of substance.[7]   A woman by her conduct assumes to possess magical
powers: this of itself is a "pretence", for "it is not necessary that the
false pretence should be made in express words, if the idea is conveyed",
and "her acting as 'a cunning woman', coupled with all that passed", and
her "conduct and conversations" evidence such a pretence.[8]   Two
curious cases of the utilisation of ambiguous objects of sense, as instruments of misrepresentation, are the following.   A man sent to a public
place for the sale of bullocks and heifers three animals, one a bullock,
one a heifer, and the third a hermaphrodite, or *lusus naturae*, having

---

[1] *Blair v. Bromley* (1847), 2 Ph. 354; *Moore v. Knight*, [1891] 1 Ch. 547; *Thorne v. Heard and Marsh*, [1895] A.C. 495, H.L. (*per* Lord DAVEY at p. 506).

[2] *Re Murray, Dickson v. Murray* (1887), 57 L.T. 223.

[3] See paras. 349 *et seq.*, Chapter XVI, *post.*

[4] See para. 377, Chapter XVII, *post.*

[5] See paras. 143 and 170, *post.*

[6] *Montefiori v. Montefiori* (1762), 1 Wm. Bl. 363.

[7] *O'Herlihy v. Hedges* (1803), 1 Sch. & Lef. 123.

[8] *R. v. Giles* (1865), 34 L.J. M.C. 50, *per* BLACKBURN J. at p. 53.

some of the properties of a male and others of a female.   This was held a representation by conduct that the third animal was either a bullock or a heifer.[1]   So, the sale of an article by a dealer in antiques was regarded as in itself, and apart from the express statements accompanying the act, an implied representation that the article was a curio of some kind.   The article itself was a "silent asserter", and it was a case of *res ipsa loquitur*.[2]

65   Of course no implication of a representation from acts and conduct arises where the only statement which can be implied does not fulfil the other conditions and requisites of a representation, as stated in Chapter II, either because the implied statement is not a statement to the effect alleged,[3] or because it is not a statement to the alleged representee, or to any person in particular, such as the simulation of wealth by "keeping up appearances",[4] or the miser's pretence of distress and penury,[5] which, without more, no individual could claim to have been a statement to himself, or one on the faith of which, as so made, he acted to his detriment.

---

[1] *Gill* v. *M'Dowell*, [1903] 2 I.R. 463, *per* Lord O'BRIEN C.J. at p. 467, and GIBSON J., who, at p. 469, says (rather unkindly to the wretched freak, who, after a brief, miserable, and blameless life, must needs be defamed in death): "the animal was misleading, a sort of living lie. . . . the beast told its own lie: it was a machine of fraud which the defendant utilised".

[2] *Patterson* v. *Landsberg & Son* 1905, 7 F. (Ct. of Sess.) 675, *per* Lord KILLACHY at p. 681; *Edgar* v. *Hector*, [1912] S.C. 348.

[3] *Beattie* v. *Ebury (Lord)* (1874), L.R 7 H.L. 102, was a case of this kind.   See the observations of Lord CAIRNS L.C. at pp. 109–112, Lord CHELMSFORD at p. 121, and Lord HATHERLEY at p. 128.

[4] See *Burnes* v. *Pennell* (1849), 2 H.L. Cas. 497 *per* Lord BROUGHAM at pp. 531–533.

[5] Instances will readily occur to any one, from ordinary life and history, of professional men or tradesmen rashly drawing, from a display of all the outward and visible signs of poverty by wealthy and mean men and women, inferences which induce them to make reductions in their charges, or to grant time, or consent to compromises of their claims; inferences of their own drawing from mere general appearances, and on which, therefore, they could found no cause of action.

CHAPTER IV

What is Misrepresentation?

Misrepresentation defined

66   A representation which when made, or, in the case of a continuing representation, when acted upon by the representee, was false in fact, is in law a misrepresentation (see Article 10).   This involves consideration of the questions of (1) the constituents of falsity, (2) the date or dates at which the falsity must be shown, and (3) the canons of construction applied for the purpose of determining whether a representation is to be deemed false or true.

What constitutes falsity in fact

67   For the purposes of the present discussion, which relates solely to the definition, nature and extent of *misrepresentation*, the knowledge or belief of the representor is wholly irrelevant. That topic has its relevance, and indeed its importance, at the stage when, misrepresentation being already demonstrated, it becomes necessary to distinguish between *innocent* and *fraudulent* misrepresentation.[1]   While in the domain of ethics the knowledge or belief of the representor may be all-important,[2] what we are now considering is what the law deems to be a misrepresentation.

Falsity in fact is all that need be established to show a misrepresentation.   A man may unintentionally make a misstatement.   He may also unintentionally make a correct statement, and, in so doing, behave "like white witches, mischievously good".[3]   But neither is the former repre-

---

[1] See note 5 on p. 80, *infra*.

[2] See Jeremy Taylor, *Ductor Dubitantium*, Bk. III, Ch. II, Rule 5, para. 4: "sometimes a man may speak that which is the truth, and yet be a liar at the same time in the same thing.   For he does not speak truly because the thing is true; but he is a liar because he speaks it when he thinks it is false."

[3] Dryden in *The Medal*, aiming at Lord Shaftesbury.

sentation thereby made true, nor the latter false. The modest claim of Autolycus that he is "sometimes honest by chance"[1] may be a difficult one to make good; but it is quite certain that a man may tell the truth sometimes by chance. And, if he does tell the truth, however much he intended to lie, he has made no statement which can ever be actionable (or indictable, either, as a false pretence), or as to which, therefore, there can ever be any occasion to institute the further inquiry which otherwise would follow, as to the state of the representor's mind, the inducement to the representee, and the like, inasmuch as the first condition of all has not been satisfied. "Although the accused," said BRETT L.J. in a criminal case, "had a criminal intent and believed his statement was false, yet if *in fact* by chance the statement was not incorrect, the charge is not supported".[2] So, in a civil case, where the defendant had made an implied representation that the plaintiff would have the right to sell liquor off the premises, if he acquired them, the representation which, so far as he knew, was false (there being, to his knowledge, restrictive covenants in a previous conveyance), turned out to have been, *malgré lui*, true all the time, because no one during a period of 26 years since the date of the conveyance had interfered with the sale of liquor off the premises, and the defendant, on that ground, was held entitled to judgment.[3] To the question—misrepresentation or no misrepresentation —the nice distinctions which philosophers or philologists draw between objective and subjective truth, or, as Lord BRAMWELL put it, between "absolute" and "contingent" truth,[4] and all considerations of the personal equation, are wholly immaterial. Objective, not subjective, truth is alone relevant. The *falsum*, not the *falsus*, is, at this stage, the sole subject of the inquiry.[5]

---

[1] *Winter's Tale*, Act IV, scene 3.

[2] *R. v. Aspinall* (1876), 2 Q.B.D. 48, C.A., at p. 58.

[3] *Hepworth v. Pickles*, [1900] 1 Ch. 108. So, in *Re Tiedemann and Ledermann Frères*, [1899] 2 Q.B. 66, the implied representation of a certain person that he had a principal who was in a position to assume the obligations of his contract, turned out, *malgré* the representor, to be true.

[4] *Derry v. Peek* (1889), 14 App. Cas. 337, H.L., at p. 348.

[5] But the state of mind of the *falsus* may be in the highest degree relevant at a later stage of the inquiry; for, in determining whether the false statement *was fraudulently made*, the test is to be found in the meaning which the representation had in the mind of the representor— *Akerhielm v. De Mare*, [1959] 3 All E.R. 485; [1959] A.C. 789; P.C.; "If James *intended the letters to convey* the impression that the company was a going concern, or was willing that a recipient should get that impression, clearly he was guilty of fraud, because he knew very well that it was not a going concern. But although that is, in my view, the impression that the letters read together would naturally create, James cannot be held guilty of fraud unless he *intended or was willing* that they should be read in this way"—*per* CROSS L.J. in *Gross v. Lewis Hillman, Ltd*, [1970] Ch. 445, C.A. at p. 459. See, further, Chapter V, para. 98, *post*.

Onus of proving falsity

68 Since in any form of proceeding a misrepresentation must be established, it follows that the burden of alleging and proving falsity in fact, which alone turns a representation into a misrepresentation, rests on the party who sets it up, whatever the form of proceeding may be.[1] Whether a representation is false or not, if there is any evidence, is of course a question of fact.[2]

Substantial falsity essential

69 Falsity and truth are, for the purposes of the law, opposites and mutually exclusive. What is not true is false, and what is not false is true. The question therefore—what is falsity?—depends on the question which, though in another application, "jesting Pilate" asked *ex cathedra*, but "stayed not for an answer". That answer, for the purposes of the law of misrepresentation, has been given by English jurisprudence in reasonably plain terms. Truth, as has already been pointed out, is not truthfulness: verity is not veracity. Neither is it mathematical truth. In science, absolute exactitude alone is truth, and a departure from it by a hair's breadth is error. But, in the case of communications between man and man for the purpose of influencing conduct, there are necessarily degrees of truth and falsity. The facts may correspond with the statement entirely, or partially, or not at all. The important features may be correctly described, whilst the unimportant details are misstated, or *vice versa*. Yet since, for the purpose of determining legal liability, law must resort to dichotomy and set over against one another the two cate-

---

[1] *Vernon* v. *Keys* (1810), 12 East, 632, affirmed (1812), 4 Taunt. 488, Ex. Ch. where, after verdict for the plaintiff, judgment was arrested on the ground that no unequivocal falsehood had been proved; *Legge* v. *Croker* (1811), 1 Ball & B. 506, *per* Lord MANNERS L.C. (Ir.) at p. 515; *Hallows* v. *Fernie* (1868), 3 Ch. App. 467, *per* Lord CHELMSFORD, L.C., at p. 477 ("the precise representation must be distinctly stated"); *Bodger* v. *Nicholls* (1873), 28 L.T. 441, where there was no proof of the unsoundness of the animal, assuming there to have been an implied representation of its soundness; *Melbourne Banking Corporation* v. *Brougham* (1882), 7 App. Cas. 307, P.C., at pp. 314, 315; *Smith* v. *Chadwick* (1884), 9 App. Cas. 187, H.L. (*per* Lord SELBORNE L.C. at pp. 190–192); *Goldstein* v. *Salvation Army Assurance Society*, [1917] 2 K.B. 291, Div. Ct. (*per* ROWLATT J, at p. 294). *Cf.* the criminal cases, such as *R.* v. *Perrott* (1814), 2 M. & S. 379, where, there being no allegation that any *specific* material pretence was false, the indictment was held bad, and *R.* v. *Aspinall* (1876), 2 Q.B.D. 48, *per* BRETT L.J. at p. 57. And see generally the cases cited in the notes to this chapter.

[2] For whether the fact corresponds with the statement, must, obviously, and *ex vi terminorum*, be a question of fact, but, on the other hand, it is a question of law whether there is any evidence of facts either contradicting, or supporting the statement, as the case may be. Further, when the representation is said to be implied from acts and conduct, "it must in every case depend upon the nature of the transaction whether the fact not disclosed is such that it is impliedly represented not to exist; and that must generally be a question of fact proper for a jury": *Lee* v. *Jones* (1864), 17 C.B. N.S. 482, Exch. Ch. (*per* BLACKBURN J. at p. 506).

gories of falsity and truth, in one or other of which every representation
is to be included, it follows that some criterion, other than the scientific
(which is obviously inapplicable), must be adopted for deciding which
of the only two possible characters must be assigned to any particular
representation.   That criterion (see Article 11) is fixed by reference to
the effect of the statement on the mind of the representee.   The question
is—was it, *as between him and the representor*, true or false?   The answer
depends on whether the *material* particulars were correctly or incorrectly
stated.   That is to say, if the discrepancy between the facts as represented,
and the facts as they existed, is such as would have reasonably influenced
the mind of a normal representee in considering whether or not to alter
his position as he did, the representation is false; if otherwise, true.   This
is one way of stating the rule.   Another (which is perhaps the commoner
form, but amounts to exactly the same thing) is to say that falsity *in
substance* is, on the one hand, necessary, and, on the other, adequate, to
establish misrepresentation; for "substance" is here applied to those
features in the statement which were intended to have, and had, an
effect on the representee, or, in other words, which to him appeared—
reasonably appeared, of course—material.   The two forms of the rule are
combined in its statutory application to contracts of marine insurance.[1]

Inaccuracy in unimportant details

70   It results from the above that where the entirety of a representation forms a faithful picture or transcript of the facts, its truth is established, and is not affected by any number of inaccuracies in unimportant
details.   These are matters of mere fringe and superficies, the sort of
"errors" which "like straws upon the surface flow".   "He who would
search for" falsity "must dive below".   On the other hand, if the general
impression conveyed is false, the utmost precision and the most punctual
and scrupulous accuracy in a number of immaterial minutiae will not
avail to stamp the misrepresentation with the sign of truth: on the
contrary it may be treated as part and parcel of the misrepresentation,
and as an instrument of fraud as well. In prospectuses of companies,

> "large print, little print, italics, red ink, and other attractive devices in
> other parts of the prospectus to lead the unwary from the true path of
> inquiry are only specimens of the art of deceiving, and an apparent candour
> may be a more potent engine of deception."[2]

---

[1] See s. 20 (4) of the Marine Insurance Act 1906 (6 Edw. 7, c. 41): "a representation as to
matter of fact is true, if it be substantially correct, that is to say, if the difference between what
is represented and what is actually correct would not be considered material by a prudent
insurer."

[2] BYRNE J. at p. 634 of *Watts* v. *Bucknall*, [1902] 2 Ch. 628, a passage cited with approval on
appeal, [1903] 1 Ch. 766, C.A., by COLLINS M.R. at p. 777.

The difference in this respect between a misrepresentation and a breach of warranty, where exact correspondence between statement and fact is the very thing contracted for, was insisted upon by Lord MANSFIELD,[1] and, since his time, there have been numerous illustrations in the books of the rule that proof of falsity in the substance (understood as above) of a representation is proof of its having been a misrepresentation. Less than this will not suffice: more is not required.[2]

Falsity must go to the very fact represented

71   No falsity is "substantial" which does not amount to falsity in relation to the very fact actually or impliedly stated. In the case of statements of intention, opinion, or law, which involve or presuppose only a very limited statement of fact, as has already been indicated, this proposition (which, as applied to other types of statement, may seem a truism) becomes of great importance.[3] In such cases, the existence of the intention, opinion, belief, or expectation being the only fact which is stated, and also in cases where the representor qualifies his statement by "so far as I know", or similar expressions, the only falsity which can be shown necessarily involves dishonesty also. Bad faith is untruth, and similarly innocence is truth.[4] This in no way negatives the statement that the representor's condition of mind is irrelevant to the question of falsity

---

[1] *Pawson* v. *Watson* (1778), 2 Cowp. 785, at pp. 788–790. *Cf.* the other authorities cited in note 2 on p. 131, *post*.

[2] *Dobson* v. *Sotheby* (1827), Mood. & M. 90 (a fire insurance case, in which the premises had been described as a barn, where Lord TENTERDEN C.J. at p. 92, directed the jury to consider whether the description, though not strictly accurate, was substantially so, having regard to its effect on the mind of the insurer in estimating the risk); *Adamson* v. *Evitt* (1830), 2 Russ. & M. 66 (in which LEACH M.R. considered a statement "substantially" correct which referred to a man as having an annual income of "about £1000", though in fact he had only £900); *Denton* v. *Macneil* (1866), L.R. 2 Eq. 352 (inaccurate statements as to an invention held by ROMILLY M.R. not to have been substantial or material, and action accordingly dismissed); *Bear* v. *Stevenson* (1874), 30 L.T. 177, P.C. (where the representation was that only one incumbrance existed on certain sheep and wool: in fact there were two others, but the instruments created by them had been handed back by the incumbrancers to the representors, on the understanding that they should be, as they afterwards were, satisfied out of the advance then being negotiated for: held not false in substance, though not literally true); *McKeown* v. *Boudard-Peveril Gear Co.* (1896), 65 L.J. Ch. 735, C.A. (where as to certain of the representations, there were "inaccuracies" merely, or "trifling errors", or "trivial" mistakes, which, therefore, did not make the representations false: *per* LINDLEY L.J. and LOPES L.J. at p. 736, and RIGBY L.J. at p. 737); *Seddon* v. *North-Eastern Salt Co.*, [1905] 1 Ch. 326 (where JOYCE J. at p. 335 held that there was no proof that a balance sheet showing a certain result was substantially, though it was strictly, incorrect); *Brookes* v. *Hansen*, [1906] 2 Ch. 129 (*per* JOYCE J. at pp. 137, 138).

[3] See para. 16, *ante*, as to statements of intention: para. 30, *ante*, as to statements of opinion; and para. 37, *ante*, as to statements of law. See also para. 96, *post*.

[4] See, again, para. 96, *post*. This rule, as applied to representations in marine insurance, is neatly expressed in s. 20 (5) of the Marine Insurance Act 1906 (6 Edw. 7, c. 41): "a representation as to a matter of expectation or belief is true if it be made in good faith."

or truth in fact, because it so happens that, in the class of case under consideration, the representor's belief or intention is the fact which is either truly or untruly represented—the curtain *is* the picture.

Inconsistency not falsity

72 Falsity is not established by shewing inconsistencies between different statements made by the representor: it is of no use to urge that both, or all, such statements cannot be true, if it is not proved that some one of them is contrary to the fact.[1]

When the falsity must be shown to have existed

73 It is commonly said that the representation must be shown to have been false when made. But this is not quite correct. The only real issue is: was it true or false when it was acted upon?[2] The question is whether the representee was deceived, misled, or damaged. And this question can be answered only by reference to the point of time at which he altered his position on the faith of the representation. If at this point of time, assuming it to be later than the date when it was made, the statement (which in that event would be a continuing one) was not a true portrait or transcript of the facts *then* existing, the representee is injured, however closely that statement may have corresponded with the facts existing at the date when it was made. Conversely, however false when made, the representation, if true when acted upon, would leave the representee without any possible cause of action or ground of complaint. The incorrect mode of stating the proposition with which this paragraph begins comes down to us from a simpler age when it almost invariably happened either that the making of the statement and the acting upon it were synchronous, or that the facts were the same at both dates. The inexactitude does no practical harm when applied to such cases, but, in relation to continuing representations, where the facts are not the same at the two dates, it has a distinct tendency to mislead. A continuing representation is deemed to be made and repeated during every moment of the interval of time which separates the first statement from the representee's alteration of position, where there is any such appreciable interval. Like a continuing offer, in the case of a contract,[3] it may be withdrawn alto-

---

[1] *Goldstein* v. *Salvation Army Assurance Society*, [1917] 2 K.B. 291 (*per* ROWLATT J. at pp. 293, 294).

[2] This passage in the text received the express approval of Lord TUCKER in *Briess* v. *Woolley*, [1954] A.C. 333, H.L. at pp. 353–354; see also the speech of Lord OAKSEY at p. 344.

[3] *Cf.* (amongst numerous other cases) *Carlill* v. *Carbolic Smoke Ball Co.*, [1893] 1 Q.B. 256, C.A., *per* LINDLEY L.J. at p. 262.

gether or modified at any time before it is acted upon, but, unless so withdrawn or modified, and, if modified, subject to the modification, it endures until that time.[1]   And any revocation or correction must be in the
most clear and explicit terms.[2]

Supervening alteration of facts represented

74   During the abovementioned intervening period the situation may
be altered in two ways.   The representor may discover that what he
believed to be true when making the statement was in fact at that time
untrue;   or circumstances may supervene which render a statement,
true when made, untrue when acted upon.   The former class of case is
discussed elsewhere[3]; it has no concern with the present discussion,
inasmuch as, in such cases, no question of supervening falsity arises;
what was originally false remains false, and the representor's subsequent
discovery can only have the effect (if anything) of turning innocence into
fraud.   But, in the latter class, the subsequent events convert a true
representation into something which, whether to be regarded as fraudulent or not,[4] is at all events a misrepresentation in fact, unless the representor supplements it by such timely modifications as will render it in
accord with the new facts.[5]   The doctrine is not limited to contracts

---

[1] See *Smith* v. *Kay* (1859), 7 H.L. Cas. 750, where the acceptance of certain bills was procured
by misrepresentation, for which bills a bond was afterwards substituted, and, in answer to
the argument that the plaintiff was not induced to execute *the bond* by any false statement, Lord
CHELMSFORD, at p. 769, said: "It is a continuing representation. The representation does not
end for ever when the representation is made. The . . . young man . . . in stating his case,
would say, Before I executed the bond I had been led to believe, and I therefore continued to
believe, that . . . etc." *Cf. Meluish* v. *Milton* (1876), 3 Ch.D. 27, C.A. (*per* MELLISH L.J. at
p. 35: "when the lady went through the ceremony of marriage with the testator, she in effect
represented to him that she was capable of becoming his lawful wife, and, *every day when they
were living together*, she must be taken as continuously representing that she was his lawful wife").
As to the right of the representor to withdraw or modify within the limits of the interval
mentioned, see *Holland* v. *Manchester and Liverpool District Banking Co., Ltd.* (1909), 25 T.L.R.
386 (as to an erroneous entry in a pass-book which, it was there held, can be set right by the
banker at any time before the customer draws upon his supposed balance, but unless and until so
corrected, is a continuing representation), with which compare (as applied to marine insurance)
the Marine Insurance Act 1906 (6 Edw. 7, c. 41), s. 20 (6): "a representation may be withdrawn or corrected before the contract is concluded". Article 9 of the Code gives a definition
of a continuing representation.
[2] See the observations of Lord HALSBURY L.C. at p. 370, COTTON L.J. at pp. 371, 372, and
LINDLEY L.J. at p. 373 of *Arnison* v. *Smith* (1889), 41 Ch.D. 348, C.A.
[3] *Vide* para. 103, *post.* Both classes are referred to by FRY J. at p. 475 of *Davies* v. *London and
Provincial Marine Insurance Co.* (1878), 8 Ch.D. 469.
[4] See paras. 101–104, *post.*
[5] *With* v. *O'Flanagan*, [1936] Ch. 575, C.A. On p. 584 Lord WRIGHT M.R. referred to
"the duty which rests upon the party who has made the representation not to leave the other
party under an error when the representation has become falsified by a change of circumstances".

uberrimae fidei, or to any cases in which owing to confidential relationship there is a peculiar duty of disclosure, but is applicable to cases in which, if the representor had been silent from the beginning, there would have been no duty to speak at all.[1]

Where a bankrupt's interest in certain property was subject to (*inter alia*) his wife's life interest, and was correctly so described by one who was negotiating with the bankrupt's assignees for the purchase of that interest, but, before the contemplated purchaser contracted to purchase, the wife died, without any disclosure of this fact by him, the description was false, at the date of the purchase, and Lord ELDON L.C. set aside the sale[2]; where an applicant for an insurance policy had truly stated in the proposal form that he was not insured against accident or disease in any other office, but before the issue of the policy had so insured himself, it was held that the company had a good defence to a claim on the policy,[3] and a similar decision was given in the case of an applicant who had failed to correct a true statement as to his latest medical adviser which was rendered false by his consultation of a specialist in the interim[4]; and where, in a case of a fire insurance, the party had added a third storey to the premises after his original statement (which merely described the premises as they then existed), the representation became false when acted upon, and the policy was held not enforceable.[5] So, if directors of a company, announced as such in the prospectus, retire before allotment, the representation is false at the latter, which is the only material, date[6]:

---

[1] *Per* Lord WRIGHT M.R. in *With* v. *O'Flanagan* (*supra*) at p. 585, adverting in this regard to a dictum of BENNETT J. in the judgment then under appeal, as to the effect of *Traill* v. *Baring* (1864), 4 De G.J. & Sm. 318.

[2] *Turner* v. *Harvey* (1821), Jac. 169.

[3] *Re Marshall and the Scottish Employers' Liability and General Insurance Co., Ltd.* (1901) 85 L.T. 757.

[4] *British Equitable Insurance Co.* v. *Great Western Rail. Co.* (1869), 38 L.J. Ch. 314.

[5] *Sillem* v. *Thornton* (1854), 3 El. & Bl. 868, at pp. 882–884, where it was said that the "warranty" (the language used would equally apply to a representation) was a "continuous one". There seems some reason to think that the court may have intended to go even further than the proposition in the text, and may have thought that the warranty or representation would continue during *the currency of the policy*, that is, beyond the expiration of the interval mentioned. If so, and to that extent, the decision is overruled by *Thompson* v. *Hopper* (1858), E.B. & E. 1038, Ex. Ch., at p. 1049. The representation most certainly does not last a minute beyond the act whereby the representee has irretrievably altered his position in the manner alleged. See the case cited in note 1 on p. 87, *post*.

[6] *Re Scottish Petroleum Co., Anderson's Case* (1881), 17 Ch.D. 373, *per* MALINS V.-C. at p. 377, distinguishing the case cited in the next note; *Re Scottish Petroleum Co., Wallace's Case* (1883), 23 Ch.D. 413, C.A., where the Court of Appeal, disagreeing on this point with KAY J., held that the contract to take shares was voidable by reason of the representation having become false before allotment (see the observations of BAGGALLAY L.J. at p. 432, LINDLEY L.J. at p. 435, and FRY L.J. at p. 438).

not so, however, where the retirement is after allotment.[1] Again, a statement, true when made, in the course of negotiations for a compromise between a judgment debtor and a judgment creditor, that the former's father had always refused, and still refused to assist him, is rendered false by the fact, known to the party, that between that date and the effecting of the compromise the father had died intestate, leaving only the son and his widow to share the estate, which was of some value, and the compromise entered into on the faith of the continuing representation is accordingly vitiated.[2] On the same principle, where a man sells a horse by auction, describing it truly as his property, but, while the auction is proceeding, it is sold privately, and the vendor, notwithstanding, authorises the sale to continue, he is deemed to continue therewith his description of the horse as his property, and the person who eventually purchases on the faith of his continuing representation is entitled to rescind the contract[3]; and the same view was taken of the position of one who, having truly described the state of his health in his proposal for a life insurance, failed to record a material change in his physical condition which afterwards took place before the conclusion of the contract.[4]

75 Conversely, a representation which was false when made may in virtue of supervening facts become true when acted upon, in which case there is no falsity at the only material date, and therefore no misrepresentation. Thus, where a statement in a prospectus that more than half the shares had been subscribed for, which was untrue at the date of the issue of the prospectus, became true before allotment to the representee, and even before his application, the shareholder obtained no relief.[5]

---

[1] *Hallows* v. *Fernie* (1868), 3 Ch. App. 467 where Lord CHELMSFORD L.C. at p. 472, pointed out that the retirement of the directors in question *after* allotment could not possibly make the representation false, even as a continuing representation.

[2] *Gilbert* v. *Endean* (1878), 9 Ch.D. 259, C.A. (*per* BRETT L.J. at p. 268).

[3] *Whurr* v. *Devenish* (1904), 20 T.L.R. 385. With the cases cited under this section, the authorities on the liability by estoppel of a partner who retires from a firm without notifying his retirement may be compared; see those cited in the various treatises on partnership, and particularly *Goode and Bennion* v. *Harrison* (1821), 5 B. & Ald. 147, *per* BAYLEY J. at p. 158, who speaks of the retiring partner in that case "having done nothing to correct the mistake", and of his "suffering that delusion *to continue*", and points out that such a person "may protect himself from the consequences *of that misrepresentation* by giving notice", etc. On the whole, it is submitted that the date at which alone falsity is material, in the case of a continuing representation, is correctly stated in Article 10 of the Code.

[4] *Harrington* v. *Pearl Life Assurance Co.* (1914), 30 T.L.R. 613.

[5] *Ship* v. *Crosskill* (1870), L.R. 10 Eq. 73, *per* ROMILLY M.R. at pp. 85, 86. Contrast *Tofts* v. *Pearl Life Assurance Co., Ltd.*, [1915] 1 K.B. 189, C.A., where the misrepresentation, if it ever became true at all, certainly did not become so until after it had been acted upon (*per* PHILLIMORE L.J. at p. 194).

Canons of construction

76 In Article 12 of the Code three rules of construction are set out, which are to be applied where the falsity or truth of any representation is in issue. The first of these relates to the sense in which the words, or other signs constituting the representation, are to be understood; the second, to the effect of omission and silence; the third, to the necessity of considering any complex representation as a whole, and not piecemeal.

Representation is deemed prima facie to have been understood in its natural meaning

77 A representation is understood in the sense in which it was reasonably understood by the representee. What the representor professes to have meant or intended, when making it, is wholly immaterial.[1] But the representee cannot establish falsity by putting an unnatural or strained interpretation upon the words used, however clearly he may prove that in fact he so understood them. *Prima facie* the meaning deemed to have been conveyed is the primary, i.e. the natural, customary, and ordinary meaning—that which would be conveyed to a normal person.[2] It is no more sufficient to prove an understanding in a particular sense, unless that sense was a possible one, than it is to prove a natural sense, without also proving that in fact the representation was understood in that sense.

But secondary meaning can be specially proved

78 But, as in the case of the law of defamation,[3] though the representee is in the absence of special circumstances assumed to have accepted the

---

[1] See *Greenwood* v. *Leather Shod Wheel Co.*, [1900] 1 Ch. 421, C.A., *per* LINDLEY M.R. p. 434. *Cf. Glasier* v. *Rolls* (1889), 42 Ch.D. 436, C.A., where KEKEWICH J. at p. 454, said that the representee having construed the representation in the sense alleged and proved by him, which was a reasonable sense, and in which it was false, it was no answer to say that the representor meant by his own statement something else, which would have been true. The C.A., who reversed the judge on another ground, did not disagree with him on this point. See also *Angus* v. *Clifford*, [1891] 2 Ch. 449, C.A.

[2] The primary meaning is not necessarily the literal meaning; it is not so where the customary sense is different. Paley (*Principles of Moral and Political Philosophy*, Bk. III, Pt. I, Ch.xv) has some judicious observations on this head: "As there may be falsehoods which are not lies, so there may be lies without direct or literal falsehood. An opening is always left for this species of prevarication, where the literal and grammatical signification of a sentence is different from the popular and customary meaning . . . it is absurd to contend for any sense of words in opposition to usage, for all senses of all words are founded upon usage, and upon nothing else."

[3] These rules are stated and commented upon in Mr Spencer Bower's *Code of Actionable Defamation*, Part IV. Every canon of construction there stated for the purpose of determining whether matter published is defamatory or not is applicable, *mutatis mutandis*, to the determination of questions as to the falsity of representations.

statement in its ordinary or primary meaning, it is nevertheless open to either party to allege and prove the existence of such special circumstances, and that in virtue thereof, a secondary, i.e. a trade, technical, conventional, or wholly unnatural sense, was conveyed to the mind of the representee.   Such secondary sense may operate either to render false what otherwise would be true, or to render true what otherwise would be false.

And apart altogether from technical, trade, or conventional meanings,[1] it may be shown that the representor wished and intended the representee to affix, and that the representee did in fact affix, a special and unnatural sense to the expressions used.[2]

Ambiguous representations

79   The immediately preceding paragraphs are applicable to representations to which only one sense (if a primary one) is applicable, or (if secondary) is sought to be applied.   More difficult questions arise when the words are *ancipitis sensus*, genuinely and reasonably susceptible of more than one meaning.   In all such cases, no less than when a single secondary sense is assigned, the burden both of allegation and of proof is on the representee, who must first aver, and then prove, in what sense he understood the expressions used, and that the representation was false in that sense.   The stringency of this rule has been long recognised, and is illustrated by a considerable chain of examples.   Indeed, in one instance, so necessary was it considered by the pleader to allege the meaning put upon the words of the representation (which was that certain designs of silk handkerchiefs had been registered) that an elaborate "innuendo", spread over 13 lines of print, was pleaded in the declaration,[3] whereupon it was solemnly argued for the defendant (as if the case had been one of defamation) that the innuendo was heavier than the words could carry, on which the court observed that "the objection that the innuendo is larger than the representation is answered by the remark that no innuendo is required".[4]   Nor was it, perhaps, in that particular case; but equally no innuendo is necessary in an action of defamation, if the plaintiff is content to stand or fall by the single primary sense of the words.   Where, however, there are two possible meanings, it is essential, both in the one class of action and in the other, to allege, as well as to prove, which of

---

[1] As, *e.g.*, *Woodhouse* v. *Swift* (1836), 7 C. & P. 310, where ALDERSON B. received evidence as to the conventional meaning in the trade of "sound timber".

[2] *Piggott* v. *Stratton* (1859), 1 De G.F. & J. 33, at p. 50.

[3] *Barley* v. *Walford* (1846), 9 Q.B. 197, at p. 199.

[4] *Ibid.*, p. 209.

the two meanings is relied upon, particularly if, in the other meaning, the words are innocent of any defamatory or deceptive effect respectively. Though in the one case it is, and in the other it is not, usual to apply to such an averment the term "innuendo", this can make no difference in principle; so that the pleading referred to, though quaint and startling at the first blush, was in reality based on a sound analogy.

Instances

80 The rule stated in the preceding paragraph has been applied in the following circumstances. A statement by the representor that his intended partners would not give more than a named sum for a certain property might mean either that they had in fact refused to do so, or that they were not likely to do so in the future; it was for the plaintiff to prove the former meaning, in which alone the statement would have been an unequivocal falsehood, and, as he had not done so, his action failed.[1] Words in a prospectus capable of being construed either as a description of the present intention of the company to start business with a certain equipment of steamships, or as an engagement to provide itself with them in the future, were not alleged by the plaintiff to have been construed by him in the present tense, and he was therefore held not to have established any misrepresentation.[2] Where the vendors in London of a cargo of rye at Gibraltar advertised it as "in perfect condition", and added, "by telegram", it was held that the representee had no right to assume that this meant that the cargo had been inspected, but only that a telegram stating its condition had in fact been received, which was true.[3] A prospectus stated that no remuneration was to be given *by the company* to the directors. According to the plain meaning of the words this was true, because the directors, though they received remuneration, did not receive it from the company, but from the promoters. Assuming, however, that the representation might reasonably be construed as negativing the receipt of remuneration from any one concerned with the company, it was held to be for the plaintiff to prove that he so understood it.[4] Another representation in a prospectus that "the present value of the turnover or output of the entire works is over £100,000 per annum", was capable of importing either that the works had in some year in fact produced the amount stated, or that they were capable of

---

[1] *Vernon* v. *Keys* (1810), 12 East, 632, *per* Lord ELLENBOROUGH C.J. at p. 636.
[2] *Hallows* v. *Fernie* (1868), 3 Ch.App. 467, *per* Lord CHELMSFORD L.C. at pp. 476, 477 ("if the words are susceptible of a different meaning, he is deceived, not by the words, but by his construction of them").
[3] *Schroeder* v. *Mendl* (1877), 37 L.T. 452, C.A.
[4] *Arkwright* v. *Newbold* (1881), 17 Ch.D. 301, C.A., *per* COTTON L.J. at pp. 324, 325.

doing so. In the former sense it was false; in the latter, true. The plaintiff, however, refused to say what sense he put upon the words, stating in answer to an interrogatory directed to the point, that he "understood the meaning to be that which the words obviously conveyed", and that he was "unable to express in other words what he understood to be the meaning thereof". If there had been only one reasonable meaning of the words, this would have been a proper and sufficient answer; but since there were two possible senses, and the plaintiff nevertheless elected to stand or fall by his supposed single and obvious sense, he found himself in the position of having refused even to attempt to discharge the burden which the House of Lords, affirming the C.A., held to lie upon him, of, first, assigning a meaning, and then proving that he understood, and was induced by, the representation in that sense, and that in that sense it was false.[1] On the other hand, when a similarly ambiguous statement in a prospectus that "the business had paid 17 per cent. upon the capital employed in it" was false, if the company's premiums were included in the capital, but true, if they were not, and the plaintiff put the former sense, which was a reasonable one, upon the statement, and proved that he so understood it, it was held that a misrepresentation had been proved, and the burden of proof had been discharged.[2] *A fortiori* is this the case when it is shewn that the representor himself construed his representation in the sense alleged by his opponent, and not in the sense in which it would have been true.[3] A statement, in answer to a question which the representor was under no obligation to answer, as to the incumbrances on certain property of a third person, might under the circumstances, mean either that there was no such incumbrance in fact, or that there was none so far as the representor could remember: it was held that the onus was upon the representee of showing that the representation had been construed, and reasonably (not necessarily) construed, by him in the former sense, in which it would have been false, and not in the latter, in which it would have

---

[1] *Smith* v. *Chadwick* (1884), 9 App. Cas. 187, H.L., *per* Lord SELBORNE, L.C. at pp. 190–192, and Lord BLACKBURN at pp. 197–201.

[2] *Glasier* v. *Rolls* (1889), 42 Ch.D. 436, C.A. The view stated in the text was that of KEKEWICH J. at p. 454, and was not dissented from by the C.A., who reversed his decision solely on the ground that the misrepresentation was not fraudulent, whilst agreeing that there had been a misrepresentation in fact. In *Capel & Co.* v. *Sim's Ships Composition Co., Ltd.* (1888), 58 L.T. 807, the same learned judge, at pp. 808, 809, expressed the same opinion as to the onus which rests on the plaintiff, where the statement is capable of more than one interpretation, to allege and prove a particular sense, and that he *reasonably* understood it in that sense.

[3] *Glicksman* v. *Lancashire and General Assurance Co., Ltd.*, [1925] 2 K.B. 593, C.A., *per* SCRUTTON L.J. at pp. 606–608. The decision of the Court of Appeal was affirmed in the Lords—[1927] A.C. 139; but on a different point, and this dictum does not seem to have been referred to.

been true; in other words, of establishing an unequivocal misrepresentation. This he failed to do, and the judgment accordingly went against
him.[1] Where, in a "passing off" case, it was contended that the use of
the words "Trade Mark" in the advertisements of an article involved a
statement to the public that the mark had been registered, it was thought
to be incumbent on the party, either to establish by evidence that the
public would *reasonably* regard the representation as involving the statement in question, or, in the absence of such evidence, to show that the
implication alleged was a necessary one.[2]

Ambiguity designed by representor

81 The type of ambiguity which we have been discussing is inherent
in the terms of the representation. Its consequence is to throw a
difficulty in the way of the representee; for it places upon him the onus
of demonstrating the representation to be reasonably capable of being
understood in the sense relied upon, and proving moreover that he
understood it in that sense. But there is another type of ambiguity in
representation which counts against the representor, and where the onus
is on him, and not on the representee. We find this type when there is
evidence of the representor having resorted to ambiguous, which then
becomes ambidextrous, language for the express purpose of afterwards
falling back on the literal, or it may even be the plain and ordinary,
interpretation of the words, though he well knew and intended that the
representee should take them in another and perhaps less natural sense.
The contrast is between natural and spontaneous ambiguity, and that
which is artificial and premeditated. In the latter class of case, every
presumption is made against him who uses dubious phraseology as an
instrument of fraud. *Fortius verba accipiuntur contra proferentem* is, as
Bacon justly observes, "a rule drawn from the depths of reason",[3]
and there can be no juster application of the principle than to the interpretation of the statements of him who, without expressly or literally
lying, or concealing truth, *fallendi causa obscure loquitur.* "If", said Lord
Eldon L.C. "one man understands an expression in one sense, and
another in a different sense, though the court would impute to both that
they understood it in the right sense, yet . . . if the expression used by

---

[1] *Low* v. *Bouverie*, [1891] 3 Ch. 82, C.A., *per* Lindley L.J. at p. 101, and Bowen L.J. at
p. 106.

[2] *Sen Sen Co.* v. *Britten*, [1899] 1 Ch. 692, *per* Stirling J. at p. 698, who, in reference to the
earlier case of *Lewis's* v. *Goodbody* (1892), 67 L.T. 194, the report of which seems to indicate a
decision *en sens contraire*, observed that he had made inquiries, and, as the result, had "some
reason to believe", that evidence *was* there adduced.

[3] Bacon's *Maxims of the Law*, Reg. III, vol. vii, p. 333 (Spedding and Ellis's edition).

one party has at all misled the other''—by which phrase he must have been referring to independent evidence that the first party intended to mislead—''it is always material in considering what a court of equity will do with the case''.[1] Lord BLACKBURN similarly, but more strongly, expresses the view that the ambiguity of a representation may be a badge of fraud, from the consequences of which it is for the representor to escape if he can, and that he cannot do so by the mere plea that the representee ought to have taken it in the other of the two possible senses.[2] To the same effect, LINDLEY L.J. in reference to ambiguous conditions of sale,[3] and Lord HALSBURY L.C. on the ''ambidextrous language'' of a prospectus.[4] The canon thus enunciated has been applied in a variety of cases,[5] the most illustrative perhaps of which is one where, in the course of a negotiation for an underlease of land by the sea, the representor, answering the representee's question whether there would be an un-impeded sea view from the house she was proposing to build on the land, replied, with absolute accuracy in the literal sense of the words, that he was bound by the superior lease not to build on the intervening land. Having regard, however, to what he must have gathered from the lady's question as to her apprehensions, it was held that he deliberately framed his answer so as to remove them, and must, therefore, be taken to have intended her to understand by it that she was safe in taking the house from any such interruption as she feared, and that the representation, so construed, was false because she was not in fact protected from the event which afterwards happened, *viz.* the making by the representor

---

[1] At p. 176 of *Turner* v. *Harvey* (1821), Jac. 169. See para. 74, *ante*, for the facts of this case.

[2] *Smith* v. *Chadwick* (1884), 9 App. Cas. 187 H.L., at p. 201: ''if with intent to lead the plaintiff to act upon it, they put forth a statement which they know may bear two meanings, one of which is false to their knowledge, and thereby the plaintiff putting that meaning on it is misled, I do not think they can escape by saying he ought to have put the other. If they palter with him in a double sense it may be that they lie *like* truth; but I think they lie, and it is a fraud''.

[3] At p. 28 of *Terry and White's Contract* (1886), 32 Ch.D. 14, C.A.

[4] *Aaron's Reefs, Ltd.* v. *Twiss*, [1896] A.C. 273, H.L., at pp. 282, 283. *Cp.* the observations of KAY L.J. at p. 113 of *Low* v. *Bouverie*, [1891] 3 Ch. 82, C.A.: ''if there was fraud, and the statement was intended to mislead, its ambiguity would not be a defence''.

[5] *Turner* v. *Harvey* (1821), Jac. 169; *Piggott* v. *Stratton* (1859), 1 De G.F. & J. 33; *Coulson* v. *Allison* (1860), 2 De G.F. & J. 521; *Dendy* v. *Cary* (1863), 9 Jur. N.S. 845; *Scott* v. *Snyder Dynamite Projectile Co., Ltd.* (1892), 67 L.T. 104, C.A., *per* LINDLEY L.J., at p. 106: ''the prospectus is catchy and misleading in nine-tenths of its paragraphs. It *suggests* that the company have acquired an existing patent, though it is possible, by subjecting it to a microscopic examination, to *say* that that is not what is really meant. Like the well-known introduction to the Ingoldsby Legends'' (the reference is to Canon Barham's two humorously mystifying prefatory letters addressed ''to Richard Bentley, Esq,.''—there is no Introduction) ''it appears to say a great deal, whilst not saying anything''; *Aaron's Reefs, Ltd.* v. *Twiss*, [1896] A.C. 273, H.L.

of other arrangements with his lessor, whereby he became no longer subject to any restrictions as to building.[1]

Falsity by omission, silence or inaction

82 It has been shrewdly said, though the poet has put the words into the mouth of a fool, that there are "those That therefore only are reputed wise For saying nothing".[2] It is certain that there are others who, for the like reason, are reputed in law misrepresentors. Apart from cases of pure non-disclosure in the strictest sense of the term, when no falsehood is told, but some absolute duty of disclosure imposed by considerations of public policy is violated, there are cases where a man may positively lie by saying nothing, and where the circumstances are such that reticence or concealment may amount to active misrepresentation. One (and the more obvious) of the two main types of such reticence is the omission from a statement of all reference to qualifying facts, leaving what is stated to stand as an absolute, and therefore a false, representation. The other is to be found in those who "do a wilful stillness entertain", when their previous declarations or acts bid them speak, in order to remove a delusion for the creation of which they are themselves responsible. Both these classes are intended to be comprised in Article 12, Rule 2, of the Code.

Omission of essential qualifying or modifying facts

83 The law requires from a representor not only that he adds nothing which makes false what would otherwise have been true; he must not willingly omit anything which is required to render true, or to preserve as true, what would without the qualification be false. Such an omission amounts to that form of *suppressio veri* which not merely is equivalent to, but which actually is, *suggestio falsi*. To state a thing which is true only with qualifications or additions known to, but studiously withheld by, the representor, is to say the thing which is not. Such a statement is a "lie", and one of the most dangerous and insidious forms of lie. "If a man", says CHAMBRE J. "professing to answer a question, select

---

[1] *Piggott* v. *Stratton* (1859), 1 De G.F. & J. 33; *Re General Provincial Life Assurance Co., Ex. parte Daintree* (1870), 18 W.R. 396; *Re Banister, Broad* v. *Munton* (1879), 12 Ch.D. 131, C.A.; *Re Marsh and Earl Granville* (1882), 24 Ch.D. 11, C.A. *Cf.* the story, referred to by Paley (*Moral and Pol. Philos.*, Bk. III, Pt. I, ch. v), when dealing with deceptive promises, of the general (Temures) who promised the garrison of Sebastia that, if they would surrender, no blood would be shed, and, on their surrendering, buried them all alive, and the similar stories told in I Kings ii, 8, 9, and in Thuc., *Hist.* III, 34.

[2] *Merchant of Venice*, Act I, scene 1.

those facts only which are likely to give a credit to the person of whom he speaks, and keep back the rest, he is a more artful knave than he who tells a direct falsehood''.[1]

84 It is not because a statement is incomplete, that it is to be deemed a misrepresentation, any more than a report of a trial is deemed to fall short of a "fair and accurate report" merely because it is an abbreviated version of the proceedings. But both in the one case and in the other, he who summarises does so at his peril. If his summary is a faithful portrait, it is none the worse for being a miniature; if, however, the incompleteness is one-sided and partial—if the artist *ita mentitur, sic veris falsa remiscet*, that the picture presented is out of perspective and distorted, then the pretended transcript is untrue in the one case, and "unfair" in the other.[2] The rule is best expressed by Lord CHELMSFORD and Lord CAIRNS respectively in two of the cases arising out of the Overend and Gurney disaster. The language used by the former was:

> "it is said that everything which is stated in the prospectus is literally true, and so it is. But the objection to it is, not that it does not state the truth as far as it goes, but that it conceals most material facts with which the public ought to have been made acquainted, the very concealment of which gives to the truth which is told the character of falsehood".[3]

Lord CAIRNS describes the process as "such a partial and fragmentary statement of fact, as that the withholding of that which is not stated makes that which is stated absolutely false".[4] In accordance with the above rule, the following statements, from which the following qualifying or otherwise material facts were respectively omitted or withheld, were deemed misrepresentations, in relation to contracts (mostly of

---

[1] At p. 372 of *Tapp* v. *Lee* (1803), 3 Bos. & P. 367, cited with approval by PARK J. at p. 403 of *Foster* v. *Charles* (1830), 6 Bing. 396. It is a remarkable, though seldom remarked, fact in the story of Ananias and Sapphira (Acts v, 1–11), that whilst the latter told a lie (though inferentially only, even in her case), Ananias, who has gone down the ages as the type of the Liar, made no representation at all, but "lied unto God" purely by silence.

[2] See such cases as *Frescoe* v. *May* (1860), 2 F. & F. 123, where the pretended report "put forward what is inculpatory, withholding what is exculpatory", and was held entirely unprotected.

[3] *Oakes* v. *Turquand*; *Peek* v. *Same* (1867), L.R. 2 H.L. 325, at pp. 342, 343.

[4] *Peek* v. *Gurney* (1873), L.R. 6 H.L. 377, at p. 403. Cp. the observations of POLLOCK C.B. at p. 160 of *Cazenove* v. *British Equitable Assurance Co., Ltd.* (1860), 29 L.J. C.P. 160: ("it is trifling to say that that is a true answer which requires something to be added to it to make it true"); those of JAMES L.J. at p. 318 of *Arkwright* v. *Newbold* (1881), 17 Ch.D. 301, C.A. ("supposing you state a thing partially, you make a false statement as much as if you misstated it altogether. Every word may be true, but if you leave out something which qualifies it, . . . that is an actual misstatement"); and those of Lord MACNAGHTEN at p. 251 of *Gluckstein* v. *Barnes*, [1900] A.C. 240, H.L. ("everybody knows that sometimes half a truth is no better than downright falsehood").

sale and purchase):—declaration in proposal for a life policy that the proposer was resident in a certain town, without mentioning that he was "resident" there only in the sense that he was in the county goal of that town for debt[1]; particulars of an annuity, which were quite accurate as far as they went, without adding that the annuity was terminable in five years[2]; a statement that lands were held under an agreement for four lives, without adding that the four lives dated from the expiration of the present tenant's lease, which would not happen for 19 years[3]; reference to a case submitted to counsel by the representor, without any mention of the opinion itself, which was then before him, and was adverse[4]; a statement that certain farms were let, without stating that the tenants had given notice to quit[5]; a plan of an estate which was correct in every respect, except that it omitted certain particular trees, though showing an indiscriminate mass of trees as intended to pass[6]; a description of the property sold as being subject to a life interest, without mentioning the fact that it was also subject to three mortgages[7]; particulars of sale which were silent as to a ground rent to which the property was subject[8]; a statement by the defendant's solicitor that he did not know of any restrictions on the use of certain premises, without adding that he had never looked at the deeds to see if there were any[9]; a description of property as "leasehold business premises", without mentioning that the lease contained restrictive covenants against certain specified businesses[10]; a statement of the existence of an off-licence in respect of certain premises, which was true, omitting to add that there were covenants in a previous conveyance to the representor's predecessors in title against the user of them as an inn, tavern, or beerhouse[11]; a recital in a deed of sale omitting all reference to a certain mortgage[12]; an advertise-

---

1 *Huguenin* v. *Rayley* (1815), 6 Taunt. 186.

2 *Coverley* v. *Burrell* (1821), 5 B. & Ald. 257.

3 *Martin* v. *Cotter* (1846), 3 Jo. & Lat. 496.

4 *Reynell* v. *Sprye* (1852) , 1 De G.M. & G. 660 (*per* Lord CRANWORTH L.J. at pp. 703-705).

5 *Dimmock* v. *Hallett* (1866), 2 Ch. App. 21 (*per* TURNER and CAIRNS L.JJ.).

6 *Denny* v. *Hancock* (1870), 6 Ch. App. 1. See particularly the observations of MELLISH L.J. at p. 14: "it really almost requires, to my mind, some charity . . . to suppose that he did not prepare his plan with a view of leading a purchaser to suppose the trees to be included, and omit these particular trees, in order that he might be able to say afterwards—'these were not intended to pass'".

7 *Torrance* v. *Bolton* (1872), 8 Ch. App. 118.

8 *Jones* v. *Rimmer* (1880), 14 Ch.D. 588; *per* JESSEL M.R. at p. 591, who held this to be a misrepresentation, though an innocent one, particularly having regard to the extreme precision with which all the items of receipt and profit had been stated.

9 *Nottingham Patent Brick and Tile Co.* v. *Butler* (1886), 16 Q.B.D. 778, C.A.

10 *Re Davis and Cavey* (1888), 40 Ch.D. 601, *per* STIRLING J. at p. 605.

11 *Hepworth* v. *Pickles*, [1900] 1 Ch. 108, *per* FARWELL J. at pp. 111, 112.

12 *Dixon* v. *Winch*, [1900] 1 Ch. 736, C.A.

ment of land as "capital freehold *building* land", without any reference to the fact that the local authority had, under byelaws, prohibited building thereon until all the refuse with which certain excavations had been filled up should have been removed[1]; and a proclamation of the sale of land as at the instance of the mortgagees, without any reference to the incumbrances which amounted to a sum in excess of the utmost value of the land.[2]   And there are other miscellaneous illustrations of concealment in this class of transaction.[3]

> "In all cases of sale, it is the obvious duty of the vendor . . . to describe everything which it is material to know in order to judge of the nature and value of the property. It is not for him just to tell what is not actually untrue, leaving out a great deal that is true, and leaving it to the purchaser to inquire whether there is any error or omission in the description or not".[4]

A second, and very fruitful, nursing ground of the type of misrepresentation under consideration is the company prospectus, and it is to these documents, perhaps, that the occasion most frequently arises to apply the rule that an omission may render the entire document so partial and fragmentary as to be positively false.[5]   Another species of case

---

[1] *Baker* v. *Moss* (1902), 66 J.P. 360.

[2] *Mahomed Kala Mea* v. *A.-V. Harperink* (1908), 25 T.L.R. 180, P.C.

[3] Such as *Smith* v. *Harrison* (1857), 26 L.J. Ch. 412; *Piggot* v. *Stratton* (1859), 1 De G.F. & J. 33; *Dendy* v. *Cary* (1863), 9 Jur. N.S. 845.

[4] Per KINDERSLEY V.-C. at p. 430 of *Brandling* v. *Plummer* (1854), 2 Drew. 427. *Cf.* the observations of FRY J. at p. 136 of *Re Banister, Broad* v. *Munton* (1879), 12 Ch.D. 131, C.A.

[5] *New Brunswick and Canada Railway and Land Co.* v. *Muggeridge* (1860), 1 Dr. & Sm. 363; *Arkwright* v. *Newbold* (1881), 17 Ch.D. 301, C.A.; *Oakes* v. *Turquand*; *Peek* v. *Same* (1867), L.R. 2 H.L. 325, per Lord CHELMSFORD L.C. at pp. 341–345, and Lord CRANWORTH at p. 368, in which the prospectus concealed the true state of the affairs of Overend, Gurney & Co., whilst stating nothing actually false: see note 3 on p. 95; *Peek* v. *Gurney* (1873), L.R. 6 H.L. 377 (the same prospectus, and the same decision, so far as the question of misrepresentation is concerned): see note 4 on p. 95; *Jury* v. *Stoker* (1882), 9 L.R. Ir. 385, C.A.; *Edgington* v. *Fitz-maurice* (1885), 29 Ch.D. 459, C.A., where DENMAN J., who was affirmed by the C.A., expressed the view, at p. 472, that the concealment of the real object of the issue (which was to pay off pressing liabilities) was sufficient to render the prospectus as a whole such a "partial and fragmentary" statement as to amount to positive falsity; *Re Mount Morgan (West) Gold Mine, Ltd., Ex parte West* (1887), 56 L.T. 622, where the prospectus stated that the company was formed to acquire 14 acres of the famous Mount Morgan, in Queensland, and contained glowing reports of the value of the Mount Morgan property, but omitted to add that the 14 acres did not belong to the proved auriferous portion of Mount Morgan to which alone the reports related, and KAY J., accordingly, at p. 623, pronounced the prospectus to be both false and fraudulent; *Derry* v. *Peek* (1889), 14 App. Cas. 337, H.L. (a statement that the company had power to use steam on their tramways, without adding that this power was subject to the consent of the Board of Trade, and two local authorities); *Scott* v. *Snyder Dynamite Projectile Co., Ltd.* (1892), 67 L.T. 104, C.A. (reference to "firing experiments" with a projectile, without adding that the experiments took place five years previously, and related to a different patent); *Aaron's Reefs, Ltd.* v. *Twiss*, [1896] A.C. 273, H.L., where the prospectus omitted reference to the contents of certain material contracts, through satisfying the bare statutory requirements of the law by inserting the dates and names of the parties thereto, and it was held that the whole prospectus was thereby rendered false *at common law*, per Lord WATSON, at

inviting the application of the rule consists of imperfect and incomplete statements as to the credit and dealings of a third person[1]; and there are other, and miscellaneous, illustrations of the principle.[2]

---

p. 287, and Lord DAVEY, at pp. 293, 294, and where documents were referred to which described the state of the mine, without mentioning that the condition described was that of the mine several years back,—see observations of Lord HALSBURY L.C. at pp. 282, 283, as to this "ambidextrous language"; *Re Dunlop-Truffault Cycle and Tube Manufacturing Co.*, *Ex parte Shearman* (1896), 66 L.J. Ch. 25, where it was held by KEKEWICH J. that the representation (implied from the company's name) that a Dunlop was connected with the company, which was true, unaccompanied by any statement that this Dunlop had no connection whatever with the famous Dunlop Pneumatic Tyre Co., amounted to a misrepresentation; *Components' Tube Co.* v. *Naylor*, [1900] 2 I.R. 1, where there is to be found a luminous discussion of the whole question by PALLES C.B. at pp. 37–60, and where, the jury having found, in answer to one of the questions left to them, that certain omissions were material, and such as to render the prospectus "as a whole, substantially misleading and calculated to deceive", the court refused to disturb the verdict; *Cackett* v. *Keswick*, [1902] 2 Ch. 456, C.A., per ROMER L.J. at p. 476: "Wholly apart from the provisions of sect. 38, in my opinion, in common fairness to the intending investor, to whom a prospectus of this kind is issued, such a contract as we have had to deal with ought to be specified and referred to in the prospectus"; *R.* v. *Lord Kylsant*, [1932] 1 K.B. 442, C.C.A. in which at pp. 448–449 it was said: "The falsity in this case consisted in putting before intending investors, as material on which they could exercise their judgment, figures which apparently disclosed the existing position, but in fact hid it . . . This inference (of solvency) would be drawn particularly from the statement that dividends had been regularly paid over a term of years, though times had been bad—a statement which was utterly misleading when the fact that those dividends had been paid, not out of current earnings, but out of funds which had been earned during the abnormal period of the war, was omitted."

[1] *Tapp* v. *Lee* (1803), 3 Bos. & P. 367; *Ames* v. *Milward* (1818), 8 Taunt. 637, where an assertion by the representor that one Bates had paid him well, which was literally true as regards a certain agreement between these parties, was held substantially false, by reason of the representor's silence as to his dealings with Bates generally, and the security he held of him; *Lee* v. *Jones* (1864), 17 C.B. N.S. 482, Ex.Ch., per SHEE J. at p. 498, who based his decision on the ground that the creditors had been guilty of such a "partial, inaccurate, and subdolous setting forth . . . of facts within their knowledge, material for the proposed sureties to be informed of as, along with the communication of other facts material for them to know, amounted to a misrepresentation", and in the Court of C.P. below, (1863), 14 C.B. N.S. 386, per BYLES J. ("pregnant with the *assertion* that", etc.), and KEATING J. ("active misrepresentation"), at p. 398.

[2] Such as *Stevens* v. *Adamson* (1818), 2 Stark, 422; 20 R.R. 707, where the representor sold premises without informing the representee that only the day before the contract he had been served with notice of re-entry by the superior landlord unless certain repairs were executed in a specified time; *Flight* v. *Booth* (1834), 1 Bing. N.C. 370, where premises were let on the representation that there were restrictions on the use of them for the purposes of any offensive trade, and two other named trades, which was held to be a clear implied representation that there were no restrictions as to any inoffensive business except the two specified, the fact being that a large number of other inoffensive callings were prohibited (see pp. 377, 378); *Carlish* v. *Salt*, [1906] 1 Ch. 335 (concealment of the fact that the vendor had, two days before the contract, been apprised of a party-wall award against him in respect of the premises sold). See also *Greenwood* v. *Greenwood* (1863), 2 De G.J. & Sm. 28; *Brooke* v. *Lord Mostyn* (1864), 2 De G.J. & Sm. 373, where the production of several relevant documents, coupled with the keeping back of a certain very material valuation, was held a misrepresentation justifying the setting aside of the compromise founded thereon; *Gilbert* v. *Endean* (1878), 9 Ch.D. 259, C.A., another compromise case, where the solicitor of the defendants stated to the plaintiff's solicitor that one of the defendants was penniless, and had refused to assist, but omitted to add that his father had died intestate, and was reputed to be possessed of some property: which was held by BRETT L.J. at p. 268, and COTTON L.J. at p. 270, to amount to an absolute misrepresentation; *Mackay* v. *Commercial Bank of New Brunswick* (1874), L.R. 5 P.C. 394, where, in the

85   On the other hand, unless the omission makes the residue false, though the representor may thereby render himself obnoxious to some other rule of statutory or common law, the representation is not only devoid of fraud,[1] but it is not a misrepresentation at all.

> "If a person relies, as a ground for rescission of a contract, on the omission of a statement, he must show that the omission of that statement makes what is stated misleading".[2]

Silence considered in conjunction with something previously said or done

86   It is now necessary to consider the other class of case above-mentioned, where silence, though not in itself a misrepresentation, may, in conjunction with something previously said or done, help to convert truth into falsehood.   This class comprises the three species in the next three paragraphs respectively discussed.

Necessity to say more arising from something already said

87   Where a man has unnecessarily said something, a duty may at

---

Colonial Court, the jury had been directed that the sending of a telegram to the plaintiff in the name of one Lingley, which stated truly that certain moneys had been remitted, amounted to a misrepresentation, by reason of the omission to notify the plaintiff that the telegram had not been sent by Lingley, and that Lingley was insolvent and had absconded, and where, though it was not necessary to pronounce expressly upon the point, the Judicial Committee assumed, and clearly thought, that the direction was right; *Emma Silver Mining Co.* v. *Grant* (1879), 11 Ch.D. 918 (*per* JESSEL M.R. at pp. 933–936); *Boyd and Forrest* v. *Glasgow and South Western Rail. Co.* (1911), 13 S.C. 33, which was reversed, *sub nom. Glasgow and South Western Rail. Co.* v. *Boyd and Forrest, No. 1*, [1913] A.C. 404, H.L., but not on any ground affecting the question now under discussion, where "a journal of bores" was put forward for railway contractors to tender upon, without stating that the bores had been taken by the company's servants, and that the "journal" had been added to, altered, and edited, to suit the company's purposes, by their engineer (pp. 62–74); *Nocton* v. *Lord Ashburton*, [1914] A.C. 932, H.L. (*per* Lord DUNEDIN, at p. 962).   In *Cazenove* v. *British Equitable Assurance Co., Ltd.* (1860), 29 L.J.C.P. 160 the Court of Exchequer Chamber held that an assured who had in a proposal for assurance answered the question "How often has medical attendance been required?"—"One year ago", when there were several occasions of medical attendance, had made a false representation, notwithstanding that every word was true.   So too, in *Australia*, in *Guardian Assurance Co., Ltd.* v. *Condogianis* (1919), 26 C.L.R. 231 the High Court of Australia held a similar evasive answer in a proposal for fire insurance to be a misrepresentation entitling the company to avoid the policy.   This decision was affirmed by the Judicial Committee—[1921] 2 A.C. 125.

   1 "No mere silence will ground the action of deceit", *per* JAMES L.J. at p. 318 of *Arkwright* v. *Newbold* (1881), 17 Ch.D. 301, C.A.

   2 *Per* RIGBY L.J., at p. 736, of *McKeown* v. *Boudard-Peveril Gear Co.* (1896), 65 L.J. Ch. 735. *Cf. Heymann* v. *European Central Rail. Co.* (1868), L.R. 7 Eq. 154, at p. 164; *Re Coal Economising Gas Co., Gover's Case* (1875), 1 Ch.D. 182, C.A. (*per* BRETT J., at p. 199: "for a mere non-disclosure . . . which has not the effect of rendering that which was disclosed or stated a misrepresentation . . . there was no remedy, either at law or in equity"), *Bentley & Co., Ltd.* v. *Black* (1893), 9 T.L.R. 580, C.A. (where it was held that the mere non-disclosure of the figures on which an accountant's certificate was based did not render the certificate a mis-representation); *Re Christineville Rubber Estates, Ltd.* (1911), 81 L.J. Ch. 63 (*per* EVE, J., at p. 66).

once arise to say more, in which case, if he violates this duty, his reticence thenceforth becomes an implied misrepresentation, though complete silence in the first instance would not have been misrepresentation or even actionable non-disclosure.[1] It has already been seen that this duty arises in the case of a continuing representation where, before it is acted upon, facts come to the notice of the representor falsifying a statement which when made was true.[2] But there are other cases where in the course of the negotiations the party has let fall something which, whether he so intended or not, he immediately perceives to have a delusive effect on the mind of the representee, and where, by not correcting the delusion, he is deemed to confirm and perpetuate it, and so to mis-represent.[3] In a curious case[4] relating to the sale of oats by sample which were in fact new oats, but which the purchaser believed to be old, and, therefore, commanding a higher price, BLACKBURN J. laid it down that, if the purchaser had believed not merely that the oats were old, but that

---

[1] *Davies* v. *London and Provincial Marine Insurance Co.* (1878), 8 Ch.D. 469, *per* FRY J., at p. 475: "in ordinary contracts"—sc. such as are not *uberrimae fidei*—"the duty may arise from circumstances which arise during the negotiation". He then instances such cases as subsequent discovery of falsity in the original representation, and the supervening of events which falsify facts which were true when stated. *Cf.* the subsequent observations of the same authority to the same effect at pp. 310, 311 of *Arkwright* v. *Newbold* (1881), 17 Ch.D. 301, C.A. See also what is said by Lord CAMPBELL L.C. at pp. 723, 724 of *Walters* v. *Morgan* (1861), 3 De G.F. & J. 718, as to the "duty to say more" being created by even "a single word, or (I may add) a nod, or a wink, or a shake of the head, or a smile, from the purchaser", and by Lord SELBORNE L.C. at p. 236 of *Coaks* v. *Boswell* (1886), 11 App. Cas. 232, where, after stating that mere silence is not deceit, unless the party "undertakes or professes to communicate" the facts withheld, he adds: "this, however, he may do, if he makes some other communication which, without the addition of those facts would be necessarily, or naturally and probably, misleading". See also the general statements (which would apply equally to all the forms of reticence mentioned in this part of the text) of KNIGHT-BRUCE V.-C. at p. 104 of *Stikeman* v. *Dawson* (1847), 1 De G. & Sm. 90 ("a fraudulent suppression or a fraudulent concealment may be, and sometimes is, equivalent, civilly, to a false assertion fraudulently made in express terms"); of Lord ROMILLY at p. 114 of *Central Rail. Co. of Venezuela* v. *Kisch* (1867), L.R. 2 H.L. 99 ("the suppression of a fact will often amount to misrepresentation"); and of ROMER L.J. at p. 792 of *Seaton* v. *Heath*, [1899] 1 Q.B. 782, C.A. ("misrepresentation might undoubtedly be made by concealment").

[2] See for instance para. 74, *ante*.

[3] *Nicholson* v. *Hooper* (1838), 4 My. & Cr. 179, *per* Lord COTTENHAM L.C. at pp. 185, 186: "if Hooper had no such right"—sc. to deposit certain warrants, and give the defendants a good title to sell them for repayment of moneys advanced—"it was the duty of the plaintiff, when informed of his having assumed it, and that the defendants had on the faith of it advanced a large sum of money, to have apprised them of his intention to dispute it. Not only did he not do so, however, but . . . he confirmed them in the error into which they are supposed to have fallen, and himself derived benefit from the delusion so perpetuated"; *Andrew* v. *Aitken* (1882), 31 W.R. 425 (*per* FRY J. at p. 426: "without in any way imputing to the solicitors of the plaintiff the slightest intention to deceive, I hold that, by their silence, they authorised the defendant's solicitors to consider that the assumption in their marginal note was correct, and therefore misrepresented the nature of the covenant").

[4] *Smith* v. *Hughes* (1871), L.R. 6 Q.B. 597.

the seller was contracting to sell them as old[1]—to which HANNEN J. added that the seller must also be shown to have believed that the purchaser so believed,[2]—the purchaser's refusal to pay, and consequently his defence to the action, would have been justified; *not*, however, on the ground of misrepresentation by silence on the part of the vendor, but because the parties in that case would not have been *ad idem*, and the invalidating cause would thus have been "mistake" in the strict technical sense of the word.

Necessity to speak arising from something said by another

88 A misrepresentation may be made by silence, when either the representee, or a third person in his presence, or to his knowledge, states something false, which indicates to the representor that the representee either is being, or will be, misled, unless the necessary correction be made. Silence, under such circumstances, is either a tacit adoption by the party of another's misrepresentation as his own, or a tacit confirmation of another's error as truth. Thus, where the plaintiff called for orders at the office of a certain firm called Edward Gandell and Co., and one Edward Gandell, who was managing the business as clerk to Thomas Gandell, the sole member of that firm, presented himself in answer to his inquiry, and handed to him a card of "Thomas Gandell and Co.," and then ordered goods to be invoiced and sent to "Edward Gandell & Co.," knowing that the firm which the plaintiff was desirous of, and thought he was doing business with, was the Gandell & Co. at whose office the interview was taking place, and withheld the fact that he was carrying on a separate and distinct business with one Todd at another place, where he and Todd intended to obtain delivery and possession of the goods ordered, this suppression was treated as a misrepresentation[3]; and so also was the conduct of a party in leaving uncorrected the form in which letters were addressed to him, as and for a person of good repute of somewhat similar name to his own in the same street, for whom he knew he was being mistaken by the party on whom he was attempting to foist the contract.[4] In addition to these cases of personation by silence, there

---

[1] *Smith* v. *Hughes* (1871), L.R. 6 Q.B. 597, at p. 608.

[2] *Ibid.*, at p. 611.

[3] *Hardman* v. *Booth* (1863), 1 H. & C. 803.

[4] *Cundy* v. *Lindsay* (1878), 3 App. Cas. 459, H.L., where Lord CAIRNS L.C. at p. 465, says that "they"—the jurors—"have found that by the form of the signatures to the letters which were written by Blenkarn, by the mode in which his letters and applications to the respondents were made out, and *by the way in which he left uncorrected the mode and form in which, in turn, he was addressed by the respondents*; that by all these means he led and intended the respondents to believe that the person with whom they were communicating was not Blenkarn, the dishonest

are illustrations of a violated duty to correct a delusion being held tantamount to misrepresentation, where a person stands by and allows in silence an erroneous statement made by a third person to, or in the presence and hearing of, the representee.[1]

Necessity to speak of unusual features in well-known types of transaction

89 Lastly, there are cases which are usually classed as belonging to the province of non-disclosure, pure and simple, and not to that of misrepresentation, but which, nevertheless, certain very learned authorities have preferred to treat as examples of positive misrepresentation to be implied from silence. It has been held that the mere entering into any transaction of a well-known business type, without revealing matters which would be considered unusual and abnormal in such transaction, amounts to a representation that there are no such matters, and therefore (if it be proved that in fact such matters did exist, and that the

---

and irresponsible man, but was a well-known and solvent house of Blenkiron & Co., doing business in the same street.''

[1] In *Pilmore* v. *Hood* (1838), 5 Bing. N.C. 97, the defendant made a misrepresentation to a third person who (to the defendant's knowledge) communicated it to the plaintiff, the defendant meanwhile standing by and saying nothing, and this reticence was held (*per* TINDAL C.J. and VAUGHAN J. at p. 107) to constitute a misrepresentation *to the plaintiff*. *Cf. North British Insurance Co.* v. *Lloyd* (1854), 10 Exch. 523, where ALDERSON B. at p. 529, expresses the view that one who knows that a misrepresentation is being made by a third person, and "allows it in silence", is himself misrepresenting. See also the observations of Bramwell B., at p. 798 of *Russell* v. *Thornton* (1859), 4 H. & N. 788 ("Mr Honyman says silence gives consent. In some cases it may; for instance, when there is a duty to speak, and the party does not, an assent may be inferred from his silence"); of BLACKBURN J. at p. 673 of *Polak* v. *Everett* (1876), 1 Q.B.D. 669 ("if a man stands by, and allows another to act without objecting, when, from the usage of trade or otherwise, there is a duty to speak, his silence would preclude him as much as if he proposed the act himself"); and of Lord ESHER M.R. at p. 788 of *Nottingham Patent Brick and Tile Co.* v. *Butler* (1886), 16 Q.B.D. 778, C.A.

The topic was more recently explored in *Bradford Third Equitable Benefit Building Society* v. *Borders*, in the judgment of the court *per* CLAUSON L.J. in the Court of Appeal at [1940] 1 All E.R. 302; [1940] Ch. 202 and in the Lords at [1941] 2 All E.R. 205. The Court of Appeal sustained the counterclaim, overruling BENNETT J., the trial judge; but the Lords reversed the decision and restored the judgment of BENNETT J., holding that an amendment made to the pleadings in the Court of Appeal should not have been made, and that fraud by the plaintiffs (defendants) on the counterclaim had not been made out on the facts. There are some useful dicta in the Lords, however, on the question raised in the text above. At p. 211 Viscount MAUGHAM said that a *representation of fact* "will include a case where the defendant has manifestly approved and adopted a representation made by some third person"; and Lord WRIGHT said at p. 220: "I do not question that, if a person knowingly and deliberately profits by another's fraud, he may be properly held to have participated in the fraud and to be liable for the damage. This may happen where a continuing false representation has been made by a person, on the basis of which the transaction is concluded. I am prepared to assume here that, not only may that person be guilty of fraud (*With* v. *O'Flanagan*, [1936] 1 All E.R. 727; [1936] Ch. 575), but so also may any person who, though not a party to the fraudulent original representation, afterwards learns of it and deliberately and knowingly uses the delusion created by the fraud in the injured party's mind in order to profit by the fraud".

transaction was not of the regular and normal description which from the representor's silence the representee was entitled to expect), a false representation.[1]

Except as above, silence is not a representation

90   In no class of case other than those already mentioned is silence tantamount to a representation, or actionable in law or equity *as such*, however amenable it may be to the civil consequences of a breach of the duty of disclosure which arises in transactions *uberrimae fidei*, under another head of jurisprudence, or however censurable it may be *in foro conscientiae*. It is not silence, or reticence, which in itself can amount to a misrepresentation. It must be *concealment*, or *suppressio veri*. And these terms import the existence of a duty. A man cannot be said to conceal what he is not bound to reveal, suppress what he is under no duty to express, or keep back what he is not required to put forward. There must be a duty of some sort to speak, arising out of the circum-

---

[1] *Hamilton* v. *Watson* (1845), 12 Cl. & Fin. 109, a suretyship case, *per* Lord CAMPBELL at p. 119: "I should think that this might be considered as the criterion whether the disclosure ought to be made voluntarily, namely, whether there is anything that might not naturally be expected to take place between the parties who are concerned in the transaction"; *Evans* v. *Edmonds* (1853), 13 C.B. 777, where, in an action by a trustee of a separation deed for payment of the allowance covenanted to be paid by the husband, it was held that the proved concealment by the plaintiff of the fact that he had seduced the wife, and that the object of the deed was not the usual and ordinary object of a separation deed, but to give the plaintiff access to the wife and opportunities for continuing his clandestine intrigue, amounted to a fraudulent mis-representation (*per* JERVIS C.J. at p. 784, and MAULE J. at pp. 785, 786; *Evans* v. *Carrington* (1860), 2 De G.F. & J. 481 (*per* Lord CAMPBELL L.C. at p. 493); *North British Insurance Co.* v. *Lloyd* (1854), 10 Exch. 523, a suretyship case (*per* ALDERSON B. at p. 527, and PARKE B. at p. 529); *Lee* v. *Jones* (1864), 17 C.B. N.S. 482, Exch. Ch., another suretyship case, where at p. 500, SHEE J. cites the above dictum of Lord CAMPBELL, and BLACKBURN J. at pp. 503, 504, says: "I think, both on authority and on principle, that, when the creditor describes to the proposed surety the transaction proposed to be guaranteed (as in general a creditor does), that description amounts to a representation, or at least is evidence of a representation that there is nothing in the transaction that might not naturally be expected to take place between the parties to a transaction such as that described. And, if a representation to this effect is made to the intended surety by one who knows that there is something not naturally to be expected to take place between the parties to the transaction, and that this is unknown to the person to whom he makes the representation, and that, if it were known to him, he would not enter into the contract of suretyship, I think it is evidence of a fraudulent representation on his part"; *Harrower* v. *Hutchinson* (1870), L.R. 5 Q.B. 584, Exch. Ch. (*per* MARTIN B. at p. 594, and CLEASBY B. at p. 595); *Phillips* v. *Foxall* (1872), L.R. 7 Q.B. 666 (where BLACKBURN J. again observes, at p. 679: "I still adhere to the opinion that I expressed in *Lee* v. *Jones*, that if such a transaction as is alleged in the plea had taken place before the defendant entered into the contract of suretyship, and had been concealed from him, it would have furnished evidence of a false representation to the surety that no such thing existed"); *Cavendish Bentinck* v. *Fenn* (1887), 12 App. Cas. 652, H.L., a case involving the question of the duty of disclosure owed by an agent to his principal, where Lord MACNAGHTEN, at p. 671, discusses the position of the agent who is alleged to have concealed his interest, "and *so to have represented* that he was not interested in the property, and that it belonged to other persons who were not connected with the scheme"; *Oelkers* v. *Ellis*, [1914] 2 K.B. 139 (*per* HORRIDGE J. at pp. 147, 148).

Actionable Misrepresentation

stances, in accordance with the principles set out in the text, before
the representee can legally complain of the representor's silence.
Tacit acquiescence in the self-delusion of another, if nothing is said or
done to mislead, or silence which does not make that which is stated
false, draws with it no legal liability.

> "Mere silence as regards a material fact which the one party is not under an
> obligation to disclose to the other, cannot be a ground for rescission, or a
> defence to specific performance"[1];

much less, of course, can it constitute a cause of action for damages for
fraudulent misrepresentation.[2] The most familiar illustrations of this
principle are the cases where a purchaser buys at the price of grazing or
prairie land from an ignorant native owner land which he knows to con-

---

[1] Fry, *Specific Performance* para. 705, and Story, *Eq. Jurispr.* Vol. I paras. 204, 385; *Horsfall* v.
Thomas (1862), 1 H. & C. 90, *per* BRAMWELL B. at pp. 99, 100 (no duty to communicate
defect in cannon sold, therefore no misrepresentation, the defect not having been proved to
have been concealed or covered up so as to deceive the purchaser, who never inspected);
Smith v. *Hughes* (1871), L.R. 6 Q.B. 597, where BLACKBURN J. at p. 607 says: "I agree that
even if the vendor was aware that the purchaser thought that the article possessed that quality,
and would not have entered into the contract unless he had so thought, still the purchaser is
bound, unless the vendor was guilty of some fraud or deceit upon him, and that a mere absti-
nence from disabusing the purchaser of that impression is not fraud or deceit, for, whatever
may be the case in a court of morals, there is no legal obligation on the vendor to inform the
purchaser that he is under a mistake not induced by the misrepresentation of the vendor";
with which compare HANNEN J. at pp. 610, 611 ("a belief on the part of the plaintiff that the
defendant was making a contract to buy the oats under the mistaken belief that they were old
would not relieve the defendant from liability unless the mistaken belief was induced by some
misrepresentation of the plaintiff, or concealment of a fact which it became his duty to communicate"), and COCKBURN C.J. at p. 603 ("the question is whether . . . the passive acquiescence of the seller in the self-deception of the buyer will entitle the latter to avoid the contract.
I am of opinion that it will not"); *Coaks* v. *Boswell* (1886), 11 App. Cas. 232, H.L., *per* Lord
SELBORNE at pp. 235, 236: "inasmuch as a purchaser is (generally speaking) under no ante-
cedent obligation to communicate to his vendor facts which may influence his own conduct
or judgment when bargaining for his own interest, no deceit can be implied from his mere
silence as to such facts, unless he undertakes or professes to communicate them"); *Seddon*
v. *North Eastern Salt Co.*, [1905] 1 Ch. 326 (*per* JOYCE J. at pp. 334, 335). *Bell* v. *Lever Brothers,
Ltd.*, [1932] A.C. 161, H.L. *per* Lord ATKIN at p. 228—"It is said that there is a contractual
duty of the servant to disclose his past faults. I agree that the duty in the servant to protect
his master's property may involve the duty to report a fellow servant whom he knows to be
wrongfully dealing with that property. The servant owes a duty not to steal, but, having
stolen, is there superadded a duty to confess that he has stolen ? I am satisfied that to imply
such a duty would be a departure from the well established usage of mankind and would be to
create obligations entirely outside the normal contemplation of the parties concerned. If a
man agrees to raise his butler's wages, must the butler disclose that two years ago he received a
secret commission from the wine merchant; and if the master discovers it, can he, without
dismissal or after the servant has left, avoid the agreement for the increase in salary and recover
back the extra wages paid? If he gives his cook a month's wages in lieu of notice can he, on
discovering that the cook has been pilfering the tea and sugar, claim the return of the month's
wages ? I think not. He takes the risk; if he wishes to protect himself he can question his
servant, and will then be protected by the truth or otherwise of the answers." *Cf.*
per Lord THANKERTON at pp. 231–232.
[2] *Per* Lord CAMPBELL L.C. at p. 724 of *Walters* v. *Morgan* (1861), 3 De G.F. & J. 718.

tain valuable minerals,[1] or through which he has privately ascertained that a railway authorised by Parliament is intended to pass, with the possible result of enhancing its value[2]; or buys an "old master", or a rare manuscript, from a peasant who thinks it rubbish, and sells it as such[3]; or, conversely, where a vendor sells land with a mine under it which he knows to be nearly worked out, or where a patentee grants a licence to work a patented invention which, to his knowledge, has no validity or value,[4] or where a lessor demises premises which he knows to be ruinous or unsafe,[5] or an employer is silent as to the difficulties which the contractor will experience by reason of the nature of the soil to be excavated.[6] In all these instances, assuming that no single word has been let fall which might mislead, and no device of any sort employed, reticence is innocuous. It is often simply a case of one man bringing his knowledge, experience, skill, or technical judgment to bear upon the

---

[1] *Fox* v. *Mackreth* (1788), 2 Cox, 320; 2 Bro. C.C. 400; *per* Lord THURLOW L.C. at p. 321: "Let us put this case. Suppose A., knowing of a mine on the estate of B., and knowing at the same time that B. was ignorant of it, should treat and contract with B. for the purchase of that estate at only half its real value; can a court of equity set aside this bargain? No; but why is it impossible? Not because the one party is not aware of the unreasonable advantage taken by the other of this knowledge, but because there is no contract existing between them by which the one party is bound to disclose to the other the circumstances which had come within his knowledge . . . It is therefore not only necessary that great advantage should be taken in such a contract, and that such an advantage should arise from a superiority of skill or information; but it is also necessary to show some obligation binding the party to make such a disclosure. Therefore, the question is, not whether the transaction be such as a man of honour would disclaim and disdain, but it must fall within some settled definition of wrong recognised by this Court"; *Turner* v. *Harvey* (1821), Jac. 169, *per* Lord ELDON L.C. at p. 178: "the purchaser may use his own knowledge, and is not bound to give the vendor information of the value of his property . . . if an estate is offered for sale and I treat for it, knowing that there is a mine under it, and the other party makes no inquiry, I am not bound to give him any information of it; he acts for himself, and exercises his own sense and knowledge"; *Smith* v. *Hughes* (1871), L.R. 6 Q.B. 597, *per* COCKBURN C.J. at pp. 603, 604: "the question is not what a man of scrupulous morality or nice honour would do under such circumstances. The case put of the purchase of an estate, in which there is a mine under the surface, but the fact is unknown to the seller, is one in which a man of tender conscience or high honour would be unwilling to take advantage of the ignorance of the seller; but there can be no doubt that the contract for the sale of the estate would be binding."

[2] *Edwards* v. *Meyrick* (1842), 2 Hare 60 (*per* WIGRAM V.-C. at pp. 73–75).

[3] See *Phillips* v. *Homfray* (1871), 6 Ch. App. 770, where Lord HATHERLEY L.C. at p. 779 observes: "I apprehend it would be an error to say generally that you cannot enforce a contract in this court where the one party knows more of the value than the other does. It happens frequently in the purchase of pictures, for instance, that one party knows a great deal more of the value than the other, and yet the bargain is perfectly good."

[4] *Smith* v. *Scott* (1859), 6 C.B. N.S., 771, *per* WILLIAMS J. at p. 780, WILLES J. at p. 782, and BYLES J. at p. 783, as to the insufficiency of the plea of fraud.

[5] *Keates* v. *Earl of Cadogan* (1851), 10 C.B. 591; *Cavalier* v. *Pope*, [1906] A.C. 428 H.L., *per* Lord MACNAGHTEN at p. 430; *Ryall* v. *Kidwell & Son*, [1914] 3 K.B. 135, C.A.

[6] *Ranger* v. *Great Western Rail. Co.* (1854), 5 H.L. Cas. 72, *per* Lord CRANWORTH L.C. at pp. 86, 87.

transaction, and using the weapons with which, perhaps at great cost of time, labour and money, he has equipped himself for the business of life.[1] No doubt, such dealings would be repugnant to a man of high honour and delicacy, who might think that in him who has a giant's strength, "'tis tyrannous To use it like a giant", that *minimum decet libere cui multum licet*, that it is not always right to exercise a right, and that knowledge, like wealth, is power, which may be abused, as well as used. Into these considerations, however, it is obvious that the law cannot enter. The only concern of jurisprudence must always be to declare under what circumstances, and in whom, a right is vested, and not to inquire whether the exercise of that right is conformable to the higher standards of refined ethics. But the law nevertheless so acutely appreciates the importance and value of "justifying its ways", whenever it is possible, to the moral sense of the community, that it has again and again cast a powerful searchlight over the entire *res gestae* of any case to see whether anything is to be found in them to prevent this right of reticence from operating, or to destroy it if it has begun to do so. Thus Lord ELDON L.C., after laying down the general principle, as already stated, is careful to add:

"but a very little is sufficient to affect the application of that principle. If a word, if a single word, is dropped which tends to mislead the vendor, the principle will not be allowed to operate".[2]

And to this "single word" Lord CAMBPELL L.C. adds "a nod, or a wink, or a shake of the head, or a smile from the purchaser", as facts which may make all the difference.[3] Accordingly, in a case where a purchaser

---

[1] It will be observed that the expression *caveat emptor*, very commonly used a summary statement of the proposition enunciated in the text, has been studiously avoided. In the first place, in common with all similarly abbreviated maxims,—those "short dark oracles" which, according to Bacon, "give little light or direction", and "are but as proverbs, and many times plain fallacies", such as "the law favours the heir", "estoppels are odious", *in jure proxima causa spectatur*, *de minimis non curat lex*, "the greater the truth the greater the libel", and the like,—the maxim is too absolute to be either of any utility in practice, or scientifically correct in theory; and, in the second place, this particular phrase is more than ordinarily misleading, inasmuch as it seems to imply that it is only a purchaser who takes all risks, and has no rights against the reticent vendor, whereas, in the like absence of positive misrepresentation or breach of duty to disclose, a vendor is equally without protection against the reticent purchaser. Lastly, *caveat* gives no information at all. Where the one party is under no duty to disclose, it is for the other party *cavere*; but where there is such a duty, it is for the first party, and not for the other, *cavere*. So that *caveat emptor* is as utterly meaningless an expression as *caveant omnes* or *caveat unusquisque*. Every one who enters upon any business must take care of himself in respect of all matters as to which he has no right to insist that another shall take care of him. As to when he has, and when he has not these rights, the phrase in question affords little if any guidance.

[2] *Turner* v. *Harvey* (1821), Jac. 169 (at p. 178).

[3] At p. 724 of the case cited in the next note.

had concealed from the vendor of land the fact that it contained minerals of a far greater value than, to his knowledge, the vendor supposed, and had further been guilty of acts and conduct indicating an intention to deceive, specific performance was refused.[1]   The like consequence attended a purchaser's suppression of the fact that he had been secretly abstracting coal from the mine offered for sale, which fact gave the vendor rights against him of a different nature from, and of a larger pencuniary value than, the mere vendor's right to the price of the coal; in that case Lord HATHERLEY L.C. was of opinion that there had been acts and conduct of his own which cast upon the purchaser a duty of disclosure which otherwise would not have arisen,[2] and he likened it to the case of one "killing a man's horse and then making an offer to buy it, leaving him to suppose that it is still alive",[3] adding by way of further illustration, that where

> "a picture-dealer, employed to clean a picture, scrapes off a part of the picture to see if he can discover a mark which will tell him who is the artist, and then finds a mark showing it to be the work of a great artist; that would not be a legitimate mode of acquiring knowledge for the purpose of enabling him to buy the picture at a lower price than the owner would have sold it for had he known it to be the work of that artist".[4]

In other words, suppression by a purchaser of facts affecting the value of the property which are not merely within his own knowledge, but the issue of his own volition and wrongful action, is equivalent to a misrepresentation.   So also, where a man, in treaty with another for the purchase of a policy on the life of a third person, is in the course of the negotiations apprised of an accident to the "life", he may lawfully keep silence as to the incident if he has never made any representation at all in the first instance, but if he should thereafter insinuate in the slightest degree that the health of the "life" continues as before, his silence

---

[1] *Walters* v. *Morgan* (1861), 3 De G.F. & J. 718.
[2] *Phillips* v. *Homfray, No. 1* (1871), 6 Ch.App. 770, at pp. 778–780.
[3] *Ibid*, at p. 777.
[4] *Ibid*, at p. 780. *Cf. Lowther* v. *Lord Lowther* (1806), 13 Ves. 95, where a picture-dealer, with whom a "Mars and Venus" had been deposited for sale, and who therefore stood in a fiduciary relation to the depositor, discovered that it was a Titian, of the value of £5000, and thereupon, without revealing this fact to his principal, himself became the purchaser of it for £300 (*per* Lord ERSKINE L.C. at p. 103).   This case may have been in Lord HATHERLEY's mind when he gave the illustration above cited. See also *R.* v. *Boucher* (1842), 3 Q.B. 641, where a charter of incorporation was obtained from the Crown by a petition which referred, *inter alia*, to the "condition of the gaol", when in fact there was then no borough gaol in existence; and the observations of Lord HALSBURY L.C. at p. 283 of *Aaron's Reefs, Ltd.* v. *Twiss*, [1896] A.C. 273, H.L., as to a person negotiating with a bank for a loan on mortgage of his house, without disclosing that he was not the owner of the house.

would become "under the circumstances equivalent to an active mis-representation".[1]

> "Though a person may be deceived by another with the knowledge of a third person, *if that third person is not party to the deceit, and owes no legal duty or obligation to the party deceived, and does nothing but preserve silence,* however morally blameworthy . . . he cannot be held liable . . . at the instance of the party deceived,"

but where the party is not a mere "passive spectator", and "actively assists in the deceit", it is otherwise.[2]

But it is one thing simply to say nothing, and no more; it is another to take any active step to conceal what might without that step have been more readily noticeable. Silence, taken in conjunction with any such positive conduct, may become capable of being regarded as a representation, when without it it could not be so regarded.[3]

Where there are several statements regard must be had to the effect as a whole

91 Where a number of statements form one entire complex representation, the primary principle of construction is that all the statements or documents, if connected by express reference or identity of subject-matter, but not otherwise, must be considered in their interrelation and bearing upon one another, in order to ascertain whether the conjoint effect of the whole is a true or a false transcript of the facts. This rule, which is Rule 3 of Article 12 in the Code, is applied both to a series of statements comprised in one document,[4] or to a number of documents, such as a bundle of correspondence,[5] or the particulars and plan of a property to be sold,[6] or, in the case of companies, a prospectus accompanied by a covering letter,[7] or followed by a telegram printed in

---

1 *Per* WALSH M.R. (Ireland) at p. 113 of *Thompson* v. *Lambert* (1868), 17 W.R. 111.

2 *Per* ROMER J. in *Marnham* v. *Weaver* (1899), 80 L.T. 412.

3 *Baglehole* v. *Walters* (1811), 3 Camp. 154.

4 *Cargill* v. *Bower* (1878), 10 Ch.D. 502, per FRY J. at p. 516; *Re Metropolitan Coal Consumers Association, Ltd. Wainwright's Case* (1890), 63 L.T. 429, C.A.; *Scott* v. *Snyder Dynamite Projectile Co., Ltd.* (1892), 67 L.T. 104, C.A.,—see the passage cited in note 5 on p. 93, *ante*; *Aaron's Reefs, Ltd.* v. *Twiss*, [1896] A.C. 273, H.L., *per* Lord HALSBURY L.C. at p. 281; *Components' Tube Co.* v. *Naylor*, [1900] 2 I.R. 1, where amongst the questions held to have been properly left to the jury, was this: "was the prospectus *as a whole* misleading and calculated to deceive?" The document containing the several statements was, in each of the above cases, a prospectus; *R.* v. *Lord Kylsant*, [1932] 1 K.B. 442, C.C.A. at p. 445 (summing-up of WRIGHT J.) and pp. 448–449 (judgment of the Court of Criminal Appeal *per* AVORY J.)

5 *Oelkers* v. *Ellis*, [1914] 2 K.B. 139 (*per* HORRIDGE J. at pp. 147, 148); *Gross* v. *Lewis Hillman Ltd.*, [1969] 3 All E.R. 1476; [1970] Ch. 445, C.A.

6 *Dykes* v. *Blake* (1838), 4 Bing. N.C. 463; *Denny* v. *Hancock* (1870), 6 Ch. App. 1; *Re Arnold, Arnold* v. *Arnold* (1880), 14 Ch.D. 270, C.A.; *Eastwood* v. *Ashton*, [1914] 1 Ch. 68, C.A.

7 *Drincqbier* v. *Wood*, [1899] 1 Ch. 393.

the newspapers, alleged to have come from the scene of the company's operations,[1] or in connection with other documents to which it refers.[2] Such an examination may result either in rendering the entirety of the complex representation false, though the component statements taken by themselves may be true,[3] or in rendering the entirety true, though some of the component statements, taken separately, may be false.[4] Or the complex representation may be so homogeneous in its falsity, that, of necessity, the whole is as false as every constituent part, and every part is as false as the whole.[5]

92　　The above general rule is, however, subject to this qualification, that if one out of the several statements or documents, not inseparably or necessarily inter-connected with the other statements or documents alleged to make up the compound representation, has a clear and definite meaning, and is clearly and definitely false, the representee is entitled to rely on this one statement, or document, by itself as a misrepresentation, and it is no answer to say that, if he had carefully examined the other statements or documents, he might have discovered something which would have led him to the truth.[6]　Conversely, if the representor can

---

[1] *Andrews* v. *Mockford*, [1896] 1 Q.B. 372, C.A.

[2] *Cargill* v. *Bower* (1878),10 Ch.D. 502.

[3] As in *Re Metropolitan Coal Consumers Association, Ltd., Wainwright's Case* (1890), 63 L.T. 429, C.A., where two of the statements in the prospectus were (1) that a large part of the capital had been *privately taken up*, and (2) that 2000 noblemen had approved of the objects of the company, and a large number of them had *subscribed to the capital*. Each of these, standing by itself, was literally true, but it was held that their conjoint effect was that the "noblemen" had "privately taken up" the capital, and had "subscribed to the capital" in that sense, and not in the ordinary sense of sending in application forms for the shares. *Cf. Scott* v. *Snyder Dynamite Projectile Co.* (1892), 67 L.T. 104, and the passage from the judgment of LINDLEY L.J. at p. 106, which is cited in note 5 on p. 93, *ante*, and *Drincqbier* v. *Wood*, [1899] 1 Ch. 393, where the prospectus stated that a site had been acquired for the company's works at Edmonton, and the letter covering the prospectus spoke of "the assets of the company" as including its "freehold land", etc.　Both these statements, taken separately, were true, but BYRNE J. held that they must be construed in the light of one another, and that, when so interpreted, they amounted to a representation that the "site" was "freehold land", which was false.

[4] *Bartlett* v. *Salmon* (1855), 6 De G.M. & G. 33 *per* Lord CRANWORTH at pp. 41–42.　*Cf. Cargill* v. *Bower* (1878), 10 Ch.D. 502; *Clements* v. *Conroy*, [1911] 2 I.R. 500; *Golding* v. *Royal London Auxiliary Insurance Co.* (1914), 30 T.L.R. 350.

[5] *Brandling* v. *Plummer* (1854), 2 Drew 427, 430–431; *Denny* v. *Hancock* (1870), 6 Ch. App. 1, 11–12, 13–14; *Andrews* v. *Mockford*, [1896] 1 Q.B. 372, 377–378, 382, 383.

[6] *White* v. *Cuddon* (1842), 8 Cl. & Fin. 766, where the conditions under which fines were payable by the custom of a manor were distinctly misrepresented, though the actual amount of income derived was not over-stated; *Torrance* v. *Bolton* (1872), 8 Ch. App. 118, when the bidder at an auction was held entitled to rely upon a plain misrepresentation in the advertisement of the property for sale, and the representor was not allowed to excuse himself by reference to the particulars and conditions of sale in which the truth appeared, not having proved that these were brought to the notice of the representee; *Re Arnold* (1880), 14 Ch.D. 270, C.A., *per* BAGGALLAY L.J. at p. 282, and BRAMWELL L.J. at p. 284, where, the plan being false, it

point to some one statement which presents the material facts truthfully and candidly, the representee cannot rely on the necessary imperfection and incompleteness of some other statement which does not purport to do more than refer him to the first statement, such as a marginal note, or index.[1]

Questions of law and fact

93 Where the representation is contained in a document, or its terms (if orally made) are admitted, and where it is self-contained and self-luminous (as it were), that is to say, where there are no surrounding circumstances, or *res gestae*, of such a nature as to suggest an artificial or special meaning, or the possibility of several meanings, the question of the sense to be assigned to the representation is one of law to this extent, that the court is entitled, and bound, to pronounce whether it is capable of the meaning alleged, or of any other meaning than that alleged, or of any meaning in which it would be false, or true, as the case may be.[2]

---

was in vain that the vendor urged that if the purchaser had looked at the particulars in conjunction with the plan, he must have discovered that there was a blunder somewhere; *Redgrave* v. *Hurd* (1881), 20 Ch.D. 1, C.A. *per* JESSEL M.R. at p. 14. See Ch. XI, paras. 190 *et seq.*, *post*, and some of the cases cited thereunder, where it was held that references in a prospectus to other documents which, on examination, might enable the applicant for shares to discover the falsity of some plain misrepresentation in the prospectus itself, are of no avail to prove the affirmative plea of knowledge, if the representor did not in fact choose to make the examination.

[1] This was what happened in *Moore* v. *Explosives Co., Ltd.* (1887), 56 L.J. Q.B. 235, C.A., where in the body of a prospectus it was stated that "the completion of the works will enable the company to increase their *present capacity for manufacture* from 400 to 1000 tons of explosives *per annum*," and to this paragraph there was affixed a marginal note in red ink—"Increase of *present manufacture*." The paragraph stated the absolute truth, but the plaintiff claimed to read it, in conjunction with the marginal note, as meaning that the company's *actual present manufacture* was 400 tons per annum, which would have been untrue. It was held, however, that the marginal note, the office of which was merely that of an index finger or clue-word to the paragraph, could not possibly have the effect of adding to, or detracting from, its meaning (*per* Lord ESHER M.R. and FRY L.J.). *Quaere*, however, as to the soundness of this decision, having regard to the undoubted rule of construction in analogous cases of defamation, where the jury is at liberty to consider whether a heading, or marginal note, or an index-entry, does not contain defamatory matters in itself, apart from the body of the book, chapter, paragraph, or contents to which it relates. See *Buckingham* v. *Murray* (1825), 2 C. & P. 46.

[2] *Bellairs* v. *Tucker* (1884), 13 Q.B.D. 562, Div. Ct., *per* DENMAN J. at p. 575, disagreeing with the view taken by LOPES J. at the trial: "I think it was for the judge and not for the jury to say whether, with reference to the surrounding circumstances, the statements in question were expressions of hope and belief only, or statements of existing facts". But *quaere*, whether, having regard to the recognition by DENMAN J. himself of "surrounding circumstances", it was not for the jury to determine what sense, *in the light of those circumstances*, was to be attributed to the statements in the prospectus. Having regard to subsequent decisions of the C.A. and the H.L. (see cases cited in note 4 on p. 111) it seems clear that LOPES J. took the only proper and safe course, and that DENMAN J.'s opinion was wrong, though, but for the existence of the surrounding circumstances, it may have been right. It is curious to find that, three years later, DENMAN J. even in the absence of any surrounding circumstances, took the same course

Subject to the above, every question as to the meaning conveyed to the mind of the representee is an issue of fact; and, in the case of a suggested special or secondary sense, evidence may be admissible, or even necessary. Thus it is a question of fact what "sound timber" means in a representation describing certain timber as such, and evidence is receivable on the point[1]; where particulars are given to a life insurance company of the health and physical history of a "life", to which is appended a reference to papers containing similar particulars on a previous application to another society, it has been held a question of fact whether, by this reference, the representation was intended to convey that the health of the assured was the same as it had been at the previous date, in which case it would have been false, or merely that his health at the earlier date was as it was then described to be, in which construction it would have been true,[2] and to this issue evidence of surrounding facts (conversations and oral statements, etc.) may be relevant[3]; and, where prospectuses of companies are concerned, the exact meaning of paragraphs, clauses, and expressions therein, upon the ascertainment of which the whole question of falsity or truth may depend, has, in every case of reasonable doubt, always been considered a matter of fact.[4] Similarly, the question whether the mere use of the words "Trade Mark" in advertisements of an article constitute an implied representation to the public that such a mark has been registered, must be treated as one of fact,

---

in another prospectus case as he had criticised Lopes J. for taking when there did exist such circumstances, but the C.A. (Lord Esher M.R. and Fry L.J.) disagreed with him on this point, holding that the paragraph there in question was capable of only one meaning, and that he ought not to have left it to the jury to say what the meaning was, or whether a marginal note affixed to the paragraph had any and what effect in altering it: *Moore v. Explosives Co., Ltd.* (1887), 56 L.J. Q.B. 235. So also, in *Bentley & Co., Ltd. v. Black* (1893), 9 T.L.R. 580, C.A., Lord Esher M.R. said that there the proper construction to be put upon the words of the prospectus "was for the Court". *Cf. Oelkers v. Ellis,* [1914] 2 K.B. 139 (*per* Horridge J. at p. 147, as to a bundle of correspondence).

[1] *Woodhouse* v. *Swift* (1836), 7 C. & P. 310.
[2] *Foster* v. *Mentor Life Assurance Co.* (1854), 3 E. & B. 48, *per* Coleridge J. at pp. 71–74, and Lord Campbell C.J. at pp. 77–81.
[3] *Ibid., per* Lord Campbell C.J. at pp. 78, 79.
[4] *Clarke* v. *Dickson, No. 2* (1859), 6 C.B. N.S. 453, where the falsity or truth of a statement in the prospectus depended on the question to whom the expression "the proprietors" was intended to apply, and Cockburn C.J. at pp. 469–471, said that this question had been rightly left to the jury; *Charlton* v. *Hay, No. 2* (1875), 32 L.T. 96, where the prospectus stated that the produce of the company's mills was 800 barrels a day, and the profits £100,000 a year, and referred to certain vouchers and documents from which those figures were taken, and Cockburn C.J. (somewhat charitably to the defendants) left it to the jury to say whether this meant merely that the directors had these documents in their possession, showing the above figures, and that they had no reason to doubt their genuineness,—on which construction the representation was true,—or that the produce and profits in fact were as stated,—in which case it was false; *Smith* v. *Chadwick* (1884), 9 App. Cas. 187, H.L. *per* Lord Blackburn at p. 195.

to be established (if at all) by evidence of mercantile witnesses as to the meaning which the words in question would have conveyed to their minds.[1]

---

[1] *Sen Sen Co.* v. *Britten*, [1899] 1 Ch. 692, *per* STIRLING J. at p. 696: "I have no evidence before me as to the effect which the representation has had upon anybody. I have nothing before me but the bare fact that these words appear upon the packages." See also the cases cited in the notes to Ch. XVII, para. 377, *post*. The canons of construction stated in this section are precisely the same as those applied to the determination of the meaning of alleged defamatory matter: see Article 16 (5), (6), and (7), of Mr Spencer Bower's *Code of the Law of Actionable Defamation*, and the cases cited in the notes thereto, particularly *Capital and Counties Bank, Ltd.* v. *Henty & Sons* (1882), 7 App. Cas. 741, H.L., *per* Lord BLACKBURN, at pp. 769–778.

CHAPTER V

What Constitutes Fraudulent, and Innocent, Misrepresentation Respectively

Introductory

94 The last chapter examined representations in relation to the facts which they purport to represent. It remains to investigate representations, first from the point of view of the belief and mental attitude of the representor, and, next, in their effect upon the mind and material interests of the representee. This chapter is concerned with the former, and the next two chapters with the latter, of these questions. The former, it is true, only becomes material in certain of the various possible proceedings for misrepresentation, and is wholly irrelevant to others, as will be seen hereafter,[1] whereas the topics subsequently to be discussed, such as inducement and materiality, like all those which have preceded this part of the text, are vital to every form of action or defence which is based upon misrepresentation.[2] But, in tracing the progress of false-hood from its source to its destination, with a view of establishing how and when it becomes actionable, it seems desirable to observe the order of time, which in this case is also the logical and psychological order; and, if so, the next stage in the progress is obviously the mind of the representor.

---

[1] See Chapters X and XI, *post.*

[2] The action in damages for negligent misrepresentation, dealt with in Chapter XIX, is no exception to this rule. Though this action, as is pointed out in that chapter, is one in negligence, and not strictly an action founded on misrepresentation, yet materiality and inducement must be shown before it can be held proved that the negligence of the representor caused loss or injury to the plaintiff in respect of which he is entitled to damages.

Fraudulent Misrepresentation

95   In certain cases,[1] the party complaining of having been misled by
a representation to his injury has no effective remedy unless the representation was not only false, but fraudulent.   Fraud, no less than falsity,
is a question of fact,[2] and the burden of establishing this fact, in every
such case, is on the representee.[3]   The question, however, of what are
the constituent elements of fraud, as applied to a representation, is a
question of law in the sense that it has been settled by judicial authority,
which it is now proposed to examine.

Fraud as distinguished from mere falsity

96   It is well established that fraud in law, and fraud in equity, are
one and the same.[4]   And it is also clear that nothing short of actual fraud
will support an action for deceit, and that the law does not recognise
any such things as "imputed", "constructive", "technical", or "artificial" fraud, if these terms are used to support a suggestion that anything short of actual fraud will suffice.   So much follows from Lord
HERSCHELL's analysis of the matter in *Derry* v. *Peek*.[5]

"Every deceit comprehends a lie, but a deceit is more than a lie".[6]
There cannot be a fraudulent misrepresentation which is not false, but
there can be a misrepresentation which is not fraudulent.   Except in
those cases where the very fact expressly or impliedly represented is the
knowledge or belief or other state of mind of the representor, and where,
therefore, it so happens that falsity is conterminous with fraud, and
truth with innocence,[7] untruth does not of itself import a dishonest

---

[1] See Chapters IX, X and XI, *post*.   Since the passing of the Misrepresentation Act 1967 the
classes of case in which the sufferer from an innocent misrepresentation is denied all remedy
are much smaller than when Mr Spencer Bower's text was originally written.

[2] See, generally, the cases cited in the notes to this and succeeding paragraphs, and also in
the notes to Chapter X, *post*.

[3] See Chapter X, *post*.

[4] *Le Lievre* v. *Gould*, [1893] 1 Q.B. 491, C.A., *per* Lord ESHER M.R. at p. 498; *cf. Derry* v.
Peek (1889), 14 App. Cas. 337, H.L. Though *Le Lievre* v. *Gould* now stands overruled, as to its
principal point, by *Hedley Byrne & Co., Ltd.* v. *Heller & Partners, Ltd.*, [1963] 2 All E.R. 575;
[1964] A.C. 465, H.L., it was not disapproved on this point.

[5] (1889) 14 App. Cas. 337, H.L. at pp. 359–360.

[6] BULLER J. at p. 56 of *Pasley* v. *Freeman* (1789), 3 Term Rep. 51.

[7] It has been seen—see paras. 16, 30 and 37, *ante*, that expressions of intention, belief,
opinion, etc., constitute an implied statement of the fact that the representor has the intention,
belief, or opinion which he professes to have.   If, therefore, such implied statement is false,
it must necessarily be fraudulent also.   So also, where the representor expressly adds such
qualifications as "so far as I know", "to the best of my belief", etc; see *Milne* v. *Marwood*
(1855), 15 C.B. 778.   Illustrations of innocence, in this class of case, being exactly equivalent
to truth, are: *Horsfall* v. *Thomas* (1862), 1 H. & C. 90, *per* BRAMWELL B. at pp. 100, 101;
Bodger v. *Nicholls* (1873), 28 L.T. 441, *per* BLACKBURN J. at p. 445; *Melbourne Banking Corporation* v. *Brougham* (1882), 7 App.Cas. 307, at pp. 319, 320, with which compare, as applied

mind any more than, conversely, an intention to deceive necessarily involves that the statement made was untrue in fact.[1]   "In an action of deceit", said Lord HERSCHELL,

> "it is not enough to establish misrepresentation alone.   It is conceded on all hands that something more must be proved . . . though it has been a matter of controversy what additional elements are requisite".[2]

Non-belief in truth renders misrepresentation fraudulent

97   What then are the "requisite additional elements" referred to by Lord HERSCHELL ?   On examination these are reduced to one—*viz.*, the absence of honest belief by the representor at the material time that the statement made by him was true.   Non-belief covers everything.   It is often said that a misrepresentation is fraudulent when the representor (1) knew it to be false, or (2) believed it to be false, or (3) did not know or believe it to be true, or (4) made it in reckless indifference as to its truth or falsity.   This is as unscientific a classification as a division of the animal creation into horses, vertebrates, and animals, would be.   It is obvious, as Lord HERSCHELL points out in his famous judgment,[3] that (4) is the same thing as (3), with a needlessly added term of opprobrium[4]; and equally obvious that (2) is an *a fortiori* case of (3), and (1) of (2), and that all four cases are comprehended in the formula that "a fraudulent misrepresentation is a misrepresentation which, when made, or (in the case of a continuing representation) when acted upon, the representor

---

to marine insurance, the rule stated in the Marine Insurance Act 1906 (6 Edw. 7, c. 41), s. 20(5): "a representation as to matter of . . . belief is true if it be made in good faith".   See also para. 71, *ante.*

1 See para. 67, *ante.*

2 *Per* Lord HERSCHELL at p. 359 of *Derry* v. *Peek* (1889), 14 App. Cas. 337, H.L.

3 At p. 374 of *Derry* v. *Peek* (1889), 14 App. Cas. 337, H.L.

4 In many of the cases on the subject it will be noticed that judges have thought it necessary to characterise the putting forth of a statement without belief in its truth as a thing done "recklessly", or with culpable "indifference" as to its truth or falsity, or "in a gambling spirit".   All these *purpurei panni*, and rhetorical supplements, are entirely unnecessary, and (what is worse) they tend to mislead, as will be seen in paras. 107–109, *post*, where it is shown that the heresy of assimilating negligence in belief to absence of belief is the outcome of the confusion in thought between want of care in arriving at the belief, and the making of a representation without belief, and without caring whether it is true or not,—a confusion which could never have arisen if the expressions in question had not been tacked on to the phrase "absence of belief".   If in fact the representor does not honestly believe his representation to be true, it is utterly immaterial in what spirit—speculative, reckless, or deliberate—he propounds it.   The mere propounding it is the fraud.   But the terms in question would lead the unwary to suppose that, if the absence of belief is not characterised by the gambler's spirit, it does not indicate fraud.   This delusion is encouraged by the inveterate practice of pleaders, whose tendency it is never to desert a phrase, however unnecessary or erroneous, of which they have once become enamoured.

did not in fact honestly believe to be true".[1] And, though he had previously, in deference to current modes of expression, mentioned (1),
(2), and (4) as so-called classes of fraudulent representation, this was
the opinion finally expressed by Lord HERSCHELL: "to prevent a false
statement being fraudulent, there must, I think, always be an honest
belief in its truth.   And this probably covers the whole ground".[2]   In
other words, it "covers the whole ground" to say that, where this
"honest belief in its truth" is not to be found, the misrepresentation is
fraudulent; where it is, it is innocent. The expression "honest belief"
imports that there may be an actual and real belief which yet will not
save the misrepresentation from being fraudulent. This happens when
the belief itself is generated by a resolution to avoid all sources and means
of information which would lead to suspicion,—by a wilful and sedulous
abstention from, or curtailment of, investigation for the express purpose of putting the representor in a position to say that he in fact believes
what he professes to believe,—by that "diligence in ignorance" (to use
the felicitous expression of KNIGHT-BRUCE L.J.) in order not to ascertain the truth, or have any doubt thrown on what he desires, and is
determined, to believe, which plays so important a part in the doctrine of
constructive or imputed notice. A belief so engendered may be as
much a badge of fraud as the absence of any belief at all. The qualification of "honesty" is mentioned in several of the authorities, without
any apparent meaning being attached therein to the term "honest",
other than "actual" or "real"[3]; but Lord HERSCHELL expresses his
view that it has a precise and important signification, which he describes
thus:

> "if I thought that a person making a false statement had shut his eyes to the
> facts, or purposely abstained from inquiring into them, I should hold that
> honest belief was absent, and that he was just as fraudulent as if he had
> knowingly stated that which was false".[4]

Although in many of the decisions the words "recklessness", "indifference", and other like words are to be found used characterising the

---

[1] This is Article 13 of the Code.

[2] *Derry* v. *Peek* (*supra*) at p. 374.

[3] See, for instance, *Shrewsbury* v. *Blount* (1841), 2 Man & G. 475, *per* ERSKINE J. who, at p.
507, uses the expressions "really believed in their truth", and "honestly believed the representations to be true", as if they were convertible; *Harward* v. *Guardians of the Poor of Hackney
Union* (1898), 14 T.L.R. 306, C.A., where A. L. SMITH L.J. at p. 307, says: "a dishonest
satisfaction would be no satisfaction at all".

[4] *Derry* v. *Peek* (*supra*) at p. 376.

state of mind of the representor,[1] it is submitted that these indicia are irrelevant and inessential; the test is simply whether the representor had or had not an honest belief in the truth of the representation as he understood it.[2] In *New Zealand*, in *Foley's Creek Extended Co. v. Cutten and Faithful*[3] WILLIAMS J. had to consider the case where a promoter of a company, though himself "honestly believing in the truth of the particulars" given, misrepresented them in such a way as would lead those who read his report to come to a certain conclusion, "not with the intention of conveying that meaning", but "negligently, without considering the meaning his words would be likely to convey". In these circumstances he exonerated the defendant from liability for fraud.

The mind of the representor

98 It has been emphasised in the previous chapter that the falsity or truth of a representation is to be tested exclusively by the meaning which the actual words used reasonably conveyed to the mind of the particular representee. It is no defence to a charge of *falsity* that the representor used the words in the belief and with the intention that they would convey a different meaning, in which sense they were true. But at the next stage of the cause of action, where the inquiry is whether the representation was *fraudulently made*, a different test altogether is appropriate. What we are now investigating is not the effect of the words upon the representee, but the state of mind of the representor when he uttered them. *In deciding whether the representation was fraudulently made*, the question is not whether the representor honestly believed it to be true in the sense assigned to it by the court, or by an objective consideration of its truth or falsity, but whether he honestly believed it to be true in the sense in which he understood it, albeit erroneously, when it was made. This statement of principle no doubt has some limitations. For instance, the meaning placed on the representation by the representor may be so far removed from the sense at which it would be understood by any reasonable person as to make it impossible to hold that the representor honestly understood it to bear the meaning claimed by him, and

---

[1] See, for instance, *Behn v. Burness* (1863), 3 B. & S. 751 Ex.Ch. (*per Cur.* at p. 753, where the phrase "reckless ignorance whether it may be true or untrue" is for the first time introduced); *Arkwright v. Newbold* (1881), 17 Ch.D. 301, C.A. (*per* COTTON L.J. at p. 320 "reckless disregard"); *Angus v. Clifford*, [1891] 2 Ch. 449, C.A. (where BOWEN L.J. describes the "indifference" of the representor as "the moral obliquity which consists in the wilful disregard of the importance of truth"); *Coats, Ltd. v. Crossland* (1904), 20 T.L.R. 800 (SWINFEN EADY J. at pp. 803–806 "reckless" non-belief).

[2] It is the representation *as understood by the representor* in which he must be shown not to have had an honest belief—see next chapter.

[3] (1903), 22 N.Z.L.R. 759, at pp. 762–763.

honestly believed it in that sense to be true. But subject to the limitation impose by such extreme cases, the principle is clear: the proof of
fraud involves an examination of the representation in the sense in which
the representor *bona fide* understood it.[1]

Intention and motive of the representor

99 It is a *sine qua non* of fraud that the representor intend that the
representee should act upon the representation in the way in which he
did eventually act.[2] So in *Peek* v. *Gurney*[3] the plaintiff failed in an action
for damages for fraud based upon representations contained in a prospectus inviting members of the public to subscribe for shares. The
plaintiff never became such a subscriber; he purchased shares through
the Stock Exchange from persons who had already subscribed for them
and who were consequently upon the company's register, and was left
without an action for fraud, since he did not act on the faith of the representations in the way which was or must be deemed to have been the
intention of the representors.

100 This topic, however, will be developed more fully in the next
chapter.[4] Here it is sufficient to observe that although fraud necessarily
involves an intention on the part of the representor that the representee
shall act in the way in which he does eventually act, yet there is no
necessity to prove any intention further or more remote than this—and
certainly the *motive* of the representor is quite irrelevant.[5] It is immaterial that the plaintiff may or may not be able to show, for instance, that
the representation was made with the intention or motive of damaging
the representee,[6] or of benefiting himself, or a third person[7]; or even

---

[1] The greater part of this paragraph is taken almost *verbatim* from the judgment of the Privy
Council *per* Lord JENKINS in *Akerhielm* v. *De Mare*, [1959] A.C. 789, at p. 805. See further
per CROSS L.J. at p. 459 of his judgment in the Court of Appeal in *Gross* v. *Lewis Hillman, Ltd.*,
[1969] 3 All E.R. 1476; [1970] Ch. 445, C.A. *Cf. per* Lord PORTER in *Bradford Third
Equitable Benefit Building Society* v. *Borders*, [1941] 2 All E.R. 205, at p. 228. The High Court of
Australia has recently discussed the same topic in *John McGrath Motors (Canberra) Pty., Ltd.* v.
Applebee (1964), 110 C.L.R. 656.
[2] See Chapter VI, paras. 114 *et seq., post.*
[3] (1873), L.R. 6 H.L. 377. How far the observations of their Lordships would be applied
to a similar case today has been doubted, in view of the changes in current commercial practice
in the sharemarkets—see Gower, *Modern Company Law* (3rd edn.) 320. But the principle, in so
far as the materiality of intention goes, remains unshaken.
[4] See Chapter VI, paras. 114 *et seq., post.*
[5] *Derry* v. *Peek* (1889), 14 App. Cas. 337, *per* Lord HERSCHELL at p. 374 ("if fraud be proved,
the motive of the person guilty of it is immaterial").
[6] *Edgington* v. *Fitzmaurice* (1885), 29 Ch.D. 459, at p. 462; *Arnison* v. *Smith* (1889), 41
Ch.D. 348, at p. 368, *per* Lord HALSBURY L.C.; *United Motor Finance Co.* v. *Addison & Co.,
Ltd.*, [1937] 1 All E.R. 425, P.C.
[7] *Pasley* v. *Freeman* (1789), 3 Term Rep. 51 *per* BULLER J. at p. 58.

that it is shown that his intention or motive was possibly even to benefit the representee, but that the scheme went awry.[1]   A false representation made without honest belief in its truth will be fraudulent if made with intention that the representee act upon it, even if it be made without any demonstrable motive or intention whatever.[2]

When the non-belief must be shown to have existed

101   In paras. 97 *et seq.* above it has been seen that the prime essential of a fraudulent misrepresentation is an absence of honest belief in its truth on the part of the representor.   In ordinary cases—that is, when there is either no appreciable interval of time between the making of the misrepresentation and the representee's alteration of position on the faith of it, or where no change in the situation takes place during such interval—it may be said that to establish fraud it is necessary and sufficient to prove that the representor, *when making the misrepresentation*, did not believe in its truth.   But where there is such an interval—that is, in the case of a continuing representation[3]—and there is some alteration of the circumstances in that interval, the time at which the representor's state of mind becomes material to the question of fraud or innocence is, it is conceived, the later, and not the earlier, of the above two dates.

Two possible cases

102   The change in the situation may happen in one of two ways.   It may come to the knowledge of the representor, during the interval, that his original statement was false, when made, though he then believed it to be true.   Or, though the representation, when made, was not only believed to be, but was in fact, true, it may become, by reason of events supervening in the course of the interval, in substantial discrepancy with the facts existing at the date of the representee's alteration of position, and, therefore, as has already been seen,[4] false in fact.   Both types

---

[1] *Smith* v. *Chadwick* (1884), 9 App. Cas. 187, H.L. *per* Lord BLACKBURN at p. 201—"The defendants might honestly believe that the shares were a capital investment, and that they were doing the plaintiff a kindness by tricking him into buying them.   I do not say that is proved; but if it were, they are civilly responsible as for a deceit".   *Cf.* what JESSEL M.R. said in the same case in the Court of Appeal (20 Ch.D. 27 at p. 44)—"He cannot be allowed to escape merely because he has good intentions".   *Cf. Re McCallum, McCallum* v. *McCallum* (1901), 83 L.T. 717, at pp. 718, 725.   See, further, *United Motor Finance Co.* v. *Addison & Co., Ltd., supra.*

[2] See *Richardson* v. *Silvester* (1873), L.R. 9 Q.B. 34 *per* BLACKBURN J. at p. 36; *Wilkinson* v. *Downton*, [1897] 2 Q.B. 57 *per* WRIGHT J. at p. 58.   *Cf. Weir* v. *Bell* (1878), 3 Ex.D. 238, C.A. *per* BRAMWELL L.J. at p. 243.

[3] Defined in Article 9 of the Code; see p. 5, *ante.*

[4] See Chapter IV, para 74, *ante.*

of case are mentioned in a frequently quoted passage from a judgment of FRY J. and in both he expresses the view that there rests on the one party "an obligation to disclose to the other the change of circumstances".[1] But, in the case before him, which was one of rescission, it was not necessary for FRY J. to decide, nor did he expressly decide, whether the failure to discharge such obligation would render the misrepresentation fraudulent when the change of circumstances, to the knowledge of the representor, takes place, and thenceforth until acted upon by the representee.[2] This is the question which it now becomes necessary to consider.

Representor's duty when he discovers statement made bona fide was in fact false

103   As to the former class of case, where the representor discovers, before his misrepresentation is acted upon, that it was false when made, and does not immediately correct it in the amplest and clearest language,[3] there has never been any question. It is obvious that, if when the representee alters his position, the representor knows that his representation was untrue when made, he cannot displace the allegation of fraud by saying that he originally believed it to be true. Since at least 1818, this

---

[1] *Davies* v. *London and Provincial Marine Insurance Co.* (1878), 8 Ch.D. 469, at p. 475: "Again, in ordinary contracts",—he had just been dealing with the duty of disclosure in relations and contracts *uberrimae fidei*—"the duty may arise from circumstances which occur during the negotiations. Thus, for instance, if one of the negotiating parties has made a statement which is false in fact, but which he believes to be true, and which is material to the contract, and during the course of the negotiations he discovers the falsity of that statement, he is under an obligation to correct his erroneous statement; although, if he had said nothing, he very likely might have been entitled to hold his tongue throughout. So, again, if a statement has been made which was true at the time, but which in the course of the negotiations becomes untrue, then the person who knows that it has become untrue is under an obligation to disclose to the other the change of circumstances."

[2] In this case one of the parties had (impliedly at least) represented to the other at an interview that a third person was liable to a criminal prosecution. At a subsequent interview, though in the meantime facts had occurred (such as the advice of counsel) showing that the success of such proceedings was highly doubtful, these intervening facts, of which the party was aware, were not disclosed, and, on the faith of the original and uncorrected representation, the other party entered into a certain contract, which FRY J. accordingly ordered to be rescinded. It was not a case of damages, and therefore the question of fraudulent representation which would be relevant to such a case alone (see Ch. X) did not strictly arise.

[3] *Arnison* v. *Smith* (1889), 41 Ch.D. 348, C.A., *per* Lord HALSBURY L.C. at p. 370, COTTON L.J. at pp. 371, 372, and LINDLEY L.J. at p. 373 (a case in which the directors, on ascertaining the falsity of the prospectus, sent out an ambiguous circular so framed as "to avoid bringing to the mind of the plaintiff the real facts of the case, whilst stating enough to enable the defendant to say that the plaintiffs were informed of those facts". Contrast the cases in which the representor was held to have made the necessary correction unambiguously and in good time, such as *Re Edwards to Daniel Sykes & Co., Ltd.* (1890), 62 L.T. 445, and *Golding* v. *Royal London Auxiliary Insurance Co.* (1914), 30 T.L.R. 350.

has never been doubted in any authority, either at common law,[1] or in equity.[2] The rule has been expressed in unambiguous and emphatic terms by Lord BLACKBURN:

> "when a statement or representation has been made in the *bona fide* belief that it is true, and the party who has made it afterwards comes to find out that it is untrue, and discovers what he should have said, he can no longer honestly keep up that silence on the subject after that has come to his knowledge, thereby allowing the other party to go on, upon a statement which was honestly made at the time when it was made, but which he has not now retracted when he has become aware that it can be no longer honestly persevered in. *That would be fraud*".[3]

104 On principle, and in accordance with the general current of authority, it would seem equally clear that a misrepresentation becomes fraudulent in the second of the two classes of case abovementioned, *viz.* where the representor fails to reveal to the representee the occurrence of supervening events which have come to his notice in the interval, in virtue of which the statement which was, when made, in substantial accordance with the material facts then existing, becomes in substantial disaccord with the material facts existing at the time when the representee alters his position on the faith of the representation. For if, as has been shewn,[4] it is the characteristic of a continuing representation that it is, in contemplation of law, repeated at each successive moment from the *terminus a quo*, when it was put forth as an inducement, to the *terminus ad quem* when the inducement operates and materialises, for the purpose of determining whether it is false or true at the latter date, it surely follows that the mental state of the representor must be carried along with the representation in its passage between the two termini, for the further purpose of determining whether, at such latter date, it is also fraudulent or not. It is clear that the representation under such circumstances becomes false when acted upon, so as to entitle the representee to avoid the transaction.[5] On what possible theory can it be

---

[1] *Jarrett* v. *Kennedy* (1848), 6 C.B. 319, *per* WILDE C.J. at p. 323 (discovery by directors before allotment, that all the statements in the prospectus were false when made, was not revealed to applicants, and plaintiff obtained damages accordingly as for a fraudulent suppression and misrepresentation).

[2] *Edwards* v. *M'Leay* (1818), 2 Swan. 287 (*per* Lord ELDON L.C. at p. 289, affirming GRANT M.R. at p. 313 of G. Cooper, 308); *Reynell* v. *Sprye*; *Sprye* v. *Reynell* (1852), 1 De G.M. & G. 660, *per* Lord CRANWORTH L.J. at p. 709 ("this, from the date of the discovery"—sc. of the fact that the plaintiff's interests under a will were much larger than the defendant had originally represented or supposed—"becomes, in the contemplation of this court, a fraudulent misrepresentation, even though it was not so originally"); *Arnison* v. *Smith* (1888), 41 Ch.D. 348, C.A.

[3] *Brownlie* v. *Campbell* (1880), 5 App. Cas. 925, H.L., at p. 950.

[4] See *ante*, Chapter IV, para. 74.

[5] *With* v. *O'Flanagan*, [1936] 1 All E.R. 727; [1936] Ch. 575, C.A. is a more recent authority to support this proposition.

supposed that it does not become fraudulent also, for the purpose of entitling the representee to damages? If the representor is to be regarded as saying at the last moment of the interval, "what I originally stated is in accordance with the facts *now* existing", why is he not to be also responsible in damages, as for a fraudulent, and not merely false, representation, if (as, *ex hypothesi*, is the case) he not only does not believe in the truth of that which he so asserts, but knows or believes the contrary? It would not have been thought necessary to labour this point, were it not that a high authority, JAMES L.J., once (without, however, giving any reasons) expressed a distinctly contrary view to that now put forward.[1] It is submitted that the *dictum* in question—for it is nothing more—is opposed to sound reason, and also to the main current of authority, both at common law,[2] and in equity[3]; and that the very class

---

[1] At p. 329 of *Arkwright* v. *Newbold* (1881), 17 Ch.D. 301, C.A., where, after delivering his judgment and hearing those of COTTON and LUSH L.JJ., JAMES L.J. supplemented his own by stating: "I think it right to add that I entirely agree with what Lord Justice COTTON has said, that we cannot accede to the suggestion made by counsel for the plaintiffs, that the persons issuing a prospectus are liable to an action of deceit" (which they could not be except in the case of a *fraudulent* misrepresentation—see Ch. XI), "because they do not mention a fact coming to their knowledge before the allotment of shares, which falsifies a statement in the prospectus". But COTTON L.J., who is thus vouched as a party to this positive expression of opinion, had not in fact gone so far. All he had said (at p. 325), after mentioning the question "how far the plaintiff could have obtained any relief if the statement in the prospectus had, to the knowledge of the directors, become untrue before the contract had been completed", was this:—"on this point I give no opinion, but I must not be considered as acceding to the view that the coming into existence of a fact which would have made a statement in the prospectus untrue, if it had existed at the time of the issuing of the prospectus, would, in an action of deceit, entitle the plaintiff to relief". That is to say, he neither accedes, nor differs, but reserves his opinion. This is a very different thing from expressing a final and definite adverse view. LUSH L.J. did not mention the point at all. So that the doctrine rests entirely on the statement of JAMES L.J. not supported by any reasoning, and quite unnecessary to the decision, which was in favour of the defendants on other grounds.

[2] See *Adamson* v. *Jarvis* (1827), 4 Bing. 66, which neatly raises the point: for the action there was for damages for *fraudulent* misrepresentation of authority from the owner to sell. The statement was true when the representor made it, but at the time of the auction sale it had ceased to be so, he no longer having that authority. BEST C.J. at p. 74, delivering the judgment of the Court of Common Pleas, said: "for this injury the plaintiff is entitled to compensation, *whether the affirmation was false or true at the time it was made*. If the defendant had authority to sell at the time he employed the plaintiff, but ceased to have that authority at the time of the sale, he should have informed the plaintiff of this change in his situation". So, also, in *Denton* v. *Great Northern Rail. Co.* (1856), 5 E. & B. 860, it was held that the company's announcement in their time-table that a certain train ran at a certain time, which was true when first made, became subsequently fraudulent, when the train was taken off, as against anyone, who, like the plaintiff, acted on the faith of the uncorrected time-table as a continuing representation of the truth: *per* Lord CAMPBELL C.J. at pp. 866, 867, and WIGHTMAN J. at p. 867. *Cf.* the observations of LINDLEY L.J. at p. 773 of *Canning* v. *Farquhar* (1886), 16 Q.B.D. 727, C.A.: "if he had paid the money without disclosing to the office the fact that his statements, which were true when he made them, were so no longer, he would have done that which would have been plainly dishonest".

[3] *Traill* v. *Baring* (1864), 4 De G.J. & Sm. 318, where there was an implied representation by one insurance company to another that they had the intention of taking a third of the risk, and procuring another company to take another third, if the representees would take the re-

of case now under consideration clearly falls within the comprehensive statement by Lord BLACKBURN which immediately follows the passage (relating to representations subsequently discovered to have been false *when made*) which is cited above[1]:

> "I go on further still to say, which is perhaps not so clear, but certainly it is my opinion, that, where there is a duty and an obligation to speak, and a man in breach of that duty or obligation holds his tongue and does not speak, and does not say the thing he was bound to say, if that was done with the intention of inducing the other party to act upon the belief that the reason why he did not speak was because he had nothing to say, I should be inclined myself to hold that that was fraud also",[2]

—by which last words it is evident that he was intending to distinguish this species of case, or a class which includes it, from, and to add it to, the species which he had just been considering, and which answers to the first of the two types of continuing misrepresentation above indicated.

Innocent misrepresentation

105 Fraudulent and innocent misrepresentations constitute two opposite and mutually exclusive categories, just as much as true and false representations. For purposes of legal proceedings, a representation can no more be compounded of dishonesty and honesty, than it can be of untruth and truth. It follows that *a misrepresentation is innocent when at the material date the representor did in fact honestly believe it to be true.*[3] What "honest" belief is, has already been considered.[4] It remains to examine the nature of "belief in fact".

Honest actual belief the test of innocence

106 Honest belief in the truth of the misrepresentation is the test of its innocence. Less than this, as we have seen, will not suffice; but, on the other hand, more is not required. This proposition has been accepted ever since the famous exposition of the subject by Lord HER-

---

maining third, and it was held by KNIGHT-BRUCE and TURNER L.JJ. that, assuming the representors *bona fide* had this intention when making the representation, it was their duty to inform the representees of their subsequent change of mind before the latter acted upon it as originally made, and that their failure to do so constituted, "in the eyes of this court", a fraudulent misrepresentation; *British Equitable Insurance Co.* v. *Great Western Rail. Co.* (1869), 38 L.J. Ch. 314 (*per* GIFFORD L.J. at p. 316: "There cannot be a doubt that the suppression of that fact was fraudulent").

[1] Para. 103, *ante*.
[2] *Brownlie* v. *Campbell* (1880), 5 App.Cas. 925, H.L., at p. 950.
[3] This is Article 15 of the Code: see p. 7, *ante*.
[4] See para. 97, *ante*, and notes thereon.

SCHELL in *Derry* v. *Peek*,[1] the *locus classicus*.[2] Belief, not knowledge, is the criterion.[3] It is no more necessary to constitute innocence that the representor should *know* the stated fact to be true, than it is necessary to constitute fraud that he should know it to be false. "Justification by faith" is a doctrine which applies to the law of misrepresentation, as much as to the Articles of Religion, and faith is not knowledge for the former purpose, any more than for the latter,[4] nor need it be rational, or based on sound premises; it may, indeed, be violently opposed to reason and good sense,[5] but it must be *good* faith, that is to say, it must be sincere.[6]

Negligence, absence of reasonable grounds, etc., compatible with innocence

107 Care, skill, and competence being irrelevant to the question of whether a misrepresentation is innocent or fraudulent, it follows that any statement which fulfils the one condition of innocence above stated, is not rendered fraudulent

> "by the mere fact that the belief was unreasonable, or was based upon inadequate materials, information, or inquiry, or arose from negligence, forgetfulness, inadvertence, or incompetence".[7]

It is the existence and genuineness of the representor's belief on which alone rests his *moral* qualification to be free of any imputation of fraud. By what *mental* processes he arrived at the conclusion, or whether his mind was sluggish or active, suspicious or credulous, rational or irrational,

---

1 *Derry* v. *Peek* (1889), 14 App. Cas. 337, H.L.

2 But as early as 1844, TINDAL C.J. had held, delivering the judgment of the Court of Exchequer Chamber in *Collins* v. *Evans* (1844), 5 Q.B. 820, at pp. 827, 830, that "a statement or representation, which is false in fact, but not known to be so by the party making it, but on the contrary made honestly, and in the full belief that it is true" is not the subject of an action for damages—in other words, is not to be deemed fraudulent.

3 *Derry* v. *Peek*, *supra*, at pp. 359–380. At pp. 359, 360, Lord HERSCHELL distinguishes proceedings for rescission, and "making good", and also cases of estoppel, in none of which is the question of fraud or innocence relevant. At pp. 360–363, he criticises the judgments of the Lords Justices, which the House was reversing. At pp. 363–374, he makes a "close and critical examination of the earlier authorities", and at pp. 374–376 lays down the principles which he deduces from them, when purged of their occasional errors.

4 *Derry* v. *Peek* (*supra*); in *New Zealand*, see *Foley's Creek Extended Co.* v. *Cutten and Faithful* (1903), 22 N.Z.L.R. 759, at pp. 762–763.

5 "Faith is not knowledge, no more than three is four, but eminently contained in it; so that he that knows believes, and something more; but he that believes many times does not know—nay, if he doth barely and merely believe, he doth never know"—Chillingworth's *Religion of Protestants*, p. 412. *Cf.* the patristic dictum: *apparentia non habent fidem, sed agnitionem*.

6 On the *credibile quia absurdum* principle of Tertullian (*De Carne Christi*, cap. 5).

7 This is Article 16 of the Code. *Cf.* the definition of "good faith" in s. 90 of the Bills of Exchange Act 1882 and s. 62 (2) of the Sale of Goods Act 1893: "A thing is deemed to be done in good faith, when it is in fact done honestly, whether it be done negligently or not".

prone to investigate or ready to take everything for granted, are questions which, *per se*, have no relevance. This proposition has now been clearly and finally established by the decision of the House of Lords above referred to, but, before that decision, there had been, as Lord HERSCHELL points out in reviewing the authorities,[1] occasional unguarded judicial observations which, particularly when divorced from their context, might have encouraged the view that certain things, if otherwise grossly culpable, might be deemed to amount to fraud while not meeting the requirement which he had postulated. But these must since *Derry* v. *Peek* be regarded as heresy.

Even gross negligence is not fraud

108 Thus, negligence, however gross, is not fraud. Indeed, it may be said to be its direct *antitheton*. This is now well established[2]; but it has often been said that negligence may be so gross as to amount to evidence of fraud.[3] In its literal sense, this proposition is of course quite inaccurate. Negligence no more indicates fraud, than it constitutes it. White cannot be evidence of black, any more than it is black. But the *alleged* white may be of so exceedingly dingy a hue that any person called upon to decide whether it is black or white, there being no middle colour possible, may be justified in saying that the thing described as white is in fact black. So on a plea of actual, though negligent belief, the tribunal which has to decide as to the existence and reality of the belief may be forced to the conclusion that the suggested negligence, if it were a case of negligence, would be so outrageous and abnormal that the theory of want of care must be rejected in favour of the alternative hypothesis of no belief at all. As an elliptical mode of expressing the above attitude, the phrase—"gross negligence may amount to evidence of fraud",—can be accepted, but in no other sense, and to no further extent. The proper amplification of this misleading brachylogy is to be found in judgments of Lord CRANWORTH,[4] and BOWEN L.J.[5]; but even

---

[1] *Derry* v. *Peek* (1889), 14 App. Cas. 337, H.L. at pp. 363–374.

[2] *Derry* v. *Peek* (1889), 14 App. Cas. 337, H.L. at p. 361; *Angus* v. *Clifford*, [1891] 2 Ch. 449, C.A. per LINDLEY L.J. at pp. 462–468; *Le Lievre* v. *Gould*, [1893] 1 Q.B. 491 per BOWEN L.J. at p. 501.

[3] For instance, at pp. 188, 190, 191 of *Evans* v. *Bicknell* (1801), 6 Ves. 174 (per Lord ELDON L.C.), and at pp. 216, 217 of *Martinez* v. *Cooper* (1826), 2 Russ. 198.

[4] At p. 168 of *Western Bank of Scotland* v. *Addie* (1867), L.R. 1 Sc. & Div. 145, H.L. "if a little more care and caution must have led the directors to a conclusion different from that which they put forth, this may afford *strong evidence to show that they really did not believe in the truth of what they stated*, and so that they were guilty of fraud".

[5] *Le Lievre* v. *Gould*, *supra*, at p. 500: "if the case had been tried with a jury the judge would have pointed out to them that gross negligence might amount to evidence of fraud, if it was

in the expositions of these accurate jurists the unfortunate term "evidence" is used.   It is suggested that the best statement of the principle, which considers this terminological pitfall, and is characterised by both literal and substantial accuracy and completeness, may be that of FRY J. in a case which involved the question of what degree of wilful avoidance of the truth amounts to constructive notice.   He there observes,

> "It has been said that there may be negligence which amounts to fraud. That language has always seemed to me not strictly accurate.   Fraud imports design and purpose.   Negligence imports that you are acting carelessly, and without that design.   But what is meant is this—that conduct which might be negligent, or might be attributable to negligence, is really attributable to a design not to know more".[1]

It is partly owing to the above ambiguity of expression, and partly to the confusion between intellectual carelessness in forming an opinion, and the moral carelessness involved in putting forward a statement without any belief at all one way or the other,[2] that the notion ever gained ground that an innocent misrepresentation can be rendered fraudulent by mere proof of negligence.

---

so gross as to be incompatible with the idea of honesty, but that even gross negligence in the absence of dishonesty did not of itself amount to fraud."

[1] At p. 706 of *Kettlewell* v. *Watson* (1882), 21 Ch.D. 685.   *Cf.* a similar adverse criticism by him of the modified view, "gross negligence is evidence of fraud", at pp. 489, 490 of *Northern Counties of England Fire Insurance Co.* v. *Whipp* (1884), 26 Ch.D. 482, C.A.

[2] Lord HERSCHELL, at p. 361 of *Derry* v. *Peek* (1889), 14 App. Cas. 337, H.L., in the course of his criticism of the views expressed in the C.A. by COTTON L.J. says: "to make a statement careless whether it be true or false, and therefore without any real belief in its truth, appears to me to be an essentially different thing from making, through want of care, a false statement, which is nevertheless honestly believed to be true.   And it is surely conceivable that a man may believe that what he states is the fact, though he has been so wanting in care that the court may think that there were no sufficient grounds to warrant his belief".   So also BOWEN L.J. at p. 501 of *Le Lievre* v. *Gould, supra*, observes: "there seems to have been some sort of an idea that when a jury was asked the . . . question, whether the man had made the representation not knowing and not caring whether his statement was true or false, the expression 'not caring' had something to do with his not taking care"—(a very natural idea, it may be added, the naturalness of which illustrates forcibly the harm done by the needless introduction of rhetorical phrases as fringe and supplement to the simple "non-belief" which is adequate to all the requirements of the rule)—"but that expression did not mean not taking care to find out whether the statement was true or false; it meant not caring in the man's own heart and conscience whether it was true or false,—and that would be wicked indifference and recklessness".   A third reason, or historical explanation, of the confusion between the two ideas is given by the Lord Justice, at p. 500 of the same case, *viz.* "the fact that Equity judges had to decide questions of law and fact together.   An Equity judge, when he had to deal with a question of fraud, discussed his reasons for coming to the conclusion that there had been fraud, and it very often happened that an Equity judge decided that there was fraud in a case in which gross negligence had been proved . . . Cases of gross negligence, in which the Chancery judges decided that there had been fraud, were piled up one upon another, until at last a notion came to be entertained that it was sufficient to prove gross negligence in order to establish fraud.   That is not so.   In all those cases fraud and dishonesty were the proper *ratio decidendi*".

Irrational or ill-founded belief cannot support a charge of fraud

109   In like manner, and for the same reasons, irrational or ill-founded belief is not the same thing as the absence of belief, nor can it be said to be indicative thereof, except in some such elliptical form of words as has been used in reference to negligence.   A representor may have acted on inquiry and materials which would not have satisfied a person of normal intelligence, much less a trained judge of evidence; but this goes for nothing if the belief—the individual being what he was— really and truly existed.   Belief is none the less belief because it is irrational.   Innocence is not negatived by proof of the representor's stupidity, but only by proof of his bad faith.   The notion that absence of reasonable grounds for a belief which actually existed can convert innocence into fraud, or into something equivalent thereto, in contemplation of law, though apparently underlying certain dicta in the earlier cases,[1] was never expressed in plain terms until 1867 by Lord CHELMSFORD L.C.,[2] and then was promptly disavowed and dissented from by Lord CRANWORTH.[3]   These, moreover, were individual opinions: there was no actual decision of any court to the above effect until that of the Court of Appeal in *Peek* v. *Derry*,[4] which was overruled by the House of Lords, *sub nom. Derry* v. *Peek*.[5]   Here, however, as in the case of negligence, the alleged unreasonableness of any belief may be so glaring that a court would be justified in inferring that the belief could never really have existed, and that the supposed believer was not so irrational, incompetent, or foolish, as, for his own purposes he may profess to be when an attempt is made to saddle him with responsibility for the consequences of his misrepresentation.[6]

---

[1] For instance, the expressions used by MAULE J. at p. 507, of *Shrewsbury* v. *Blount* (1841), 2 Man. & G. 475: "it would be an answer to the action that he had *good reason to believe* the representations which he had made", and again, "belief *reasonably well grounded*", and "*well founded* belief".

[2] At p. 162 of *Western Bank of Scotland* v. *Addie* (1867), L.R. 1 Sc. & Div. 145, H.L.: "if an untrue statement is made founded upon a belief which is destitute of all reasonable grounds, or which the least inquiry would immediately correct, I do not see that it is not fairly and correctly characterised as misrepresentation and deceit".

[3] At p. 168 of the case last cited: "if persons . . . make statements . . . which they *bona fide* believe to be true, I cannot think they can be guilty of fraud because other persons think, or the court thinks, or your Lordships think, that there was no sufficient ground to warrant the opinion which they had formed".

[4] (1887), 37 Ch.D. 541, C.A.

[5] (1889), 14 App. Cas. 337, H.L., acted upon and applied immediately afterwards by the C.A. in *Glasier* v. *Rolls* (1889), 42 Ch.D. 436, C.A.   As regards prospectuses of companies, the law has been altered by statute: *vide* Ch. XVI, paras. 329 *et seq.*, *post.*

[6] See the observations of Lord HERSCHELL at p. 369 of *Derry* v. *Peek* (1889), 14 App. Cas. 337, H.L.: "I think there is here some confusion between that which is evidence of fraud, and

Forgetfulness will not support a charge of fraud

110 A man may believe in the truth—that is, the complete truth—of his representation, by reason of his not remembering a qualifying circumstance which at one time he had known. This forgetfulness, again, does not, *per se*, negative innocence. Once more, the only question is—had he really and truly forgotten the circumstance ? In an action for fraudulent misrepresentation, he cannot be punished for a bad memory, any more than in the other cases discussed above he can be punished for want of diligence in inquiry, or soundness in judgment.[1] Of course in any proceeding in which it is enough to establish an innocent misrepresentation, the mere circumstance that the omitted fact was not present to the mind of the representor at the time does not excuse him if the omission was such as to render his statement false.[2] And, again, if the representation is one which asserts positively that a thing was certainly so, and the fact be that the representor does not recollect whether it was so or not, the imperfection of his recollection will not excuse him, since he chose to take upon himself the responsibility of a positive

---

that which constitutes it. A consideration of the grounds of belief is no doubt an important aid in ascertaining whether the belief was really entertained. A man's mere assertion that he believed the statement he made to be true is not accepted as conclusive proof that he did so. There may be such an absence of reasonable ground for his belief as, in spite of his assertion, to carry conviction to the mind that he had not really the belief which he alleges''. Again, at pp. 375, 376, Lord HERSCHELL says: ''I can conceive many cases where the fact that an alleged belief was destitute of all reasonable foundation would suffice of itself to convince the court that it was not really entertained, and that the representation was a fraudulent one''. So, at p. 380: ''the statements of witnesses are by no means to be accepted blindfold. The probabilities must be considered. Whenever it is necessary to arrive at a conclusion as to the state of mind of another person, and to determine whether his belief under given circumstances was such as he alleges, we can only do so by applying the standard of conduct which our own experience of the ways of men has enabled us to form; by asking ourselves whether a reasonable man would be likely under the circumstances so to believe''. It will be noticed that both Lord CRANWORTH and Lord HERSCHELL, though the context puts their meaning beyond doubt, use the unfortunate expression ''evidence'' which, but for that context, would, it is submitted, tend to mislead. See para. 108, *ante*, as to the use of the term in connection with negligence.

[1] *Bain* v. *Fothergill* (1874), L.R. 7 H.L. 158 (*per* Lord HATHERLEY, at p. 212); *Mathias* v. *Yetts* (1882), 46 L.T. 497, C.A. (*per* LINDLEY L.J. at p. 506); *Low* v. *Bouverie*, [1891] 3 Ch. 82, C.A. (*per* LINDLEY L.J. at p. 101, and BOWEN L.J. at p. 106). In the last case, it was held that, of the two authorities which would appear to lay down a different doctrine, *Burrowes* v. *Lock* (1805), 10 Ves. 470 (*per* GRANT M.R.), and *Slim* v. *Croucher* (1860), 1 De G.F. & J. 518, the former can only be supported on the ground of estoppel, where of course no fraud need be shown, and the latter on no ground. The same principle is applied to actions for money had and received on the ground of ''mistake'': see *Kelly* v. *Solari* (1841), 9 M. & W. 54.

[2] See the cases cited in the last note, particularly *Mathias* v. *Yetts*, *supra*, *per* JESSEL M.R. at p. 502 (where he says that ''forgetting a fact'' does not prevent a representation being fraudulent ''in law'', by which he means an innocent misrepresentation, but one which is amenable to proceedings for rescission), and see Sir James HANNEN, at p. 504.

assurance, knowing that the representee would be likely to act upon the faith of it.[1]

Negligence in making a representation may nevertheless support an action for damages

111   Until 1964 the distinction between fraudulent misrepresentation and innocent misrepresentation, which has been examined in this chapter, was decisive on the question whether an action for damages would lie. But this is no longer the law. In the first place, the provisions of the Misrepresentation Act 1967 now give to the representee an action for damages for innocent misrepresentation, subject to a special statutory defence, in cases in which he has been induced by the representation to enter into a contract to his detriment. These provisions are considered in Chapter XII. In the second place, the decision of the House of Lords in *Hedley Byrne & Co., Ltd.* v. *Heller & Partners, Ltd.*[2] in 1964 made it clear that *some* negligent misrepresentations can be used as the foundation of an action for damages *in negligence*. What the circumstances are, in which such an action will lie, is a question to be considered separately in another chapter.[3]

---

[1] *Brownlie* v. *Campbell* (1880), 5 App. Cas. 925, H.L., *per* Lord SELBORNE L.C. at p. 936, Lord HATHERLEY at p. 945, and Lord BLACKBURN at p. 953.

[2] [1963] 2 All E.R. 575; [1964] A.C. 465, H.L.

[3] Chapter XIX, *post*.

CHAPTER VI

Inducement and Materiality

Introductory

112 The previous chapter dealt with the legal consequences of the representor's state of mind in making a representation. It now becomes necessary to deal with the representee's state of mind when receiving it. Of the two inquiries the latter is of the greater importance because it is of universal application, whereas the former is important only in certain forms of proceeding. Whether damages or rescission be sought, the plaintiff is out of court unless he establishes *inducement* and *materiality*[1]; but it is only where deceit is alleged that the question of the representor's fraud or innocence has any relevance.[2]

Both inducement and materiality essential

113 Inducement and materiality are two quite separate ingredients of any actionable misrepresentation. Both must be established[3]; it is of no avail to show that the representee was in fact induced to act to his prejudice by a falsehood, unless that falsehood was of a nature to induce a normal person so to act in the circumstances of the case; whilst, on the other hand, it is useless to show the *a priori* probability of its operating as an inducement, unless it is shown that it did in fact induce. It is true that in certain extreme cases inducement may be inferred as a fact from materiality[4]; and, as will later be seen,[5] proof of actual inducement, including (a) intention to induce and (b) resultant alteration of position by the representee may, in the particular circumstances of the case, without more in the way of actual evidence directed to the point, give

---

[1] *Vide post*, Chapters XI–XVI.

[2] While in the examination of Inducement and Materiality it is the state of mind of the representee which is primarily under scrutiny, it should not be overlooked that in the consideration of Inducement the state of mind of the representor is still relevant; for an intention on his part to induce must necessarily be proved or imputed. See paras. 115–118, *post*. It must also be noticed that since the passing of the Misrepresentation Act 1967 the reasonable belief of the representor in the truth of the representation affords a defence to the new action for damages for innocent misrepresentation.

[3] *Smith* v. *Chadwick* (1884), 9 App. Cas. 187, H.L., *per* Lord SELBORNE L.C. at p. 190.

[4] See note 1 on p. 138; also paras. 133–134, *post*.

[5] See note 5 on p. 143, *post*.

rise to a legitimate inference of materiality.[1]   But all this does not nega-
tive the existence of the clear distinction between the two *alleganda et probanda*, each of which must be separately established as a fact.[2]

Actual inducement necessary

114 Inducement in fact, as distinguished from a tendency to induce
(which is materiality), is, *ex vi termini*, a question of fact,[3] and the burden
of proving it is, as already stated, on the representee.   However likely a
misrepresentation may have been to influence an average individual—
however "calculated" (in both senses of the word) it may have been to
lead a normal representee to take just the steps which he did take—
however inconceivable even it may be that he could have remained
insensible to the allurements held out—yet, if in fact he was not induced,
the misrepresentation is not actionable.[4]   It now becomes necessary to
consider what are the precise elements in this burden of proof, and what
are the content and limits of the conception of "inducement".

---

[1] See para. 115, *post*.

[2] Warranty, or an express condition or term in a contract, of course, renders irrelevant all considerations of inducement or materiality: *Pawson* v. *Watson* (1778), 2 Cowp. 785 (*per* Lord MANSFIELD C.J. at pp. 788–790); *Newcastle Fire Insurance Co.* v. *Macmorran & Co.* (1815), 3 Dow. 255 H.L. (*per* Lord ELDON L.C. at pp. 262, 265); *Attwood* v. *Small* (1838), 6 Cl. & Fin. 232 (*per* Lord BROUGHAM at p. 444); *Anderson* v. *Fitzgerald* (1853), 4 H.L. Cas. 484 (*per* Lord CRANWORTH L.C. at pp. 503–505); *Towle* v. *National Guardian Assurance Co.* (1861), 30 L.J. (Ch.) 900; *Thomson* v. *Weems* (1884), 9 App. Cas. 671, H.L. (*per* Lord BLACKBURN at pp. 683, 684, and Lord WATSON at p. 689); *Hambrough* v. *Mutual Life Insurance Co. of New York* (1895), 72 L.T. 140, C.A. (*per* RIGBY L.J. at pp. 141, 142); *Dawsons, Ltd.* v. *Bonnin*, [1922] 2 A.C. 413, H.L. (*per* Lord HALDANE at pp. 423, 424, Lord CAVE at pp. 432, 433, and Lord DUNEDIN at p. 435); *Paxman* v. *Union Assurance Society Ltd.* (1923), 39 T.L.R. 424 (*per* McCARDIE J. at p. 426); *Condogianis* v. *Guardian Assurance Co., Ltd.*, [1921] 2 A.C. 125 at p. 129, following *Newcastle Fire Insurance Co.* v. *Macmorran & Co.* (supra).   Contrast *Mutual Life Insce. Co. of New York* v. *Ontario Metal Products Co., Ltd.*, [1925] A.C. 344, P.C.

[3] See paras. 133–134, *post*; *Smith* v. *Chadwick* (1884), 9 Ch.App. 187, 196.

[4] For instance, nothing could have been more calculated to induce the representee to purchase shares than the prospectus and scrip-certificates in *Shrewsbury* v. *Blount* (1841), 2 Man. & G. 475, but the jury chose to find that in fact he was not so induced, and the Court of C.P. refused to disturb the verdict.   Again, in *Smith* v. *Chadwick* (1884), 9 App. Cas. 187, H.L., it was obvious that a statement in the prospectus as to a certain person being one of the directors (which was false) must have made a deep impression on any person of ordinary business habits and experience acquainted with the particular trade and locality, and both Lord SELBORNE L.C. at p. 190, and Lord BLACKBURN at p. 194, expressed no little astonishment that the plaintiff had not professed to rely upon it: but, so far from doing so, he admitted in cross-examination that in fact he was not influenced by any of the names on the "front page" (see p. 194), but solely by statements in the body of the prospectus as to output and profits, which were ambiguous, and to which he steadily refused to assign any particular meaning; being unable, therefore, on his own admission, to prove that he was in fact induced by the only misrepresentation which was both intended, and likely to, mislead him, he failed in his claim.

Two aspects of inducement

115   Inducement in fact is shown by proof that the representation was
made both with the object, and with the result, of inducing the representee to alter his position.[1]   Neither element suffices without the other.
To prove the representor's intention to produce the effect comes to
nothing, unless the effect itself be proved; and to establish the result is
idle, unless it be shown that the representor actually, or presumptively,
intended to bring it about.[2]   The representor is presumed to have so
intended, if he wilfully used language calculated, or of a nature, to induce
a normal person in the circumstances of the case to act as the representee
did.   It follows that the topic of materiality and that of the presumptive
intent of the representor are much involved *inter se*, and the authorities
cited on one topic will often be found to be very much in point on the
other.

Intention insufficient if actual inducement not shown

116   The proposition that there is nothing actionable in a mere intention to induce which fails of its effect altogether would seem to be
sufficiently obvious.   "An action cannot be supported for telling a bare
naked lie", as was said by BULLER J. in one of the earliest of the misrepresentation authorities,[3] or, to apply the equitable metaphor of a
later judgment, "a man may with impunity lie in gross . . . but he
cannot . . . tell a lie appurtenant".[4]   The class of case, however, where
the representee was undoubtedly moved by something, but where there
are several possible motives and inducements besides the misrepresentation, has occasioned some doubt and difficulty, which is the justification
for the large number of decisions dealing expressly with the point, and
for the many successive restatements of the rule, in more or less elaborate
terms, by various judges from Lord BROUGHAM L.C. to Lord SELBORNE
L.C.   The former of these Lords Chancellors expressed his views on the
question with the utmost precision and detail: "Thirdly and chiefly",

---

[1] See Article 17 of the Code.   This is supposed to be expressed by the common formula:
"the representation must be one *dans locum contractui*".   But this expression is not very
felicitous or exact: *dans locum* is too broad, since it would obviously include any sort of contracts for the making of which a representation may give the *occasion or opportunity*, which is a
very different thing from inducement; and *contractui* is too narrow, because the rule applies
to many modes of altering a man's position on the faith of a representation, besides the entering
into a contract with the representor, or with any one.

[2] See paras. 116–118, *infra*.

[3] In *Pasley* v. *Freeman* (1789), 3 Term. Rep. 51, *per* BULLER J. at p. 56.

[4] *Per* NORTH J. in *Archer* v. *Stone* (1898), 78 L.T. 34.   He defines a "lie appurtenant" as
follows: "that is to say, if he tells a lie relating to any part of the contract, or its subject-
matter, which induces another person to contract", etc.

he says, after enumerating two of the ingredients in any proceeding for misrepresentation, "it should be this false representation which gave rise to the contracting of the other party. *Dolus dans locum contractui* is the language of the civil law, not *dolus malus* generally; not the mere fraudulent conduct of the party trying to overreach his adversary; nor mere misconduct and falsehood throughout, unless *dedit locum contractui*"[1]; then, after reviewing the previous decisions, he proceeds:

> "Now, my Lords, what inference do I draw from these cases? It is this, that general fraudulent conduct signifies nothing; that attempts to over-reach go for nothing; that an intention and design to deceive may go for nothing, unless all this dishonesty of purpose, all this fraud, all this intention and design, can be connected only with the particular transaction, and not only connected with the particular transaction, but must be made to be the very ground upon which this transaction took place, and must have given rise to this contract. If a mere general intention to overreach were enough, I hardly know a contract, even between persons of very strict morality, that could stand; we generally find the case to be that there has been an attempt of the one party to overreach the other, and of the other to overreach the first; but that does not make void the contract. It must be shown that the attempt was made, and made with success, *cum fructu*. The party must not only have been minded to overreach, but he must actually have overreached . . . and, moreover, the representations so made must have had the effect of deceiving the purchaser; and moreover, the purchaser must have trusted to these representations, and not to his own acumen, not to his own perspicacity, not to inquiries of his own."[2]

And to the same effect, but in much terser language, Lord SELBORNE L.C. observes, in reference to a case where the representee was a vendor—in the last case the representee was a purchaser—that

> "if the vendor was not *in fact* misled, the contract could not be set aside, because a *dolus* which neither induced nor materially affected the contract is not enough".[3]

Accordingly, whenever the representee has failed to discharge the burden of establishing that he was *in fact* induced, he has failed altogether. This failure may arise from proof or admission that he relied *solely*[4] on something other than the misrepresentation on which his action or defence is founded, whether that "something" be an assurance or certificate or warranty which he insisted on obtaining, and obtained,[5] or a statement

---

[1] *Attwood* v. *Small* (1838), 6 Cl. & Fin. 232, H.L., at p. 444.

[2] *Ibid.*, at pp. 447, 448.

[3] *Coaks* v. *Boswell* (1886), 11 App.Cas. 232, H.L., at p. 236.

[4] Mere proof that he relied on something *in addition to* the misrepresentation sued upon does not negative the fact of inducement, if otherwise proved: see para. 120, *infra*.

[5] As in *Flinn* v. *Headlam* (1829), 9 B. & C. 693, where the jury found that the plaintiff relied solely upon a certificate of seaworthiness, which he insisted on and obtained, and not on the alleged misstatement as to the vessel's cargo.

in the prospectus or document the subject of the proceedings other than the particular representation alleged to have been the inducing cause,[1] or the representee's own skill or judgment,[2] or his own general knowledge of business, or faith in the venture, or special inquiries or researches[3] or actual knowledge of the truth.[4]   Or, without the representor proving out of the representee's own mouth, or otherwise, any of such affirmative matters—and there is no onus on him to do so—the representee may simply fail to establish what is incumbent on him, either because he cannot even swear that he saw or read the document alleged to contain the misrepresentation,[5] or that it was addressed to, or intended for him, or a class of which he was a member[6]; or because he never examined the article, the active concealment of defects wherein is alleged to have constituted the misrepresentation[7]; or because he determined to take the risk, whatever it was[8]; or for other reasons.[9]

1 As in *Re Northumberland and Durham District Banking Co., Ex parte Bigge* (1858), 28 L.J. (Ch.) 50, where the shareholder was not misled by the reports and accounts of the company, which was the case set up by him, but solely by the oral statements of an individual director.   He had never even seen these reports and accounts.   So, also, in *Baty* v. *Keswick* (1901), 85 L.T. 18, the plaintiff was shewn to have relied on the names of the directors, and not on the statements in the body of the prospectus, as alleged by him in his claim.

2 As in *Hill* v. *Balls* (1857), 2 H. & N. 299 (purchase of glandered horse).   In *Australia*, *A.-G. of N.S.W.* v. *Peters* (1924), 34 C.L.R. 146 (H. Ct. of Aus.), for which see next note.

3 See *Bellairs* v. *Tucker* (1884), 13 Q.B.D. 562, Div. Ct., *per* MANISTY J. at p. 582 (as to "personal knowledge of business", and "faith in the product", etc.); and, as regards reliance by the representor on his own investigation and skill, see the last sentence of the passage cited in the text from Lord BROUGHAM's judgment in *Attwood* v. *Small, supra.* In *Australia*, *A.-G. of N.S.W.* v. *Peters* (1924) 34 C.L.R. 146 (H. Ct. of Aus.) where (p. 152) "the fact or the amount of the contractors' loss *was considered immaterial*, and the Government (which in the action was claiming rescission) had entered into the contract 'for public reasons'".

4 See Chapter XI, paras. 190 *et seq., post.*

5 As in *Re Northumberland, etc. Co., Ex parte Bigge, ubi sup.*

6 As in *Salaman* v. *Warner* (1891), 65 L.T. 132, C.A. (the report of this case in [1891] 1 Q.B. 734, C.A., does not deal with the defects in the statement of claim, but only with a preliminary point of practice), where the addressing of the prospectus to the class of purchasers in the market, of whom the plaintiff was one, and the consequent inducement, was not alleged, or not sufficiently alleged; *Sleigh* v. *Glasgow and Transvaal Options, Ltd.* 1904, 6 F. (Ct. of Sess.) 420, where the prospectus had not been issued to the public

7 This was the case in *Horsfall* v. *Thomas* (1862), 1 H. & C. 90 (see the observations of BRAMWELL B. at p. 99, who there points out that "the defendant never examined the gun, and therefore it is impossible that an attempt to conceal the defect could have had any operation on his mind or conduct.   If the plug which it was said was put in to conceal the defect had never been there, his position would have been the same".

8 *Seddon* v. *North Eastern Salt Co.*, [1905] 1 Ch. 326 (*per* JOYCE J. at p. 335).

9 See *Attwood* v. *Small* (1838), 6 Cl. & Fin. 232, H.L.; *Shrewsbury* v. *Blount* (1841), 2 Man. & G. 475; *Vigers* v. *Pike* (1842), 8 Cl. & Fin. 562, H.L.; *Way* v. *Hearn* (1862), 13 C.B. (N.S.) 292 (*per* ERLE C.J. at pp. 302, 303, WILLIAMS J. at p. 305, and BYLES J. at p. 307); *Central Rail. Co. of Venezuela* v. *Kisch* (1867), L.R. 2 H.L. 99, 125; *Mathias* v. *Yetts* (1882), 46 L.T. 497, C.A. (*per* JESSEL M.R. at p. 502, and Sir James HANNEN at p. 504); *Bellairs* v. *Tucker* (1884), 13 Q.B.D. 562, Div.Ct. (where DENMAN J. at p. 578 expressed the view that the jury's finding that the plaintiff had been materially induced was against the weight of the evidence); *Wasteneys* v. *Wasteneys*, [1900] A.C. 446, P.C. (at p. 451, where it was said to be "impossible to believe that the respondent was induced to execute the deed by representations

The necessity for proving actual inducement as a fact, however, does not mean that it cannot be inferred as a fact from the same evidence as has been adduced to prove intention to induce, and materiality. But the inference so made is one of fact and not of law.[1]

Intention to induce also necessary

117 The complementary proposition—that intention to induce, beside actual inducement, is essential—is not less well-established by authority, or less obvious in principle. It stands to reason that it is not every false statement by which another is *in fact* induced to alter his position for the worse, which is actionable, for, as Lord DENMAN C.J. pointed out,

> "if every untrue statement which produces damage to another would found an action at law, a man might sue his neighbour for . . . having a conspicuous clock too slow, since the plaintiff might be thereby prevented from attending to some duty, or acquiring some benefit",[2]

or, to adopt the illustration put by COLERIDGE J. in a later case, if "a person coming from abroad publishes a false account of a mining district . . . a party going out in consequence, and suffering loss", would on that theory "be entitled to sue"[3]; or, as DENMAN J. said in later authority, in which it was held that an incorrect entry in Lloyd's Register did not give a cause of action to a person to whom it was not expressly or impliedly intended to be put forward as an inducement to do anything:

> "it would be . . . almost as great a stretch to say that if, in a public directory, there were the statement of an address of a firm which was inaccurate . . . that then any one of the public who had to pay a large sum for a journey to go to that place to do business with that firm would have a cause of action against the proprietors of that directory for that statement".[4]

---

as to his wife's chastity"); *Stevens* v. *Hoare* (1904), 20 T.L.R. 407 (*per* JOYCE J. at p. 408); *A. W. Gamage Ltd.* v. *Charlesworth*, 1910 S.C. 257 (where the company's manager was not called to prove the inducement, but only an assistant counting-house manager).

[1] *Smith* v. *Chadwick* (1884), 9 App. Cas. 187 *per* Lord BLACKBURN at page 196.

[2] At p. 208 of *Barley* v. *Walford* (1846), 9 Q.B. 197.

[3] Put in the form of a *reductio ad absurdum* to counsel arguing for the plaintiff, at p. 485 of *Gerhard* v. *Bates* (1853), 2 E. & B. 476, to which, however, a perfectly sound answer was given, that the representor in the case put would be liable if, but not unless, there were an *intention* to produce the result mentioned, and the result followed; and this (it was contended, an ultimately established) was the case then before the court. Counsel for the defendant, at a later stage (p. 486), seized upon the illustration of COLERIDGE J. and put it in a more general form: "a lecturer might just as well be liable to every one who heard him, if he stated an untruth", to which Lord CAMPBELL C.J. made the same answer that the plaintiff's counsel had made to the above question of COLERIDGE J., *viz.* that the lecturer undoubtedly would be liable if, but only if, the statement were "fraudulently made, and with the *intent* to produce the evil".

[4] *Thiodon* v. *Tindall* (1891), 65 L.T. 343, Div. Ct., at p. 348.

There must clearly be a *purpose* on the part of the representor to induce the particular representee, or a class of which he forms one, to act upon the representation, as well as the fact that he did act upon it. The representor must have at least had this person, or class of person, in his mind, and must have foreseen the probability of his, or their, being induced, in order to render him liable. There must not only have been a *suasio*, but also an *animus suadendi*. Where the statement is made, if it can be said to be made at all, to the representee[1] *alio intuitu*, as in the case put of the owner of the clock, the lecturer, or the proprietor of a registry or directory, the representor, *if nothing more is shown*, cannot be responsible, however clearly it be demonstrated that some person did in fact rely upon it, and however heavy the loss which resulted from such reliance. That is to say, no intent is presumed from such representations in themselves. To make them actionable an express intent must be alleged and proved, as well as the *fructus*, as Lord BROUGHAM puts it.[2] In every case where there has been no such allegation, the declaration or statement of claim has been held bad on demurrer, or struck out[3]; where there has, the pleading has been held good.[4] Similarly, where there has been no proof at the trial of this necessary averment, the representor has failed[5]; where there has, he has succeeded.[6]

---

1 See Chapter IX.

2 In *Attwood* v. *Small* (1838), 6 Cl. & Fin. 232, H.L., at pp. 444, 447, 448. The passage is cited in para. 116, *supra*.

3 In *Salaman* v. *Warner* (1891), 65 L.T. 132, C.A., the plaintiff did not allege in his statement of claim either an intention on the part of the defendants to induce him to purchase the shares, or that he was in fact induced; the statement of claim was accordingly struck out.

4 The demurrer to the declaration in both *Barley* v. *Walford*, *supra*, and *Gerhard* v. *Bates*, *supra*, was overruled.

5 *Way* v. *Hearn* (1862), 13 C.B. N.S. 292, where the defendant (who set up the plaintiff's misrepresentation as an affirmative defence to the action) failed to prove that the plaintiff had any intention to deceive or mislead him, or any intention other than to conceal a certain indebtedness from his wife (*per* ERLE C.J. at pp. 302, 303, WILLIAMS J. at p. 305, and BYLES J. at p. 307); *New Brunswick and Canada Railway and Land Co.* v. *Conybeare* (1862), 9 H.L. Cas. 711, where it was held that the communication by the appellant company's secretary was not made "with any reference to any statement of the respondent that he wished to buy shares", and could not, therefore, be supposed to have been intended to influence him, or to bind the company; *Thiodon* v. *Tindall*, *ubi sup.*; *Baty* v. *Keswick* (1901), 85 L.T. 18, where FARWELL J. thought that no intention had been shown to induce underwriters, of whom the plaintiff was one, as distinct from investors, to underwrite shares by the alleged misrepresentations in the body of the prospectus; *Sleigh* v. *Glasgow and Transvaal Options, Ltd.* 1904, 6 F. (Ct. of Sess.) 420, where it was not proved that the directors had ever issued the prospectus to any one but certain business friends, or could therefore have thereby intended to induce the plaintiff, who was not one of these specific addressees, to subscribe for shares; *A. W. Gamage, Ltd.* v. *Charlesworth*, as to which see note 9 on pp.134–5, *supra*; *Tackey* v. *McBain*, [1912] A.C. 186, P.C.

6 In *Andrews* v. *Mockford*, [1896] 1 Q.B. 372, C.A., it was distinctly alleged that the defendants by the prospectus which they issued, and by a subsequent fabricated telegram which they caused to be published in the financial papers, intended to, and did, induce the plaintiff to purchase shares *in the market*. This express and actual intention (for none such could be implied from the mere issue of the prospectus, the office of which is ordinarily exhausted on allotment)

Representation may be spent

117A Though a representation may be made with the intention of causing a representee to alter his position in a given way, yet supervening events may prevent him from ever taking the action which it was intended by the representor that he should be persuaded to take. The result of this supervening impossibility of actual inducement will be that the representation is regarded as spent; and if later the representee enters into a different transaction from that contemplated as a result of which he suffers loss, it will be impossible for him to use the original representation, now spent, as a ground for a claim or a defence against the original representor. So in *Gross* v. *Lewis Hillman, Ltd.*,[1] A, having entered into a firm contract to purchase real property relying on the representations of the vendor X, subsequently allowed B to take the benefit of his agreement to purchase upon the payment to him of a commission. On the direction of A, X accordingly conveyed the legal estate in the property directly to B, who was assumed by the Court of Appeal to have been aware of the representations upon which A had relied in entering into the original agreement. These representations were false, and it was contended that they were fraudulent; and when B became aware of their untruth he issued proceedings against X, claiming rescission of the executed conveyance and a refund of the purchase money. The allegation of fraud was disallowed by the trial judge, and the plaintiff failed in the court of first instance on that ground; but on appeal the judgments of the Court of Appeal proceeded on the assessment that fraud might have been found proved. The claim of B for rescission of the contract was rejected, however, on the ground that on this set of facts the representations of X, even if fraudulent, were spent at the moment when the original firm contract for sale between X and A was executed.

Intention may be imputed

118 In many, indeed most, of the cases founded on misrepresentation in the courts, the proof of intention to induce occupies little place; this

---

of course had to be proved, and was proved. The question of intention to induce was one of those left to the jury specifically by Lord RUSSELL C.J. and was answered by them in the affirmative, and the C.A. held that there was abundant evidence on which the jury could so find. Similarly in the curious case of *Gordon* v. *Street*, [1899] 2 Q.B. 641, C.A., where the defendant set up as a defence to the action that the plaintiff, a notorious usurer, had misrepresented and suppressed his identity, BUCKNILL J. was careful to leave to the jury the question whether the plaintiff intended to, as well as whether he did in fact, induce the defendant to contract with him, and, again the C.A., the jury having found both of these issues in favour of the defendant, refused to disturb the verdict.

[1] *Gross* v. *Lewis Hillman, Ltd.*, [1969] 3 All E.R. 1476; [1970] Ch. 445 C.A. *Cf. Peek* v. *Gurney* (1873), L.R. 6 H.L. 377, a case where the representations in a prospectus were held "spent" on the allotment of the shares.

ingredient in the cause of action, essential though it is, goes by default in the normal course of litigation, in which the circumstances of the case may so point to an intention to induce as to make it vain for anyone to contend to the contrary.[1] But to say this is to say no more than that the law will not insist on a subjective examination of the actual state of mind of the representor, but may infer his intention from the circumstances in which the representation was made, where this inference is a legitimate one.

Instances may easily be called to mind, however, where the circumstances will not so easily give rise to an inference of intention to induce, or may tend to support the opposite conclusion, even though the representee may actually have been induced by the representation to alter his position to his detriment. In such cases proof of actual intention to induce on the part of the representor becomes essential.[2] So, in the circumstances posed as illustrations by Lord DENMAN C.J., COLERIDGE J. and DENMAN J. in the cases mentioned in para. 117, *supra*, if it be supposed that the owner of the "conspicuous clock" is asked the time by a rival trader, who, to his knowledge, will receive a valuable order if he punctually keeps a certain appointment (the order otherwise probably coming to himself), and, in answer to the question, silently points to his clock which he knows to be a quarter of an hour too slow, and which, if relied upon, would result in the rival trader being too late for the appointment, it cannot be doubted that an express intention to induce would be established. The same result would follow if the lecturer or traveller mentioned by COLERIDGE J., though, to all appearance, merely instructing his audience in the mineralogy or geology of a mining district,

---

[1] See, for instance, *Smith* v. *Chadwick* (1884), 9 App. Cas. 187, H.L., *per* Lord SELBORNE L.C. at p. 190 ("the intention which the law justly imputes to every man to produce those consequences which are the natural results of his acts" is stated to be one of the tests by which "actual fraud" must be "judged"); *Coaks* v. *Boswell* (1886), 11 App. Cas. 232, H.L., where Lord SELBORNE L.C. at p. 236, again insists, in relation to the making of "a communication which would be necessarily, or naturally and probably, misleading", that "if it is a fair conclusion that he did this intentionally, and with a view to mislead in any material point, that is fraud. *A man is presumed to intend the necessary or natural consequences of his own words* and acts, and the *evidentia rei* would therefore be sufficient *without other proof of intention*"; *Arnison* v. *Smith* (1889), 41 Ch.D. 348, C.A., *per* LINDLEY L.J. at p. 372; *Wilkinson* v. *Downton*, [1897] 2 Q.B. 57, *per* WRIGHT J. at p. 59 ("it is difficult to imagine that such a statement . . . could fail to produce grave effect under the circumstances upon any but an exceptionally indifferent person, and *therefore an intention to produce such an effect must be imputed*"). *Cf.* in *Australia* the observations of CUSSEN A.C.J. in *Nicholas* v. *Thompson*, [1924] V.L.R. 554, at p. 564, a case in which this ingredient had not been made the subject of a question to the jury. The decision is subjected to some criticism by the present editor in note 2 to para. 128, *post*.

[2] In *Bradford Third Equitable Benefit Building Society* v. *Borders*, [1941] 2 All E.R. 205, the Lords found fraud not proved on a variety of grounds; Lord WRIGHT at p. 220 referred to this point when he said that "nothing short of the wicked or guilty mind will serve the plaintiff". *Cf. Tackey* v. *McBain*, [1912] A.C. 186, P.C., at pp. 191–192.

or in the social conditions of a newly discovered country, or in the scientific or mechanical points of a newly invented machine, were found to be materially interested in the mining or farming estates, or in the discovery or invention, the merits of which he had been describing, and knew or foresaw that his audience would immediately subscribe for shares in a company formed to develop or exploit these properties; or, if the proprietors of the shipping register, in the last of the above three cases, had been shown also to have owned the vessels, and to have sent out a false description of them to specific persons known to be likely buyers.

Representation made where there can be no obligation to speak truly

119   It has been argued that there may be a type of situation in which, notwithstanding that a false misrepresentation is made with the know-ledge of its falseness, with intent that it shall be acted upon, it will still fall short of a cause of action, though the representee indeed act upon it, where the moral duty of the representor may be to tell a lie—e.g. in a case where information is sought by one who intends to use it for the commission of a crime.[1]   It has been suggested, moreover, that the same principle may apply to other situations where there is no moral duty to speak the truth—e.g., where a busybody has officiously asked a question to which he had no right to expect a truthful answer.[2]

Co-existence of other inducing causes irrelevant

120   It is sufficient to prove that the representation was *an* inducing cause.   It is not necessary to establish that it was *the* inducing cause. Whether, if a full disclosure of the truth had been made, the representee would or would not have altered his position in the manner in which he did, is a question to which the law does not require an answer.   It is enough if a full and exact revelation of the material facts *might* have pre-vented him from doing so—if it would have "given him pause".[3]   As

---

[1] See, for instance, the dictum of BRAMWELL B. in *Cave* v. *Mills* (1862), 7 H. & N. 913, at p. 930.   *Cf. per* POLLOCK C.B. in *Collins* v. *Cave* (1859), 4 H. & N. 225, at p. 232.   This decision was affirmed in the Exchequer Chamber (1860), 6 H. & N. 131.

[2] See *Tackey* v. *McBain*, [1912] A.C. 186, P.C., at pp. 191–192.

[3] *Reynell* v. *Sprye, Sprye* v. *Reynell* (1852), 1 De G.M. & G. 660, *per* Lord CRANWORTH L.J. at p. 708; *Re London and Leeds Bank, Ltd., Carling's Case* (1887), 56 L.J. Ch. 321, *per* STIRLING J. at pp. 323, 324.   The views on this point expressed by ROMILLY M.R. at p. 96 of *Pulsford* v. *Richards* (1853), 17 Beav. 87, and again at pp. 238, 239 of *Jennings* v. *Broughton* (1853), 17 Beav. 234, cannot now be accepted as law.   In New Zealand, *Smith* v. *Mackenzie* (1883), 1 N.Z.L.R. 1, C.A. at p. 32—"if a fraudulent misrepresentation by the defendant has caused damage to the plaintiff, it is no answer to say that something else has contributed to the mischief"; *Klingen-stein* v. *Walters* (1885), 3 N.Z.L.R. 18, C.A. at p. 24.

against the wrong-doer, when once it is proved that the representation had an influence upon the mind and conduct of the representee, no burden is placed upon the latter, or right conferred upon the former, of conjecturing what would have happened if certain things had been said which, in fact, have not been. "Can it be permitted", said Lord CHELMSFORD L.C., "to a party who has practised a deception, with a view to a particular end which has been attained by it, to speculate on what might have been the result if there had been a full communication of the facts?"[1]   Again, "I do not think", said JAMES V.-C., "a Court of Equity is in the habit of considering that a falsehood is not to be looked at because, if the truth had been told, the same thing might have resulted"[2]; or, as it was put by BYRNE J. in a prospectus case, "'would you have taken the shares if something had been left out, and something else put in?' is an extremely difficult question to answer",[3] and one which the representor is not entitled to ask, and to which the representee can give a perfectly adequate reply by saying "I cannot say; I have never seen such a prospectus".

It follows that, when once it is shown that the misrepresentation was an inducing cause of the alteration of the position, it is no answer to set up and prove that other matters, being in the nature of *res inter alios*, co-existed and co-operated in producing the result.[4]

The entirety of statements or documents (where more than one) to be considered

121   In the case of what may be called a complex representation, that is to say, a representation which is compounded of several more or less interconnected statements contained in one document (such as a prospectus, an advertisement, particulars of sale, and the like), or made at one conversation or interview, or in the case of a representation

---

[1] *Smith* v. *Kay* (1859), 7 H.L. Cas. 750, at p. 759, a passage cited, and applied, by A. L. SMITH L.J. at p. 646 of *Gordon* v. *Street*, [1899] 2 Q.B. 641, C.A.

[2] *Re Imperial Mercantile Credit Association, Williams' Case* (1869), L.R. 9 Eq. 225, n., at p. 226 n.

[3] *Drincqbier* v. *Wood*, [1899] 1 Ch. 393, at p. 404.

[4] This is expressed in Article 17 (i) of the Code—see p. 8, *ante*. See *Attwood* v. *Small* (1838), 6 Cl. & Fin. 232, H.L. (*per* Lord BROUGHAM at p. 448); *Re Royal British Bank, Nicol's Case* (1859), 3 De G. & J. 387 (*per* Lord CHELMSFORD L.C. at p. 422); *Higgins* v. *Samels* (1862), 2 John & H. 460 (*per* PAGE-WOOD V.-C. at p. 468); *Mathias* v. *Yetts* (1882), 46 L.T. 497, C.A. (*per* JESSEL M.R. at p. 502); *Edgington* v. *Fitzmaurice* (1885), 29 Ch.D. 459, C.A. (*per* COTTON L.J. at pp. 480, 481, BOWEN L.J. at pp. 483, 484, and FRY L.J. at p. 485, agreeing with the opinion of DENMAN J. expressed at pp. 466, 471, 472); *Re London and Leeds Bank, Ltd. Carling's Case, ubi sup.*, *Drincqbier* v. *Wood, supra* (*per* BYRNE J. at pp. 404, 405); *Paul and Vincent, Ltd.* v. *O'Reilly* (1913), 49 I.L.T. 89 (*per* PALLES C.B. at pp. 91, 92). In *New Zealand, Smith* v. *Mackenzie* (1883), 1 N.Z.L.R. 1, C.A. at p. 32; *Klingenstein* v. *Walters* (1885), 3 N.Z.L.R. 18, C.A., at p. 25.

the effect of which is to be gathered from a number of documents or conversations, related to one another by express reference or community of subject-matter, it is a primary rule that, for the purpose of determining the issue of inducement, the effect on the representee's mind of the entirety of the statements, conversations or documents must be considered, rather than the effect of any particular passage, statement, or document, apart from the others.[1]   Thus where a shareholder had given general evidence that he was induced by a prospectus to take shares in the company, and was then asked to point out the particular passages in the prospectus on which he relied, KINDERSLEY V.-C., with reference to this situation, observed:

> "He [the shareholder] says, 'I decline to answer the question; the documents speak for themselves'.   I think he was justified in that.   He is not obliged to enter into any argument to prove on what particular passages in the prospectus he forms the impressions which he states he drew".[2]

Similarly, but with more emphasis and elaboration, Lord HALSBURY L.C., sitting in the Court of Appeal, has said:

> "It is an old expedient, and seldom successful, to cross-examine a person who has read a prospectus, and ask him, as to each particular statement, what influence it had on his mind, and how far it determined him to enter into the contract.   This is quite fallacious; it assumes that a person who reads a prospectus, and determines to take shares on the faith of it, can appropriate among the different parts of it the effect produced by the whole.   This can rarely be done even at the time, and for a shareholder thus to analyse his mental impressions after an interval of several years, so as to say what representation in particular induced him to take shares, is a thing all but impossible.   A person reading the prospectus looks at it as a whole . . . and on the whole he forms his conclusion.   You cannot weigh the elements by ounces".[3]

This rule was later restated by Lord HALSBURY in the House of Lords,[4] and has been freely cited and applied by the courts generally in other prospectus cases.[5]   Again, in the case of two documents such as, first, a

---

[1] This is Article 17 (ii) of the Code; see p. 8, *ante.*   As to the necessity of considering the entirety of a complex representation for the purpose of determining its truth or falsity, see para. 91, Chapter IV, *ante.*

[2] At pp. 379, 380 of *New Brunswick and Canada Railway and Land Co.* v. *Muggeridge* (1860), 1 Drew & Sm. 363.

[3] At p. 369 of *Arnison* v. *Smith* (1888), 41 Ch.D. 348, C.A.

[4] E.g., at p. 344 of *Derry* v. *Peek* (1889), 14 App. Cas. 337, H.L. ("I do not believe that any one can so far analyse his mental impressions as to say what particular fact in a prospectus induced him to subscribe"), and again at p. 280 of *Aaron's Reefs, Ltd.* v. *Twiss*, [1896] A.C. 273, H.L. ("I must protest against its being supposed that, in order to prove . . . that a certain course of conduct was induced by it"—sc. a fraud—"a person is bound to explain with exact precision what was the mental process by which he was induced to act").

[5] See the observations of Lord HERSCHELL at p. 291 of *Aaron's Reefs, Ltd.* v. *Twiss*, *supra* ("the question to be determined was what idea would be conveyed to an ordinary man by a

prospectus, and then a telegram sent to the financial press from the mine to which the prospectus related, for the purpose of "strengthening the effect" of that prospectus, though it did not expressly refer to it, A. L. SMITH L.J. delivered a decided opinion in these terms:

> "Upon these findings there was proved against the defendants a *continuous fraud* on their part, commencing with the sending of the prospectus to the plaintiff, and culminating in the direct lie told in the telegram which was intended by the defendants to operate upon the plaintiff's mind . . . *It is not taking the correct view of the case to sever it into parts* . . . and to argue that the prospectus by itself would not support a cause of action, and that the telegram by itself would not do, and since two nothings make nothing, the combination of the two does not support a cause of action. *The case must be taken as a whole*".[1]

In a case much more recently decided in the Court of Appeal,[2] though the plaintiff's claim failed on another point, all the members of the court adverted to the necessity of reading the letters "together" in which the representations appeared, in order properly to assess the effect of them on the mind of the representee.

122   Where, however, there is no express reference in one of two documents or statements to the other, and the two neither purport to be, nor are, qualifications upon, or supplementary to, one another, the representee is entitled to allege, and prove, if he can, that he relied on one of the two, without reference to, or without even having seen or heard, the other at all, though, if he had paid any attention to that other, the conjoint effect of both would have been such as to prevent any possibility of inducement[3]; or, in any such case, he may say that he was influenced separately and independently by each of the two statements, so that an affirmative defence disentitling him to relief in respect of one of them may be entirely unavailing for that purpose in respect of the other.[4]

---

perusal of this prospectus, *viewing every statement contained in it in the light of the other statements to be found there*"); BYRNE J. at p. 404 of *Drincqbier* v. *Wood*, [1899] 1 Ch. 393, and COLLINS M.R. at p. 551 of *McConnel* v. *Wright*, [1903] 1 Ch. 546, C.A. ("though the plaintiff had very great difficulty in fastening upon any particular misrepresentation which he could aver had influenced him in taking shares, still it was a question *whether he was misled by the prospectus as a whole*").

   [1] *Andrews* v. *Mockford*, [1896] 1 Q.B. 372, C.A., at p. 382. *Cf.* what RIGBY L.J. says at p. 383.

   [2] *Gross* v. *Lewis Hillman, Ltd.*, [1969] 3 All E.R. 1476; [1970] Ch. 445, C.A.

   [3] *Cf.* Chapter XI, para. 190, *post*, and the cases there cited, as to when a representor is, and when he is not, entitled to exculpate himself by reference to other statements and documents.

   [4] *Re London and Provincial Electric Lighting and Power Generating Co.*, *Ex parte Hale* (1886), 55 L.T. 670 (*per* CHITTY J.).

Where representee must assign the meaning upon which he relied

123 It has already been explained that where a representation fairly admits of more than one meaning, it is incumbent on the representee to state and prove in which of its possible meanings he understood it, and that it was false in the sense in which he relied upon it.[1] The authorities cited in support of the above proposition[2] are also authorities for the proposition (which is the same, but in an inverted form) that the burden is on the representee of showing, in such cases, that he was induced by the representation in the sense in which it was false, or fraudulent, or otherwise actionable, according to the circumstances. Thus Sir George JESSEL M.R. said:

> "It is for him to say, 'I relied on the statement in this meaning, that is the meaning I took; if it is ambiguous, it is the fault of the defendant, and relying on that I entered into the contract'. But if the plaintiff will not tell us what he relied on; if he says to the court, 'Please to find out the meaning; I relied on the statements in the prospectus, and I relied upon them according to their meaning, whatever that meaning is'; surely that will not do. How can the court find out that he has been deceived at all ? The court may think it means the very thing the plaintiff did not think it meant, and then are they to say he has been deceived because he took it in the wrong sense ? That, of course, is impossible".[3]

The representee cannot put himself in the position of the prisoner who, on being asked whether he was guilty or not guilty of the offence charged, disclaimed any preconceived opinion on the subject, and modestly replied: "That is what I want you gentlemen to tell me". Where there is only one possible sense, he is entitled to point to what is, in that only possible sense, and on the face of it, a plain untruth,

> "but, if he cannot do this . . . he must prove a particular sense, and that he understood the representation, and *acted on it, in that sense*, and further that he reasonably so understood".[4]

Materiality

124 Materiality is a thing distinct from inducement. Each is a question of fact, and each must be separately proved.[5]

---

[1] See Chapter IV, paras. 77 *et seq., ante.*

[2] See the cases cited in the notes to para. 80, *ante.*

[3] JESSEL M.R. at p. 45 of *Smith* v. *Chadwick* (1882), 20 Ch.D. 27, C.A., approved by the House of Lords (1884), 9 App. Cas. 187, H.L.

[4] KEKEWICH J. at pp. 808, 809 of *Capel & Co.* v. *Sim's Ships Composition Co., Ltd.* (1888), 58 L.T. 807. See Article 17 (iii) of the Code.

[5] Though, in extreme cases, inducement may be inferred as a fact from materiality, or at least from the same evidence as is tendered to show materiality—see para. 133, *post.* As to the inference of materiality from inducement see para. 128, *post*, and particularly note 2 thereto.

What materiality means

125 A representation is material when its tendency, or its natural and probable result, is to induce the representee to enter into the contract or transaction which in fact he did enter into, or otherwise to alter his position in the manner in which he did in fact alter it.[1] The proposition has been variously expressed,[2] but the above is the substance of it. The representation must be shown to have been capable of inducing, as well as the actual precursor of, the inducement, in order to satisfy the definition; just as, in the analogous sphere of defamation, a publication must not only have in fact injured a person's reputation, but must also have had a defamatory tendency.[3]

126 For the purpose of determining the question of materiality in any case, as distinct from inducement, the views of either of the parties are (with the exception to be mentioned presently) of no importance whatever. If in any ordinary case a representation was not material, the fact that the representee thought at the time, or says at the trial, that it was, cannot make it so[4]; on the other hand, the fact that the representee at the time considered a material representation to be immaterial, does not negative its *materiality*, though of course it destroys all prospect of establishing actual inducement. Still less, in any normal case, has the opinion of the representor any significance. If the statement by means

---

[1] This is Article 18 of the Code.

[2] "Of such a nature as would induce a person to enter into the contract, or would tend to induce him to do so", is the language of JESSEL M.R. at p. 44 of *Smith* v. *Chadwick* (1882), 20 Ch.D. 27, C.A., whilst, in the same case in the House of Lords (1884), 9 App. Cas. 187, H.L., Lord BLACKBURN, at p. 196, uses the expression—"of such a nature as would be likely to induce a person to enter into a contract". *Cf. Greenwood* v. *Greenwood* (1863), 2 De G.J. & Sm. 28 (*per* TURNER L.J. at p. 43); *Traill* v. *Baring* (1864), 4 De G.J. & Sm. 318 (*per* TURNER L.J. at p. 330); *Re Marshall and The Scottish Employers' Liability and General Insurance Co., Ltd.* (1901), 85 L.T. 757 (*per* WRIGHT J. at p. 758); *Mutual Life Insurance Co. of New York* v. *Ontario Metal Products Co., Ltd.*, [1925] A.C. 344, 350–352, P.C. (life insurance). As applied to marine insurance, a "material representation" is defined in s. 20 (2) of the Marine Insurance Act 1906 (6 Edw. 7, c. 41), as "a representation which would influence the judgment of a prudent insurer in fixing the premium, or determining whether he will take the risk."

[3] See *Capital and Counties Bank, Ltd.* v. *Henty & Sons* (1882), 7 App. Cas. 741 (*per* Lord BLACKBURN at pp. 769–778). *Cf.* the text on the same topic in the authors' *Law of Estoppel by Representation* (2nd edn.) pp. 91–92.

[4] See *Holliday* v. *Lockwood*, [1917] 2 Ch. 47 (*per* ASTBURY J. at pp. 53–55). In *Beachey* v. *Brown* (1860), E.B. & E. 796, an action for breach of promise of marriage, to which the defendant set up that he had been induced to make the promise by the lady's fraudulent concealment of certain material facts, CROMPTON J. says at p. 803: "I do not think that the non-disclsoure of a fact which is material *in the mind of the defendant* is enough". This view would of course apply to a case of a positive misrepresentation as much as to one of concealment. The question of materiality arose sharply in *Angus* v. *Clifford*, [1891] 2 Ch. 449, C.A., a case reviewed in some detail in note 3 on p. 149, *post*. The point referred to in the text above will be found discussed by the trial Judge, ROMER J., at p. 456 of the report, and by KAY L.J. at pp. 480–481.

of which he in fact induced another to alter his position ~~with~~
to produce that result in the ordinary course of events, su~~ch~~
tendency cannot be affected by any allegation (even if bel~~ieved by the~~
representor that he did not, or does not, regard his repre~~sentation as~~
having that nature or tendency.[1]

The natural result must be to induce the particular representee

127 It must be remembered, that a tendency to induce means a
tendency to induce the particular representee in the particular circumstances of the individual case. Where there are no special circumstances,
it is necessary and sufficient to prove that, in the ordinary course of
events, having regard to the relation of the parties and the nature of the
business or transaction, the natural and probable effect of the representation was to influence the mind of a normal representee in the manner
alleged. But, to the knowledge of the representor, the representee
may be an abnormal person, influenced by particular fancies, fads, or
superstitions[2]; or it may be that, again to the knowledge of the representor, there are circumstances of a character such that any statement
respecting them, though it might be utterly inoperative on the mind of
any other person, will make all the difference in the world to the particular representee to whom he addresses it; in which type of case it is
obvious that the special susceptibility of the representee, and the representor's knowledge of it, may be of importance, because these facts will

---

[1] Where there is a duty of disclosure, it is no excuse that the party failing in such duty considered the undisclosed matters not material, if in fact they were so: *Lindenau* v. *Desborough*
(1828), 8 B. & C. 586 (*per* BAYLEY J. at p. 592, and LITTLEDALE J. at p. 593); *Dalglish* v.
Jarvie (1850), 2 Mac. & G. 231 (*per* ROLFE B. at p. 243); *London Assurance* v. *Mansel* (1879),
11 Ch.D. 363 (*per* JESSEL M.R. at p. 368). Still less would such a belief be an answer in the
case of a misrepresentation of an actually material fact. Similarly, in defamation, the intention
and meaning of the defamer is wholly irrelevant, as explained in Article 17 (5) of Mr Spencer
Bower's *Code of the Law of Actionable Defamation*, and note (e) thereto.

[2] It is a matter of history, and common observation, that the acutest minds have been, and
are, subject to the domination of special prejudices, antipathies, predilections, and superstitions; and that those whose life is spent in tempting fate *per mare per terram,*—soldiers, and
"they that go down into the sea in ships, and have their business in great waters,"—and other
classes, such as the theatrical profession, are peculiarly under such influences. Suppose that a
representor knows that his representee will never sign a contract, or do any business, on a
Friday, or on the 13th of a month, or enter upon any enterprise in which an individual believed
to bring him ill-luck is concerned, and, with this knowledge, misrepresents the date of a contemplated or past transaction, or the *personnel* of those interested therein, it would seem that,
on principle (no such extreme case has yet been the subject of any report), such a misrepresentation would be material as between the parties,—material, that is, *to the inducement,* which
(see para. 129) is all that is required to be established.

make a representation material which would not be material in other circumstances.[1]

Two cases: 1 Where there are no special circumstances

128 In the case where there are no special circumstances to be taken into account in assessing the likely impact of the representation on the representee, and the question of materiality resolves itself simply into an assessment of the impact of the representation on the mind of a normal representee, little difficulty occurs in practice. For where there are no special circumstances, and the actual representee is a "normal" representee, the case must be hard to imagine in which, once intention to induce and actual resultant inducement be proved, there is room for a submission that the representation was not a material one.[2]

2 Where there are special circumstances

129 But the decisions in cases in which special circumstances have been proved, making the actual representee particularly susceptible to

---

[1] *Higgins* v. *Samels* (1862), 2 John & H. 460, PAGE-WOOD V.-C. at p. 468 ("he admits that he knew the lime would be useless to the defendant unless it was fit for the London market",—which knowledge would deprive the representor of his right to contend that, if the lime was good and merchantable, the question of a particular market was immaterial); *Archer* v. *Stone* (1898), 78 L.T. 34, where the plaintiff had falsely represented to the defendant that he was not purchasing for a certain individual, and NORTH J., in giving judgment for the defendant, based it on the fact that the plaintiff knew that the particular individual was so distasteful to the defendant that he would not have sold his land to him, or his "party", or to any one through whom it would eventually get into his hands; *Gordon* v. *Street*, [1899] 2 Q.B. 641, C.A., where A. L. SMITH L.J., at p. 648, lays stress on the fact that the plaintiff himself was thoroughly aware of the importance in his own interest of suppressing his identity, which fact tended to establish and confirm the view taken by the Court of Appeal, and the jury in the court below, that the plaintiff's misrepresentations as to his personality were, as between the parties, material to the *inducement*; *Whurr* v. *Devenish* (1904), 20 T.L.R. 385, where it was proved in evidence, to the satisfaction of Lord ALVERSTONE C.J., that the defendant knew of the materiality of the representation made by him, at the sale of a horse by auction, that the horse was a private gentleman's property (his own), and not that of a horse-dealer, and where it was further proved that a statement of that character to a buyer under the circumstances would tend to establish a belief in "the *bona fides* and genuineness of the sale", and "yield better prices".

[2] The question was seriously posed in a decision of the Full Court of Victoria in 1924, whether materiality was indeed separately necessary to be proved in an action for fraud, in a case where intention to induce actual inducement had been found by a jury. In *Nicholas* v. *Thompson*, [1924] V.L.R. 554 CUSSEN A.C.J. (a judge whose scholarly and thoughtful judgments are held in high respect in Australia) and MCARTHUR J. went the length of disagreeing expressly with the text of Mr Spencer Bower's first edition (and indeed with the corresponding passage in *Halsbury*), and of deciding that materiality was not a separate essential ingredient in the cause of action for fraud. "Supposing defendant had admitted", said CUSSEN A.C.J. at p. 566, "that the representation was made in order to induce, and that it did induce, could he insist that plaintiff was bound to prove in addition, something not expressly alleged, namely that it was material. I do not think so". It is submitted, however, that the answer is as stated in the text above. If intention to induce, and resultant alteration in position, are proved, the court *may* without more, in the circumstances of a particular case, infer materiality, and will do so in many cases; but it will not *necessarily* do so.

certain representations, have sometimes given rise to nice questions. These have arisen for the most part in cases in which the materiality, as between the parties, of a representation as to the personality, identity or status of any individual, or as to the ownership of any property to which it relates, has been debated.   Putting aside statements as to the position, credit, character, or business of one contemplated as the person with whom the representee is to contract, or whom he is to accept as his debtor, or to trust, or as to the personality of a proposed tenant or occupant of lands or premises, the subject of the contract induced by the misrepresentation,[1] or as to the *personnel* of the directorate or management of a company or concern in which the representee is induced to take an interest—all which are of manifest materiality,[2] and come rather within the first class—there are several examples in the books of representations as to personality which, though of no conceivable importance under ordinary circumstances, have, on proof of the knowledge by both parties of special circumstances, been held material.   Thus, in the absence of any special circumstances, it is a matter of no concern to the vendor, or to the purchaser, of property, to know who is the particular individual for whom such property is to be bought, in the one case, or

---

[1] *Feret* v. *Hill* (1854), 15 C.B. 207, in which case it was held that a lease completed by actual possession could not be avoided, or treated as a nullity, though it had been induced by a fraudulent misrepresentation, but it was recognised that the statement as to the intended user of the premises for a perfumery business was a material one, which would have justified the representee in refusing to grant the lease, or give possession, in the first instance; *Canham* v. *Barry* (1855), 15 C.B. 597, where the plaintiff, knowing that the defendant could not assign the lease in question without his lessor's consent, and would not, therefore, do so, unless one Morris, the intended occupant of the farm, was a responsible person, fraudulently stated that Morris answered this description, with the object and result of inducing the defendant to sell his leasehold interest, and it was held that this misrepresentation was not "collateral" (a very stupid expression, used in *Feret* v. *Hill*), or "foreign", the term used by WILLIAMS J. (see pp. 615, 621): in other words, it was material (*per* MAULE J. at p. 616, who distinguished *Feret* v. *Hill*, at pp. 611, 612); *Cundy* v. *Lindsay* (1878), 3 App. Cas. 459, H.L., where the misrepresentation of the intended debtor and contractor as being the honest and solvent firm of Blenkiron and Co. (whereas in truth it was the dishonest and impecunious firm of the name of Blenkarn in the same street) was of obvious materiality; *Morrisson* v. *Robertson* 1908 S.C. 332, where the representor, a person whom the pursuer would not have trusted, stated himself to be the son, and the agent, of a person whom the pursuer did trust. *Cf.* the other cases of personation in the notes to Chapter III, paras. 60 and 61, *ante*.

[2] *Re Life Association of England, Ltd., Blake's Case* (1865), 34 Beav. 639, *per* ROMILLY M.R. at p. 642; *Hallows* v. *Fernie* (1868), 3 Ch.App. 467; *Bevan* v. *Adams* (1870), 22 L.T. 795; *Re Scottish Petroleum Co., Anderson's Case* (1881), 17 Ch.D. 373; *Re Same Co., Maclagan's Case* (1882), 51 L.J. Ch. 841; *Re Same Co., Wallace's Case* (1883), 23 Ch.D. 413, C.A.; *Smith* v. *Chadwick* (1884), 9 App.Cas. 187, H.L. (*per* Lord SELBORNE L.C. at p. 190, and Lord BLACKBURN at p. 194); *Re Metropolitan Coal Consumers' Association, Wainwright's Case* (1890), 63 L.T. 429, C.A. *Cf.* the cases such as *Re Bank of Hindustan, China and Japan, Ltd., Rogers' Case* (1871), 25 L.T. 406; *Re Imperial Mercantile Credit Assn., Payne's Case* (1869), L.R. 9 Eq. 223; *Re Discoverers' Finance Corporation, Ltd., Lindlar's Case,* [1910] 1 Ch. 312, in which a misrepresentation of the status or position of a proposed transferee of shares in a company was held a material inducement to the directors to sanction the transfer.

for whom it is being sold, in the other; but where it is known to the representor that, in fact, for whatever reason or caprice, the personality of the principal is so odious and objectionable to the representee that he would never enter into the contract if such personality were disclosed to him, then whether the "Dr Fell" in question be a purchaser, or a vendor, any misrepresentation as to this matter becomes a material one.[1] On the other hand, where it is not shown clearly that the representee would not have entered into the contract on the same terms with any one else, and where the identity of the purchaser or vendor is neither of the essence of the contract, nor part of the consideration for it,[2] or where it is not proved that the representor told any falsehood, but only that (not being under any duty to disclose the truth) he kept silence,[3] no materiality is

---

[1] *Phillips* v. *Duke of Buckingham* (1683), 1 Vern. 227; *Smith* v. *Wheatcroft* (1878), 9 Ch.D. 223, where the principle was recognised by FRY J. at p. 230, though the representee in that case did not bring himself within it; *Archer* v. *Stone* (1898), 78 L.T. 34, *per* NORTH J. See, further, *Said* v. *Butt*, [1920] 3 K.B. 497 (McCARDIE J.); *Dyster* v. *Randall & Sons*, [1926] Ch. 932 (LAWRENCE J.); *Lake* v. *Simmons*, [1927] A.C. 487, H.L., *per* Viscount HALDANE at p. 501.

[2] *Fellowes* v. *Lord Gwydyr* (1829), 1 Russ. & M. 83, which was a case of a misrepresentation of the personality of *a vendor*, not a purchaser, and which took the form, not of a suppression of the identity of an unacceptable individual, but of a false allegation that the representor had a principal, and that this principal was Lord Gwydyr, a *persona grata* to the representee; whereas he had no principal, and had bought the Coronation fittings and decorations in question from Lord Gwydyr, and was reselling them at a profit, and Lord Gwydyr (so it was urged), if he had been the vendor, would not have entered into the transaction with any such commercial view, or allowed the representee to be a loser by it; here Lord LYNDHURST L.C. said that, if it had been shown that the representee would not have treated with any one but Lord Gwydyr, he would have been entitled to relief, but as this was not clearly made out, he was not; *Smith* v. *Wheatcroft* (1878), 9 Ch.D. 223, *per* FRY J. who, at p. 230, after citing Pothier on the effect of *error personae*, says: "I ask myself here whether the defendant has shewn that any personal consideration entered into the contract. Has he shewn that he would have been unwilling to enter into a contract on the same terms with any one else? I say distinctly that he has failed to produce any such effect on my mind, and, that being so, I think the second branch of the defence" (which was based on an alleged misrepresentation that the plaintiff was buying the land for his own use, and not for that of a certain colliery company) "fails, as well as the first."

[3] *Nash* v. *Dix* (1898), 78 L.T. 445, which was decided shortly after *Archer* v. *Stone* (1878), 78 L.T. 34, and by the same judge (NORTH J.): the claim (specific performance by the purchaser against vendor), and the defence (misrepresentation by the plaintiff that he was buying for himself, and not for a particular individual or class to whom the representee objected) was the same in both cases, but in *Nash* v. *Dix* the plaintiff had not (as the plaintiff in *Archer* v. *Stone* had) told any falsehood whatever, for, though he knew that the defendant objected to sell to Roman Catholics, and though he had entered into a contract to resell at a profit to persons of that faith, he was in a position to say with truth (as he did) that he was not buying for them, or as their agent, and there was no duty to reveal the intended and agreed resale. So in *Dyster* v. *Randall & Sons*, [1926] Ch. 932, LAWRENCE J. said at p. 939; "The real question therefore is whether C's silence, in the circumstances, amounted to a misrepresentation which renders the agreement unenforceable in this court. In my judgment mere nondisclosure as to the person entitled to the benefit of a contract for the sale of real estate does not amount to misrepresentation, even though the contracting party knows that, if the disclosure were made, the other party would not enter into the contract; *secus*, if the contract were one in which some personal consideration formed a material ingredient—see *Nash* v. *Dix* and *Said* v. *Butt*." The last-mentioned case is reported in [1920] 3 K.B. 497.

established.   Again, under ordinary circumstances, if a man is willing to
borrow money on certain terms, it is a matter of no moment whatever to
him who the intended creditor is ; but if it is known to the representor
that the representee has (again, whether for good reason or bad, does not
signify) such a horror or dislike of a particular person that he would not
at any price incur any liability to him, and, knowing this, he suppresses
and misrepresents the identity of the creditor so objected to, whether it
be himself or another, the misstatement is material.[1]   In a recent case the
defendant, then called AR, was convicted of permitting disorderly
conduct in a tearoom.   Wishing to obtain a lease of other premises for
use as a restaurant, she applied for such a lease using the name of AP,
and then, to give matters as correct an appearance as possible, she executed a deed poll purporting to effect or record a change of her name to
AP.   It was held that she had represented herself as a person other than
AR, and that the representation was material.[2]

Other representations which illustrate the subject under discussion
are statements that a specified person is independent of other persons or
influences, when in fact he is not so, or *vice versa*,[3] and statements as to

---

[1] *Smith* v. *Kay* (1859), 7 H.L. Cas. 750, where it was urged that the representee would equally
have been ready to execute the securities he did in favour of any one who would give him the
terms to which he willingly became subject, and that it did not matter that Smith (the representor) bought up these securities, or how he became the owner of them, but the contention
was rejected by Lord CHELMSFORD L.C. (at pp. 758, 759), and Lord CRANWORTH (at pp.
769, 770); *Gordon* v. *Street*, [1899] 2 Q.B. 641, C.A., where a notorious moneylender, "the
hottest and bitterest" of his tribe, according to his own description of himself, had, by fraudulently misrepresenting and concealing his own identity under an alias or pseudonym, induced a
necessitous person to borrow money of him on extortionate terms, which (as the representee
alleged and proved) he would, to the representor's knowledge, never have consented to do,
had he been aware that he was dealing with this particular usurer, and it was held that the
misrepresentation was material *to the inducement*, if not to the contract,—*per* A. L. SMITH L.J.
who cites, at p. 646, *Smith* v. *Kay* (1859), 7 H.L. Cas. 750, and, at pp. 647–649, deals with FRY
J.'s judgment, and the passage from Pothier referred to by him, in *Smith* v. *Wheatcroft* (1878),
9 Ch.D. 223—see note 2 on p. 148—and shews how the same principles which justified FRY J.
in refusing the representee relief in that case required the Court of Appeal to grant it in the
case before them.   See also *Said* v. *Butt*, [1920] 3 K.B. 497, 501, *per* McCARDIE J. and the
comments thereupon of LAWRENCE J. in *Dyster* v. *Randall & Sons.*, [1926] Ch. 932 at p. 939.

[2] *Sowler* v. *Potter & ors.*, [1939] 4 All E.R. 478, [1940] 1 K.B. 271 (TUCKER J.).

[3] *Fellowes* v. *Lord Gwydyr* (1829) 1 Russ. & M. 83—see note 2 on p. 148—was the case of a
man representing himself to be an agent of another, when in reality he was independent of him,
being a purchaser from him.   On the other hand *Moens* v. *Heyworth* (1842), 10 M. & W. 147
(representation that goods had been "invoiced to sellers as of first shipping quality" by shippers
having a distinct and independent position, whereas they were agents or partners of the representors), *Smith* v. *Wheatcroft*, cited in note 2 on p. 148, *Archer* v. *Stone*, cited in note 3, *ibid*,
and *Gordon* v. *Street*, cited in note 1, *supra*, were cases of the converse type, sc. of statements by
the representor of his separate individuality, when in fact he was identical with, or the agent of,
another person.   A curious point, which should be noticed under this head, arose in *Angus* v.
Clifford, [1891] 2 Ch. 449, C.A., where the question was mooted, though it became unnecessary to decide it, whether an express or implied statement as to a report of an expert being
independent and disinterested, when in fact it was prepared at the instance and in the interests
of a third person, is or is not, capable of being considered material, when there is no mis-

the ownership, or late ownership, of certain kinds of property, such as horses, or pictures, and the like[1]; all which representations, under the conditions above stated, but not otherwise, may be material.   In such

representation in the report itself.   ROMER J. whose view of the case rendered it incumbent on him to decide the point, held (pp. 456–458) that such a representation might be, and in that case was, most material (that is, to the inducement), and he instanced the cases of a valuation of a surveyor, or the opinion of a patent expert, as to which it might be most important for the representee to know whether it had been prepared on behalf of the vendor, or the purchaser, of the land or invention, or was independent of either.   The Court of Appeal differed from ROMER J. as to the meaning of the representation contained in the prospectus in that case, which, in their view, conveyed merely that the report referred to had been prepared "for the directors" in the sense of "for submission to the directors", and not (as ROMER J. had held) in the sense of "under the instructions of the directors", in which former sense the statement was true, and it was not necessary to express any decisive opinion as to the materiality of the representation on the construction put upon it in the court below; but LINDLEY L.J. (pp. 468, 469), expressed some doubt on the point, though he was careful to preface his remarks by describing it as "a matter on which I do not intend to rest my judgment", whilst BOWEN L.J. (p. 475), said: "as to the materiality of the misrepresentation I will say nothing. It is a difficult point", and KAY L.J. (at p. 480): "I am not satisfied that *in this case* the statement is proved to be sufficiently material", any more than, in his view, a statement that it was reported by a particular mining engineer that a certain mine existed in a certain place, and the mine did exist there, though the report had not been made by the specified engineer, could be considered material, but, later, at p. 181, when dealing with the question of damage (which, for the purposes of that case, and his observations thereon, is not distinguishable in principle from the question of inducement), KAY L.J. seems to realise that such a type of misrepresentation at least *might* be material: "I can quite conceive it might, by way of argument, be put in this way . . . '*I should not have taken the shares at all* if it had not been for this statement, and having taken the shares now, . . . damage has resulted to me,'" and he concludes, "I am not quite convinced in my own mind at present, and I will not give any decided opinion upon it, that there is a damage which results directly from the false statement".   It is submitted that the decision—for it was a decision—of ROMER J. was quite sound, and that it has in no way been overruled by the faint expressions of doubt contained in the dicta—for they amounted to no more—of LINDLEY and KAY L.JJ.

[1] Generally speaking, the value of a picture gallery, library, stable, or collection of curios, is independent of the question who owns them, or has lately owned them, but it is well known by auctioneers and agents for sale that in many cases a representation that such property comes from private hands is a great inducement to purchase, and that the fact that a horse, or a collection, belongs to, or has come from, a dealer, would debar many persons from having anything to do with the sale.   Statements of the above character as to the ownership, or recent ownership, of "goods and chattels" generally, wines, pictures, or horses, were considered material, as between the parties, in the following: *Bexwell* v. *Christie* (1776), 1 Cowp. 395 ("sale of goods and effects of a *gentleman deceased, at his house in the country*, by order of the executors" was the announcement, which was untrue, and Lord MANSFIELD C.J. described it as a fraud on the public, and mentions, by way of illustration, the then well-known case of the sale of "a gentleman's wines"—the reporter in a note gives his name as Bradshaw—"where large quantities had been sent in belonging to other persons, and all sold at a very high price, under an idea they were his. The consequence was, most of the buyers were taken in"); *Hill* v. *Gray* (1816), 1 Stark. 434 (where the only point correctly decided, or assumed, by Lord ELLENBOROUGH C.J. was that a representation, if it had been made, that the pictures there being sold were being sold for Sir Felix Agar, might have been a material representation); *Whurr* v. *Devenish* (1904), 20 T.L.R. 385 (a case of a sale of a horse, in which Lord ALVERSTONE C.J. held that a false statement as to the horse being the property of the defendant, a private gentleman, whereas at the moment of the sale it was owned by a jobmaster, was material, for it tended to induce a belief in the *bona fides* of the sale, and to fetch better prices).   With the last case cf. *R.* v. *Kenrick* (1843), 5 Q.B. 49, where a representation to the same effect was held a false pretence.

cases it is idle to urge that the representation was immaterial to the contract, because this presupposes that the contract has already been entered into, and so begs the question. The point is whether, but for the statement, the representee would have ever entered into the contract at all, or, in other words, whether the statement was material, not to the contract, but to the inducement.[1]

130 Representations that an infant is of full age[2] are of obvious materiality, when made to one who, to the representor's knowledge, would not advance money or give credit to, or contract with, the minor, if believed by him to be so.[3] This sort of materiality, however, belongs rather to the first of the two classes abovementioned, inasmuch as representations of the character indicated must necessarily be material in all ordinary commercial transactions, and do not require the existence of special conditions, and the representor's knowledge of such conditions, to make them so.

Burden of proof as to materiality

131 From what has already been said, and the authorities generally on misrepresentation, it is quite clear that, unless expressly or impliedly admitted (as it very frequently is), materiality must be established by the representee in addition to, and apart from, actual inducement.[4] Of course the same evidence which proves inducement may readily lead to an inference of materiality; and again in many cases the burden of proof will be found to be discharged simply by a comparison of the representation itself with the proved or admitted circumstances of the case. Where the statement, in relation to those circumstances, is alleged to disclose *ex facie* its own materiality, the matter is the subject of argument only, when once the circumstances are shown. But, there will be cases (e.g. where the representation is only an implied one, say, from the external appearance of an object) in which it may be necessary to produce some evidence of the tendency of the representation to deceive, which

---

[1] This point was insisted upon by Lord ELDON L.C. in *Sibbald* v. *Hill* (1814), 2 Dow. 263, who decided against the representor, "not on the ground that the misrepresentation affected the nature of the risk, but because it induced a confidence without which the party would not have acted" (p. 267), and by A. L. SMITH L.J. at pp. 645, 646 of *Gordon* v. *Street*, [1899] 2 Q.B. 641, C.A.

[2] See Chapter XI, paras. 218–219, and notes thereto.

[3] It is a very different, and a very difficult, question how far, and under what conditions, and in what form, such representations, when made by the infant himself, are actionable. This is the subject of Chapter XI, paras. 218–219, *post*.

[4] *Per* JESSEL M.R. at p. 502, and Sir James HANNEN at p. 504 of *Mathias* v. *Yetts* (1882), 46 L.T. 497, C.A. *Cf. Cackett* v. *Keswick*, [1902] 2 Ch. 456 (*per* FARWELL J. at pp. 463, 464).

will not in all cases be presumed, as a matter of course, on the *res ipsa loquitur* theory.[1]

Inducement and materiality questions of fact

132 Both inducement and materiality are *prima facie* questions of fact.[2] But as appears in other parts of the text, the intention of the representor to induce, a resultant alteration of position by the representee, and the materiality of the representation, may each in proper cases be inferred from other circumstances of the case without any evidence specifically directed to it and to it alone.[3] The inferences so to be made, however, are always inferences of fact,[4] and are not made as a matter of law. The point is well illustrated, as to *inducement*, by *Arnison* v. *Smith*. In that case where, out of a large number of plaintiffs in an action based on misrepresentations in a prospectus, twelve did not appear at the trial, and afterwards appealed against the judgment which was necessarily given against them (the others, who did appear, having succeeded), the Court of Appeal had no alternative but to dismiss their appeal, Lord HALSBURY L.C. observing that

> "it certainly is in the highest degree improbable that these plaintiffs did not see the prospectus, or that they were not influenced by the representation contained in it; but we are all of opinion that there is *no evidence of those facts upon which a court of justice can act*".[5]

And it is no less well established that *materiality* is an issue of fact, to be left to the jury, if there is one,[6] and to be found as a fact by the judge, if

---

1 Thus, in *London General Omnibus Co., Ltd.* v. *Lavell*, [1901] 1 Ch. 135, C.A., it was held that the judge was not entitled to infer a tendency to deceive from a mere inspection of the external appearance of the rival omnibuses, but that evidence was necessary to establish it. On the other hand, in the "hermaphrodite" case, and the "antique" case, cited in notes 1 and 2 on p. 78, *ante*, it was thought that the malformed animal, in the former, and the curio, in the latter, "told its own lie", and bore on its face the evidence of its capacity to induce and mislead.

2 See Article 19 (1) of the Code, and the authorities referred to in the text to the earlier part of this chapter, and particularly to *Andrews* v. *Mockford*, [1896] 1 Q.B. 372, C.A., at p. 374 (as to the questions left to the jury—see Questions 4 and 11); *Hulton* v. *Hulton*, [1917] 1 K.B. 813, C.A.; *Mutual Life Insurance Co. of New York* v. *Ontario Metal Products Co., Ltd.*, [1925] A.C. 344, at pp. 350, 351, P.C.

3 See paras. 113, 116 *ante*; para. 133, *post*.

4 *Smith* v. *Chadwick* (1884), 9 App. Cas. 187, *per* Lord BLACKBURN at p. 196.

5 *Arnison* v. *Smith* (1889), 41 Ch.D. 348, C.A. at p. 374.

6 In *Flinn* v. *Headlam* (1829), 9 B. & C. 693, the question was left to the jury; and in *Andrews* v. *Mockford, supra*, it appears from p. 374 that, besides the two questions referred to in note 2, *supra*, addressed to the issue of inducement, Lord RUSSELL C.J. left to the jury the further question (Question 10) of materiality ("was it [the telegram] *calculated to bring about the result* that the plaintiff and others would buy shares in the market ?"). In *Flinn* v. *Headlam, supra*, the jury found that the representation was *not* material, and the court considered this finding so unreasonable that they ordered a new trial, but no one suggested that it was not a

there is not[1]; and where the judge has taken upon himself to withhold this issue from a jury, the conditions not being such as are described in para. 134 (*post*), he has been held to have usurped the functions of the jury, and a new trial has been ordered.[2] In relation to marine insurance, this rule finds a place in the provisions of the statute which codifies the law on this subject.[3]

Inducement and materiality separate questions

133 It has already been emphasised[4] that inducement and materiality are *separate* questions of fact, requiring independent proof. This does not mean, of course, that evidence directed, for instance, to the demonstration of materiality may not be used also to establish inducement, or *vice versa*; but it does mean that where the evidence proves one of these *probanda*, but not the other, the misrepresentation will not be established. It may often happen, it is true, that the probability of inducement is so great, or, in other words, the materiality is so palpable, that actual inducement may be found with little, or even in some extreme cases with no, further evidence; just as, in cases of malicious prosecution, the absence of reasonable and probable cause may be so gross and glaring as to justify the further step of finding malice as an inference of fact from this circumstance alone. But, in the one class of the case as in the other,

---

question for a jury to determine. So, also, in *Cazenove* v. *British Equitable Assurance Co., Ltd.* (1860), 29 L.J. C.P. 160, Ex. Ch., the court refused to disturb the jury's finding that a certain fact was not material, though they decided in favour of the defendants on another ground.

[1] In *Re Universal Non-Tariff Fire Insurance Co., Forbes & Co.'s Claim* (1875), L.R. 19 Eq. 485 (see pp. 493, 494, 496), *Capel & Co.* v. *Sim's Ships Composition Co., Ltd.* (1888), 58 L.T. 807 (see pp. 809, 810), and *Whurr* v. *Devenish* (1904), 20 T.L.R. 385, a judge, sitting without a jury, determined the issue of materiality *as a fact*.

[2] *Bevan* v. *Adams* (1870), 22 L.T. 795, where, the representation being that half the first issue of shares in a company had been subscribed for, which was taken to imply a further statement that the deposits had been paid, BEST C.J. took upon himself to withdraw from the jury the question of whether the payment of the deposits was material or not, and to hold, as matter of law, that it *could not be so.* This was held to be wrong, and a new trial was ordered. Similarly, in *Charlton* v. *Hay* (1874), 31 L.T. 437, a demurrer to a count of the declaration which set up s. 38 of the Companies Act 1867 on the ground that the omitted contract could not be material, was overruled. On the other hand, in *Hill* v. *Gray* (1816), 1 Stark. 434 Lord ELLENBOROUGH C.J., ignoring the jury, took upon himself to rule that the representation as to the ownership of the picture *was* material, and must have induced the representee, who was setting up the misrepresentation as a defence, and he non-suited the plaintiff accordingly. This procedure would probably not be followed under modern jury practice. With the above cases, all decided more than ninety years ago, it is interesting to compare *Nicholas* v. *Thompson,* [1924] V.L.R. 554, a more modern decision of the Full Court of Victoria, cited in note 2 on p. 146, *ante*. There CUSSEN A.C.J. and MCARTHUR J., in like circumstances, took it on themselves on appeal to hold materiality established as a matter of law.

[3] See s. 20 (7) of the Marine Insurance Act 1906 (6 Edw. 7, c. 41); "whether a particular representation be material or not is, in each case, a question of fact."

[4] In para. 113, *ante*.

the two things are distinct issues. A theory, indeed, was prevalent in the earlier stages of the history of the law of misrepresentation—a theory which was the natural outcome of the law of evidence then existing,[1] and which even in recent times, when such excuse had ceased to be admissible, received the embarrassing *imprimatur* of no less an authority than JESSEL M.R.[2]—that from proved materiality the court is at liberty to infer actual inducement, *as matter of law*, without any evidence whatsoever. This heresy has now been effectually exploded, or explained away, by the highest authorities, who have placed beyond doubt that only in rare instances should such an inference be drawn at all, and that, when it is drawn, it is still an inference of *fact*,[3] and has, even then, no

---

[1] Before the passing of the Evidence Act 1851 (14 & 15 Vict. c. 99), whereby (see s. 2) the parties in an action were for the first time allowed to give evidence, the representee obviously could not prove inducement as a fact otherwise than by evidence of materiality as a fact. It was natural, therefore, that in those days, the two issues should be confounded. Accordingly, whilst we find a great deal of discussion in the early authorities as to materiality, we find very little importance attached to inducement, except as involved in, and consequent upon, if not identical with, materiality. See the observations of Lord BLACKBURN on this point, cited *infra* in note 3.

[2] The deliverance in question (which has necessitated so much subsequent explanation with a view to showing that JESSEL M.R. could not have meant what he appears to have said, or correction on the assumption that he did) is to be found on p. 21 of *Redgrave* v. *Hurd* (1881), 20 Ch.D. 1, C.A.: "when a person makes a material representation to another to induce him to enter into a contract, and the other enters into that contract, it is not sufficient to say that the party to whom the representation was made does not prove that he entered into the contract relying upon the representation. If it is a material representation calculated to induce him to enter into the contract, it is an inference of law that he was induced by the representation to enter." Notwithstanding such criticism as is contained in Mr Spencer Bower's text, and has been repeated in other subsequent statements of the true principle, the dictum of Sir George JESSEL M.R. "yet anon repairs his drooping head"; see, for instance, *per* HILBERY J. in *Bellotti* v. *Chequers Developments, Ltd.*, [1936] 1 All E.R. 89, at p. 93. But perhaps the point of dispute has now become of academic importance only; see the observations of the present editor in para. 134 of the text, *infra*.

With the cases noted above compare the decision of the Full Court of Victoria in *Nicholas* v. *Thompson*, [1924] V.L.R. 554, in which, faced with the reverse position, CUSSEN A.C.J. and McARTHUR J. inferred materiality as a matter of law from inducement. The decision is the subject of some criticism by the present editor in note 2 on p. 146, *supra*.

[3] *Smith* v. *Chadwick* (1882), 20 Ch.D. 27, C.A., where, at p. 44, JESSEL M.R. states the rule correctly: "the inference" (sc. of fact—this is clear from what follows) "is, if he entered into the contract, that he acted on the inducement so held out; *but even then you may show that in fact he did not so act;*" *Mathias* v. *Yetts* (1882), 46 L.T. 497, C.A., *per* JESSEL M.R. at p. 502 (who here again tacitly revokes his previous error), Sir James HANNEN at p. 504, and LUSH L.J. at p. 507; *Smith* v. *Chadwick* (1884), 9 App. Cas. 187, H.L., affirming the decision of the C.A. reported as above, where Lord BLACKBURN, at p. 196, says: "I do not think it is necessary . . . that the plaintiff always should be called as a witness to swear that he acted on the inducement. At the time when *Pasley* v. *Freeman* was decided, he could not be so called", and then, after referring to the language of JESSEL M.R. in the Court of Appeal, as cited above, and approving it, he proceeds: "in *Redgrave* v. *Hurd*, the late Master of the Rolls is reported to have said that it was an inference of law"—(and not merely, as Lord BLACKBURN held it to be, " a fair inference of fact"). "If he really meant this, he retracts it in his observations in the present case. I think it is not possible to maintain that it is an inference of law . . . I quite agree that, being a fair inference of fact, it forms evidence proper to be left to a jury that he was so in-

further operation than to move the burden from the shoulders of the representee to those of the representor; that is to say, that when once the former has established a case of obvious materiality, he may thereby have established at the same time a strong *prima facie* case of inducement also, such a case as makes it incumbent on the latter to prove the absence thereof,[1] but not an irrebuttable case, which would be the corollary of any rule that the implication is one of law. And, even in such circumstances, the fact that the representee does not choose to go into the witness-box is some evidence tending to qualify the conclusion which might otherwise result from proof of palpable materiality, and ought to be taken into consideration from this point of view by the tribunal to whom it falls to adjudicate on the issue.[2]

Diminishing importance of this rule

134 The proposition that materiality and inducement require to be separately proved derived its importance initially from the fact that misrepresentation cases were formerly tried by jury. Where this is the form of trial it becomes necessary to ascertain the facts by submitting specific issues to which the jury give answers; and where in a jury trial some fact essential to the cause of action is not made the subject of a question to the jury, and consequently is not the subject of any specific finding, it will be impossible, except where the parties have made an

---

duced''; *Smith* v. *Land and House Property Corporation* (1884), 28 Ch.D. 7, C.A., *per* BOWEN L.J. at p. 16: "I cannot quite agree with the remark of the late Master of the Rolls in *Redgrave* v. *Hurd* that,'' —he then quotes the passage cited in the last note,—''and I think that probably his Lordship hardly intended to go so far as that, though, there may be strong reason for drawing such an inference, as an inference of fact''; *Hughes* v. *Twisden* (1886), 55 L.J. Ch. 481, where, after discussing the above-cited authorities, and remarking that JESSEL M.R. could not have meant what he is reported to have said in *Redgrave* v. *Hurd*, NORTH J. concludes: "looking at all these cases . . . I come to the conclusion that it is not a presumption of law, but an important piece of evidence, from which, *if there is nothing else*, the court may draw the inference *of fact* that the plaintiff was induced by the statement to enter into the contract''; *Arnison* v. *Smith* (1889), 41 Ch.D. 348, C.A., *per* Lord HALSBURY L.C. at p. 369, where he endorses the statement of the law contained in the passages above cited from the judgment of JESSEL M.R. in the Court of Appeal in *Smith* v. *Chadwick*, *supra.*, and not the statement made by him in *Redgrave* v. *Hurd*, *supra.* For the application of the above principles to the statutory cause of action in relation to prospectuses, see Ch. XVI.

[1] See the passages cited in the last note from the judgments of NORTH J. and Lord HALSBURY L.C. In *Moss & Co., Ltd.* v. *Swansea Corporation* (1910), 74 J.P. 351, CHANNELL J. inferred inducement as a fact, though the plaintiff, when in the box, had said nothing about it.

[2] Lord BLACKBURN, at p. 196 of *Smith* v. *Chadwick* (1884), 9 App. Cas. 187, H.L., almost immediately after the passage cited in note 3, *supra*, proceeds: "but whenever that" (sc. the question what inference of fact ought to be drawn) "is a matter of doubt, I think the tribunal which has to elicit the fact should remember that now, and for some years past, the plaintiff can be called as a witness on his own behalf, and that if he is not so called, or, being so called, does not swear that he was induced, it adds much weight to the doubt whether the inference was a true one. I do not say it is conclusive''.

agreement to meet such a case, for the trial judge subsequently to supplement the jury findings by making himself the supplementary finding of fact without which the plaintiff cannot succeed.[1] The result of an application for judgment for the defendant (or in jurisdictions where such a result is possible, for a non-suit) in such an event is rather like that on a demurrer application, and instances are not lacking where it has been equally fatal to a plaintiff with a good claim on the merits; but in a day in which jury trials of civil actions have become a rarity, questions of fact as well as questions of law have increasingly fallen to be determined by the trial judge, and the difficulty has largely disappeared. For a judge sitting alone may make such findings as the evidence justifies, right up to the moment of judgment. The result is an increasing relevance in the cases which illustrate the proposition that though materiality and inducement are indeed separate questions, the same evidence which proves one may in a proper case go far to prove the other, and in an extreme case may actually establish it.[2]

What are questions of law in relation to inducement and materiality

135 It is a question of law whether, in the ordinary course of events, or in the proved special circumstances of the individual case, the representation is *capable* of being regarded as material:

> "it may be that the misstatement is . . . so trivial that the court will be of opinion that it *could not* have affected the plaintiff's mind at all, or induced him to enter into the contract".[3]

Similarly, in relation to the issue of inducement, as in the case of any other issue of fact, the question may at any time arise, whether there is any evidence thereof at all, or (where it has been *prima facie* proved by the representee) any evidence to the contrary; and these are questions of law.

All the circumstances to be considered

136 In determining, as a fact, whether any representation was of a nature to induce, or did actually induce, the representee to alter his position, "all the circumstances must be considered".[4] Amongst these

---

1 This was the point of *Nicholas* v. *Thompson*, [1924] V.L.R. 554 referred to in note 2 to para. 128, *ante*.

2 This topic is dealt with in para. 134, *supra*. *Whurr* v. *Devenish* (1904), 20 T.L.R. 385 seems to be an early illustration of what has become the usual practice; sitting without a jury, the judge determined the issue of materiality as a fact.

3 JESSEL M.R. at pp. 45, 46 of *Smith* v. *Chadwick* (1882), 20 Ch.D. 27, C.A.

4 Lord HALSBURY L.C. in *Bloomenthal* v. *Ford*, [1897] A.C. 156, H.L., at p. 162.

circumstances are: the character of the document in which the representation is contained; the nature of the transaction, contract or business
into which it is alleged that the representee was induced to enter; the
kind of property passing by any contract of sale or mortgage; the profession, trade, skill, experience, or position in life of the representee; and
the present and past relation of the parties to one another.[1] Thus, as has
been already noticed, a prospectus, or an advertisement after the modern
flamboyant manner, will not be judged with quite the same severity,
nor will quite so much literal accuracy be expected of it, as in the case of
conditions of sale, for instance, or a formal instrument, or a business
letter.[2] Again, it has been considered, in prospectus cases, of importance
that the representee "was a person well acquainted with dealings in
shares of companies, with prospectuses, and Stock Exchange transactions",
and, so, "not likely to look upon a prospectus with more unquestioning
faith than the rest of mankind",[3] or,

> "a man of business who had himself turned his own business into a company,
> and taken shares in other companies, and was quite competent to form an
> opinion for himself"[4]

or a person with general and particular experience (as a broker) of
company promotions and undertakings,[5] or an underwriter, and not an
investor, to which two classes of subscribers different considerations
might appeal.[6]

---

[1] This passage in the text was expressly approved by the New Zealand Court of Appeal in
Easterbrook v. *Hopkins*, [1918] N.Z.L.R. 428, at p. 443.

[2] See para. 49, *ante*, and the notes thereto.

[3] DENMAN J. at p. 577 of *Bellairs* v. *Tucker* (1884), 13 Q.B.D. 562; *cf. Stubbs* v. *Slater*,
[1910] 1 Ch. 632, at p. 642, C.A., where, in the case of one who professed to have been misled
by the Stock Exchange term "net rate", notice was taken of his previous history as a speculator
and gambler.

[4] Lord BLACKBURN, at p. 197 of *Smith* v. *Chadwick* (1884), 9 App. Cas. 187, H.L.   *Cf.* Lord
SELBORNE L.C. at p. 190, who described the plaintiff as "an intelligent man of business, aware
of the current prices at that time of bar and plate iron" (matters most relevant to the representation in that case, which related to the yield and profits of a business of this nature).

[5] KEKEWICH J. at p. 809 of *Capel & Co.* v. *Sim's Ships Composition Co., Ltd.* (1888), 58 L.T.
807. So in *Shrewsbury* v. *Blount* (1841), 2 Man. & G. 475, TINDAL C.J. at p. 504, drew attention to the fact that the plantiff in that case, who claimed to have been deceived by the statement
of a mining company as to its affairs, "was an attorney", and "that his knowledge of the world
and experience must have taught him how little reliance is to be placed upon representations of
such a nature".

[6] "The investor wants a sound concern; the underwriter wants an attractive prospectus";
per FARWELL J. in *Baty* v. *Keswick* (1901), 85 L.T. 18.   In other words, the ordinary applicant
for shares is influenced by representations as to the inherent merits and business features of the
undertaking, whereas the underwriter is comparatively indifferent as to these, and is concerned
mainly with (as a modern financier pithily expressed it) "the front page of the prospectus",
and the chances of the names appearing therein attracting at once (whatever happens afterwards) a response from the public sufficient to relieve him from liability, and secure his
commission.

CHAPTER VII

Alteration of Position and Damage

Introductory

137 Whatever be the form of proceeding, or the nature of the relief sought, in respect of a misrepresentation, it is incumbent on the representee to establish that he was induced thereby, not to change his mind in the sense of abandoning or adopting or varying a mere belief or opinion either on some general question or as to a particular individual or concern, but to *alter his position* in a manner affecting his material, temporal, or physical interests, as explained below.

Alteration of position

138 The alteration of position may be brought about by the representee entering into a contract or binding transaction with the representor himself, in which case that contract or transaction may be the subject of either rescission or (if the representee elects, or is compelled, to adhere to it) an action for damages; or it may consist in the representee entering into a contract or transaction with a third person, or in his doing, or abstaining from, any act whatsoever which he is not compellable by law to do, or abstain from doing,[1] in which latter event, there is no remedy other than an action for damages, and resultant damage therefore must be proved, as well as the act constituting the alteration of position,[2] whereas, in any case in which avoidance only is sought, damage is wholly irrelevant.[3] Therefore the first of the three rules enunciated by Lord HATHERLEY, then Sir W. PAGE-WOOD V.-C. and so often since approved

---

[1] See Article 20 of the Code. As to physical acts, such as using chattels or land expressly or impliedly represented to be safe, see para. 143, *post.*

[2] See paras. 141 *et seq., post.*

[3] See Chapter XIII, para. 230, *post.*

and cited, though adequate to the subject-matter of the case before him, requires some qualification and explanation to make it acceptable as a proposition of universal application. It runs as follows: "Every man must be held responsible for the consequences of a false representation made by him to another upon which that other acts, and, so acting, is injured or damnified".[1] As applied to the class of proceeding wherein damage is the gist of the action—which was the case then before him— his statement is accurate, but not as applied to a claim to rescind. Again, "acting" must be understood as limited to acts having some bearing on the representee's temporal interests[2]; and, lastly, in an action of deceit, it is now the law that it is sufficient that the representee has *suffered* an alteration of position, producing physical injury, without having done any act at all.[3]

The alteration of position, whether pecuniary loss accompanies it or not, must be a change in the business or practical affairs or condition of the representee. It is submitted that a representation will not be actionable *merely* because it has influenced someone, for instance, to join, or leave, a particular religious community or political party or social club,[4] or to adopt or abandon philosophical or scientific tenets or doctrines. Neither, so it is submitted, will a lie told by a politician to his electors to secure support give any cause of action, nor the kind of statement sometimes made by practical jokers, where nothing more results than that the representee is rendered ridiculous in greater or lesser degree, whatever may be the judgment to be passed on such falsehoods *in foro conscientiae*.

Other classes of transactions constituting alteration of position

139   The entering into a contract either with the representor himself,[5] or with a third person,[6] or class of persons,[7] are the two most common and obvious types of what is understood by alteration of position. But there are also other relations, involving liability present or contingent, which the representee may be induced to assume, and which, though

---

[1] *Barry* v. *Croskey* (1861), 2 John. & H. 1, at pp. 22–23.

[2] See para. 139, *infra*.

[3] See para. 143, *post*.

[4] In *Chamberlain* v. *Boyd* (1883), 11 Q.B.D. 407, C.A., it was considered that the loss of a chance of being elected to a club was not temporal damage sufficient to render actionable a slander which was not so otherwise.

[5] For this class of case, see Chapters XII and XIII, *post*.

[6] See, e.g., *Skidmore* v. *Bradford* (1869), L.R. 8 Eq. 134 (where the representee was induced to contract with a third person to purchase his warehouse). And see generally the misrepresentation of authority cases referred to in Chapter X, paras. 182–3, *post*.

[7] *Barry* v. *Croskey* (1861), 2 John. & H. 1.

not amounting in strictness to contracts, nevertheless constitute an alteration in his position, in respect of which he has a right to maintain an action. These it will be convenient to call "transactions".[1] They include such unilateral acts as gifts,[2] licences and consents,[3] condonations of matrimonial offences,[4] forbearances,[5] and renunciations,[6] and also acts, of whatever kind, the effect of which is to render the representee civilly responsible to some third person,[7] including, perhaps, even an act which renders him amenable to the criminal law, but which would not have done so if the statement on the faith of which he committed it had been true.[8]

Burden of proof: questions of law and fact

140 The onus is on the representee to allege and prove the particular mode in which his position was altered, and that the representor, actually or presumptively, intended him to act upon the representation in that manner, and that he did so act; and it is not sufficient to prove even that damage was caused to the representee unless it came through the

---

[1] See the definition of the term in Article 20 of the Code.

[2] *Haygarth* v. *Wearing* (1871), L.R. 12 Eq. 320, *per* WICKENS V.-C. at p. 329, in setting aside a sale induced by fraudulent misrepresentation, "the same conclusion would, I conceive, have resulted from the same view of the evidence in other respects if I had held that the true transaction was intended as substantially a gift by Miss Haygarth, and not a sale; for . . . I conceive that the evidence could not support a gift obtained from Miss Haygarth on the footing of certain representations, without showing those representations to be true"); *Re Glubb, Bamfield* v. *Rogers*, [1900] 1 Ch. 354, C.A., where it was held that a gift can be recovered by the donor, on discovery of the true facts, from a donee who had innocently misrepresented them.

[3] As to consents to judgments, see Chapter XVII, *post*.

[4] *Roberts* v. *Roberts and Temple* (1917), 33 T.L.R. 333 (*per* HILL J. at pp. 334, 335).

[5] *Firbank's Executors* v. *Humphreys* (1886), 18 Q.B.D. 54, C.A., where the deceased was induced to continue carrying out his contract with the railway company without pressing for cash, which he otherwise would have done: *per* LINDLEY L.J. at p. 61.

[6] *M'Carthy* v. *Decaix* (1831), 2 Russ. & M. 614 (*per* Lord BROUGHAM L.C. at pp. 620–623; a case of renunciation of marital rights). Formal and express releases, compromises, and receipts in full discharge and satisfaction, of course fall within the class of contracts proper: see *Stewart* v. *Great Western Rail. Co.* (1865), 2 De G.J. & Sm. 319; *Lee* v. *Lancashire and Yorkshire Rail. Co.* (1871), 6 Ch. App. 527; *Hirschfield* v. *London, Brighton, and South Coast Rail. Co.* (1876), 2 Q.B.D. 1; *Gilbert* v. *Endean* (1878), 9 Ch.D. 259, C.A. Compare the cases of rescission of deeds of compromise and settlement cited in the notes in Chapter XIII, para. 251, *post*.

[7] See *Adamson* v. *Jarvis* (1827), 4 Bing. 66, where the representee, an auctioneer, was induced to sell certain goods, whereby he rendered himself liable to the true owner; *Eyre* v. *Smith* (1877), 2 C.P.D. 435, where the "transaction" was a resolution to liquidate the affairs of a bankrupt by arrangement under the old bankruptcy law. *Cf.* also the cases of registration of transfers of shares induced by the misrepresentation of the applicant.

[8] *Burrows* v. *Rhodes*, [1899] 1 Q.B. 816, Div.Ct., where one of the matters complained of in the statement of claim, which was held to have been well pleaded, was that the plaintiff had been taken prisoner by the South African Republic, and was liable to summary execution in that State, and also to severe punishment in England, and where the objection that he was suing in respect of a criminal act was overruled, inasmuch as, if the representation on which he so acted as to incur criminal liability had been true, it would not have been a criminal act.

medium of an alteration of position induced by the misrepresentation.[1] Whether there is any sufficient averment,[2] or proof,[3] of such matters is a question of law. Subject to the above, and subject also to the principle of law that a man is presumed to intend the natural consequences of his acts and statements, all matters connected with alteration of position are issues of fact.

Damage

141   Where the representee elects, or is compelled, to affirm a contract with the representor into which he was induced to enter by misrepresentation, or where his alteration of position consisted in some act or result other than the entering into a contract, and as to which therefore no question of either avoidance or affirmance can arise, his only remedy is an action in damages. In such an action it is essential to prove not only that he acted on, or suffered in consequence of, his belief in the truth of the representation, but that such action or suffering resulted in damage cognizable by the law.[4] It is of no more use in such cases to prove alteration of position without damage, than (as has already been seen) it is sufficient to prove damage without alteration of position.

What constitutes actionable damage

142   The only damage of which the law takes cognizance, in an action for misrepresentation, is actual and temporal damage—that is, some loss either of money or money's worth, or some physical injury, capable of being pecuniarily compensated, or some present or contingent liability, or tangible detriment, which admits of being quantified and assessed. Such damage does not include mere mental distress, or the mere loss of social advantages to which no money value can be attached[5]; and there

---

[1] See the cases, generally, which are cited in this chapter, and, particularly *Tallerman* v. *Dowsing Radiant Heat Co.*, [1900] 1 Ch. 1, where STIRLING J. dismissed the action because, though damage was caused to the plaintiff by misrepresentations alleged to constitute a "passing off", yet "the statements complained of were not intended to be acted on by the plaintiffs, and have not been acted upon by them" (pp. 5, 6). Where it is a case of *suffering* an alteration of position, of course no act need be averred or proved, but only the consequences which the representee had to endure, and the damage caused thereby; as to which, see para. 143, *post*.

[2] In *Behn* v. *Kemble* (1859), 7 C.B. N.S. 260, the third count of the declaration did not allege either any intention on the part of the representor that the representee should act on the representation, or that the representee did so act: it was accordingly held bad. So also, in the more modern case of *Salaman* v. *Warner* (1891), 65 L.T. 132, C.A., the statement of claim was struck out on the ground (amongst others) that no such averments appeared in it.

[3] See the cases cited in this chapter, generally.

[4] This is Article 21 of the Code, *q.v.* As to when a representee is compelled in law by certain circumstances to adhere to a contract with the representor which otherwise he might have rescinded, see Chapter XIV, *post*.

[5] See *Chamberlain* v. *Boyd* (1883), 11 Q.B.D. 407, C.A., a case of slander not actionable except upon proof of actual temporal damage, and which therefore is in point, where it was held that the loss of a chance of admission to a social club did not amount to such damage.

is no such thing, in proceedings of the nature in question, as the presumptive damage which the law takes notice of in certain classes of action, such as defamation. Proof of damage is essential.[1]

143 Damage of the nature indicated may consist, firstly, in entering into or carrying out a contract or transaction which involves pecuniary injury to the extent of the difference between what is paid and payable thereunder and the lesser value—if it be lesser—of what is received and receivable,[2] or it may take the form of payments to a third person, or to the representor himself,[3] or loss of profits, appointments, or earnings,[4] or trouble and expense, or detriment of any kind to which a money value can be attached.[5] Secondly, as in the "trap" and "invitation" cases, which are usually dealt with under the head of negligence, though it is conceived that at least with equal propriety they may be said

---

[1] Per STARKE J. in *Potts* v. *Miller* (1940), 64 C.L.R. 282 (High Court of Aus.) at p. 287: "In an action for deceit, the proof of real damage is essential. It is not a question of nominal damages; the foundation or gist of the action is real damage, though it is quite true that if the real damage proved be small the verdict will also be small".

[2] See Chapter XI, paras. 203 *et seq., post*, for the rules for the quantification of the damages.

[3] Moneys paid to the representor himself are usually sued for in the form of an action for money had and received: but they may be regarded as damages, and none the less because the amount is liquidated: see *Kettlewell* v. *Refuge Assurance Co., Ltd.*, [1908] 1 K.B. 545, C.A., *per* Lord ALVERSTONE C.J. at p. 550.

[4] *Barley* v. *Walford* (1846), 9 Q.B. 197 (loss of profits on a design for silk handkerchiefs); *Denton* v. *Great Northern Rail. Co.* (1856), 5 E. & B. 860 (missing an appointment); *Burrows* v. *Rhodes*, [1899] 1 Q.B. 816, Div. Ct. (loss of pay and earnings and capacity to earn).

[5] In *Barley* v. *Walford, supra*, besides his loss of profits, the plaintiff was put to the trouble and expense of making inquiries, and communicating with the parties who had been falsely stated by the defendant to be the registered owners of the design, and to have the intention of prosecuting the plaintiff. In *Milne* v. *Marwood* (1855), 15 C.B. 778, the plaintiff was put to the expense of fitting up the ship, which had been misrepresented to be sound, for a voyage to Australia. In *Richardson* v. *Silvester* (1873), L.R. 9 Q.B. 34, the plaintiff spent money and time in going to see the farm advertised. In *Wilkinson* v. *Downton*, [1897] 2 Q.B. 57, apart from the physical injuries mentioned in note 1 on p. 164, the plaintiff paid the railway fares of certain persons whom she sent to see after her husband, and WRIGHT J. held that there could be no question as to her right to recover this sum as damage (p. 58). In *Burrows* v. *Rhodes, supra*, amongst other heads of damage claimed was the expense of seven surgical operations which the plaintiff had to undergo. In *Pritty* v. *Child* (1902), 71 L.J. K.B. 512, Div. Ct., the plaintiff claimed and recovered the expense of sinking a well on the spot indicated by the "water-finder". As to other kinds of detriment, see *Mullett* v. *Mason* (1866), L.R. 1 C.P. 559, where the plaintiff recovered the value not only of the diseased cow which had been fraudulently misrepresented as sound, but of five others with which it was placed, and which also died of the disease. *Cf. Carlill* v. *Carbolic Smoke Ball Co.*, [1893] 1 Q.B. 256, C.A., where it was held that the mere trouble of sniffing the smoke-ball at the stated intervals was sufficient "detriment or inconvenience" to constitute a consideration for the contract sued upon (*per* LINDLEY L.J. at pp. 264, 265, and BOWEN L.J. at p. 271), and, for the same reason, the same trouble and inconvenience would, no doubt, in an action of misrepresentation or any other tort, constitute legal damage sufficient to support the action, however exiguous the pecuniary value of that damage might be.

to be founded on fraudulent misrepresentation by conduct,[1] the damage may consist in doing an act which results in personal and physical injury.[2] Thirdly, it has been decided, quite in accordance with the principles of the law of misrepresentation (though WRIGHT J. seemed to doubt whether he was not extending them), that if a fraudulent misrepresentation is made by one to another, which that other is intended to, and does,

---

[1] All the elements of fraudulent misrepresentation are present in this type of case. By his conduct in "setting the trap", that is, in leaving the dangerous cavity unfenced, unlighted, and unwarned against, or by pulling up the train short of, or past, the platform (to take the common examples), the party, silently but none the less effectually, represents that the place is safe, that there is no hole, or that there is no danger in alighting. This is a statement by conduct as it was expressly put by Lord CAIRNS L.C. at p. 15 of *North Eastern Rail. Co.* v. *Wanless* (1874), L.R. 7 H.L. 12: "it appears to me that the circumstance that the gates at this level crossing were open at this particular time, amounted to a statement, and a notice to the public, that the line at that time was safe for crossing". It appears, further, from all the negligence cases of this description—see particularly *Brass* v. *Maitland* (1856), 26 L.J. Q.B. 49, *Clarke* v. *Army and Navy Co-operative Society, Ltd.*, [1903] 1 K.B. 155, C.A. (*per* COLLINS M.R. at pp. 164, 165, and ROMER L.J. at p. 166), *Blacker* v. *Lake and Elliot, Ltd.* (1912), 106 L.T. 533, Div. Ct., *White* v. *Steadman*, [1913] 3 K.B. 340 (*per* LUSH J. at pp. 348, 349), and *Bates* v. *Batey & Co. Ltd.*, [1913] 3 K.B. 351 (*per* HORRIDGE J. at pp. 355, 356),—that when, and only when, such an implied statement is not merely false, but made with a knowledge of its falsity—which is precisely what the law means by fraudulent (see Chapter V, para. 97, *ante*)—it is the subject of an action for damages at the suit of any person who acted on the faith of its being true, unless he knew *aliunde* of the danger, which knowledge again—see Chapter XI, paras. 190–192, *post*—is a good affirmative plea to an action of deceit, because the plaintiff is thereby shown not to have been deceived, or "entrapped".

The effect of the Contributory Negligence Act 1945 on this kind of claim should perhaps here be adverted to; it seems to have escaped notice in many of the texts. Where *personal injury* is caused by fraudulent misrepresentation of the type above referred to, and the injured person, though not *aware* of the danger, would have become aware of it, and could have avoided injury, if he had exercised due care for his own safety, it is conceived that the provisions of the Contributory Negligence Act will be applicable to reduce or even to extinguish his claim. If this be so, such a case will be an exception to the unqualified pronouncement of Mr Spencer Bower in earlier editions of this work (published of course before the passing of the Contributory Negligence Act) that "actual and personal knowledge (of the danger) must be proved . . . there is absolutely no exception to this rule"—para. 192, *post*.

[2] Illustrations of physical injury resulting from the act of using a chattel, or real property, the qualities or condition of which had been *expressly* misrepresented are: *Levy* v. *Langridge* (1838), 4 M. & W. 337, Ex. Ch.; *Longmeid* v. *Holliday* (1851), 6 Exch. 761 (where, however, the plaintiff failed, because the representation was not deemed to have been made to him); *Burtsal* v. *Bianchi* (1891), 65 L.T. 678 (where the plaintiff claimed in respect of the illness caused by his taking a house with defective drains on the faith of a representation by the defendant that they were in good order, but, it not being proved that the representation was fraudulent, as well as false, the action failed). In a curious case of *Southern* v. *How* (1618), Cro. Jac. 468, the defendant delivered a stone, stating it to be a genuine jewel, to the plaintiff, a factor, for delivery to the King of Barbary. The plaintiff proceeded to Barbary, and delivered the stone to the king, who, however, declared it to be counterfeit, and promptly arrested and imprisoned the plaintiff, who sued the defendant for damages for deceit. The court was "inclined to be against" the plaintiff, because it did not clearly appear that the defendant knew that the stone was not genuine, and the suit did not proceed further: but, if it had, the damages presumably would have included a sum to compensate the plaintiff for his imprisonment. In *Victoria*, in *Nicholls* v. *Taylor*, [1939] V.L.R. 119 (Full Ct. of Vict.) a purchaser of a second-hand motor car, to whom the vendor had fraudulently misrepresented that the tyres were new, recovered damages for personal injury caused by the capsize of the car though a tyre blowing out.

believe to be true, and which is of a nature to cause not merely mental distress, but also consequent physical injury to a normal person so believing, then, though the representee *does* nothing on the faith of it, but only endures something, the pecuniary equivalent for the bodily suffering is damage of which the court must take notice in an action based on such misrepresentation.[1] Mere "moral and intellectual" damage—that is personal distress of mind, unaccompanied by physical effects—will not do.[2]

144   The above being the *nature* of the damage which is required to be established, where damage is a necessary ingredient in the cause of action, it remains to examine what relation between the misrepresentation and the damage is necessary and sufficient to render such misrepresentation actionable in this respect. The relation obviously must be a causal one, and not one of mere succession or sequence. The *propter hoc* as well as the *post hoc* must be proved. It is not enough to show that damage followed, or even that it was caused by, the misrepresentation, unless it was of such a nature that the representor did in fact, or (if he had thought of the matter at all) must have contemplated it as the, or a,

---

[1] *Wilkinson* v. *Downton*, [1897] 2 Q.B. 57, where (see the preliminary statement of the facts by WRIGHT J. at p. 58) "the defendant, in the execution of what he seems to have regarded as a practical joke, represented to the plaintiff that he was charged by the husband with a message to her to the effect that her husband was smashed up in an accident, and was lying at the Elms at Leytonstone with both legs broken, and that she was to go at once in a cab with two pillows to fetch him home. All this was false. The effect of the statement on the plaintiff was a violent shock to her nervous system, producing vomiting and other more serious and permanent physical consequences, at one time threatening her reason, and entailing weeks of suffering and incapacity to her as well as expense to her husband for medical attendance". The above decision was followed, and applied to the case of a man frightening a woman with threats in the falsely assumed character of a detective from Scotland Yard, in *Janvier* v. *Sweeney*, [1919] 2 K.B. 316, C.A. It would also bring within the scope of actionable misrepresentation the kind of lie which plays so prominent a part in drama and fiction, as to the death, arrest, conviction, engagement, or marriage of a person in whom the representee is interested.

[2] The judgment of WRIGHT J. in the case last cited, which was afterwards cited with approval by Lord SHAW at p. 13 of *Coyle* v. *John Watson, Ltd.*, [1915] A.C. 1, H.L., and by BANKES L.J. at p. 322 of *Janvier* v. *Sweeney*, *supra*, is occupied (at pp. 58–61) with an examination of the question whether illness resulting from fright, or shock, can be considered to come within the description of physical injury at all, a question which was answered by him in the affirmative for the purpose of that case at any rate, and, afterwards for all purposes, in *Dulieu* v. *White & Sons*, [1901] 2 K.B. 669 (see the very interesting and philosophical judgments of KENNEDY J. and PHILLIMORE J. who, though agreeing in the result, arrive at it by somewhat different trains of reasoning). *Mere* "moral and intellectual" damage of course will not do: as Lord WENSLEY-DALE said at p. 598 of *Lynch* v. *Knight* (1861), 9 H.L. Cas. 577, "mental pain or anxiety the law cannot value, and does not pretend to redress, when the wrongful act complained of causes that alone, though when a material damage occurs and is connected with it", it is otherwise. To the above authorities, cited in the second edition of this work, there should perhaps be added *Hambrook* v. *Stokes Brothers*, [1925] 1 K.B. 141 and *Schneider* v. *Eisovitch*, [1960] 1 All E.R. 169, [1960] 2 Q.B. 430.

probable result. The rule may be expressed in two ways, accordingly as causality, or intention, is taken as the standard. On the one hand, it is correct to say that the damage must be shown to have been the natural and probable, or else the actually intended, result of the misrepresentation being believed and acted upon, or (in the case of physical suffering) being believed. On the other hand, it is equally correct, and comes to the same thing, to say that the damage must be shown to have been intended, actually or presumptively, and that a representor is presumed to have intended the natural and probable consequences of his misrepresentation, that is to say, the consequences which he actually foresaw, or which he ought to have foreseen, as likely to ensue, either in the ordinary course of events, or in the special circumstances of the case. One of two things, therefore, must always be established: either a necessary, or at least natural, relation of causality between the two events or facts, or else an actually intended connection.[1] Unless such a connection is made out, the representee, though he may prove that he did in fact sustain the damage alleged by reason of his belief in the truth of the representation, must fail[2]; when it is made out, he succeeds.[3] Of course,

---

[1] *Cf.* what was said by Lord DENMAN C.J. delivering the judgment of the Court of Queen's Bench, at p. 209 of *Barley* v. *Walford* (1846), 9 Q.B. 197, in a passage cited in para. 117, *ante*, in relation to the question of inducement to which it is equally relevant: "it is not true to say that any false statement which produces damage is actionable; for, if every untrue statement which produces damage to another would found an action at law, a man might sue his neighbour for having a conspicuous clock too slow".

[2] *Collins* v. *Cave* (1860), 6 H. & N. 131, Exch. Ch., *per* WIGHTMAN, J. at p. 134 ("the difficulty is to say that the damage necessarily resulted from the fraudulent misrepresentation"); *Barry* v. *Croskey* (1861), 2 John. & H. 1 (demurrer allowed); *Dashwood* v. *Jermyn* (1879), 12 Ch.D. 776; *Angus* v. *Clifford*, [1891] 2 Ch. 449, C.A., where KAY L.J. at pp. 480, 481, expressed a doubt whether the damage alleged was sufficiently made out, though the decision in favour of the defendants proceeded on other grounds; *Ajello* v. *Worsley*, [1898] 1 Ch. 274, *per* STIRLING J. at pp. 281–283. A good example of the absence of a natural causal connection is put, in the course of the argument, by PAGE-WOOD V.-C. in *Barry* v. *Croskey*, *supra*, at pp. 18, 19: "Your argument", he observes, addressing counsel for the plaintiffs, and referring to *R.* v. *De Berenger* (1814), 3 M. & S. 67, "would show that every person who, in consequence of De Berenger's frauds upon the Stock Exchange, was induced to purchase shares at an advanced price, in reliance upon the false rumours he had circulated that peace was concluded, was entitled to maintain an action against De Berenger for the increase in price. Would not such consequences be too remote to form ground for an action?" These observations were approved and applied by Lord CAIRNS, at pp. 412, 413, of *Peek* v. *Gurney* (1873), L.R. 6 H.L. 377, and approved in, but held inapplicable to the circumstances of, *Andrews* v. *Mockford*, [1896] 1 Q.B. 372, C.A., by A. L. SMITH L.J. at p. 381, and RIGBY L.J. at pp. 384, 385, and (as appears from p. 385) by Lord RUSSELL C.J. at the trial.

[3] As in *Polhill* v. *Walter* (1832), 3 B. & Ad. 114, a case of misrepresentation of authority to accept a bill of exchange, where Lord TENTERDEN C.J. delivering the judgment of the King's Bench, said, at pp. 123, 124: "the defendant must be *taken to have intended* that all such persons" (sc. "all to whom the bill may be offered in the course of circulation") "should give credit to the acceptance, and then act upon the faith of that representation, *because that, in the ordinary course of business, is its natural and necessary result*"; *Barley* v. *Walford*, *supra*, *per Cur.*, at pp. 206–209; *Mullett* v. *Mason*, cited in note 5 on p. 162, *ante*; *Wilkinson* v. *Downton*,

whenever the representee is in a position to allege and prove that the
representor in fact intended the precise kind of damage which resulted,
the question of whether such damage was the probable result of the
misrepresentation, which is only of importance when the plaintiff is
compelled to resort to the theory of *presumed* intention, becomes wholly
immaterial.[1]

Those dicta which seemed to insist that the damage must be "proximate", "immediate", or "direct" do not, it is submitted, add any
further requirement to those stated above.   No great harm has been done
by the rather loose use of such expressions, since all lawyers, by the
expression "too remote", as applied to damage, understand damage
which is not the natural and proper result of the wrong, and by the terms
"proximate" or "immediate" damage which is.   The test, despite the
use of such terms, remains as first stated—is the damage (a) such as was
actually intended ?   Or (b) such as was the natural and probable result
of the misrepresentation ?[2]

---

supra, per WRIGHT J. at p. 59 (" it is difficult to imagine that such a statement, made suddenly
and with apparent seriousness, could fail to produce grave effects under the circumstances
upon any but an exceptionally indifferent person, and *therefore an intention to produce such an
effect must be imputed,* and it is no answer in law to say that more harm was done than was
anticipated, for that is commonly the case with all wrongs").

1 In *Milne* v. *Marwood* (1855), 15 C.B. 778, where the plaintiff (unnecessarily, perhaps)
had averred that the defendant actually intended him to incur the expense which he did in
fitting up for a voyage to Australia the vessel which had fraudulently been represented to be
sound, WILLIAMS J. at pp. 781, 782, and MAULE J. at p. 783, doubting whether this was "general" damage, that is, damage flowing in the ordinary course of events from the wrong, thought
that there should be a new trial to clear up the point, which the first jury may not have had in
their minds, whether, as pleaded, such damage had in fact been intended; but in *Andrews* v.
Mockford, [1896] 1 Q.B. 372, C.A., it was held that there was abundant evidence of the alleged
actual intention of the defendants, by their fabricated and published telegram, not only to
strengthen the effect of the fraudulent prospectus, which was addressed of course only to
possible allottees, but also to cause the public to purchase shares in the market, and to sustain
the precise damages which they did; and, whilst recognising, in accordance with Lord
HATHERLEY's observations cited in note 2 on p. 165, *ante,* that this result was not the natural
and probable one in ordinary circumstances, the Court of Appeal was of opinion that the circumstances of that case disclosed an intention in fact on the part of the defendants to produce it,
which rendered it unnecessary to consider whether such intention could otherwise have been
imputed to them.

2 In the second edition Mr Spencer Bower has a lengthy passage at this point in the text,
devoted to the destructive criticism of the propositions of Lord HATHERLEY, then Sir W.
PAGE-WOOD V.-C., in *Barry* v. *Croskey* (1861), 2 John. & H. 1 where he said:

"First.   Every man must be held responsible for the consequences of a false representation
made by him to another, upon which that other acts, and, so acting is injured or damnified.

Secondly.   Every man must be held responsible for the consequences of a false representation made by him to another, upon which a third person acts, and, so acting is injured or
damnified—provided it appear that such false representation was made with the intent
that it should be acted upon by such third person in the manner that occasions the injury
or loss . . .

Thirdly.   But, to bring it within the principle, the injury, I apprehend, *must be the*

Burden of proof and questions of law and fact

145 All questions of damage are questions of fact, the burden of establishing which is upon the representee,[1] subject to the following which are questions of law, *viz.* (i) whether there is any evidence of any temporal damage having been sustained at all, (ii) whether the alleged damage amounts to what the law regards as damage, (iii) whether there is any evidence that the alleged damage was caused by the representee's belief in the truth of the alleged misrepresentation, and (iv) whether the proved damage, though shown to have been produced by the proved misrepresentation, was its natural and probable, or (as the case may be) its actually intended, consequence.[2]

---

immediate, and not the remote, consequence of the representation thus made. To render a man responsible for the consequences of a false representation made by him to another, upon which a third person acts, and, so acting, is injured or damnified, it must appear that such false representation was made *with the direct intent* that it should be acted upon by such third person in the manner that occasions the injury or loss.''

It was to the words which are shown above as italicised in the text of the judgment of PAGE-WOOD V.-C. that Mr Spencer Bower took particular exception, as apparently adding a gloss to the accepted test of natural and probable result; the present author is inclined to regard the passage more leniently, as adverting to no more than the limits which the practical difficulties of proof will always impose upon such *probanda* as the extent of damage, and the persons who can be shown to be within the class to whom representations are deemed to have been made. (See note 4 to para. 168, Chapter IX, *post.*)

[1] *Smith* v. *Chadwick* (1884), 9 App.Cas. 187, H.L: see the judgment of Lord BLACKBURN at pp. 195–196. If no actual damage is proved, the representee fails altogether: for there is no legal presumption of nominal damage, as in cases of breach of contract, or the infringement of a personal right or title: See *Hyde* v. *Bulmer* (1868), 18 L.T. 293.

[2] See, generally, the cases already cited in the notes to the text, and add to them: *Vernon* v. *Keys* (1810), 12 East. 632 (*per* Lord ELLENBOROUGH C.J. at p. 638, in the Court of C.P., *affd.* (1812), 4 Taunt. 488, Ex.Ch.); *Eastwood* v. *Bain* (1858), 3 H. & N. 738; *Bear* v. *Stevenson* (1874), 30 L.T. 177, P.C.; *Clydesdale Bank* v. *Paton*, [1896] A.C. 381, H.L. (*per* Lord DAVEY at pp. 397, 398); *Tallerman* v. *Dowsing Radiant Heat Co.*, [1900] 1 Ch. 1; *Stevens* v. *Hoare* (1904), 20 T.L.R. 407, *per* JOYCE J. at p. 409. See, as to the proof of damage in the statutory action against directors of companies in respect of prospectuses, Chapter XVI.

CHAPTER VIII

Who are deemed Parties to a Representation—I: The Representor

Introductory

146 In any proceeding of whatever nature in which misrepresentation is set up, either as a cause of action or ground of complaint, or as an affirmative plea or answer, the only person liable is the representor, subject however to the rules of procedure as to transmission of liability by reason of death, insolvency, or the like, or as to the right or duty of certain persons to defend on behalf, or as representing the estate, of any person under disability.[1] It is convenient, accordingly, before discussing in detail the various remedies and forms of relief available to representees,[2] to ascertain precisely who are the persons deemed in law to be representors.

Representor defined

147 A representor is described in Article 1 of the Code[3] as a person by whom or on behalf of whom a representation is made. The following is a general statement, elaborated in the succeeding paragraphs of this chapter, of the rules for determining which persons are deemed "representors", and responsible as such.[4] In the first place, only he who actually makes the representation is liable for its consequences, if there was no principal or partner on whose behalf he made it; but if there was any

---

[1] These rules, as regards actions for damages, proceedings for rescission, and affirmative defences, are stated or referred to in Chapters XI, XIII, and XIV, *post*, respectively.

[2] See Chapters XI, XII, XIII, XIV, *post*.

[3] See p. 3, *ante*.

[4] These rules are stated in Article 22 of the Code; see pp. 10–11, *ante*.

person by whose express or implied authority he purported to, and did, make it, such latter person is deemed the representor, or one of the two representors, as the case may be.[1] Secondly, one of two co-agents, or a sub-agent, does not, merely as such, render the other co-agent, or the intermediate agent, respectively, liable as a principal for his misrepresentations.[2] Thirdly, all who concur in making any misrepresentation are jointly responsible to the representee for the consequences of its untruth, and, where it was fraudulent, those who are deemed to have participated in the fraud are jointly and severally responsible.[3]

Principal and agent

148 Any person, whether principal or partner, and whether generally, or for the purposes of a particular transaction, by whose express or implied authority a representation has been made, is accountable to the representee, in proceedings instituted by him for rescission or analogous relief, if the representation turns out to be false; and for this purpose, it makes no difference that the prinicipal is a corporation.[4]

It is not possible to state quite so general a principle, however, as applicable to proceedings where damages are claimed, since in these the state of mind of the representor becomes relevant, and distinctions may be made between the state of mind of the principal and that of the agent. As to such proceedings special considerations arise, which are dealt with later in this chapter. But at least this can be said, that where (i) the agent in making the representation does so within the scope of his authority, express or implied, and (ii) the circumstances are such that the agent would himself be liable in damages in respect of the misrepresentation, the principal will also be liable in damages.[5] There may be other situations, in which, though the agent could not be sued for fraud, the principal will be liable; these are discussed in para. 152 below.

In determining whether the agent in making the representation acted

---

[1] See paras. 148 *et seq., post.*
[2] See para. 150, *post.*
[3] See para. 157, *post.*
[4] See para. 151, *post. Bradford Third Equitable Benefit Building Society* v. *Borders,* [1941] 2 All E.R. 205, H.L. *per* Viscount MAUGHAM L.C. at p. 211—"A corporation, which must act through its agents, is as responsible as any other principal for any wrongful act committed by an agent acting within the scope of his employment, and not the less where the wrongful act is a fraud . . ."
[5] See paras. 151 *et seq., post.*

within the scope of his authority, no difficulty arises when the authority is express. The court has merely to construe its words. But where implied authority is set up, the question must be determined in each case in accordance with the principles of the law of agency, or of partnership, which for this purpose is only a branch of the law of agency.[1]

Agents of a company

149 In relation to the liability of a company for the misstatements of its agents, ROMER J. has made some useful observations, which can easily be adapted so as to admit of general application.[2] He classifies the agents who can bind a company by such misrepresentations as follows: (1) general agents, e.g. the directors, acting at a board meeting, or otherwise as a board; (2) special agents, e.g. persons expressly authorised to procure subscriptions for shares, or whose acts in so doing are afterwards adopted and ratified by the company; (3) persons who, with or without authority, have obtained contracts to take shares by misrepresentations, of the making and the falsity of which representations the company becomes aware before the contracts are completed; and (4) persons who, without authority, or even before the company has been incorporated, have issued a prospectus or other document, where the company knows of the issue, and knows that applications for shares have been based on representations contained in such prospectus or document, and, though ignorant in the first instance of the nature of the representations, discovers, before the contracts are completed, what they were, and that they were false. Wherever the alleged agent has been shown to have had the implied authority of the alleged principal, and to have purported to act thereunder, such principal has, in accordance with the above and other principles applicable to the determination of

---

1 The text reverts to this topic in paras. 157 *et seq., post.* See, as to the various classes of agents 1 Halsbury's Laws (4th edn.) pp. 424 *et seq.* An example of a partner of an actual representor being liable in damages for his fraudulent representation made in the course of the partnership business is to be found in *Re Collie, Ex Parte Adamson* (1878), 8 Ch.D. 807, C.A. *Cf.* in *New Zealand, Smith* v. *Mackenzie* (1883), 1 N.Z.L.R., C.A. 1.

2 *Lynde* v. *Anglo-Italian Hemp Spinning Co.,* [1896] 1 Ch. 178, at pp. 182, 183. In *Collins* v. *Associated Greyhound Racecourses, Ltd.,* [1930] 1 Ch. 1, LUXMOORE J. adopted ROMER J.'s classification; but he pointed out at p. 22 that the headnote to the report of *Lynde's case* summarised the fourth class of cases incorrectly. LUXMOORE J.'s decision was unanimously affirmed in the Court of Appeal—*ibid.,* p. 28. It is submitted that the text above incorporates the correction proposed by LUXMOORE J.

this question, been held liable as a representor[1]; where otherwise, he has been held not so liable.[2]

Co-agents and Sub-agents

150 One of several agents of the same principal does not, *as such*, by any representation which he may make, render his co-agent liable to the representee for the consequences thereof.[3] Some express authority must be shown *in hac re*, if such a result is to follow.[4] The only persons liable in such cases, failing proof of particular instructions, are (1) he who actually made the representation; (2) those who concurred in it, or took part in it; and (3) the principal for whom the agent, in the formance of his duties as agent, made it.[5]

A sub-agent may render the ultimate principal liable for his representations, on the basis of implied authority, if the proved circumstances are such that it must be deemed to have been intended and agreed by and between the principal and the agent, that the latter should appoint a substitute for the purpose of discharging in his stead, but on behalf of the former, duties including or involving the making of representations of the character of that sued upon.[6] Otherwise, direct intervention and express authority on the part of the ultimate principal must be shown by

---

[1] As in *Re Metropolitan Coal Consumers Association, Karberg's Case*, [1892] 3 Ch. 1, C.A. (*per* LINDLEY L.J. at p. 13); *Re Metal Constituents, Ltd., Lord Lurgan's Case*, [1902] 1 Ch. 707, where the company would have been held liable on the principle of the last case but for the fact that the applicant had disabled himself from relying on the point by having signed the memorandum of association (see pp. 709, 710). Both the above were cases where the company knew of the prospectus, and of the misstatements therein, before they were acted upon, though it had been issued by persons who were not, and (since the company had not then been registered) could not have been its agents at the time.

[2] As was the case in *New Brunswick and Canada Railway and Land Co. v. Conybeare* (1862), 9 H.L. Cas. 711 (secretary of company held to have no implied authority to make representations as to the value of its shares); *Western Bank of Scotland v. Addie* (1867), L.R. 1 H.L. Sc. & Div. 145, *per* Lord CRANWORTH, at pp. 166–168; *Thorne v. Heard and Marsh*, [1895] A.C. 495, H.L., where it was held that the alleged agent was not in law the agent of the alleged principals, the mortgagees, but of the mortgagor, *per* Lord HERSCHELL, L.C., at p. 502, and Lord DAVEY at p. 506; *Levy v. Scottish Employers Insurance Co.* (1901), 17 T.L.R. 229, Div. Ct.; *Banbury v. Bank of Montreal*, [1918] A.C. 626, H.L. There is a curious Australian case, *Johnston v. Friends Motor Co., Ltd.* (1910), 10 C.L.R. 365 (High Ct. of Aus.) in which a company was sued by one of its shareholders, who was also a director, for rescission of a contract under which he had been allotted shares, on the ground of misrepresentation. The alleged misrepresentation was contained in a document drawn up by the plaintiff himself, with others, as promoters. *Held*: that no suit would lie, as the plaintiff could not in these circumstances claim that he had been deceived by any statement attributable *to the company*; if he had been deceived, it was by his co-promoters in circumstances which did not render the company responsible to him.

[3] *Weir v. Bell* (1878), 3 Ex.D. 238, C.A. (*per* BRAMWELL L.J. at p. 245, and COCKBURN C.J. at pp. 247, 248, 250). *Cf. Re Denham & Co., Ltd.* (1883), 25 Ch.D. 752, at pp. 764, 765.

[4] *Cargill v. Bower* (1878), 10 Ch.D. 502, *per* FRY J. at pp. 513, 514.

[5] *Ibid.*, *per* FRY J. at p. 514. *Cf. Bear v. Stevenson* (1874), 30 L.T. 177, P.C.

[6] *De Bussche v. Alt* (1878), 8 Ch.D. 286, C.A., at pp. 310, 311.

evidence.¹ In no other way can the principal become responsible as a representor.

Fraudulent misrepresentation: Liability of principal and agent

151 In the preceding paragraphs the respective liability of principal and agent for misrepresentation has been considered from the point of view of contract.² The same question gives rise to greater difficulty where the relief sought is damages for fraud, for here not only the falsity of the representation, but the state of mind of the representor is relevant; not only must the principal, in a word, be bound by the false representation itself, as if he had himself uttered it, but the utterance which the law deems to be his must be shown to have been made with a *fraudulent mind*.³ Though for long there was doubt as to how far the law would impute this fraudulent mind to the principal where the utterances were exclusively those of an agent, or where two or more agents of the same principal shared between them the utterances and the state of mind which together in either of them would have been sufficient to make that one guilty of fraud, it is now possible to state simply the rules by which the courts will be guided in such situations.

No difficulty arises, in general, where the person who makes the representation has himself the necessary *mens rea*, i.e. has himself no honest belief in its truth. In such a case he himself will be personally liable in fraud, whether he be principal or agent; and if he be an agent, his principal will also be liable if he has made his representation, within the scope of his authority express or implied.⁴ And the principal may be liable even if the fraudulent representation was made by the agent before the agency commenced, if, being a continuing representation, it continued after the commencement of the agency, and then had the effect of inducing the plaintiff to enter, through the agent, into a contract with the principal.⁵ For in such a case it is the agent's duty, having made false

---

¹ Such intervention and direct relation was proved in *Powell and Thomas v. Evan, Jones & Co.*, [1905] 1 K.B. 11, C.A. (*per* COLLINS M.R. at pp. 17, 18, STIRLING L.J. at p. 20, and MATHEW L.J. at pp. 22, 23).

² In para. 148, above, the liability of the representor in rescission proceedings was being considered; and an action for rescission is properly considered as an action in contract.

³ See Chapter V, *ante*.

⁴ DEVLIN J. considers this kind of question in *Kwei Tek Chao v. British Traders and Shippers, Ltd.*, [1954] 2 Q.B. 459 at p. 470; for an example of one *partner* being held liable in damages for the fraudulent misrepresentations of another partner made in the course of the partnership business, see *Re Collie, Ex parte Adamson* (1878), 8 Ch.D. 807, C.A. In New Zealand, *cf. Smith v. Mackenzie* (1883), 1 N.Z.L.R., C.A. 1.

⁵ *Briess v. Woolley*, [1954] 1 All E.R. 909; [1954] A.C. 333, H.L. A director of company A had conducted preliminary negotiations, without any authority from his company or his co-directors to do so, for the sale of its shares to company B. He made some fraudulent misrepresentations in the course of these negotiations. When matters had advanced to the stage

representations, to correct them before the other party acts upon them to his detriment, and it is his failure, acting as agent, to do so which carries liability to the principal.

A person may become liable for the fraud of another in entering into a contract purportedly on his behalf, where the latter is at the time of making his representation not his agent at all, if he subsequently adopts that contract as his own and takes the benefit of it.[1]

Divided responsibility

152 In all of the cases discussed in the preceding paragraph the person who actually makes the representation has done so with a fraudulent mind. He is himself, by definition, guilty of fraud; the question discussed was whether his principal should be held fraudulent also. But where either principal or agent makes a misrepresentation honestly, while the other has the state of mind necessary to make it fraudulent, the question of liability becomes more difficult.

Where a false representation is made honestly by the agent, the principal, but not the agent, having no honest belief in the truth of what is represented, it is of course clear that the agent will not be liable in fraud, for, by definition, his part in the transaction has been an honest one. The principal in such case will be liable in fraud only if (a) he has expressly authorised the making of the representation complained of, or (b) if he

---

where it seemed that an acceptable offer might be obtained, he requested and received from his co-shareholders authority to negotiate a sale. He did this; the ultimate outcome was an action against the shareholders of company A for damages for the fraud of the director as their agent. On the assumption (for the matter was apparently not made certain by the evidence) that no new fraudulent representation had been made after his appointment as agent of the shareholders to sell the shares, the question was, whether they were liable for his fraud. It was held by the Lords that they were liable, on the ground that once his fraudulent representations had been made, he was under a duty to the representees to withdraw them, and his action in allowing them to remain uncorrected amounted to fraud, for which those appointing him were vicariously responsible. See, especially, *per* Lord REID at p. 349; *per* Lord TUCKER at pp. 353–354; *per* Lord COHEN at p. 359. *Cf.* in *Australia*, *Bosaid* v. *Andry*, [1963] V.R. 465, 477 (SHOLL J.).

1 *Wilson* v. *Tumman* (1843), 6 Man. & G. 236 *per* TINDALL C.J. at p. 242; *Keighley Maxsted & Co.* v. *Durant*, [1901] A.C. 240, H.L. *per* Lord MACNAGHTEN at pp. 246–247, citing *Wilson* v. *Tumman, supra. Cf. Story on Agency*, para. 452 ("the principal is not liable for the torts or negligences of his agent in any matters beyond the scope of his agency, unless he has expressly authorised them to be done, *or he has subsequently adopted them for his own use and benefit*"), a passage cited with approval by BLACKBURN J. at p. 145 of *M'Gowan & Co., Ltd.* v. *Dyer* (1873), L.R. 8 Q.B. 141, and by Lord MACNAGHTEN at pp. 736, 737 of *Lloyd* v. *Grace, Smith & Co.*, [1912] A.C. 716, H.L. The view of KEKEWICH C.J. to the contrary in *Hoole* v. *Speak*, [1904] 2 Ch. 732 at pp. 735–736 is now discredited. See also *Burdett* v. *Horne* (1911), 28 T.L.R. 83, C.A. But *quaere*: can the defendant become liable, by an election, unless when he adopts the contract as his own he knows of the fraudulent misrepresentation by which it was induced? The question was raised by Lord OAKSEY in his judgment in *Briess* v. *Woolley*, [1954] A.C. 333, H.L. at p. 344.

has been guilty of some conduct identifying himself with the making of the representation, sufficient to convict him of fraud—e.g., employing the agent with the intention that he shall make the representation in ignorance of the true facts.[1]   This rule dates from 1840, when *Cornfoot* v. *Fowke*[1] was decided in the Exchequer Chamber.   ROLFE B. said:

> "If the plaintiff,[2] knowing of the nuisance, expressly authorised Clarke to say that it did not exist, or to make any statement of similar import, or if he purposely employed an agent, ignorant of the truth, in order that the agent might innocently make a false statement believing it to be true, and might so deceive the party with whom he was dealing, in either of those cases he will be guilty of fraud."[3]

And ALDERSON B. went on to say:

> "And I think it impossible to sustain a charge of fraud, when neither principal nor agent has committed any—the principal, because, *though he knew the fact, he was not congizant of the representation being made*, nor ever directed the agent to make it; and the agent because, though he made a misrepresentation, he did not know it to be one at the time when he made it, but gave his answer *bona fide*."

Cornfoot v. *Fowke* passed subsequently through a period of adversity, but has ultimately survived to rank as a leading statement of a well-recognised principle of the law of agency as it at present stands[4]; and it can now be

---

[1] *Cornfoot* v. *Fowke* (1840), 6 M. & W. 358 Ex.Ch.; *Ludgater* v. *Love* (1881), 44. L.T. 694, C.A.

[2] It was a claim for damages for breach of an agreement to take a lease, and fraud was raised as a defence.

[3] At p. 370.   The citation from ALDERSON B. is from p. 371.   *Cf.* to the same effect, *per* PARKE B. at pp. 372–373.

[4] In *Pearson & Son, Ltd.* v. *Dublin Corporation*, [1907] A.C. 351, H.L., the Earl of HALSBURY on pp. 357–358 referred to it as a decision depending solely upon a point of pleading.   That case was the subject of an enthusiastic exposition by Mr Spencer Bower in the second edition of this work (1927) at pp. 166–167.   The authority of *Cornfoot* v. *Fowke*, weakened by *Pearson* v. *Dublin Corporation*, was for the moment almost destroyed by the subsequent decision of the Court of Appeal in *London County Freehold and Leasehold Properties, Ltd.* v. *Berkeley Property and Investment Co., Ltd.*, [1936] 2 All E.R. 1039, C.A., in which ROMER L.J., citing from the speech of Lord LOREBURN L.C. in *Pearson* v. *Dublin Corporation* (*supra*) that "the principal and agent are one, and it does not signify which of them made the incriminated statement, or which of them had the guilty knowledge", went on to hold that where "the principal, though having no knowledge that the representation is made, knows that it is untrue" he "is as much liable as though he had himself made the representation knowing it to to be untrue".

But this heretical doctrine did not last long.   The following year the same question was debated before ATKINSON J. in *Anglo-Scottish Beet Sugar Corporation* v. *Spalding U.D.C.*, [1937] 3 All E.R. 335; [1937] 2 K.B. 607.   ATKINSON J. pointed out that *Cornfoot* v. *Fowke* and *Pearson* v. *Dublin Corporation* were concerned with widely different sets of facts; in *Cornfoot* v. *Fowke* the agent who made the representation made it honestly, and the principal, who knew the truth, did not authorise the representation, or know that it was being made.   In *Pearson* v. *Dublin Corporation*, on the other hand, two agents, working in conjunction if not actually in collusion, together made the representation and possessed the "guilty knowledge" which all the Lords expressly referred to.   ATKINSON J. refused to follow *London County Freehold and Leasehold Properties, Ltd.* v. *Berekeley Property and Investment Co., Ltd.*   The decision was not stated with confidence that "there is no way of combining an innocent principal and agent so as to produce dishonesty".[1] To quote the words of DEVLIN J. as the judge of first instance in *Armstrong* v. *Strain*[2]:

> "It is precisely that conscious knowledge—whether it be termed 'mens rea', a 'wicked mind' or a 'dishonest purpose' which can never be present in the case of an innocent division of ingredients."

153 Notwithstanding all that has been said above as to cases in which neither principal nor agent is himself guilty of fraud, because the conduct of neither contains both the essential ingredients, it must be emphasised that if the agent himself makes a fraudulent misrepresentation (i.e. so as himself to be guilty of fraud) acting on behalf of the principal within the scope of his authority, real or apparent, the principal will always be liable[3]; and he will be liable even if he himself,[4] or another agent,[5] has been the innocent instrument by which the fraudulent agent's misrepresentation has been transmitted to the representee. It will not avail the principal as a defence (for the ordinary rules as to agency are here applied) that he did not know that the representation was likely to be made, or that he had disapproved of its being made, or even had forbidden its making, if it is made by one who is in fact his agent, acting

---

appealed from; but the later decision of the Court of Appeal in *Armstrong* v. *Strain (infra)* has since put the matter beyond any doubt. In *New Zealand* see *Whinray* v. *Public Trustee*, [1943] N.Z.L.R. 239 (CALLAN J.); *Stratford Borough* v. *J. H. Ashman (N. P.) Ltd.*, [1960] N.Z.L.R. 503, 520-1, C.A.

[1] *Armstrong* v. *Strain*, [1952] 1 K.B. 232, C.A. *per* DEVLIN J., the trial judge, approved by BIRKETT L.J. at p. 246.

[2] [1952] 1 K.B. 232, at p. 246. It may be noted that the Court of Appeal had previously followed *Cornfoot* v. *Fowke* in the earlier case of *Gordon Hill Trust, Ltd.* v. *Segall*, [1941] 2 All E.R. 379, and this fact is recalled by ROMER L.J. in his judgment in *Armstrong* v. *Strain* at p. 249.

[3] *Barwick* v. *English Joint Stock Bank* (1867), L.R. 2 Exch. 259, Ex.Ch., at p. 265: "With regard to the question whether a principal is answerable for the acts of his agent in the course of his master's business, and for his master's benefit, *no sound distinction can be drawn between the case of fraud and the case of any other wrong. The general rule is, that the master is answerable for every such wrong of the servant or agent as is committed in the course of the service, and for the master's benefit, though no express command or privity of the master be proved.*" The above rule, as formulated by the Exchequer Chamber, has been cited and applied in all the subsequent cases—e.g. *Lloyd* v. *Grace, Smith & Co.*, [1912] A.C. 716, H.L. (in which it was held that it need not be for the master's benefit); *Bradford Third Equitable Benefit Building Society* v. *Borders*, [1941] 2 All E.R. 205, H.L., where at p. 211 Viscount MAUGHAM said "A corporation, which must act through its agents, is as responsible as any other principal for any wrongful act committed by an agent acting within the scope of his employment, and not the less where the wrongful act is a fraud...'

[4] *Pearson & Son, Ltd.* v. *Dublin Corporation*, [1907] A.C. 351, H.L. (I), as explained by ATKINSON J. in *Anglo-Scottish Beet Sugar Corporation* v. *Spalding U.D.C.*, [1937] 3 All E.R. 335; [1937] 2 K.B. 607.

[5] *London County Freehold and Leasehold Properties, Ltd.* v. *Berkeley Property and Investment Co., Ltd.*, [1936] 2 All E.R. 1039, as explained by ATKINSON J. in *Anglo-Scottish Beet Sugar Corporation* v. *Spalding U.D.C.*, [1937] 3 All E.R. 335; [1937] 2 K.B. 607.

within the real or apparent scope of his authority.[1]   And the principal
will be liable even if he derived no benefit, and was intended to derive
none, from the transaction, which was entered into solely for the benefit
of the agent.[2]

Fraud by a corporation

154   The guilty mind of an artificial person is a conception calculated
to trouble any careful thinker; and some have wondered how such
principles as are expounded in the text above can be usefully applied to
cases in which it is sought to hold a corporation liable in fraud.   It may
be argued that a corporation can never know anything except in the
minds of its agents; and consequently that it cannot be convicted of
fraud except by the process of attributing to it the knowledge possessed
by one or more of them.   But if the knowledge of an agent of the corporation, derived in the course of his agency, is to bind the corporation, then
it follows that a corporation may be held guilty of fraud if one agent,
acting within the scope of his authority, innocently makes a false representation, the true factual position having been brought to the knowledge of another agent of the corporation while acting as such agent.[3]
The courts have refused, however, so to hold; and it appears clear that a
corporation will not be held liable in fraud on such a state of facts and
no more.[4]

It will no doubt often be found that the evidence brings the actual
case within the dicta of SINGLETON L.J. in *Armstrong* v. *Strain*[5] where he
said:

> "Difficulties may arise in a claim against a company which can only speak or
> act through its agents or officers, but if an officer of a company writes and
> represents that which is untrue when many other officers of the company
> know the true facts, it may well be found that he made the representation
> without belief in its truth, or that he made it recklessly, careless whether it
> was true or false.   That must depend on the evidence."

---

[1] This is the ordinary rule in Agency; and as was held in *Barwick* v. *English Joint Stock Bank*
(1867), L.R. 2 Exch. 259, Ex.Ch. at p. 265 (and has been law ever since) "no sound distinction can be drawn between the case of fraud and the case of any other wrong".

[2] *Swire* v. *Francis* (1877), 3 App. Cas. 106, P.C. at p. 113; *Hambro* v. *Burnand*, [1904]
2 K.B. 10; *Lloyd* v. *Grace, Smith & Co.*, [1912] A.C. 716, H.L.

[3] This is what was for some time thought to have been held, first by the House of Lords in
Pearson & Son, Ltd. v. *Dublin Corporation*, [1907] A.C. 351, H.L. (I), and then by the Court of
Appeal in *London County Freehold and Leasehold Properties, Ltd.* v. *Berkeley Property and Investment
Co., Ltd.*, [1936] 2 All E.R. 1039, C.A.   But in his masterly analysis of these decisions ATKIN-
SON J. demonstrated in *Anglo-Scottish Beet Sugar Corporation* v. *Spalding U.D.C.*, [1937] 3 All
E.R. 335; [1937] 2 K.B. 607 that neither decision went so far as had been supposed.

[4] *Anglo-Scottish Beet Sugar Corporation* v. *Spalding U.D.C.* (supra); *Armstrong* v. *Strain*, [1952]
1 All E.R. 139; [1952] 1 K.B. 232, C.A.

[5] *Armstrong* v. *Strain* (supra).

If the evidence supports such a conclusion, then the agent making the representation will by definition himself be guilty of fraud, and if he has made the representation as agent within the scope of his authority, the corporation will be liable. But if so much cannot be proved? It is here submitted that there will be *some* cases in which the corporation must be deemed to have the knowledge which is possessed by the agent not making the representation. This may depend, it is submitted, on the position of this agent within the corporation. Is he an "agent to know"?[1] If, for instance, the managing director, fully acquainted with all the material facts, causes or authorises another servant of the company innocently to make a false representation, could it be doubted that the company would be liable, just as the managing director himself would have been liable had the transaction been his and not the company's?

Corporation sole

155 The liability of a corporation sole is co-extensive with that of a corporation aggregate, and the same considerations apply.[2]

Fraudulent agent continues liable notwithstanding liability of principal

156 An agent making a fraudulent misrepresentation whereby he becomes himself personally liable for fraud does not rid himself of liability in tort by reason of the fact that his principal is held liable. He incurs no personal liability under the contract into which he has entered as agent, being regarded for the purposes of the law of contract merely as a pipe through which the contractual tie has passed from one principal party to the other. But in tort he remains personally liable, notwithstanding the concurrent liability of his principal,[3] subject only to the limiting factor that the defrauded party, though he may recover judgment for damages against both, may not enforce the judgments which he obtains so as to be paid the same damages twice.[4]

Notwithstanding that in an action for fraud the plaintiff has claimed, or even has obtained,[5] against the principal an order for rescission, he may still have judgment against the agent by whom the fraudulent misrepresentations were actually made, for such sum as may be recoverable

---

[1] DEVLIN J. considers this kind of question in *Kwei Tek Chao* v. *British Traders and Shippers, Ltd.*, [1954] 2 Q.B. 459 at pp. 471–2.

[2] In *New Zealand, Whinray* v. *Public Trustee*, [1943] N.Z.L.R. 239 is an example of an attempt to hold a corporation sole liable in fraud, which foundered on the decision of ATKINSON J. in *Anglo-Scottish Beet Sugar Corporation* v. *Spalding U.D.C.*, [1937] 3 All E.R. 335; [1937] 2 K.B. 607.

[3] *Eaglesfield* v. *Marquis of Londonderry* (1878), 26 W.R. 540, H.L. *per* Lord BLACKBURN at p. 541; *Goldrei Foucard & Son* v. *Sinclair*, [1918] 1 K.B. 180, C.A.

[4] See the authors' *Res Judicata* (2nd edn.) p. 385.

[5] As in *Ship* v. *Crosskill* (1870), L.R. 10 Eq. 73.

by him in his judgment against the principal as part of the *restitutio in integrum* ordered by the judgment[1]; but such sums may be recovered against the agent only in so far as they have not been recovered against the principal, and no further sum may be claimed against the agent, in such a case, beyond the amount which the principal must pay as part of the process of restitution.[2]

Damages for innocent misrepresentation: liability of principal and agent

156A The preceding paragraphs have examined the liability of a principal for damages for *fraud* where an allegedly fraudulent misrepresentation has been made, not by the defendant himself, but by his agent. The case will now be considered where damages are claimed from a principal for his agent's misrepresentation, but fraud is either not alleged, or is not satisfactorily proved; the misrepresentation is accordingly an innocent one. Before the passing of the Misrepresentation Act 1967 it was impossible to fix the principal with liability for damages for such misrepresentations, for no action lay in damages in the absence of fraud[3]; but since the passing of that Act an action for damages will lie, in cases in which an innocent misrepresentation has resulted in the representee entering into a contract upon the faith of it, subject however to the defence which the Act makes available to the representor, that the person making the representation had reasonable ground to believe, and did believe, up to the time the contract was made, that the facts represented were true.

There is as yet little authority on this subject; but it is submitted that the following rules may be found to govern the position, in cases in which the agent, in making the representation, does so within the scope of his authority, express or implied:

(1) Where the *agent* cannot prove that he had reasonable grounds to believe, and did believe, up to the time the contract was made, that the facts represented were true, he will himself be liable in damages.

(2) In such a case the principal will also be liable in damages, upon exactly the same principle as renders a principal liable for damages for the fraud of his agent, though he himself may have been innocent of any

---

1 It would so appear from the judgment of Lord ROMILLY M.R. in *Ship* v. *Crosskill* (1870), L.R. 10 Eq. 73 at pp. 82–83; there the claim failed on the facts, but the dictum has generally been accepted as authority on principle.

2 In the Australian case of *Sibley* v. *Grosvenor* (1916), 21 C.L.R. 469 (High Ct. of Aus.) the majority of the court held that damages *ultra* could be awarded against the agent; but it is here submitted that the dissenting judgment of ISAACS J. may be preferred.

3 The position is stated perhaps over-simply, no attention being paid to the *Hedley Byrne* type of action, as to which see the next paragraph.

fraud, and may in fact have generally believed in the truth of the representation which the agent, fraudulently, made within the scope of his authority.

(3) Where the agent can and does prove that he had reasonable grounds to believe, and did believe, up to the time the contract was made, that the representation was true, he will not himself be liable in damages. His principal will also escape liability, unless guilty of conduct amounting to fraud; for there seems no reason why he should be visited with responsibility for a misrepresentation innocently and *bona fide* made by his agent, in the absence of conduct on his part such as would make him liable for fraud in accordance with the rules set out in para. 156 above.

Liability of a principal for an agent's negligent misrepresentations

156B   It remains to mention the case of the liability of the principal *in negligence* for the consequences of the *negligent* misrepresentation of his agent, made within the scope of his authority, in cases in which, following the decision of the House of Lords in *Hedley Byrne & Co., Ltd.* v. *Heller & Partners, Ltd.*,[1] an action for damages will lie. Where the special relationship between plaintiff and defendant is proved, which is necessary to found such an action, the liability of the principal for the agent's negligence in making the representation will be governed by the ordinary principles of the law of agency. There are already ample illustrations in the Reports; and the cases will be found considered in some detail in Chapter XIX, *post*.

Implied authority

157   Where a principal is sought to be made liable, as a representor, for the misrepresentation of his agent, it is not often that an express command or authority can be proved, and the representee is generally compelled to resort to the doctrine of implied authority. This doctrine has been expressed in various language, but the substance and meaning, behind all the forms of words which have been used, is one and the same, and the principle is quite plain and clear, though its application to the facts of any particular case may be a matter of considerable nicety. A man is said to have the implied authority of another to make the representation which, being false, or false and fraudulent (as the case may be), is to render that other answerable for its consequences to the representee, when that representation was, and purported to be, made in the course

---

[1] [1963] 2 All E.R. 575; [1964] A.C. 465, H.L.

and within the scope and for the purposes of his service or employment or (where it is a case of partnership, which is mutual agency) of the partnership business or undertaking.[1]

So it was said by Lord BLACKBURN in *Houldsworth* v. *City of Glasgow Bank*,[2] referring to the decision of the House of Lords in *Barwick* v. *English Joint Stock Bank*,[3]

> "The substantial point decided was, as I think, that an innocent principal was civilly responsible for the fraud of his authorised agent acting within his authority, to the same extent as if it was his own fraud."

Of this observation Lord MACNAGHTEN said, in the later case of *Lloyd* v. *Grace, Smith & Co*.[4]:

> "I think, too, that the expressions 'acting within his authority', 'acting in the course of his employment', and the expression 'acting within the scope of his agency', (which *Story* uses) as applied to an agent, speaking broadly, mean one and the same thing. What is meant by those expressions is not easy to define with exactitude. To the circumstances of a particular case one may be more appropriate than the other."

In applying this principle to actual facts, the nature of the service, employment, business, or undertaking must first be proved (unless admitted), and the question then is whether making representations at all is within "the class of acts" which the alleged agent or partner is employed, or engages, to perform; and, if so, the further inquiry may become necessary whether the representation sued upon belongs to the class of representations which he is employed, or which it is part of the partnership business, to make.[5] If the proper answer to these questions is in the affirmative, the principal is liable as a representor; if either of them is answered in the negative, he is not.[6]

---

[1] *Barwick* v. *English Joint Stock Bank* (1867), L.R. 2 Exch. 259, Ex.Ch.

[2] (1880), 5 App. Cas. 317, at p. 339.

[3] (1867), L.R. 2 Exch. 259 Ex.Ch.

[4] [1912] A.C. 716, H.L., at p. 736.

[5] *Barwick* v. *English Joint Stock Bank* (1867), L.R. 2 Exch. 259, Ex.Ch. at p. 266: "He has put the agent in his place to do that class of acts, and he must be answerable for the manner in which the agent has conducted himself in doing the business which it was the act of the master to place him in." In *Australia*, see *Australasian Brokerage, Ltd.* v. *Australian and New Zealand Banking Corporation, Ltd.* (1934), 52 C.L.R. 430 (High Ct. of Aus.) *per* STARKE J. at p. 441; *per* DIXON, EVATT and McTIERNAN JJ. at p. 451.

[6] In most of the cases already cited above the implied authority was established, in accordance with the principles stated in the text: see particularly *Barwick* v. *English Joint Stock Bank*, *supra*; *Mackay* v. *Commercial Bank of New Brunswick* (1874), L.R. 5 P.C. 394; *Lloyd* v. *Grace, Smith & Co.*, [1912] A.C. 716, H.L. It is not necessary to cite these over again: it is more important, for the purpose of illustrating the above principles and the mode in which they have been applied to various kinds of employment and agency, to call attention to some of the cases where the implied authority was *not* established, such as: *Burnes* v. *Pennell* (1849), 2 H.L. Cas. 497 (director of company), *per* Lord CAMPBELL at pp. 519, 520; *Wheelton* v. *Hardisty* (1857), 8 E. & B. 232, Exch. Ch. (medical attendant and referee of assured not agents to make the

Forgery by agent

158 It has been suggested that whatever may be the position as to other fraudulent misrepresentations made by an agent pursuant to his actual or implied authority, a principal can never be liable for an agent's *forgery* unless he has expressly authorised it, the making and uttering of a forged document being a crime, as to the commission of which no agency can be imputed by law. This proposition was strenuously argued in a 1939 case,[1] in which C, the managing clerk in a solicitor's branch office, had defrauded a Building Society by the presentation of forged title deeds. It was held by ATKINSON J., and again (unanimously) by the Court of Appeal that there could be no difference in this regard between a fraudulent misrepresentation involving forgery and one which did not involve the commission of a crime; in both cases the question was simply whether the making of the representation was a matter as to which, on the facts of the case, the court would impute authority.[2]

Ratification

159 The act of a person in purporting to enter into a contract as agent for another, by whom he had not in fact been given the necessary authority, may be ratified by the person on whose behalf he purported to contract; and in the case of such a ratification the agent is deemed for the

---

contract, or therefore, to affect him by fraudulent misrepresentation), at pp. 260, 268–274, and 301, 302; *Re Northumberland and Durham District Banking Co., Ex parte Bigge* (1858), 28 L.J. Ch. 50 (a director of company), *per* KINDERSLEY V.-C.; *Re Liverpool Borough Bank, Duranty's Case* (1858), 26 Beav. 268 (another company case); *Re National Patent Steam Fuel Co., Ex parte Worth* (1859), 28 L.J. Ch. 589 (again a company case); *Re Royal British Bank, Ex parte Frowd* (1861), 30 L.J. Ch. 322 (bank clerk); *New Brunswick and Canada Railway and Land Co.* v. *Conybeare* (1862), 9 H.L. Cas. 711 (secretary of company); *Swift* v. *Jewsbury* (1874), L.R. 9 Q.B. 301, Exch. Ch. (bank manager), *per* Lord COLERIDGE C.J. at pp. 313–315; *Newlands* v. *National Employers' Accident Association Ltd.* (1885), 54 L.J. Q.B. 428, C.A. (secretary of a company), *per* BRETT M.R. at p. 430, and BOWEN L.J. at p. 431; *British Mutual Banking Co., Ltd.* v. *Charnwood Forest Rail. Co.* (1887), 18 Q.B.D. 714, C.A. (secretary of a company); *Lynde* v. *Anglo-Italian Hemp Spinning Co.*, [1896] 1 Ch. 178 (agent of company), *per* ROMER J. at pp. 184, 185; *Biggar* v. *Rock Life Assurance Co.*, [1902] 1 K.B. 516 (insurance agent) at pp. 524, 525; *Hoole* v. *Speak*, [1904] 2 Ch. 732 (a prospectus case); *M'Millan* v. *Accident Insurance Co., Ltd.*, 1907 S.C. 484 (insurance agency); *Hindle* v. *Brown* (1908), 98 L.T. 791, C.A. (auctioneer). In *Australia, Maye* v. *Colonial Mutual Life Assurance Society, Ltd.* (1924), 35 C.L.R. 14 (High Ct. of Aus.) (life assurance proposal).

1 *Uxbridge Permanent Benefit Building Society* v. *Pickard*, [1939] 1 K.B. 266 (ATKINSON J.); on appeal, [1939] 2 All E.R. 344; [1939] 2 K.B. 248, C.A.

2 In the report of the decision at first instance in [1939] 1 K.B. 266 ATKINSON J. said at p. 274: "It seems to me that in (*Ruben* v. *Great Fingall Consolidated*, [1906] A.C. 439, H.L. and *Kreditbank Cassel G.m.b.H.* v. *Schenkers, Ltd.*, [1927] 1 K.B. 826, C.A.) you have two authorities of the plainest kind showing that forgery is just like any other fraud. If it is committed within the ostensible authority of an agent the principal is liable". The decision was upheld by the Court of Appeal. Needless to say, it is not to be read as imposing any criminal liability upon the principal.

purposes of the contract to have received his authority as on the date when he purported to enter into the contract.[1]   An act constituting a tort may likewise, at least in the case of proprietary torts, be adopted by a person who takes the benefit of it—e.g. by him who ratifies the tort of conversion, himself enjoying or consuming the chattel converted.[2]

It has been suggested that he who elects to take the benefit of a contract induced by a fraudulent misrepresentation made by a person purporting (but without the necessary authority) to contract as his agent must take that benefit subject to liability for damages for the misrepresentation which induced it.[3]   So in *Lloyd* v. *Grace, Smith & Co.*[4]   Lord MACNAGHTEN said :

> "The only difference in my opinion between the case where the principal receives the benefit of the fraud and the case where he does not, is that in the latter case the principal is liable for the wrong done to the person defrauded by his agent acting within the scope of his agency, and in the former case he is liable on that ground and also on the ground that by taking the benefit he has adopted the act of his agent : he cannot approbate and reprobate."

But it is submitted that there is a distinction between ratifying the act of the agent in entering into the contract, and ratifying his fraudulent misrepresentation.[5]   If the facts about the representation are all known to the principal when he makes his election to ratify the contract, then doubtless he will be taken to have elected to accept the benefit of the contract subject to liability for the representation, and the words of Lord MACNAGHTEN quoted above will be given full weight.[6]   But election

---

[1] 1 Halsbury's Laws (4th Edn.) 452; *Keighley Maxsted & Co.* v. *Durant*, [1901] A.C. 240, H.L. at pp. 246–247, adopting *Wilson* v. *Tumman* (*infra*); *Koenigsblatt* v. *Sweet*, [1923] 2 Ch. 314.

[2] *Wilson* v. *Tumman* (1843), 6 Man. & G. 236 *per* TINDAL C.J. at p. 242 : "That an act done, for another, by a person, not assuming to act for himself, but for such other person, though without any precedent authority whatever, becomes the act of the principal, if subsequently ratified by him, is the known and well-established rule of law.   In that case the principal is bound by the act, whether it be for his detriment or his advantage, and whether it be founded on a tort or a contract, to the same extent as by, and with all the consequences which follow from, the same act done by his previous authority".

[3] Mr Spencer Bower so states in the second edition of this work para. 169 when he says : "A man may become liable as principal for the misrepresentation of another by adoption or ratification".   So, too, *Story on Agency* para. 452 : "The principal is not liable for the torts or negligences of his agent in any matters beyond the scope of his agency, unless he has expressly authorised them to be done, or he has subsequently adopted them for his own use or benefit"— a passage cited with approval by BLACKBURN J. at p. 145 of *McGowan & Co., Ltd.* v. *Dyer* (1873), L.R. 8 Q.B. 141 and by Lord MACNAGHTEN in *Lloyd* v. *Grace, Smith & Co., Ltd.*, [1912] A.C. 716, H.L., quoted in the text above.   *Cf. Burdett* v. *Horne* (1911), 28 T.L.R. 83, C.A.

[4] [1912] A.C. 716, H.L. at p. 738.

[5] The awkwardness involved in the proposition that a non-proprietary tort may be ratified is referred to by *Bowstead on Agency* (13th edn.) 37.

[6] See, for instance, the facts in *Burdett* v. *Horne* (1911), 28 T.L.R. 83, C.A.

always requires full knowledge by the elector; and if, in deciding to ratify the contract, he does so in ignorance of the fraudulent misrepresentation, it is difficult to see how the principal can be said to have elected to ratify this misrepresentation.[1]

Lord Tenterden's Act

160 By the provisions of Lord Tenterden's Act[2] no action may be brought whereby to charge any person upon or by reason of any representation made concerning the character, conduct or credit of any other person, to the intent or purpose that such other person may obtain money, credit, or goods thereupon, unless such representation is in writing, signed by the party to be charged therewith. This has been held to mean that a principal will not be liable upon such a representation by his agent, even if in writing and signed by the agent, if the principal has not himself signed.[3]

Lord Tenterden's Act, though available as a defence in actions in damages for fraudulent misrepresentations which are signed only by agents, has no application to actions for damages for negligence based on innocent misrepresentations of the type illustrated by *Hedley Byrne & Co., Ltd.* v. *Heller & Partners, Ltd.*[4]

Burden of proof and questions of fact and law

161 The burden is on the representee of establishing that the representation was made by the person charged as representor, or by his authority, where he did not personally make it. Where either personal representation or express authority is alleged, the issue is entirely one of

---

[1] In *Briess* v. *Woolley*, [1954] 1 All E.R. 909; [1954] A.C. 333, H.L. Lord OAKSEY found himself face to face with this difficulty when he said at p. 344: "My Lords, I think that on the authorities, and particularly in the judgments of the Court of Appeal in *Marsh* v. *Joseph*, [1897] 1 Ch. 213, it cannot be said that the shareholders ratified Rosher's agency up to October 14th 1948, as it was not proved that they had full knowledge of all the facts, or that there is sufficient evidence to make it clear that they intended to ratify whatever he had done".

[2] Statute of Frauds Amendment Act 1828 (9 Geo. IV, c. 14). For a fuller discussion of the effect of this Act see paras. 197 *et seq.*, Chapter XI, *post.*

[3] *Banbury* v. *Bank of Montreal*, [1918] A.C. 626, H.L. *Cf.* more recently *Hedley Byrne & Co.* v. *Heller & Partners, Ltd.*, [1963] 2 All E.R. 575; [1964] A.C. 465, H.L. and *W. B. Anderson & Sons, Ltd.* v. *Rhodes (Liverpool), Ltd.*, [1967] 2 All E.R. 850.

[4] [1963] 2 All E.R. 575; [1964] A.C. 465, H.L.

fact,[1] subject to the question of law whether there is any evidence at all of such representation or authority. Where, however, implied authority is alleged, though, subject as above,[2] it is a question of fact what the nature and terms of the employment or business in the particular case were, and what were the duties of the alleged agent,[3] it is a question of law whether, from the proved or admitted facts in relation to these matters, the authority is to be implied,[4] and, where the terms of the employment are wholly contained in any document, it is for the court to construe that document.

---

[1] It will be found that it was so treated in all the cases cited in this chapter in which express authority was alleged, and the matter was one of dispute—see, for example *Ludgater* v. *Love* (1881), 44 L.T. 694, C.A., where, on both trials of the action, it was left to the jury to say whether the defendant had authorised his son to make the representation he had made.

[2] *Thorne* v. *Heard and Marsh*, [1895] A.C. 495, H.L., *per* Lord HERSCHELL L.C. at p. 502: "it appears to me perfectly clear that, in order to charge any person with a fraud which has not been personally committed by him, the agent who has committed the fraud must have committed it while acting within the scope of his authority, while doing something and purporting to do something on behalf of the principal . . . if the person, although he has been employed as agent, is not, in the transaction which is the wrongful act, acting for or purporting to be acting for the principal, it seems to me impossible to treat that as the fraud of the principal. Now, in this case there is no pretence for saying"—(this expression may be regarded as equivalent to "there is no evidence")—"that in what he did that was fraudulent . . . Searle was acting for the respondents."

[3] In *Newlands* v. *National Employers' Accident Association, Ltd.* (1885), 54 L.J. Q.B. 428, C.A., it was pointed out that no "practice or regular course of business" of the society had been proved by evidence, which would support the averment that its secretary had authority to make a representation of the kind which he in fact made (implying, that the issue was one of fact, on which evidence was receivable), and that, as there was no such evidence, it was a conclusion of law that no implication of authority could be made (*per* BRETT M.R. at p. 430, and BOWEN L.J. at p. 431). See also *British Mutual Banking Co., Ltd.* v. *Charnwood Forest Rail. Co.* (1887), 18 Q.B.D. 714, C.A., where it had been left to the jury at the trial to say whether the secretary of the company had been held out as a person to answer inquiries, and the jury had answered in the affirmative, but the C.A. held that from the whole of the facts proved and found no authority could be inferred in law (*per* Lord ESHER M.R. at pp. 716, 717, and BOWEN L.J. at pp. 717–719).

[4] See pp. 415, 416 of *Mackay* v. *Commercial Bank of New Brunswick* (1874), L.R. 5 P.C. 394, and the two authorities cited in the last note.

CHAPTER IX

Who are deemed Parties to a Representation—II: The Representee

Introductory

162 In order to sustain any action or proceeding in respect of misrepresentation, it is as essential to show that the representation was made to one whom the law deems to be a representee, as it is to prove that it was made by one whom the law deems to be a representor. Having then in the previous chapter discussed who is legally accountable as a representor, we must now consider what persons may in law claim relief as representees.

Representee defined

163 A representee is described in Article 1 of the Code as including any person either to whom the representation is directly and immediately made, or to whose notice, though not so made to him, it is intended to come, and does come. This intention may be proved to have been expressed by the representor, when making the representation, to the person to whom he made it in the first instance, as when he is shewn to have requested or authorised that person to pass it on or repeat it to the person whom it was intended to reach, who then becomes the representee. Or such intention may be inferred from the representor's proved knowledge, when making the representation, that any statement he made as to the subject-matter of the transaction would be so passed on, and from all the circumstances of the case. It results from this general rule that there are three classes of persons to whom a representation may be deemed to have been made: (i) the person to whom it was physically and directly made, or his principal, or partner; (ii) a specific person, not being the person to whom the representation was immediately made, nor his principal or partner, but whom the representor, either expressly or presumptively, intended it to reach and affect; and (iii) any member of the public, or of a section or class of the community, who acts upon any representation addressed in the first instance not to any specific individual, but to such public, or section or class, and who accordingly thereupon becomes a representee.[1]

The person to whom the representation is actually made, or his principal or partner

164   The first of the three classes of representee above referred to is an obvious one.   If the representation is made to A solely and directly, with no other person in contemplation, A is plainly the sole representee. It is equally manifest that, if it is made by the representor to A, with knowledge that A is merely the agent of B to receive the communication, or the agent for that purpose of some one who, though not disclosed at the time, afterwards turns out to be B, or if without there being any such knowledge on the part of the representor, A is in fact for that purpose agent of B who afterwards intervenes as principal, and enters into a contract with the representor on the faith of the representation,—then, in any of such cases, the representee, and the only representee, is B, and the person to whom the statement is immediately and physically made is merely the agent to convey it to such representee, or the medium or messenger through whom the transmission is effected, just as if he were a telegraphic or telephonic instrument.[2]   On the other hand, the representation may be made to B through A, but still with the intention that A shall also be influenced by it, and act upon it, or with the knowledge that B is A's partner or joint contractor or associated with him in the business in question, or is about to be so associated, in either of

---

[1] *Swift* v. *Winterbotham* (1873), L.R. 8 Q.B. 244, where Cockburn C.J. at p. 253, includes the three classes mentioned in the text in his statement of the rule: "it is now well established that, in order to enable a person injured by a false representation to sue for damages, it is not necessary that the representation should be made directly; it is sufficient if the representation is made to a third person to be communicated to the plaintiff, or to be communicated to a class of persons of whom the plaintiff is one, or even if it is made to the public generally, with a view to its being acted on, and the plaintiff, as one of the public acts on it, and suffers damage thereby." The soundness of the above proposition was in no way impugned or affected by the Exchequer Chamber, when, *sub nom. Swift* v. *Jewsbury* (1874), L.R. 9 Q.B. 301, Exch. Ch., they reversed the actual decision in this case, on the ground that the alleged *representor* could not be so deemed in law.

[2] For instance, in *Haycraft* v. *Creasy* (1801), 2 East 92, the defendant made the misrepresentation to the plaintiff's son, and afterwards to his brother, in answer to inquiries made by these two persons professedly on behalf of the plaintiff; and in *Gilbert* v. *Endean* (1878), 9 Ch.D. 259, C.A., the solicitor of one party made the representation to the solicitor of the other.

which cases both A and B may become the representees, if both act upon the representation.

Questions of considerable nicety may arise where, for instance, the representations are made to an agent for an undisclosed principal. Where, in such a case, an agent has contracted in circumstances importing that he is the real and only principal, the result will be that the principal cannot sue on the contract; and, not being able to sue on the contract, he may not sue for rescission of the contract into which, influenced by the misrepresentation, his agent has entered on his behalf. In such a case the only person able to obtain rescission is the agent; and in order to succeed he must prove that he was himself induced by the representations to enter into the contract.[1]

Any person to whom the representor actually or presumptively intended the representation to be passed on

165   But, further, even where B is not known or believed to be, and is not in fact, the principal or partner of, or otherwise associated with A, the representor may yet either accompany his representation to A with a direct instruction or authority to repeat it to B, or make it with an implied intent that it shall come to the notice of B, and be acted on by him—such implication being made from the representor's express declarations or admissions, or from his making the representation with knowledge that A intends to pass it on to B, for him to act upon,[2] or with knowledge subsequently acquired, but before B has acted upon it, that A has so passed it on to B for that purpose.[3]   In any such case B is deemed

---

[1] *Collins* v. *Associated Greyhound Racecourses, Ltd.*, [1930] 1 Ch. 1 (LUXMOORE J.) at pp. 19–20. The decision was affirmed in the Court of Appeal—*ibid.*, p. 28.

[2] This was the case in *Langridge* v. *Levy* (1837), 2 M. & W. 519; in error, *Levy* v. *Langridge* (1838), 4 M. & W. 337, Exch. Ch., where the plaintiff's father, to whom the representation (that the gun sold had been made by Nock, and was a good and safe gun) had been addressed, expressly told the defendant that the gun was intended for the use of himself and his sons (see pp. 520, 521, and 530, 531, of the report of the case in the Court of Exchequer), and it was held that the plaintiff, who lost his hand in consequence of the gun exploding, was entitled to recover. Similarly, in *Swift* v. *Winterbotham* (1873), L.R. 8 Q.B. 244, the nature of bank business, as proved by evidence at the trial, was such that it must have been "within the contemplation of the defendants when the representation was made, that it would or might be communicated to the customer of the bank on whose behalf it was sought". Though the decision was reversed by the Exchequer Chamber, the reversal was on grounds which left the above statement quite unimpeached. *Cf. Parsons* v. *Barclay & Co., Ltd.* (1910), 103 L.T. 196, C.A.; *Wells* v. *Smith*, [1914] 3 K.B. 722; *Paul and Vincent, Ltd.* v. *O'Reilly* (1913), 49 I.L.T. 89.

[3] As in *Pilmore* v. *Hood* (1838), 5 Bing. N.C. 97, where the defendant, in order to induce one Bowman to take a lease of a public house, had told him a falsehood, and afterwards, Bowman being unable to complete, and the defendant accepting the plaintiff as his lessee in his stead, Bowman, to the defendant's knowledge, passed on the fraudulent representation to the plaintiff

to be the representee, if and as soon as the representation has been so passed on to him, and he has altered his position on the faith of it, whether A is or is not also to be accounted a representee, which depends upon the question whether he was intended *solely* as the living medium of communication, or as a person himself to be influenced by the statement, as well as the transmitter of the influence to B, which again depends upon all the circumstances of the individual case.[1] Whenever such intention is neither established directly by evidence, nor as an implication from the proved or admitted facts, B is not in law the representee[2]; A, of course, is; but, in most of the cases which raise the question, he fails on the ground that he was not the person injured.[3]

In *New South Wales* it has been held that a representation made to the promoter of a company not yet formed, with the intention that it should be passed on to, and acted upon by, the company when formed, is to be deemed a representation *to the company*.[4]

A member of a class of persons to whom the representation is addressed

166 In a certain class of action on contract, the futile objection has frequently been raised that a man "cannot contract with the world", to which the obvious answer is that, assuming this to be so, it is nevertheless true that you can make a proposal to the public, or to a class of the community, or to a body of undesignated persons, which proposal any individual member of the public, or of the class or body in question, by word or act, may accept, and that, on his doing so, a valid contract is

---

which was held enough to entitle the latter to recover, as the representee (*per* TINDAL C.J. at pp. 105, 106, and BOSANQUET J. at pp. 108, 109). *Cf. Gross v. Lewis Hillman, Ltd.*, [1970] Ch. 445, C.A., particularly *per* CROSS L.J. at p. 461.

[1] To take an illustration from a familiar type of case, A may hand or address a prospectus, circular, or announcement of any kind, to B (i) with express instructions not to communicate it to any one else, but to regard it as private and personal, or (ii) for the sole purpose of his passing it on, as a mere distributing agent, to C, or a class of which C is one, or (iii) with the intention that B shall act upon it, and also pass it on to his friends, of whom C is one, or to a class to which both B and C belong, as in *Levy v. Langridge, supra*. In case (i), B is ordinarily held to be the sole representee but not necessarily so, if the circumstances of the case, in their entirety, point to a different conclusion, as e.g. in the case cited in note 4 to para. 166, *post*; with which contrast *Edinburgh United Breweries, Ltd. v. Molleson*, [1894] A.C. 96, H.L., where it was not alleged or proved that the misrepresentation made to Dunn was intended to be, or was in fact, "passed on" to the pursuer company, and where it was clear that whatever implied representation Dunn made to the company was not a transmitted, but an independent and different representation (*per* Lord HERSCHELL L.C. at pp. 109–112); in case (ii) C is the sole representee, as in *Gerhard v. Bates*, as to which see note 5 to para. 166, *post*; in case (iii), both B and C are representees.

[2] See the cases cited in the notes to paras. 167–170, *post*.

[3] See the same cases.

[4] *Leslie Leithead Pty., Ltd. v. Barber* (1965), 65 N.S.W.S.R. 172.

created between him and the proposer[1]; and, on the same principle, a representation, no less than an offer, may be made to a class, with the object of inducing as many members of it as possible to take a certain course, whereupon any individual belonging to the class who can prove that he in fact acted upon the representation so made, acquires rights (all other ingredients in the particular cause of action being also established) against the representor[2]; for, as has been well said,

> "it is not a bad rule that any one who makes a fraudulent representation, which is intended to be generally circulated, should be liable to any person injured by acting upon it, however remote the consequences may be".[3]

Consequently, any person who by a prospectus, circular, report, or other similar document addressed to the public, is induced to subscribe for shares or debentures in a public undertaking,[4] or by any advertisement or like document, issued when the company is a going concern, is induced to purchase such shares or debentures in the market,[5] or by any

---

[1] *Carlill* v. *Carbolic Smoke Ball Co.*, [1893] 1 Q.B. 256, C.A., *per* LINDLEY L.J. at p. 262, BOWEN L.J. at pp. 268, 269, and A. L. SMITH L.J. at p. 274.

[2] In fact, any person whose practice or profession depends for its success upon delusive statements prefers to operate upon the multitude, rather than upon specific persons, whether the statements are addressed orally to an assembly, or in print through e.g. newspapers. Mr Spencer Bower, in earlier editions, adds a scholarly note which ranges from Herodotus to Coleridge.

[3] *Per* BRAMWELL B. at p. 548 of *Bedford* v. *Bagshaw* (1859), 4 H. & N. 538.

[4] *Re Royal British Bank, Ex parte Brockwell* (1857), 26 L.J. Ch. 855, where the plaintiff took three shares in the Bank issued under a second charter, which they had recently acquired, on the faith of a half-yearly report, and it was held *per* KINDERSLEY V.-C. at p. 862, that "the representation was intended not only to delude existing shareholders, but to induce *the public* to take new shares just issued", and none the less because the report was headed, "For the use of the proprietors only".

[5] *R.* v. *De Berenger* (1814), 3 M. & S. 67, where Lord ELLENBOROUGH C.J. at p. 73, described the offence charged (spreading rumours of the death of Napoleon, and the imminent conclusion of peace) as "a fraud levelled against all the public"; but see para. 171, *post*, as to the doubts which have been expressed by high authority whether any of such persons would have had a civil remedy against De Berenger; *Shrewsbury* v. *Blount* (1841), 2 Man. & G. 475, where, as the jury found, the plaintiff had been induced to purchase shares by misrepresentations contained in the company's scrip-certificates and advertisements; *Gerhard* v. *Bates* (1853), 2 E. & B. 476, where the second count of the declaration alleged that the defendant had made fraudulent misrepresentations *to the Stock Exchange*, "with intent to injure and deceive *the public*", and that "the defendant, by means of the said false and fraudulent representations, *induced the plaintiff* to become the *purchaser* and bearer of" the shares in question; and it was held on demurrer that this count was good, or, in other words, that the plaintiff had sufficiently *averred* that he was a representee (whatever difficulties he might afterwards encounter *in proof*, having regard to the fact that the document said to have contained the misrepresentations was a prospectus); *Scott* v. *Dixon* (1859), 29 L.J. Ex. 62 n., where copies of a report containing a false statement that profits had been earned by a banking company which were available for a dividend, and that the shares were a safe investment, were left by the directors at the bank premises for distribution to any broker or other member of the public who came to make inquiries, and it was held that though the report was originally issued to the shareholders, who were primarily the representees, it was also addressed, in the manner described, to any member of the public; *R.* v. *Aspinall* (1876), 2 Q.B.D. 48, C.A., a criminal case, but, according to

published misrepresentation is induced to do either or both of such things, if the misrepresentation was intended or calculated to bring about either or both of such results,[1] is, immediately on so acting, deemed a representee. So also, any member of the public to whom a negotiable instrument "may be offered in the course of circulation",[2] or to whom an advertisement offering a situation is published,[3] or who is invited by public announcement to attend an auction sale,[4] or to whom a time-table of trains is issued by a railway company,[5] is in like manner, and under the like conditions, entitled to all the rights which any person might claim to whom the representation had been made directly and individually.

Questions of law and fact

167 The question whether the party claiming relief in respect of any misrepresentation was, or was not, the representee, or one of the representees, is a question of fact, and the subject, therefore, of evidence[6]; but the question whether there is any evidence of this fact, and also the question whether, on the proved and admitted facts of the case, the repre-

---

BRETT J.A. at pp. 57, 59, the same rules as to allegation and proof apply to both civil and criminal proceedings for fraudulent misrepresentation made to the public;—but as to this dictum see paras. 171 and 174 below; *Scott* v. *Brown, Doering, McNab & Co.*, [1892] 2 Q.B. 724, C.A., where, by acts and conduct ("rigging the market"), the parties had made fraudulent misrepresentations as to the value of the shares to induce members of the public to purchase in the market.

1 In *Andrews* v. *Mockford*, [1896] 1 Q.B. 372, C.A., where it was held that the prospectus issued by the directors, and a fabricated telegram, purporting to come from the mine, were intended to produce conjointly a double effect, *viz.* on the one hand, to induce subscriptions for the shares by "strengthening" the prospectus, and, on the other, to induce purchases in the market.

2 *Polhill* v. *Walter* (1832), 3 B. & Ad. 114, *per cur.* at pp. 123, 124, where it was held that the statement by a man that he has authority to accept a bill of exchange "is made to all to whom the bill may be offered in the course of circulation, and is *in fact intended to be made to all*, and the plaintiff is one of them"; *West London Commercial Bank* v. *Kitson* (1884), 13 Q.B.D. 360, C.A., where a similar representation was held to have been made to any member of the class of persons who might discount the bill (*per* BRETT M.R. at pp. 361–2).

3 *R.* v. *Silverlock*, [1894] 2 Q.B. 766, where a count in an indictment was held good, which averred that an advertisement for a housekeeper was a false pretence to *all his Majesty's subjects*, by means of which "the accused" did unlawfully obtain from *the prosecutrix* certain property.

4 *Robinson* v. *Wall* (1847), 2 Ph. 372 *per* Lord COTTENHAM L.C. at pp. 374, 375; and see Chapter XV, *post.*

5 *Denton* v. *Great Northern Rail. Co.* (1856), 5 E. & B. 860.

6 In *Swift* v. *Winterbotham* (1873), L.R. 8 Q.B. 244, evidence was given of the practice of one bank making communications to another bank, for the purpose of their being transmitted to a customer of such other bank; and, in *Bedford* v. *Bagshaw* (1859), 4 H. & N. 538, there was similar evidence as to the practice of the Stock Exchange Committee, and rules of the Stock Exchange (see p. 545).

sentation must, or must not, be deemed to have been made to the alleged representee, are questions of law.[1]

Burden of proof

168   It is incumbent on the party who asserts a right to relief in respect of a misrepresentation to allege,[2] and, having so alleged, to prove, that he was the representee, or one of the representees.[3]   Where the representation was made, if at all, directly and immediately to the alleged representee, little or no difficulty is experienced, as a rule, in discharging the burden.   It is when the communication is said to have been made in the first instance, not to the alleged representee, but to a third person, with intent that it should be "passed on", or to have been addressed to a class of whom the alleged representee claims to be one, that nice questions arise, and the burden may be peculiarly heavy.[4]   But, whether onerous or light, the duty of sustaining it is clear, and in every case where the evidence, or the proper inference to be drawn from it, was not adequate for the purpose, the party setting up the misrepresentation has been held disentitled to relief.

169   Thus, in reference to the case of a specific individual whom the representor is alleged to have intended his representation to reach and influence and mislead, though made directly to a third person, the allegation requires very cogent and precise proof, which in many cases has not been forthcoming, whereupon either the fact has been found against

---

[1] For instance, in *Gerhard* v. *Bates* (1853), 2 E. & B. 476, which was a demurrer, *Bedford* v. *Bagshaw, supra, Swift* v. *Winterbotham, supra, R.* v. *Aspinall* (1876), 2 Q.B.D. 48, C.A., *Salaman* v. *Warner* (1891), 65 L.T. 132, C.A., *R.* v. *Silverlock*, [1894] 2 Q.B. 766, *Andrews* v. *Mockford*, [1896] 1 Q.B. 372, C.A., and in many others of the cases cited in this section, the question of law was, whether the facts alleged in the declaration, statement of claim, or indictment, or proved at the trial, sufficiently disclosed a cause of action, or offence, that is, constituted *any* evidence that the plaintiff was the person, or one of the persons, to whom the false representation or pretence had been made.

[2] Amongst the other omissions which made a count of the declaration in *Behn* v. *Kemble* (1859), 7 C.B. N.S. 260, bad in law, was the omission "to aver that any representation was made *to the plaintiff*".

[3] See *Collins* v. *Associated Greyhound Racecourses, Ltd.*, [1930] 1 Ch. 1 *per* LUXMOORE J. at p. 20; on appeal, *per* Lord HANWORTH M.R. at p. 31.

[4] Lord HATHERLEY (then WOOD V.-C.) must have been intending to refer to the greater precision and difficulty of proof in cases of transmitted representation than in those where the representation was direct, when drawing the distinction which he apparently did between the *alleganda et probanda* in his first rule and the necessary elements of proof in his second and third rules,—a distinction which (except as here explained) there is some reason to think unjustified: the point is dealt with in the 2nd edition, p. 157.

the alleged representee, or, if found in his favour, the court has held that there was no evidence to justify such a finding.[1]

170   Again, where the representation is made to a class of which the alleged representee claims to be a member, difficult problems frequently present themselves. In all such cases "there must always be this evidence against the person to be charged, namely, that the plaintiff was one of the persons to whom he contemplated that the representation should be made".[2]   And, further, unless there is direct evidence of the representor's declarations and admissions of his intention on that behalf, which is not often available, the nature of the representation must be carefully examined; for, on such examination, in the light of not only any evidence which is necessary and admissible but also such ordinary practices in the affairs of life as the courts will take judicial notice of,[3] it is often found that, though a class of persons was obviously intended to be deceived thereby, the class in question was not a class to which the alleged representee belongs, in which case the burden of proof is not discharged; as, for instance, where a plaintiff claims to have been induced to purchase shares in the market by a prospectus or other document the primary office and nature of which is to induce, not purchases, but applications for allotment,[4] or, conversely, to subscribe for shares

---

[1] Thus, in *Longmeid* v. *Holliday* (1851), 6 Exch. 761, the misrepresentation as to the lamp which injured the plaintiff was made not to her, but to her husband, who had not brought to the notice of the defendant, nor was the defendant otherwise proved to have known, that it was intended for the plaintiff's use, and it was accordingly held that the plaintiff had not proved that she was the representee, or a representee (*per* PARKE B. delivering the judgment of the court at p. 776). This case may be usefully contrasted with *Langridge* v. *Levy*, cited in note 2 to para. 165, *ante*, where the father of the plaintiff *had* expressly informed the representor that the gun was intended for the plaintiff's use, which of course makes all the difference, for, as was afterwards pointed out by the court at pp. 1052, 1053 of *Blakemore* v. *Bristol and Exeter Rail. Co.* (1858), 8 E. & B. 1035, "if in that case a friend of the father or son, by their permission, had used the gun and sustained the accident, we apprehend . . . no action could have been maintained by him", and still less, as observed by WOOD V.-C. at pp. 17, 18, 24 of *Barry* v. *Croskey* (1861), 2 John & H. 1, would a stranger, finding the gun, and using it without permission, and sustaining injury in consequence, have had any cause of action as a representee. See also *Collins* v. *Cave* (1860), 6 H. & N. 131, Exch. Ch., at p. 134 ("it is alleged that the representation was made with a view to induce Charles Collins"—not the plaintiff, who was William Collins—" . . . we do not see that the damage which the plaintiff alleges himself to have sustained arose from the acts of the defendant").

[2] *Bedford* v. *Bagshaw* (1859), 4 H. & N. 538 *per* POLLOCK C.B. at p. 548. Though it may be doubted—see para. 172, *infra*—whether the rule so stated was correctly applied to the facts in that case, no-one has doubted the soundness of the rule itself.

[3] *Polhill* v. *Walter* (1832), 3 B. & Ad. 114 (*per cur.* at p. 124): "the plaintiff must be taken to have intended that all such persons should act upon the faith of that representation, because that, *in the ordinary course of business*, is its natural and necessary result".

[4] Ordinarily, the function of a prospectus is exhausted when the application-lists are closed, and subscriptions have, or have not, been secured by the representations contained therein, and a subsequent purchaser of shares in the market cannot, without cogent and express evidence,

by a representation obviously intended to induce only a purchase[1]; or where a shareholder complains of a misrepresentation made by a director of the company to brokers improperly seeking to elicit from him information as to the company's affairs[2]; or where a member of the public, as such, claims to have sustained injury in consequence of an implied misrepresentation addressed to a more limited class to which he does not belong[3]; or, where a company complains of its agents' fraudulent statements not to it, but to the public.[4]

"*Stock Exchange*" *misrepresentations*

171 There is a group of cases which ought in conclusion to be mentioned, in which persons have brought it about, in one way or another, that those dealing in certain kinds of securities, particularly upon the Stock Exchange, should be persuaded of the happening of some event, or the fulfilment of some condition, upon the happening or fulfilment of which some given issue of securities, or the market in general, would be likely to rise or fall, whereupon such persons have bought or sold the securities in question upon the faith of the false

---

be heard to say that the prospectus formed an inducement to him to effect such purchase, or contained any representation addressed to him with that object, or otherwise : *Peek* v. *Gurney* (1873), L. R. 6 H.L. 377 (*per* Lord CHELMSFORD at pp. 395–400, and Lord CAIRNS at pp. 410–413); *Salaman* v. *Warner* (1891), 65 L.T. 132, C.A. But it must be remembered that nothing was decided in the above cases beyond this, that a connection between the prospectus and the purchase by the alleged representee, who claims in that character, will not be presumed, but must be proved. Where such connection is distinctly alleged, as it was in *Gerhard* v. *Bates* (1853), 2 E. & B. 476, or clearly established by evidence, as it was in *Andrews* v. *Mockford*, [1896] 1 Q.B. 372, C.A., the burden of allegation in the one case, and of proof in the other, is discharged.

1 *Re National Patent Steam Fuel Co.*, *Ex parte Worth* (1859), 28 L.J. Ch. 589, where it was held that no representation had been made to the plaintiff in the character of an applicant for allotment of shares, in which character he claimed, but only a representation to him as a contemplated purchaser, from a director, of a particular block of shares.

2 *Tackey* v. *McBain*, [1912] A.C. 186, P.C.

3 In *Blakemore* v. *Bristol and Exeter Rail. Co.* (1858), 8 E. & B. 1035, the defendants, in providing a crane for the unloading of goods by consignees, were held to have made an implied representation (by acts and conduct) to the class of consignees, and their employees, but not to the public at large. One Harvey was a consignee, and, with two assistants in his regular employ, used the crane for the above purpose, and, in so doing, called in the plaintiff, a member of the public, to help his assistants, and the plaintiff, when so engaged, was injured, and sued on the theory and averment that the defendants had "professed *to the public*" that the crane was safe : but the court held that the only "profession" made was to Harvey, as a consignee, and the two assistants he brought with him, and that the burden was on the plaintiff to show that the defendants knew, or *must* have known, that Harvey would require further assistance from outside, and that, this burden not having been discharged, the action failed. *Cf.* the cases considered in the text in paras. 171–175, *infra*.

4 *Vigers* v. *Pike* (1842), 8 Cl. & Fin. 562, *per* Lord COTTENHAM L.C. at pp. 646, 647; *Overend and Gurney Co.* v. *Gibb* (1872), L.R. 5 H.L. 480, *per* Lord CHELMSFORD at p. 501; *Re Ambrose Lake Tin and Copper Mining Co.*, *Ex parte Taylor*, *Ex parte Moss* (1880), 14 Ch.D. 390, C.A., *per* BRETT L.J. at p. 397, and COTTON L.J. at p. 399.

information, thereby suffering loss. *R.* v. *De Berenger*[1] the first of these
to be considered, was a prosecution for criminal conspiracy, in which
it was alleged that De Berenger and seven others had conspired together
to spread rumours generally among the public that Napoleon Bonaparte
had been killed, and that peace between France and England was imminent. Though it was held that what had been done was "a fraud levelled
against all the public",[2] it does not seem to the author of this edition to
be a case of much significance in the present treatise[3]; for it seems to
him doubtful whether any member of the public could have had a *civil*
claim by reason of what was done by the conspirators.[4]

172 *Bagshaw* v. *Seymour*[5] and *Bedford* v. *Bagshaw*[6] are the next two
cases in this group. The former is mentioned only by way of introduction to the latter, in which *Bagshaw* v. *Seymour* was treated as a binding
authority.[7] In *Bedford* v. *Bagshaw* the defendant, who was chairman of the
board of directors of a company, was alleged to have falsely represented
to the Committee of the Stock Exchange that the requisite proportion of
the company's share capital had been subscribed in cash, which was a
condition precedent to the obtaining of an official listing of the shares
of the company on the Stock Exchange; so that any one apprised of the
fact that the shares were officially listed would be led (so it was argued)
to believe that the necessary subscription had in fact been made. This
was held by the Court of Exchequer to be an implied representation not
only to the members of the Stock Exchange Committee directly, but
also indirectly and inferentially, to "all persons buying shares on the
Stock Exchange", who "must be considered as persons to whom it was
contemplated that the representation would be made".[8] It is to be observed that the Chief Baron had, before applying it to the particular
circumstances, first laid down the general rule to be followed in all such

---

[1] (1814), 3 M. & S. 67.

[2] By Lord ELLENBOROUGH C.J. at p. 73.

[3] Though discussed by Mr Spencer Bower at some length in earlier editions.

[4] This view is not the present author's alone; Lord HATHERLEY, then Sir W. PAGE WOOD
V.-C., expressed the same opinion in *Barry* v. *Croskey* (1861), 2 John & H. 1 at pp. 18–19;
and RIGBY L.J. in *Andrews* v. *Mockford*, [1896] 1 Q.B. 372, C.A. at pp. 384–385. See, too,
Salaman v. *Warner* (1891), 65 L.T. 132, C.A.

[5] (1856), 18 C.B. 903.

[6] (1859), 4 H. & N. 538.

[7] Mr Spencer Bower in the 2nd edition, pointed out that *Bagshaw* v. *Seymour* had a very
curious history, in that it appears to have been decided in the House of Lords *without argument*.
For this reason he treated it as of questionable authority, and proceeded to consider whether
Bedford v. *Bagshaw*, which had been fully argued, had been correctly decided.

[8] (1859), 4 H. & N. 538 *per* POLLOCK C.B. at p. 548.

cases in carefully guarded terms,[1] which have already been cited in this text,[2] and which were pointed and emphasised by his further remark that he was

> "not prepared to lay down as a general rule that, if a person makes a false representation, every one to whom it is repeated, and who acts upon it, may sue him",

and by the illustration given by BRAMWELL B. that

> 'it would be a strong thing to hold that if a man makes a verbal untrue statement to any person, as for instance, that the shares in a particular company are a valuable security, if that person buys and recommends his friends to buy, that he is to be liable to any one who buys on the faith of that representation".[3]

It was held by the Court of Exchequer that the facts of the case before them satisfied the conditions specified in the rule, and were not like those of the illustration, which failed to do so. From this decision, so far as regards the particular application of the rule in that case (not the rule itself) and also from the result of *Bagshaw* v. *Seymour*, Lord CHELMSFORD, in the later case of *Peek* v. *Gurney*,[4] expressed the strongest possible dissent ("the decisions, and the grounds on which they proceeded, appear to me to be extraordinary, and I cannot bring my mind to agree with them").

The statement in the heading of *Peek* v. *Gurney* that the House of Lords overruled these two decisions, says Mr Spencer Bower in commenting on the latter case,[5] is "absolutely incorrect". Noticing that Lord CAIRNS in his judgment in *Peek* v. *Gurney* makes no express criticism of *Bedford* v. *Bagshaw*, and recalling the observations upon the case by BRETT J.A.[6] and AMPHLETT J.A.[7] "in a case where the circumstances were precisely the same",[8] and those of A. L. SMITH L.J. in "a still

---

[1] *Ibid.*

[2] In para. 170, *ante.*

[3] Both the further observation of POLLOCK C.B., and the illustration of BRAMWELL J., are at p. 548.

[4] (1873), L.R. 6 H.L. 377, at p. 397.

[5] 2nd edn., p. 188.

[6] At p. 57 of *R.* v. *Aspinall* (1876), 2 Q.B.D. 48, C.A. *R.* v. *Aspinall* is discussed a little later in the text above. Though the *facts* were similar, it is submitted by the present author that a prosecution for criminal conspiracy does not furnish any adequate test of the definition of a representee.

[7] *Ibid.*, at p. 65.

[8] "The only difference", says Mr Spencer Bower in a footnote to the second edition at p. 188, "was in the form of proceeding"; the misrepresentation being charged in the one case as a civil wrong and in the other as a criminal offence. But is this not a distinction of importance? The present author adverts to it in the text above.

more recent case'',[1] he concluded that the decision in *Bedford* v. *Bagshaw* may be regarded as sound.

To the mind of the author of this edition the matter seems more doubtful. It seems to him that it is impossible to dispense with the essential requirement that a plaintiff must be at the least a member of a class of persons to whom the representation was addressed, and that having reached him it caused him to incur damage intended or actually or imputedly foreseen by the representor. It is not sufficient, he submits, that the plaintiff should have been induced to incur damage, albeit of a kind which would naturally flow from the representations of the defendants, if he has acted, not upon the faith of any representations by them, but by reason of conduct, or the separate representations, of other persons to whose notice the original representations actually came.

For this reason he prefers the view of Lord CHELMSFORD in *Peek* v. *Gurney* to those of the other authorities which Mr Spencer Bower mentioned in earlier editions. It does not seem to him that it was really possible, on the evidence in *Bedford* v. *Bagshaw* as it is reported, to hold that the representations of the defendants ever went further than the committee of the Stock Exchange; and it would appear to him that whatever action the plaintiff took was taken on the faith of what the committee did, and not on the faith of any repetition to him of the original representation.

Barry v. *Croskey: Peek* v. *Gurney*

173 In *Barry* v. *Croskey*,[2] a case which has already been cited in an earlier chapter,[3] the facts appear to have been very similar to those in *Bedford* v. *Bagshaw*; but it was a demurrer case, and in this case again it does not appear to have been argued, at least so far as the Report goes, that there had been no effective representation made *to the plaintiffs*, as distinct from the Committee of the Stock Exchange. The approval by PAGE WOOD V.-C. of the judgment of POLLOCK C.B. in *Bedford* v. *Bagshaw* must be read as having been made without reference to this point.

---

[1] *Scott* v. *Brown, Doering, McNab & Co.*, [1892] 2 Q.B. 724, C.A. The passage from the judgment of A. L. SMITH L.J. is set out in the text in para. 175. What he said, when considered against the background of the facts in that case, was undoubtedly good law; for in that case the representations (of a fictitious price for the shares) had been made, via the Stock Exchange list, *to the public*. But in *Bedford* v. *Bagshaw* it is submitted that no representation was made to the public, and that the representation made to the Committee was spent when the Committee acted upon it and listed the shares of the company.

[2] (1861), 2 John & H. 1.

[3] Chapter VII, note 2 on p. 166, *ante*.

In *Peek* v. *Gurney*[1] the plaintiff, who had purchased shares on the market from an original allottee thereof, suffered loss when they were discovered to be worth less than he had paid for them. He alleged that he had relied upon misrepresentations contained in the prospectus which the promoters of the company had issued to prospective subscribers. It was held that it was necessary for him to show some direct connection between the promoters and himself in the communication of the prospectus, and that in this case the prospectus, being issued as a representation to intending subscribers only, could not be regarded as a representation upon which the plaintiff could rely, as a purchaser from such a subscriber. It was in this case that Lord CHELMSFORD, referring to *Bagshaw* v. *Seymour* and *Bedford* v. *Bagshaw* said[2] that

> "the decisions, and the grounds on which they proceeded, appear to me to be extraordinary, and I cannot bring my mind to agree with them".

174   *R.* v. *Aspinall*[3] decided in 1876, was another criminal case, which is mentioned here for the sake of completeness only. For the reasons given above in the discussion of *R.* v. *De Berenger*[4] it is submitted here that the essentials of a prosecution for criminal conspiracy may be satisfied with less than is necessary to found a civil action for fraud, in that actual communication to and inducement of a "representee" as defined in these pages may not be necessary.[5]

Salaman v. *Warner*; *Scott* v. *Brown, Doering, McNab & Co.*

175   *Salaman* v. *Warner*,[6] decided by the Court of Appeal in 1891, was a case characterised by execrable pleading, and the consequent exasperation of the members of the Court of Appeal may have been responsible for a measure of obscurity in the texts of their judgments. But the point is made again in all the judgments that while proof of conspiracy to do an illegal act may support a conviction on a criminal charge, the same evidence will not necessarily give rise to a civil claim, for damage of the nature discussed in Chapter VII, suffered by a repre-

---

[1] (1873), L.R. 6 H.L. 377.
[2] At p. 397.
[3] (1876), 2 Q.B.D. 48.
[4] (1814), 3 M. & S. 67.
[5] See the cases cited in note 4 on p. 194, *supra*. It is submitted that nothing in the modern doctrine of conspiracy, as laid down in *Crofter Hand Woven Harris Tweed Co., Ltd.* v. *Veitch*, [1942] 1 All E.R. 142; [1942] A.C. 435, H.L. touches the principles applicable to the kind of cases which are discussed in the text above.
[6] (1891), 65 L.T. 132, C.A.

sentee as defined in the present chapter, is essential to support a claim for damages.

> "If two persons agree to do an unlawful act, or agree to do a lawful act by unlawful means, they commit an indictable offence. The gist of the offence is the agreement, and they may be found guilty although that agreement did not result in any act. An action may be brought against several defendants who have agreed to do an act which results in the infringement of the legal right of the plaintiff, but the cause of action there is not the agreement, but the infringement of the legal rights of the plaintiff resulting in injury to him. In the present case I can find no infringement of the legal right of the plaintiff. The injury of which he complains is too remote, and on that ground I think the statement of claim so far as the conspiracy is concerned fails, and I am of opinion, therefore, that this appeal should be dismissed."[1]

Scott v. *Brown, Doering, McNab & Co.*[2], decided in 1892, was a very different type of case. There the defendants "rigged the market". By faked sales of shares between themselves, purporting to have been entered into in the ordinary course of business on the Stock Exchange, they brought about the quotation of a fictitious price for the shares in which they were dealing in the official pricelist issued by the Stock Exchange. The question before the court in that case was quite different from that which we have been discussing—it was whether the faked contract was an illegal contract, in respect of which the court would refuse either party a cause of action upon it. But A. L. SMITH L.J. in the course of his judgment adverted *obiter* to the point which has been under discussion in the present text and said[3]:

> "Test it in this way. Suppose a purchaser induced to purchase shares of the plaintiff or McNab by means of the fictitious premium created by them solely for the purpose of inducing such purchaser and others to buy, could he or not have successfully sued either or both for a false and fraudulent misrepresentation? I say that he could . . ."

—clearly because the conduct of the parties was directed to the production of a representation *to the public*, though the official list of the Stock Exchange, that the securities in question had been genuinely sold on the open market for the quoted amount. Such a representation made directly to the public could, no doubt, if acted upon by a member of the public to his loss, form the basis of a claim for damages for fraud, in accordance with the principles which are to be found set down in the text above.

---

[1] At p. 136, *per* LOPES L.J.
[2] [1892] 2 Q.B. 724.
[3] At p. 734.

CHAPTER X

When Misrepresentation is Actionable

Introductory

176   Having discussed in order all the several matters which are, or may be, necessary ingredients in proceedings founded on misrepresentation, we are now in a position to state generally when, and under what conditions, fraudulent and innocent misrepresentations respectively become amenable to civil remedy and relief, and what is the nature of such remedy and relief in the two classes of case.

Proceedings to which fraudulent misrepresentation is amenable

177   A fraudulent misrepresentation whereby the representor has induced the representee to alter his position in some manner otherwise than by entering into a contract or transaction with the representor, may be the subject of an action for damages, either at common law or in equity; and the representee, on proof of the several matters mentioned in Chapter XI, is entitled to the kinds of remedy therein specified, but to no other relief.   Where, however, such alteration of position on the faith of the fraudulent misrepresentation is to be found in his having entered into a contract with the representor, the representee is entitled either to adhere to the contract, and maintain an action for damages as above, or to repudiate it, and, if the repudiation is resisted, to sue for the avoidance or annulment thereof; or to set up the misrepresentation as an affirmative defence to any action to enforce the contract, subject to the conditions set forth in Chapters XIII, XIV and XV respectively,[1] but, in such case, the two rights are strictly alternative to one another; the representee cannot, unless they are pleaded avowedly and expressly

---

[1] This is Article 24 of the Code.

as alternatives, pursue both remedies, either simultaneously[1] or in succession,[2] or, as it was put by CROMPTON J.

> "if you are fraudulently induced to buy a cake, you may return it and get back the price; but you cannot both eat your cake and return your cake",[3]

which, in more formal language, means that a representor, under such circumstances, cannot both approbate and reprobate. But, though he has no more than a right to choose, on the other hand, he has no less; and if, therefore, he elects to sue for rescission, not having lost his right to do so,[4] it is no valid objection to his suit, that he might have sued for damages, or, conversely if he elects to sue for damages, not having lost his right to do so,[5] it is no answer to his action that he might or ought first to have avoided the contract, or taken proceedings to avoid it, or that the course which he has preferred to take may result in more serious consequences to the representor than if he had sued for rescission.[6]

---

[1] In *Lemprière* v. *Lange* (1879), 12 Ch.D. 675, JESSEL M.R., after granting the plaintiff part of the relief prayed by him (*viz.* a declaration that the lease in question was void, having been procured by misrepresentation, and an injunction), refused to grant the residue (*viz.* mesne profits and damages), pointing out (at p. 679) the inconsistency between the two claims. *Cf. Stoddart* v. *Union Trust, Ltd.*, [1912] 1 K.B. 181, C.A. The "making good" theory—now discarded,—referred to in para. 180, *post*, similarly offends against this rule, based as it is on a hazy idea that an amalgam of elements selected from each of the two inconsistent and alternative remedies referred to in the text may, somehow, be the subject of simultaneous equitable relief. There is no objection, however, to claiming *alternatively* these inconsistent remedies in one and the same action: see *Greenwood* v. *Leather Shod Wheel Co.*, [1900] 1 Ch. 421, C.A.; *Goldrei, Foucard & Son* v. *Sinclair*, [1918] 1 K.B. 180, C.A.

[2] In *Ship* v. *Crosskill* (1870), L.R. 10 Eq. 73, the plaintiff had already had his name removed from the register of shareholders, and so had obtained a statutory annulment of his contract with the company, and, but for the fact that the actual misrepresentors were agents of the company, and therefore for purposes of fraudulent misrepresentation severally as well as jointly liable, and the further fact that the company was insolvent, and therefore the plaintiff could not get restitution in full from it of the money paid to it, such avoidance would have been a bar to the action. But, as this case shows, a subsequent claim will lie against the actual misrepresentor for anything the representee has failed to get under his order for rescission against the other contracting party, being the principal of such actual representor. In *Australia cf. Sibley* v. *Grosvenor* (1916), 21 C.L.R. 469; *Ivanof* v. *Phillip M. Levy, Pty., Ltd.*, [1971] V.R. 167, where a majority of the High Court of Australia went further still, and awarded damages against the agent beyond what was recoverable against the principal in an action for rescission. In *New Zealand* see *Hazeldine* v. *Milligan and Lindsay*, [1922] N.Z.L.R. 872.

[3] *Clarke* v. *Dickson* (*No. 1*) (1858), E.B. & E. 148, at p. 152.

[4] As he may, by affirmation, express or implied, or inability to make complete specific restitution, etc., see Chapter XIV, *post*. In that case, his title to relief, if any, is limited to damages against the representor.

[5] This he might have done by accepting a voluntary cancellation of the contract, if accompanied by complete restoration of everything he had paid thereunder, but not otherwise: see Chapter XI, para. 196, *post*, and *Ship* v. *Crosskill, supra*.

[6] In *Arnison* v. *Smith* (1889), 41 Ch.D. 348, C.A., the plaintiff's counsel contended (see p. 367) that "the cases show that an action to rescind, and an action for deceit, are perfectly independent, and there is not a trace of authority in support of the position that you must resort to the former before resorting to the latter". This contention the C.A. accepted (*per* COTTON L.J. at p. 371).

And an election to rescind as against a party with whom the representee has contracted will not necessarily bar an action against another co-representor, not a party to such contract (e.g. the agent actually making the representation) claiming (for instance) a refund of a deposit which it has proved impossible to recover from the actual payee.[1]

Proceedings to which innocent misrepresentation is amenable

178   Until the passing of the Misrepresentation Act 1967[2] an innocent misrepresentation could found no action in damages, unless such a duty of care was owed by the representor as to give rise to a claim *in negligence* by a person suffering damage by reason of the representation.[3] By s. 2 of that Act, however, it is now provided that where any person has entered into a contract after a misrepresentation has been made to him by another, and has thereby suffered loss, the court may award damages at his suit, though the misrepresentation be an innocent one, in cases in which before the Act such damages could have been claimed if the representation had been fraudulent, unless the representor proves (and this is a good defence to such a claim) that he had reasonable ground to believe, and did believe, up to the time that the contract was made, that the representation was true.

It is also provided by the same section that where the representee claims rescission, and but for the Act would be entitled to rescind, the court is given power to declare the contract subsisting, and to award damages in lieu of rescission, if of opinion that such a course is equitable, having regard to the circumstances.

The essential ingredients of the action for damages for innocent misrepresentation created by the Misrepresentation Act 1967, and the possible limits of such a claim, are discussed more fully in Chapter XII, *post*.

Quite separately from the cause of action created by the Act, an action in negligence, under which damages may be claimed, may be founded upon a misrepresentation innocently, but negligently, made, in circumstances in which a special relationship is demonstrated between the parties, as a result of which a duty of care in making the representation is owed by the representor to the claimant. This is the action some-

---

[1] In *Australia Sibley* v. *Grosvenor* (1916), 21 C.L.R. 469 (H. Ct. of Aus.); *Ivanof* v. *Phillip M. Levy, Pty., Ltd.*, [1971] V.R. 167.

[2] The Act is reproduced *in extenso* in Appendix C, *post*.

[3] This is the *Hedley Byrne* action, alluded again a little later in the text above.

times known as the *Hedley Byrne* action, from the name of the case[1] in
which the House of Lords laid down the principle in 1963; it is fully
discussed in Chapter XIX. But as will be seen in that chapter, this is an
action *in negligence*. The plaintiff need not be a representee, so long
as he is a person suffering loss through the representation being made,
who was or should have been in the contemplation of the representor
when he made his representation. The *Hedley Byrne* action is mentioned
here for the sake of completeness only; it will not be dealt with further
in this chapter, or in Chapter XII, as a remedy available for *misrepresentation*, and its further examination will be deferred until in Chapter XIX
it is considered in detail as a completely separate topic.

Innocent misrepresentation giving rise to right to rescind

179 In the case of an innocent misrepresentation if, but not unless,
the representee's alteration of position consisted in his entering into a
contract or transaction with the representor, the representee is entitled,
subject to the provisions of the Misrepresentation Act 1967, to the
remedies and relief, by way of active proceedings or affirmative defence,
for the purposes of avoiding such contract or transaction or having it
treated as a nullity, that form the subjects of Chapters XIII, XIV and XV
respectively.

But, as is pointed out in the preceding paragraph, the court is by s. 2
of that Act empowered, where the equity of the case indicates such a
course, to declare the contract subsisting and to award damages in lieu
of rescission.[2]

180 Except as mentioned above in general terms, to be elaborated
in Chapters XI to XV and Chapter XIX, misrepresentation as defined
in this work cannot be made the subject of any non-statutory action or
civil proceedings whatever. It is particularly to be mentioned that those
old cases in which the "equitable doctrine" of "making good" is hinted
at, or mentioned, are not, in today's state of the law, to be understood as
supporting any action, whether as plaintiff or defendant, founded on
misrepresentation, save alone those which have already been mentioned,
or such relief as may be founded on estoppels arising from the misrepresentation in question.[3]

---

[1] *Hedley Byrne & Co., Ltd.* v. *Heller & Partners, Ltd.*, [1963] 2 All E.R. 575; [1964] A.C. 465,
H.L.

[2] The measure of damages is the subject of a note in para. 226, *post*.

[3] In earlier editions of this work, Mr Spencer Bower devoted several pages at this point in
the text to denouncing the "heresy" of "making good" in characteristically forthright style;
see, for instance the 2nd edn. pp. 191–198.

Compensation in specific performance cases

181   It should perhaps be recalled at this point that there is another kind of case, not mentioned in the review which has been made above, in which a representee may be awarded compensation, if not damages, flowing from a representation which has induced him to enter into a contract with the representor.   This is the case in which the representor, having by a misrepresentation induced a contract, seeks specific performance, and the court holds the misrepresentation not sufficiently substantial to give the representee a right to rescind.   In such a case the court may order specific performance, but subject, if it so thinks fit, to the representor accepting liability to pay to the representee an amount in compensation.[1]

But this is not to say that where it is the representee who sues for specific performance he may at the same time maintain a claim for compensation—e.g., in reduction of the purchase price, if he be a purchaser, for the damage which he has suffered by reason of the misrepresentation. It has been held that the representee, if his contract is still executory, must elect whether to rescind, or to enforce his contract; and that if he choose the latter course he must accept performance by the other party without compensation in respect of any misrepresentations by which he was induced to enter into the contract.[2]

This topic is discussed further in more detail in Chapter XV, paras. 319 *et seq.*, *post.*

Misrepresentation of authority

182   A misrepresentation of authority, whether express or implied from the conduct of the representor in assuming to contract or act as if he had such authority, is actionable, when fraudulent, under the same

---

[1] Specific performance was granted subject to such terms in *Scott* v. *Hanson* (1829), 1 Russ & M. 128; *King* v. *Wilson* (1843), 6 Beav. 124 and *Hughes* v. *Jones* (1861), 3 De G.F. & J. 307. In the last-mentioned case the amount of the compensation was made the subject of a reference. But as is pointed out in Chapter XV, paras. 319 *et seq.*, where this topic is discussed in rather more detail, the representee has no absolute right to any order directing such compensation to be paid; it is no more than a condition which a court of Equity may think it proper to require the representor to accept if he asks for a decree.

[2] Cases in which a representee was plaintiff are mentioned in the notes to para. 320, Chapter XV, *post.*   A recent decision in which the court declined to make an order for specific performance coupled with an abatement in the price which the plaintiff must pay, is *Gilchester Properties, Ltd.* v. *Gomm*, [1948] 1 All E.R. 493 (ROMER J.).   In *New Zealand Mackenzie* v. *Belcher* (1909), 28 N.Z.L.R. 7; *Rollo* v. *Leineweber* (*No. 2*) (1909), 29 N.Z.L.R. 133; *Schmidt and Bellshaw* v. *Greenwood* (1912), 32 N.Z.L.R. 241, C.A.

conditions as any other fraudulent misrepresentation.[1]   But it is undoubted law that damages can be recovered for an innocent, as well as for
a fraudulent, misrepresentation of authority,[2] and the opinion, formerly
entertained, to the contrary has been discarded.[3]   At first sight, therefore,
this would seem to be an anomaly, and an exception to the general rule
before the passing of the Misrepresentation Act that innocent misrepresentation would not be the subject of an action for damages; and
indeed for a time it was so considered.[4]   But the modern doctrine is now
clear, *viz.*, that when regard is had to the true theory of representations of authority, the right to recover damages for misrepresentation of
such authority, though not fraudulent, involves no such exception.[5]

Theory of the doctrine

183   The theory of this modern doctrine is as follows.   There never
was, and never can be, any question but that a representation as to the
existence or extent of authority conferred upon any representor to enter
into a proposed contract or binding transaction with the representee
may be a most material one, may actually induce the representee to
contract on the faith of it, and may result in loss or injury to him.   So far,
there is no reason why the ordinary principles of the law of misrepresentation should not apply to any such case; but, inasmuch as the application
of these principles would of necessity deny to any one who has trusted
to an innocent representor's unwarranted assumption of authority all
remedy whatever either against the alleged principal or the representor,[6]
the law found it necessary to devise a doctrine in virtue of which, without
impinging on the rules relating to misrepresentation, relief in such cases

---

1 *Polhill* v. *Walter* (1832), 3 B. & Ad. 114; *Smout* v. *Ilbery* (1842), 10 M. & W. 1 (*per cur.*
at p. 9); *Randell* v. *Trimen* (1856), 18 C.B. 786 (*per* JERVIS C.J. at pp. 793, 794); *Starkey* v.
Bank of England, [1903] A.C. 114, H.L.

2 See the authorities cited in note 1 on the next page.

3 In *Smout* v. *Ilbery*, *supra*, it was distinctly held that the misrepresentation of authority
must constitute a wrong, in order to entitle the representee to relief (pp. 9–11), but this
opinion was held erroneous, and overruled in *Collen* v. *Wright* (1857), 8 E. & B. 647, Exch.
Ch., as was pointed out by KEKEWICH J. at pp. 349, 350 of *Halbot* v. *Lens*, [1901] 1 Ch. 344,
and by the C.A. in *Yonge* v. *Toynbee*, [1910] 1 K.B. 215, C.A. (*per* BUCKLEY L.J. at p. 226).

4 LINDLEY L.J. at p. 61 of *Firbank's Executors* v. *Humphreys* (1886), 18 Q.B.D. 54, C.A., so
describes it, *per incuriam*, and an argument in support of this view was one of the two alternative
contentions presented to the House of Lords, though unsuccessfully, in the case cited in the
next note.

5 *Starkey* v. *Bank of England*, [1903] A.C. 114, H.L., *per* Lord HALSBURY L.C. at pp. 117, 118,
and Lord DAVEY at pp. 118, 119.

6 There could be no remedy against the alleged principal in contract, because *ex hypothesi*,
no contract was in fact or law made with him; nor against the representor for misrepresentation, either by way of rescission (for the contract did not purport to be made with him, and so
there is no contract to rescind), or for damages (for the representor was innocent).

might be given.   By viewing the assumption of authority as an implied warranty, undertaking, promise, or contract, as well as an implied representation that the party has the authority which he professes to have, the courts made it possible to treat the non-existence of the authority assumed as a breach of warranty or contract, as well as a misrepresentation, and, since in the former case it is wholly immaterial whether the breach was fraudulent or innocent, the desired result was thus achieved.[1]

---

[1] *Collen* v. *Wright* (1857), 8 E. & B. 647 Ex.Ch.;   *Dickson* v. *Reuter's Telegram Co., Ltd.* (1877), 3 C.P.D. 1, C.A., per BRAMWELL L.J. at p. 5, BRETT L.J. at p. 8 and COTTON L.J. at p. 8;   *Firbank's Executors* v. *Humphreys*, *supra*, per Lord ESHER M.R. at p. 60, and LINDLEY L.J. at p. 61;   *Halbot* v. *Lens*, *supra*;   *Starkey* v. *Bank of England*, *supra*, per Lord HALSBURY, L.C., at pp. 116, 117;   *Salton* v. *New Beeston Cycle Co.*, [1900] 1 Ch. 43 (*per* STIRLING J. at p. 49); *Bank of England* v. *Cutler*, [1907] 1 K.B. 889 (*per* A. T. LAWRENCE J. at p. 907);   *Yonge* v. *Toynbee*, *supra*., per BUCKLEY L.J. at pp. 226, 227, and SWINFEN-EADY J. at pp. 231–233; *Simmons* v. *Liberal Opinion, Ltd.*, *Re Dunn*, [1911] 1 K.B. 966, C.A.;   *Edwards* v. *Porter*, [1925] A.C. 1, H.L. (*per* Lord ATKINSON at pp. 21–23).   See, generally, on this topic, 1 Halsbury's Laws (4th Edn.) title "Agency", para. 857.

CHAPTER XI

The Action for Damages for Fraudulent Misrepresentation

Introductory

184   On proof of the several matters specified below, an action, or counterclaim,[1] is maintainable at the suit of the representee to recover damages in respect of *fraudulent* misrepresentation.[2]   Such action is founded *in tort*, and the same principles of law and rules of evidence are applicable in whatever division of the High Court the proceedings be instituted.[3]

Ingredients of the cause of action

185   In any action for damages for *fraudulent* misrepresentation,[4] the burden is on the representee of alleging, with all necessary particulars,[5]

---

[1] See *Redgrave* v. *Hurd* (1881), 20 Ch.D. 1, C.A.; *Bradford Third Equitable Benefit Building Society* v. *Borders*, [1941] 2 All E.R. 205, H.L., and some of the cases cited in Chapter XV, *post*, in which counterclaims for damages were set up by the defendant.   In speaking of actions, plaintiffs, and defendants, in the course of this chapter it will be understood that these expressions are intended to include counterclaims, defendants counterclaiming, and plaintiffs resisting such counterclaims, respectively.

[2] Actions for damages founded on *innocent* misrepresentations are dealt with in Chapter XII; the action in negligence founded on a *negligent* misrepresentation is examined in Chapter XIX.

[3] The action at common law was originally known, and is still often described, as an "action on the case for deceit", or (more shortly) an "action of deceit", or "for deceit".   A bill for the same purpose in equity used formerly to be called an equitable claim for damages; but it has always been recognised that, whatever the tribunal, or the name, the principles of substantive law applicable to the two forms of proceeding, and the nature of the remedy and relief obtainable, are precisely the same: *Peek* v. *Gurney* (1873), L.R. 6 H.L. 377 (*per* Lord CHELMSFORD at p. 384, and Lord CAIRNS at p. 390); *Arkwright* v. *Newbold* (1881), 17 Ch.D. 301, C.A. (*per* COTTON L.J. at p. 320); *Smith* v. *Chadwick* (1884), 9 App. Cas. 187, H.L. (*per* Lord BLACKBURN at p. 193); *Schroeder* v. *Mendl* (1887), 37 L.T. 452, C.A. (*per* COTTON L.J. at p. 454); *Derry* v. *Peek* (1889), 14 App. Cas. 337, H.L. (*per* LORD HERSCHELL at p. 360).

[4] This chapter is concerned only with the action for damages for *fraudulent* misrepresentation; damages for *innocent* misrepresentation is the topic of Chapter XII, and the *Hedley Byrne* action for *negligence* is dealt with in Chapter XIX.

[5] See Chapter XVIII, *post*, as to particulars of fraud.

and, having so alleged, of establishing, each of the following matters,[1] except so far as any of them may be expressly or impliedly admitted before or at the trial[2]:

    (i) That the alleged representation consisted of something said, written, or done, which amounts in law to a representation:

    (ii) That the defendant was the representor:

    (iii) That the plaintiff was the representee:

    (iv) Inducement and Materiality:

    (v) Falsity:

    (vi) Alteration of Position:

    (vii) Fraud:

    (viii) Damage.

On establishing all the above issues, or such of them as are challenged, the plaintiff is entitled to relief in the form of damages; if he fails in any one of them, his action fails altogether. The first six are common to all forms of proceeding in respect of misrepresentation,[3] and have already been fully discussed. The seventh, fraud, is peculiar to actions of the class now under consideration.[4] Damage is an essential constituent of this cause of action, and also of the action for damages for innocent misrepresentation, described in the next chapter, and of the action in negligence described in Chapter XIX, *post*.

186 From the earliest times it has been recognised that the concurrence of fraud and damage is essential to, and a distinguishing mark of,

---

[1] This is Article 28 of the Code. As to the special *alleganda et probanda* in statutory proceedings for misrepresentation, see Chapter XVI, *post*.

[2] Perhaps the nearest approach to a full judicial exposition of the constituent elements of a cause of action for damages for misrepresentation is to be found in *Shrewsbury* v. *Blount* (1841), 2 Man. & G. 475 (*per* ERSKINE J. at p. 498), *Denton* v. *Great Northern Rail. Co.* (1856), 5 E. & B. 860 (*per* Lord CAMPBELL C.J. at pp. 866, 867, and WIGHTMAN J. at pp. 867, 868), *Smith* v. *Chadwick*, *supra* (*per* Lord SELBORNE L.C. at p. 190, and Lord BLACKBURN at pp. 195–197), and *Arnison* v. *Smith* (1889), 41 Ch.D. 348, C.A. (*per* Lord HALSBURY L.C. at pp. 367, 368). Viscount MAUGHAM attempted a useful brief summary in *Bradford Third Equitable Benefit Building Society* v. *Borders*, [1941] 2 All E.R. 205, H.L. when he said at p. 211 that ''not attempting to make a complete statement of the law of deceit, but only to state the main points which a plaintiff must establish'' he would enumerate these as (1) a misrepresentation of fact made by words or conduct, (2) made with the knowledge that it was false or at least in the absence of any genuine belief that it was true, (3) with the intent that it should be acted upon by the plaintiff or a class of persons of whom he is one in the manner which resulted in damage to him, (4) with the result that the plaintiff so acted upon it and sustained damage.

[3] Except that, as appears in Chapter XIX, it is not necessary in a *Hedley Byrne* action for the plaintiff to be a representee.

[4] See Chapter II as to what amounts to a representation in law, and Chapter III as to how such a representation must be proved to have been made; Chapter VIII as to who is a representor; Chapter IX as to who is a representee; Chapter VI as to inducement and materiality; Chapter IV as to falsity; Chapter VII as to alteration of position, and damage; Chapter V as to essentials of fraud.

a claim for damages for fraudulent misrepresentation.[1] Indeed, the very names of this cause of action, "action of deceit", and "action for damages", connote respectively the two elements. The necessity for proving damage has been dealt with already.[2] The necessity for establishing fraud would, at first sight, appear to be so obvious as to occasion amazement that it could ever have been the subject of the anxious consideration which it has received, or the many decisions to which it has given rise[3]; but, once the fact is appreciated that the term "fraud", as used by judges and jurists until *Derry* v. *Peek*,[4] was in a state of continual flux, at one time meaning one thing and at other times other things, the wonder is perhaps that the authorities have not been more numerous than they have. One clear result, however, emerges from a consideration of the cases, *viz.* that at all periods in the history of our jurisprudence up to the date of the passing of the Misrepresentation Act 1967, a misrepresentation which was not alleged, or was not proved, to be also fraudulent, whatever that term may at the time have been deemed to include, was held not to be the subject of an action for damages.[5] In

---

[1] *Baily* (or *Bayly* or *Bailie*) v. *Merrell* (or *Merrel* or *Merrill*) (1615), 3 Bulstr. 94 (*per* CROKE J. at p. 95: "damage without fraud gives no cause of action, but where these two do concur and meet together, then an action lieth"); *Pasley* v. *Freeman* (1789), 3 Term Rep. 51 ("the foundation of this action is fraud and deceit in the defendant, and damage to the plaintiff": *per* BULLER J. at p. 56, who cites the above statement of CROKE J. but not quite accurately); *Levy* v. *Langridge* (1838), 4 M. & W. 337, Exch. Ch. (at p. 338).

[2] See Chapter VII.

[3] This surprise was frequently expressed by BOWEN L.J. e.g. at pp. 499, 500 of *Le Lievre* v. *Gould*, [1893] 1 Q.B. 491, C.A. ("a plaintiff cannot succeed in an action of deceit or fraud without proving that the defendant was fraudulent. That any doubt should ever have been cast upon that proposition seems to me strange . . . There must be fraud in order to found an action of fraud"). *Cf. Candler* v. *Crane, Christmas & Co.*, [1951] 1 All E.R. 426; [1951] 2 K.B. 164, C.A.; *Bradford Third Equitable Benefit Building Society* v. *Borders*, [1941] 2 All E.R. 205, H.L. *per* Lord WRIGHT at p. 220, the passage being quoted *verbatim* in note 5, below. With the extension to the field of misrepresentation of the action for damages for negligence first recognised by *Hedley Byrne & Co., Ltd.* v. *Heller & Partners, Ltd.*, [1963] 2 All E.R. 575; [1964] A.C. 465, H.L., and the introduction of claims for damages for innocent misrepresentation by s. 2 of the Misrepresentation Act 1967, such statements lose much of their former importance; but they are still perfectly valid in the field of claims for *fraudulent* misrepresentation.

[4] (1889), 14 App. Cas. 337, H.L.

[5] Section 2 of the Misrepresentation Act 1967 is dealt with shortly in para. 188, below, and in more detail in Chapter XII. A modern statement of the necessity for fraud in an action for deceit is that of Lord WRIGHT in *Bradford Third Equitable Benefit Building Society* v. *Borders*, [1941] 2 All E.R. 205, H.L., at p. 220: "Fraud involves deliberate intent, which is called *mens rea.* Nothing short of the wicked or guilty mind will serve, as this House held in most striking circumstances in *Derry* v. *Peek* . . ." In the following cases at common law the declaration or statement of claim was held bad on the ground that fraud was not sufficiently alleged, as well as falsity: *Chandelor* v. *Lopus* (1603), Cro. Jac. 4; 1 Dyer, 75, n., Exch. Ch. (*per* POPHAM C.J.: "if I have any commodities which are damaged and I, *knowing them to be so*, sell them for good, and affirm them to be so, an action upon the case lies for the deceit; but although it be damaged, if I, *knowing not that*, affirm them

every case where it was so alleged, or was so alleged and proved, as the case might be, the plaintiff succeeded, or, if he failed, he failed on grounds independent of the fraudulent character of the misrepresentation.[1]

---

to be good, still no action lies, without I warrant them to be good". In this case, all that was averred was that the defendant affirmed a certain stone to be a Bezoar stone "*ubi re vera* it was not", and "all the justices and barons besides" (meaning "except") ANDERSON J. held that, no *scienter* being alleged, nor any warranty, the declaration disclosed no cause of action); *Hill* v. *Balls* (1857), 2 H. & N. 299 (*per* POLLOCK C.B. at p. 302, MARTIN B. at p. 304, and BRAMWELL B. at pp. 305, 306); *Behn* v. *Kemble* (1859), 7 C.B. N.S. 260 (*per* ERLE C.J. at p. 267; "the count does not allege any fraudulent misrepresentation by the defendant, nor any *scienter*"); *Childers* v. *Wooler* (1859), 2 E. & E. 287, 306, 307; *Thiodon* v. *Tindall* (1891), 65 L.T. 343, Div. Ct. In the following common law cases, there being no *proof* of fraud, in addition to falsity, either the plaintiff was non-suited, or judgment entered for the defendant at the trial, or *in banco*: *Haycraft* v. *Creasy* (1801), 2 East, 92; *Pickering* v. *Dowson* (1813), 4 Taunt. 779; *Ames* v. *Milward* (1818), 8 Taunt. 637 (where an award in favour of the plaintiff was set aside, because the arbitrator had specifically found that the misrepresentation was not fraudulent, though the evidence clearly pointed in the opposite direction); *Horncastle* v. *Moat* (1824), 1 C. & P. 166; *Freeman* v. *Baker* (1833), 5 B. & Ad. 797 (at pp. 805, 807); *Shrewsbury* v. *Blount* (1841), 2 Man. & G. 475; *Taylor* v. *Ashton* (1843), 11 M. & W. 401 (*per* PARKE B. at p. 413); *Collins* v. *Evans* (1844), 5 Q.B. 820, Exch. Ch. (at pp. 827–830); *Ormrod* v. *Huth* (1845), 14 M. & W. 651, 664, Exch. Ch.; *Longmeid* v. *Holliday* (1851), 6 Exch. 761 (*per cur.* at p. 766); *Dickson* v. *Reuter's Telegram Co., Ltd.* (1877), 3 C.P.D. 1, C.A. (at pp. 6, 7); *Schroeder* v. *Mendl* (1877), 37 L.T. 452, C.A.; *Joliffe* v. *Baker* (1883), 11 Q.B.D. 255, Div. Ct.; *Bellairs* v. *Tucker* (1884), 13 Q.B.D. 562, Div. Ct. (*per* DENMAN J. at p. 576, and MANISTY J. at pp. 580–582); *Bishop* v. *Balkis Consolidated Co.* (1890), 25 Q.B.D. 512 (*per cur.* at p. 521); *Burtsal* v. *Bianchi* (1891), 65 L.T. 678; *Parsons* v. *Barclay & Co., Ltd.* (1910), 103 L.T. 196, C.A.; *Tackey* v. *McBain*, [1912] A.C. 186, P.C.; *Heilbut, Symons & Co.* v. *Buckleton*, [1913] A.C. 30, H.L.; *Glasgow and South Western Rail. Co.* v. *Boyd and Forrest (No. 1)*, [1913] A.C. 404, H.L.; *Lawrence* v. *Hull* (1924), 41 T.L.R. 75; *Bradford Third Equitable Benefit Building Society* v. *Borders*, [1941] 2 All E.R. 205, C.A.; *Akerhielm* v. *De Mare*, [1959] 3 All E.R. 485; [1959] A.C. 789, P.C. In *Australia, John McGrath Motors (Canberra) Pty., Ltd.* v. *Applebee* (1964), 110 C.L.R. 656 (H. Ct. of Aus.); In *New Zealand, Foley's Creek Extended Co.* v. *Cutten and Faithful* (1903), 22 N.Z.L.R. 759 at pp. 762–763; *Whinray* v. *Public Trustee*, [1943] N.Z.L.R. 239.

The following are equity cases in which, fraud not being proved or (in some cases) even alleged, the action failed: *Evans* v. *Bicknell* (1801), 6 Ves. 174 (*per* Lord ELDON L.C. at pp. 188, 191, 192; *Rashdall* v. *Ford* (1866), L.R. 2 Eq. 750, 754; *Ship* v. *Crosskill* (1870), L.R. 10 Eq. 73; *Redgrave* v. *Hurd* (1881), 20 Ch.D. 1, C.A. (where the counterclaim, so far as it claimed damages, was dismissed, because there was no proof of fraud; so far as it claimed rescission, where such proof was unnecessary, it succeeded: *per* JESSEL M.R. at p. 12); *Derry* v. *Peek* (1889), 14 App. Cas. 337, H.L. (*per* Lord HERSCHELL at p. 374); *Glasier* v. *Rolls* (1889), 42 Ch.D. 436, C.A.; *Angus* v. *Clifford*, [1891] 2 Ch. 449, C.A. (*per* LINDLEY L.J. at pp. 462–468, BOWEN L.J. at p. 471, KAY L.J. at p. 479); *Low* v. *Bouverie*, [1891] 3 Ch. 82, C.A.; *Coleman* v. *North* (1898), 47 W.R. 57; *Manners* v. *Whitehead* 1898, 1 F. (Ct. of Sess.) 171; *Lagunas Nitrate Co.* v. *Lagunas Syndicate*, [1899] 2 Ch. 392, C.A. (*per* LINDLEY M.R. at pp. 427–431).

[1] The cases cited in the last preceding note are of more importance, as testing the principle of law for which they are cited, than the cases now to be mentioned; but it may nevertheless be of some use to give a roughly classified list (according to the subject matter of the representation) of some of the more important decisions. The groups are as follow: (1) *Representations on sale of interests in land*—*Richardson* v. *Silvester* (1873), L.R. 9 Q.B. 34: in *Australia, Holmes* v. *Jones* (1907), 4 C.L.R. 1692 (H. Ct. of Aus.); *Brooksby* v. *Lightowler*, [1938] V.L.R. 112 (Full Court of Victoria), (2) *Representations on sale of chattels*—*Levy* v. *Langridge* (1838), 4 M. & W. 337, Exch. Ch.; *Wright* v. *Crookes* (1840), 1 Scott N.R. 685 Exch. Ch.; *Udell* v. *Atherton* (1861), 7 H. & N. 172; *Mullett* v. *Mason* (1866), L.R. 1 C.P. 559; *Waddell* v.

Standard of proof

187 It was for long a matter of discussion, if not of actual controversy, how far, if at all, the proof of fraud involved a standard of proof

---

Blockey (1879), 4 Q.B.D. 678, C.A.; *Ludgater* v. *Love* (1881), 44 L.T. 694, C.A.; *Gill* v.
McDowell, [1903] 2 I.R. 463; *Malcolm, Brunker & Co., Ltd.* v. *Waterhouse & Sons* (1908),
24 T.L.R. 854; *Hornal* v. *Neuberger Products, Ltd.*, [1956] 3 All E.R. 970; [1957] 1 Q.B. 247,
C.A. In *Australia, Nicholls* v. *Taylor*, [1939] V.L.R. 119. (3) *Representations in prospectuses,
and similar documents, issued by companies, as to their undertakings, property, and affairs:* Clarke v.
Dickson (No. 2) (1859), 6 C.B. N.S. 453; *Scott* v. *Dixon* (1859), 29 L.J. Ex. 62 n.; *Bedford* v.
Bagshaw (1859), 4 H. & N. 538; *Peek* v. *Gurney* (1873), L.R. 6 H.L. 377; *Weir* v. *Bell* (1878),
3 Ex.D. 238, C.A.; *Edgington* v. *Fitzmaurice* (1885), 29 Ch.D. 459, C.A.; *Knox* v. *Hayman*
(1892), 67 L.T. 137, C.A.; *Andrews* v. *Mockford*, [1896] 1 Q.B. 372, C.A.; *Gerson* v. *Simpson*,
[1903] 2 K.B. 197, C.A.; *J. and P. Coats, Ltd.* v. *Crossland* (1904), 20 T.L.R. 800. In *Australia,
Potts* v. *Miller* (1940), 64 C.L.R. 282 (H. Ct. of Aus.). In *New Zealand, Cleave* v. *McDonald*,
[1925] N.Z.L.R. 311, C.A. (4) *Representations by firms or individuals as to takings, earnings,
profits, etc. of a business or undertaking*—*Pilmore* v. *Hood* (1838), 5 Bing N.C. 97, *Richardson* v.
Dunn (1860), 8 C.B. N.S. 655; *Briess* v. *Woolley*, [1954] 1 All E.R. 909; [1954] A.C. 333,
H.L. (method of trading); *Doyle* v. *Olby (Ironmongers) Ltd.*, [1969] 2 All E.R. 119; [1969] 2
Q.B. 158, C.A. In *Australia, Neal* v. *Ayers* (1940), 63 C.L.R. 524 (H. Ct. of Aus.); *Toteff* v.
Antonas (1952), 87 C.L.R. 647 (H. Ct. of Aus.); *Cooke* v. *Caldwell's Wines, Ltd.* (1925),
25 N.S.W. S.R. 161. In *New Zealand, Easterbrook* v. *Hopkins*, [1918] N.Z.L.R. 428, C.A.;
Jack v. *Peters*, [1941] N.Z.L.R. 153. (5) *Representations as to validity of transactions, authority
and power to do certain acts, genuineness of instruments, etc.*—*Barley* v. *Walford* (1846), 9 Q.B. 197;
Eastwood v. *Bain* (1858), 3 H. & N. 738; *West London Commercial Bank* v. *Kitson* (1884), 13
Q.B.D. 360, C.A.; *British Mutual Banking Co., Ltd.* v. *Charnwood Forest Rail. Co.* (1887), 18
Q.B.D. 714, C.A.; *Marnham* v. *Weaver* (1899), 80 L.T. 412; *Kettlewell* v. *Refuge Assurance Co.,
Ltd.*, [1908] 1 K.B. 545; *United Motor Finance Co.* v. *Addison & Co. Ltd.*, [1937] 1 All E.R.
425, P.C. (regularity of hire purchase agreements); *Uxbridge Permanent Benefit Building Society*
v. *Pickard*, [1939] 2 All E.R. 344; [1939] 2 K.B. 248, C.A. (validity of mortgage transactions;
forgery). In *Australia, Hatcher* v. *White* (1953), 53 N.S.W. S.R. 285 (building permit);
In *New Zealand, Smith* v. *Mackenzie* (1883), 1 N.Z.L.R. 1, C.A. (establishment of ferry service).
(6) *Representations as to a third person's credit or respectability*—*Pasley* v. *Freeman* (1789), 3 Term
Rep. 51; *Tapp* v. *Lee* (1803), 3 Bos. & P. 367; *Hamar* v. *Alexander* (1806), 2 Bos. & P.
N.R. 241; *Biddle and Loyd* v. *Levy* (1815), 1 Stark. 20; *Foster* v. *Charles (No. 1)* (1830), 6 Bing.
396; *Foster* v. *Charles (No. 2)* (1830), 7 Bing. 105; *Corbett* v. *Brown* (1831), 8 Bing. 33;
Barwick v. *English Joint Stock Bank* (1867), L.R. 2 Exch. 259; *Ramshire* v. *Bolton* (1869), L.R. 8
Eq. 294; *Leddell* v. *McDougal* (1881), 29 W.R. 403, C.A.; *Paul and Vincent, Ltd.* v. *O'Reilly*
(1913), 49 I.L.T. 89; and the cases of fraudulent misrepresentation of credit, orally made,
which failed only because of the statutory objection, cited in the notes to paras. 197–202, *post*.
(7) *Representations as to personality and identity*: see several of the cases cited in the notes to para.
129, Chapter VI, *ante*. This kind of representation, if fraudulently made, may, if damage
flowing from it can be substantially proved, lead to a successful action in fraud; it may also in
particular circumstances have another quite different consequence, *viz*. that no valid contract
ever came into existence. These two quite different aspects of the same set of facts sometimes
lead in practice to bewildering complications; see e.g. in *New Zealand, Fawcett* v. *Star Car
Sales, Ltd.*, [1960] N.Z.L.R. 406, C.A. (8) *Representations of the status of infancy*; as to which
see paras. 218–219, *post*. (9) *Representations as to the safety of a place, a chattel, or an investment*: see,
as to the two former species, some of the cases cited in the notes to para. 143, Chapter VII;
and as to the safety of investments, *Ingram* v. *Thorp* (1848), 7 Hare, 67; *Smith* v. *Pococke* (1854),
2 Drew. 197. (10) *Miscellaneous representations: Denton* v. *Great Northern Rail. Co.* (1856),
5 E. & B. 860 (railway time-table), *Burrows* v. *Rhodes*, [1899] 1 Q.B. 816, C.A. (misrepresentation that the "Jamieson Raid" had the sanction and approval of Her Majesty); *Pritty* v.
Child (1902), 71 L.J. K.B. 512, Div. Ct. (water-finder); *Dott* v. *Brickwell* (1906), 23 T.L.R. 61
(misrepresentation by a money-borrower inducing an unregistered money-lender to make a
loan); *S. Pearson & Son, Ltd.* v. *Dublin Corporation*, [1907] A.C. 351, H.L. (misrepresentation
on plan of existence and position of a certain wall); *Tackey* v. *McBain*, [1912] A.C. 186, P.C.

higher than the ordinary standard in civil actions involving charges of lesser gravity—e.g. of negligence. Fraud, it was contended, approximated to crime, if indeed in given cases it did not actually amount to a criminal offence; and there were some who contended consequently that the criminal standard of proof should apply. These doubts were resolved by the decision of the Court of Appeal in *Hornal* v. *Neuberger Products, Ltd.*[1] Citing in support *dicta* of Lord SUMNER in *Lek* v. *Mathews*,[2] DENNING L.J., delivering the leading judgment, with which HODSON L.J. and MORRIS L.J. concurred, held that the proof of fraud in a civil action required no more than proof according to the ordinary civil standard. In applying this rule, however, the court will remember that the standard of proof in a civil action depends upon the nature of the issue. The more serious the allegation, the higher the degree of probability that is required; but it need not, in a civil case, reach the very high standard required by the criminal law.[3]

Though the standard used by the courts, in trying an issue of fraud on a civil claim, is not the very high standard which the criminal courts require, yet it is a high standard. And the high standard of evidentiary proof made requisite by the gravity of the allegation is reflected in the attitude of the Court of Appeal upon a submission in that court attacking the conclusion of fact in the court below. It may in a proper case sometimes be possible to engage the attention of the Court of Appeal on a submission that the trial judge should not on the evidence have found fraud in a case where he has actually done so; only in rare cases has that court been persuaded to find fraud proved where the trial judge has declined on the evidence before him to find it.[4]

---

[1] [1956] 3 All E.R. 970; [1957] 1 Q.B. 247, C.A.

[2] (1927), 29 Ll.L.Rep. 141.

[3] At p. 258. HODSON L.J. at pp. 263–264 cited and followed an earlier *dictum* of DENNING L.J., to the same effect, in *Bater* v. *Bater*, [1951] P. 35. Here DENNING L.J. had said at pages 36–37: "So also in civil cases, the case may be proved by a preponderance of probability, but there may be degrees of probability within that standard. The degree depends on the subject-matter. A civil court, when considering a charge of fraud, will naturally require for itself a higher degree of probability than that which it would require when asking if negligence is established. It does not adopt so high a degree as a criminal court, even when it is considering a charge of a criminal nature; but still it does require a degree of probability which is commensurate with the occasion." MORRIS L.J. held to the same effect at p. 266. The *dicta* in *Hornal* v. *Neuberger Products, Ltd.* have been widely approved and followed. In *New Zealand* see, e.g., *Fenton* v. *Kenny*, [1969] N.Z.L.R. 552; on appeal, [1971] N.Z.L.R. 1, C.A.

[4] *Coghlan* v. *Cumberland*, [1898] 1 Ch. 704, C.A., and, more notably, *Spence* v. *Crawford*, [1939] 3 All E.R. 271 may be cited as exceptions to prove the rule. In the latter case the House of Lords found fraud proved, though the trial judge had declined to do so, and the (Scottish) Court of Appeal was equally divided on the point. The reluctance of Appeal Judges to substitute their own impressions—albeit very strong ones—for those of the trial judge can

Effect of the Misrepresentation Act 1967

188　As will be seen in the next chapter, s. 2 of the Misrepresentation Act 1967[1] now provides for an action for damages for innocent misrepresentation where the effect of the representation has been to induce the representee to enter into a contract thereby suffering loss, in circumstances in which the representation would have given an action for damages if made fraudulently. But it is provided in the same section that it is a defence if the representor proves affirmatively that he had reasonable ground for believing and did believe that the representation was true.

This new action is separately dealt with in Chapter XII, *post*. It might perhaps be thought on a first impression of the matter that the new cause of action could have been appropriately considered in the present chapter, the statute being treated simply as having extended the definition of fraud; but second thoughts will show that the new statutory provision is not to be regarded simply as an extension of the definition of fraudulent misrepresentation by which an existing action for damages for fraud is given in respect of innocent misrepresentations of which the representor cannot prove that they were not made fraudulently. The new Act, having thus extended the definition of fraudulent misrepresentation, also limits the claims under the extended definition to cases in which, as a result of the representation the representee *has entered into a contract*. These two important, and quite different, aspects of the amendment to the law made by the Misrepresentation Act seemed to the present author to render it convenient that the new action for damages for innocent misrepresentation should be considered separately, and it is dealt with accordingly in a separate chapter—Chapter XII, *post*.

Affirmative defences specially available in actions for damages for fraud

189　Mr Spencer Bower, at this point in the text of earlier editions, dealt at length with certain affirmative defences specially available in actions for damages for fraud, as distinct from those affirmative defences,

---

frequently be noted in the modern decisions: see, for instance, *Gross* v. *Lewis Hillman, Ltd.*, [1970] Ch. 445, C.A. at pp. 459–460 *per* Cross L.J., at pp. 462, 463 *per* Harman L.J. In *Akerhielm* v. *De Mare*, [1959] 3 All E.R. 485; [1959] A.C. 789, H.L. the Lords expressly stated that where a defendant has been acquitted of fraud in a court of first instance that decision should not be altered on appeal except upon the clearest grounds. In *New Zealand* see *Kenny* v. *Fenton*, [1971] N.Z.L.R. 1 C.A. at pp. 14–15; pp. 32–34; pp. 35–36.

[1] See Appendix C, *post*, for the full text of the Act.

such as release,[1] illegality,[2] estoppel *per rem judicatam*,[3] and statutory limitation[4] which are available in actions for tort generally. The affirmative defences so specially dealt with were: (1) the representee's knowledge of the truth, (2) agreement between the parties excluding liability for misrepresentation, (3) previous avoidance of the contract resulting in loss, (4) (as to representations as to credit, etc.) Lord Tenterden's Act.

As will presently be seen, the author of this edition inclines to the view that the first of these is not truly an affirmative defence at all[5]; and as to

---

[1] Article 29 of the Code states the several affirmative pleas to actions for damages. Where release is set up, the exact terms and limits of the instrument must be scrutinised: thus, in *Turquand* v. *Marshall* (1869), 4 Ch. App. 376, where the liquidator had released a shareholder from all claims against him as such shareholder, or as a contributory, this was held to be no release of the liquidator's claims against him as a director for fraud.

[2] This plea is of no avail when the very misrepresentation consisted either in a fraudulent misrepresentation of the law (see Chapter II, para. 42, *ante*), or in a statement of facts which, if true, would have rendered the transaction legal: *Burrows* v. *Rhodes*, [1899] 1 Q.B. 816, Div. Ct. See, too, *In Re Mahmoud and Ispahani*, [1921] 2 K.B. 716, C.A. *per* BANKES L.J. at p. 726, SCRUTTON L.J. at p. 730 (representation that of existence of a valid licence to deal in linseed oil); *Siveyer* v. *Allison*, [1935] 2 K.B. 403 (representation that representor was free to contract a valid marriage). In *Australia*, *Hatcher* v. *White* (1953), 53 N.S.W. S.R. 285, where a builder who had carried out work in respect of which the necessary building permit had not been obtained, and for which he was consequently not entitled to recover payment, successfully claimed damages for deceit based on the owner's fraudulent representation that he had obtained, and actually held, the necessary permit.

But again in *Australia*, in *Walsh* v. *Commercial Travellers' Association of Victoria*, [1940] V.L.R. 259, where a plaintiff had entered into a contract of employment at young persons' rates of remuneration, fraudulently misrepresenting his age as being under twenty-one years, and then claimed the full adult remuneration from his employer, the Full Court of Victoria held that public policy precluded him from being estopped from setting up his true age in support of his (statutory) claim to the higher remuneration; and also that the same reasoning stood in the way of the employer counterclaiming against him for fraud, based on his fraudulent misrepresentation as to his age.

In *Dott* v. *Brickwell* (1906), 23 T.L.R. 61 a moneylender who, being unregistered, could not recover the amount of his loan, the contract being illegal, was nevertheless held entitled to sue for damages for a fraudulent misrepresentation whereby he was induced to advance the money; and a plea of illegality to such an action is bad.

A different class of case is that in which the representation is as to the fruits of a contemplated illegal course of action; it is submitted that no action for deceit can successfully be founded upon a fraudulent misrepresentation of this kind. The point arose in *Australia* in *Neal* v. *Ayers* (1940), 63 C.L.R. 524 (H. Ct. of Aus.) and in *New Zealand* in *Jack* v. *Peters*, [1941] 60 N.Z.L.R. 153; both were cases of sales of licensed premises, and the representations in each case were as to total turnover, which to the knowledge of both parties included sales of liquor after licensed hours.

[3] But if the *judgment* was itself obtained by fraud there is no estoppel; see the author's *Doctrine of Res Judicata* (2nd Edn.) Chapter XIII, paras. 370 *et seq.* As to setting aside judgments so obtained, see Chapter XVI, *post.*

[4] The statutes of limitation afford no answer to a case of fraud against a trustee—Limitation Act 1939, s. 19; in *New Zealand* Limitation Act 1950, s. 21. As to the period of limitation running from the representee's discovery of the truth see Limitation Act 1939, s. 26; in *New Zealand* Limitation Act 1950, s. 28. Fraudulent misrepresentation cannot be "an act done in pursuance of a public duty", within the meaning of the Public Authorities Protection Act 1893: *S. Pearson & Son, Ltd.* v. *Dublin Corporation*, [1907] A.C. 351, H.L.

[5] See para. 193, *infra.*

the second of them, it is now largely, if not entirely, taken away by s. 3 of the Misrepresentation Act 1967.[1] It is only the third and fourth of the defences, therefore, which are given a place of any importance in this edition.

Special defences—I : Representee's knowledge of the truth

190 A representee who knows the truth is not deceived. Proof, therefore, by the representor of such knowledge on the representee's part is a good answer in whatever form of proceeding the representee may set up the misrepresentation, whether in a form which necessitates the establishment of fraud[2] as in the kind of action now under consideration, or otherwise for damages, or by way of claim to avoid a contract,[3] or of an affirmative plea to an action brought to enforce it.[4] It is

---

[1] See para. 194, *infra*.

[2] It has been thought convenient to deal in this place, once and for all, with the affirmative plea in question, since it is common to all forms of proceeding for misrepresentation, and, when describing hereafter the affirmative pleas to rescission, and the affirmative replies to a defence setting up misrepresentation—see Chapter XIV and Chapter XV hereafter—it will be sufficient merely to refer to the present statement. It is clear from the many cases cited in the notes immediately following that, where a case of actual and full knowledge is made out, the defence is complete; but the paucity of the reported decisions in which the plea has succeeded is some evidence of the extreme difficulty in discharging the very serious burden imposed on the representor, as stated in the next three paragraphs of the text. Possibly the only example of the success of the plea in this jurisdiction is *Eaglesfield* v. *Marquis of Londonderry* (1878), 26 W.R. 540, H.L. (*per* Lord HATHERLEY at p. 541, who refers to the plaintiff's full knowledge of the acts and circumstances of the company, as one among other reasons why his action ought to fail). In *Australia*, however, *Holmes* v. *Jones* (1907), 4 C.L.R. 1692 (H. Ct. of Aus.) may be pointed to as an example of the success of the plea. But that case may equally well stand upon the proposition that the representee had not in fact been influenced by the representation, but had relied exclusively on his own judgment—see observations in note 6 on pp. 216–19, *infra*.

[3] Examples of proved knowledge of the truth constituting a bar to an action or analogous proceeding for rescission are: *Attwood* v. *Small* (1838), 6 Cl. & Fin. 232 (*per* Lord COTTENHAM L.C. at p. 390, and Lord BROUGHAM at pp. 448–450); *Vigers* v. *Pike* (1842), 8 Cl. & Fin. 562 (*per* Lord COTTENHAM L.C. at p. 648); *Lumley* v. *Desborough* (1870), 22 L.T. 597; *Begbie* v. *Phosphate Sewage Co., Ltd.* (1875), L.R. 10 Q.B. 491 (*per cur.*, at pp. 498, 499); *Re British Burmah Lead Co., Ltd., Ex parte Vickers* (1887), 56 L.T. 815; *Wasteneys* v. *Wasteneys,* [1900] A.C. 446, P.C. (a very curious case, in which it was proved (see p. 449) that the plaintiff, who professed to have been deceived by his wife's asseverations of chastity into executing a deed of separation, did not in fact believe a word of them, and positively so stated orally, when executing the deed, and afterwards in a letter to the alleged fraudulent misrepresentor: "you and I know it to be false": it is not often that, from the representee's own contemporaneous and subsequent declarations, evidence of such a complete and convincing character is available to establish the plea of knowledge); *Howarth* v. *Pioneer Life Assurance Co., Ltd.* (1912), 107 L.T. 155, Div. Ct. In *Nelson* v. *Stocker* (1859), 4 De G. & J. 458, where a misrepresentation of majority was set up as a reply to a defendant's plea of infancy, it was proved that the intended wife knew the truth, though her solicitor to whom the representation was made did not. Held that this constituted a good answer to the plea.

[4] *Dyer* v. *Hargrave* (1805), 10 Ves. 505, where the representee's complete knowledge of the property he was purchasing, having lived there all his life and having had its situation specially pointed out to him, was held to be an answer both to his affirmative defence to the vendor's action for specific performance, and also to his cross-bill to set aside the contract:

immaterial to the success of this plea whether the misrepresentation was fraudulent or innocent.   In all cases alike the representee cannot be heard to say that he was misled by a statement which was intended to, but did not in fact, mislead him, or to complain even of a deliberate and proved perversion of facts of the exact truth of which he had complete information and cognizance.   It is an *a fortiori* case where the truth is positively incorporated in the very contract which it is sought to impeach,[1] or where the representee not only knows the truth, but incites the representor to pervert it.[2]

191   It is sufficient, in order to make good the plea to prove either that the facts were within the knowledge of the representee when the statement was made, or that they were subsequently made known to him from other sources of information, or disclosed by the representor himself, before the representation was acted upon[3]; for, as has been seen,[4] every representation is a continuing one during the interval, if there is an interval, between the making of it and the representee's alteration of position.   If the representor's disclosure is made after the latter date, it is entirely ineffectual, unless accompanied by complete restitution or compensation, or at least an offer thereof.[5]

Knowledge must be actual knowledge, and complete

192   The knowledge must be clearly proved to have been full and complete.   Partial and fragmentary information, or mere suspicion, will

---

per GRANT M.R. at pp. 508, 509; *Bawden* v. *London, Edinburgh and Glasgow Assurance Co.*, [1892] 2 Q.B. 534, C.A., where the defendants set up, as a defence to an action on an accident policy, the fraudulent misrepresentation of the plaintiff that he had no physical infirmity, whereas in fact he was a one-eyed man; but, inasmuch as the company, through their agent, had ocular cognizance of this palpable fact, the defence failed; *Keeling* v. *Pearl Assurance Co., Ltd.* (1923), 129 L.T. 573.   Contrast *Levy* v. *Scottish Employers' Insurance Co.* (1901), 17 T.L.R. 229, Div. Ct.

[1] As in *Clements* v. *Conroy*, [1911] 2 I.R. 500 (*per* HOLMES and CHERRY L.JJ. at p. 531).

[2] The practice of money-lenders to solicit declarations of majority by infants in order to get an estoppel against them, is struck at by s. 4 of the Betting and Loans (Infants) Act 1892 (55 Vict., c. 4).

[3] See the cases referred to in notes 2 and 3 on p. 214, in some of which the knowledge was derived *aliunde*; in others, from the representor; in others, both from him and from outside sources.

[4] Chapter IV, paras. 73 *et seq., ante.*

[5] *Arnison* v. *Smith* (1889), 41 Ch.D. 348, C.A. (*per* Lord HALSBURY L.C. at pp. 369, 370, COTTON L.J. at pp. 371, 372, and LINDLEY L.J. at p. 373).

not do.[1] Moreover, actual[2] and personal[3] knowledge must be proved.
Constructive,[4] or imputed,[5] notice is entirely out of the question.[6]

---

[1] *Martin* v. *Cotter* (1846), 3 Jo. & Lat. 496 (at pp. 507, 508, *per* Lord St. Leonards, then
Sir Edward Sugden L.C. of Ireland); *Wilson* v. *Short* (1848), 6 Hare, 366 (*per* Wigram
V.-C. at p. 376, who points out that the onus is on the representor to prove clear and distinct
notice); *Hughes* v. *Jones* (1861), 3 De G.F. & J. 307 (notice must be as "clear, precise, and
definite" as the misrepresentation, *per* Knight-Bruce L.J. at p. 312); *Higgins* v. *Samels*
(1862), 2 John & H. 460 (where the misrepresentation was that limestone in a certain quarry
would produce lime "fit for the London market", and the representor set up, as an answer,
that the representee had looked at the stone in the quarry, but Wood V.-C. at p. 468, pointed
out that this was no proof that knowledge of the incapacity of the stone to produce the lime
was brought home to the representee, who was not a lime-burner); *Aberaman Ironworks* v.
Wickens (1868), 4 Ch. App. 101 (*per* Lord Cairns L.C. at pp. 107, 108); *Redgrave* v. *Hurd*
(1881), 20 Ch.D. 1, C.A. (*per* Jessel M.R. at pp. 15–17).
[2] As distinguished from "constructive".
[3] As distinguished from "imputed".
[4] Constructive notice is the name usually given by equity lawyers to that kind of notice which
is deemed to arise in contemplation of law from wilful blindness, or as Knight-Bruce L.J.
termed it, "diligence in ignorance".
[5] Imputed notice is that notice with the law imputes to a principal through his agent, if he
is his agent to know, or to be informed as to, the matters in question; or the notice which the
law infers of facts and documents from proved actual notice of a fact or document pointing to
their existence. Mr Spencer Bower's original text, to which this edition has adhered, is
dogmatic on the point; but it must be remembered, in accepting it, that it may be thought
necessary to read it subject to some gloss when the case of notice to a corporation is being
considered. A corporation can be given notice of the truth only through its directors, officers,
agents, or servants. No doubt the proof that such notice has been adequately given may have its
difficulties; but it is here submitted that it may not be *impossible*, because the corporation is not a
natural person, to give it effective notice. See, for examples of the kind of situation in which
this point may arise, *Bawden* v. *London, Edinburgh and Glasgow Assurance Co.*, [1892] 2 Q.B. 534,
C.A., referred to in note 6, below; with this case may be contrasted *Newsholme Brothers* v. *Road
Transport and General Insurance Co., Ltd.*, [1929] 2 K.B. 356, C.A. In this last case it was contended that notice given orally to an agent of an insurance company, who filled in the proposal
for the proponent, was notice to the company; though the agent for the company to obtain
business, the Court of Appeal held that he was the proponent's agent, and not that of the
company, for the purpose of filling in the form, and on this account the plea of notice to an agent
failed. But it appears from the judgments that had the agent been the agent of the company
for the purpose of completing the proposal, the plea of notice might have been acceptable.
So at p. 373 Scrutton L.J. said: "If the person having authority to bind the company by
making a contract in fact knows of the untruth of the statements and yet takes the premium,
the question may be different . . .".
In *Australia*, *Holmes* v. *Jones* (1907), 4 C.L.R. 1692 (H. Ct. of Aus.), a case which is critically
noticed in note 6 below; *cf. Maye* v. *Colonial Mutual Life Assurance Society, Ltd.* (1924), 35
C.L.R. 14 (H. Ct. of Aus.).
In *New Zealand* the ways in which an agent may be constituted an "agent to know" are discussed in *Blackley* v. *National Mutual Life Association of Australasia, Ltd.*, [1972] N.Z.L.R. 1038,
C.A.
[6] A lengthy footnote in the second edition here recapitulates the essential facts in a number
of decisions which are here only enumerated: *Dyer* v. *Hargrave* (1805), 10 Ves. 505; *Dobell* v.
Stevens (1825), 3 B. & C. 623; *Pearson* v. *Wheeler* (1825), Ry. & M. 303; *Bowring* v. *Stevens*
(1826), 2 C. & P. 337; *Harris* v. *Kemble* (1831), 5 Bligh N.S. 730; *Reynell* v. *Sprye*, *Sprye* v.
Reynell (1852), 1 De G.M. & G. 660; *Price* v. *Macaulay* (1852), 2 De G.M. & G. 339;
Brandling v. *Plummer* (1854), 2 Drew 427; *Rawlins* v. *Wickham* (1858), 3 De G. & J. 304;
Central Rail. Co. of Venezuela v. *Kisch* (1867), L.R. 2 H.L. 99; *Torrance* v. *Bolton* (1872), 8 Ch.
App. 118; *Caballero* v. *Henty* (1874), 9 Ch. App. 447; *Re Arnold, Arnold* v. *Arnold* (1880),
14 Ch.D. 270.
Later cases in the same note are *Redgrave* v. *Hurd* (1881), 20 Ch.D. 1, C.A., where Jessel

There is no exception to this rule,¹ except in cases to which the Con-

---

M.R. gives a very lucid exposition of the principles stated in the text above as to the insuf-ficiency of proof of mere means of knowledge, perfunctory inquiry, partial discovery, etc., and takes occasion to make some criticism of FRY J.'s reading of *Attwood* v. *Small* (1838), 6 Cl. & Fin. 232; *Mathias* v. *Yetts* (1882), 46 L.T. 497, C.A. (*per* JESSEL M.R. at p. 502, and Sir JAMES HANNEN at p. 504, to the same effect as in the last case); *Re London and Staffordshire Fire Insurance Co.* (1883), 24 Ch.D. 149 (where PEARSON J. held, at pp. 154, 156, that the onus is on the representor to show that he *actually* brought home knowledge of the truth to the representee, and not that he did so by means which, in accordance with the statutory provisions of Table A, would, in all ordinary matters of business of the company, which this was not, have been deemed to amount to notice); *White* v. *Haymen* (1883), Cab. & El. 101 (*per* MATHEW J. at p. 103, who held that a mere reference in a prospectus to other documents, assuming it to amount to constructive notice, would no more avail the representor than any other form of constructive notice); *Arnison* v. *Smith* (1889), 41 Ch.D. 348, C.A. (where Lord HALSBURY L.C. at p. 370 points out that "it obviously lies on those who rely on a subsequent explanation to show that such explanation was quite clear", and then shows how, in the particular case, the representors had carefully wrapped up their pretended explanation in order "to *avoid* bringing to the notice of the plaintiffs the real facts of the case, whilst stating enough to enable the defendants to say that the plaintiff was informed of these facts"; to the same effect COTTON L.J. at pp. 371, 372, and LINDLEY L.J. at p. 373); *Moss & Co., Ltd.* v. *Swansea Corporation* (1910), 74 J.P. 351; *Nocton* v. *Lord Ashburton*, [1914] A.C. 932, H.L. (*per* Lord DUNEDIN at p. 962: "no one is entitled to make a statement which on the face of it conveys a false im-pression, and then excuse himself on the ground that the person to whom he made it had available means of knowledge", or that "he could have pieced out for himself the true state of matters"); *Wells* v. *Smith*, [1914] 3 K.B. 722 (*per* SCRUTTON J. at pp. 725, 726).

It might be argued that *Bawden* v. *London, Edinburgh and Glasgow Assurance Co.*, [1892] 2 Q.B. 534, C.A. was an instance of the agent's knowledge being imputed to the company "whose agent he was to know"; but the facts in that case, which is further discussed in the next note, were indeed unusual, and the decision itself is now perhaps best to be regarded as one on these special facts. In *Newsholme Brothers* v. *Road Transport and General Insurance Co., Ltd.*, [1929] 2 K.B. 356, C.A. a set of facts only a little less dramatic led the Court of Appeal to an opposite result—see note 1 below.

In the *Australian* case of *Holmes* v. *Jones* (1907), 4 C.L.R. 1692 (H. Ct. of Aus.), ISAACS J. refers in the course of his judgment to *Bawden* v. *London, Edinburgh and Glasgow Assurance Co.* (*supra*) and says at p. 1715 that "the principle is plain that if once a person constitutes another his agent to stand in his place, he takes the responsibility of that person doing his duty to his principal" (and passing on to him the information which is brought to his notice). This seems to the present author to go rather too far; the decision in *Holmes* v. *Jones* is perhaps better to be regarded as based on the proposition that the purchasers were shown on the whole of the facts to have relied not on the representations of the vendor at all, but on a later inspection by their own agents made with a view to purchase. With this case may be compared the decision of the same court in *Maye* v. *Colonial Mutual Life Assurance Society, Ltd.* (1924), 35 C.L.R. 14.

¹ The cases in which judges have dilated on the subject-matter of the misrepresentation being an "object of sense" form no exception to the rule: for, on a close examination of these, it will be apparent that in every one of them except, perhaps, *Baily* v. *Merrell* (1615), 3 Bulstr. 94 (where the plaintiff failed because he *might have* weighed the load), the fact that was really found, and on which the decision was based, was that the representee had actual knowledge of the properties or situation or quantity of the land or the qualities of the article, and the fact that the thing was palpable to the sense of any person who used them went a long way to induce such a finding, but there was always *some* evidence beyond this to justify it; see *Dyer* v. *Hargrave* (1805), 10 Ves. 505, the first case cited in the last note. So, in *Bawden* v. *London, Edinburgh and Glasgow Assurance Co.*, [1892] 2 Q.B. 534, C.A., the defendants, being a corporation, could only see an "object of sense" with the eyes of an "agent to know", and it was proved that the person who took the policy, being an agent of this kind, saw that the assured had only one eye: in other words, this was actual knowledge in only way in which a company can have actual knowledge. On the other hand, see *King* v. *Wilson* (1843),

tributory Negligence Act applies.[1] Thus, it is of no avail to show merely
that the representee had the means of knowledge within his reach, the
use of which would have enabled a person of ordinary business habits and
normal sagacity to discover the real facts, and this, though the representor
may himself have supplied such materials; nor is it even sufficient to
show that the representee, "with all appliances and means to boot", had
in fact made a cursory, or even a diligent, use of them, unless it be also
proved that such investigation led to a revelation of the entire truth.[2]
The good sense of this is obvious. A man who has told even an innocent
untruth, by which he has induced another to alter his position,—much
more one who has fraudulently lied with that object and result,— has
debarred himself from ever complaining in a court of justice, any more
than he could in a court of morals, that the representee acted on the faith
of his misstatement in the manner in which he, the representor, intended
that he should. He can never be heard to resent the fact that another
believed the lie that was told for the very purpose of inspiring that belief,
or plead as an excuse that, if the representee had not been such a fool as to
trust such a knave, no harm would have been done.[3] The representee

---

6 Beav. 124 (where it was strongly urged that the representee, being positively in occupation of
the property, must have known its depth, but Lord LANGDALE M.R. declined to impute any
such knowledge to him, and there being no proof that he had actually measured it, the representor's contention failed: "I see no reason", he says at p. 129, "why he was to test the
reiterated representation by an actual admeasurement"); *Levy* v. *Scottish Employers' Insurance Co.*
(1901), 17 T.L.R. 229, Div. Ct.; *Biggar* v. *Rock Life Assurance Co.*, [1902] 1 K.B. 516, where
WRIGHT J. at p. 526, distinguished *Bawden* v. *London, Edinburgh and Glasgow Assurance Co.*, *supra*;
M'Millan v. *Accident Insurance Co., Ltd.*, 1907 S.C. 484, where, in Scotland, this case was openly
dissented from, though it was not really necessary to do so for the purposes of the decision. In
Newsholme Brothers v. *Road Transport and General Insurance Co., Ltd.*, [1929] 2 K.B. 356, C.A.
the Court of Appeal "distinguished" *Bawden's* case, and in a set of facts admittedly a little less
dramatic dismissed the plea of notice to the representee of the true facts. So in *Mackintosh
and Dwyer* v. *Marshall* (1843), 11 M. & W. 116 it was of no avail to urge that the representee
might have found out the truth from Lloyd's List, or in *Re Puckett and Smith's Contract*, [1902]
2 Ch. 258, C.A. that he *might* have inspected the adjoining lands. In *Shepherd* v. *Croft*, [1911]
1 Ch. 521, 528, 529, the representee *might* have peered out of the hole in the garden, and so
have discovered the watercourse; but she did not and was not bound to. *Cf. Central Rail. Co.
of Venezuela* v. *Kisch* (1867), L.R. 2 H.L. 99, 123–124.

1 Mr Spencer Bower wrote the sentence in his text in earlier editions, "There is *absolutely
no exception* to this rule". But he wrote before the Contributory Negligence Act, and it is
conceived by the author of this edition that this Act must modify the original author's absolute
rule in cases in which fraudulent misrepresentation has been the cause of injury to the person.
For everyone is under a duty to take reasonable care for his own safety, and if by taking reasonable care the injured person could have become aware of the danger, and have avoided injury,
his neglect of his own safety must surely be "fault" which will operate to reduce his award
in damages, and even in some cases possibly to extinguish the claim altogether.

2 See *Redgrave* v. *Hurd* (1881), 20 Ch.D. 1, C.A.; in *New Zealand*, *Young* v. *Butler* (1902),
22 N.Z.L.R. 407 (a rescission case, but the principle is the same.)

3 See *Barley* v. *Walford* (1846), 9 Q.B. 197 (*per cur.* at p. 209: "the defendant has no right
to say that the plaintiff was wrong in giving him credit for what he said"): *Wilson* v. *Short*
(1848), 6 Hare, 366 (*per* WIGRAM V.-C. at p. 377: "where A, dealing with B, makes a

never owed any duty to the representor to be circumspect, or to be active in suspicion, or diligent in detective research; and, even if he ever had been under such a duty, it was the very office and effect of the misrepresentation to discharge him of it, and to put his mind at rest.[1]

---

particular and distinct representation, material to the interests of B, I cannot admit that A has a right to say to B that he, B, should have doubted A's word, by reason of any general statement made by A, in which a cautious man might possibly have detected an inconsistency with the particular and distinct representation''); *Reynell* v. *Spyre, Spyre* v. *Reynell* (1852), 1 De G.M. & G. 660 (*per* Lord CRANWORTH L.J. at p. 710: ''no man can complain that another has too implicitly relied on the truth of what he has himself stated''); *Price* v. *Macaulay* (1852), 2 De G.M. & G. 339 (*per* KNIGHT-BRUCE L.J. at pp. 346, 347: ''no man can be heard to say that he is to be assumed not to have spoken the truth''); *New Brunswick and Canada Railway and Land Co.* v. *Muggeridge* (1860), 1 Drew & Sm. 363 (*per* KINDERSLEY V.-C. at p. 382); *Central Rail. Co. of Venezuela* v. *Kisch* (1867), L.R. 2 H.L. 99 (*per* Lord CHELSMFORD L.C. at pp. 120, 121: ''when once it is established that there has been any fraudulent misrepresentation or wilful concealment by which a person has been induced to enter into a contract, it is no answer to his claim to be relieved from it to tell him that he might have known the truth by proper inquiry. He has a right to retort upon the objector, 'You, at least, who have stated what is untrue . . . for the purpose of drawing me into a contract, cannot accuse me of want of caution because I relied implicitly upon your fairness and honesty'''); *Hunter* v. *Walters* (1871), 7 Ch.App. 75 (*per* JAMES L.J. who, at p. 86, ridicules the notion that the representor is to be excused because the representee *might* have discovered this, that, and the other: ''it appears to me that the proper place for such an argument would be some satirical work ridiculing, by clever exaggerations, the doctrines of the Court of Equity with reference to constructive notice''); *Mathias* v. *Yetts* (1882), 46 L.T. 497, C.A. (*per* JESSEL M.R. at p. 502); *Gluckstein* v. *Barnes*, [1900] A.C. 240, H.L. (*per* Lord MACNAGHTEN at pp. 251, 252: ''but then, says Mr Gluckstein, . . . if you had only distrusted us properly, and read the prospectus with the caution with which all prospectuses ought to be read, and sifted the matter to the bottom, you *might* have found a clue to our meaning . . . My Lords, I decline altogether to take any notice of such an argument''). Similarly, as regards representation, for the purposes of estoppel, in *Bloomenthal* v. *Ford*, [1897] A.C. 156, H.L., Lord HALSBURY L.C. has some equally pungent and emphatic observations, at pp. 161, 162, on the idea that ''it is competent for him''—the representor—''to turn round and say, 'You should have observed certain circumstances; and, if you had done that you would have been better advised than to have advanced the money','' or that ''it is open to the person who made the representation to say, 'I told you so-and-so, but you ought not to have believed me. You were too great a fool. I had a right to mislead you, because you were too great a fool''' ; and Lord HERSCHELL, at p. 168, delivers himself to the same effect: ''the very person who makes a statement of that sort has put the other party off making further inquiry. He has produced on his mind an impression as a result of which further inquiry is thought to be unnecessary or useless''. *Cf.* also *Betjemann* v. *Betjemann*, [1895] 2 Ch. 474, C.A., a case of concealed fraud in relation to a plea of a statute of limitations, and the observations of LINDLEY L.J. at p. 479, and RIGBY L.J. at p. 482 (''what is the duty of a man to inquire? To whom does he owe this duty? Certainly not to the person who has committed the concealed fraud'').

1 And this, whether the misrepresentation was fraudulent or innocent. In several of the cases cited in the immediately preceding notes it was innocent, or not alleged to be otherwise. The representor is in this dilemma, even on the assumption,—for which, however, there is no foundation,—that the representee owed any duty whatever to him to exercise care and caution: either the representor knew the truth, when he told the untruth, in which case he was fraudulent, and it does not lie in the wrong-doer's mouth to complain of the result which, by his fraud, he intended to bring about; or he believed what he said, and was innocent, in that he had not himself discovered the truth, in which case the observations of JAMES L.J. at p. 281 of *Re Arnold, Arnold* v. *Arnold* (1880), 14 Ch.D. 270, C.A., a case where the misrepresentation was assumed to be innocent, apply with unanswerable force: ''if a man makes a description calculated to mislead, I do not think that it is well for him to say, 'If you had been very careful,

Alternative theory of this ground of defence

193   If it be asserted by way of affirmative defence that the representee
was fully aware of the true facts, and this assertion is positively proved by
the evidence, is not this exactly the same as negativing the representee's
assertion (made as part of his case on the claim) that he was induced by
the fraudulent representations of the representor ?   It seems to the editor
of this edition that too much can be made of the representee's knowledge
of the facts as an *affirmative defence*; it might be thought more logical to
acknowledge the importance of this aspect of the matter when considering
the representee's claim.   In considering the elements of a cause of action in
deceit we have already stated, as a positive requirement to be proved by
the representee, *inducement—viz.*, that he was actually induced, by the
representation and on the faith of it, to alter his position to his detriment.
If he was fully aware of the true facts, it seems to the author of this
edition that, not having believed the representation complained of,
because he knew the true position, he cannot assert that he was induced
by it.[1]

Special defences—II: Agreements excluding liability for misrepresentation

194   Mr Spencer Bower, at this point in the text, dealt at length with
the next of the alternative defences which he had listed, at the time of his
earlier editions,[2] as effective to rebut a claim for damages for fraud.
This was an agreement between the parties express or implied,[3] "to
waive inquiry, take all risks, or accept all the faults, assume facts, etc.".
   While no doubt such an agreement, if satisfactorily proved, would at
the time when Mr Spencer Bower wrote have constituted a sufficient
defence to a claim for rescission for innocent misrepresentation, it must
be considered at least doubtful whether it could ever have been effective
as a defence to an action for *fraudulent* misrepresentation.[4]   But the

---

you would have found out the blunder'.   How was it that he did not himself find it out ?
How can the vendors be heard to say that the purchaser ought to have found out for them this
very blunder which they never found out for themselves ?"   *Cf.* the observations of GRANT
M.R. at p. 317 of *Edwards* v. *M'Leay* (1815), G. Cooper 308, and those of A. T. LAWRENCE J.
at p. 509 of *Scriven Brothers & Co.* v. *Hindley & Co.*, [1913] 3 K.B. 564.

   [1] This point is particularly brought out in the Australian case of *Holmes* v. *Jones* (1907),
4 C.L.R. 1692 (H. Ct. of Aus.)
   [2] The last previous edition (the 2nd) was published in 1927.
   [3] Mr Spencer Bower emphasises the difficulty of satisfactorily proving an *implied* agreement,
and says that his researches failed to provide a single instance of a successful defence based on
implied agreement (2nd Ed., para. 214, note 1).
   [4] The second edition contains a number of references to decided cases of which it may be
useful to append a reference here to the principal decisions.   It may be noted that none of them
affords an instance of a judgment for the defendant in an action for damages for fraud, based on

provisions of the Misrepresentation Act 1967 have now rendered such agreements ineffective by statute, except in so far as the court or arbitrator may allow, as a matter of fairness, as a defence to an action for damages either in fraud or for innocent misrepresentation, or to an action for rescission, or as a rejoinder to a defence based upon misrepresentation, fraudulent or innocent. Section 3 of the Misrepresentation Act provides:

> "3. If any agreement (whether made before or after the commencement of this Act) contains a provision which would exclude or restrict—
>
> > (a) any liability to which a party to a contract may be subject by reason of any misrepresentation made by him before the contract was made; or
> >
> > (b) any remedy available to another party to the contract by reason of such a misrepresentation;
>
> that provision shall be of no effect except to the extent (if any) that, in any proceedings arising out of the contract, the court or arbitrator may allow reliance on it as being fair and reasonable in the circumstances of the case."

195   In what circumstances, if at all, the court may now be induced to allow agreement to operate to nullify the effect of a *fraudulent* representation has not been the subject of consideration by a court of high authority since the passing of the Misrepresentation Act. It is submitted, however, that though the courts may well decide in appropriate cases to allow such an agreement to nullify the effect of an innocent misrepresentation, it will be difficult to persuade them to do so in any case where the representation is proved a fraudulent one. Even before the passing of the Act, it was fairly generally accepted, though there was little high authority expressly so deciding in any case where such a decision was necessary, that an agreement such as is now under consideration lost any validity

---

this defence. The principal references are: *Baglehole* v. *Walters* (1811), 3 Camp. 154 (ship sold expressly "with all faults"; fraud alleged. Lord ELLENBOROUGH said "In a contract such as this I think there is no fraud unless the seller by positive means renders it impossible for the purchaser to detect latent faults". Evidence was tendered to prove artifice, but plaintiff's case of fraud was held to fail on the facts); *Pickering* v. *Dowson* (1813), 4 Taunt. 779 (another case of a ship sold "with all faults". Although fraud was alleged, it was expressly held that there was "no evidence of any fraud at all"); *Schneider* v. *Heath* (1813), 3 Camp. 506 (another case of a ship sold "with all faults". But there had been a fraudulent misrepresentation. Lord MANSFIELD C.J. said "The words are very large to exclude the buyer from calling upon the seller for any defect in the thing sold; but if the seller was guilty of any positive fraud in the sale, the words will not protect him. There must be such fraud, either in a false representation, or in using means to conceal some defect". Both were held proved on the facts, and the plaintiff succeeded in his claim for refund of the deposit). In *Ward* v. *Hobbs* (1878), 4 App. Cas. 13, H.L., fraud was not proved, and the claim failed on that account; but Earl CAIRNS L.C. said at p. 21 that if it could have been proved that the seller had known of the taint, an action would have lain for deceit notwithstanding the stipulation in the contract that the animals were taken "with all their faults".

which it purported to cover was shown to have been fraudulently made.[1]

The effect of the decisions before the Act may be summed up as being that an express agreement to sell with all faults, though it protects the representor from liability if there are faults, even to his knowledge, is no protection whatever if, besides knowing of those faults, he used positive means and devices to cover them up, or hide them away.[2] Indeed, every such manoeuvre or artifice, since it amounts of itself to a falsehood by conduct, as has already been shown,[3] may be regarded as a new and independent misrepresentation, to which the term requiring the representee to put up with "all faults" has no application. *Fraus est celare fraudem.* So where the representor expressly refuses to warrant the soundness of what he sells, or to sell otherwise than with all faults, but yet chooses to add a fraudulent statement that, so far as he knows and believes, the subject of the sale is free from this or that specified fault, the express term in the contract, and the express refusal to warrant, go for nothing, and he loses the protection they would otherwise give him;[4] but such statement must be shown to be as clear and explicit and direct as the express term or refusal.[5] And, in cases of sales of land, where there is a condition that the purchaser shall take such title as the vendor has, or shall assume certain facts, or where, in the case of a prospectus, the

---

[1] The authorities usually cited in support of this proposition are *S. Pearson & Son, Ltd.* v. *Dublin Corporation,* [1907] A.C. 351, H.L. and *Boyd and Forrest* v. *Glasgow and South Western Rail. Co.,* 1911 S.C. 33 in the judgment of the Lord Justice-Clerk at p. 61. The decision went to appeal in [1913] A.C. 404, and was reversed, the Lords holding fraud not proved; but the decision in the Lords does not advert to the point now under discussion. In the Tenth Report of the Law Reform Committee (1967), which is reprinted in Appendix B to this treatise, it is said in para. 23 that "The decision in the House of Lords in *Boyd and Forrest* v. *Glasgow and South Western Rail. Co.,* 1915 S.C. (H.L.) 20 leaves little doubt that the parties are at present free to contract out of liability for misrepresentation *unless it can be shown to have been fraudulent, in which case the agreement will be disregarded as being contrary to public policy*".

[2] *Baglehole* v. *Walters* (1811), 3 Camp. 154 (per Lord ELLENBOROUGH C.J. at p. 157, "unless the seller by positive means renders it impossible for the purchaser to detect secret faults": in that case, however, the plaintiff failed to prove the use of such "positive means"; *Schneider* v. *Heath* (1813), 3 Camp. 506, where the representee succeeded on proof that the representor had removed the vessel, which was to be "taken with all faults", from the ways in which she lay, and had kept her continuously afloat, so that her bottom and keel were always concealed until the moment when the representee was given possession of her); *Ward* v. *Hobbs* (1878), 4 App. Cas. 13 H.L. (where, at p. 27, Lord O'HAGAN refers to, and adopts the proposition of Lord ELLENBOROUGH C.J. cited *supra,* but points out that, in the case before the House, "it has not been pretended that he"—the defendant—"was guilty of any contrivance" to conceal or disguise the disease from which the pigs were suffering). See para. 58, and the cases cited thereto, *ante.*

[3] See para. 58, Chapter III, *ante.*

[4] *Per* Lord CAIRNS at pp. 20, 21, of *Ward* v. *Hobbs* (1878), 4 App. Cas. 13, H.L.

[5] *Ibid.,* at pp. 22–23 *per* Lord CAIRNS.

applicant is required to waive his right to complain of the nondisclosure of material contracts, or where in the case of a contract to execute works there is a term that the contractors shall accept the accuracy of plans drawings or particulars furnished by the engineers, the condition or term is no bar to the representee's claim to relief if the representor, pretending not to know of any defect in title or inaccuracy of description, or of any material contract, is shown to have been all the time cognizant thereof;[1] and, so far from being a defence to an action for damages for misrepresentation, constitutes strong evidence of the fraud which is required to establish it. So also, a "covered clause" in a marine insurance policy protects the assured from the consequences of an accidental or mistaken, not a designed, misdescription of the subject of the insurance.[2]

Special defences—III: Avoidance of contract

196 Where the representee's alteration of position consisted in the entering into a contract with the representor, it is a good defence to an action or counter-claim for damages to allege and prove that, before writ issued or counter-claim pleaded, such contract had in fact been avoided by mutual consent[3] or by judgment of a court,[4] just as, conversely, in proceedings for rescission, it is a good defence to allege and prove that before the commencement thereof the representee had in fact affirmed such contract;[5] for in either case the election to pursue one, rather than the other, of the two alternative remedies, is shown to have been

---

[1] *Re Banister, Broad* v. *Munton* (1879), 12 Ch.D. 131, C.A., where Jessel M.R. at pp. 142, 143, BRETT, L.J. at pp. 145, 147, and COTTON L.J. at pp. 149, 150, point out that a vendor is not entitled to set up, as an answer to the action, a term or condition of this nature in respect of anything which the vendor knows not to be true, but only in respect of some fact of which he knows nothing; *Brownlie* v. *Campbell* (1880), 5 App. Cas. 925, H.L., where the rule is recognised by Lord SELBORNE L.C. at pp. 936, 937 though in this case no fraud was proved; *Greenwood* v. *Leather Shod Wheel Co.*, [1900] 1 Ch. 421, C.A. (a case of alleged waiver, pursuant to a waiver-clause in a prospectus wherein it was stated that "there *may be* contracts" which the statute then in force would require to be disclosed, implying that the representors did not know of any, whereas it was proved that they were cognizant of several, of the most vital materiality: held that the clause constituted no defence at all; see, especially, the observations of LINDLEY M.R. at pp. 435–437); *Cackett* v. *Keswick*, [1902] 2 Ch. 456, C.A. (the like); *S. Pearson & Son, Ltd.* v. *Dublin Corporation*, [1907] A.C. 351, H.L. (an action for damages for fraudulent misrepresentations in plans, drawings, and specifications: Lord LOREBURN L.C. at pp. 353, 354, Lord HALSBURY at p. 356, Lord ASHBOURNE at pp. 359, 360, Lord JAMES at p. 362, and Lord ATKINSON at pp. 364, 366).
[2] *Hewitt Brothers* v. *Wilson*, [1915] 2 K.B. 739, C.A.
[3] This was impliedly recognised in *Arnison* v. *Smith* (1889), 41 Ch.D. 348, C.A.
[4] See *Ship* v. *Crosskill* (1870), L.R. 10 Eq. 73, where this was assumed.
[5] See Chapter XIII, *post.*

definitely exercised before the initiation of the proceedings.[1] But such consent is not shown by mere proof of an offer not accepted—still less by mere disclosure or admission of the fact that a misrepresentation has been made, unaccompanied by such an offer.[2] A clear offer not only of rescission, but of complete restitution and indemnity, must be proved to have been made.[3] And it must be remembered that this applies only to a case where the contracting party was the actual representor; where the representation was, in fact, made by the agent of the contracting party (the directors of a company, for instance), the representee has still a right to recover against the agent, notwithstanding that the contract (whether by consent, or judgment) has been avoided, any damage he may have sustained by reason of his not having in fact obtained, or being able to obtain, from the contracting party the full restitution which had been agreed, or adjudged, to be made.[4] If he has in fact recovered such full restitution, he has sustained no damage, and, on this ground, since damage is a necessary ingredient in the cause of action,[5] his claim fails.[6]

Special defences—IV: Lord Tenterden's Act

197 Since the passing of the Statute of Frauds Amendment Act 1828,

---

[1] See Chapter X, *ante*, as to this right of election, and as to the impossibility of assuming the two inconsistent attitudes of affirmation and repudiation.

[2] *Arnison* v. *Smith* (1889), 41 Ch.D. 348, C.A., where the directors of a company, after the issue of a fraudulent prospectus, sent an "ambidextrous" circular to the applicants, by which they pretended at the trial that they had corrected their misrepresentations and revealed the truth; but it was held by the C.A., affirming KEKEWICH J. that not only had there been no such full and clear disclosure, but, even if there had been, the circular made no offer to restore the money paid, and, therefore, there was no ground for reducing the damages even, much less any defence to the action.

[3] *Arnison* v. *Smith*, *supra*, per Lord HALSBURY L.C. at pp. 369, 370: "if the directors had sent to each of the plaintiffs a notice to this effect, 'We have deceived you, and, if you like, you can have your money back', the case would have stood very differently, and I reserve my opinion as to what would then have been the right course for the court to take. It may be that in such a case it would be held not reasonable for the plaintiffs to go on with their eyes open, and incur further damage". To the same effect COTTON L.J. at p. 372, and LINDLEY L.J. at p. 373.

[4] For instance, in *Ship* v. *Crosskill* (1870), L.R. 10 Eq. 73, the plaintiff had already succeeded in obtaining an order of the court for the rectification of the register of the company by the removal of his name therefrom, but, the company being in liquidation, he was unable to obtain the moneys which, by the same order, had been ordered to be repaid to him by the company. He subsequently sued the directors for the damage so sustained, and no one suggested that he had not the right to do so, but, as was pointed out by Romilly, M.R., only if, as in any other action for damages, he could prove that the misrepresentation was fraudulent (which, when applying for rectification, was not necessary), and this he failed to do. *Cf.* in *Australia, Sibley* v. *Grosvenor* (1916), 21 C.L.R. 469; *Ivanof* v. *Phillip M., Levy, Pty., Ltd.*, [1971] V.R. 167; In *New Zealand, Hazeldine* v. *Milligan and Lindsay*, [1922] 41 N.Z.L.R. 872.

[5] See Chapter VII.

[6] And, if some loss has been incurred before the offer to make full restoration has been made, the damage will be confined to such loss, and will not extend to further damage incurred by a representee "with his eyes open". See *Arnison* v. *Smith* as cited in note 3, *supra*.

usually cited as Lord Tenterden's Act, there has been available to the representor a special affirmative defence to any action for damages based upon a fraudulent representation[1] relating to the credit of a third party where the representation is not in writing and signed personally by the representor.[2]   The short title of the statute appears to reflect the notion that its object was to extend the operation of the Statute of Frauds (29 Car. 2, c. 3), but this was certainly not its only object, as appears from its long title ("an Act for rendering a written memorandum necessary to the validity of certain *promises and engagements*").   There is no doubt, however, that one of its objects was to supplement the earlier statute in certain directions, where the experience of 150 years had shown it to be defective.   It consists of ten sections, whereof s. 6 is the section now to be considered.   The Act does not extend to Scotland,[3] but a provision to the same effect as the section in question, except in one important respect, and more clearly and artistically expressed, is contained in a statute introduced 28 years later to meet the special mercantile requirements of that part of the United Kingdom.[4]

198   The section is as follows:

> "No action shall be brought whereby to charge any person upon or by reason of any representation or assurance made or given concerning or relating to the character, conduct, credit, ability, trade, or dealings of any other person, to the intent or purpose that such other person may obtain credit, money, or goods (upon), unless such representation or assurance be made in writing, signed by the party to be charged therewith."

The drafting leaves something to be desired;[5] and the word "upon", nowadays generally shown in brackets, has been the despair of courts of construction.[6]   But the section has been effective as a defence in most of

---

[1] See note 3 on the next page.

[2] It relates only to actions for damages: an action or other proceeding for rescission of a contract induced by misrepresentation cannot be said to be an action "whereby to charge any person" within the meaning of s. 6.   As to actions for money had and received, see para. 199, *post*.

[3] See s. 9 of the Act of 1828.

[4] This is s. 6 of the Mercantile Law Amendment (Scotland) Act 1856.

[5] Mr Spencer Bower writes a blistering note on this subject in earlier editions, instancing the obscurity attendant upon the use of the expressions "any representation or assurance", and "concerning or relating to", and noticing that the phrase "trade or dealings" would *prima facie* seem to have a much wider application than was actually intended by the Legislature, or has been given to it by courts of construction.

[6] Three theories of the genesis of the blunder are put forward in *Lyde* v. *Barnard* (1836), 1 M. & W. 101—(1) that "credit" and "money or goods upon" were somehow transposed, per GURNEY B. at p. 104, ALDERSON B. at pp. 109, 110, and PARKE B. at pp. 115, 116; (2) that after "upon", the words "such representation or assurance" had been accidentally omitted or erased, per PARKE B. at pp. 115, 116; and (3) that the word was originally "there-

the reported cases in which it has been put forward,[1] or but for circumstances not connected with the nature of the plea itself, would have been so.[2] The representations affected by the section have been held by the highest authority to be fraudulent representations only.[3] They are not confined to representations of a character similar to those affected by s. 4 of the Statute of Frauds,[4] nor to those made solely for the purpose of obtaining credit for a third person, as distinguished from those made for that purpose and also for fraudulent purposes of the representor's own,[5] nor to those by which it is intended to benefit such third person, as

---

upon", which would make quite good sense, and that it was afterwards thought that, though the word was sensible, it was unnecessary, and that, in preparing the roll for Parliament, the person instructed to delete the word hastily passed his pen through the first part of it only, leaving the remainder—"upon"—standing, *per* Lord ABINGER C.B. at pp. 123, 124. Whatever be the correct explanations, it is certain that, with the one consent, the courts have treated the word as meaningless and non-existent.

[1] See *Lyde* v. *Barnard* (1836), 1 M. & W. 101 (where, the Court of Exchequer being equally divided, the non-suit by Lord ABINGER C.B. at the trial stood); *Haslock* v. *Fergusson* (1837), 7 Ad. & El. 86; *Swann* v. *Phillips* (1838), 8 Ad. & El. 457; *Devaux* v. *Steinkeller* (1839), 6 Bing. N.C. 84; *Williams* v. *Mason* (1873), 28 L.T. 232; *Swift* v. *Jewsbury* (1874), L.R. 9 Q.B. 301, Exch. Ch.; *Pearson* v. *Seligman* (1883), 48 L.T. 842, C.A.; *Clydesdale Bank* v *J. and G. Paton*, [1896] A.C. 381, H.L.; *Hirst* v. *West Riding Union Banking Co.*, [1901] 2 K.B. 560, C.A.; *Parsons* v. *Barclay & Co., Ltd.* (1910), 103 L.T. 196, C.A.

In *Banbury* v. *Bank of Montreal*, [1918] A.C. 626, H.L. the plea was rejected; but that was not an action for damages for *fraud*, but one based on negligence in giving advice, the duty of care alleged being one arising from *contract*. It was held that Lord Tenterden's Act has no application to such a claim, and this decision has since been followed in *W. B. Anderson & Sons, Ltd.* v. *Rhodes (Liverpool), Ltd.*, [1967] 2 All E.R. 850 (CAIRNS J.), and in *Mutual Life and Citizens Assurance Co., Ltd.* v. *Evatt*, [1971] 1 All E.R. 150; [1971] A.C. 793, P.C. None of these cases, however, was a claim for damages for fraud.

[2] In *Tatton* v. *Wade* (1856), 18 C.B. 371, Exch. Ch., where there were two representations, one oral and the other in writing, no one doubted that, if the plaintiff had been proved to have relied on the former alone, the plea would have succeeded: but the jury found, on what the Exchequer Chamber held to be a proper direction, that the plaintiff did not rely on the oral representation alone (*per* POLLOCK C.B. at p. 385, WIGHTMAN J. and CROMPTON J. at p.387, and BRAMWELL B. at p. 388).

[3] *Banbury* v. *Bank of Montreal, supra* (*per* Lord FINLAY L.C. at pp. 639–641, Lord ATKINSON at pp. 690–694, Lord PARKER at pp. 706–708, and Lord WRENBURY, at pp. 711–713). The reason, of course, was that these were the only representations which at the time of the decisions would support an action for damages for misrepresentation. It is certain that *Banbury* v. *Bank of Montreal*, [1918] A.C. 626, H.L. is an authority for the proposition that Lord Tenterden's Act does not apply to *Hedley Byrne* actions; see *per* Lord PARKER OF WADDINGTON at p. 708, *per* Lord WRENBURY at p. 713. Whether it may now apply, notwithstanding these *dicta*, to the action for damages for innocent misrepresentation now permitted by the Misrepresentation Act 1967 is not so certain—see Chapter XII, para. 225, for some discussion of this topic.

[4] *Devaux* v. *Steinkeller, supra, per* TINDAL C.J. at p. 88, and BOSANQUET J. at p. 89, where it is pointed out that it is not until s. 7 of the statute is reached that any mention is made of the Statute of Frauds at all.

[5] *Clydesdale Bank* v. *J. & G. Paton, supra, per* Lord WATSON at pp. 390, 391, Lord HERSCHELL at pp. 393, 394, and Lord DAVEY at pp. 396, 397, with regard to the (in this respect) similar clause of the Scottish statute referred to in note 4 to para. 197, *ante*.

as distinguished from those intended only for the representor's own benefit.[1]

199   The section provides the representor with a defence, if he chooses to avail himself of it, to all actions for the recovery of damages, or, whether strictly they can be so regarded or not, all actions for money had and received, founded on fraudulent misrepresentation,[2] but not to actions for rescission, or for money had and received merely as part of the restitution and relief consequential upon such rescission.[3]   The burden of proof, and of allegation, is upon the representor, and, if there are two representations as to credit, one oral and the other written and signed, an additional burden rests upon the representor to show that the representee relied solely on the former.[4]

200   The signature required to defeat this plea is a personal one, and signature by an agent is not sufficient.[5]   This plainly appears from a comparison of the language of the section, and also that of s. 1 of the same statute,[6]—in both of which the words, "or his agent thereunto lawfully authorised", are significantly omitted,—with the language of certain sections of the Statute of Frauds, where they are as significantly inserted.   It must be thought to follow that, as there can be no personal physical signature by a corporate body, such body can always successfully plead the statutory plea to any action for damages based upon misrepresentation as to a third person's credit, whether oral or written, made by any of its agents.[7]

---

[1] *Pearson* v. *Seligman* (1883), 48 L.T. 842, C.A.

[2] *Haslock* v. *Fergusson* (1837), 7 Ad. & El. 86, where the action was so framed, in the hope of getting round the statute.

[3] See note 2 to para. 197, *ante*.

[4] See *Tatton* v. *Wade* (1856), 18 C.B. 371, Exch. Ch.

[5] *Williams* v. *Mason* (1873), 28 L.T. 232; *Swift* v. *Jewsbury* (1874), L.R. 9 Q.B. 301, Exch. Ch.; *Hirst* v. *West Riding Union Banking Co.*, [1901] 2 K.B. 560, C.A.

[6] *Hyde* v. *Johnson* (1836), 2 Bing. N.C. 776, was a similar decision on the similar words in s. 1 of the statute.

[7] In the 2nd edition Mr Spencer Bower expresses this opinion and cites in support *Hirst* v. *West Riding Union Banking Co.* (*supra*) and *Banbury* v. *Bank of Montreal*, [1918] A.C. 626, H.L. *per* Lord PARKER at p. 708, and Lord WRENBURY at pp. 713–714.   But these authorities do not appear to the present author completely to support the proposition in the text.   The first of them goes only so far as to decide that a corporation is a "person" within the meaning of the section, and that it is not to be held liable upon a representation made, albeit in writing, *by its agent*.   The passages cited from the second case decide that a corporation is a "person".   But may not a corporation itself "sign" a document containing a representation?   Such an eventuality is perhaps unlikely; but what of a representation in writing *under seal*?

201　As to the six, or (counting "trade or dealings" as one phrase) the five, possible subject-matters of the class of representation falling within the section, "credit" explains itself; but the other terms, with the exception of "conduct", have received judicial interpretation. Thus, a representation as to a man's "ability" was held by two members of the Exchequer Chamber to include a representation as to incumbrances on that person's property,[1] though the other two members differed, being of opinion that such a representation relates only to a fund.[2] A statement as to a third person's "ability" or "credit" is none the less so, because the representor adds other facts, furnishing a reason why the person may be trusted.[3] "Character" has been confined to "character for paying promptly";[4] and the expression "trade or dealings", which, construed in the ordinary and literal meaning of the words, would include every sort of commercial transaction, has been held not to apply to such dealings as have no direct relation to the question of a third person's credit.[5]

The expression "another person" in the section contemplates of course some third person, physically and legally distinct from both the representor and the representee.[6] A company in which the representor might be the largest, or practically the sole, shareholder would still be "another person",[7] and, though a firm is not a person, yet if A makes a representation as to the credit of a firm consisting of himself and B, he is making a representation about "a third person", *viz.* B, and none the less because he is also making one about himself.[8]

202　Where the statutory plea is raised, it has been said that, in cases of oral—as distinct from written but unsigned—representations, it is the preferable course for the court to obtain a finding from the jury (if the case is tried before a jury) as to the matters to which the oral statement was intended to relate, if this question fairly admits of doubt,

---

[1] Lord ABINGER C.B. and GURNEY B. in *Lyde* v. *Barnard*, cited in note 1 on p. 226, *ante*.

[2] *Ibid.*, *per* ALDERSON and PARKE BB.

[3] *Swann* v. *Phillips* (1838), 8 Ad. & El. 457, *per* LITTLEDALE J. at p. 461, and PATTESON J. at p. 462.

[4] This was the kind of "character" which was the subject of *Haslock* v. *Fergusson*, cited in note 7, *ante*.

[5] *Bishop* v. *Balkis Consolidated Co.* (1890), 25 Q.B.D. 512, C.A., *per cur.* at p. 522, differing from VAUGHAN WILLIAMS J. who in the court below had held that an oral representation that certain documents had been lodged with a company on a transfer of shares was a representation within the section.

[6] *Hirst* v. *West Riding Union Banking Co.*, [1901] 2 K.B. 560, C.A. *per* STIRLING L.J. at pp. 563–564; *Banbury* v. *Bank of Montreal*, [1918] A.C. 626, H.L. at pp. 708, 713–714.

[7] See, for instance, in a quite different context, *Lee* v. *Lee's Air Farming, Ltd.*, [1960] 3 All E.R. 420; [1961] A.C. 12, P.C.

[8] *Devaux* v. *Steinkeller* (1839), 6 Bing. N.C. 84.

and then to rule on the question of law whether, accepting the finding of fact, the representation is within the section or not.[1]   In cases of written but unsigned, or not personally signed, representations, or where, in the case of any oral representation, there is no dispute or difficulty either as to the substance or the meaning of the words used, all questions raised by the statutory plea are questions of law.

Damages

203   In an action of deceit, or its equitable equivalent, the relief to which a successful plaintiff is entitled is damages, and damages only. There can be no question of undoing any contract or transaction, since the action is instituted and maintained on the basis that the representee has elected, or is compelled by the application of certain rules of law, to adhere to such contract or transaction; from which it follows that he can be put back in the position in which he was before he altered it on the faith of the fraudulent misrepresentation (which is the purpose of all civil relief) only by the recovery of a gross sum in money, which is to compensate him (so far as money can) for the loss which he has suffered down to the date of trial, and also for such loss (if any) as he must necessarily suffer in the future under the provisions of the contract which he is fixed with, or otherwise.

Principles of assessment—General

204   What "damage" means in law, and what causal connection must be established between it and the misrepresentation, are subjects which have already been discussed;[2] but there are also certain principles of law upon which, where damage exists, the amount thereof is to be computed.

The governing principle is that the sum to be awarded must represent neither more nor less than the total amount of the moneys irrevocably paid away, and the value of property irrevocably parted with by the representee through having altered his position in the manner proved,[3]

---

[1] *Lyde* v. *Barnard* (1836), 1 M. & W. 101, *per* ALDERSON B. at p. 111, and PARKE B. at p. 112.   The other course, *viz.* after a full and proper direction as to what legal consequences flow from what facts, to leave it to the jury to find for the defendant or the plaintiff, is quite permissible, and, as in cases of malicious prosecution, where "reasonable and probable cause" is in question, or in cases of defamation, where the dispute is as to whether the publication is protected or not, judges frequently adopt it in preference to the first.

[2] See Chapter VII, *ante*.

[3] Where the fraudulent misrepresentation has resulted, not in the representee entering into a contract, but in loss in some other way, the measure of damages will be the measure generally applicable in actions in tort—proper compensation for the loss suffered. Thus *Mafo* v. *Adams*, [1970] 1 Q.B. 548, where the representee had been induced by a fraudulent representation to vacate premises, he was held entitled to compensation for the loss of his protected tenancy, and "in addition, upon accepted principles, to compensation for the physical inconvenience suffered."

and also, since the damage must be assessed once for all,[1] the present
value of all moneys payable and property transferable by virtue of any
liability assumed in consequence of such alteration of position, less the
amount of moneys or value of property received, and receivable, by the
representee under any contract or transaction induced by the misrepresentation.

Principles of assessment—I: One-sided account

205   The simplest type of case is that in which there is only one side
to the account, that is to say, where the representee has sustained a loss
of a specific chattel,[2] or where he has paid, or is liable to pay, a definite
sum of money, and has received nothing, provided, of course, that the
property or sum so delivered or paid is irrecoverable in law,[3] or in fact,
by reason of the insolvency of the deliveree or payee,[4] and if it is a case of
liability to pay, provided that there are no valid grounds for disputing it.[5]
In such cases, it is simply a matter of addition, coupled (in the case of
liability to future periodical payments) with an estimate, according to
well-known mathematical and accountancy rules, of the present value
of such liability, and no balance has to be struck.

It may be doubted whether a claim for damages may be sustained in
respect of loss attributable to performance of a legal duty, where the
decision to perform it and not to default therein is induced by a fraudulent misrepresentation.   In Australia it has been held that no such claim
is maintainable.   In *Australasian Brokerage, Ltd.* v. *Australian and New
Zealand Banking Corporation, Ltd.*[1] the point was dealt with in the joint
judgment of DIXON, EVATT, and McTIERNAN, JJ., in which it was said:[1]

> "(The averment was) that the plaintiff company was induced to perform
> the agreement, a thing it appears on the averments contained in the count
> to be legally compellable to do, and that in performing the agreement it
> incurred expenses and thus lost sums of money.   'In the eye of the law a
> man is not injured by being beguiled into the doing of a thing which he is
> already bound to do.   Where this happens the deceitful artifice is not a
> ground even for the avoidance of a contract, and *a fortiori*, it does not
> afford a ground for an action of deceit'—T. A. Street's *Foundations of Legal
> Liability* (1906) Vol. I, p. 416.   For this reason the count is bad."

---

[1] *Clarke* v. *Yorke* (1882), 52 L.J. Ch. 32 (*per* PEARSON J. at p. 34).
[2] As in *Mullett* v. *Mason* (1866), L.R. 1 C.P. 559 (loss of cows by disease).
[3] Examples of such cases are *Richardson* v. *Sylvester* (1873), L.R. 9 Q.B. 34 (expenses incurred), *Wilkinson* v. *Downton*, [1897] 2 Q.B. 57 (*quoad* the sums paid for railway fares).
[4] As in *Mackay* v. *Commercial Bank of New Brunswick* (1874), L.R. 5 P.C. 394.
[5] See *Polhill* v. *Walter* (1832), 3 B. & Ad. 114; *Pontifex* v. *Bignold* (1841), 3 Man. & G. 63, 82.
[6] (1934), 52 C.L.R. 430 (H. Ct. of Aus.).
[7] At p. 448.

Principles of assessment—II: Where fraud has induced contract

206   It is where the representee's alteration of position has assumed the form of a contract with the representor, or with a third person, and where usually there are two sides to the account, and a balance has to be struck, that nice questions as to the quantification of damages have generally arisen.   But the rules applicable may now be said to be established.   On one side of the account must be placed everything that the representee has paid, and the proved value of everything he is compellable to pay in the future, including the value (to be assessed) of any property or advantages, estimable in money, which he has transferred, or is compellable to transfer in the future, pursuant to the terms of the contract. On the other side is to be placed all money, or the value of all property which he has received, or is entitled in the future to receive (here again the present value is to be estimated), under the same contract.[1] If the real value of the items on the credit side of the account is *nil*, which has not infrequently been found to be the case,[2] the representee is entitled to the whole amount of the items on the other side, which is "the ultimate, final, highest standard of his loss".[3]

On the other hand, if the credit items are a complete equivalent, he has sustained no damage at all.[4]

207   An interesting variation on this theme is furnished by the case where two parties exchange land or goods at agreed "values" recited in the agreement no money (or no substantial sum) passing between them, and one subsequently sues for damages for a fraudulent misrepresentation

---

[1] See *McConnel* v. *Wright*, [1903] 1 Ch. 546, C.A., *per* COLLINS M.R. at pp. 554, 555, where a lucid exposition of the general rule is to be found.   In *Australia*, *Holmes* v. *Jones* (1907), 4 C.L.R. 1692 (H. Ct. of Aus.);   *Cooke* v. *Caldwell's Wines, Ltd.* (1925), 25 N.S.W. S.R. 161, 168.   In *Toteff* v. *Antonas* (1952), 87 C.L.R. 647 (H. Ct. of Aus.) it was argued for the defendant in a fraudulent misrepresentation case involving the sale of a business that the only misrepresentation proved having been one as to the value of the stock, the damages should be limited to the difference between the value of the stock and the price paid for the stock, neglecting the loss which the purchaser sustained on other items purchased, such as goodwill, as to which there had been no misrepresentation.   This contention was rejected by the High Court of Australia, which assessed the damage as the loss sustained on the transaction as a whole.

[2] See *Twycross* v. *Grant (No. 1)* (1877), 2 C.P.D. 469, C.A. and *Goldrei, Foucard & Son* v. *Sinclair*, [1918] 1 K.B. 180, C.A. where the jury so found, and *Jury* v. *Stoker* (1882), 9 L.R. Ir. 385, and *Thomson* v. *Lord Clanmorris*, [1900] 1 Ch. 718, C.A., where the judge so found.

[3] *McConnel* v. *Wright*, *supra*, at pp. 554, 555.

[4] *Ibid.*, at p. 555.   In *Australia* see *Holmes* v. *Jones* (1907), 4 C.L.R. 1692 (H. Ct. of Aus.). This was one of the grounds on which the appeal succeeded.   On the other hand it is equally true to say, if the credit items are nil, that the representee's loss will be the gross sum expended.   See in *New Zealand*, *Easterbrook* v. *Hopkins*, [1918] N.Z.L.R. 428, C.A. at p. 445, and *Jack* v. *Peters*, [1941] 60 N.Z.L.R. 153, for examples in which the goodwill of a business purchased has been held to be worthless, and the full amount of the purchase price paid has been awarded in damages accordingly.

affecting a part only of the property acquired by him. In a *Victorian* case[1]
A transferred to B a farm, a team of bullocks and tackle, and an interest
as equitable purchaser in a block of grazing land subject to an outstanding
liability for a balance of purchase money. In return B transferred to A
forty-three blocks of suburban residential land. Each of the properties
was "valued" in the exchange contract, a sum being specified as the
agreed value of each. A sum of £100 was paid in cash by A to B to
balance the account. It was represented by B to A that the suburban
blocks were not subject to flooding. Subsequently, when it was found
that the blocks in fact flooded, A sued B for damages for fraudulent
misrepresentation. The trial judge found fraud proved. He awarded
damages, assessing them by deducting the market value of the flooding
land, ascertained as at the date of the transaction between the parties,
from the sum fixed in the agreement as its value. It was contended, on
the authority of *Holmes* v. *Jones*,[2] that he should have valued *all* the property passing each way, as at the material date, and should have assessed
damages on the foundation afforded by such a calculation. The Full
Court of Victoria rejected this proposition, saying[3]:

> "In a contract of exchange cannot it be said:—If the property taken by the
> plaintiffs was not subject to flooding it is worth £X, which is the same
> value as the property given by them to the defendants (i.e. the price paid
> by the plaintiffs), but, because it is not flood-free, it is worth only £X
> minus £99, and, as the plaintiffs paid the equivalent of £X they suffer
> damage to the extent of £99? We think it can and, if there is evidence
> to support his finding of the difference in values, that the learned Judge's
> assessment should not be disturbed."

Principles of assessment—how value to be calculated

208 The soundness of these propositions is generally accepted[4]; but
questions have arisen, and have provoked discussions of a solemnity and
length quite disproportionate to the merits or plausibility of the arguments advanced, as to what "value" must be taken to mean, when applied
to the property or benefits acquired by the representee under the contract,
and also as to the date at which these values must be ascertained.

---

[1] *Brooksby* v. *Lightowler*, [1938] V.L.R. 112 (Full Court of Victoria).
[2] (1907), 4 C.L.R. 1692 (H. Ct. of Aus.).
[3] At pp. 117–118.
[4] Lord ATKIN doubted, in *Clark* v. *Urquhart*, [1930] A.C. 28 (H.L: I.) at p. 68 whether
they may not have been expressed "in too rigid terms", and reserved the right to reconsider
the statement in *McConnel* v. *Wright* if occasion should arise. See, e.g. the questions raised in
para. 213, *infra*. In New Zealand MACARTHUR J. set out a useful summary of the principles in
New Zealand Refrigerating Co., Ltd. v. *Scott*, [1969] N.Z.L.R. 30.

It is now well settled that the value of any property or rights or benefits received by the representee means their real or actual value, to be
determined by reference to the evidence adduced,[1] and without reference to current or market prices in the case of marketable securities,
where such prices are wholly artificial, and the mere manufacture and
creation of the very company or persons whose fraud has given the representee his right to damages; or, in other words, "value" means the
price which the shares or other property would have fetched as between
reasonable and honest sellers and purchasers, if the whole truth of the
facts which the representors had perverted or concealed had been within
the knowledge of those fixing the price.[2]   The ascertainment of the
real value, in this sense, usually results in reducing the figure to be de-
ducted, and proportionately enhancing the damages,[3] but it sometimes
operates in the opposite direction, and it is the representor who adduces
the evidence with the view of aggravating the former sum and mini-
mizing the latter.[4]

209   The date at which this real value is to be assessed is the date at
which the property was acquired, or (in the case of shares or other like
securities) the date of allotment or transfer.[5]   The representee is not

---

[1] *Pearson* v. *Wheeler* (1825), Ry. & M. 303 (a case of fraudulent misrepresentation of the
takings of a public house, *per* ABBOTT C.J. at p. 304); and the authorities cited in the next note.
It has been held in *New Zealand* in *Canavan* v. *Wright*, [1957] N.Z.L.R. 790, C.A. that
where there is positively no satisfactory evidence of value as at the material date, the claim
must fail.

[2] *Twycross* v. *Grant (No. 1)* (1877), 2 C.P.D. 469, C.A., *per* Lord COLERIDGE C.J. at
pp. 489–491, in the C.P.D., and *per* BRAMWELL L.J. at pp. 503–505, and COCKBURN C.J.
at pp. 542–546, in the C.A.; *Jury* v. *Stoker* (1881), 9 L.R. Ir. 385; *Arkwright* v. *Newbold*
(1881), 17 Ch.D. 301, C.A., *per* FRY J. at pp. 312, 313 (it was not necessary for the C.A. to
consider the question, because they reversed the judgment given by FRY J. in favour of the
plaintiff); *Peek* v. *Derry* (1887), 37 Ch.D. 541, C.A., *per* COTTON L.J. at pp. 591–593, and
Sir James HANNEN and LOPES L.J. at p. 594 (the discussion as to damages, and the principles
laid down by the C.A. with reference thereto are of course unaffected by the subsequent
reversal of the decision itself by the H.L.); *Glasier* v. *Rolls* (1889), 42 Ch.D. 436, C.A., *per*
KEKEWICH J. at p. 455 (here again the rule laid down is in no way impeached by the subsequent
reversal by the C.A.); *McConnel* v. *Wright*, [1903] 1 Ch. 546, C.A., *per* COLLINS M.R. at
pp. 552–555, ROMER L.J. at pp. 556–558, and COZENS-HARDY L.J. at p. 559; *Cackett* v.
Keswick, [1902] 2 Ch. 456, C.A., *per* FARWELL J. at p. 468, whose decision was affirmed by the
C.A.; *Shepheard* v. *Broome*, [1904] A.C. 342, H.L., *per* Lord LINDLEY at pp. 347, 348, approving what had been said on this subject in the courts below, reported *sub nom. Broome* v. *Speak*,
[1903] 1 Ch. 586, C.A., *per* BUCKLEY J. at p. 605, and, in the C.A., COLLINS M.R. at pp. 622,
623, and COZENS-HARDY L.J. at p. 630.

In *New Zealand*, *Cleave* v. *McDonald*, [1925] N.Z.L.R. 311, C.A.

[3] As in all the cases cited in the last note.

[4] As in *Pearson* v. *Wheeler* (1825), Ry. & M. 303, where ABBOTT C.J. admitted the evidence
of the defendant's surveyors to reduce the damages.

[5] *Peek* v. *Derry*, *Glasier* v. *Rolls*, *Cackett* v. *Keswick*, *McConnel* v. *Wright*, and *Shepheard* v.
Broome, *supra*, at the pages respectively cited in note 2, *supra*.   In *Australia*, *Potts* v. *Miller*

bound to sell on discovery of the fraud, or at any time afterwards, but if he chooses to do so, the sum which he in fact receives on the sale stands in the place of the sum which the tribunal would otherwise have to assess as the actual money's worth of the property when acquired, and no question of valuation or value arises.[1] This rule, however, is subject to the obvious qualification that, if the representee sells in the market or otherwise after the lapse of more than a reasonable time from the date of his discovery of the truth, though he is always bound to give credit for at least that sum, it does not follow that, as against the representor, he may not be bound to give credit for more, or that the real value of the property at the date of acquisition is no longer to be considered; for if the price has been depreciated in the interval from causes entirely independent of the representor's fraud, and not arising (in the case of shares) from the intrinsic defects in the company's undertaking and affairs which were the subject of the misrepresentation, the price actually obtained on the sale, if less than the real value at the date of allotment or purchase, is deemed wholly irrelevant to the inquiry.[2]

210 We have seen in the preceding paragraph that credit must be given for *at least* the actual value realised by the representee on sale, for it is his net loss that is being assessed, and this must be calculated by giving credit for all that has actually been recouped. But in the case where the representee has elected not to sell, or simply has not yet sold at the date of the inquiry, the value of the property at the date of the transaction induced by the fraudulent misrepresentation must be assessed by valuation. How far, if at all may such a valuation take into account subsequent happenings by which the damage thought at first to have been suffered has in the event later been diminished? May, (for instance), the *subsequent* unexpected development of the neighbourhood, by reason of which the land purchased has in fact risen in value, after the event, be taken into account? This difficulty is one extending to the assessment of all kinds of claims for damage; and an apposite example in another class of case is the case of the widow suing under the Fatal Accidents Act who has in fact remarried before the trial. In such a case the *possi-*

(1940), 64 C.L.R. 282 (H. Ct. of Aus.) *per* STARKE J. at pp. 289–290 and *per* DIXON J. at pp. 296–300. In *New Zealand, Canavan* v. *Wright*, [1957] N.Z.L.R. 790, C.A., furnishes an example of a claim for damages failing because there was positively no satisfactory evidence of the value of the land at the time of the sale.

[1] *Peek* v. *Derry* (1887), 37 Ch.D. 541; passage quoted in note 2 on p. 233.

[2] *Waddell* v. *Blockey* (1879), 4 Q.B.D. 678, C.A.; *Peek* v. *Derry*, as cited in note 2, on p. 233. In *Australia, Potts* v. *Miller* (1940), 64 C.L.R. 282 (H. Ct. of Aus.).

bility of remarriage, always to be taken into account in such cases as a factor in diminution of damage, can at least no longer be dismissed from account; and so in the case of fraud, if supervening events have in fact lessened the consequences of the fraud, the court cannot shut its eyes entirely to what has actually happened.[1]

211   It is the duty of the representee to minimise the damages in the interests of both parties, if the representor offers him a real opportunity of so doing.   Thus a defrauded shareholder who elects to keep his shares, and is bound therefore to pay calls on them, would not be justified in heaping up the damages by continuing to pay such calls with his eyes open, after a sincere and *bona fide* offer by the company, or its directors, to avoid the contract, and restore everything received by them under it; but a mere half-hearted and ambiguous admission of misstatements in a prospectus, unaccompanied by such an offer, would clearly leave the representee entitled, and bound, to go on meeting all payments due under the contract, and adding them to the damages.[2]   Still more unavailing, either to extinguish or to reduce the damages, is the mere fact that shortly after the date when the representee acquired the shares the company made good its representation, for the material date, as already stated, is the date when the representee took the shares, and "the damage might have been assessed there and then".[3]

212   It is important to bear in mind that, even in those cases where there is no necessity to assess or calculate values, and the sums sought to be recovered are fixed sums ,[4] or where the damages have, so to speak, liquidated themselves,[5] the relief sought is still, in contemplation of law,

---

[1] See, in *Australia*, *Potts* v. *Miller* (1940), 64 C.L.R. 282 (H. Ct. of Aus.) where this general topic is discussed by STARKE J. at pp. 289–290, and by DIXON J. at p. 298, and it is said: "This reasoning (in *Twycross* v. *Grant* (1877), 2 C.P.D. 469, at p. 544) makes it necessary to distinguish between the kinds of cause occasioning the deterioration or diminution in value. If the cause is inherent in the thing itself, then its existence should be taken into account in arriving at the real value at the time of purchase. If the cause be 'independent' 'extrinsic' 'supervening' or 'accidental', then the additional loss is not the consequence of the induce-ment".   In *Mallett* v. *Jones*, [1959] V.R. 122 after the representee had discovered fraud he affirmed his contract reserving his action for damages; but he later made default in perfor-mance, with the result that the representor rescinded for breach.   It was held by the Full Court of Victoria that the court could, and should, take these facts into consideration in assessing the damages; but in the actual result of the case they were held to make no difference to the assessment.

[2] See *Arnison* v. *Smith* (1889), 41 Ch.D. 348, C.A., *per* Lord HALSBURY L.C. at pp. 369–370.

[3] *McConnel* v. *Wright*, [1903] 1 Ch. 546, C.A., *per* COLLINS M.R. at p. 553.

[4] As in the cases cited in the notes to para. 206, *ante*.

[5] As in the authorities cited in note 2 on p. 231, *ante*.

nothing but damages.[1]   Thus, where the value of the property acquired under a contract is *nil*, so that the plaintiff has nothing to give credit for, and sues simply for the liquidated sums he has paid, he cannot by labelling his action "money had and received" alter its intrinsic nature, or escape the disabilities attaching to an action of deceit, such as incapacity to sue for an innocent misrepresentation, or to recover from the estate of a deceased representor.[2]   On the other hand, the application of this principle sometimes operates for the benefit of the representee, and not to his detriment.   For instance, where, as in the case of a completely executed contract, it may be necessary to establish that the real object of the action is to recover damages, and not to rescind (which might not be permissible in such a state of the facts), it is obviously of vital importance in the interests of the representee to invoke the aid of the rule which says that a sum, though liquidated, may nevertheless be damages, whether capable of being also called "money had and received", or not.[3]

"Consequential damages"

213   Although in the majority of cases damages for fraud may be calculated simply in accordance with the foregoing rules, there remains a class of cases in which there is a place in the assessment for what have been called "consequential damages".[4]   The damages flowing from the fraudulent sale of a business, for instance, may not be adequately represented by the difference between the price paid for it and the amount which the sale of it realises after the fraud is discovered.   There may, for instance, be losses of the expenses of moving in and out, and operating losses during the period when the purchaser was vainly trying to make the business pay.   If these are shown to be the direct result of the fraud, and to have been reasonably incurred, they may be added to the claim assessed according to the rules already enunciated;   for fraud, like any other tortious injury, gives rise to a claim for all damage directly arising from the tortious act, and it will not lie in the mouth of the fraudulent

---

[1] See *Stoddart* v. *Union Trust, Ltd.*, [1912] 1 K.B. 181, C.A.

[2] Statutes passed since Mr Spencer Bower penned this passage have invalidated both of the illustrations which he gave.   He cited *Ship* v. *Croskill* (1870), L.R. 10 Eq. 73, and *Manners* v. *Whitehead* 1898, 1 F. (Ct. of Sess.) 171, as to the former incapacity; and, as to the latter, *Re Duncan, Terry* v. *Sweeting*, [1899] 1 Ch. 387, *per* ROMER J. at pp. 390 and 392.

[3] *Kettlewell* v. *Refuge Assurance Co.*, [1908] 1 K.B. 545, C.A., *per* Lord ALVERSTONE C.J. at p. 550.   This passage, again, is now of little more than historical interest since the passing of the Misrepresentation Act 1967.

[4] The term used by Lord DENNING M.R. in *Doyle* v. *Olby (Ironmongers), Ltd.*, [1969] 2 All E.R. 119; [1969] 2 Q.B. 158, C.A. at p. 167.

representor to say that such damages could not reasonably have been foreseen.[1]

Exemplary damages

214   There appears to be no decision reported in which exemplary damages have been deliberately awarded on a claim for fraudulent misrepresentation; but it has been said that Lord DEVLIN's speech in *Rookes* v. *Barnard*[2] is wide enough to cover an award of exemplary damages for deceit in a proper case.[3]

215   It is conceived that the above rules state the utmost limit of the damages which can be recovered in an action of deceit.   It is quite clear that such an action "is not an action of contract, and, therefore, no damage in respect of prospective gains which the person contracting was entitled to expect comes in".[4]   To take a simple case: I give £40 for a chattel, which is fraudulently misrepresented to me to have no defects. I prove that when I took delivery of the chattel, its real value was £5. I am entitled to £35 damages.   I am not entitled to go into evidence to show that, if the chattel had been as represented to be, I was at that time in the favourable position of being able to resell it for £100, nor can I recover this anticipated profit of £60, much less both the £60 and the £35. In the one case, I am applying to an action of tort the measure of damages applicable only to breaches of contracts.   In the other, I am seeking to get the benefit of both measures at once.   Attempts, however, have from time to time been made, not indeed to obtain the latter or cumulative form, but the former, or substituted, kind of relief, under the guise of a supposed but wholly untenable theory that the law can award as

---

[1] *Doyle* v. *Olby (Ironmongers), Ltd.* *(supra) per* Lord DENNING M.R. at p. 167; *per* WINN L.J. at pp. 168–169.   It is generally thought that it was to "consequential damage" that Lord ATKIN was referring in his dictum in *Clark* v. *Urquhart*, [1930] A.C. 28 at pp. 67–68 cited in note 4 on p. 232, *ante*.

Doyle v. *Olby (Ironmongers), Ltd.* *(supra)* must in the respectful opinion of the author be regarded as containing some most unsatisfactory *dicta*.   The decision was given extempore, and while the result can hardly be criticised, the reasoning is at times at least doubtful.   Compare, for instance, the statement of WINN L.J. at p. 168 that damages should be assessed by comparing the position of the representee after the representation with his position before it, with the measure sponsored by Lord DENNING M.R. at p. 167 that "The object of damages is to put the plaintiff in as good a position, as far as money can do it, as if the promise had been performed"!   Yet WINN L.J. found himself able to say, at p. 167, that he "agreed entirely" with the judgment which had been delivered by Lord DENNING M.R. The judgment of SACHS L.J. may be thought to have been phrased with some reserve.   The case should be used only after careful reading.

[2] [1964] 1 All E.R. 367; [1964] A.C. 1129, H.L.

[3] *Mafo* v. *Adams*, [1969] 3 All E.R. 1404, C.A.

[4] *McConnel* v. *Wright*, [1903] 1 Ch. 546, C.A., *per* COLLINS M.R. at p. 554.

damages the difference between what the property was worth, and what it would have been worth if it had answered to the description, which is neither more nor less than to turn the representee into a purchaser, the representor into a vendor, and the action of deceit into an action for a breach of a contract of sale. Such attempts, therefore, which are really an offshoot of the "making good" heresy,[1] have always failed,[2] though diligent search may extract occasional unguarded expressions from some of the authorities, which, by themselves, and regardless of the context or subject-matter, would tend to encourage such a delusion.[3]

216 In actions of deceit, as in all other actions for damages or the recovery of unliquidated sums, any difficulties which arise in the quantification of the damages from the fraud or fault of the defendant operate to his disadvantage, and not to that of the plaintiff, on the sound principle of *omnia praesumuntur contra spoliatorem*. If he has deliberately destroyed, or carelessly complicated, the means of arriving at an accurate result, it is he who must suffer. The law will presume the most, and the

---

[1] "For long periods in the history of our jurisprudence", says Mr Spencer Bower in the second edition of this work at p. 191, "an erroneous belief prevailed, and persisted with singular pertinacity, that under cover of the nebulous and mystic expression 'making good', there lurks a special form of equitable relief in cases of misrepresentation which is neither damages, nor rescission, but a compound of some of the ingredients of each, with a flavour of rectification and specific performance thrown in". This theory he proceeds to dispose of with characteristic vigour at pp. 192–197 in a passage which has not been reproduced in this edition.

[2] Thus one of the many impossible arguments as to the measure of damage which were unsuccessfully urged upon the C.A. in *Twycross* v. *Grant* (*No. 1*) (1877), 2 C.P.D. 469, C.A., was the contention that the proper measure was the difference (if any) between the real value of the plaintiff's shares when he acquired them, and the value which they would have had if the representations in the prospectus had been true. This was put forward in the interests of the representor, the suggestion being that the shares would have been equally valueless if the facts represented had existed. On the other hand, a similar contention was raised in the interests of the representee in *Cassaboglou* v. *Gibb* (1883), 11 Q.B.D. 797, C.A., and met with the like fate, the plaintiff in vain contending that, his agent having misrepresented to him that a contract had been made on his behalf with a third person, he was entitled to recover the loss of profits which he would have made on such contract, if it had been entered into; which, it was held, was to treat the action as if it were an action for breach of contract by vendor against vendee, and was wholly erroneous, the only damages recoverable being the expenses to which the plaintiff had been put by reason of acting on the misrepresentation. *Cf. Johnston* v. *Braham and Campbell*, [1916] 2 K.B. 529, Div. Ct. (a similar decision).

[3] See *Pontifex* v. *Bignold* (1841), 3 Man. & G. 63, where the plaintiff, who had been induced by the fraudulent misrepresentation as to its affairs of a life insurance society to effect an insurance, sued for damages, stating in the declaration that "the policy was of much less value to the plaintiff than if the said representations had been true". On demurrer, the court held that this was good, and MAULE J., at p. 82, put his decision on the ground that the policy "may not be equally secure, and may be of different value", an expression which would seem to support the erroneous view mentioned in the text, but which probably meant no more, or at any rate could not correctly have meant any more, than that the present value of the future premiums payable might be greater than the present value of the prospect of recovering the policy money on the death of the insured.

worst[1]; but this is subject to the requirement that the plaintiff must assiduously put forward in support of his case such evidence as is reasonably available to him.

217   It not infrequently happens in practice that the court is left to assess damages for fraud on evidence which is less than completely satisfactory.   Plaintiffs sometimes present their cases on a mistaken view of the principles of quantum, and adduce insufficient evidence of the value of the property acquired by the representee at the date of its acquisition. In such cases defendants, better aware of the true principles to be used in assessment, have been known to offer no evidence as to damage, and at the end to make a plea that the action should fail altogether for lack of proof of damages.   The courts lean against such a result when it can be avoided, and will in such a case endeavour, if there is any evidence at all upon which to act, to make an intelligent estimate of the loss sustained.[2] But if there is no evidence at all to assist such an attempt, the plaintiff must fail for lack of proof.   "The absence of proper evidence of actual loss is a reason why the jury's verdict cannot be allowed to stand."[3] The assessment of damage cannot be left entirely to conjecture.

Infancy

218   Though an infant has been consistently held by the courts, and declared by the legislature, incapable of binding himself by a contract, it has always been the law of England that he is civilly responsible for the consequences of a pure, or "naked" tort, that is, for a wrong which cannot reasonably be treated as a mere breach of contract, or as "connected in any sense with a contract".[4]   Where, however, the tort is not a

---

[1] See *Armory* v. *Delamirie* (1722), 1 Sm. L.C. 396, and the cases cited in the notes thereto in that treatise, and *Leeds (Duke)* v. *Amherst (Earl) (No. 2)* (1850), 20 Beav. 239, for the principle in its general application to wrongful acts, whether at common law or in equity.   The first case was one of detinue at common law; the second was one of equitable waste, in which a very curious and interesting judgment, profusely garnished with quotations from Ovid, the Digest, the New Testament, and Sir Edward Coke, was delivered by SHADWELL V.-C.

[2] See, for instance, in *Victoria*, *Mallett* v. *Jones*, [1959] V.R. 122 (Full Court of Victoria) *per* DEAN and SMITH JJ. at p. 129: "Courts have often to deal with problems of assessment of damage where it is clear that some damage has been suffered, but no firm evidence exists as to the precise extent of it".   *Cf.* in a case not involving fraud, *Joseph* v. *National Magazine Co., Ltd.*, [1958] 3 All E.R. 52, where HARMAN J. said at p. 54: "The question of damages in such a case is and must remain more or less a matter of guesswork"; but this did not prevent an assessment from being made.

[3] *Per* DIXON J. in *Australia* in *Potts* v. *Miller* (1940), 64 C.L.R. 282 (H. Ct. of Aus.) at p. 301. *Cf.* in *New Zealand*, *Canavan* v. *Wright*, [1957] N.Z.L.R. 790, C.A.

[4] This is the expression used by KNIGHT-BRUCE V.-C. at p. 109 of *Stikeman* v. *Dawson* (1847), 1 De G. & Sm. 90.   Instances of "naked" torts for which the infant has been held liable are: *Bristow* v. *Eastman* (1794), 1 Esp. 172 (action for recovery of moneys embezzled by

"naked" one, or (to borrow a phrase from the law of real property) is not a tort "in gross", but is in some way "appurtenant" to a contract,[1] the infant is not liable, any more than if he were being sued for the enforcement, or for damages for the breach, of an express contract.[2] In applying this principle, the courts have always looked to the substance of the alleged wrongful act, and have disregarded the language employed by ingenious pleaders for the purpose of emphasising, or covering up (as the case may be), the contractual aspect or incidents of the case.[3]

In the application of this rule as to an infant's torts in general to the particular tort of fraudulent misrepresentation, it is obviously difficult to imagine a case where an infant's fraudulent misstatement (made as it almost invariably is for the purpose of inducing a money-lender or tradesman to advance money or supply goods in the belief that he is of full age) can possibly be described as "not connected in any sense with a contract". Certainly there is no record of a minor's fraudulent misrepresentation, as distinguished from other forms of fraud, being regarded as a naked tort, either at law or in equity, and though it has sometimes been laid down by judges that, should such a case ever arise, the infant will be held liable,[4] the fact remains that no such case has arisen yet, nor have

---

an infant apprentice); *Burnard* v. *Haggis* (1863), 32 L.J. C.P. 189, where the infant having hired a horse for use on the road, but not for jumping, rode it at a fence on which it was impaled and killed (*per* WILLES J. at p. 391: "what was done by the defendant was not an abuse of contract, but the doing of an act which he was expressly prohibited by the owner to do with the animal. The act of riding this horse at the place where it met its death is just as much a trespass as if the defendant without any hiring, and without the plaintiff's leave, had mounted the plaintiff's horse and gone with it into the field and used it as this horse was in fact used"); *Walley* v. *Holt* (1876), 35 L.T. 631 (a similar case to the last); *Re Seager, Seeley* v. *Briggs* (1889), 60 L.T. 665 (a similar case to *Bristow* v. *Eastman, supra*).

1 NORTH J., in *Archer* v. *Stone* (1898), 78 L.T. 34, distinguishes between "a lie in gross" and "a lie appurtenant", which he describes as "a lie relating to any part of the contract or its subject-matter, which induces another person to contract".

2 See *Jennings* v. *Rundall* (1799), 8 Term Rep. 335, where the infant was held not liable for damages for the reckless riding of a mare which had been delivered to him "to be moderately ridden", on the ground that the action was in substance an action for the breach of a hiring contract.

3 Thus, in *Bristow* v. *Eastman, supra*, Lord KENYON C.J. said at p. 172 that "an infant was liable *ex delicto*, though not *ex contractu*; and though the action was in form an action of the latter description, yet it was of the former in point of substance"—a view adopted, and acted upon by WILLES J. in *Burnard* v. *Haggis, supra*, by KELLY C.B. and HUDDLESTON B. in *Walley* v. *Holt, supra*, by KAY J. in *Re Seager, supra*, and by PHILLIMORE J. in *Cowern* v. *Nield*, [1912] 2 K.B. 419, Div. Ct. at pp. 423, 424. On the other hand, in *Jennings* v. *Rundall, supra*, an action framed as one of tort was held to be in substance one of contract (*per* Lord KENYON C.J. at pp. 336, 337).

4 As, for instance, by KNIGHT-BRUCE V.-C. at p. 109 of *Stikeman* v. *Dawson* (1847), 1 De G. & Sm. 90, and by PHILLIMORE J. at p. 424 of *Cowern* v. *Nield*, [1912] 2 K.B. 419, Div. Ct., where an infant trader, having sold goods to the plaintiff, received the price, and refused to deliver the goods, was sued for breach of contract, or alternatively for money had and received, and the court, whilst holding that the action, as framed, was not maintainable, nevertheless

any of those judges suggested how it ever could arise. In the earliest, which is still also the leading, authority on the question, very strong language was used by the Court of King's Bench in pronouncing the utter impossibility of treating an infant's fraudulent assertion of majority as a pure tort, or the subject of an action[1]; and it has since been held that, in such cases, the plea of infancy cannot be defeated by resort to the doctrine of estoppel[2] any more than it can be rebutted in an action.

219 It has from time to time been suggested that relief of an equitable character may be obtained against an infant's fraudulent misrepresentation, though inducing, or connected with, a contract. The authorities on this head require careful scrutiny, upon which it will appear that, apart from dark hints and dubious dicta, there has been no judicial enunciation of any wider proposition than that an infant who has made a fraudulent misrepresentation of his majority, or of any other fact, with the object and result of obtaining from the representee property *in specie*, or a traceable specific fund, may be compelled in equity to restore, or account for, such specific property or fund to the representee.[3] There is, certainly, one decision which went beyond these limits,[4] but it was given in the administration of assets in bankruptcy, to which special considerations apply, and on this ground it has always in modern times been held to be anomalous.[5] As soon as attempts were made to extend

---

ordered a new trial in order to give the plaintiff an opportunity of turning his claim into one of tort, if he could, being obviously under the impression,—for otherwise the course adopted would have been a cruel kindness to the plaintiff,—that it was possible to frame the action *ex delicto*, but how, the court did not state, nor is it easy to conceive.

[1] *Johnson* v. *Pye* (1665), 1 Keb. 905, 913.

[2] *Bartlett* v. *Wells* (1862), 1 B. & S. 836; *De Roo* v. *Foster* (1862), 12 C.B. N.S. 272; *Miller* v. *Blankley* (1878), 38 L.T. 527 (*per* GROVE J. at pp. 528, 529, and LINDLEY J. at p. 530); *Levene* v. *Brougham* (1909), 25 T.L.R. 265, C.A.

[3] *Cory* v. *Gertcken* (1816), 2 Madd. 40 (*per* PLUMER V.-C. at pp. 49–51); *Overton* v. *Banister* (1844), 3 Hare, 503 (*per* WIGRAM V.-C. at p. 506); *Stikeman* v. *Dawson* (1847), 1 De G. & Sm. 90 (*per* KNIGHT-BRUCE V.-C. at p. 111); *Wright* v. *Snowe* (1848), 2 De G. & Sm. 321 (*per* KNIGHT-BRUCE V.-C. at p. 324); *Nelson* v. *Stocker* (1859), 4 De G. & J. 458 (*per* KNIGHT-BRUCE L.J. at p. 463, and TURNER L.J. at pp. 464–466); *R. Leslie, Ltd.* v. *Sheill*, [1914] 3 K.B. 607, C.A. (*per* Lord SUMNER at p. 618).

[4] This was *Re King, Ex parte Unity Joint Stock Mutual Banking Association* (1858), 3 De G. & J. 63, where the Association filed a proof in the bankruptcy of an infant, based upon a claim to recover money lent upon the security of a policy of insurance issued to the infant in reliance upon his fraudulent assertion of majority, and KNIGHT-BRUCE and TURNER L.JJ., though with great reluctance, and yielding only to the supposed authority of Lords COWPER, HARDWICKE, and THURLOW, refused to expunge the proof (see pp. 68, 69).

[5] *Miller* v. *Blankley* (1878), 38 L.T. 527 (*per* GROVE J. at p. 529, and LINDLEY J. at p. 530); *Re Jones, Ex parte Jones* (1881), 18 Ch.D. 109, C.A. (*per* JESSEL M.R. at p. 120); *R. Leslie, Ltd.* v. *Sheill*, [1914] 3 K.B. 607, C.A. (*per* Lord SUMNER at pp. 615, 616, KENNEDY L.J. at pp. 624, 625, and A. T. LAWRENCE J. at p. 628).

the equitable rule above stated so as to cover the case of general pecuniary relief, in other than bankruptcy proceedings, they were defeated.[1]

---

[1] *R. Leslie, Ltd.* v. *Sheill, supra,* where the C.A., reversing the decision of HORRIDGE J. and also overruling that of LUSH J. in *Stocks* v. *Wilson,* [1913] 2 K.B. 235, which HORRIDGE J. had followed, both these actions having been brought to obtain equitable relief (the common law claims were obviously hopeless) in respect of an infant's fraudulent misrepresentation of full age, held that whatever may be the equitable rule as to restitution, and accountability for, *the very* property, or sum, obtained by the infant's fraud, it is quite wrong to extend that rule so as to embrace mere pecuniary compensation, or repayment of, not the same, but an equivalent sum of money (*per* Lord SUMNER at pp. 618, 619, after a careful analysis and elucidation of the authorities at pp. 613–618, and *per* KENNEDY L.J. at pp. 622–625).

CHAPTER XII

The Action for Damages for Innocent Misrepresentation

Introductory

220 Until 1967 there was no action for damages for misrepresentation unless the misrepresentation was fraudulent.[1] (The *Hedley Byrne*
action for negligence,[2] founded on a representation made in breach of a
duty to take care, is, as is pointed out in Chapter XIX not, strictly
speaking, an action for misrepresentation at all). But by the provisions
of s. 2 of the Misrepresentation Act 1967 an action in damages was for
the first time given to representees for loss suffered by reason of representations innocently made to them.

The Misrepresentation Act 1967

221 Section 2 of the Misrepresentation Act 1967 provides:

"(1) Where a person has entered into a contract after a misrepresentation
has been made to him by another party thereto and as a result thereof he
has suffered loss, then, if the person making the misrepresentation would
be liable to damages in respect thereof had the misrepresentation been
made fraudulently, that person shall be so liable notwithstanding that the
misrepresentation was not made fraudulently, unless he proves that he had
reasonable ground to believe and did believe up to the time the contract
was made that the facts represented were true.

(2) Where a person has entered into a contract after a misrepresentation
has been made to him otherwise than fraudulently, and he would be entitled,
by reason of the misrepresentation to rescind the contract, then, if it is

---

[1] *Derry* v. *Peek* (1889), 14 App. Cas. 337, H.L.; *Heilbut, Symons & Co.* v. *Buckleton*, [1913]
A.C. 30, H.L.; *Rutherford* v. *Acton-Adams*, [1915] A.C. 866, P.C.; *Gilchester Properties, Ltd.*
v. *Gomm*, [1948] 1 All E.R. 493, C.A.

[2] *Hedley Byrne & Co., Ltd.* v. *Heller & Partners, Ltd.*, [1963] 2 All E.R. 575, [1964] A.C. 465,
H.L.

claimed, in any proceedings arising out of the contract, that the contract ought to be or has been rescinded the court or arbitrator may declare the contract subsisting and award damages in lieu of rescission, if of opinion that it would be equitable to do so, having regard to the nature of the misrepresentation and the loss that would be caused by it if the contract were upheld, as well as to the loss that rescission would cause to the other party.

(3) Damages may be awarded against a person under subsection (2) of this section whether or not he is liable to damages under subsection (1) thereof, but where he is so liable any award under the said subsection (2) shall be taken into account in assessing his liability under the said subsection (1)."

Representees entering into contract essential

222   It will be seen that not all damage suffered through acting upon the truth of an innocent misrepresentation is sufficient to support an action for damages.   It is only where the representation has *induced the representee to enter into a contract* that the representor will be liable; and then only in cases in which the representor *would have been liable in damages if the representation had been fraudulently made.*[1]

Affirmative defence available

223   Beside the other affirmative defences available in a claim for damages for innocent misrepresentation[2] the Statute provides that it shall be a defence if the representor affirmatively proves that he had reasonable grounds to believe, and did believe up to the time when the contract was made, that the facts represented were true.

It will be seen that false representations which were formerly readily divisible into two classes—fraudulent and innocent—now fall into three: (1) Those in which the representor has no honest belief in their truth; these are fraudulent.   (2) Those in which, while the representee cannot prove them fraudulent, the representor cannot affirmatively prove that he had an honest belief; these are innocent misrepresentations which will support an action for damages.   (3) Those in which the representor can prove that he believed that the facts represented were true; here no action for damages will lie.

Damages in lieu of rescission

224   Beside giving representees the action for damages instituted by s. 2 (1), the Statute[3] allows damages to be awarded in lieu of rescission in

---

[1] For the essentials of such an action see Chapter XI.
[2] See para. 225, *post.*
[3] Section 2 (2) and 2 (3).

actions in which rescission is sought on the ground of innocent mis-representation, if the court[1] is of opinion that it is equitable so to do.

Just what criteria the courts will use in exercising the discretion which Statute confers, in determining whether it is equitable to refuse rescission and to award damages in lieu thereof, it is impossible to predict with certainty until sufficient decisions of courts of high authority are available on the subject. The topic receives some attention in the next chapter—see para. 230, *infra*.

It is to be noticed that damages may be awarded in lieu of rescission under sub-s. (2) and (3) notwithstanding that all the requirements of sub-s. (1) may not be met. It is obvious that the *first* requirement of sub-s. (1)—that the representee has entered into a contract on the faith of the representation—must be met, for it is expressly so provided; and moreover it is only in actions for rescission of such a contract that the relief given by sub-ss. (2) and (3) can be granted. But the statute envisages that damages may be awarded in lieu of rescission for innocent misrepresentation in some cases in which, had the representation been fraudulent, it would not in the event have supported a claim for damages. It may be thought that this rather curious provision may have been inserted to provide for a case in which the court may see fit to refuse the remedy of rescission where a contract is still executory where it appears that the consequences of rescission may be out of all proportion to the injury suffered by the representee.[2]

Special defences

225 Since the action for damages given by s. 2 (1) is given only in cases in which, had the representations been fraudulent, it would have supported a claim for damages, it follows that all the affirmative defences which will afford an answer to a claim for damages for fraud will be available to a defendant in an action brought under the section. These are dealt with in the previous chapter,[3] and only two of them need be mentioned here. The first is the defence of agreement to take with all faults, or to forgo any right to remedy for misrepresentation, such as for instance may follow from the insertion of an "exemption clause" in the contract of the parties. In earlier editions of this work Mr Spencer Bower expressed the opinion that at least in the case of non-fraudulent

---

[1] Or an arbitrator.
[2] See the Tenth Report of the Law Reform Committee (1962) para. 13; the Report is reprinted in full in Appendix B, *post*.
[3] See paras. 189 *et seq*, *ante*.

misrepresentation such an agreement could afford a good defence;[1] but
s. 3 of the Misrepresentation Act 1967 now provides that

> "If any agreement (whether made before or after the commencement of
> this Act) contains a provision which would exclude or restrict—
>
> (a) any liability to which a party to a contract may be subject by reason
>   of any misrepresentation made by him before the contract was made;
>   or
>
> (b) any remedy available to another party to the contract by reason of such
>   a misrepresentation;
>
> that provision shall be of no effect except to the extent (if any) that, in any
> proceedings arising out of the contract, the court or arbitrator may allow
> reliance on it as being fair and reasonable in the circumstances of the case."

The other defence, discussed in the previous chapter, which should
here be noticed, is the last of the special defences there listed—the
defence given by Lord Tenterden's Act. Notwithstanding that it has been
expressly held by courts of the highest authority[2] that this defence is
available only in actions for fraudulent misrepresentation, it is submitted
that the express terms of the statute may now make it available in actions
brought under s. 2 (1).

Measure of damages

226 The Misrepresentation Act 1967 is silent as to the measure of
damages to be given in an action for damages for innocent misrepresentation. But there seems no reason to think that the measure of damages
in such an action will be in any way different from that in an action on
facts similar in all other respects, except that the representation was
innocent and not fraudulent.[3]

The same rules will not necessarily govern the measure of damages to
be awarded in lieu of rescission; for as to these it is expressly provided
by s. 2 (3) that damages may be awarded against a representee under 2.
2 (2) even though he might not have been liable for damage under s. 2 (1).
Such a situation might arise, for example, in a case where, though there
had been a material but innocent misrepresentation which had induced
the representee to enter into the contract, which before the Act would
have entitled him as of right to rescission, yet the court found that the
circumstances as a whole rendered it equitable to declare the contract

---

[1] e.g., 2nd end. (1927), pp. 210, *et seq.*

[2] e.g., *Banbury* v. *Bank of Montreal*, [1918] A.C. 626, H.L.

[3] "In civil causes and trespasses, the law doth rather consider the damage of the party
wronged, than the malice of him that was the wrongdoer"—*Bacon's Maxims of the Law*, Reg. VII.

subsisting. If in any such circumstances it happened that the representee suffered no loss, judging the matter as if there had been a fraudulent misrepresentation, yet the court would be empowered by the Act to make such an award as might be thought just in all the circumstances, having regard to the loss by the representee of his right to rescind. But it is clear from sub-s. 3 that the two separate statutory claims for damages are not to be the occasion for an award of a sum greater than the total loss suffered; in assessing liability under sub-s. 1 the court must take into account any award made under sub-s. 2.

Act does not extend to Scotland and Northern Ireland

227   The provisions of the Misrepresentation Act 1967 do not extend to Scotland or to Northern Ireland.[1]

---

[1] Section 6 (3) and 6 (4); for full text see Appendix C, *post*.

CHAPTER XIII

Rescission and Consequential or Analogous Relief—I: The Claim for Such Relief

Introductory

228   In every department of the law, where the nature of the case admits of it, a party who has suffered an *injuria* may be righted either directly or indirectly.   Thus, in cases of injunction, the order may assume a negative or prohibitory form, or a mandatory and positive one;   and, where a contract is sought to be enforced, the object may be attained indirectly by pecuniary compensation, or (in a proper case) directly by specific performance.   The same alternative remedies are available, where the aid of the court is invoked to get rid of a contract, or its consequences, on any grounds recognised by law;   and misrepresentation is one of those grounds.   That is to say, the relief may be indirect, in the shape of an award of a lump sum as damages, or direct in the form of judicial annulment of the contract, and mutual restitution *in specie*.   In the one case, the past is accepted and recognised, but compensated for by an equivalent in money;   in the other, the past is undone, and the *status quo* is restored *ad integrum*.   The former of these alternative modes of relief has been dealt with in the preceding chapter;   it is now proposed to discuss the latter.

Rescission for fraudulent misrepresentation

229   It will be convenient, in discussing the availability of the remedy of rescission, to consider separately the cases of fraudulent and of innocent misrepresentation.   In this paragraph an attempt will be made to state shortly the availability of rescission where there has been fraud;

the rest of the chapter will be concerned, for the most part, with the consequences in the same regard of innocent misrepresentation.

A material fraudulent misrepresentation which has induced a contract or transaction[1] will *always*[2], on the discovery of the fraud, entitle the representee to repudiate the contract or transaction, even if it has been completely performed or executed,[3] unless by reason of such performance or execution *restitutio in integrum* has become impossible; and if on being notified of such repudiation, the representor refuses to accept the position, the representee may institute proceedings for the judicial annulment thereof, with all necessary and appropriate consequential relief.[4] On establishing the several matters as to which the burden of allegation and proof rests upon him,[5] unless the representor can establish any of the countervailing pleas hereafter mentioned,[6] the representee will be entitled to succeed in such proceedings.

230   Subject to what appears in the next succeeding paragraphs, once misrepresentation, whether fraudulent or innocent, is proved the representee's right to rescind the contract is absolute. Damage is irrelevant. The relative advantages or disadvantages of adhering to, or of repudiating, a contract induced by an incorrect statement are matters exclusively for the consideration of the representee. He is the sole judge of the expediency or propriety of getting rid of the relations between himself and the representor. It is no answer to his claim, if otherwise good, to

---

[1] As to what "transaction" means, see Chapter VII, para. 139, *ante*. A gift is the most familiar illustration; see *Re Glubb, Bamfield v. Rogers,* [1900] 1 Ch. 354, *per* LINDLEY M.R. at pp. 361–362.

[2] Since the passing of the Misrepresentation Act 1967 it appears that the representee will be able to elect whether to pursue his remedy for fraud, which gives him an absolute right of rescission, or whether to claim rescission on the ground of misrepresentation in respect of which he does not undertake to prove fraud. If he chooses the latter (and easier) course, however, he will be faced with the possibility that the court, notwithstanding due proof of misrepresentation, may in its discretion refuse rescission. How likely it is that it will do so, in circumstances which indicate fraud, though fraud is not actually alleged, is the subject of some discussion in para. 232, *post*.

[3] Instances are: *Edwards v. M'Leay* (1818), 2 Swan. 287; *Sturge v. Sturge* (1849), 12 Beav. 229; *Reynell v. Sprye, Sprye v. Reynell* (1852), 1 De G.M. & G. 660; *Garrard v. Frankel* (1862), 30 Beav. 445; *Harris v. Pepperell* (1867), L.R. 5 Eq. 1; *Lindsay Petroleum Co. v. Hurd* (1874), L.R. 5 P.C. 221; *Hart v. Swaine* (1877), 7 Ch.D. 42; *Paget v. Marshall* (1884), 28 Ch.D. 255. In *Feret v. Hill* (1854), 15 C.B. 207, though common law had then no jurisdiction to give relief, the estate having passed, it seems to have been recognised that it might have been otherwise in equity. In *Charter v. Trevelyan* (1844), 11 Cl. & Fin. 714 (a non-disclosure case), a conveyance was rescinded after thirty-seven years. In *Australia* see *Alati v. Kruger* (1955), 94 C.L.R. 216 (H. Ct. of Aus.).

[4] See paras. 248 *et seq.*, *infra*.

[5] See paras. 245–247, *infra*.

[6] See Chapter XIV, *post*.

point to the most irrefragable evidence that the contract, if affirmed, will work out to his benefit, and not to that of the representor, or will be to the common advantage of both, and that any person of ordinary business sagacity would recognise that, though misled, the representee has been misled into a lucrative, and not a detrimental, alteration of position.   The rationality of his motives for insisting on avoidance is wholly immaterial.   To the representor's question,—"why should you capriciously and wantonly abandon a business which is demonstrably for your advantage ?"—he is entitled to reply, with Shylock, "it is my humour". It may be a matter of honour, and not of interest, with him.   Having seen cause to regret his association with an undesirable individual, company, or enterprise, and finding subsequently that the law gives him a right to sever the association, he may be anxious to avail himself of that right, irrespective of any immediate or tangible gain or loss.[1]   The sole relevant question is as to the right to rescind; if the right does not exist, *cadit quaestio*; if it does, the law no more concerns itself with the reasons which move the representee to exercise his right, than it concerns itself with the motives which influence a party to insist on any other right of property, or action, to which he may be entitled.[2]   The representor has no voice in the matter, and he can neither be heard to speculate, nor invite the court to speculate, on the supposed inadequacy or insagacity of such reasons or motives.

Innocent misrepresentation now gives qualified right to rescind only

231   Until 1967 the law made no distinction between fraudulent and innocent misrepresentations as giving rise to a right to rescind,[3] provided that the contract was still executory.   "It is now well established",

---

[1] *Hulton* v. *Hulton*, [1917] 1 K.B. 813, C.A. (*per* SWINFEN EADY L.J. at p. 822); *Goldrei, Foucard & Son* v. *Sinclair and Russian Chamber of Commerce in London*, [1918] 1 K.B. 180, C.A. *per* SARGANT L.J. at p. 182.

[2] See the observations of Lord CAIRNS L.C. at p. 108 of *Aberaman Ironworks* v. *Wickens* (1868), 4 Ch. App. 101. So in non-disclosure cases "it is not necessary to show that . . . loss afterwards took place in consequence of these transactions": *per* Lord LANGDALE M.R. at p. 84 of *Gillett* v. *Peppercorne* (1840), 3 Beav. 78. And, in cases of contract generally, the party who has contracted for one thing is not bound to accept another, and a different, thing, though most people might think it more valuable, and though it may have involved greater expense to the other party: *Forman & Co. Pty., Ltd.*, v. *The Liddesdale*, [1900] A.C. 190, at p. 197, 201, P.C.

[3] If the possible distinction between the consequences of fraudulent and innocent misrepresentation resulting from *Kennedy* v. *Panama, New Zealand and Australian Royal Mail Co., Ltd.* (1867), L.R. 2 Q.B. 580 be for the moment omitted from consideration. For some discussion of the effect of this case see below.

wrote Mr Spencer Bower in the second edition of this work,[1] "that for the purposes of rescission the question, which is of such vital importance in actions for damages, whether the representation was fraudulent or innocent, is wholly immaterial".[2] But the provisions of the Misrepresentation Act 1967, while removing the difference between the consequences of fraudulent and innocent misrepresentations in one respect (i.e. providing that in future both might give rise to actions in damages) made a difference between them, in another respect, which was not there before. By s. 2 (2) of that Act it is now provided that:

> "Where a person has entered into a contract after a misrepresentation has been made to him otherwise than fraudulently, and he would be entitled, by reason of the misrepresentation, to rescind the contract, then, if it is claimed, in any proceedings arising out of the contract, that the contract ought to be or has been rescinded, the court or arbitrator may declare the contract subsisting and award damages in lieu of rescission, if of opinion that it would be equitable to do so, having regard to the nature of the misrepresentation and the loss that would be caused by it if the contract were upheld, as well as to the loss that rescission would cause to the other party."

The Act does not expressly lay down any criteria by which courts are to judge whether it is equitable to allow the representee to rescind, and as yet there has been insufficient time for authoritative decisions to furnish any reliable guide. But some attempt may be deemed to pre-

---

[1] 2nd edn., p. 239. Mr Spencer Bower's rather sweeping statement must be taken to have been qualified by the later statement on p. 250 of the same edition, of the rule (as the law then stood) that innocent misrepresentation could not give a right to rescind an executed contract, while fraudulent misrepresentation would do so. For the availability of the right to rescind for innocent misrepresentation where a contract has been executed, since the passing of the Misrepresentation Act 1967, see para. 232, *infra*.

[2] The decisions cited in support of this proposition were *Clermont* (*Viscount*) v. *Tasburgh* (1819), 1 Jac. & W. 112 (*per* PLUMER M.R. at p. 118); *Re Deposit and General Life Assurance Co.*, *Ayre's Case* (1858), 27 L.J. Ch. 579, *per* ROMILLY M.R. at p. 583; *Ross* v. *Estates Investment Co.* (1868), 3 Ch. App. 682, *per* Lord CAIRNS L.C. at p. 685, describing the representations in that case as "made *either* fraudulently, *or* in such a way as entitled the plaintiff, when he discovered their inaccuracy, to repudiate his shares"; *Redgrave* v. *Hurd* (1881), 20 Ch.D. 1 C.A., *per* JESSEL M.R. at pp. 12, 13; *Re Denham & Co., Ltd.* (1883), 25 Ch.D. 752, *per* CHITTY J. at pp. 766, 767; *Derry* v. *Peek* (1889), 14 App. Cas. 337, H.L. *per* Lord HERSCHELL at p. 359; *Re Metropolitan Coal Consumers' Association, Ltd.*, *Wainright's Case* (1890), 63 L.T. 429, C.A., *per* COTTON L.J. at p. 431 ("this case is not like an action of deceit . . . A man who has been induced to enter into a contract by material misrepresentation is entitled to be relieved from it, even if the representations are made innocently"); *Stewart* v. *Kennedy* (*No. 2*) (1890), 15 App. Cas. 108, *per* Lord WATSON at pp. 121, 122; *Ferguson* v. *Wilson* 1904, 6 F. (Ct. of Sess.) 779, at p. 783; *Mair* v. *Rio Grande Rubber Estates, Ltd.*, [1913] A.C. 853, H.L. (*per* Lord SHAW, at p. 870); *Goldrei, Foucard & Son* v. *Sinclair*, [1918] 1 K.B. 180, C.A. (*per* SARGENT J. at p. 192); *Abram S.S. Co., Ltd.* v. *Westville Shipping Co., Ltd.*, [1923] A.C. 773, H.L.; *MacKenzie* v. *Royal Bank of Canada*, [1934] A.C. 468, P.C. *per* Lord ATKIN at p. 475—"a contract . . . is liable to be avoided if induced by material misrepresentation of an existing fact, *even if made innocently*". See, too, *Senanayake* v. *Cheng*, [1965] 3 All E.R. 296; [1966] A.C. 63, P.C.

dict the principles by which courts may possibly be expected to resolve the question, and one test which may well be put forward for consideration is the requirement that the representation complained of must "go to the root of the contract".

Before the Judicature Acts it had been held that at common law, while fraud always gave a right to rescind, an innocent misrepresentation did not give such a right unless it went to the root of the contract.[1] Equity, however, never accepted this principle; and when by virtue of the Judicature Acts every court became a court of Equity the former common law rule was thought to have gone by the board.[2] Though this gradually came to be regarded as settled, murmurs were heard from time to time from those—and some in high places—who remembered the old common law rule with respect;[3] and when the Law Reform Committee in its famous Tenth Report,[4] recommended that for the future the right of rescission should be one in the discretion of the court, it expressly related the proposal to the point now under discussion. It said, in considering the position which might obtain if the Committee's recommendations were adopted:

> "It is true that an independent misrepresentation on a matter which does not go to the root of the contract will continue to give a right to rescission, whereas a corresponding statement incorporated in the contract will be a warranty for breach of which damages alone can be awarded. But as the court will have a discretion (if our recommendation is adopted) to award

---

[1] *Kennedy* v. *Panama, New Zealand, and Australian Royal Mail Co.* (1867), L.R. 2 Q.B. 580, at p. 587.

[2] But see the cases mentioned in the next note, in which it is clear that the old rule died hard. In *New Zealand* the New Zealand Court of Appeal held in *Riddiford* v. *Warren* (1901), 20 N.Z.L.R. 572, C.A. that the section in the Sale of Goods Act which provides that "the rules of the common law including the law merchant and in particular the rules relating to . . . the effect of misrepresentation . . . shall continue to apply to contracts for the sale of goods" was sufficient to preserve, in that jurisdiction, the rule laid down in *Kennedy* v. *Panama, New Zealand and Australian Royal Mail Co.* as regards misrepresentations affecting contracts for the sale of goods. *Cf.* in *Victoria, Watt* v. *Westhoven*, [1933] V.L.R. 458 to the same effect. This proposition has not been accepted by English courts.

[3] In *Lever Brothers, Ltd.* v. *Bell*, [1931] 1 K.B. 557, at p. 588, SCRUTTON L.J., in the Court of Appeal, had expressed it as his opinion that *Kennedy* v. *Panama, New Zealand and Australian Royal Mail Co.* was no longer law; but this dictum cannot be taken as surviving the speech of Lord ATKIN in the same case in the Lords (where the decision of the Court of Appeal was reversed)— *Bell* v. *Lever Brothers Ltd.*, [1932] A.C. 161, at pp. 219–220. In his judgment in *Watt* v. *Westhoven*, [1933] V.L.R. 458, LOWE J. (in *Victoria*) cited at p. 466 Lord ATKIN's speech as demonstrating that Mr Spencer Bower's text in the second edition of this work at p. 239 was "too sweeping" and ventured the observation that *Kennedy's* case was still "at least an authoritative exposition of the law regarding the nature of the error necessary to avoid a contract on the ground of mistake induced by innocent misrepresentation".

[4] Tenth Report of the Law Reform Committee (1962) para. 26. The report is reproduced in full in Appendix B, *post*.

damages instead of rescission, we believe that what may appear to be an anomaly will be of small importance in practice''.

While the courts can hardly be expected to accept these words as determining the construction of the statute which was ultimately passed, albeit in the terms generally recommended by the Report, yet the reform may be thought sufficiently related to the question here under consideration to warrant the conclusion that the court will be likely, in cases in which an innocent misrepresentation is set up as supporting an election to rescind, to inquire, at least as one of the questions which may go to the equity of the matters: does the representation complained of "go to the root of the contract"?

This consideration appears particularly applicable to the case, to which the 1967 Act extends the right to rescind for innocent misrepresentation, of an *executed* contract for the sale of goods.

"A car," (says the Report of the Committee[1]) "might be returned to the vendor (after delivery and acceptance) because of a misrepresentation about the mileage done since the engine was last overhauled, or a transfer of shares rescinded on account of an incorrect statement about the right to receive the current dividend."

Such representations could be regarded as not going to the root of the contract; and they might seem likely in the new dispensation, to be regarded by the courts as proper to be remedied by damages.[2]

Executed contracts

232 Until 1967 it was accepted as a rule of general application, though the matter was not entirely free from doubt, that *innocent* misrepresentation would not support a claim for rescission where the contract had been completed by conveyance or otherwise fully performed on both sides.[3] *Wilde* v. *Gibson*[4] afforded ample authority for the rule as it affected

---

[1] *Ibid*, para. 11.

[2] This topic is explored in more detail in the next paragraph of the text.

[3] On this ground the representee was denied relief of the character in question in *Attwood* v. *Small* (1838), 6 Cl. & Fin. 232; *Wilde* v. *Gibson* (1848), 1 H.L. Cas. 605; *Brownlie* v. *Campbell* (1880), 5 App. Cas. 925, H.L.; *Soper* v. *Arnold* (1887), 37 Ch.D. 96, C.A., affirmed (1889), 14 App. Cas. 429, H.L.; *May* v. *Platt*, [1900] 1 Ch. 616; *Debenham* v. *Sawbridge*, [1901] 2 Ch. 98; *Re Metal Constituents, Ltd., Lord Lurgan's case*, [1902] 1 Ch. 707, at p. 709; *Seddon* v. *North Eastern Salt Co., Ltd.*, [1905] 1 Ch. 326; *Milch* v. *Coburn* (1910), 27 T.L.R. 170; *Angel* v. *Jay*, [1911] 1 K.B. 666, Div. Ct. (where a lease was vainly sought to be distinguished from a conveyance); *Glasgow and South Western Rail. Co.* v. *Boyd and Forrest, No. 2*, [1915] A.C. 526, H.L.; *Rutherford* v. *Acton-Adams*, [1915] A.C. 866, at p. 869. The provisions of the Misrepresentation Act do not of course affect the law as it has been understood in Australia and New Zealand, in which jurisdictions the old cases will still regulate the rights of the parties—see, for instance, *Kramer* v. *Duggan* (1955), 55 N.S.W. S.R. 385.

[4] (1848), 1 H.L. Cas. 605.

conveyances of land; and the same rule was subsequently held to apply to leases.[1] The extension of the doctrine to other classes of contracts rested upon rather less firmly established authority,[2] and cases in recent years show signs of dissatisfaction by the courts with any general principle such as has been referred to.[3] But all this is now of historical interest only, for the Law Reform Committee, after reviewing the cases, recommended, in 1962, the abolition of the rule;[4] and by s. 1 of the Misrepresentation Act 1967[5] it was provided that:

> "Where a person has entered into a contract after misrepresentation has been made to him, and . . . the contract has been performed, . . . then, if otherwise he would be entitled to rescind the contract without alleging fraud, he shall be so entitled, subject to the provisions of this Act, notwithstanding the matters mentioned in paras. (a) and (b) of this section".

Paragraph (b) specifies the case where "the contract has been performed".

It is to be noted that in their Tenth Report of 1962[6] the Law Reform Committee did not recommend quite so sweeping a change as that actually made by the statute. After noticing and commenting upon the confused state of the law as it affected contracts other than those for the sale of an interest in land, the Committee recommended that the so-

---

[1] *Angel* v. *Jay*, [1911] 1 K.B. 666; *Edler* v. *Auerbach*, [1949] 2 All E.R. 692, [1950] 1 K.B. 359.

[2] *Seddon* v. *North-Eastern Salt Co., Ltd.*, [1905] 1 Ch. 326 is the one usually cited; but when its text is examined the decision appears really to rest on election by conduct to affirm the contract. Indeed it may be doubted whether JOYCE J. found misrepresentation proved at all. Many of the other decisions called in aid appear when examined to stand upon equally doubtful ground—e.g. those in *Rawlins* v. *Wickham* (1858), 3 De G. & J. 304; *A.-G.* v. *Ray* (1874), 9 Ch. App. 397; *Redgrave* v. *Hurd* (1881), 20 Ch.D. 1 and *Newbigging* v. *Adam* (1886), 34 Ch.D. 582. In *MacKenzie* v. *Royal Bank of Canada*, [1934] A.C. 468, P.C. the Judicial Committee made no difficulty about the rescission of what appears to have been an executed contract where *restitutio in integrum* was completely possible; and see the cases in the next note below. It has not always been easy to discern whether a given contract should be regarded as "executed" or "executory"—indeed it has been questioned whether contracts *must* fall into one or other class. The issue has tended to become confused with the question whether *restitutio in integrum* is possible. See, for instance, in this regard *MacKenzie* v. *Royal Bank of Canada* (*supra*); *Senanayake* v. *Cheng*, [1965] 3 All E.R. 296; [1966] A.C. 63, P.C.; and, in *New Zealand, Root* v. *Badley*, [1960] N.Z.L.R. 756. In *Australia Alati* v. *Kruger* (1955), 94 C.L.R. 216 (High Court of Australia).

[3] *Armstrong* v. *Jackson*, [1917] 2 K.B. 822 (MCCARDIE J.); *Lever Brothers, Ltd.* v. *Bell*, [1931] 1 K.B. 557 at p. 588 (SCRUTTON L.J.); *Solle* v. *Butcher*, [1950] 1 K.B. 671, C.A. at p. 695 (DENNING L.J.); *Leaf* v. *International Galleries*, [1950] 2 K.B. 86, C.A. at pp. 90–91 (DENNING and JENKINS L.JJ.); *Curtis* v. *Chemical Cleaning and Dyeing Co.*, [1951] 1 K.B. 805, C.A. (DENNING L.J.).

[4] In para. 5 of their Report the Jenkins Committee said that "the evidence which we have received leaves us in little doubt that there are cases where the inability to rescind a contract after it has been executed can work serious injustice".

[5] The full text of the Act is set out in Appendix C, *post*.

[6] The Report is set out in full in Appendix B, *post*.

called rule in *Seddon* v. *North-Eastern Salt Co.*[1] should be abrogated to the extent that it should be competent for the court to declare *such contracts* rescinded for innocent misrepresentation, notwithstanding that they had been performed; but the Committee recommended at the same time that the rule in *Wilde* v. *Gibson*,[2] disallowing the rescission of executed contracts for the sale of interests in land, should stand untouched.[3] The Legislature, however, abolished both rules.

It is of course particularly to be noticed, that though the remedy of rescission becomes available, by virtue of s. 1, notwithstanding that the contract has been executed, there is still a saving provision in s. 2 (2). The remedy given by s. (1) is given expressly "subject to the provisions of this Act"; and s. 2 (2) provides that in the case of *innocent* misrepresentations the court, notwithstanding that the representee may be entitled by reason of the representation to rescind, may declare the contract subsisting, and award damages, if of opinion that it is equitable so to do.

In deciding whether it is equitable to declare a contrast subsisting and award damages, no doubt the court may take into account as an important consideration the fact that the contract has been carried into effect wholly or partly; and it may be expected in examining this consideration to inquire whether, and to what degree, the execution of the contract has rendered *restitutio in integrum* difficult or even impossible.[4] In weighing these matters, many of the earlier decisions may well be found still to retain some substantial degree of relevance, and even of importance. They may seem to have been well founded on considerations of reason and convenience.[5] Though the Legislature has included contracts affecting land, with others, in a general abrogation of the old rule, it must be recognised that in doing so it has still left the court with a discretion. It is here suggested that while in the future the courts will be ready in proper cases to order rescission, the remedy will be given only where justice appears to require it; and it may be found that, the provisions of the new statute notwithstanding, rescission will not be

---

[1] [1905] 1 Ch. 326.
[2] (1848), 1 H.L. Cas. 605.
[3] Para. 6 of the Report.
[4] The difficulty, if not impossibility, of logically separating these topics, is seen in *MacKenzie* v. *Royal Bank of Canada* (supra) and *Senanayake* v. *Cheng* (supra). In *Australia* their mutual impact is illustrated in the judgment in *Alati* v. *Kruger* (1955), 94 C.L.R. 216, H. Ct. of Aus. In *New Zealand* see *Root* v. *Badley*, [1960] N.Z.L.R. 756.
[5] The point is explored in the Jenkins Report, reprinted in Appendix B, *post*; see paras. 6–7 of the Report. It is noted in the Australian case of *Svanosio* v. *McNamara* (1956), 96 C.L.R. 186 *per* DIXON C.J. and FULLAGAR J. at p. 199 and *per* McTIERNAN, WILLIAMS and WEBB JJ. at pp. 206–207.

granted as of course in cases in which conveyance or lease has followed after a deliberate investigation of title.

Fault as a factor

233 A factor which the courts may well decide to treat as important in determining whether to allow rescission for innocent misrepresentation is fault on the part of the representor. If fraud on the part of the representor is alleged, and proved, rescission, as has already been seen, will follow as a matter of course.[1] In cases in which, though fraud is not alleged, the facts demonstrate or suggest its existence, it can hardly be doubted that in the new dispensation the courts will be ready as a matter of justice to grant, or at least seriously to consider, rescission. There may be cases, moreover, in which, while fraud neither is alleged nor can be proved, the representor is clearly at fault in making the false representation upon which the representee has relied; the case which at once springs to mind is that in which the representor has taken insufficient care to ascertain the truth, perhaps readily ascertainable by him. In such cases it is conceived that the courts will incline to regard the negligence of the representor as a factor influencing them to grant rescission. In the Tenth Report of the Law Reform Committee to which reference has already been made it is recommended that the right to damages for innocent misrepresentation should depend on this factor;[2] and this representation was carried forward into the legislation in s. 2 (1). The Act is silent as to the role of fault in founding a right to rescind, but there seems no reason to doubt that the courts may regard it as a factor of importance, notwithstanding this omission.

Innocent misrepresentation subsequently incorporated into contract

234 An innocent misrepresentation which is material and which has induced the representee to enter into a contract will (as we have seen) entitle the representee, but subject to the provisions of the Misrepresentation Act 1967, to rescission. But before the passing of the Misrepresentation Act there had been some authority[3] for the proposition that if the misrepresentation which induced the contract had been itself incorporated into that contract as a term the representee no longer had a

---

1 See para. 229, *ante.*
2 See para. 17 of the Report the full text of which appears in Appendix B, *post.*
3 Tenth Report of the Law Reform Committee, reprinted in Appendix B, *post.*; in *Pennsylvania Shipping Co.* v. *Compagnie Nationale de Navigation*, [1936] 2 All E.R. 1167, at p. 1171; *Leaf* v. *International Galleries*, [1950] 1 All E.R. 693; [1950] 2 K.B. 86.

right to rescind, his rights being limited to an action in damages for breach of the term which had been so incorporated in his contract. By Section 1 (a) of the Misrepresentation Act 1967 it is now provided that

"Where a person has entered into a contract after a misrepresentation has been made to him and . . . the misrepresentation has become a term of the contract . . . then, if otherwise he would be entitled to rescind the contract without alleging fraud, he shall be so entitled, subject to the provisions of this Act",

notwithstanding that the representation has been incorporated into the contract as a term.

Contracts induced by misrepresentation are voidable, not void

235   It is now well established that, except where the misrepresentation fundamentally misrepresents the nature and effect of the contract itself, or is one as to the identity of the alleged contractee,[1] any contract procured by misrepresentation is valid unless and until disaffirmed, and is not invalid *ab initio*; in other words such contracts are not void but voidable.[2] It may be doubted whether, in the earlier stages of our jurisprudence, the enormous importance of the distinction between voidability and *ipso facto* invalidity was fully appreciated, or, assuming it to have been so, was always adequately expressed.[3] But at the present time there is no question either as to the mutually exclusive character of these

---

[1] For the effect of such misrepresentations, see paras. 240 *et seq.*, *post*. The exceptional result which follows in such cases (in which the contract is void *ab initio*, not voidable) is discussed by EDWARDS J. in the *New Zealand* case of *Berridge* v. *Public Trustee* (1914), 33 N.Z.L.R. 865.

[2] *Clough* v. *London and North Western Rail. Co.* (1871), L.R. 7 Exch. 26, Ex. Ch., *per Cur.* at p. 34 ("the fact that the contract was induced by fraud did not render the contract void, or prevent the property from passing, but merely gave the party defrauded a right, on discovering the fraud, to elect whether he would continue to treat the contract as binding, or would disaffirm the contract, and resume his property, . . . and we further agree that the contract continued valid until the party defrauded had determined his election by avoiding it"); *Erlanger* v. *New Sombrero Phosphate Co.* (1878), 3 App. Cas. 1218, *per* Lord BLACKBURN at pp. 1277, 1278; *Re Scottish Petroleum Co.*, *Wallace's Case* (1883), 23 Ch.D. 413, C.A., *per* BAGGALLAY L.J. at pp. 430–432; *Aaron's Reefs, Ltd.* v. *Twiss*, [1896] A.C. 273, H.L. *per* Lord Watson at pp. 290, 291, and Lord DAVEY at p. 294; *Re Glubb, Bamfield* v. *Rogers*, [1900] 1 Ch. 354, C.A., *per* LINDLEY M.R. at pp. 361, 362, as to a gift; *United Shoe Machinery Co. of Canada* v. *Brunet*, [1909] A.C. 330, P.C., at p. 339 ("a contract into which a person may have been induced to enter by false and fraudulent representation is not void, but merely voidable at the election of the party defrauded, after he has notice of the fraud. Unless and until he makes his election, and by word or act repudiates the contract . . . the contract remains as valid and binding as if it had not been tainted with fraud at all").

[3] A note in the 2nd edn. instances *Duffell* v. *Wilson* (1808), 1 Camp. 401 (as to which, *cf.* *Kettlewell* v. *Refuge Assurance Co., Ltd.*, [1908] 1 K.B. 545, C.A. *per* Sir GORELL BARNES at p. 548); *Hill* v. *Gray* (1816), 1 Stark. 434; *Noble* v. *Adams* (1816), 7 Taunt. 59; *Flight* v. *Booth* (1834), 1 Bing. N.C. 370, at pp. 376–377; *Central Rail. Co. of Venezuela* v. *Kisch* (1867), L.R. 2 H.L. 99, at p. 123.

two legal incidents, or qualities, or as to the serious practical bearing of
the proposition above stated on the interests and rights both of the
representee[1] and of the representor[2] in any proceedings for rescission.

Representee has right of election

236 It follows from the above, that in the first instance the representee's only right is one of election, whether to affirm or disaffirm the
contract.[3] He has no right, at any subsequent moment most convenient
to himself and most inconvenient to the representor without having said
or done anything in the interim declaratory of his intention or attitude
in the matter, to insist that the contract was a nullity from the beginning.
Still less, on the other hand, can any representor, who may find that the
contract which he has brought about by misrepresentation is turning out
to the representee's benefit and not to his own, take advantage of his own
wrong, and claim that by reason of that wrong it never had any efficacy
at all—which course, if it had been void *ab initio*, he clearly could adopt.[4]
This latter consideration, indeed, furnishes the most forceful illustration
possible of the absurdities and injustice which would result from holding
that any such contract is void, or is defeasible at the option of either party,
instead of being, as it clearly is, defeasible at the option of the representee
only. This means that, having discovered that he was induced to contract
by a false representation, the representee may choose between three
courses: (1) if the contract appears to him to be working out to his
advantage, or whether it so appears or not, and from whatever motive,
he may do nothing, and the representee cannot compel him to do anything, with a view to its avoidance; (2) he may repudiate it; if the
representation be fraudulent, his right to do so is absolute, but if it be
innocent his right to repudiate is subject to the power of the court to
order that the contract shall stand, and that he shall have damages in lieu
of rescission; (3) he may be content to adhere to it. If he does so, and
the contract has resulted or thereafter results in loss, he may, as we have

---

[1] For, except in certain classes of case, no representee can invoke the aid of the court, to
annul judicially what is already void in law.

[2] If the contract were void *ab initio*, all the affirmative defences and answers based on the
representee's conduct or inaction subsequent to his discovery of the truth, would not be—as
they undoubtedly are—available to the representor.

[3] Com. Dig. *Election*, C.2 and *Clough* v. *London and North Western Rail. Co.* (1871), L.R. 7
Exch. 26, at p. 34, Ex. Ch. (the passage cited in note 2 on p. 257). *Morrison* v. *Universal Marine
Insurance Co.* (1873), L.R. 8 Exch. 197, at p. 204, *et seq.* In *Victoria*, *Nicholas* v. *Thompson*,
[1924] V.L.R. 554. The topic of election is considered in some detail in the authors' *Law
relating to Estoppel by Representation* (2nd edn.) Chapter XIII.

[4] See e.g. *Goode and Bennion* v. *Harrison* (1821), 5 B. & Ald. 147, at p. 159.

already seen, if the representation be fraudulent, sue for a cash sum in damages compensating him for such loss,[1] and even if the representation be innocent, he may in circumstances set out in the Misrepresentation Act 1967 be successful in a similar claim.[2]

Even after failing in a claim for rescission he may still, if he is still in a position to satisfy the necessary conditions, maintain an action for damages against the representor.[3]

Representee not bound to elect at once, or within any particular time

237   The representee is not bound to make any election within any particular time. He may postpone the exercise of his right for any period he pleases, though such omission or delay may expose him to serious risks of a nature to be explained hereafter.[4] But as will later be seen,[5] unless he acts so as to be taken as having affirmed the contract, on the one hand, or, not so acting, yet delays matters so that *restitutio in integrum* becomes impossible, mere delay will not of itself extinguish his right to elect to rescind.

The right to rescind once exercised is exhausted

238   The election to rescind or to affirm, once exercised, is exercised for ever.[6] *Quod in electionibus semel placuit, amplius displicere non potest.*[7] The representee may keep the sword of Damocles suspended over the contract as long as he pleases; but if he takes it from its place, he can never put it back again; and if, on the other hand, he cuts the thread and lets the sword fall, whether he destroys the contract or not, he loses the sword. If he once affirms he can never afterwards avoid;[8] and, if he once avoids, he can never afterwards either for his own pur-

---

[1] See Chapter XI.

[2] See Chapter XII.

[3] Thus, the representee who, in *Clarke* v. *Dickson*, *(No. 1)* (1858), E.B. & E. 148, failed to obtain relief by way of rescission against the cost-book mining company, succeeded, in *Clarke* v. *Dickson*, *(No. 2)* (1859), 6 C.B. N.S. 453, in recovering damages against the directors who made the representation, which was shown to be fraudulent.

[4] *Clough* v. *London and North Western Rail. Co.* (1871), L.R. 7 Ex. 26; *Kwei Tek Chao* v. *British Traders and Shippers, Ltd.*, [1954] 2 Q.B. 459, 474–475, *per* DEVLIN J.; see, further, Chapter XIV, *post*.

[5] See Chapter XIV.

[6] *Clough* v. *London and North Western Rail. Co.* (1871), L.R. 7 Exch. 26, Ex. Ch. In *Australia, Bosaid* v. *Andry*, [1963] V.R. 465, at p. 478 (SHOLL J.).

[7] Co. Litt. 146a.

[8] *Clough* v. *London and North Western Rail. Co.* (supra) at p. 36.

poses be allowed to affirm,[1] or, on the suggestion of the representor, be deemed to have affirmed, the contract.[2] There is no *locus poenitentiae* in either case.

Communication of election

239   If a right to rescind is a right of election (and it is) then principle seems to require that to exercise that right effectively it must be necessary to communicate the decision to rescind to the other party to the contract.[3]   In most proceedings for rescission such communication is easily proved; but at least two cases may be imagined which are worth some consideration—*viz.*, (1) Where the decision to rescind is first communicated to the representor by the commencement of the proceedings praying for rescission, and (2) Where the other party to the contract has disappeared, and communication to him of the decision to rescind is therefore not possible.

Unless it is already too late to rescind for one of the reasons mentioned in para. 237 *supra*, it is a sufficient communication to the representor of an election to rescind if the representee's election is sufficiently plainly set forth in the statement of claim or other document supporting the proceedings claiming rescission.   No earlier communication to the representor is necessary.[4]

If reliance is placed upon rescission simply by virtue of the pleadings, of course the representor may meet this plea by proving, by way of affirmative defence, some earlier election on the plaintiff's part to adhere to the contract.[5]   But the onus will lie upon him to prove such an earlier

---

1 *Ibid.* at the same page.   All the passages referred to in this and in notes 6 and 8 above were cited at length, adopted, and applied by the Exchequer Chamber in the non-disclosure case of *Morrison* v. *Universal Marine Insurance Co.* (1873), L.R. 8 Exch. 197, Ex. Ch. (at pp. 203–207).

2 *Re Thomas Edward Brinsmead & Sons, Tomlin's Case,* [1908] 1 Ch. 104, where the rule operated to the detriment of the representor, who set up conduct of the representee amounting to affirmation of the contract, and for the benefit of the representee; the latter was in a position, however, to point to a definite exercise of his election to avoid prior to the acts and conduct in question, which otherwise would have clearly barred his title to relief, WRIGHT J. holding (at p. 109) that "election once made is made for ever, and cannot be revoked even if the party wishes".   Cf. *Sparenborg* v. *Edinburgh Life Assurance Co.,* [1912] 1 K.B. 195.

3 Communication as an essential element in election between two courses of action is considered in the authors' *Law Relating to Estoppel by Representation* (2nd edn.) 321 *et seq.*

4 *Clough* v. *London and North Western Rail. Co.* (1871), L.R. 7 Exch. 26, (at p. 36); *Capel & Co.* v. *Sim's Ships Composition Co., Ltd.* (1888), 58 L.T. 807 (KEKEWICH J.) at p. 811; in Australia, *Nicholas* v. *Thompson,* [1924] V.L.R. 554 (Full Court of Victoria).   *Garnac Grain Co. Inc.* v. *H.M.F. Faure and Fairclough, Ltd.,* [1967] 2 All E.R. 353; [1968] A.C. 1130, H.L. is an illustration of pleadings which did not sufficiently unequivocally express an election.

5 See Chapter XIV.

election, except in certain classes of case.[1]   It may be thought a prudent course in the representee's own interests, however, in order to anticipate any such affirmative plea, to make some positive declaration of his attitude as soon as practicable; and in the majority of cases this precautionary step is taken.

As to the second of the two cases which we have mentioned above, the Courts have recently shown some reluctance to deny to an innocent defrauded party to a contract the power to rescind it, simply because the representor has been able effectively to conceal his whereabouts, and thus to avoid communication of a rescission.   In a recent case[2] a vendor of a motor car gave possession, and title, on the purchaser's representation that his cheque was valid for its amount.   By the time it had been discovered that his bank account was without funds, the purchaser had disappeared.   The vendor at once complained to the police and to the Automobile Association, and invoked their assistance in looking for the car.   It was duly located, some days later, in the hands of a purchaser for value to whom it had been sold, of course without any notice of any defect in title,[3] by the original purchaser.   Lord DENNING M.R., sitting as an additional judge at first instance, held that the vendor had done all that he could, and that in the circumstances he had effectively rescinded the contract of sale when he complained to the police.   He held that the property in the car then revested in him, and that the ultimate purchaser acquired no interest in it.   This decision was affirmed in the Court of Appeal.   The members of that court thought the case a logical exception to the general rule requiring express communication.   Where a fraudulent representor, they said, has deliberately put it out of the representee's power to communicate with him it cannot be necessary expressly to communicate an election to rescind.[4]

It seems to the writer of this edition, with respect, that this decision is open to some criticism.   Any decision as to a matter of commercial law the headnote of the report of which reads (as the report of Lord DENNING's decision read) "dictum of Lord BLACKBURN not followed"[5] may be thought to bear its own danger-signal; and if the decisions of the two courts in this case are admirable from the point of view of the

---

[1] As, for instance, in the case mentioned in Chapter XIV, para. 298, *post*.
[2] *Car and Universal Finance Co., Ltd.* v. *Caldwell*, [1965] 1 Q.B. 525.
[3] pp. 527–528.
[4] *Per* SELLERS L.J. at p. 550; *per* Lord UPJOHN at p. 555; *per* DAVIES L.J. at p. 558.
[5] In the All England Reports at [1963] 2 All E.R. 547.   The dictum of Lord BLACKBURN was from *Scarf* v. *Jardine* (1882), 7 App. Cas. 345 at p. 361, H.L.   The headnote in the official reports puts the matter rather more discreetly as "dictum of Lord Blackburn considered".

defrauded vendor, what may be imagined to have been the views of the unfortunate ultimate purchaser upon them? Where title has passed there may be difficulty in principle in holding that an election to rescind can effectively revest title in the vendor unless upon notice of rescission effectively given—perhaps constructively, but nevertheless effectively given—to the purchaser. What *Car and Universal Finance Co., Ltd.* v. *Caldwell* must be taken to decide is that in the particular case the fraudulent representor had impliedly agreed to be affected by constructive communication.[1]

An apparent exception

240 The rule above set out (*viz.* that the effect of misrepresentation is to make a contract voidable, but not void) is subject to one apparent (but it is not a real) class of exceptions. This comprises cases where the effect of the misrepresentation is to prevent any contract arising from the words or acts of the parties, though without the representation the same words and acts would have bound them in contract one to the other. It is because no contract ever arises in such cases,[2] that they do not constitute a real exception to the general rule.

There are two kinds of case where a misrepresentation may produce such an exceptional effect—(1) cases of mistaken identity and (2) cases of *non est factum*. These will now be separately considered.

The impersonation cases

241 The first of the two kinds of case constituting an apparent (but not real) exception to the rule that misrepresentation makes a contract voidable but not void *ab initio* is found in the cases of impersonation and mistaken identity. There are in the reports cases in which A has addressed an offer to B, which has been accepted (but not to A's knowledge) by C, posing as B. Where these are the facts there is no contract at all; the elementary rules of offer and acceptance preclude the formation of one, for the offer has not been accepted by the offeree.[3]

---

[1] Subsequent decisions have shown that even if *Car and Universal Finance Co., Ltd* v. *Caldwell* (*supra*) be accepted, the ultimate innocent purchaser for value may not be left without some ground on which to stand, furnished by sections 2 and 9 of the Factors Act; see *Newtons of Wembley, Ltd.* v. *Williams*, [1964] 2 All E.R. 135 (DAVIES L.J.); affirmed on appeal, [1964] 3 All E.R. 532; [1965] 1 Q.B. 560 (SELLERS, PEARSON and DIPLOCK L.JJ.). For a critique of these decisions see 27 Modern Law Review 472.

[2] See *per* BUCKLEY J. in *Whitehorn Brothers* v. *Davison*, [1911] 1 K.B. 463, C.A. at p. 481.

[3] These were the facts in *Boulton* v. *Jones* (1857), 2 H. & N. 564 (offer posted to Brockle-hurst, accepted by Boulton). *Cf. Cundy* v. *Lindsay* (1878), 3 App. Cas. 459, H.L. (offer posted by Blenkarn in circumstances, including address, calculated to induce the belief that it was

But the facts are not always as clear as this. What of the case where A sells a chattel (say a motor car) to B, taking B's cheque in payment, on the faith of B's representation that he is C, a well known citizen of substance ?

If A deals face to face with B, does he not effectively contract with and sell to *him*, however deeply he is deceived as to his *identity* ?[1] The offeree is the person who accepts; it is the offeror himself who has made the offer. The cases whose facts are between the two set out above merge imperceptibly into one another;[2] and it has so far been found impossible to formulate a thoroughly satisfactory universal test upon which any given case shall be adjudged. It is necessary to resist the temptation to discuss this subtle problem further in this work, and it will be reserved accordingly for some legal philosopher writing a treatise on the law of contract.[3] It is sufficient here to note the existence of this class of case.

If the representor is able to surmount this obstacle, and to show that the parties entered into a contract one with the other, though that contract was entered into on the faith of a misrepresentation as to the identity of the representor, such a representation will, speaking generally, enable the representee to rescind exactly as in a case of any other material representation. But the misrepresentation must in this event be shown to be *material*; and, as has already been pointed out, materiality does not necessarily follow as a matter of course where the representation is one as to identity.[4]

The plea of non est factum

242   The question whether a person is conclusively bound by an instrument in writing which he has signed, or whether he may, notwith-

made by Blenkiron; offer accepted in this belief—no contract). Other cases of a not dissimilar type are *Hardman* v. *Booth* (1863), 1 H. & C. 803; *Sowler* v. *Potter*, [1940] 1 K.B. 271.

[1] This was the decision in *Phillips* v. *Brooks, Ltd.*, [1919] 2 K.B. 243; *cf. Lake* v. *Simmons*, [1927] A.C. 487, H.L., and *Ingram* v. *Little*, [1960] 3 All E.R. 332; [1961] 1 Q.B. 31, where the majority of the court held that there was no contract; it is here respectfully suggested that there was something to be said for the dissenting view of DEVLIN L.J. See, further *Lewis* v. *Averay*, [1971] 3 All E.R. 907; [1972] 1 Q.B. 198, C.A., perhaps a rather better authority.

[2] A number of the cases are discussed by Professor Goodhart in (1941), 57 L.Q.R. 228. Cases decided since that article include *Ingram* v. *Little, supra, Lewis* v. *Averay* (*supra*) and, in New Zealand, *Fawcett* v. *Star Car Sales, Ltd.*, [1960] N.Z.L.R. 406, C.A., a case with a very curious set of circumstances, not the least of which was that it was the vendor, not the purchaser, of the chattel, who misrepresented his identity. In *Australia*, see *Porter* v. *Latec Finance (Queensland) Pty., Ltd.* (1964), 111 C.L.R. 177, in which the High Court of Australia was divided 3 : 2.

[3] *Anson* treats of the topic in the 22nd edn. at pp. 274 *et seq.*; *Cheshire and Fifoot* 6th edn. at pp. 207 *et seq.*

[4] See Chapter VI, *ante*, where the topic of materiality is discussed, with specific reference, in para. 129, to representations as to identity.

standing his signature, contend that he is not so bound and that the document was a nullity *ab initio* (as distinct from contending that he may elect
to avoid it for misrepresentation) is raised by a plea of *non est factum*.[1]
Until 1970 it was generally accepted that this plea succeeded or failed on
the simple test, whether the misrepresentation alleged went to the nature
or character of the instrument. If the representee could prove that he
had executed the instrument on the faith of a misrepresentation as to the
nature or character of the document signed, that document was held
void *ab initio*, for

> "the mind of the signer did not accompany the signature; in other words
> he never intended to sign, and therefore, in contemplation of law, never did
> sign, the contract to which his name is appended".[2]

The essence of every contract is mutual consent, and, of every deed, an
intention to be bound by it, and when these are lacking neither law nor
equity will attribute efficacy to what has been signed. As BUCKLEY L.J.
said in a lucid exposition of the theory[3]

> "The true way of ascertaining whether a deed is a man's deed, is, I conceive,
> to see whether he attached the signature with the intention that which
> preceded his signature should be taken to be his act and deed. It is not
> necessarily essential that he should know what the document contains; he
> may have been content to make it his act and deed, whatever it contains . . .
> If, on the other hand, he is materially misled as to the contents of the docu-
> ment, then his mind does not go with his pen. In that case it is not his
> deed".

On the other hand when the misrepresentation related only to the legal
effect, or object, or to the "contents" (in the sense of the particular
terms and provisions), of the instrument, the contract contained in, or
recorded by, such instrument was held not void, but voidable only, because in that case the representee intended to enter into *some* contract of

---

1 *Thoroughgood* v. *Cole* (1582), 2 Co. Rep. 9a and *Foster* v. *Mackinnon* (1869), L.R. 4 C.P.
704 are the two cases generally referred to as the earlier leading decisions on this topic. But
these are now to be read in the light of *Saunders* v. *Anglia Building Society*, [1970] 3 All E.R.
961, H.L. referred to in detail in the text.

2 *Foster* v. *Mackinnon* (*supra*) per BYLES J. at p. 711. *Cf.* for a similar result, *Thoroughgood* v.
Cole (1582), 2 Co. Rep. 9a (a release of property misrepresented to the signatory as a mere
acquittance for arrears of rent); *Vorley* v. *Cooke* (1857), 1 Giff. 230, at p. 236 (a mortgage
deed misrepresented as a deed on behalf of a purchaser at a sale); *Bagot* v. *Chapman*, [1907] 2
Ch. 222 (mortgage deed misrepresented as a mere paper to facilitate the raising of money in
the remote future); *Carlisle and Cumberland Banking Co.* v. *Bragg*, [1911] 1 K.B. 489, C.A.
(guarantee misrepresented as an insurance paper).

3 *Carlisle and Cumberland Banking Co.* v. *Bragg* (*supra*) at pp. 495–496. This case was overruled by the Lords in *Saunders* v. *Anglia Building Society*, [1970] 3 All E.R. 961; [1971] A.C,
1904, H.L., but the dictum of BUCKLEY L.J. seems to be worth salving.

the nature described, whereas, in the other type of case, he had no such intention.[1]

It has at times been suggested that the plea of *non est factum* is available only to those who through blindness or other physical, mental, or educational handicap are unable to exercise normal faculties of discrimination in appreciating the effect of what they have signed;[2] but this limitation is now accepted as too narrowly restricting the application of the doctrine.[3]

Saunders v. Anglia Building Society

243   In *Saunders* v. *Anglia Building Society*[4] the tests previously accepted for the applicability of the plea were reviewed first by the Court of Appeal and then by the Lords, and were adjudged by both tribunals to be too artificial.   The Lords abandoned the old tests, and substituted another, broader, one, by which the question should hereafter be decided. Any special position of the blind or illiterate signatory was disapproved. Lord REID said:

> "Originally this extension appears to have been made in favour of those who were unable to read owing to blindness or illiteracy and who therefore had to trust someone to tell them what they were signing.   I think it must also apply in favour of those who are permanently or temporarily unable through no fault of their own to have without explanation any real understanding of the purport of a particular document, whether that be from defective education, illness or innate incapacity".[5]

For the old test, which inquired whether the misrepresentation went to the nature and character of the document as distinguished from its effect, the Lords substituted the inquiry, whether the document "was fundamentally different from what the signatory supposed it to be".[6]

---

[1] The authority generally given for the distinction is the judgment of WARRINGTON J. in *Howatson* v. *Webb*, [1907] 1 Ch. 537, in which he reviewed many of the existing authorities. This judgment was affirmed in the Court of Appeal: [1908] 1 Ch. 1, C.A.

[2] *Per* Lord REID in *Saunders* v. *Anglia Building Society*, [1970] 3 All E.R. 961, H.L. at p. 963, in the passage cited in para. 243 of the text. Mr Spencer Bower comments in the second edition of this work that in none of the cases which he had there cited was the representee either illiterate or blind, except in *Thoroughgood* v. *Cole (supra)* where "goodman Thoroughgood" is described as "a layman not lettered".

[3] *Foster* v. *MacKinnon* (1869), L.R. 4 C.P. 704 opened the door wider; the relevant passage on pp. 711 *et seq.* from the judgment of the court *per* BYLES J. was expressly approved by Lord HODSON in his speech in *Saunders* v. *Anglia Building Society*, *(supra)* at p. 969.

[4] [1970] 3 All E.R. 961, H.L.

[5] At p. 963.

[6] This is the wording proposed in the speech of Lord PEARSON at p. 979.   Lord REID said at p. 964: "There must, I think, be a radical difference between what he signed and what he thought he was signing—or one could use the words 'fundamental' or 'serious' or 'very

In some of the pre-1970 cases the question had been discussed, how far a signatory might be precluded by estoppel from raising the plea of *non est factum* against an innocent assignee who had *bona fide* acquired an interest. MELLISH L.J. had adverted to the possibilities of such an argument in his judgment in *Hunter* v. *Walters*[1] when he said:

> "In my opinion, it is still a doubtful question at law, on which I do not wish to give any decisive opinion, whether, if there be a false representation concerning the contents of a deed, a person who is an educated person, and who might by very simple means have satisfied himself as to what the contents of the deed really were, may not, by executing it negligently, be estopped as between himself and a person who innocently acts upon the faith of the deed being valid, and who accepts an estate under it."

In *Carlisle and Cumberland Banking Co.* v. *Bragg*,[2] however, the Court of Appeal dismissed a submission of estoppel, holding that while such a submission might possibly be tenable in the case of a negotiable instrument, it could not succeed in other cases. The decision in *Carlisle and Cumberland Banking Co.* v. *Bragg* was the subject of some criticism, however, and it was apparent that the last word had not yet been spoken on the subject.[3]

In *Saunders* v. *Anglia Building Society*[4] the law on this topic was reviewed; and it is now clear that the doctrine of estoppel may be considered irrelevant to the plea of *non est factum*[5] except in special cases, of which negotiable instruments may be an instance.[6] The Lords thought that any carelessness (for they did not like the term "negligence" in this regard) on the part of the signatory (as regards the likely consequences of signing, should the document pass into the hands of a third party) should be treated simply as a factor of importance to be taken into account in

---

substantial'." Lord HODSON said at p. 965 that the difference must be one "which goes to the substance of the whole consideration or to the root of the matter". Viscount DILHORNE at p. 967 said that "it must be shown that the document was radically different in character from that which the signer thought it was", or, at p. 969, "fundamentally different from that which it was thought to be". Lord WILBERFORCE at p. 972 thought that it should be shown that "the transaction which the document purports to effect is essentially different in substance or in kind from the transaction intended".

1 (1871), 7 Ch. App. 75, C.A. at p. 87.

2 [1911] 1 K.B. 489, C.A.

3 See, for instance, the present author's *Law of Estoppel by Representation* (2nd edn.) pp. 67–68; Cheshire & Fifoot, *Law of Contract* (7th edn.) pp. 230 *et seq.*; *Muskham Finance, Ltd.* v. *Howard*, [1963] 1 All E.R. 81; [1963] 1 Q.B. 904, C.A. Other criticism by contemporary authors is referred to by Lord PEARSON in his judgment in *Saunders* v. *Anglia Building Society*, [1970] 3 All E.R. 961, H.L. at p. 982.

4 [1970] 3 All E.R. 961, H.L.

5 Lord Pearson expressly dismissed estoppel at p. 982.

6 The possible special position of negotiable instruments is alluded to by Lord WILBERFORCE at p. 973.

deciding whether the interests of justice require or permit the acceptance of the plea.[1]

As a result of *Saunders* v. *Anglia Building Society* the law as it now stands may be summarised as follows. The plea, though not confined to blind and illiterate persons, is one to be kept within narrow limits. Carelessness in signing a document will generally, if not inevitably, preclude the availability of the plea. If a person for *sufficient* permanent or temporary reasons fails to understand the document which he signs, at least to the point of detecting a fundamental difference between the actual document and the document which he supposes it to be, he may succeed with the plea, in which case the document will be void *ab initio*, not only as against the immediate grantee, but as against others taking under it also.

Misrepresentation as to exemption clauses

244   A place must here be found for a short note on misrepresentation as to the effect of exemption clauses—i.e. clauses in a contract purporting to exempt one party from liability for acts or omissions (e.g. involving negligence) for which he would at common law be responsible. When such a contract has been signed by the other party, albeit under the influence of a misrepresentation as to its effect, that party cannot avail himself of the plea of *non est factum*, at least in the absence of extraordinary circumstances, for he has actually signed the provision, by which it is contended that he is now bound. This is clear at least since *Saunders* v. *Anglia Building Society*,[2] and it is submitted that the same result would have followed as the law previously stood.[3] It has been argued that in such a case the contract between the parties being good, and the clause not being void *ab initio*, the clause itself could not be disallowed if the rest of the contract has been performed, in cases where the representation is non-fraudulent.[4] This argument may have lost some of its

---

[1] *Per* Lord PEARSON at p. 982.

[2] [1970] 3 All E.R. 961, H.L.

[3] See, e.g., *L'Estrange* v. *Graucob*, [1934] 2 K.B. 394, at p. 403 *per* SCRUTTON L.J. But incautious dicta seem to persist, indicating that the clause is void *ab initio*, which cannot be so—see, for instance, *per* SOMERVELL L.J. in *Curtis* v. *Chemical Cleaning and Dyeing Co.*, [1951] 1 K.B. 805, C.A., at p. 808—" In these circumstances, owing to that misrepresentation, this exemption never became part of the contract between the parties".

[4] Before the passing of the Misrepresentation Act 1967 it was generally accepted (though the matter was not entirely free from doubt) that innocent misrepresentation would not entitle the representee to rescind when the contract had been executed. The authorities usually given for this proposition were *Wilde* v. *Gibson* (1848), 1 H.L. Cas. 605, *Brownlie* v. *Campbell* (1880), 5 App. Cas. 925, H.L., and *Seddon* v. *North-Eastern Salt Co.*, [1905] 1 Ch. 326. The point is dealt with in para. 231, *ante*; but it is of little importance since the passing of the Misrepresentation Act 1967, s. 1 of which provides that an innocent misrepresentation which will support rescission will still do so, although the contract has been executed.

strength in view of the provisions of s. 1 of the Misrepresentation Act 1967.[1] But before the passing of that section the courts had found a way round this position, and had treated exemption clauses as special cases, in which notwithstanding that the rest of the contract had been executed, they could nevertheless refuse to allow a party guilty of a misrepresenta-tion as to the effect of the clause, whether fraudulent or innocent, from setting up the clause as an exemption from liability.[2]

Exemption clauses exonerating representor from effects of misrepresentation

245   The preceding paragraph dealt with the remedy of a representee to whom the effect of an exemption clause, *of whatever nature*, had been misrepresented, but fraud had not been established. It remains to deal with a quite different topic—the effectiveness of exception clauses pur-porting to exempt either party to a contract *from liability for representa-tions made to the other* in respect of the subject-matter of the contract. Such a clause is

> "of no effect except to the extent (if any) that, in any proceedings arriving out of the contract, the Court or arbitrator may allow reliance on it as being fair and reasonable in the circumstances of the case".[3]

But this topic is dealt with in other chapters of this work.[4]

What must be proved in proceedings for rescission

246   In any proceedings instituted for the purpose of obtaining rescission, the onus is on the representee of alleging, and (unless expressly or impliedly admitted at or before the trial) proving, each and every of the facts and matters required to be established in an action for damages,[5] except fraud and damage.

Though in some of the authorities there are loose expressions to be found suggestive of the idea that it is part of the representee's burden of proof to establish that some notice or act of repudiation was given or done by him before commencing the proceedings, it is clear that this is not so,

---

[1] For the full text of the Act see Appendix C, *post*.

[2] See *Curtis* v. *Chemical Cleaning and Dyeing Co.*, [1951] 1 K.B. 805, C.A. *per* DENNING L.J. at p. 870.

[3] Misrepresentation Act 1967, s. 3. The full text of the Act is given in Appendix C, *post*.

[4] See Chapter XI, para. 195; Chapter XII, para. 225, Chapter XIV, para. 284, which pas-sages deal with defences available to the representor in actions seeking relief in respect of mis-representations.

[5] See Chapter XI.

and that the action itself is sufficient to signify his election.[1] The onus is on the representor to prove, by way of affirmative defence, a previous election on the representee's part to adhere to the contract,[2] and not on the representee to prove a previous election to avoid it, except in certain special classes of case[3]; though of course it is always wise in the representee's own interests, and in order to anticipate such affirmative plea, to make some previous declaration of his attitude,[4] and, in the majority of cases, this precautionary step is taken.

247   It must appear that there is something upon which a judgment or order can operate, for the undoing of which judicial intervention is requested.   That is to say, there must be a subsisting contract or transaction which, unless and until avoided by the court, is and will remain valid and binding on the parties.   In strictness, the court, which does not make unnecessary orders,[5] may decline to interfere when its aid is invoked to rescind that which in fact, or in contemplation of law, does not exist, as, for instance, an alleged contract which is shown never to have been made, either because it was never concluded,[6] or because it was not made by or with a person having the requisite authority in that behalf,[7] or because the misrepresentation was such as to produce fundamental

---

[1] *Clough* v. *London and North Western Rail. Co.* (1871), L.R. 7 Exch. 26, Ex. Ch., *per cur.* at p. 36; *Capel & Co.* v. *Sim's Ships Composition Co., Ltd.* (1888), 58 L.T. 807, *per* KEKEWICH J. at p. 811. *Cf.*, as to voidable contracts and transactions generally, *Hyde* v. *Watts* (1843), 12 M. & W. 254, *per cur.* at p. 270: "we all think that no act or intimation of election on the part of the plaintiff to avoid the deed was necessary before bringing the action. The deed is void against the plaintiff if he chooses to treat it as such, by bringing an action on the original debt." See also cases referred to in note 4 on p. 260, *ante*.

[2] See Chapter XIV, para. 288, *post*.

[3] As for instance in the case mentioned in Chapter XIV, paras 298 *et seq.*, *post*.

[4] See Chapter XIV, para. 308, *post*.

[5] See *Reeve* v. *Gibson*, [1891] 1 Q.B. 652 (*per* VAUGHAN WILLIAMS J. at p. 657, and WILLS J. at p. 659, as to the unwisdom of this course).

[6] As in *Re Etna Insurance Co., Slattery's Case* (1872), I.R. 7 Eq. 245, where the alleged shareholder had withdrawn his application before allotment, and there was, therefore, no concluded contract. *Re Scottish Petroleum Co., Wallace's Case* (1883), 23 Ch.D. 413, C.A., was a case in which the shareholder attempted to show (1) that the allotment had not been made by the requisite number of directors, and (2) that the company had not unqualifiedly accepted his application, but had made a counter-proposal, which he had not accepted, and, though he failed to make good either suggestion, it was recognised by the Court of Appeal (see pp. 431, 432, 438) that, if he had succeeded in so doing, he would have established his right to have his name removed from the register on the ground, not of the voidability, but the voidness, or rather, non-existence, of the contract. So also, in *Re Thomas Edward Brinsmead & Sons, Tomlin's Case*, [1898] 1 Ch. 104, where it turned out on the evidence that there had probably been no concluded contract, a similar result might have followed but for the omission of the shareholder to set it up in the first instance.

[7] This was the first of the two points raised by the shareholder in *Re Scottish Petroleum Co., Wallace's Case*, *supra*.

error of the character already described,[1] or a contract which, though originally made, was determined by the parties before the proceedings were instituted,[2] or was a nullity *ab initio* by reason of its contravention of a principle of common law or a statutory enactment.[3] In many of such cases, however, relief will be granted *ex abundanti cautela*, if the matter is not perfectly clear, or if no objection is taken by either of the parties[4]; and it will always be granted *ex debito justitae* where a statutory register or other public document stands on record as *prima facie* evidence against the applicant, and where, therefore, it is just as necessary to get the entry complained of expunged or rectified in the case of a void or non-existent contract as in the case of one which is voidable only, the relief being given, not against the contract which does not exist, but against the statutory register or other document which incorrectly declares that it does. And, as will be seen hereafter,[5] where the representor is in physical possession of an instrument not obviously void on its face, and which may still be used to harass the representee, the court will make an order for its delivery up to be physically cancelled or destroyed.

Misrepresentation and marriage

248 That which is more than a contract can no more be rescinded for misrepresentation than that which is less than a contract, or is no contract at all. For instance, matrimony, which, if in any true sense it can be regarded as a contract at all,[6] is certainly a good deal more, inas-

---

[1] See paras. 241–243, *supra*.

[2] As, for instance, by forfeiture, pursuant to the articles of association of a company: *Re Home Counties and General Life Assurance Co., Woollaston's Case* (1859), 4 De G. & J. 437 (*per* KNIGHT-BRUCE and TURNER, L.JJ.); *Re London and Mediterranean Bank, Wright's Case,* (1871), L.R. 12 Eq. 334n.; *Re Same, (No. 2)* (1871), 7 Ch. App. 55; *Aaron's Reefs, Ltd.* v. *Twiss,* [1896] A.C. 273, at p. 293, H.L. The rule of course assumes that the forfeiture was *bona fide.* Where it was a fraudulent device of the shareholder in collusion with the company's secretary, the contract was held not to have been put an end to: *Re London and Provincial Starch Co., Gowers' Case* (1868), L.R. 6 Eq. 77 (*per* GIFFARD V.-C. at p. 81: "the so-called forfeiture was mere machinery for enabling them to get rid of their liability"). *New Zealand* case: in *Young* v. *Butler* (1902), 22 N.Z.L.R. 407 EDWARDS J. at p. 413 queried (without deciding the point) the claim for rescission of a purchaser of a lease who had already made default in performing obligations of the essence of the contract before he discovered the falsity of the representations upon which he had relied.

[3] Contracts, the object of, or consideration for, which is illegal, or immoral, or against public policy, or which, though not indictable or illegal, are made void by statute.

[4] e.g., in *Lee* v. *Angas* (1866), 7 Ch. App. 79 n; *cf. Kennedy* v. *Green* (1834), 3 My. & K. 699; *Vorley* v. *Cooke* (1857), 1 Giff. 230.

[5] See para. 254, *post.*

[6] Which, according to the best authorities, it cannot be: see *Sottomayer* v. *De Barros* (1879), 5 P.D. 94 (*per* HANNEN P. at p. 101). *Matrimonium* is the act of conveyance, or *traditio,* whereby the contract of betrothal is completed, not a contract in itself. One reason for its ever having been regarded as a contract is the fact that all the formal declarations of the marriage

much as it confers status and legitimacy, or, in the words of the Book of
Common Prayer a "holy estate", is not voidable on the ground of misrepresentation at the option of the party misled. It is not thought necessary here to traverse the circumstances in which a decree of nullity may
be obtained in the Divorce jurisdiction by a party to a ceremony of
marriage on the grounds, for instance, that there has been misrepresentation as to the identity of the other spouse, or as to the nature of the
ceremony.[1] Such matters are dealt with in detail in the standard texts
on divorce. But here it may be conveniently noticed that even a settlement made in consideration of marriage is not to be nullified for any
other cause than one for which the marriage itself can be declared null.[2]
A *contract to marry*, on the other hand, as distinguished from the mis-
called *contract of marriage*, may be the subject of a valid rescission or of a
defence to any action to enforce the promise, if that contract was brought
about by material misrepresentation, in the same way as any other contract.[3] And so also may a deed of separation.[4]

Form and extent of relief

249 The primary purpose of all proceedings for rescission, as contrasted with that of actions for damages, is to restore the *status quo*, to
bring back the original position by undoing all that has intervened
between it and the present. From this main principle certain very
important derivative rules necessarily follow. In the first place, the
restitution must be *in specie*, for, if it cannot be so effected, rescission
cannot be granted, any more than, if it were a question of enforcing the
contract directly, instead of annulling it directly, relief could be given
if the parties were not in a position to perform it *in specie*. In the next
place, it must be mutual—that is, if the representee is still in possession
of any property or rights derived by him under the contract or trans-

---

ceremony are based upon the *sponsiones* and *responsiones* of the Roman contract of *stipulatio*, as is
pointed out by Dr W. E. Ball in an interesting discussion of this topic at pp. 46–49 of his
St Paul and the Roman Law.

[1] A decree of nullity was granted on the first of these two grounds in *Hall* v. *Hall* (1908),
24 T.L.R. 756, and on the second of them in *Wilson* v. *Horn* (1904), 41 Sc.L.R. 312 and in
Ford v. *Stier*, [1896] P. 1.

[2] *Evans* v. *Carrington* (1860), 2 De G.F. & J. 481 (*per* Lord CAMPBELL L.C. at pp. 488, 489);
J. v. *J.* (1884), 53 L.J. (Ch.) 1014 (*per* PEARSON J. at pp. 1015, 1016). Contrast *Coulson* v.
Allison (1860), 2 De G.F. & J. 521, where a settlement was set aside on the ground of fraudu-
lent assertion of the legality of the marriage.

[3] This was recognised in *Hall* v. *Wright* (1859), E.B. & E. 746, Ex. Ch.; *Beachey* v. *Brown*
(1860), E.B. & E. 796; *Baker* v. *Cartwright* (1861), 10 C.B. N.S. 124.

[4] *Hulton* v. *Hulton*, [1917] 1 K.B. 813, C.A.

action sought to be avoided[1]; for it is obviously of the essence of the equity that in such cases both parties, and not one only, should be reinstated.[2] Thirdly, though the contract has always been voidable only until declared void or avoided by order of the court, yet that declaration or order, when once made, relates back to the date of the contract, so as to nullify all mesne dispositions of property and acts consequential upon the contract which have taken place during the intervening period,[3] which may be compared to the "period of relation back" in cases of insolvency of individuals or companies. Lastly, the rescission must be *in toto*, or not at all,[4] unless there are separate and severable covenants or stipulations, or several parties or interests, to be dealt with, or the instrument sought to be avoided is one that has two objects and may be put in suit in two characters; in any of which cases, if the other circumstances justify such an order, the court may rescind one of such covenants or stipulations without interfering with the others,[5] or set aside the con-

---

[1] If the representee has nothing to restore, the rule of course has no application. In that event, his remedy is an action of the nature considered in para. 263, *infra*. But if the representee has received money or property under the contract, there must be a *restitutio in integrum* of the defendant to his original position. See the next note, and paras. 257 *et seq.*, *post*, where this topic is further developed.

[2] Here, again, the analogy of actions for specific performance holds. In such actions the order is made only subject to the plaintiff's making out a good title, or otherwise performing his part of the contract. The observations of Lord WRIGHT in *Spence* v. *Crawford*, [1939] 3 All E.R. 271 may be called to mind. At p. 288 he said: "If a plaintiff who has been defrauded seeks to have the contract cancelled and his property or money restored to him, it would be inequitable if he did not also restore what he had got under the contract from the defendant. Though the defendant has been fraudulent he must not be robbed, nor must the plaintiff be unjustly enriched, as he would be if he got back what he had parted with and kept what he had received in return".

[3] *Reese River Silver Mining Co., Ltd.* v. *Smith* (1869), L.R. 4 H.L. 64, per Lord HATHERLEY L.C. at pp. 73, 74, Lord WESTBURY at pp. 77, 78, and Lord CAIRNS at p. 81; *Abram S.S. Co., Ltd.* v. *Westville Shipping Co., Ltd.*, [1923] A.C. 773, H.L. (per Lord ATKINSON at pp. 781–783). And this rule applies also to the restitution which the representee has to make as the condition of relief against the representor: see *Murray* v. *Palmer* (1805), 2 Sch. & Lef. 474, per Lord REDESDALE L.C. (Ir.) at p. 485. In *Australia*, *Alati* v. *Kruger* (1955), 94 C.L.R. 216 (H. Ct. of Aus.) at p. 224.

[4] *Myddleton* v. *Lord Kenyon* (1794), 2 Ves. 391, per Lord ELDON L.C. at p. 408; *Viscount Clermont* v. *Tasburgh* (1819), 1 Jac. & W. 112 (per PLUMER M.R. at pp. 119–122); *Beaumont* v. *Dukes* (1822), Jac. 422 (per PLUMER M.R. at p. 426: "it must stand or fall to the full extent"); *Clarke* v. *Dickson* (1858), E.B. & E. 148 (per CROMPTON J. at p. 155: "the plaintiff must rescind *in toto* or not at all"); *United Shoe Machinery Co. of Canada* v. *Brunet*, [1909] A.C. 330, P.C. (at p. 340)—in *Australia*, see *Alati* v. *Kruger* (*supra*) as an authority for the rescission by the party aggrieved of a contract induced by fraud, even though precise *restitutio in integrum* is not possible, if the situation is such that, by the exercise of its powers including the power to take accounts of profits and to direct inquiries as to allowances proper to be made for deterioration, the court can do what is practically just between the parties and thereby restore them *substantially* to the *status quo*. In *New Zealand*, see *Smith* v. *Crook* (1905), 24 N.Z.L.R. 532 (STOUT C.J.).

[5] As to a deed containing several distinct covenants, which for that purpose may be regarded as two deeds written on one parchment, see Com. Dig. Fait, B.2, on the authority of which SWINFEN EADY J. in *Bagot* v. *Chapman*, [1907] 2 Ch. 222, held that the mortgage-deed before

tract against one of such parties in respect of some partial and severable interest of the representee without affecting the position of the others or requiring them to be joined[1]; or allow the instrument to stand in one of its characters, for instance as a security, whilst rescinding it in the character in which it is put forward, e.g. a conveyance.[2]   Conversely, if there are two contracts or transactions in question which may fairly be regarded as complicated with one another, or interdependent, the proper relief may be to rescind both of them.[3]

250   The above are the root principles upon which relief by way of avoidance is granted, or refused, in whichever of the various possible forms of proceeding that relief may be sought.   These forms (and it is submitted that the list is exhaustive[4]) comprise (1) the ordinary action for rescission, (2) the action for money had and received, or for delivery up of property, where the representee has nothing to restore in exchange for the money or property which he seeks to recover, and which recovery, therefore, is the only remedy which concerns his interests, (3) the proceedings authorised by statute for rectification of a company's register of members, in cases of contracts to take shares therein, and the like proceedings to vary the list of contributories, where the company is in liquidation, (4) applications to be discharged from a contract of sale and purchase under the direction of the court in a pending matter and (5) physical recapture and resumption of the property the subject of the contract, wherever it may be found, without invoking any judicial interposition at all.   It now remains to consider these variations on the theme of rescission separately, and in order.

---

him might be regarded as good *quoad* one of the covenants, and "*ab initio* void for the residue" (pp. 227, 228).   In *Howatson* v. *Webb*, [1908] 1 Ch. 1, C.A., though it was doubted whether the application of the principle to the circumstances of *Bagot* v. *Chapman* was justified (see the observations of FARWELL L.J. at p. 2, and COZENS-HARDY M.R. at pp. 2, 3), the validity of the principle itself was not disputed.

[1] See the opinion to this effect of Lord LANGDALE M.R. at pp. 356, 357 of *Henley* v. *Stone* (1840), 3 Beav. 355.

[2] Thus in *Haygarth* v. *Wearing* (1871), L.R. 12 Eq. 320, WICKENS V.-C. made a declaration that the deed there in question was void as a conveyance, but good as a security.   So, in *Re Gomersall* (1875), 1 Ch.D. 137, C.A., affirmed *sub nom. Jones* v. *Gordon* (1877), 2 App. Cas. 616, H.L., the bills of exchange which were the subject of the proceedings were held to be good as securities for certain portions of their face value, but void as to the residue.

[3] *Dykes* v. *Blake* (1838), 4 Bing. N.C. 463 (*per* TINDAL C.J. at p. 477).   Contrast *Holliday* v. *Lockwood*, [1917] 2 Ch. 47 (*per* ASTBURY J. at pp. 51–55), where the unity of the two contracts was not established.   On the former case, see Fry, *Specific Performance* (6th edn.) p. 385.

[4] The vendor and purchaser procedure authorised by s. 49 of the Law of Property Act 1925, brought forward from the Vendor and Purchaser Act 1874, is not available for the decision of any question relating to the *validity* of the contract—see the text of s. 49.

Action for rescission

251   An action for rescission is the usual and normal form of proceeding for obtaining a judicial annulment of a contract induced by misrepresentation.   It is impossible to set out an exhaustive list of the kinds
of contracts or transactions which may form the subject matter of such
an action, but important instances are found in contracts relating to:
sales, mortgages or leases of land[1]; the sale or transfer of goods or securities[2]; insurance[3]; sales of a business, a partnership interest, a practice,
and the like[4]; compromises[5]; applications for shares in companies[6]; and

[1] Examples of successful actions for rescission of contracts of this type are to be found in
Cooper v. *Phibbs* (1867), L.R. 2 H.L. 149; *Torrance* v. *Bolton* (1872), 8 Ch. App. 118; *Lindsay
Petroleum Co.* v. *Hurd* (1874), L.R. 5 P.C. 221; *Hart* v. *Swaine* (1877), 7 Ch.D. 42; *Lempriere*
v. *Lange* (1879), 12 Ch.D. 675; *Re Arnold, Arnold* v. *Arnold* (1880), 14 Ch.D. 270, C.A.;
Smith v. *Land and House Property Corporation* (1884), 28 Ch.D. 7, C.A. (counter-claim);
Nottingham Patent Brick and Tile Co. v. *Butler* (1886), 16 Q.B.D. 778, C.A.; *Whittington* v.
Seale-Hayne (1900), 82 L.T. 49; *Jacobs* v. *Revell*, [1900] 2 Ch. 858; *Re Hare and O'More's
Contract*, [1901] 1 Ch. 93; *Baker* v. *Moss* (1902), 66 J.P. 360; *Mahomed Kala Mea* v. *A.V.
Harperink* (1908), 25 T.L.R. 180, P.C.; *Lee* v. *Rayson*, [1917] 1 Ch. 613; *Bellotti* v. *Chequers
Developments, Ltd.*, [1936] 1 All E.R. 89; *Sowler* v. *Potter*, [1939] 4 All E.R. 478, [1940] 1
K.B. 271; In *Australia, Sibley* v. *Grosvenor* (1916), 21 C.L.R. 469. In *New Zealand, Young* v.
Butler (1902), 22 N.Z.L.R. 407; *Power* v. *Atkins*, [1921] N.Z.L.R. 763; *Duncan* v. *Rothery*,
[1921] N.Z.L.R. 1074; *Oudaille* v. *Lawson*, [1922] N.Z.L.R. 259; *Fulton* v. *Reay*, [1926]
N.Z.L.R. 195; *Blanch* v. *Miller*, [1931] N.Z.L.R. 839.

[2] For illustrations of this class see *Moorhouse* v. *Woolfe* (1882), 46 L.T. 374 (a bill of sale):
Mathias v. *Yetts* (1882), 46 L.T. 497, C.A. (stock); *Whurr* v. *Devenish* (1904), 20 T.L.R. 385
(a horse); *Spence* v. *Crawford*, [1939] 3 All E.R. 271, H.L.; *Brown* v. *Raphael*, [1958] 2 All
E.R. 79; [1958] Ch. 636; *Car and Universal Finance Co., Ltd.* v. *Caldwell*, [1965] 1 Q.B. 525,
C.A. In *New Zealand* it was held as long ago as 1901 in *Riddiford* v. *Warren* (1901), 20 N.Z.L.R.
572, C.A. that a contract for the sale of goods may not be rescinded for innocent misrepresentation unless that representation is of the type defined in *Kennedy* v. *Panama etc. Mail Co., Ltd.*
(1867), L.R. 2 Q.B. 580; this decision has never been overruled in New Zealand, either by
any later decision or by statute. *Cf.* in *Australia Watt* v. *Westhoven*, [1933] V.L.R. 458.

[3] See *Fenn* v. *Craig* (1838), 3 Y. & C. Ex. 216; *Traill* v. *Baring* (1864), 4 De G.J. & Sm.
318; *Life and Health Assurance Association, Ltd.* v. *Yule* 1904, 6 F. (Ct. of Sess.) 437. The
great majority of insurance cases are cases in which the misrepresentation is set up as a defence
to a claim brought by the policy holder—see Chapter XIV, *post.*

[4] *Stainbank* v. *Fernley and Robinson* (1839), 9 Sim. 556; *Rawlins* v. *Wickham* (1858), 3 De
G. & J. 304; *Redgrave* v. *Hurd* (1881), 20 Ch.D. 1, C.A. (counter-claim). *With* v. *O'Flanagan*,
[1936] 1 All E.R. 727; [1936] Ch. 575, C.A.; *Brown* v. *Raphael*, [1958] 2 All E.R. 79; [1958]
Ch. 636 (sale of interest in a trust fund); *Senanayake* v. *Cheng*, [1965] 3 All E.R. 296; [1966]
A.C. 63, P.C. (sale of interest in partnership). In *New Zealand*, see *Stanley Stamp Co.* v.
Brodie (1914), 34 N.Z.L.R. 129, C.A. (sale of business); *Root* v. *Badley*, [1960] N.Z.L.R.
756; *Fenton* v. *Kenny*, [1969] N.Z.L.R. 552; on appeal *sub nom. Kenny* v. *Fenton*, [1971] N.Z.L.R.
1 C.A. (sale of motel business).

[5] *Davis* v. *Chanter* (1855), 3 W.R. 321; *Brooke* v. *Lord Mostyn* (1864), 2 De G.J. & Sm.
373; *Fane* v. *Fane* (1875), L.R. 20 Eq. 693; *Re Roberts, Roberts* v. *Roberts*, [1905] 1 Ch. 704,
C.A. (counter-claim).

[6] *Central Rail. Co. of Venezuela* v. *Kisch* (1867), L.R. 2 H.L. 99; *Henderson* v. *Lacon* (1868),
L.R. 5 Eq. 249; *Kent* v. *Freehold Land and Brickmaking Co.* (1868), 3 Ch. App. 493; *Ross* v.
Estates Investment Co. (1868), 3 Ch. App. 682; *Reese River Silver Mining Co., Ltd.* v. *Smith* (1869),
L.R. 4 H.L. 64; *Re London and Leeds Bank, Ltd., Carling's Case, Carling* v. *London and Leeds Bank,
Ltd.* (1887), 56 L.J.Ch. 321; *Capel and Co.* v. *Sim's Ships Composition Co., Ltd.* (1888), 58 L.T.
807; *Scott* v. *Snyder Dynamite Projectile Co., Ltd.* (1892), 67 L.T. 104, C.A.; *Greenwood* v.
Leather Shod Wheel Co., [1900] 1 Ch. 421, C.A.; *Components Tube Co., Ltd.* v. *Naylor* (1900),

miscellaneous subject-matters not admitting of classification.[1]   Action, of course, includes counter-claim.[2]

Contents of order to be made

252   The object of the action being to avoid both the contract or transaction itself, and also the consequences which have flowed, and which, but for its avoidance, would thereafter flow from it, it follows that the relief granted must comprise, first, a declaration, or at least a decision, that the contract or transaction is void, and must be deemed to have been so *ab initio*[3]; secondly, an order for the setting aside or cancellation of such contract or transaction, and, in certain cases, for the physical surrender of the instrument of contract to the representee[4]; thirdly, provisions for the repayment or retransfer to the representee of all moneys, property, or benefits, if any, which the representor has received under the contract or transaction, on the terms of the like restitution to the representor of all moneys, property, or benefits, if any, which the representee has received thereunder[5]; and, lastly, such terms, if any, as may be reasonably required in order to protect the parties from future enforcement by either of them against the other of any rights derived therefrom.[6]

253   Though this is not strictly necessary, it is not unusual to prefix to the order for rescission a formal and express declaration that the contract is void,[7] which, as has been pointed out,[8] means that it is declared

---

[2] I.R. 1; *Taylor* v. *Oil and Ozokerite Co.* (1913), 29 T.L.R. 515; *Mair* v. *Rio Grande Rubber Estates Ltd.*, [1913] A.C. 853, H.L.   In *Australia*, *Haas Timber and Trading Co., Pty., Ltd.* v. *Wade* (1954), 94 C.L.R. 593; in *New Zealand*, *Colonial Land Settlement of New Zealand Co., Ltd.* v. *Bohan* (1885), 3 N.Z.L.R. 98, at p. 100–101.

[1] Such as *Cooper* v. *Joel* (1859), 1 De G.F. & J. 240 (guarantee); *A.-G.* v. *Ray* (1874), 9 Ch. App. 397 (annuity); *Abram S.S. Co., Ltd.* v. *Westville Shipping Co., Ltd.*, [1923] A.C. 773, H.L. (assignment of benefit of contract); *Mackenzie* v. *Royal Bank of Canada*, [1934] A.C. 468, P.C. (contract of guarantee); *Spence* v. *Crawford*, [1939] 3 All E.R. 271, H.L. (sale of shares and indemnity).   In *New Zealand*, *Kerr* v. *Rhodes* (1888), 6 N.Z.L.R. 515 (sale of interest in patent).

[2] In *Redgrave* v. *Hurd*, *Smith* v. *Land and House Property Corporation*, and *Components Tube Co.* v. *Naylor*, *supra*, the relief was granted to a counter-claiming defendant.   In *Reynell* v. *Sprye*, *Sprye* v. *Reynell* (1852), 1 De G.M. & G. 660, which was decided before counter-claims were introduced, Sprye obtained an order for rescission by cross-bill.

[3] See para. 253, *infra*.

[4] See para. 254, *infra*.

[5] See para. 255, *infra*.

[6] See para. 256, *infra*.   The various kinds of relief obtainable in an action for rescission form the subject of Article 38 of the Code—see p. 13, *ante*.

[7] This was done in most of the cases cited in the text above.   In *Australia*, *Alati* v. *Kruger* (1955), 94 C.L.R. 216, at p. 217, p. 226.

[8] In para. 249, *ante*.

to have been a nullity from the commencement. Such a declaration is a convenient preface to, and the logical justification of, the judicial orders and directions which follow it.[1]   Like the preamble to a statute which *incipit a jussione*, it can be dispensed with, since the order for rescission necessarily involves and presupposes a judicial determination to the same effect as that which is directly pronounced by a declaration; but, for the prevention of subsequent disputes as to the meaning and grounds of the judgment (if, for instance, *res judicata* should be set up), it may serve a useful purpose, just as a preamble may, in cases of doubtful construction, be used as a key to the interpretation of the express provisions of a statute. And there may even be cases where such a declaration is substantially the sole remedy which for the moment is required.[2]

254   The order for rescission relates to the contract or transaction in question, whether in writing (as is ordinarily the case) or oral.   If in writing the contract may consist of, or be contained in, more than one document, in which case every one of such documents is the subject of the order, and conveyances or other instruments executed for the purpose of completing or carrying out, or otherwise consequential upon, the contract may be set aside, as well as the contract itself.[3]   Further, in any case where there is a statutory register or book the entries in which are declared by the legislature to be *prima facie* evidence of any contract or title purporting to be recorded therein, such as the register of members under the Companies Act 1948 the court will, as part of the relief granted, where there is statutory jurisdiction to do so, direct that such entry be expunged or rectified.[4]   "Rescission", though its literal meaning is "tearing up", is ordinarily understood in a metaphorical or symbolic sense.   Strictly, however, the representee is entitled to "rescis-

---

[1] See *Hulton* v. *Hulton*, [1917] 1 K.B. 813, C.A.

[2] An example of such a case is *Brooke* v. *Lord Mostyn* (1864), 2 De G.J. & Sm. 373, where TURNER and KNIGHT-BRUCE L.JJ., reversing ROMILLY M.R., made a declaration that a compromise of a suit for the recovery of a legacy, and the order of the court approving it, were not binding on the plaintiff, to whom they gave liberty to prosecute such suit as he might be advised.

[3] Mr Spencer Bower's original text said that "in some cases" conveyances might be set aside, presumably with *Seddon* v. *North Eastern Salt Co., Ltd.*, [1905] 1 Ch. 326 and similar cases in mind; but since the passing of the Misrepresentation Act 1967 it is conceived that the text above states the law as it now stands.

[4] Thus, as part of the relief granted *in the action*, the register of members was ordered to be rectified in *Kent* v. *Freehold Land and Brickmaking Co.* (1868), 3 Ch. App. 493; *Henderson* v. *Lacon* (1867), L.R. 5 Eq. 249; *Reese River Silver Mining Co., Ltd.* v. *Smith* (1869), L.R. 4 H.L. 64; *Re London and Leeds Bank, Ltd., Carling's Case, Carling* v. *London and Leeds Bank, Ltd.* (1887), 56 L.J. Ch. 321; *Greenwood* v. *Leather Shod Wheel Co.*, [1900] 1 Ch. 421, C.A.; *Components Tube Co., Ltd.* v. *Naylor*, [1900] 2 I.R. 1.

sion" in both senses. On the one hand, where the instrument is in the physical possession or control of the representor, he will be required by the court to deliver it up to be physically destroyed or cancelled, as well as to submit to an order for rescission, unless the defect or invalidity of the instrument appears on the face of it, and even in such a case he may be ordered to do so, if his conduct is proved to have been of such a character as to render it probable that he may in the future make an unconscionable use of the instrument by harassing and vexatious (even though hopeless) litigation, or if in any way it may, in the hands of the representor, or of third parties to whom he may transfer it, constitute "a cloud upon the title" of the representee, or otherwise hamper him in the enjoyment of his rights,[1] though in early times Equity judges seem to have been rather chary of exercising their jurisdiction in this respect, deeming it apparently something of a profanity to lay violent hands upon a solemnly executed instrument and hesitating, as Portia did in a memorable case, to "tear the bond", unless with the consent of the parties. On the other hand, a representee who has by redelivery or otherwise regained physical possession of the instrument is not by that fact alone deprived of his right to an order for cancellation by the court.[2]

255 Once rescission is decreed, the next step in the remedial procedure is to provide for the undoing of the past on both sides by mutual restoration *in specie* of all benefits received by either party under the contract.[3] In the more usual case where the representor is vendor, and it is a purchaser who is asking for rescission, the representor must repay

---

[1] See *Bromley* v. *Holland* (1802), 7 Ves. 3 (*per* Lord ELDON L.C. at p. 21); *Jackman* v. *Mitchell* (1807), 13 Ves. 581 (*per* Lord ELDON L.C. at pp. 585–587); *Ryan* v. *Mackmath* (1789), 3 Bro. C.C. 15 (*per* Lord THURLOW L.C. at p. 16); *Duncan* v. *Worrall* (1822), 10 Price, 31 (at p. 42); *Simpson* v. *Lord Howden* (1837), 3 My. & Cr. 97 (*per* Lord COTTENHAM L.C. at p. 102); *Cooper* v. *Joel* (1859), 1 De G.F. & J. 240 (*per* Lord CAMPBELL L.C. at pp. 245, 246); *Onions* v. *Cohen* (1865), 2 Hem. & M. 354 (*per* PAGE-WOOD V.-C. at p. 360); *Hoare* v. *Bremridge* (1872), 8 Ch. App. 22 (*per* Lord SELBORNE L.C. at p. 26); *Brooking* v. *Maudslay, Son and Field* (1888), 38 Ch.D. 636 (*per* STIRLING J. at pp. 643, 644, 646). In *Moorhouse* v. *Woolfe* (1882), 46 L.T. 374, the bill of sale there in question was ordered to be delivered up by the representor moneylender as a matter of course, without cavil or question on his part.

[2] *London and Provincial Insurance Co.* v. *Seymour* (1873), L.R. 17 Eq. 85 (*per* BACON V.-C. at pp. 90, 91: "the plaintiffs to whom the policies have been delivered are entitled, not only to retain possession of them, but to a decree of the court that they be now cancelled").

[3] "Benefits" here of course do not include moneys paid under a liability which existed irrespective of the contract: *Hulton* v. *Hulton*, [1917] 1 K.B. 813, C.A. If the representor has received nothing, or if neither party has received anything, this kind of relief is not required. On the other hand, if the representee has received nothing, but the representor has acquired under the contract money or chattels capable of manual delivery, the representee's remedy is of the kind described in paras. 263, *et seq.*, *post.*

all moneys which he has received,[1] and, unless the circumstances are exceptional, with interest.[2]   Where the representor is purchaser,[3] and it is a vendor who is claiming rescission, the representor will be ordered to reconvey or retransfer or redeliver all property or rights, whether in possession or in action, which he has received in the transaction,[4] executing appropriate instruments where necessary.[5]   It is not unusual to order him to deliver up documents of conveyance to be cancelled.[6] Whatever order is made as against the representor, it will be on terms that the representee on his part makes to him a similar *restitutio in integrum*.[7] In working out the necessary order in detail all necessary accounts and inquiries will be directed.[8]

The order for rescission will in appropriate cases include an order for the defendant to pay any conveyancing costs and stamp duty which the plaintiff has had to pay in the course of completing the transaction before the date when he gave notice of his rescission.[9]

---

[1] No difficulty ever arises as to the order for repayment of money, which is common form. Almost any case cited in the notes to these paragraphs will be found to include such an order.

[2] There is no doubt about the representee being entitled in all ordinary cases to interest on such moneys from the date on which they were paid to the representor up to the date of judgment, such interest being regarded, of course, as restitution, and not as damages.   For illustrative cases see *Re Metropolitan Coal Consumers' Association, Karberg's Case*, [1892] 3 Ch. 1, C.A. at p. 17; *Stepney* v. *Biddulph* (1865), 13 W.R. 576; *Re Hare and O'More's Contract*, [1901] 1 Ch. 93; *Abram S.S. Co., Ltd.* v. *Westville Shipping Co., Ltd.*, [1923] A.C. 773; *Bellotti* v. *Chequers Development, Ltd.*, [1936] 1 All E.R. 89; *Spence* v. *Crawford*, [1939] 3 All E.R. 271, H.L. In *Australia, Alati* v. *Kruger* (1955), 94 C.L.R. 216, at p. 226.   In cases, however, which involve no mutual restoration or adjustment between representor and representee, and the representee's action is therefore for moneys had and received, a different rule applies—see note 6 on p. 287, *infra*.

[3] This is the less usual case—see *Spence* v. *Crawford*, [1939] 3 All E.R. 271, H.L. *per* Lord THANKERTON at p. 279; *per* Lord WRIGHT at p. 289.   But "the principles are the same"— *per* Lord WRIGHT on same page.

[4] This also is ordinary practice.   See, for instance, *Addis* v. *Campbell* (1841), 4 Beav. 401; *Aberaman Ironworks* v. *Wickens* (1868), 4 Ch. App. 101; *Spence* v. *Crawford, supra*, at p. 285.   In *Australia, Alati* v. *Kruger* (1955), 94 C.L.R. 216, at pp. 217–229.

[5] e.g. in *Spence* v. *Crawford, supra*, at p. 285.   If necessary the order will direct some officer of the court to execute the necessary document if the defendant fails to do so—*ibid*, p. 285. In *Australia, Alati* v. *Kruger, supra*, at p. 217.

[6] See *Edwards* v. *M'Leay* (1818), 2 Swan. 287; in *Australia, Alati* v. *Kruger* (1955), 94 C.L.R. 216, at p. 217.

[7] This topic is developed at some length below in paras. 258 *et. seq.*

[8] See, for instance, *Edwards* v. *M'Leay* (1818), 2 Swan. 287; *Addis* v. *Campbell* (1841), 4 Beav. 401; *Haygarth* v. *Wearing* (1871), L.R. 12 Eq. 320.   In *Spence* v. *Crawford*, [1939] 3 All E.R. 271, H.L. an order for accounts was not necessary, for the parties had agreed on the figures subject to the question of rescission being determined by the court; but it is plain from the speech of Lord THANKERTON at p. 284 that there must have been an order if the necessary information had not been put before their Lordships by agreement.   In *Australia, Alati* v. *Kruger* (1955), 94 C.L.R. 216 (H. Ct. of Aus.) at p. 229.

[9] e.g. in *Edwards* v. *M'Leay* (1818), 2 Swan. 287; *Re Hare and O'More's Contract*, [1901] 1 Ch. 93 (JOYCE J.) *Carlish* v. *Salt*, [1906] 1 Ch. 335.   In *Australia* see *Alati* v. *Kruger* (1955), 94 C.L.R. 216, at p. 217, 230.   In *New Zealand, Fulton* v. *Reay*, [1926] N.Z.L.R. 195 at p. 197.

256   For the purpose of replacing the representee in the position which he occupied before the transaction, the representor will be ordered not only to restore any property itself of which he has had possession during the pendency of the transaction, but to bring into account all moneys which he has derived from that property while it has been in his possession—e.g., the rents of realty,[1] or dividends received on shares.[2] Such an adjustment is made not by way of damages but simply as a necessary step in effecting complete restoration of the original position.

The vexed questions of compensation for depreciation, where the vendor is plaintiff, and compensation for improvements effected by a purchaser during his period of occupation, are dealt with in a subsequent paragraph.[3]

The representor must indemnify the representee against all payments made by him pursuant to obligations under which he came in virtue of the contract, but not against payments made pursuant to obligations or matters "arising out of the contract", for this expression, if construed literally, would be wide enough to include damages, which clearly cannot be awarded in rescission proceedings, except to the limited extent countenanced by the provisions of the Misrepresentation Act 1967.[4]

257   Where it is necessary to protect the representee from possible attempts in the future on the part of the representor to enforce against him any term of the rescinded contract, or to deal with property acquired thereunder as if there had been no rescission, a perpetual injunction will be granted at the trial in terms adequate to meet the particular mischief apprehended, as, for instance, to restrain a representor from transferring

---

[1] *Stepney* v. *Biddulph* (1865), 13 W.R. 576; *Haygarth* v. *Wearing* (1871), L.R. 12 Eq. 320. In *Australia*, *Alati* v. *Kruger* (1955), 94 C.L.R. 216 at p. 229.

[2] *Addis* v. *Campbell* (1841), 4 Beav. 401; *Spence* v. *Crawford*, [1939] 3 All E.R. 271. In *New Zealand*, *Mackenzie* v. *Belcher* (1909), 28, N.Z.L.R. 7.

[3] See paras. 260, 261, below.

[4] See s. 2 of the Act, which is reprinted in full in Appendix C, *post*. It is plain that, apart from the operation of this provision, the representee has a right of election—always a right to choose one of two *mutually exclusive* courses of action—between repudiation, or rescission, on the one hand, and affirmation, with damages concurrently, on the other. The distinction between payments made pursuant to obligations *in virtue of* the contract, and those made pursuant to obligations *arising out of* the contract is well illustrated in *Newbigging* v. *Adam* (1886), 34 Ch.D. 582; *per* Cotton L.J. at p. 589; *per* Bowen L.J. at p. 594; see also *Whittington* v. *Seale-Hayne* (1900), 82 L.T. 49. In *New Zealand* see *Power* v. *Atkins*, [1921] N.Z.L.R. 763; *Duncan* v. *Rothery*, [1921] N.Z.L.R. 1074 and *Blanch* v. *Miller*, [1931] N.Z.L.R. 839.

shares,[1] or making calls,[2] in company cases, or parting with furniture obtained under a lease which has been set aside.[3] Further, a representee is entitled, on proper terms, to an interlocutory injunction restraining the representor until the trial of the action from forfeiting property of the representee under powers conferred by the contract sought to be rescinded, which contract the representee has repudiated, and cannot, therefore, consistently with the attitude he has taken up, recognise. By such an order an ingenious device of companies, in shareholders' actions, may now be checkmated,[4] the only case in which it succeeded having been overruled.[5]

Restitutio in integrum

258 The object to be achieved by rescission is the restoration of both parties as nearly as may be to the position which each occupied before the transaction. This object is expressed in the Latin *restitutio in integrum*, a phrase more particularly used by the courts, however, in referring to the restoration to his original position of the *defendant-representor*. Though he has been at fault, and even fraudulent, yet he must not be robbed, nor must the plaintiff-representee be unjustly enriched, as he would be if he received back all that he had parted with and also kept what he had received in return. The cases therefore emphasise the restoration of the defendant-representor to his pre-contract position, less often

---

[1] *Walsham* v. *Stainton* (1863), 1 De G.J. & Sm. 678.

[2] *Henderson* v. *Lacon* (1868), L.R. 5 Eq. 249.

[3] *Lempriere* v. *Lange* (1879), 12 Ch.D. 675.

[4] The device was of this nature. The shareholder, on discovery of the untruth of the representation whereby he was induced to subscribe for his shares, repudiates his contract, and sues for rescission, which involves the necessity of refusing to pay calls, since such payment would be evidence of affirmation—see para. 288, Chapter XIV, *post*—whereupon, pursuant to the contract between the parties contained in the articles of association, the company purports to forfeit the shares, with the view of doubly entrenching themselves; the idea being that, even if the representee succeeds, they are no worse off by reason of the forfeiture, whilst, if he fails, and seeks to retain the benefits which he acquired under a contract not invalidated by any misrepresentation, they will be in a position to retort upon him that the contract has been determined pursuant to its terms. To meet this manoeuvre, it was decided by NEVILLE J. in *Lamb* v. *Sambas Rubber and Gutta Percha Co., Ltd.*, [1908] 1 Ch. 845, and by the C.A. in *Jones* v. *Pacaya Rubber and Produce Co., Ltd.*, [1911] 1 K.B. 455, C.A., that, in such circumstances, a plaintiff, on paying the amount of the calls into court and undertaking in damages, is entitled to an interlocutory injunction, so that, if he is unable to establish a case for rescission at the trial, neither his position, nor the company's, is prejudiced: he still holds his shares, and the company have in court, ready to be paid out to them, the amount of the calls, with an undertaking to satisfy any damage they may have sustained. See the observations of BUCKLEY L.J. at pp. 457, 458 of the last cited case.

[5] This case is *Ripley* v. *Paper Bottle Co.* (1887), 57 L.J. Ch. 327. NEVILLE J. declined to follow it in the first, and the C.A. expressly overruled it in the second, of the two authorities cited in the last note.

expressly insisting upon the right of the plaintiff-representee so to be restored.[1] But the plaintiff does not need the protection of the doctrine; for he himself asks for restoration *in integrum*, as regards his own position, as of the essence of his claim to rescission. In praying for rescission he will generally be found to be reasonable as to the standard of the restitution he asks[2]; for if his prayer is unreasonable it will be unlikely to succeed. But whatever order he may ask in his own behalf, he must at least be prepared to restore the defendant-representor to his original position, as a condition of the rescission which he claims.[3] And in the next chapter it will be seen that if it turns out that he is unable to comply with this condition, his inability to do so will amount to a good defence to an action for rescission.[4]

Terms of order to rescind

259 This does not mean that the plaintiff-representee is obliged absolutely to restore the defendant-representor to his original position literally and in all respects. He need not positively be put back in the *same* position as before, but the requirements of justice may be met by putting him back *into as good a position*, when some monetary adjustment makes this possible.[5] Where matters have gone so far, however, that

---

[1] *Spence v. Crawford*, [1939] 3 All E.R. 271 *per* Lord THANKERTON at p. 279; *per* Lord WRIGHT at pp. 288–289.

[2] *Ibid*, *per* Lord WRIGHT at p. 289.

[3] So in *Western Bank of Scotland* v. *Addie* (1867), 1 Sc. & Div. 145, H.L. Lord CHELMSFORD L.C. on p. 160 referred to "an event which changed the nature of the shares and prevented his returning *the very thing which he received*". And at p. 166 Lord CRANWORTH, referring to the same happening, said "unless he was in a position to restore the very thing which he was fraudulently induced to purchase, he cannot have relief by way of *restitutio in integrum*".

[4] See Chapter XIV, para. 295, *post*.

[5] *Compagnie Chemin de Fer Paris-Orleans* v. *Leeston Shipping Co., Ltd.* (1919), 36 T.L.R. 68, 69. The classic statement of the rule is that of Lord BLACKBURN in *Erlanger* v. *New Sombrero Phosphate Co.* (1878), 3 App. Cas. 1218, H.L. at p. 1278, where he said: "and I think that the practice has always been for a Court of Equity to give this relief (rescission) whenever, by the exercise of its powers, it can do what is practically just, though it cannot restore the parties precisely to the state they were in before the contract". These words were echoed in the later (dissenting) judgment of RIGBY L.J. in *Lagunas Nitrate Co.* v. *Lagunas Syndicate*, [1899] 2 Ch. 392. A more modern authority is *Spence* v. *Crawford*, [1939] 3 All E.R. 271, H.L., where at p. 279 Lord THANKERTON, citing these two passages, observed that "it is well established that the doctrine is not to be applied too literally". At p. 288 of the same case Lord WRIGHT observes that in ordering rescission "the court must fix its eyes on the goal of doing what is practically just". In *Australia*, see *Alati* v. *Kruger* (1955), 94 C.L.R. 216 (H. Ct. of Aus.), where in the joint judgment of Sir Owen DIXON C.J. and WEBB, KITTO, and TAYLOR JJ. it is said on p. 223—"but it is necessary here to apply the doctrines of equity, and equity has always regarded as valid the disaffirmance of a contract induced by fraud, even though precise *restitutio in integrum* is not possible, if the situation is such that by the exercise of its powers, including the power to take accounts of profits and to direct inquiries as to allowances proper to be made for deterioration, it can do what is practically just between the parties, and by so doing restore them substantially to the *status quo*".

no monetary adjustment can reasonably be thought to restore the representor to as good a position as the one which he previously occupied, rescission must be refused, as will be seen in the next chapter. But in less extreme cases, where, besides the return of property actually handed over, a monetary adjustment appears necessary, in order to do substantial justice, such a payment will be required as a necessary condition of an order for rescission. Fairness and justice are the principles upon which such details are settled.[1]

Thus a plaintiff-vendor who by virtue of an order for rescission obtains his property again must be prepared not only to repay the purchase price, but to pay interest upon it[2]; if the plaintiff is purchaser and prays rescission to the end that he may receive his purchase money back again, he must not only return the property purchased, but must be prepared to add rent for its use while it was in his possession[3]; and a re-transfer of shares must be accompanied by a refund of dividends received.[4] So, too, a plaintiff-purchaser of a business has been required, as a condition of rescission, to make good by a monetary adjustment a deficiency in stock-in-trade.[5]

Where as a part of the mutual adjustment necessary to bring about a proper *restitutio in integrum* it is necessary to replace stock or chattels which have been disposed of by ordinary business dealings during the

---

[1] For instance, where on the rescission of a deed of separation, at the suit of the wife, on the ground of fraudulent misrepresentation by the husband, the husband sought to require the wife, as a condition of rescission, to refund the maintenance moneys which she had received over the five years during which the deed had been operative, it was pointed out that if these payments had not been stipulated for the husband would have been bound to maintain the wife on a scale not very different, apart altogether from the provisions of the deed; and the court refused to order a refund as a condition of rescission. SWINFEN EADY L.J. said at p. 281, adopting the dictum of Lord BLACKBURN in *Erlanger's* case (1878), 3 App. Cas. 1278, 1279, that the practice of the Court of Equity had always been "to do what is practically just"; and at p. 823 BANKES L.J. observed that "equity in justice" were the aim of the court. At p. 825 SCRUTTON L.J. said that the court in deciding on the conditions to be imposed was guided by the principle that he who seeks equity must do equity—*Hulton* v. *Hulton*, [1917] 1 K.B. 813, C.A. For a more modern case, see *Senanayake* v. *Cheng*, [1965] 3 All E.R. 296; [1966] A.C. 63, P.C. where it was said by the Judicial Committee at p. 83 that the requirement was met if the plaintiff "could effect substantial restitution". *Cf. Mackenzie* v. *Royal Bank of Canada*, [1934] A.C. 468, P.C. *per* Lord ATKIN at p. 476. In *Australia* see *Brown* v. *Smitt* (1924), 34 C.L.R. 160 (High Ct. of Aus.) at p. 172.

[2] Following the same principles as those upon which a representor is required to pay interest —see para. 255 above.

[3] The same applies to rent—see para. 256 above and notes. Whether, in the circumstances, it is equitable to allow any sum for rent will be a question of fact—see, in *Australia*, the order as finally made in *Alati* v. *Kruger* (1955), 94 C.L.R. 216 (H. Ct. of Aus.) at p. 229. *Cf*, in the same jurisdiction, *Brown* v. *Smitt* (1924), 34 C.L.R. 160 at p. 174.

[4] And the same to dividends—see para. 256 above and notes.

[5] This principle is developed further in the discussion of deterioration and appreciation in para. 260, below.

interim period, it has been held *in New Zealand*[1] that judgment should go for the value of such stock or chattels as at the date of the transaction to be rescinded.   SIM J. said[2]:

> "The object of the court in exercising this jurisdiction is to do what is practically just, as Lord BLACKBURN said in *Erlanger* v. *New Sombrero Phosphate Co.* To accept the defendant's contention would be to work injustice to one side or the other in every case where a change had taken place in the market value of the property in question.   If in the present case the market price of sheep had gone down instead of up, it would have been unfair to the defendant to give him only the present market value of the sheep or to allow the plaintiffs to replace the sheep that have gone with sheep purchased today".

But it seems to the writer of this edition that such an award may do less than justice; for what is requisite is that the vendor should receive back *his stock*, placing him in the same position as before the transaction. It may be thought that such a restoration of his original position will be brought about only if he be allowed such a sum as will repurchase for him, as at the date of judgment, the same stock which has been disposed of, or equivalent stock.

260   It has been required of a successful plaintiff-vendor, as a condition upon which an order for rescission will be granted to him, restoring to him the property which he sold, that he pay for improvements *bona fide* effected by the purchaser during the pendency of the transaction to the property for the restoration of which he prays.[3]   And a purchaser who sues for rescission must be prepared to "make good", by a monetary allowance, any depreciation in its value caused by his acts while he has been in possession.[4]   *Aliter*, however, with "normal" depreciation, which has occurred in the usual order of things, or from the inherent vice of the property itself, for which the law insists on no allowance.[5]

---

[1] *Fulton* v. *Reay*, [1926] N.Z.L.R. 195.

[2] At p. 196.

[3] *Stepney* v. *Biddulph* (1865), 13 W.R. 576 where counsel in argument submitted that this rule was not to be taken so far as to allow "improving a vendor out of his estate", a phrase which was impliedly approved by WOOD V.-C., and which has been repeated in later cases.

[4] So in *Erlanger* v. *New Sombrero Phosphate Co.* (1878), 3 App. Cas. 1218 Lord BLACKBURN at p. 1278 said that the court "can take account of profits and make allowance for deterioration". See the cases in notes to para. 259 above where, for instance, stock-in-trade, or the numbers of flocks had been diminished by sales by a purchaser in possession.   Of course, if the alteration is one of sufficient degree, *restitutio* ultimately becomes impossible; *Spence* v. *Crawford*, [1939] 3 All E.R. 271, H.L. on p. 279.   But so long as a monetary adjustment produces justice, it may be ordered as a condition of rescission—*ibid*.

[5] *Western Bank of Scotland* v. *Addie* (1867), 1 Sc. & Div. 145 *per* Lord CRANWORTH at p. 166; *Adam* v. *Newbigging* (1888), 13 App. Cas. 308, H.L. *per* Lord WATSON at p. 323 and Lord HERSCHELL at pp. 330–331.   *Armstrong* v. *Jackson*, [1917] 2 K.B. 822 furnishes a striking

261   But it is important to note that the allowances which a plaintiff must be prepared to make, as a matter of equity, in restoring to his representor what the latter had before the transaction—a *sine qua non* of rescission—are not necessarily paralleled in the claims which he may himself make in asking for rescission.   It may be just that a plaintiff, who may elect whether he rescind or not, may be required, as a condition upon which he may rescind, to pay for instance a fair sum for the improvements which an innocent purchaser has made to his property.   *Restitutio in integrum* cannot otherwise be said to be achieved.[1]   But the same principle will not necessarily require the court, when giving judgment for a purchaser-plaintiff who has claimed his money back, to add to the bill which the vendor must pay a sum for improvements to the property which that vendor has not asked for.   *Edwards* v. *M'Leay*[2] is sometimes relied upon as an authority for the proposition that such a claim may be successfully made; and in Australia this case was followed, and the claim upheld, by a majority of the High Court of Australia in *Brown* v. *Smitt*.[3] It seems to the writer of this edition, with respect to that court, that the views of the minority (ISAACS and RICH JJ.) are possibly to be preferred, and that in principle such a claim will not lie.   Equity may require, as a condition of rescission, that a vendor wishing to rescind and have his

---

example of the application of this rule; there the subject matter of the contract to be rescinded was shares, which during several years had almost entirely lost their value owing to their own inherent unsoundness.   This did not prevent the court from regarding the mere return of the shares, without monetary adjustment, as a sufficient restitution.   So, too, *Spence* v. *Crawford*, [1939] 3 All E.R. 271, H.L. *per* Lord THANKERTON on p. 279.   In *Australia*, see the joint judgment of Sir Owen DIXON C.J. and KITTO and TAYLOR JJ. in *Alati* v. *Kruger* (1955), 94 C.L.R. 216 (H. Ct. of Aus.), at p. 225, where it was said "the business itself (of which the plaintiff-representee had had possession) had deteriorated, but this would not matter, for as the trial judge has found, it was not due to any fault on the respondent's part, and even at common law the necessity to return property in its original condition was qualified so as to allow for incidents for which the buyer was not responsible, such as those to which the property was liable either from its inherent nature (*Newbigging* v. *Adam* (1886), 34 Ch.D. 582, at p. 588) or in the course of the exercise by the buyer of those rights over it which the contract gave—*Head* v. *Tattersall* (1871), L.R. 7 Exch. 7.''

[1] *Haygarth* v. *Wearing* (1871), L.R. 12 Eq. 320 is an example.   See also *Trevelyan* v. *White* (1839), 1 Beav. 588.   And see the passage at p. 170 of the (dissenting) joint judgment of ISAACS and RICH JJ. in *Brown* v. *Smitt* (1924), 34 C.L.R. 160 (H. Ct. of Aus.) where these and other cases are listed and discussed.

[2] *Edwards* v. *M'Leay* (1818), 2 Swan. 287.   The various reports of this celebrated case are interestingly collated by ISAACS and RICH JJ. in their dissenting judgment in *Brown* v. *Smitt* (*supra*) at pp. 170 *et seq*.   It appears clear that though in the court below the order originally made had included compensation for improvements, Lord ELDON struck this provision out of the order in giving his judgment on appeal—but this appears to have been because it was not asked for in the pleadings.   It does not appear to have been stated, in Lord ELDON's judgment as reported, either that such an order should, or should not, be made, having regard to principle.

[3] *Brown* v. *Smitt* (1924), 34 C.L.R. 160, H. Ct. of Aus.

property back again must make an appropriate allowance for permanent improvements *bona fide* made to it. If he is unwilling to make such an allowance, he may avoid doing so by allowing the transaction to stand and claiming in damages. But the same equitable principle does not involve allowing a purchaser to ask not only that his vendor accept back the property conveyed, refunding the purchase price, but that he be compelled into the bargain willy nilly to purchase improvements upon it. It is suggested that as rescission is a matter of election, the purchaser in this position is put to his choice, whether to have rescission without compensation, or no rescission at all; but that he cannot compel his vendor to pay for improvements which he does not want.

And it is further submitted that the same principle should apply to depreciation. It may be just to require a plaintiff-representee, as a condition of rescission, to make allowance to the vendor for depreciation caused by his own acts to the property which he is compelling that vendor willy nilly to accept back[1]; but on what principle can it be argued that a plaintiff-representor who has elected in all the circumstances to rescind the transaction can ask as well that the defendant who has been in possession shall make good to him the depreciation arising from that possession ?[2]

262 The courts may be readier to relax the application of the rules as to *restitutio in integrum* in cases where a representation has been fraudulent, than in those where the right to rescission is founded on innocent misrepresentation. It may indeed be argued on principle that although when, in the case of an innocent misrepresentation, the facts are such that *restitutio in integrum* is practically impossible, the result must be that rescission must be refused, yet the same facts should not be allowed to secure to a fraudulent misrepresentor the fruits of his fraudulent conduct.[3]

---

[1] See notes to paras. 259 and 260, above.

[2] There are old cases which seem to stand as authority for the proposition that depreciation caused by the act of the purchaser may be claimed by way of compensation in a vendor's suit for rescission—e.g. *Ex parte Bennett* (1805), 10 Ves. 381, at p. 400; *Robinson* v. *Ridley* (1821), 6 Madd. 2; *Gresley* v. *Mouseley* (1859), 4 De G. & J. 78. And it was said by the majority of the court in *Brown* v. *Smitt* (1924), 34 C.L.R. 160 (H. Ct. of Aus.) at p. 164 that "where the property has been improved or deteriorated by the act of the purchaser, and yet remains in substance what it was before the contract, equity adjusts the rights of the parties by awarding monetary compensation", and *Erlanger* v. *New Sombrero Phosphate Co.* (1878), 3 App. Cas. 1218 was cited in support. But it is unnecessary to point out that Lord BLACKBURN, in the passage relied on, was in fact speaking of the other type of case—that in which the court will insist on the *plaintiff* making good, as a condition of his order for rescission. It is here submitted that in *Brown* v. *Smitt* the view of the minority (ISAACS and RICH JJ.) may possibly be preferred.

[3] See *per* Lord LINDLEY M.R. in *Lagunas Nitrate Co.* v. *Lagunas Syndicate*, [1899] 2 Ch. 392, C.A. at pp. 433–434; *per* Lord THANKERTON in *Spence* v. *Crawford*, [1939] 3 All E.R. 271, at

Action for money had and received etc.

263 Where the representee has received nothing under the contract or transaction, and has nothing therefore to restore to the representor as the condition of relief, but has paid money thereunder, or where the representor is not enforcing the contract, or attempting or intending to enforce it, or has abandoned it,[1] the representee's claim is simply for the recovery of the money which he has paid, and is the proper subject of an action for money had and received. This form of proceeding is one of those equitable remedies which Lord MANSFIELD introduced into the common law on the lines of Roman jurisprudence.[2]

264 In any such action, relief is given or withheld on precisely the same principles as in an ordinary action for rescission, of which, indeed, it is, to all intents and purposes, a species, the sole *differentiae* of the species being that the restitution is necessarily unilateral, and not bilateral, for the simple reason that on the representee's side, nothing having been received or acquired, there is nothing to restore; and also that, though relief is granted on the theory that the contract is voidable, the above circumstances render it unnecessary to ask for a formal decree of rescission.[3]

265 Accordingly in every case of money had and received founded on misrepresentation, the representee succeeds where, and only where, he alleges and proves all such matters as are required to be established in an action to set aside a contract. The moneys for the recovery of which this form of proceeding has been successfully resorted to comprise deposits

---

pp. 280–281; *per* Lord WRIGHT at p. 288. An interesting *New Zealand* example of the lengths to which the court will go where the representor has been fraudulent will be found in *Berridge* v. *Public Trustee* (1914), 33 N.Z.L.R. 865.

[1] In *Flight* v. *Booth* (1834), 1 Bing. N.C. 370, the defendant had put forward no claim on the contract before the arbitrator (see p. 373), and in *Carlish* v. *Salt*, [1906] 1 Ch. 335, the defendants had themselves treated the contract as abandoned, and had pulled down the premises the subject of the sale.

[2] See Article 36 of the Code. In *Moses* v. *Macferlan* (1760), 2 Burr. 1005, Lord MANSFIELD C.J. at p. 1012, says that "this kind of *equitable* action lies for . . . money got through imposition (implied or express)", amongst other acts which he enumerates, rendering it *contra aequum et bonum* to retain or withhold from the plaintiff money which has come to the defendant's hands.

[3] See *Flight* v. *Booth*, *supra*, *per* TINDAL C.J., delivering the judgment of the court, at pp. 375, 376, the observations of LINDLEY J., at p. 294, BRETT L.J. at pp. 309, 310, and COTTON L.J. at p. 312, of *Stone* v. *City & County Bank* (1877), 3 C.P.D. 282, C.A., and *Manners* v. *Whitehead* 1898, 1 F. (Ct. of Sess.) 171 as to the identity of the principles to be applied. As to the uselessness of rescission, see *Re Ruby Consolidated Mining Co., Askew's Case* (1874), 9 Ch. App. 664, where, in a case of fully paid shares, the court refused to rectify the register of members, such an order being unnecessary.

on contracts for the purchase of property,[1] premiums on insurance policies,[2] application and allotment moneys on subscriptions for shares in companies,[3] and the like.[4] In most of the cases where the action has succeeded, the obtaining by the representor of the money was in fact fraudulent, but it is not essential, any more than it is in actions for rescission, that fraud in so obtaining it should be shewn[5]; the "imposition" and "unconscientiousness" mentioned by Lord MANSFIELD as an ingredient in the cause of action applies to the retention of money which it is *contra aequum et bonum* in the representor to withhold, notwithstanding that the acquisition of it might have been not unrighteous, as would be the case where the misrepresentation was innocent.[6]

266   Analogous to the action for money had and received on the ground of misrepresentation, are those forms of action for the recovery or

---

[1] *Jones* v. *Edney* (1812), 3 Camp. 285 (a public house); *Schneider* v. *Heath* (1813), 3 Camp. 506 (a vessel); *Stevens* v. *Adamson* (1818), 2 Stark, 422 (leasehold premises); *Flight* v. *Booth* (1834), 1 Bing. N.C. 370 (the like); *Dobell* v. *Hutchinson* (1835), 3 Ad. & El. 355 (the like); *Hutchinson* v. *Morley* (1839), 7 Scott 341 (fixtures and fittings); *Thornett* v. *Haines* (1846), 15 M. & W. 367 (leasehold premises); *Carlish* v. *Salt*, [1906] 1 Ch. 335 (freehold property).

[2] *Blake* v. *Albion Life Assurance Society* (1878), 4 C.P.D. 94; *British Workman's and General Assurance Co., Ltd.* v. *Cunliffe* (1902), 18 T.L.R. 502, C.A.; *Kettlewell* v. *Refuge Assurance Co.*, [1908] 1 K.B. 545, C.A., "silently" affirmed by the H.L., sub nom. *Refuge Assurance Co.* v. *Kettlewell*, [1909] A.C. 243, H.L.; *Tofts* v. *Pearl Life Assurance Co., Ltd.*, [1915] 1 K.B. 189, C.A.; *Hughes* v. *Liverpool Victoria Legal Friendly Society*, [1916] 2 K.B. 482, C.A.; *Byrne* v. *Rudd*, [1920] 2 I.R. 12.

[3] *Stone* v. *City and County Bank*, *supra*; *Re Ruby Consolidated Mining Co., Askew's Case*, *supra* (in which it was recognised that the representee would have a remedy, on proof of the facts, in an action for money had and received, and, indeed, that this was his only proper course, the shares having been fully paid, and that relief in the nature of rescission by a summary order under the Companies (Consolidation) Act 1908 was out of the question until after the trial of such an action.

[4] In *Duffell* v. *Wilson* (1808), 1 Camp. 401, the money recovered was a sum paid to insure the representee against being drawn for the militia. In *Blair* v. *Bromley* (1847), 2 Ph. 354, it was a sum paid for the purpose of being invested in a mortgage. In *Moss & Co., Ltd.* v. *Swansea Corporation* (1910), 74 J.P. 351, it was a deposit paid to secure the performance of a contract for the construction of works.

[5] In *Duffell* v. *Wilson*, *Flight* v. *Booth*, and *Moss & Co.* v. *Swansea Corporation*, *supra*, the misrepresentation was assumed, and, in *Edgar* v. *Hector*, 1912 S.C. 348, it was proved, to have been innocent.

[6] This is the sense in which JESSEL M.R. thought that, in ordinary cases of rescission, even if fraud is a necessary condition of relief, the condition may be said to be satisfied; it being, in his view, dishonest to seek to *retain*, though it was not dishonest to *obtain*, property and rights acquired by a representation not known to be false at the time of making it. See *Redgrave* v. *Hurd* (1881), 20 Ch.D. 1, C.A., at pp. 12, 13. It should be noted that the question of the presence or absence of fraud has some practical bearing on the measure of relief, for interest on the sum recovered may be given if, but not unless, there was fraud in the inception: *Johnson* v. *R.*, [1904] A.C. 817, P.C. (*per* Lord MACNAGHTEN, at p. 822: "money *obtained* by fraud, and retained by fraud, may be recovered with interest, whether the proceedings be taken in a court of equity, or a court of law").

delivery up of goods or property other than money, on the like ground, which the representor has parted with under the contract without having received anything in exchange, and, therefore, without having anything to restore.[1] Here, too, the only relief required is unilateral restitution, though in this case it is property, whereas in the other it is money, which forms the subject of such restitution; and the principles applicable are accordingly identical.

Company cases

267 Where it is sought to rescind, on the ground of misrepresentation, a contract to take shares in a company, either in the case where the company is still carrying on business, or in the case where it is now in liquidation, special procedures apply, and it is necessary to obtain an order of the court either (in the first case) rectifying the register (or in the second) varying the list of contributories. The reader is referred, for these procedures, to any standard work on company law.

Relief in cases of sales by order of the court

268 Where property is sold under the direction of the court, in the course of administering a trust, partnership, or insolvent estate, or in any other cause or matter, any person who has been induced by misrepresentation to enter into a contract to purchase such property is entitled to come to the court in that cause or matter, and apply to be discharged from his purchase; and an order will be made for that purpose on proof of the facts which it would be necessary to establish in an ordinary action for rescission, and subject in all respects to the same principles and conditions.[2]

The fact that the sale is, in a sense, by the court, and that the misrepresentation, if any, is made by the officers of the court, does not in the slightest degree weaken the purchaser's title to relief, or diminish

---

[1] See *Jones* v. *Keene* (1841), 2 Mood. & R. 348 (trover for a life-policy); *Moorhouse* v. *Woolfe* (1882), 46 L.T. 374 (where the representee sued a moneylender for delivery up of a bill of sale obtained by misrepresentation, he having repaid the money lent and interest at the rate represented to be the rate habitually charged).

[2] Such orders were made at the instance of the purchaser in *Martin* v. *Cotter* (1846), 3 Jo. & Lat. 496; *Lachlan* v. *Reynolds* (1853), Kay 52; *Brandling* v. *Plummer* (1854), 2 Drew 427 (here the petition was for compensation); *Dimmock* v. *Hallett* (1866), 2 Ch. App. 21; *Whittemore* v. *Whittemore* (1869), L.R. 8 Eq. 603; *Re Banister, Broad* v. *Munton* (1879), 12 Ch.D. 131, C.A.; *Re Arnold, Arnold* v. *Arnold* (1880), 14 Ch.D. 270, C.A.; *Mahomed Kala Mea* v. *A.V. Harperink* (1908), 25 T.L.R. 180, P.C.; *Re Longvale Brick and Lime Works, Ltd.*, [1917] 1 I.R. 321, *per* Lord O'BRIEN L.C. (Ir.), at pp. 329, 330.

the vendor's liability to submit to it.[1]   Indeed, this circumstance renders the contract, if anything, more readily impeachable than if the sale had no judicial sanction or authority. "The Court", said Lord St. Leonards[2] "expects from vendors, *and particularly from officers of the court*, a clear and express statement"; for, in the language of Page-Wood V.-C.,[3] "it would be strange indeed if in sales made by the direction of the court this rule" (*sc.* the rule of good faith) "should be less stringent".   In such cases there should be, as was observed by Jessel M.R. "at least as much good faith shown towards the purchaser as, and *perhaps a little more than*, is required by ordinary vendors out of court".[4]   It is the clear duty of the court to see that its ministers are at least as honest as other people, and the no less clear right of a purchaser to rely with absolute confidence on the discharge of this duty,[5] particularly having regard to the practice of the court in all such cases to expect good faith from the purchaser.[6]

Physical resumption by recapture of property

269   There are certain cases in which the representee, without invoking the aid of any judicial tribunal to annul the contract, may obtain rescission, or rather the fruits of rescission and all the practical advantages which he could derive from it, by taking the law into his own hands, just as (for instance) a person injured by a nuisance may abate it *propria manu*, instead of resorting to the court for an injunction or damages. Where goods and chattels, the possession of which is capable of passing by manual delivery, have been parted with pursuant to a contract voidable for misrepresentation, the representee, if fortunate enough to discover them afterwards, whether in the hands of the representor, or of his trustee in bankruptcy, or other third person, may lawfully revindicate or "resume" the property in such goods and chattels by physical recapture; and this summary method of enforcing the rule *je prends mes biens ou je les trouve* operates as an implied, but a most effectual and emphatic, election

---

[1] "In my view", said Cairns L.J. at p. 29 of *Dimmock* v. *Hallett*, *supra*, "the court ought not to be less strict as to sales under its own orders than as to sales out of court."

[2] When Sir Edw. Sugden, and L.C. of Ireland, in *Martin* v. *Cotter*, *supra*, at p. 505.

[3] At p. 55 of *Lachlan* v. *Reynolds*, *supra*.

[4] At p. 141 of *Re Banister*, *supra*.; with which compare his observations to the same effect at pp. 273, 274, 277 of *Re Arnold*, *supra*, and those of Byrne, J., at p. 107 of his judgment in *Debenham* v. *Sawbridge*, [1901] 2 Ch. 98.

[5] See the very strong observations of the Privy Council on the conduct of the Indian court in *Mahomed Kala Mea* v. *A. V. Harperink*, *supra*.

[6] *Per* Lord Selborne, at pp. 236 of *Coaks* v. *Boswell* (1886), 11 App. Cas. 232, H.L.

to avoid the contract.[1] Of course there must be no incidental violence or trespass, and the *fortiter in re* must be characterised by the *suaviter in modo*[2]; further, if there is anything which under a judgment for rescission would have to be restored to the representor as part of the mutual restitution which is a condition of the relief, such restoration must be made or offered by the representee when "resuming" the possession of, and property in, the chattels in question[3]; or, if the article is found in the hands of a third party who has acquired it, or has the possession or custody of it, in good faith and for value, payment must be made or tendered by the representee of what has been paid by such third party in so acquiring it, or what has been advanced by him on the security of it, or the amount of his proper charges for warehousing and the like,[4] as the case may be. Where there is nothing to restore to the representor or pay to a third party, or where the contract is not voidable but void, so that no property ever passed at all, the representee's right is unconditional.

But in any case, like any other person who takes the law into his own hands, and assumes it to be in his favour without obtaining a judicial declaration to that effect, the representee accepts the risk (slight or

---

[1] This was the course successfully adopted by the representee in, amongst other cases, *Clough* v. *London and North Western Rail. Co.* (1871), L.R. 7 Exch. 26, Ex. Ch., where the goods were obtained by the London Pianoforte Company (who were the representees, and the real defendants to the action) from the defendant railway company, on agreeing to indemnify them (see pp. 34, 37, where the right of any representee to "resume the property which he parted with under" the contract is discussed); *Re Eastgate, Ex parte Ward*, [1905] 1 K.B. 465, where the swindled creditors of the representor, after the act of bankruptcy but before the receiving order was made, broke into the house of the debtor and recaptured the goods which they had been induced to part with by the debtor's implied false pretence of his intention to pay for them, and BIGHAM J. held that they were entitled to disaffirm the contract by this somewhat lively procedure as against the representor's trustee in bankruptcy; *Tilley* v. *Bowman, Ltd.*, [1910] 1 K.B. 745, 750, where the circumstances were the same, except that in this case the "recapture" was subsequent, not only to the act of bankruptcy but to the receiving order also, which fact, however, was considered by HAMILTON J. not to affect the application of the rule.

[2] In *Re Eastgate, supra*, BIGHAM J. (p. 467), expressed his disapproval of the manner in which the "resumption" was effected, but did not consider the representee's conduct serious enough to affect his decision.

[3] See *Clough* v. *London and North Western Rail. Co.*, *sup.*, *per Cur.* at p. 37: "No man can at once treat the contract as avoided by him, so as to resume the property which he parted with under it, and at the same time keep the money or other advantages which he obtained under it; and therefore the London Pianoforte Company were bound to restore to Adams the money and the acceptance which they had obtained from him". Here the above company were the representees, and Adams was the representor, but the non-payment of these moneys to Adams was immaterial, since Adams was the only person who could assert a right to such payment, and he (for very good reasons) was not suing.

[4] In *Tilley* v. *Bowman, Ltd.*, *supra*, the representee paid the pawnbroker the money advanced, with the interest chargeable, and so obtained possession of the goods, his right to retain which was established in the action, together with his right to be recouped by the representor the moneys so paid by way of set-off in the representor's bankruptcy.

serious, according to all the circumstances) of his acts turning out to be unjustified. And in this connection the effect since 1967 of s. 2 (2) of the Misrepresentation Act 1967 must be borne in mind; for it is now competent for the Court, if it is of the opinion that such a course would be equitable, to declare the contract subsisting and award damages in lieu of misrepresentation.[1]

Questions of law and fact in proceedings for rescission

270 As regards all those elements and ingredients which are common to both the two main types of proceedings founded on misrepresentation, it has already been pointed out which of the matters of controversy arising therein are questions of law, and which are issues of fact.[2] The questions special to proceedings for rescission, whether arising on the consideration of the representee's case, or on those of any affirmative case set up by the representor, such as whether the representee has exercised his right of election by affirming the contract before the initiation of the proceedings, or by avoiding it, or at all,—whether he is in a position to restore the property in the same physical plight as that in which he received it,—whether, by his acts and conduct, he has evinced an intention to take all risks, waive all inquiry, or not to rely on the alleged or any representation, and the like,—are questions of fact, subject to these overriding rules,—that it is a question of law, whether there is any evidence in support, or in contradiction, of any allegations of the nature indicated; and also that, in case of any agreement said to be wholly contained or recorded in documents, or to depend on undisputed facts, it is a question of law whether the alleged agreement is, or is not, contained or recorded in, or to be implied or extracted from, such documents in their proper construction, or such undisputed facts.

Parties to proceedings for rescission

271 The question of what persons are deemed in law to have been parties to the representation sued upon has already been discussed,[3] as also has the question of what persons, other than the parties to the representation, may, or (in certain cases) must, be parties to an action for damages founded on misrepresentation.[4] It remains to consider who,

---

[1] For the text of the Act see Appendix C, *post*.
[2] See Chapter XI, *ante*.
[3] See Chapters VIII and IX, *ante*.
[4] See Chapter XI, *ante*.

besides the parties to the representation, may or (in certain cases) must, be parties to proceedings for rescission.[1]

The persons entitled to initiate proceedings for rescission

272 In cases of transmission or devolution, by act or operation of law, of a cause of action for rescission, by reason of the death, insolvency, infancy, or lunacy, of the representee, the rules as to the persons who are entitled to commence, or (as the case may be) continue, proceedings against the representor, are the same as those which govern actions of contract in general, and do not call for special treatment in this place. But to cases of devolution or assignment other than the above, there are two rules specially applicable, which require to be examined.

In the first place it is well settled that, where specific property is devised or conveyed or assigned from one to another, there pass with it all such equities to rescission as the person devising, conveying, or assigning was entitled to, when so doing. So long as the right is coupled with possession, physical or constructive (as by receipt of rents), the mere initiation or maintenance of an action in relation to *the property*, though proceedings for rescission may be involved in such litigation, is in no way obnoxious to the objections of champerty or maintenance.[2] "An assignment of property is valid, even although that property may be incapable of being recovered without litigation".[3] As was said by Lord ROMILLY M.R. in a judgment which has been repeatedly cited and approved, "the right of suit is a right incidental to the property conveyed", and also "incidental to each interest carved out of it"; therefore

> "any interest which, but for the previous deed, would have been sufficient to enable a person interested to ask this court to secure this property for the benefit of the persons interested therein, would, in my opinion, enable that person to ask this court to set aside the deed obtained by fraud, which, if valid, would have prejudiced or destroyed his interest in the property purporting to be conveyed to him".[4]

---

[1] See Article 44 of the Code p. 26, *ante*.

[2] This principle was recognised by Lord ABINGER C.B. at pp. 486, 487, and 499, of *Prosser* v. *Edmonds* (1835), 1 Y. & C. 481, Ex. Ch., and applied in *Cockell* v. *Taylor* (1851), 15 Beav. 103, at pp. 116, 117. *Cf. Ellis* v. *Torrington*, [1920] 1 K.B. 399, C.A., and the non-disclosure case of *Wilson* v. *Short* (1848), 6 Hare 366 (*per* WIGRAM V.-C. at pp. 376, 384).

[3] *Dawson* v. *Great Northern and City Rail. Co.*, [1905] 1 K.B. 260, C.A., *per* COLLINS M.R. at p. 271.

[4] *Dickinson* v. *Burrell* (1866), L.R. 1 Eq. 337, at p. 342. It is to be added that if the suit is brought by a plaintiff with only a part interest, all others involved must be joined, either as plaintiffs or as defendants.

Thus a man may, under the conditions stated, devise, so as to defeat his heir, an equity to set aside a conveyance on the ground of fraud to the very person guilty of it, just as he can, with the like consequences to the heir, devise away from him any other equitable and devisable interest.[1]

But while it is possible, as pointed out above, for an assignee of specific property to avail himself, in aid of his own *enjoyment* of that property, of any right in his assignor to rescind any *previous agreement* to convey the property to a third person, it has been held that such an assignee does not take by virtue of his assignment, in aid of his *rejection* of the property, a right to rescind *the agreement to purchase it made between his assignor and his vendor*, in a case where, before the assignment, the assignor was able to rescind for misrepresentation.[2]

273 Secondly, it is no less firmly established, on grounds of public policy, that a bare right or equity to rescind on the ground of misrepresentation or on any other ground, divorced from any specific property or fund, is not saleable or assignable, for all such sales and assignments of litigated titles savour of, if not actually constituting, champerty in the one case, and maintenance in the other.[3] But the assignment of a claim to recover on the principles of rescission, and on the ground of misrepresentation or concealment, a specific fund which is earmarked and can be traced, and which may properly be described as in equity the money of the claimant, or as an equitable debt, in not exceptionable on this ground,[4] the fund in question being regarded as specific property within the meaning of the first rule. Hence it is that misfeasance claims against the delinquent directors and officers of a company have always

---

[1] *Stump* v. *Gaby* (1852), 2 De G.M. & G. 623, *per* Lord St. Leonards L.C. at pp. 630, 631. For an instance of a sale to the person against whom the relief would be obtainable, see *Re Park Gate Waggon Works Co.*, cited in note 1 on p. 294.

[2] So in *Gross* v. *Lewis Hillman, Ltd.*, [1969] 3 All E.R. 1476; [1970] Ch. 445, C.A., it was held that where B had agreed to purchase, relying on the fraudulent representation of A (although fraud was not proved, the judgments in the Court of Appeal proceeded on the assumption that it might have been) and had then allowed C to purchase directly from A on payment of commission, C could not claim rescission against A because (1) no representation had been made to C and (2) the facts were quite different from those in *Dickinson* v. *Burrell* (*supra*), and (*per* Cross L.J. at p. 460) "the right to rescind for misrepresentation does not run with the land in that way."

[3] See *Wood* v. *Downes* (1811), 18 Ves. 120, at p. 125; *Prosser* v. *Edwards* (1835), 1 Y. & C. 481, at pp. 496, 500; *Dawson* v. *Great Northern and City Rail. Co.*, [1905] 1 K.B. 260, C.A. at pp. 270–271; *Fitzroy* v. *Cave*, [1905] 2 K.B. 364, C.A. at p. 371.

[4] See *Cockell* v. *Taylor* (1851), 15 Beav. 103 (at pp. 116, 117), where the distinction is drawn between an assignment of a naked right to sue, or a bare litigated claim, which would be bad, and (as was the case there) an assignment of a claim to an interest in a specific fund actually lodged in court.

been held the proper subject of assignment and sale, whether by private treaty[1] or public auction.[2]

274 The procedure, by test action or otherwise, where several representees are seeking rescission against the same representor in respect of the same representation, is dealt with elsewhere.[3]

The persons liable to proceedings for rescission

275 The persons, other than the representor, against whom, in case of his death, insolvency, infancy, or lunacy, proceedings for rescission may be initiated, continued, or maintained, are, ordinarily, those who, according to the rules as to parties applicable to actions of contract in general, would be so liable. But in cases of assignment by voluntary act of the parties, or in any case where neither a claim under the contract, nor the property the subject thereof, passes by mere operation of law, there are certain rules which in their application to proceedings for rescission it will now be convenient to notice.

276 Where the representor has assigned a mere chose in action (as distinguished from property in possession) which he has acquired under a contract or transaction voidable for misrepresentation as against him at the instance of the representee, the assignee, though taking in good faith, for value, and without notice, stands in no better position after the assignment than the assignor before it. No rule of law is better established than that the assignee of a chose in action takes subject to all equities which before the assignment were, and but for the assignment would continue to be, enforceable against the assignor; and amongst such recognised equities is the equity to avoid on the ground of misrepresentation.

---

1 As in *Re Park Gate Waggon Works Co.* (1881), 17 Ch.D. 234, C.A. (where, the liquidator having sold *all* the property of the company to a certain person, a misfeasance claim against delinquent officers of the company was held to be comprised therein, and the proper subject of sale, notwithstanding that the purchaser was the agent of these very officers, who accordingly on this ground obtained an injunction against the liquidator proceeding with the misfeasance claim against them, though the order was made without prejudice to any application which the liquidator might make to set aside the deed of sale); *Re Anglo-Austrian Printing and Publishing Union, Lord Brabourne* v. *Same*, [1895] 2 Ch. 891, (where a misfeasance claim was assigned to the debenture holders). See also, on this topic, *Re Cyona Distributors, Ltd.*, [1966] 1 All E.R. 825.
2 As in *Wood* v. *Woodhouse and Rawson, United*, [1896] W.N. 4, where misfeasance claims were ordered by the court, in a debenture holder's action, to be put up for sale by auction.
3 See paras. 387–389, Chapter XVIII, *post*.

277   On the other hand, where property in possession (physical or constructive) passes under the assignment to one who acquires it for value, without notice, and in good faith, or (to borrow a convenient phrase from the Bills of Exchange Act 1882) to an assignee "in due course", no election to avoid on the ground of misrepresentation, or proceedings in rescission, which would have been available against the assignor, will be in the slightest degree effectual to take the property out of the hands of the assignee.   To be effective such an election must have been exercised by the representee before the assignment, either by due notice or by the institution of proceedings for rescission, in which case the assignee is simply put in possession of that which it was not in the power of the assignor to bestow; in other words he acquires nothing, for *nemo dat quod non habet*.   But where there has been no such avoidance of the voidable contract before the assignment thereunder of any chose in possession, the assignee cannot be deprived of the property unless his acquisition of it was wanting in some or more of the elements necessary to constitute "due course", that is to say, unless he gave no value, and was a mere donee or volunteer, or he took with notice, or in bad faith.

278   That the property may be taken out of the hands of an assignee who is a mere volunteer, or the recipient of bounty, whether he acted in good faith and without notice or not, has been established from the earliest times.   The rule is firmly stated in a celebrated case,[1] where the question arose whether the innocent donees of portions of the property acquired by imposition could retain what they had so been given, and where WILMOT C.J. one of the Lords Commissioners of the Great Seal, delivered himself thus:

> "there is no pretence that Green's brother or his wife was party to any imposition, or had any due or undue influence over the plaintiff; but does it follow from thence that they must keep the money?   No; whoever receives it must take it tainted and infected with the undue influence and imposition of the person procuring the gift.   His partitioning and cantoning it out amongst his relations and friends will not purify the gift and protect it against the equity of the person imposed upon.   Let the hand receiving it be

---

[1] *Bridgman (or Bridgeman)* v. *Green* (1755), 2 Ves. 627; (1757) Wilmot's Opns. and Judgmts., 58.   This case was decided by Lord HARDWICKE L.C. in 1755, as reported in Vesey Sr.; and, in 1757, it came before the Lords Commissioners of the Great Seal (WILLES C.J., Sir Sidney STAFFORD SMYTHE, and WILMOT C.J.), and it is the judgment of WILMOT C.J. on this appeal or rehearing which is reported in Wilmot's Opns. and Judgmts., *supra*.

ever so chaste, yet, if it comes through a corrupt, polluted channel, the obligation of restitution will follow it".[1]

And in numerous subsequent decisions, both of misrepresentation and of undue influence, unconscionable dealing, and non-disclosure, this doctrine, which is common to all cases of imposition and oppression, has been consistently and rigorously applied.[2] It is to be observed that, for this purpose, any person to whom property is assigned by operation of law, or by force of some statutory provision, such as an execution creditor, or a trustee in bankruptcy, is not a purchaser for value, and a representee may exercise as against him any right of avoidance or rescission (and thereby recover property otherwise distributable amongst the creditors) which he might have exercised against the execution debtor, or bankrupt.[3]

279 Secondly, if the assignee had notice of the fact which gave the representee his equity to avoid the contract and resume the property, he cannot retain such property, though he gave value, and was not guilty of any dishonesty or bad faith.[4]

280 Lastly, though the assignee gave value and in fact had no express notice of the facts which rendered the contract voidable, if he acted in bad faith, that is to say, if with fraudulent deliberation he escaped notice of that which he abundantly suspected, again he is not permitted to retain the property.[5]

---

[1] Wilmot's Opns. and Judgmts., 64.

[2] See *Huguenin* v. *Baseley* (1807), 14 Ves. 273, *per* Lord ELDON L.C. at pp. 288–290, citing and approving WILMOT C.J.'s statement of the rule; *Vaughan* v. *Vanderstegen*, *Gates's Case* (1854), 2 Drew. 363; *Same* v. *Same*, *Othwaite's Case* (1854), 2 Drew. 408; *Haygarth* v. *Wearing* (1871), L.R. 12 Eq. 320; *Babcock* v. *Lawson* (1880), 5 Q.B.D. 284, C.A. The first of these was an undue influence case, with which compare a later case of this nature, *Morley* v. *Loughnan*, [1893] 1 Ch. 736 (*per* WRIGHT J. at pp. 757, 758). The others were misrepresentation cases.

[3] See *Kennedy* v. *Green* (1834), 3 My. & K. 699; *Load* v. *Green* (1846), 15 M. & W. 216; *Madell* v. *Thomas & Co.*, [1891] 1 Q.B. 230, C.A. (*per* KAY L.J. at p. 238: "a trustee in bankruptcy or execution creditor is in privity with the bankrupt or execution debtor. He takes under the bankrupt or execution debtor, not like a purchaser for valuable consideration, and it has been decided over and over again that he only takes what was vested in the bankrupt or execution debtor"); *Re Eastgate, Ex parte Ward*, [1905] 1 K.B. 465; *Re Wallis, Ex parte Jenks*, [1902] 1 K.B. 719 (*per* WRIGHT J. at p. 720); *Tilley* v. *Bowman, Ltd.*, [1910] 1 K.B. 745, at p. 750.

[4] In *Earl of Sheffield* v. *London Joint Stock Bank* (1888), 13 App. Cas. 333, H.L., such notice was proved; on the other hand, in *London Joint Stock Bank* v. *Simmons*, [1892] A.C. 201, H.L., it was not proved.

[5] *Whitehorn Brothers* v. *Davison*, [1911] 1 K.B. 463, C.A., where, however, the alleged *mala fides* was not made out. The distinction between notice and bad faith is recognised by VAUGHAN WILLIAMS L.J. at p. 476 in the passage cited in the next note.

281   The burden of proving that the assignee was not an assignee "in due course" is on the representee; there is no burden on the assignee of proving that he was.   It has never been doubted that it is incumbent on the representee to show that the assignee gave no value for the property, or had notice of the facts in virtue of which the contract was voidable, but there was at one time some conflict of judicial opinion as to whether the onus of establishing good faith was not on the assignee.   It is now clear, however, that this is not so, and that the representee must prove the assignee's absence of good faith, just as much as he must prove the absence of either of the two other elements which are necessary to constitute "due course".[1]   Whenever the representee has either not alleged, or, having alleged, has failed to prove, the absence of some one of these three elements, his claim against the assignee has been dismissed,[2]

---

[1] *Whitehorn Brothers* v. *Davison*, *supra*, where the C.A. set aside the verdict obtained by the plaintiff in the court below, and entered judgment for the defendant, on the ground, *inter alia*, that it was for the plaintiff—the representee—to prove bad faith, as much as it was for him to prove absence of value, and notice, and that the jury had been misdirected that it was for the defendant—the assignee of the property from the representor—to prove his good faith. The rule, and the reason for it, is stated with admirable lucidity by VAUGHAN WILLIAMS L.J. at pp. 476, 477: "where you have a contract of sale which is voidable on the ground of fraud, or for any other reason, and before it is avoided by the seller, the buyer, as against whom it could have been avoided, has transferred the subject-matter of the contract to an innocent third person who has given value and has accepted the transfer without either knowledge of anything wrong, or any knowledge of such circumstances as might lead him to wish not to make any further inquiry lest he should find that there was something wrong, the contract cannot be avoided as against that person; and I am of opinion that the onus of proving that there are such circumstances as prevent the third person so purchasing from being such an innocent purchaser rests on the plaintiff who seeks to recover the subject-matter of the contract from him, and not on the defendant . . . The very statement which occurs again and again that in such cases the contract is a voidable and not a void contract, i.e. that it is valid till avoided, seems to me to indicate that the onus for the purpose of avoiding it against the third person must lie on the person who is seeking to impeach that which up to that time is a valid contract.   Common sense appears to me to point to the same conclusion".   And, one may add, common fairness too.   To take property out of the possession of another, a cause of action,—a legal justification, —must be shown.   As against the representor, such justification consists in his misrepresentation; but as against a person who did not make or join in the misrepresentation, and who never had any contractual privity or relationship of any kind with the representee, it must be shown either that, by reason of notice or bad faith, it is morally right that the third person should suffer, or that, by reason of his being a mere volunteer or donee, he will not in fact suffer, or will not in fact suffer any injury which the law can recognise.   Further, to put it in another way, a man in possession of property is presumed to be in innocent and lawful possession of it until the contrary is shown.   These aspects of the matter are insisted upon by BUCKLEY L.J. at pp. 481, 482 (who there explains that the form in which the proviso to s. 23 of the Sale of Goods Act 1893 is expressed, though at first sight lending some countenance to the opposite contention, could not have been intended to revolutionise plain principles of evidence as to the *onus probandi* in such cases), and by KENNEDY L.J. at p. 487.

[2] As in *London Joint Stock Bank* v. *Simmons*, [1892] A.C. 201, H.L., where the plaintiff failed to prove notice; in *Truman* v. *Attenborough* (1910), 103 L.T. 218 a case arising out of the same kind of misrepresentation of the same representor as in *Whitehorn Brothers* v. *Davison*, [1911] 1 K.B. 463, C.A., and where the representee relied on estoppel, and did not even allege either absence of value, or notice, or bad faith; and in *Whitehorn Brothers* v. *Davison*, *supra*, where

unless he has been in a position to rely upon some estoppel against such assignee,[1] or has been able to show that there had never been any contract at all under which any property could have passed to him.

---

again the representee did not allege, or attempt to prove, any of the above, but insisted (wrongly, as the C.A. held) that it was for the defendant to prove his good faith.

1 See *Mangles* v. *Dixon* (1852), 3 H.L. Cas. 702 (*per* Lord ST. LEONARDS L.C. at pp. 732, 733); *Truman* v. *Attenborough, supra*, where, however, the estoppel was not made out.

CHAPTER XIV

Rescission and Consequential or Analogous Relief—II: Affirmative Defences

Introductory

282 Apart from the affirmative defences which are available in the case of actions in general for the rescission of contracts, whether on statutory[1] or non-statutory[2] grounds, there are certain affirmative pleas or answers which are special to actions or other proceedings instituted for the purpose of avoiding a contract or transaction on the ground of misrepresentation,[3] and which it is now proposed to consider separately and successively. The burden of allegation and proof, in the case of each of these, is (as the name "affirmative defence" imports) on the representor who affirms,[4] and not on the representee who denies; though that burden may be discharged, in whole or in part, by the representee's admissions at or before the trial or hearing, whether express or implied, or may, in the course of the proceedings, be shifted from the shoulders of the representor on to those of the representee.

Affirmative defences—I: Representee's knowledge of the truth

283 If, when the representation was made, the representee knew the whole truth as to all the material facts, he was never deceived or misled, and he is, therefore, debarred from all relief by way of rescission, as much as he is from all relief by way of compensation or damages.[5]

---

[1] Such as, e.g. limitation.

[2] Such as, release, estoppel, and the like.

[3] These are the subject of Article 42 of the Code. See p. 24, *ante*.

[4] See the observations of the Privy Council at p. 241 of *Lindsay Petroleum Co.* v. *Hurd* (1874), L.R. 5 P.C. 221, and those of Lord DAVEY at p. 295 of *Aaron's Reefs, Ltd.* v. *Twiss*, [1896] A.C. 273.

[5] See Chapter XI, *ante*, which deals with this plea as one which is common to both of the two remedies for misrepresentation—damages and rescission.

Affirmative defences—II: Agreement by the representee to waive inquiry, etc.

284 Before the passing of the Misrepresentation Act 1967 it was a good defence to an action for rescission that the representee had either directly, by virtue of a term in the contract, or impliedly by acts or conduct, undertaken or agreed to dispense with information, or not to rely upon it, or to accept the property or rights purporting to be conveyed or transferred by the contract "with all faults", or with all defects of title, or "at all risks". Where this was the case, he could not, before the passing of the statute, be heard to complain of misrepresentation in any proceedings for rescission, any more than he could be heard to so complain in an action for damages.[1]

Since the passing of the Misrepresentation Act 1967 the defence is greatly diminished in importance, for by s.3 of that Act it is provided that

> "If any agreement (whether made before or after the commencement of this Act) contains a provision which would exclude or restrict—
>
> (a) any liability to which a party to a contract may be subject by reason of any misrepresentation made by him before the contract was made; or
>
> (b) any remedy available to another party to the contract by reason of such a misrepresentation;
>
> that provision shall be of no effect except to the extent (if any) that, in any proceedings arising out of the contract, the court or arbitrator may allow reliance on it as being fair and reasonable in the circumstances of the case."

Affirmative defences—III: Agreement by representee to waive rescission and accept compensation instead

285 Subject always to the answer now given by s.3 of the Misrepresentation Act 1967 (for which see para. 287, below) if the representor can show that the representee, without having made any such agreement as is the subject of the last-mentioned class of plea, has nevertheless undertaken not to insist on rescission, but to accept pecuniary compensation in lieu of it, it is obvious that he has, *prima facie* at all events, a valid defence to any proceedings founded on misrepresentation in so far as it is sought thereby to obtain an annulment of the contract, but no further or otherwise. Here, of course, in contrast with the type of defence referred to in para. 287, where the agreement may be implied from acts and conduct as well as expressed in terms, the undertaking relied upon must be found, if at all, in the contract itself; it must be "so nominated in the

---

[1] Again, see Chapter XI, which deals with this defence.

bond''; that is to say, the representor must be in a position to point to some clause or condition of the contract in which the renunciation of this particular form of relief is clearly declared. The question usually arises in contracts for the sale of land, a common condition of which is that the sale shall not be vitiated or annulled for any error or omission in the particulars of sale, but shall be the subject only of compensation, or allowance, in money.[1] Where such a condition forms part of the bargain of the parties, the representor has always been held entitled to succeed, unless the representee, on whom the burden of proof thereupon rests, can bring the case within one or other of the two recognised exceptions to the rule.[2]

286 These two exceptions are the outcome of the principles of interpretation which have been applied by the courts in relation to clauses and conditions of the character in question. It has been found necessary to put some reasonable limitation upon the generality of the expressions ''error'', ''mistake'', ''omissions'', ''misdescription'', ''misstatement'', ''defect in title'', etc. In the first place, a deliberate and fraudulent misrepresentation has been held not to come within the class of ''errors'' or ''mistakes'' or ''omissions'' intended by such a term in the contract, that class being meant to comprise only such misstatements as are innocent and accidental. Secondly, *error in substantialibus*, or a misrepresentation as to the essence, character, or substance of the subject-matter of the contract, is not deemed to be covered by any of the above expressions.[3] The rule is best stated by the Court of Common Pleas, in a case which has always been regarded as the foundation of the law on this topic, as follows:

''where the misdescription, although not proceeding from fraud, is in a

---

[1] There is considerable variety in the precise language employed in the various cases, but this is the substance common to them all. As to the form of condition providing that there shall be neither rescission nor compensation, see para. 287A, *infra*.

[2] In the following cases the plea prevailed, the representee failing to bring himself within either of the two exceptions: *Leslie* v. *Tompson* (1851), 9 Hare, 268; *Whittemore* v. *Whittemore* (1869), L.R. 8 Eq. 603, at pp. 605, 606; *Re Terry and White's Contract* (1886), 32 Ch.D. 14, C.A.; *Re Fawcett and Holmes' Contract* (1889), 42 Ch.D. 150, C.A. (where the vendor, applying under the Vendor and Purchaser Act 1874 for a declaration that he had made a good title, successfully set up the condition to defeat an objection by the purchaser to complete); *Debenham* v. *Sawbridge*, [1901] 2 Ch. 98; *Re Simpson and Thomas Moy, Ltd.'s Contract* (1909), 53 Sol. Jo. 376; *Shepherd* v. *Croft*, [1911] 1 Ch. 521. *In Re Belcham and Gawley's Contract*, [1930] 1 Ch. 56.

[3] See, for both exceptions, the judgment of the Court of C.P. at p. 376 (as to fraud), and p. 377 (as to misrepresentation of the substance), in *Flight* v. *Booth* (1834), 1 Bing. N.C. 370; also the observations of Lord ESHER M.R. at p. 22, and LINDLEY L.J. at pp. 28–30, of *Re Terry and White's Contract* (1886), 32 Ch.D. 14, C.A., and those of BYRNE J. at p. 109 of *Debenham* v. *Sawbridge*, [1901] 2 Ch. 98.

material and substantial point, so far affecting the subject-matter of the contract that it may reasonably be supposed, that, but for such misdescription, the purchaser might never have entered into the contract at all, in such case the contract is avoided altogether, and the purchaser is not bound to resort to the clause of compensation".[1]

This does not, however, mean that such conditions are necessarily taken to refer only to errors which are trifling and trivial in mere point of quantity or figures.[2] Where there is a "misdescription in a material or substantial point" *of any sort*, the plea has failed, though the difference in value may have been insignificant.[3] Conversely, where it has been a question of compensation only, the question of difference in character has been held immaterial.[4] In accordance with the above principles, the defence has always been defeated, and rescission has been granted notwithstanding the condition, whenever fraud, or a deliberate and wilful misstatement, has been established,[5] or where the thing tendered in discharge of the contract has been shown to materially differ in quality, or substance, or title, from that which it had been represented to be.[6]

---

[1] *Flight* v. *Booth*, supra, at p. 377; *In Re Belcham and Gawley's Contract*, supra.

[2] *Re Terry and White's Contract* (1886), 32 Ch.D. 14, C.A., per LINDLEY L.J. at p. 28; *Re Fawcett and Holmes' Contract* (1889), 42 Ch.D. 150, C.A., per Lord ESHER M.R. at p. 156; *Jacobs* v. *Revell*, [1900] 2 Ch. 858, per BUCKLEY J. at p. 865.

[3] See *Flight* v. *Booth* (1834), 1 Bing. N.C. 370, at pp. 378, 379; *Madeley* v. *Booth*, cited in note 6, *infra*.

[4] *White* v. *Cuddon* (1842), 8 Cl. & Fin. 766 (where it was admitted that the misdescription of the fines payable by the custom of the manor affected the whole substance of the contract sufficiently to entitle the purchaser to rescission, if that remedy had been asked for, but, since the purchaser was suing for specific performance with compensation, and insisting on his right to it, and since such compensation was incapable of estimation, the representee failed, the substantiality of the misdescription being irrelevant to *that* question: per Lord BROUGHAM L.C. at p. 786, and Lord COTTENHAM at p. 792); *Cordingley* v. *Cheeseborough* (1862), 4 De G. & J. 379; *Re Leyland and Taylor's Contract*, [1900] 2 Ch. 625, at p. 630; *Shepherd* v. *Croft*, [1911] 1 Ch. 521, at p. 529.

[5] As in *Dimmock* v. *Hallett* (1866), 2 Ch. App. 21; *Nottingham Patent Brick and Tile Co.* v. *Butler* (1886), 16 Q.B.D. 778, C.A.

[6] As in *Stanton* v. *Tattersall* (1853), 1 Sm. & G. 529, where the property was described as "No. 58, on the north side of Pall Mall, opposite to Marlborough House", with an access (described) to No. 57, whereas in fact it was not in Pall Mall at all, and had no such access, and where, therefore, STUART V.-C. refused to give effect to the plea, holding that "what is presented to the purchaser as the subject-matter of his contract is something so different from what must be understood by the description in the particulars of sale" (p. 536) that the condition became inapplicable. Similarly, in cases where the representee has claimed the return of his deposit, which have been decided on precisely the same principles as cases of rescission— see pp. 375, 376 of *Flight* v. *Booth*, supra, paras. 263 *et seq*., Chapter XIII, *ante*—the relief prayed has been granted, notwithstanding the condition, where there has been *error in substantialibus*, as was the case in *Flight* v. *Booth*, supra (where a property was described as one in which no offensive trade, nor either of two specified trades, could be carried on—leaving it to be inferred that any inoffensive trade, other than the two specified, was permissible; whereas in fact the tenant could be ejected by the superior landlord if he exercised any of a large number of such inoffensive trades: see pp. 377, 378); *Dobell* v. *Hutchinson* (1835), 3 Ad. & El. 355 (tenancy from year to year misrepresented as a 23 years' lease, and the property incorrectly stated to comprise a certain yard); *Dykes* v. *Blake* (1838), 4 Bing. N.C. 463 (total misdescrip-

287 Upon the very considerable body of settled law which has accumulated under this head must now be imposed s.3 of the Misrepresentation Act 1967, the text of which is to be found printed in para. 284 above. An agreement which provides that a representee shall be limited to a claim in damages, or compensation, and that he shall forego a right to rescission which a misrepresentation might give him, must be acknowledged to amount to a provision which "would exclude or restrict [a] remedy available" to him; and the Misrepresentation Act must therefore be taken to invest the court with a discretion as to how far the representor shall be allowed to rely upon such a provision.

There must be cases—and some of them have already been referred to in the text of this work—where the courts are likely to disallow to the representor the benefit of such a provision, on those grounds of unfairness which have so often formed the stuff of judgments on exemption clauses. But it is here suggested that the kind of clause which is now being discussed may well turn out to be such a well-recognised part of conveyancing law as to attract the sanction of the court if drafted in a usual form, and that the tests which the court may apply in deciding whether this particular kind of clause is to take effect according to its tenor (and we say here nothing of any other kind of clause) may well be found in the very same tests, mentioned in the preceding paragraph, which have hitherto served to govern the application of this kind of clause in particular circumstances.

---

tion of property by omission from the particulars of a right of way: *per cur.*, at pp. 474–476); *Madeley* v. *Booth* (1849), 2 De G. & Sm. 718, (a very strong case, in which KNIGHT-BRUCE V.-C. held that the difference between the residue of a term, as the interest was described, and an underlease for such residue, less three days, as in fact it was, notwithstanding that most people would consider the latter had positive advantages over the former, by reason of the absence of liability to the head-landlord, and notwithstanding that the difference in value had been assessed by an arbitrator at the nominal figure of 5s., was sufficiently vital to justify a disregard of the condition, and a decision that the representor, who was suing the representee for specific performance, not only failed in his suit, but was bound to return the deposit to the representee on the agreement being delivered up by him to be cancelled); *Re Beyfus and Masters' Contract* (1888), 39 Ch.D. 110, C.A., where, at p. 115, BOWEN L.J. expressed his agreement with *Madeley* v. *Booth*, *supra*., and rejected the adverse criticism of that case by JESSEL M.R. at pp. 760, 761 of *Camberwell and South London Building Society* v. *Holloway* (1879), 13 Ch.D. 754; *Re Davis and Cavey* (1888), 40 Ch.D. 601 (where there was a condition that no objection should be taken in respect of anything contained in the original lease, but, the premises being sold as leasehold *business* premises, it was held by STIRLING J.—see pp. 608, 609—that the representee could not be forced to take premises which turned out to be subject to covenants in the original lease restraining the carrying on thereat of various specified businesses, including that of the representee; that the condition had no application, and afforded no answer; and that the representee was entitled to have his deposit repaid to him, though there was no jurisdiction to order such repayment then and there, having regard to the form of proceeding which had been adopted, *viz.* a summons under the Vendor and Purchaser Act 1874; *Jacobs* v. *Revell*, [1900] 2 Ch. 858 (misstatement of area to which vendor had title).

287A A form of condition is occasionally used in which it is stipulated that any error or omission or misdescription shall neither vitiate a sale *nor be a ground for compensation*.[1] This is a much more rigorous clause than one which restricts the right to rescind only, leaving the representee still a claim for compensation.

> "It is obviously easier to arrive at the conclusion that the purchaser shall be compellable to take the land, and have money for the deficiency, than that he has to take less than he bargained for, and have no compensation".[2]

It is here submitted that the courts may be quick to recognise the greater rigour of such a provision, and that it may be disallowed much more readily than clauses of the milder type in the exercise of the discretion given by s. 3. Even before the passing of the Misrepresentation Act the courts showed some willingness to "get round" a clause of the more rigorous type above referred to,[3] and with the authority of the Misrepresentation Act behind them they may now be expected to go further.

Affirmative defences—IV: Affirmation of the contract

288 The three defences hitherto discussed are founded on proof of the representee's knowledge, belief, or intention at or before the time when the contract or transaction was entered into: the next affirmative plea to be considered is concerned with his state of mind and will, as evinced by his acts and conduct, after the contract and in relation to it.

Representee may elect to affirm or renounce

289 It has already been explained that, on discovery of the true facts, the representee has the right of choosing whether he will affirm or dis-

---

[1] There was a condition of this character in *Portman* v. *Mill* (1826), 2 Russ. 570; *Nicoll* v. *Chambers* (1852), 11 C.B. 996; *Cordingley* v. *Cheeseborough* (1862), 4 De G.F. & J. 379; *Whittemore* v. *Whittemore* (1869), L.R. 8 Eq. 603; *Re Terry and White's Contract* (1886), 32 Ch.D. 14, C.A.; *Nottingham Patent Brick and Tile Co.* v. *Butler* (1886), 16 Q.B.D. 778, C.A.; *Re Davis and Cavey* (1888), 40 Ch.D. 601; *Jacobs* v. *Revell, supra.*; *Re Simpson and Thomas Moy, Ltd.'s Contract* (1909), 53 Sol. Jo. 376; *Shepherd* v. *Croft*, [1911] 1 Ch. 521; *Lee* v. *Rayson*, [1917] 1 Ch. 613: *Re Courcier and Harrold's Contract*, [1923] 1 Ch. 565; *Curtis* v. *French*, [1929] 1 Ch. 253.

[2] *Per* BUCKLEY J. at p. 864 of *Jacobs* v. *Revell, infra.*

[3] See *Jacobs* v. *Revell*, [1900] 2 Ch. 858; *Lee* v. *Rayson*, [1917] 1 Ch. 613 (*per* EVE J. at pp. 617–619); *Re Courcier and Harrold's Contract*, [1923] 1 Ch. 565 (*per* SARGANT J. at pp. 572, 573). Or the vendor may get a return of his deposit, which assumes the right to rescission: see *Portman* v. *Mill* (1826), 2 Russ. 570 (*per* Lord ELDON L.C. at pp. 574, 575): *Nottingham Patent Brick and Tile Co.* v. *Butler* (1886), 16 Q.B.D. 778, C.A.; *Re Davis and Cavey* (1888), 40 Ch.D. 601, though the form of the proceedings in that case precluded STIRLING J. from giving effect to his opinion by any order on the summons before him.

affirm the contract or transaction induced by a misrepresentation of those facts, and that this option, when once exercised, is exhausted, and the representee can never afterwards resale from it.[1] It follows that, if it can be established that, with full and exact knowledge of all the facts which gave him a title to avoid the contract, the representee has definitely and unequivocally elected to adhere to it, the representor has a valid defence to any proceedings for relief by way of rescission, whether he has or has not any defence to an action for damages, which is a question depending upon other considerations.[2]

Knowledge necessary to election

290 Though the representor may prove conduct on the part of the representee amounting to affirmation, so as to establish a *prima facie* defence, the representee may still repel this inchoate plea by establishing —and the onus is from that point upon his shoulders—that, when apparently so affirming, he had not complete knowledge of all the material discrepancies between the representation and the real facts, though he may have had partial information as to some of them, sufficient, perhaps, to engender a suspicion as to the whole. This is only an application of the general principle of jurisprudence,—a principle by no means confined to the present, or to any particular, subject matter,—that there can be no election where there is no precise cognizance of the material facts (including the rights arising out of these facts) upon which that election is to operate, and from which it derives vitality and significance.[3]

Election must be unequivocal

291 Further, it is incumbent on the representor to prove an unequivo-

---

[1] See Chapter XIII, paras. 235 *et seq.*, *ante*. It must always be remembered that if the contract is not voidable, but void, it can no more be affirmed than it can be disaffirmed.

[2] See Chapters XI and XII, *ante*.

[3] "There cannot be election until there is a knowledge of the right to elect", said Lord BLACKBURN in *Kendall* v. *Hamilton* (1879), 4 App. Cas. 504, 542. For a discussion of the necessity for knowledge in Election, see the authors' *Law of Estoppel by Representation* (2nd edn.), Chapter XIII, paras. 307 *et seq.*, and *Kammins Ballrooms Co. Ltd.* v. *Zenith Investments*, [1970] 2 All E.R. 871, H.L., particularly *per* Lord PEARSON at p. 890. The reader is further referred to the following cases, cited in the second edition of this work: *Duke of Leeds* v. *Earl of Amherst* (*No. 1*) (1846), 2 Ph. 117, at p. 123; *Wilson* v. *Thornbury* (1875), 10 Ch. App. 239, at p. 248; *Murray* v. *Palmer* (1805), 2 Sch. & Lef. 474, at p. 485; *Ogilvie* v. *Currie* (1868), 37 L.J. Ch. 541; *Sharpley* v. *Louth and East Coast Rail. Co.* (1876), 2 Ch.D. 663, at p. 685; *Clough* v. *London and North Western Rail. Co.* (1871), L.R. 7 Exch. 26. In a recent case, *Allen* v. *Robles*, [1969] 3 All E.R. 154, C.A., FENTON ATKINSON L.J. at p. 157 specifies the point whether, on the facts in that case, the representee had sufficient knowledge to elect. In *Australia*, see *Elder's Trustee and Executor Co., Ltd.* v. *Commonwealth Homes and Investments Co., Ltd.* (1941), 65 C.L.R. 603, and *Coastal Estates Pty., Ltd.* v. *Melevende*, [1965] V.R. 433.

cal election by the representee to adhere to the contract.[1] It is not
necessary that this election should be indicated by express or direct
language: indeed, it is rarely, if ever, that the affirmation takes this form.
Acts and conduct, including written and spoken words, from which such
an inference may be fairly drawn, are sufficient,[2] and it is by this means
that the defence is in the vast majority of cases sought to be proved. But
the acts and conduct relied upon must be inconsistent with any attitude
of mind except that of affirmation,[3] or at all events more consistent
with an intention to affirm, than with an intention to repudiate, the
contract.[4] It is idle to point to indecisive or equivocal acts or language
which may evince no more than a state of doubt, suspicion, or suspended
judgment; in that case the representor proves, not an election, but an
abstention from election, which abstention not only does not support
the plea, but negatives it.[5]

292 Where, however, the acts and conduct relied upon indicate
with reasonable clearness a definite election to affirm, and there is no
allegation or proof on the other side that the representee's election was

---

[1] This rule is discussed in the chapter on Election in the authors' *Law of Estoppel by Representation* (2nd edn.), Chapter XIII, para. 305. The reader is referred to the cases there cited, and
to *Garnac Grain Co. Inc.* v. *H.M.F. Faure and Fairclough, Ltd. and Bunge Corporation*, [1967] 2 All
E.R. 353, H.L., *per* Lord PEARSON at p. 360. See, further, the instances in note 5, *infra*.

[2] Com. Dig., Election, C.1, and *Clough* v. *London and North Western Rail. Co.*, *supra.*, *per
Cur.*, at p. 34. In *Australia*, see *Coastal Estates, Ltd.* v. *Melevende* (*supra*). In *New Zealand*, for
an example of election by conduct, see *Gray* v. *Thomson*, [1922] N.Z.L.R. 465.

[3] See the cases in note 1 above; this is the rule as to contracts for the sale of goods, as
expressed in s. 35 of the Sale of Goods Act 1893.

[4] *Cf.* again, as to sale of goods, the above cited s. 35 of the Sale of Goods Act 1893.

[5] The representee is entitled to suspend his judgment, and to make no election at all—see
para. 237, Chapter XIII, *ante*. Positive and unequivocal acts must be proved: see *Clough* v.
London and North Western Rail. Co. (1871), L.R. 7 Exch. 26, Ex. Ch., *per Cur.*, at p. 34; *Morrison* v. *Universal Marine Insurance Co.* (1873), L.R. 8 Exch. 197, Ex. Ch. (*per Cur.*, at pp. 203–
207). Instances of acts held, or found, *not* to amount to such unequivocal exercise of election
are: *Wontner* v. *Shairp* (1847), 4 C.B. 404 (attending a meeting of shareholders for the mere
purpose of proposing the very thing which was the object of the suit); *Clough* v. *London and
North Western Rail. Co.*, *supra* (see pp. 33, 35); *Morrison* v. *Universal Marine Insurance Co.*, *supra;*
Re Metropolitan Coal Consumers' Association, Ex parte Edwards (1891), 64 L.T. 651 (where the
applicant attended only one meeting of shareholders, at which he stayed for a few minutes and
did not wait for the discussion, and on one occasion made an inquiry of the secretary as to the
price of the shares); *Torrance* v. *Bolton* (1872), 8 Ch. App. 118 *per* JAMES L.J. at p. 124); *Re
Metropolitan Coal Consumers' Association, Karberg's Case*, [1892] 3 Ch. 1, C.A. (where the applicant
was not proved to have done any act at all, but merely to have waited for some time till the
decision of the C.A. in the case of another shareholder in respect of the same misrepresentation,
which was held to be a reasonable course to adopt); *Abram S.S. Co.* v. *Westville Shipping Co., Ltd.*,
[1923] A.C. 773, H.L. (*per* Lord DUNEDIN at p. 779, and Lord ATKINSON at pp. 785–789).
In *Australia*, see *Brown* v. *Smitt* (1924), 34 C.L.R. 160 *per* ISAACS and RICH JJ. at pp. 167–168.
Their joint judgment was a dissenting one, but on this point the members of the High Court
of Australia agree—see p. 163 of the Report. See, further, *Haas Timber and Trading Co. Pty.,
Ltd.* v. *Wade* (1954), 94 C.L.R. 593 (H. Ct. of Aus.).

founded on inadequate knowledge of the material facts, the defence succeeds, and the action or other proceeding for rescission fails.[1]   Of the numerous decisions illustrative of the success of the defence now under discussion, by far the larger part are cases relating to contracts to take shares in companies.[2]

---

[1] See a number of cases in the next footnote. In *Australia, Bosaid v. Andry*, [1963] V.R. 465, at p. 478 (SHOLL J.). In *New Zealand, Gray v. Thomson*, [1922] N.Z.L.R. 465 (SIM A.C.J.).

[2] Mr Spencer Bower in the second edition of this work cites the following authorities: *Campbell* v. *Fleming* (1834), 1 Ad. & El. 40 (selling the shares after knowledge of the facts): *Pulsford* v. *Richards* (1853), 17 Beav. 87 (purchasing further shares after full knowledge); *Re Royal British Bank, Mixer's Case* (1859), 4 De G. & J. 575 (receipt of dividends on the shares: per Lord CAMPBELL L.C. at pp. 586, 587); *Re Hop and Malt Exchange and Warehouse Co., Ex parte Briggs'* (1866), L.R. 1 Eq. 483, at p. 487 (instructing broker to sell shares at a premium, though no actual sale took place); *Re Cachar Co., Lawrence's Case* (1867), 2 Ch. App. 412 (per Lord CAIRNS L.J. at pp. 423, 424: here the applicant paid a call without protest, and with knowledge from the memorandum and articles of association that the objects of the company were not as represented in the prospectus, and that his son was attending a committee of investigation in his interests); *Re Russian (Vysksounsky) Ironworks Co., Kincaid's Case* (1867), 2 Ch. App. 420 (per Lord CAIRNS L.J. at p. 426, and TURNER L.J. at p. 427), *Whitehouse's Case* (1867), L.R. 3 Eq. 790, *Taite's Case* (1867), L.R. 3 Eq. 795; *Scholey* v. *Central Rail. Co. of Venezuela* (1868), L.R. 9 Eq. 266, n. (where the plaintiff "paid a call without remonstrance, and received a dividend", upon which state of facts Lord CAIRNS L.J. at p. 267 n., observed: "if anything could affirm a voidable contract, it would be conduct of that kind. By receiving a dividend, he elected to continue a member of the company, and having done that he could not come next day, or next week, and file his bill, etc."); *Ogilvie* v. *Currie* (1868), 37 L.J. Ch. 541 (where the plaintiff, after months of suspicion did nothing at all, but relied on the promise of the company to appoint a new secretary and auditor, in the hope, as he admitted, that a compromise would result); *Re Bank of Hindustan, China and Japan, Campbell's and Hippisley's Cases* (1873), 9 Ch. App. 1 (where the applicants, after a compromise sanctioned by the judge, remained on the list of contributories, took part in the appointment of liquidators, and, without raising any objection, paid calls under balance orders); *Sharpley* v. *Louth and East Coast Rail. Co.* (1876), 2 Ch.D. 663, C.A. (where the plaintiff, after knowledge that the company's representation as to the capital necessary for making the line was false, insisted on the line not being abandoned, and took an active part in meetings of his fellow-townsmen for the purpose of urging on the company the continuance of the enterprise); *Cargill* v. *Bower* (1878), 10 Ch.D. 502, 508, 509 (where the plaintiff, having supported the petition for liquidation of the company, and got his costs in that character, and, having commenced an action against it and its directors for damages and rescission, dropped the claim for rescission); *Re Wheal Unity Wood Mining Co., Chynoweth's Case* (1880), 15 Ch.D. 13, C.A. (where the liquidator of the cost-book mining company had made calls upon the transferee, forfeited his shares, and sued him to judgment, which acts were held to amount to a clear affirmation of the transfer which was sought to be avoided on the ground of the transferor's misrepresentation, and, therefore, a bar to the liquidator's claim to settle such transferor's name on the list of contributories); *Reid* v. *London and Staffordshire Fire Insurance Co.* (1883), 53 L.J. Ch. 351 (where the plaintiff, after commencing his action for rescission and rectification of the register, gave notice of discontinuance, and did nothing until he heard that another shareholder had succeeded in the C.A. in a similar action); *Re Dunlop-Truffault Cycle and Tube Manufacturing Co., Ex parte Shearman* (1896), 66 L.J. Ch. 25 (where the applicant, after a clear notice of repudiation, paid allotment-moneys and instalments in respect of her shares, in the mistaken belief that such payment would strengthen her position, and KEKEWICH J. held that her conduct in so doing was in fact an affirmation, though she intended the exact contrary); *Re Metal Constituents Ltd., Lord Lurgan's Case*, [1902] 1 Ch. 707 (where BUCKLEY J. at pp. 710, 711, "reviewed the facts in detail, and found that Lord Lurgan had elected to keep the shares after he had become suspicious about the company"); *Seddon* v. *North Eastern Salt Co., Ltd.*, [1905] 1 Ch. 326 (where the plaintiff, after full knowledge, continued to carry on the business of the London Salt Co., and at a profit, and, was held by

293 It should be noted that the affirmation of a contract, based on the discovery of the falsity of one of two separate and distinct representations, though made in one and the same document, or at one and the same time, is no bar to a proceeding for rescission of the contract based on the subsequent discovery of the falsity of the other representation.[1] Nor will affirmation of a contract, and even recovery of damages, against one of two representors, even though they be partners, prevent the representee obtaining rescission against the other representor.[2] But where only one representation is complained of from first to last, though it may be false in two or more particulars, the representee who has once affirmed the contract with knowledge of one of such discrepancies only, is precluded from ever afterwards obtaining an order to set it aside on discovery of a fresh point of falsity in the same representation.[3]

Affirmative defences—V: Where rescission would be unjust to the representor or to third parties

294 Mutual restitution being a condition of rescission, unless the representee has nothing to restore,[4] it follows that the court will never set aside a contract or transaction in any case where complete *restitutio in integrum* on both sides, and *in specie*, where the property is specific, cannot be effected, for to do so would be unjust to the representor.[5] But, as has already been noticed, *restitutio in integrum* is a matter of substance,[6] and the court will not insist in every case that the representor be put back in precisely the same position, if by a monetary adjustment, not

---

JOYCE J. to have thereby affirmed his contract to purchase all the shares of such company); *Re Christineville Rubber Estates, Ltd.* (1911), 81 L.J. Ch. 63 (unexplained delay with full knowledge). In *Australia, Life Insurance Co. of Australia, Ltd.* v. *Phillips* (1925), 36 C.L.R. 60 *per* KNOX L.J. at pp. 74–75 (assured making application for loan under life assurance policy after he had become fully aware of alleged misrepresentation by company).

[1] *Re London and Provincial Electric Lighting and Power Generating Co., Ex parte Hale* (1886), 55 L.T. 670. In *Australia, Bosaid* v. *Andry*, [1963] V.R. 465, at p. 478 (SHOLL J.).

[2] *Rawlins* v. *Wickham* (1858), 3 De G. & J. 304 (*per* KNIGHT-BRUCE L.J. at p. 315, and TURNER L.J. at p. 322).

[3] *Campbell* v. *Fleming* (1834), 1 Ad. & El. 40; *Re Russian (Vysksounsky) Ironworks Co., Whitehouse's Case* (1867), L.R. 3 Eq. 790.

[4] In which case an order for rescission is generally unnecessary, and the remedy available is that described in Chapter XIII, paras. 263 *et seq.*, *ante*.

[5] "Though the defendant has been fraudulent, he must not be robbed, nor must the plaintiff be unjustly enriched, as he would be if he got back what he had parted with and kept what he had received in return"—Lord WRIGHT, in *Spence* v. *Crawford*, [1939] 3 All E.R. 271, at pp. 288–289. In *Australia, Gans* v. *Riley* (1912), 15 C.L.R. 731, at p. 734 (H. Ct. of Aus.). In the same jurisdiction, *A. H. McDonald & Co., Pty., Ltd.* v. *Wells* (1931), 45 C.L.R. 506 (H. Ct. of Aus.) furnishes an example of a case in which the parties had engaged in a series of transactions, some, but not all, of which it was possible to rescind; complete *restitutio in integrum* being impossible, the Court refused rescission.

[6] See Chapter XIII, para. 258 where this proposition is developed.

amounting to the award of damages, he can be restored to *as good* a position.[1] Nor will rescission be granted, even though such restitution is practicable as between the immediate parties, if the undoing of the contract would prejudicially affect the rights or interests which any third party has, in good faith and for value, acquired under it whilst it was still unavoided, because this would be obviously unjust to the third party, who would thus be punished for no fault of his own, and for the benefit of the person by whose conduct or inaction he was encouraged to acquire those rights and interests.[2]

Restoration of defendant's position impossible

295   First, as to the class of case where it is inequitable, as between the representor and the representee, to avoid the contract. As has already been indicated,[3] if it appears—and the onus of proof in this regard may be upon the representor[4]—that the representee received something specific under the contract, that is to say something other than money or securities or goods incapable of an individual character, and that by his act the nature, quality or substance—the species in fact—of this something has been destroyed or changed, the representor establishes a valid affirmative defence, since the representee is not able to satisfy the condition of *restitutio in integrum* upon which alone rescission will be granted.[5] Thus where the property acquired under the contract, such as a mine, a colliery, or a business, has been either worked out or exhausted, or so

---

[1] See para. 259, note 5, *ante*.

[2] The two classes of case are referred to in a passage from the judgment of the Exchequer Chamber in *Clough* v. *London and North Western Rail. Co.* (1871), L.R. 7 Exch. 26, Ex. Ch., at p. 35: "We think that, so long as he"—the representee—"makes no election, he retains the right to determine it either way, subject to this that *if, in the interval while he is deliberating, an innocent third party has acquired an interest in the property, or if, in consequence of his delay, the position even of the wrongdoer is affected*, it will preclude him from exercising his right to rescind".

[3] See paras. 258–262 in Chapter XIII, *ante*.

[4] Though the burden is sometimes said, or assumed, to be on the representee of showing that he is in a position to make specific restoration; see, for instance, *Stainbank* v. *Fernley* (1839), 9 Sim. 556, where, by his bill, the representee offered to retransfer the shares to the representor and repay the dividends he had received in respect of them. It seems, however, to be more sound to regard the restoration as a condition subsequent, as in cases of specific performance, where the decree is made subject to subsequent proof of title, but the defendant may by way of defence allege that the plaintiff not only has no title, but can never acquire one, in which case the onus is clearly on him. Similarly it is conceived that, in cases of rescission, if the representor does not aver, or, having averred, does not prove, impossibility of specific restitution, the order for rescission would go, subject to such restitution; and, if it turns out afterwards that the restitution cannot be effected, the order would become inoperative.

[5] "Where it has been wholly or substantially destroyed by the default of the party seeking rescission, there can be no rescission because there can be no restitution"—see the joint judgment of KNOX C.J., GAVAN DUFFY and STARKE JJ. in the High Court of Australia in *Brown* v. *Smitt* (1924), 34 C.L.R. 160, at p. 164.

dealt with as to result in an entire alteration of its physical or commercial character,[1] or where shares or securities so acquired have lost their original status, and have become shares or securities of a different legal quality, and with different legal incidents,[2] the plea prevails, and rescission is refused. But it is of no avail to show a mere depreciation or deterioration of the property arising in the ordinary course of events, or from natural decay or inherent defects, and in no wise imputable to the positive acts and conduct of the representee.[3] So, also, rescission is refused where the representee has transferred to a third person the whole benefit of the contract impeached: but if, at the hearing, he is in a position to prove that the transfer has been avoided, either by his own act, he having the right to do so, or by a judicial declaration, he regains his former right to relief, and the plea fails.[4] Further, even where the

---

[1] As in *Attwood* v. *Small* (1838), 6 Cl. & Fin. 232 (collieries, and iron works and mines, described by Lord COTTENHAM L.C. at p. 357 as "a property of this description, varying from day to day", and, therefore, peculiarly the subject of the rule in its most stringent application); *Vigers* v. *Pike* (1842), 8 Cl. & Fin. 562 (*per* Lord COTTENHAM L.C. at p. 651, a case where the representee company had worked out and exhausted the mines which it had acquired under the contract); *Clarke* v. *Dickson* (*No. 1*) (1858), E.B. & E. 148 (where the representee had worked the mine, and where ERLE J. at p. 153 likens the case to that of a man offering to return to the representor a lottery ticket which had turned up a blank, and CROMPTON J. at p. 155 to that of a butcher who had bought cattle from a grazier offering to return the carcase); *Sheffield Nickel and Silver Plating Co., Ltd.* v. *Unwin* (1877), 2 Q.B.D. 214, at pp. 223, 224 (where the position of both parties in relation to the patents and businesses the subject of the contract had been entirely changed); *Ladywell Mining Co.* v. *Brookes* (1887), 35 Ch.D. 400, C.A. (*per* LINDLEY L.J. at p. 414: 'rescission is not possible because the property acquired by the company does not belong to the company any longer"). *Lagunas Nitrate Co.* v. *Lagunas Syndicate*, [1899] 2 Ch. 392, C.A. (where, at p. 433, LINDLEY M.R. observes that "the real difficulty in the way of rescission lies in the impossibility of restoring the parties to their original position", and, at pp. 433, 434, enumerates the circumstances which resulted in this impossibility, *viz.* that the plaintiff company had called upon the defendent syndicate to make, and the syndicate had made, outlays upon the property; that the company had worked the property at a profit and received dividends; that the syndicate had sold shares received in part payment; that afterwards an entirely new board of directors had been formed, who even then claimed no rescission, and worked the business as before at a profit, etc.).

[2] *Clarke* v. *Dickson* (*No. 1*) (1858) E.B. & E. 148 (*per* ERLE J. at pp. 153, 154, and CROMPTON J. at p. 155, where, besides the working out of the mines, the additional fact is referred to that the representee, having been instrumental in getting the cost-book mining company converted into a joint stock company, had disabled himself from returning the shares in the same plight as that in which he had received them); *Western Bank of Scotland* v. *Addie* (1867), L.R. 1 Sc. and Div. 145 H.L. (where an incorporated company under the Banking Act, 7 Geo. 4 c. 67, had been put an end to, and was thereupon registered as an incorporated company under the Joint Stock Companies Acts 1856 and 1857, whereby, said Lord CRANWORTH at pp. 165, 166, the representee was not in a position to restore the very thing which he had acquired, and on this ground, quite apart from the bar constituted by the winding up, was precluded from obtaining rescission: *cf.* the observations of Lord CHELMSFORD L.C. at p. 160). Contrast *Oelkers* v. *Ellis*, [1914] 2 K.B. 139 (*per* HORRIDGE J. at p. 153).

[3] *Western Bank of Scotland* v. *Addie*, *supra*, *per* Lord CRANWORTH at pp. 165, 166; *Adam* v. *Newbigging* (1888), 13 App. Cas. 308, H.L., *per* Lord WATSON at p. 323, and Lord HERSCHELL, at pp. 330, 331. In *New Zealand*, *Stanley Stamp Co.* v. *Brodie* (1914), 34 N.Z.L.R. 129, C.A.

[4] *Abram S.S. Co.* v. *Westville Shipping Co.*, [1923] A.C. 773, H.L. (*per* Lord DUNEDIN at pp. 779, 780, and Lord ATKINSON at pp. 781–783).

defence is otherwise good, it is open to the representee to defeat it by proof that the representor has deliberately stood by and silently encouraged the acts of the representee which are alleged to have produced the alteration or extinction of the property, with full consciousness of his own misrepresentation, and for the sole purpose of providing himself with materials for the assertion of the plea, if and when his fraud should be discovered.[1] Further, the court will not refuse relief where, though not precise or punctilious, such a substantial restitution can be made as to render rescission "practically just".[2] Where there is a doubt whether the representee will or will not be able to make, or procure to be made, a restoration *in specie* to the representor, the judgment may be framed in the alternative, that is to say, for rescission, if the restoration is effected within a stated time, and, if not, for dismissal of the action.[3]

In *Australia*, *Alati* v. *Kruger*[4] furnishes a good example of a case in which the court, notwithstanding that in a number of small respects a literal *restitutio in integrum* was impossible, yet was able to decree rescission with monetary adjustments. The case was one of the sale of a business with the lease of the premises in which it was carried on, and the purchaser had taken an assignment of the lease, and had been in possession for some weeks. In the joint judgment of DIXON C.J., WEBB, KITTO and TAYLOR JJ. it was said[5]:

> "He had had possession of the premises, and although that might have sufficed at common law to preclude rescission: *Blackburn* v. *Smith*,[6] it could hardly do so in equity, since a money payment could compensate for any difference there might be between the rental value of the premises and the rent paid by the respondent to the landlords. The title to the term created by the lease had been vested in the respondent by assignment, but that was subject to any right which he had to disaffirm the transaction. The title would revest in equity when he elected to rescind, and he was in a position

---

[1] *Maturin* v. *Tredennick* (1864), 12 W.R. 740.

[2] *Erlanger* v. *New Sombrero Phosphate Co.* (1878), 3 App. Cas. 1218 (*per* Lord BLACKBURN at pp. 1278, 1279); *Hulton* v. *Hulton*, [1917] 1 K.B. 813, C.A. (*per* SWINFEN EADY L.J. at pp. 821, 822, BANKES L.J. at p. 823, and SCRUTTON L.J. at pp. 825, 826); *Spence* v. *Crawford*, [1939] 3 All E.R. 271, H.L. ("The plaintiff who seeks to set aside the contract will generally be reasonable in the standard of restitution which he requires. However the court can go a long way in ordering restitution if the substantial identity of the subject matter of the contract remains"—*per* Lord WRIGHT at p. 289). In *New Zealand*, *Root* v. *Badley*, [1960] N.Z.L.R. 756 at p. 763, where McGREGOR J. said "The court is in a position to do what is substantially just."

[3] See the form of the decree set out at p. 245 of *Lindsay Petroleum Co.* v. *Hurd* (1874), L.R. 5 P.C. 221, where there was a question whether the company, having been dissolved, could eventually, through other parties, procure the property to be reconveyed to the representors.

[4] (1955), 94 C.L.R. 216 (H. Ct. of Aus.).

[5] At pp. 224–225.

[6] (1848), 2 Exch. 783, 792.

to make a legal re-assignment with the landlords' consent. He had taken
over (as he said in evidence) about twenty pounds worth of stock, but while
of course he could not restore that to the appellant *in specie* he could pay or
allow for its value, and nothing more could in justice be required.   The
business itself had deteriorated but this would not matter, for, as the trial
judge has found, it was not due to any fault on the respondent's part, and
even at common law the necessity to return property in its original condition was qualified so as to allow for incidents for which the buyer was
not responsible, such as those to which the property was liable either from
its inherent nature (*cf. Newbigging* v. *Adam*[1]; *Adam* v. *Newbigging*[2]) or in the
course of the exercise by the buyer of those rights over it which the contract
gave: *Head* v. *Tattersall*.[3] No other change had occurred.   The case was
therefore typical of the class of cases in which a defrauded purchaser is
regarded by a court exercising equitable jurisdiction as entitled to rescind
the purchase and obtain a decree, on proper terms, declaring and giving
effect to the rescission as an avoidance of the transaction from the beginning.''

Where rescission would be unjust to innocent third parties

296 The second of the two classes of case above referred to, in
which rescission will be refused because of injustice which would result,
is that in which the representor, though not in a position to complain
of injustice to himself, yet is able to call the attention of the court to the
fact that innocent third parties who have for value acquired property or
rights under the contract will be prejudicially affected by an order for
rescission. Where the representor can do this, he may rely upon such
facts as a defence, not in the least because of the merits of the plea as
between the parties, but simply because no court will pronounce a judgment which, however equitable as between the immediate parties, must
necessarily have the effect of taking away or injuring the property or
rights of others. Whilst such a refusal of relief is an act of justice to the
third party, it cannot be deemed unjust to the representee who, though
he has actively done no injury to such third party, has, by inaction, made
it possible for him, and perhaps encouraged him, to enter into transactions, make payments, incur liabilities, give credit, or otherwise
alter his position, on the faith of the continuing subsistence and validity
of the contract which it is sought to annul. The representee is under no
obligation to make his election whether to affirm, or to avoid, the contract within any specified time, or at all: he may sit on the fence and
adopt a waiting policy for as long as he pleases, but he does so at his own
risk, and cannot complain if in the meantime rights have been acquired

---

[1] (1886), 34 Ch.D. 582, 588.
[2] (1888), 13 App. Cas. 308, 330.
[3] (1871), L.R. 7 Ex. 7, 12.

by others which must be respected, and which cannot be respected without depriving him of rights which he would otherwise have been entitled to enforce against the representor.[1]

297   The plea in question is most frequently raised, and established, where the contract sought to be rescinded is a contract to take shares in a company.   Apart from the class of case in which the company is in process of liquidation, which circumstance is a bar in itself, as will presently be seen,[2] and apart, therefore, from the question of the rights of creditors, it has always been held that a very slight delay on the part of the shareholder, after knowledge of the falsity of the representation, will disentitle him to avoid his contract,[3] the ground being that, from the moment when his name is entered on the register of members, which is a document accessible to the public, it is at least possible that other persons may have inspected that register and joined the company on the faith of such entry.[4]   No delay can be imputed to the shareholder until

---

[1] See paras. 308 *et seq.*, below, for the significance of delay in this respect.

[2] See paras. 298 *et seq.*, post.

[3] *Sharpley* v. *Louth and East Coast Rail. Co.* (1876), 2 Ch.D. 663, C.A.; and see the cases cited in the next note.   In *Australia*, see *Civil Service Co-operative Society of Victoria, Ltd.* v. *Blyth* (1913), 17 C.L.R. 601; *Haas Timber and Trading Co., Pty., Ltd.* v. *Wade* (1954), 94 C.L.R. 593.

[4] *Central Rail. Co. of Venezuela* v. *Kisch* (1867), L.R. 2 H.L. 99 (*per* Lord ROMILLY at p. 125: "a contract between a company and an individual differs from a contract between two individuals alone in this respect that, upon the faith of his being a member of the company, various persons are induced to deal with the company, and to become shareholders . . . The result is that it becomes necessary for him, in order to set aside a contract of this description, that he should come with the utmost diligence for that purpose, so that no person may be misled by the fact of his remaining a member of the association"); *Scholey* v. *Central Rail. Co. of Venezuela* (1868), L.R. 9 Eq. 266 n. (*per* Lord CAIRNS L.C. at p. 267 n: "the court would be most careful to see, in a company going on and trading, in which the rights of the shareholders and others varied from day to day, that a person coming to complain of misrepresentation of this kind, and coming to avoid a voidable contract, came within the shortest limit of time that was fairly possible in such a case"); *Ogilvie* v. *Currie* (1868), 37 L.J. Ch. 541 (*per* Lord CAIRNS L.C. at p. 546: "there was this company trading, every day of necessity involving an alteration in its position, and the position of his fellow-shareholders"); *Re Hull and County Bank, Burgess's Case* (1880), 15 Ch.D. 507 (*per* JESSEL M.R. at p. 512: "they"—the other shareholders—"acquired rights as innocent parties, which this applicant seeks to take away from them"); *Re Snyder Dynamite Projectile Co., Skelton's Case* (1893), 68 L.T. 210 (*per* STIRLING J.); *Aaron's Reefs, Ltd.* v. *Twiss*, [1896] A.C. 273 (*per* Lord DAVEY who, at p. 294, insists that the representee "must exercise his right of repudiation with extreme promptness after his discovery of the fraud or misrepresentation, for this reason: the putting of his name on the register may have induced other persons to give credit to the company, or to become members of the company"); *Re Metal Constituents, Ltd., Lord Lurgan's Case*, [1902] 1 Ch. 707 (*per* BUCKLEY J. at p. 710: "his [Lord L.'s] signature to the memorandum of association made him on registration a member of the company, and bound him not only in favour of the company, but *in favour of every other person who became a member of the company*," whence it followed that, if judgment were given for Lord L., the unjust result would be "that *every person who subsequently became a member* would be deprived of the benefit which he supposed he had by Lord L. being a member"); *First National Reinsurance Co., Ltd.* v. *Greenfield*, [1921] 2 K.B. 260, Div. Ct.   In *New Zealand*, the passage in the text was expressly approved by the Court of

he is apprised of the whole of the real facts, but where the discrepancy between the actual and the represented facts relates to the objects and business of the company, he is presumed to have had such knowledge immediately upon the registration of the memorandum and articles of association; whence it follows that, in such cases, the period during which he must act in order to preclude the possibility of the defence under discussion being raised against him, besides being of brief duration, commences at a specially early stage,[1] and, where the memorandum and articles are registered at the same time as, or before, the issue of the prospectus (which is frequently the case), it commences at once.

Affirmative defences—VI: The liquidation of the company in the case of a contract to take shares

298   Where the contract sought to be set aside is a contract to take shares in a company registered or formed pursuant to the statutory enactments in that behalf, and the company goes into liquidation, every person whose name is properly on the register of members at the date of the commencement of the liquidation is a contributory to the debts and liabilities of the company, to the extent (if any) to which his shares are not fully paid up, and the liquidator is not only entitled, but bound, to place his name on the list of contributories in discharge of his duty as an officer of the court. If such a person therefore is minded to proceed against the company for rescission of his contract, or for rectification of the register, or for the removal of his name from the list of contributories, on the ground of misrepresentation, the mere commencement of the

---

Appeal in *General Mortgage Corporation, Ltd. v. Gibbs,* [1932] N.Z.L.R. 584; but the court was equally divided on whether, on the facts, the plaintiffs were barred by their delay from the relief sought. In the same jurisdiction it was observed by WILLIAMS J. in *Nenthorn Consolidated Gold-Mining Co., Ltd., Clement's Case* (1890), 9 N.Z.L.R. 233 at p. 239 that promptitude in applying to the court for rectification was especially necessary in the case of a mining venture, where values are subject to sudden and great fluctuations.

1 By s. 20 of the Companies Act 1948 (which is a reproduction of corresponding sections in previous Companies Acts), every member is bound by the memorandum and articles of the company as if he had signed them. See the observations of Lord WESTBURY L.C. at p. 734 of *New Brunswick and Canada Rail. and Land Co. v. Conybeare* (1862), 9 H.L. Cas. 711: "when the respondent took these shares . . . in the eye of the law, and by force of the statute under which this company was formed, he must be considered to have impliedly executed this deed of association", and, therefore, to have had notice of everything contained therein. This being so, it was always held, and with particular insistence and emphasis by Lord CAIRNS L.J. that it is the duty, or at all events the business and the interests of the shareholder, if he is desirous of removing a possible or probable bar to all relief by way of rescission, to move with more than ordinary promptitude: see his observations at pp. 423, 424 of *Re Cachar Co., Lawrence's Case* (1867), 2 Ch. App. 412; at pp. 426, 427 of *Re Russian (Vyksounsky) Ironworks Co. Kincaid's Case* (1867), 2 Ch. App. 420; at pp. 540, 541 of *Re Madrid Bank, Wilkinson's Case* (1867), 2 Ch. App. 536; and at p. 684 of *Re Barned's Banking Co., Peel's Case* (1867), 2 Ch. App. 674.

winding up whilst his name is in fact, and properly, upon the register, is an absolute defence and bar to such proceedings. The representee may be in a position to prove the falsity of the representation, the inducement, and the materiality; he may even have repudiated the contract, so far as giving notice of such repudiation is concerned, and may have taken this step immediately upon, or within what would otherwise have been deemed a reasonable time after, discovery of the truth; but, if he has not in fact procured the actual physical removal of his name from the register, nor taken any of the steps, mentioned below,[1] which the law deems equivalent thereto, his name is none the less properly on the register at the date of the liquidation, and this fact is still an insuperable obstacle in the way of rescission.

299   The theory upon which the defence under discussion rests, and by which it is justified, is substantially the doctrine of the inviolability of the *jus tertii* in conjunction with, and in application to, the express provisions of company legislation.   The liquidation, by force of these statutory provisions, alters entirely the position and relation to one another of the various parties concerned.   There is no longer, except in name, a company at all; there are no longer shareholders in the same sense as before; for the winding-up order "makes the shareholders contributories, and contributories in a totally different way, in some respects, as regards the debts and liabilities of the concern, from what they were before".[2] If, in favour of any one of these contributories, rescission were to be granted, the burden on the other contributories, presumably as innocent as himself, would be proportionally increased; whilst the creditors would lose a proportionate part of the fund, or rather of the responsibility of the body of persons answerable for the satisfaction of their claims, to which, on the faith of the subsistence and validity of the contract, they had justifiably looked.[3] Each of these results being manifestly unjust, the court will not make an order which will produce both.

"The general principle is that no contract can be rescinded so as to affect

---

[1] See paras. 304–308, below.

[2] *Per* JESSEL M.R. at p. 511 of *Re Hull and County Bank, Burgess's Case* (1880), 15 Ch.D. 507.

[3] See the observations of Lord CRANWORTH at p. 366 of *Oakes* v. *Turquand, Peek* v. *Same* (1867), L.R. 2 H.L. 325: "this is obviously the reason why the new statute"—he is referring to s. 11 of the Act of 1862, which is now s. 113 of the Act of 1948—"opened the register to the inspection of all the world . . . The permission to all persons not shareholders to inspect the register, and so to ascertain who are shareholders, and to what extent they are liable would have been an unwarrantable exposure of the affairs of the company, were it not that all persons have an interest in knowing who are liable, and to what extent."

rights acquired *bona fide* by third parties under it.   It is true that the creditors and other shareholders have not acquired direct interests under the contract, but they have acquired an indirect interest.   The shareholders have got a co-contributory, the creditors have got another person liable to contribute to the assets of the concern, so that, although in the case of ordinary voidable contracts simple repudiation is enough, there must be, in the case of a voidable contract to take shares, repudiation and something more before the winding up commences'',[1]

and "equities which would be sufficient as between the shareholders and the company cannot be set up against the creditors and co-contributories".[2]

300   Of the two classes of persons concerned, the class of creditors is that which is the more seriously affected, and against which the release of a shareholder would operate with the more obvious injustice.   If A is in partnership with B, and C is a creditor of the firm, it would be a violation of the plainest principles of equity and honesty, that A should be allowed to retire from the firm, on the ground that he was induced to become a member by the misrepresentation of B, without remaining liable to C.   And, in the case of an ordinary partnership at common law, A does so remain liable, and therefore an order to set aside a contract between two persons to enter into such a partnership can properly be made, because no *jus tertii* is in the slightest degree disturbed thereby.[3] But the case of a company registered or framed under the Companies Act, which is a partnership or association legalised by the statutes only and subject to the conditions and restrictions imposed thereby, is very different;   the shares in such a company are transferable without the consent of the creditors whilst the company is a going concern, and during that period, therefore, the creditors have no right to complain of any shareholder throwing back his shares on the company for misrepresentation, or any other cause;   but, directly the company has become insolvent, a new state of things arises, and the creditors must be injured by the withdrawal of a contributory from the body of persons, now crystallised and no longer fluctuating, whose responsibility, to the extent of the forced contributions leviable upon them, is the only security they thenceforth can have for the satisfaction of their claims.[4]   This view

---

[1] *Per* FRY L.J. at p. 439 of *Re Scottish Petroleum Co., Wallace's Case* (1883), 23 Ch.D. 413, C.A.

[2] *Per* BAGGALLAY L.J. at p. 429 of the same case.

[3] *Tennent* v. *City of Glasgow Bank* (1879), 4 App. Cas. 615, *per* Lord CAIRNS L.C. at pp. 621, 622.

[4] *Ibid.*

has been acted on throughout the history of company legislation.[1] The principle has always been the same, *viz.* that every creditor has a right to look to the responsibility of any person who is at the material date on the register under a contract which, though it may be voidable, has not in fact been avoided. No relief by way of rescission will be granted which will prejudice this established right of the creditors, as after winding up it inevitably must.[2]

301 Though it is the creditors who in most cases are mainly, if not solely, interested in the withdrawal of any name from the list of contributories, it is clear that an order for rescission would, on precisely the same principle, work a similar injustice towards those who were the representee's fellow shareholders, and are now his co-contributories, since, by such withdrawal, the amount of the call to be made by the liquidator on them would be proportionately increased for the purpose

---

[1] For a historical sketch of company legislation relative to the topic dealt with in the text down to 1862, see *per* Lord CHELMSFORD L.C. at pp. 346–347 of *Oakes* v. *Turquand* (1867), L.R. 2 H.L. 325.

[2] *Oakes* v. *Turquand, Peek* v. *Same* (1867), L.R. 2 H.L. 325 (*per* Lord CHELMSFORD L.C. at p. 350: "it is true that there was no contract between the creditor and the shareholders . . .but he must be taken to have known what his rights were under the Act, and that he had the security of all the persons whose names were to be found upon the register, and who had agreed to become shareholders," and, at p. 353, "if this allottee could escape so could all the others, and the creditor would be left with no remedy except against the contributions . . . of those who were fraudulent", and Lord CRANWORTH at p. 367: "it [the Legislature] intended to put the persons whose names are on it [the register] in the same position towards creditors (subject of course to the statutory restrictions) as persons engaged in ordinary partnership, or persons trading formerly under the Act of 1844"); *Tennent* v. *City of Glasgow Bank* (1879), 4 App. Cas. 615. In *Victoria*, see *Whittlesea Land Co.* v. *Gutheil* (1892), 18 V.L.R. 557, 561.

In earlier editions Mr Spencer Bower added an interesting note on *Downes* v. *Ship* (1868), L.R. 3 H.L. 343 as follows: What happened in this curious, and almost comical, case was this. On Ship's application to have his name removed from the register of members and list of contributories, WOOD V.-C. (quite wrongly) made an order as prayed, notwithstanding the liquidation of the company: *Ship's Case* (1865), 13 W.R. 450. Thereupon one Downes, a promoter of the company who was responsible for the prospectus, asked for, and (very strangely) was granted by the Lords Justices, leave to intervene and appeal—(1865), 13 W.R. 531—the liquidator being apparently unwilling, or not having the funds to do so. Not till the appeal of this very unmeritorious person came on to be heard did it dawn upon the Lords Justices that they had acted without the slightest jurisdiction in giving leave to appeal to one who was not a party to the proceedings, and could by no possibility have any *locus standi*, and they expressed their repentance of this error by dismissing the appeal which they had themselves encouraged, and on grounds which showed that such encouragement never ought to have been given—(1865), 13 W.R. 599; 2 De G.J. & Sm. 544. Nothing daunted, Downes appealed to the House of Lords, and his appeal was again dismissed, and on the same ground: but the opinion was clearly expressed that, if the liquidator, who was the only person entitled to do so, had appealed from the order of WOOD V.-C., he would have succeeded (*per* Lord CRANWORTH at p. 356), and it was intimated that it might not be too late even then for him to take the necessary steps, and, indeed, he was almost invited to take them. But, so far as the reports are concerned, "the rest is silence".

of satisfying the creditors,[1] or (where there are sufficient assets to meet their claims) for the purposes of discharging the costs of the winding up, and the adjustment of the rights of the contributories *inter se*.[2]

302   It is immaterial whether the company is being wound up voluntarily or by the court, or subject to the supervision of the court.[3]   The date at which the liquidation is deemed to have commenced, for the purposes of the defence in question, is the date of the petition, not of the order, because by the statute the order when made relates back to the former date.[4] Further, it is not absolutely necessary that the liquidation should have formally commenced, in order to support the plea, if the company has actually stopped payment, and given public notice thereof, and closed its doors[5]; but it is not enough to prove the mere fact of insolvency, where no steps of any kind, formal or informal, have been taken towards the initiation of the winding-up, and in such circumstances relief may be given, at all events on proof that no creditor is likely to be prejudiced.[6]

303   It has been noticed that the plea may be defeated, notwithstanding that the representee's name was on the register of members at the commencement of the winding up, by proof of facts which the law deems equivalent to the removal of his name; that is to say, if, in the language of FRY L.J.,[7] the representee can show that he has "done something more than" merely repudiate his contract to take shares.   It is now well

---

1 See *Henderson* v. *Royal British Bank* (1857), 7 E. & B. 356 (*per* Lord CAMPBELL C.J. at p. 364); *Downes* v. *Ship*, *supra* (*per* Lord CRANWORTH at pp. 335, 356: "or even against other innocent shareholders"); *Ogilvie* v. *Currie* (1868), 37 L.J. Ch. 541 (*per* Lord CAIRNS L.C. at pp. 543–547); *Re Hull and County Bank, Burgess's Case* (1880), 15 Ch.D. 507 (*per* JESSEL M.R. at pp. 511–514); *Re Scottish Petroleum Co., Wallace's Case* (1883), 23 Ch.D. 413, C.A. (*per* FRY L.J. at p. 439).   In all these cases, the point of view of the fellow-shareholders and co-contributories is discussed, and the injustice done to them, apart from that done to the creditors, by an order for rescission in favour of one who was on the register at the date of the commencement of the liquidation, is insisted on.

2 In *Hull and County Bank, Burgess's Case, supra*, it was admitted that there was enough to pay all the creditors, and it was strongly, but vainly, urged upon the court that this fact made a difference.

3 Companies Act 1948, s. 211: *Stone* v. *City and County Bank* (1877), 3 C.P.D. 282, C.A., *per* BRAMWELL L.J. at pp. 305, 306, BRETT L.J. at pp. 310–312, and COTTON L.J. at pp. 313–315.

4 *Kent* v. *Freehold Land and Brickmaking Co.* (1868), 3 Ch. App. 493 (*per* Lord CAIRNS L.C. at p. 494).

5 *Tennent* v. *City of Glasgow Bank* (1879), 4 App. Cas. 615 (*per* Lord CAIRNS L.C. at pp. 622–623).

6 *Re London and Leeds Bank, Ex parte Carling* (1887), 56 L.J. Ch. 321 (*per* STIRLING J. at pp. 324–326, where he explains how very special, and unlikely to recur, the circumstances were in *Tennent* v. *Glasgow City Bank, supra*).

7 See para. 299, *ante*, and note 2 thereon.

settled what this "something more" comprises, and what it excludes. The representee must establish that, before the date of the commencement of the liquidation, he has commenced proceedings against the company for rescission, or asserted his claim to such relief in proceedings instituted against him by the company; or that the company has entered into a binding agreement with him to remove his name from the register, and is therefore in default in not having done so, in which case his name is off the register in contemplation of law; or that he has entered into an agreement with the company whereby he and it have both undertaken to be bound by the result of proceedings for rescission already commenced by some other shareholder in respect of the same misrepresentation as that in question, in which case he is in contemplation of law, as against the company, in precisely the same position as if he were a party to those proceedings.[1]

304   The theory upon which the commencement of proceedings by the representee before the liquidation operates as a good answer to the plea, and entitles him, if otherwise entitled, to have the contract set aside, or the register or list of contributories rectified or varied, is that, just as the winding-up order, if and when made, relates back to the filing of the petition, so the order for rescission, if and when made, relates back to the commencement of the proceedings, and, indeed, as has been seen,[2] to an even earlier date, *viz.* that of the contract itself, which is thereby declared void *ab initio*. And the representee is entitled to succeed, as against the defence in question, not only when he has himself been the *actor* in a suit or application against the company,[3] but also where, in an action for calls brought by the company, he has asserted his right to have the contract avoided in a counter-claim or affirmative defence,[4] or even

---

[1] All three modes of surmounting the *prima facie* bar are the subject of a comprehensive statement by KAY J. in *Re Lennox Publishing Co., Ex parte Storey* (1890), 62 L.T. 791.

[2] See *ante*, para. 252, Chapter XIII.

[3] As in *Reese River Silver Mining Co.* v. *Smith* (1869), L.R. 4 H.L. 64, and *Re Metropolitan Coal Consumers' Association, Karberg's Case*, [1892] 3 Ch. 1, C.A. (see the observations of LINDLEY L.J. at p. 10). It is to be observed that if a representee, having commenced proceedings before the winding up in respect of a specified misrepresentation, desires to amend his statement of claim after that date, he will not be allowed to do so, if the amendment consists in the assertion of another misrepresentation, and so in effect amounts to the bringing of a fresh action, for to this fresh action the liquidation would clearly be a bar; but if limited to the mere expression of the original claim in a better shape and with greater precision and detail, the amendment will be allowed, and, in that case, the liquidation will no more be a bar to the claim as amplified than it was to the claim as originally pleaded: see *Cocksedge* v. *Metropolitan Coal Consumers' Association, Ltd.* (1891), 65 L.T. 432, C.A.

[4] *Re Warren's Blacking Co., Pentelow's Case* (1869), 4 Ch. App. 178, and *Re General Railway Syndicate, Whiteley's Case*, [1900] 1 Ch. 365, C.A.

in an affidavit in answer to the company's application for summary judgment which states his intention of so counter-claiming, and on which he has obtained leave to defend.[1]

305 Secondly, if the parties have obviated the necessity of resorting to litigation at all by means of an agreement for good consideration binding the company to remove the representee's name from the register, such agreement having been definitely concluded before the commencement of the liquidation, this again is sufficient to render the plea ineffective, for the name is, in such case, not properly or *de jure* on the register.[2] But where the agreement to remove the name is made between several repudiating shareholders acting by an agent, and the particular representee seeking to have his contract to take shares set aside fails to prove that he has expressly or impliedly authorised such agent, he fails to prove the agreement so far as he is concerned, and, therefore, to obtain rescission.[3] And where the company's agreement is, not to remove the name from the register, but to allow the representee to transfer his shares to one of the directors, and the agreement has not been completed by registration of the transfer at the date of the liquidation, so that the name is then still on the register, the representee has not established what is required to authorise the plea, and no rescission can be ordered.[4]

306 The third class of case is that in which the representee, though he has neither sued the company for rescission, nor entered into any agreement with it that such rescission shall be voluntarily effected, has nevertheless done something which partakes of the nature both of a proceeding *in invitos* and a voluntary arrangement; that is to say where the representee has agreed with the company that both he and it shall be bound by the result of a pending action or application by another shareholder for rescission in respect of the same misrepresentation, which is regarded as tantamount in law to his having been a co-plaintiff or co-

---

[1] See the case last cited. The decisions in *Re Cleveland Iron Co.*, *Ex parte Stevenson* (1867), 16 W.R. 95, and *Re Etna Insurance Co.*, *Persse's Case* (1871), I.R. 6 Eq. 298, so far as they are in conflict with *Re General Railway Syndicate*, *Whiteley's Case*, supra, must be considered to have been overruled thereby.

[2] *Re Etna Insurance Co.*, *Ex parte Shiels* (1873), I.R. 7 Eq. 264 where the applicants had demanded, as of right, the removal of their names from the register on the ground of misrepresentation, and the directors had agreed to do so, and were in default in not having done so; *Re Scottish Petroleum Co.*, *Maclagan's Case* (1882), 51 L.J. Ch. 841, where a similar agreement was made between the applicant and one director of the company only, there being authority conferred by the articles on a single director to bind the company.

[3] *Re London and County General Agency Association*, *Hare's Case* (1869), 4 Ch. App. 503.

[4] *Re Anglo-Danubian Steam Navigation & Colliery Co.*, *Walker's Case* (1868), L.R. 6 Eq. 30.

applicant in such pending proceeding. In all such cases, therefore, the representee has always been held as much entitled to relief as if they fell within the first class.[1] But where such an agreement, binding both parties and concluded before the commencement of the winding up, is not alleged, or, having been alleged, is not fully proved, the plea succeeds and the representee fails.[2]

307   Whenever the representee is not in a position to bring the case within any of the three classes above mentioned, his claim to rescission has always been defeated,[3] unless, of course, he can show that his name has somehow or another, whether on the ground of misrepresentation,[4] or on any other ground, disappeared from the register before the winding up, or that his shares have been in fact forfeited for whatever cause, or that there never was any concluded or binding contract at all between him and the company to take the shares.[5]

Affirmative defences— VII: Delay as a defence

308   Mr Spencer Bower was of the decided opinion, with which most if not all modern authority agrees,[6] that *mere* delay by a representee, without more, was not a defence to a claim for rescission.[7]   There can

---

[1] As in *Re Estates Investment Co., Pawle's Case* (1869), 4 Ch. App. 497.

[2] *Re Estates Investment Co., Ashley's Case* (1870), L.R. 9 Eq. 263 (where a committee of repudiating allottees had agreed to be bound by the result of another shareholder's proceedings against the company, but Ashley failed to prove that he was a member of this committee, or a party to the agreement); *Re Scottish Petroleum Co., Wallace's Case* (1883), 23 Ch.D. 413, C.A. (where one Anderson, whilst the company was a going concern, had obtained an order for the rectification of the register, on the ground of the same misrepresentation as that of which Wallace was complaining—see *Anderson's Case* (1881), 17 Ch.D. 373—but there was no binding agreement that this case should govern those of the other repudiating allottees, and therefore no relief could be given: *per* BAGGALLAY L.J. at pp. 432–435, LINDLEY L.J. at pp. 435–437, and FRY L.J. at p. 439).

[3] As it was in (e.g.) *Re Lennox Publishing Co., Ex parte Storey* (1890), 62 L.T. 791, and *Re Central Klondyke Gold Mining and Trading Co., Thomson's Case* (1898), 5 Mans. 282.

[4] As in *Re Life Association of England, Ltd., Blake's Case* (1865), 34 Beav. 639 (where, the representee having threatened criminal proceedings, the company were only too pleased and anxious not only to repay his deposit, but to take his name off the register, before the commencement of the winding up, and the liquidator in vain sought to fix him as a contributory). The mere return of the deposit, without rectification of the register, is not enough to defeat the plea, and the two decisions of ROMILLY M.R. to the contrary in *Re Canadian Native Oil Co., Fox's Case* (1868), L.R. 5 Eq. 118, and *Re Western Insurance Co., Briggs' Case* (1869), 19 L.T. 758, are clearly bad: see the observations of LINDLEY L.J. at p. 437 of *Re Scottish Petroleum Co., Wallace's Case, supra.*

[5] See para. 247, Chapter XIII, *ante.*

[6] e.g. 26 Halsbury's Laws (3rd edn.) 887, para. 1648; *Anson* (22nd edn.) 225; *Cheshire & Fifoot* (7th edn.) 246. It is to be noted, however, that the Tenth Report of the Law Reform Committee (1962), over which Lord JENKINS presided, referred (para. 10) to delay *simpliciter* as a defence to an action for rescission; see note 8 to para. 313 below.

[7] 2nd edn. pp. 291 *et seq.*

be no doubt but that this proposition must still be applicable unreservedly for a claim for rescission based on fraud[1]; but as will be seen in a later paragraph,[2] the author of this edition submits that the proposition which could be laid down in Mr Spencer Bower's day as equally applicable, in all cases, to claims for rescission for innocent misrepresentation, may perhaps now be qualified in view of some of the implications of the Misrepresentation Act 1967. First, however, it is thought proper to record *verbatim* Mr Spencer Bower's views, expressed in a characteristically vehement text, in the next four paragraphs (paras. 309–312 inclusive).[3]

309 Delay, laches, and acquiescence (said Mr Spencer Bower in the second edition of this work)[4] are constantly referred to in connection with proceedings for rescission as if, of themselves, they constituted affirmative defences thereto. This is quite a mistake. And it is a still graver error to use these expressions (as the term "laches" in particular is frequently used) with an underlying suggestion that the representee owes a duty to the representor in the matter, the failure to discharge which renders him "guilty" of conduct which, of itself, raises a personal equity against him in favour of the representor. The only legal consequence of the representee's inaction is either to furnish some evidence, with other facts, in support of a plea of knowledge, or affirmation, against himself, or to give scope for the intervention of the *jus tertii*, or of the plea of inability to make specific restitution to the representor; but where the inaction, for however long a period it extends, is not sufficient to constitute such evidence, or where, notwithstanding the lapse of time, no innocent person has in fact acquired rights or interests under the contract sought to be set aside, and the property to be restored to the representor, as the condition of rescission, can be so restored in the same plight as that in which it was received, the delay, laches, or so-called "acquiescence" go for nothing,—which is tantamount to saying that, *per se*, these matters constitute no defence.[5]

---

1 Section 2 of the Misrepresentation Act, upon which the observations which follow in the text at para. 313 are based, has no application to fraudulent misrepresentation.

2 Para. 313, below.

3 Paras. 321–324 of 2nd edn.

4 2nd edn., para. 321.

5 See, for instance, *Allen* v. *Robles*, [1969] 3 All E.R. 154, C.A. where FENTON ATKINSON L.J. said at p. 157: "The lapse of time would only operate against them if thereby there was prejudice to the defendant or if in some way rights of third parties intervened or if their delay was so long that the Court felt able to say that the delay in itself was of such a length as to be evidence that they had in truth decided to accept liability". In *Australia, cf.* the (dissenting)

310   To take the first two of these expressions (Mr Spencer Bower continued)[1]—which in reality mean the same thing as applied to cases of rescission—"delay" indicates either the mere lapse of time (like the French *delai*),—in which sense if is obviously ridiculous to attribute it to any one as a default,—or an omission or neglect on the representee's part to avoid the contract or transaction within a reasonable time (this being also the connotation of "laches"), which again cannot be described as a default on his part unless it can be shown (which it cannot) that he owed any duty to the representor in that behalf.   A representee is neither punished for, nor prejudiced by, delay in itself; though he may be seriously prejudiced by the rights which, during his inertia and supineness, he has allowed others to acquire against him.   "I take it to be a settled doctrine of equity", said JESSEL M.R.,[2]

> "not only as regards specific performance, but also as regards rescission, that this is not an answer, unless there is such delay as constitutes a defence under the Statute of Limitations.   That, of course, is quite a different thing."

The period during which the lapse of time counts for any purpose whatever does not even begin to run until the representee's right of election accrues, that is, until he has knowledge of all the facts giving him that right[3]; and then only for the purposes mentioned.   Indeed, if he asserts his claim before knowledge of the facts, he may be deemed to have struck too soon, and in such a case "too swift arrives as tardy as too slow".[4]   It may be, however, that, after full consciousness of such rights as he ever had, he remains inactive and impassive for so long a period as to justify an inference of fact that from the first he never had any such rights as he pretends to have had, and that he never was deceived at all,[5] or that he had originally agreed to waive inquiry, or not to rely upon the

---

judgment of ISAACS and RICH JJ. (on this point the other members of the court agreed; see p. 163) at p. 167 of *Brown* v. *Smitt* (1924), 34 C.L.R. 160 (H. Ct. of Aus.); also *Haas Timber and Trading Co., Pty., Ltd.* v. *Wade* (1954), 94 C.L.R. 593.

[1] 2nd edn., para. 322.

[2] At p. 13 of *Redgrave* v. *Hurd* (1881), 20 Ch.D. 1, C.A. *Cf.* the passage from *Lindsay Petroleum Co.* v. *Hurd* (1874), L.R. 5 P.C. 221, which is transcribed in the text, *post*.

[3] *Rawlins* v. *Wickham* (1858), 3 De G. & J. 304 (*per* KNIGHT-BRUCE L.J. at p. 314, and TURNER L.J. at pp. 318–321); *Lindsay Petroleum Co.* v. *Hurd*, *supra.*, at p. 241 ("in order that the remedy should be lost by laches or decay, . . . it is necessary that there should be sufficient knowledge of the facts constituting the title to relief").

[4] This was suggested, but not established, in *Edwards* v. *M'Leay* (1815), G. Coop. 308 (*per* GRANT M.R. at p. 318), and in *Gibson* v. *D'Este* (1843), 2 Y. & C. Ch. Cas. 542 (*per* KNIGHT-BRUCE V.-C. at p. 578).

[5] See Chapter XI, paras. 190 *et seq.*, *ante*.

alleged or any misrepresentation,[1] or that, without having so agreed in the first instance, he afterwards deliberately elected to affirm the contract which, if he had chosen to do so, he might have rescinded[2]; or the representee's delay, without furnishing, or contributing to, evidence of anything, may give "room and verge" for the intervention of the *jus tertii*, or for an alteration in the character of the subject-matter of the contract, or, in company cases, the winding up of the company; and, whether in any particular case any of these events supervenes or not, it is clear that the longer the delay, the greater the peril and possibility of their so doing must be. "We think", said the Exchequer Chamber, "that, so long as he [the representee] makes no election, he retains the right to determine it either way, subject to this that, if in the interval while he is still deliberating, an innocent third party has acquired an interest in the property, or if, in consequence of his delay, the position even of the wrongdoer is affected"—that is, where the representee has incapacitated himself from restoring to the representor *in specie* that which he originally received from him *in specie*—"it will preclude him from exercising his right to rescind".[3] To the same effect it has been laid down by the Privy Council that

> "the doctrine of laches in courts of equity is not an arbitrary or technical doctrine. Where it would be *practically unjust* to give a remedy, either because the party has, by his conduct, done that which might fairly be regarded as equivalent to a waiver of it, or where, by his conduct and neglect, he has, though perhaps not waiving that remedy, yet put the other party in a situation in which it would not be reasonable to place him, if the remedy was afterwards to be asserted, in either of these cases lapse of time and delay are most material. But in every case, if an argument against relief, which would otherwise be just, is founded upon mere delay, that delay,

---

[1] See Chapter XI, paras. 194 *et seq.*, *ante*. The effectiveness of this defence has now been substantially destroyed by the provisions of s. 3 of the Misrepresentation Act 1967.

[2] *Clough* v. *London and North Western Rail. Co.* (1871), L.R. 7 Exch. 26, Ex. Ch. (at p. 34: "we think the party defrauded may keep the question open so long as he does nothing to affirm the contract"; and at p. 35: "lapse of time without rescinding will furnish evidence that he has determined to affirm the contract, and when the lapse of time is great, it probably would in practice be treated as conclusive evidence that he has so determined"); *Torrance* v. *Bolton* (1872), 8 Ch. App. 118 (*per* JAMES L.J. at p. 124); *Aaron's Reefs, Ltd.* v. *Twiss*, [1896] A.C. 273, H.L. (*per* Lord DAVEY at p. 294: "lapse of time without rescinding may furnish evidence of an intention to affirm the contract. But the cogency of this evidence depends upon the particular circumstances of the case, and the nature of the contract in question"). For cases of delay not amounting to affirmation or election, see *Mutual Reserve Life Insurance Co.* v. *Foster* (1904), 20 T.L.R. 715, H.L.; *Cross* v. *Mutual Reserve Life Insurance Co.* (1904), 21 T.L.R. 15; *Merino* v. *the Same* (1904), 21 T.L.R. 167; *Molloy* v. *the Same* (1905), 22 T.L.R. 59; *Taylor* v. *Oil & Ozokerite Co.* (1913), 29 T.L.R. 515. On the other hand, in the case of *Re Christineville Rubber Estates, Ltd.* (1911), 81 L.J. Ch. 63, unexplained delay was held fatal.

[3] *Clough* v. *London and North Western Rail. Co.* (1871), L.R. 7 Exch. 26, Ex. Ch., at p. 35.

of course, not amounting to a bar by any statute of limitations, the validity of that defence must be tried upon principles substantially equitable".[1]

311 It would appear, therefore (Mr Spencer Bower went on),[2] that where a representee is said to have been "guilty" of delay and laches, what is meant is that his delay and laches amount to waiver, or to affirmation, or that it has given rise to one of the older affirmative pleas above mentioned (in which case it is unnecessary and misleading to make use of the phrases in question at all, or any phrases other than those appropriate to characterise such pleas).   Unless this is meant, the expressions, since they point to nothing which is a defence at all, have no meaning whatsoever, except in the highly metaphorical sense in which a man may be said to have been guilty of a breach of duty to himself, or of a neglect of that regard for his own interests which is dictated by counsels of worldly wisdom and ordinary business sagacity, embodied in such proverbial philosophy as "strike while the iron is hot", or *dimidium facti qui coepit habet*, or Iago's "dull not device by coldness and delay".[3] Very frequently, indeed, as will be noticed on reference to the language used *arguendo* in the authorities, "laches" and "delay"—like many other terms of equally convenient ambiguity in meaning and laxity in use, such as the expression "arrangement", when something has to be dressed up in the guise of a contract which is not so in law—serve to indicate a consciousness on the part of the advocate that he cannot support a case of affirmation or waiver, or whatever the appropriate defence may be, but must escape from rescission, if at all, like Venus in a mist, under cover of some such large and generous terminology, for the application of which to the case in question he may find specious warrant in not a few incautious deliverances of equity judges.   Nor will he be without assistance from that unfailing resource of unsound reasoning, the "maxims of the law", of which an anthology might easily be extracted, and set out in parallel columns, capable of supporting both sides of any question. *Vigilantibus, non dormientibus, jus subvenit* is extensively relied upon in this connection by those who fail to see that this, like other maxims, is only true with the proper qualifications, and, when extended beyond these

---

[1] *Lindsay Petroleum Co.* v. *Hurd* (1874), L.R. 5 P.C. 221, *per Cur.*, at pp. 239, 240; *Erlanger* v. *New Sombrero Phosphate Co.* (1878), 3 App. Cas. 1218, H.L. (*per* Lord PENZANCE, at p. 1231). *Cf.* as to the intervention of the *jus tertii*, the judgment of CHITTY J. in *Re Murray, Dickson* v. *Murray* (1887), 57 L.T. 223.   See, further, the cases cited in note 5 on p. 322.

[2] 2nd edn., para. 323.

[3] "Generally", says Bacon, in his essay "Of Delays" (XXI), "it is good to commit the beginnings of all great actions to Argus with his hundred eyes; and the ends to Briareus with his hundred hands: first to watch, and then to speed."

limits, is demonstrably false. It is true when limited to acquiescence in the proper sense of the word, which doctrine, as has been said by a very profound jurist,[1] "applies in all cases where rights, once valid, are lost by delay, and the implied acquiescence from such delay", that is to say, in all cases where inaction and standing by amounts either to a representation which induces another to alter his position to his prejudice, or to a licence or encouragement to another to adopt or continue in a certain course of conduct, such inducement, licence, or encouragement being implied from the party's abstention from exercising the right which he knows is his, and knows is being violated by a person who is expending money in the honest belief either that there is no such right, or that it is being waived. The maxim, however, has no application to cases of misrepresentation, and, if applied literally to such cases, is totally false. The law does not, and cannot, refuse its aid and countenance to the _dormiens_, if he wakes up and demands it before the other party, or any third person, has the right to insist that it shall be refused. He may have slept as long as Rip Van Winkle, but if nothing has happened affecting his title to relief during his slumber, that relief is not to be granted or withheld accordingly as he has slept for a short or a long time. On the other hand, if something has happened affecting his title, it does not signify how brief his nap may have been. If Achilles wakes up in time to beat the tortoise at the winning-post, the law has no business to inquire how long it was before he woke up. No doubt, lapse of time, without any attempt on the part of the representee to assert his rights, besides being a peril to him in the manner and to the extent already indicated, is also calculated to excite, even _in gremio judicis_, a certain human sympathy with the misrepresentor, at all events where his misrepresentation was innocent, and a correspondingly critical attitude towards the slackness and laxity (which is all that the term "laches" means in point of etymology) exhibited by the representee in nursing a stale claim. "It has beautifully been remarked", said Lord CAMPBELL L.C.,[2]

> "with respect to the emblem of Time, who is depicted as carrying a scythe and an hour-glass, that while with the one hand he cuts down the evidence which protects innocence, with the other he metes out the period when innocence can no longer be assailed".

There is a not unnatural tendency to support, if possible, the defence of one who, after many years, is charged with misrepresentation on _prima_

---

[1] Story's _Equity Jurisprudence_, vol. ii, para. 1534.
[2] At p. 617 of _Bright_ v. _Legerton_ (1860), 2 De G.F. & J. 606. _Cf. Lawrance_ v. _Lord Norreys_ (1890), 15 App. Cas. 210, at pp. 213, 219, 221, H.L.

facie plausible grounds, where, in the course of that period, the persons and documents by which, if the accusation had been made *dum fervebat opus*, he could have established the truth of his representation, may have perished or been lost or mislaid or destroyed, and in such cases the idea of an ethical period of limitation presents some attraction to the sternest and most unbending judicial mind.[1]   But the effect of delay not amounting to, or affording evidence of, or scope for, any of the defences referred to, cannot be put higher than this, even in the case of innocent misrepresentations; whilst, in any case where the misrepresentation was fraudulent, and where the representor, so far from being an object of commiseration, has enjoyed for the period of delay an entirely unmerited good fortune, this sympathetic attitude is absolutely out of place. "No time", said Lord LYNDHURST L.C. in another case, "will assure [such persons] in the enjoyment of their plunder, but their children's children will be compelled in this court to restore it".[2]

312   Mr Spencer Bower concludes his excursus on this topic[3]: "Acquiescence", when used, as it frequently but most improperly is, as a mere synonym for "laches" or "delay", equally constitutes, of itself, no bar to relief.   The true meaning of this term has been well stated by Lord COTTENHAM L.C.:

> "if a party having a right, stands by and sees another dealing with the property in a manner inconsistent with that right, and makes no objection while the act is in progress, he cannot afterwards complain.   This is the proper sense of the word acquiescence".[4]

Acquiescence, in fact, is more than quiescence, which is all that is connoted by "delay" and "laches"; it is a quiescence in such circumstances as indicate an assent to, and encouragement and permission of, a course of conduct on the part of another.   Failing these circumstances, there is nothing but "mere lapse of time",—that is to say, nothing at all.[5] Manifestly, acquiescence has no possible meaning in relation to the right

---

[1] *Vatcher* v. *Paull* (1915), 84 L.J. P.C. 86 at p. 91.

[2] At p. 741 of *Charter* v. *Trevelyan* (1844), 11 Cl. & Fin. 714.

[3] 2nd edn., para. 324.

[4] *Duke of Leeds* v. *Earl of Amherst* (1846), 2 Ph. 117, at p. 123; *De Bussche* v. *Alt* (1877), 8 Ch.D. 286, C.A. (*per Cur.*, at pp. 312–314).   *Cf.* the passage from Story, cited in note 1 on p. 326, and the observations of TURNER L.J. at p. 74, and Lord CAMPBELL L.C. at p. 77, of *Life Association of Scotland* v. *Siddal* (1861), 3 De G.F. & J. 58.

[5] *Murray* v. *Palmer* (1805), 1 Sch. & Le F. 474 *per* Lord REDESDALE L.C. (Ir) at pp. 486–487.

to avoid a contract for misrepresentation, except when used in the above sense as the equivalent of "affirmation", as it sometimes is.[1]

Effect of the Misrepresentation Act on the above

313 With the views above expressed by Mr Spencer Bower in 1927 the writer of this edition finds himself in complete agreement in 1973, but for one thought. When the original text was written, the Misrepresentation Act 1967 was still 40 years in the future, and rescission for innocent misrepresentation was still severely restricted by reason of the so-called rule in *Seddon* v. *North Eastern Salt Co., Ltd.*,[2] which prevented rescission of executed contracts.[3] This rule has now been abrogated by statute,[4] and by a statute moreover which has thought fit, probably as a direct consequence of the abrogation of the rule in *Seddon* v. *North Eastern Salt Co., Ltd.*[5] to provide that the court shall have a final discretion to refuse rescission if the equities of the case require this course,[6] and may in such a case give damages in lieu.[7] Cases in which the contract has been executed, then, may in the opinion of the present author be found to constitute a class in which the court may choose to refuse rescission in its discretion, simply because of the time which has elapsed before purported rescission, *without more*.[8] It is as yet too early to do more than to predict that this is a point which is sure to be argued in the not distant future; perhaps all that will emerge will be that the courts may become a little more

---

[1] In *Sharpley* v. *Louth and East Coast Rail. Co.* (1876), 2 Ch.D. 663, C.A., MALINS V.-C., in the court below, though not the C.A., used "acquiescence" to denote conduct which was evidence of an election on the part of the representee to affirm the contract, and of nothing else. It should be noted that it is possible for *the representee* to rely upon the doctrine of acquiescence, *in its proper sense*, as a means of defeating the representor's plea that he (the representee) has by his acts and conduct altered the character of the property passing under the contract; see para. 295, and the case cited in note 1 on p. 311, *ante.*

[2] [1905] 1 Ch. 326.

[3] See Chapter XIII para. 231, *ante.*

[4] Misrepresentation Act 1967, s. 1. The Act is reprinted in full in Appendix C, *post.*

[5] See the Tenth Report of the Law Reform Committee (1962), paras. 10–12.

[6] Section 2 (2).

[7] *Ibid.*

[8] A case which foreshadowed future possibilities was *Leaf* v. *International Galleries*, [1950] 1 All E.R. 693; [1950] 2 K.B. 86. There the defence raised the rule in *Seddon* v. *N.E. Salt Co.*, [1905] 1 Ch. 326; but the members of the Court of Appeal were in a restless mood, and two of them questioned the applicability of that rule. Evershed M.R. preferred to shelter behind the existing rule; but the case may suggest to a careful reader that the other members of the court (DENNING and JENKINS L.JJ.) were willing, if the rule were to be discarded or departed from, to use delay *simpliciter* as an adequate defence to a claim for rescission of an executed contract on the ground of innocent misrepresentation. It may be remembered (see note 6 on p. 321, *ante*) that the committee over which Lord JENKINS later presided, in its celebrated Tenth Report (see Appendix C, *post*) seemed of the opinion (para. 10) that delay without more might be a defence to an action for rescission—and they had been considering the rule in *Seddon* v. *N.E. Salt Co.* in the immediately preceding paragraph.

sensitive to the proposition that the length of the delay in itself without more is sufficient evidence of election to affirm.[1]

---

[1] There is a hint of this in the judgment of FENTON ATKINSON L.J. in *Allen* v. *Robles*, [1969] 3 All E.R. 154, C.A., cited in note 5 on p. 322 above. It may be noticed that this was a case decided after the passing of the Misrepresentation Act, but the evidence did not bring the court to the point where it was necessary to consider the exercise of the discretion given by s. 2 (2).

CHAPTER XV

Misrepresentation as a Defence or Invalidating Cause

Introduction

314 Misrepresentation operates as an absolvent, as well as a dissolvent,—an invalidating cause, no less than a cause of action. Though more frequently used as a sword, it may serve as a shield. Hitherto it has been considered in the former capacity. It remains to examine it in the latter.

To what proceedings misrepresentation is a defence or answer

315 Subject to the qualifications and conditions hereafter mentioned[1] it may be stated broadly that wherever a representee is in a position to claim, or obtain, rescission of any contract or transaction on the ground of misrepresentation, he is also in a position to set up, or make good, respectively, an answer on the same ground to any proceeding instituted by the representor against him under or in respect of such contract or transaction,[2] whether the proceeding be for the direct, though not the specific, enforcement of the contract by recovery of a debt due thereunder,[3] or for the indirect enforcement of it by

---

[1] See paras. 317–322, below.

[2] This is Article 42 of the Code.

[3] The second edition of this work sets out a lengthy list of cases in which misrepresentation was successfully set up as an answer to proceedings in which it was sought directly though not specifically to enforce contracts. It will be sufficient here to note *Bannerman* v. *White* (1861), 10 C.B. N.S. 844 (claim for price of goods); *Hirschfield* v. *London Brighton and South Coast Rail. Co.* (1876), 2 Q.B.D. 1 (defence to affirmative plea of release)—see, on this point, *in New Zealand, Bailey* v. *Munro,* [1953] N.Z.L.R. 577; *Aaron's Reefs, Ltd.* v. *Twiss,* [1896] A.C. 273, H.L. (action to recover calls etc. on forfeited shares); *Gordon* v. *Street,* [1899] 2 Q.B. 641, C.A. (action on promissory note); *Re Marshall and Scottish Employers' Liability and General Insurance Co., Ltd.* (1901), 85 L.T. 757 (claim under an accident policy); *Edgar* v. *Hector,* 1912 S.C. 348 (claim for price of furniture).

recovery of damages for breach,[1] or for specific performance of its terms.[2]

316   Misrepresentation may in such cases be pleaded and set up either by a defendant representee as a defence to any action or proceeding instituted by a plaintiff representor, or by a plaintiff representee as a reply or answer to any counter-claim, or affirmative case, pleaded or set up by a defendant representor,[3] even when such counter-claim or affirmative case is itself one of misrepresentation, whereby it results that, in a sense, one misrepresentation is set off against another.[4]   It may be

---

[1] See *Wharton* v. *Lewis* (1824), 1 C. & P. 529, and *Foote* v. *Hayne* (1824), 1 C. & P. 545, two actions for damages for breach of promise of marriage, in both of which ABBOTT C.J. directed the jury that misrepresentation of the lady's circumstances and character would be a defence.   So in *Canham* v. *Barry* (1855), 15 C.B. 597, a plea of misrepresentation to an action for damages for breach of an agreement to deliver possession of leasehold premises was held good on demurrer.

[2] The following are illustrations of successful answers, on the ground of misrepresentation, to claims or counter-claims for specific performance: *Cadman* v. *Horner* (1810), 18 Ves. 10; *Knatchbull* v. *Grueber* (1817), 3 Mer. 124; *Viscount Clermont* v. *Tasburgh* (1819), 1 Jac. & W. 112; *Beaumont* v. *Dukes* (1822), Jac. 422; *Harris* v. *Kemble* (1831), 5 Bligh N.S. 730; *White* v. *Cuddon* (1842), 8 Cl. & Fin. 766; *Lord Brooke* v. *Rounthwaite* (1846), 5 Hare 298; *Shackleton* v. *Sutcliffe* (1847), 1 De G. & Sm. 609; *Reynell* v. *Sprye, Sprye* v. *Reynell* (1852), 1 De G.M. & G. 660; *Price* v. *Macaulay* (1852), 2 De G.M. & G. 339 (as to one of the two lots the subject of the contract); *Walters* v. *Morgan* (1861), 3 De G.F. & J. 718; *Cabellero* v. *Henty* (1874), 9 Ch. App. 447; *Redgrave* v. *Hurd* (1881), 20 Ch.D. 1, C.A.; *Smith* v. *Land and House Property Corporation* (1884), 28 Ch.D. 7, C.A.; *Archer* v. *Stone* (1898), 78 L.T. 34; *Jacobs* v. *Revell*, [1900] 2 Ch. 858; *Re Roberts, Roberts* v. *Roberts*, [1905] 1 Ch. 704, C.A.; *Taylor* v. *Oil and Ozokerite Co.* (1913), 20 T.L.R. 515; *Lee* v. *Rayson*, [1917] 1 Ch. 613; *Holliday* v. *Lockwood*, [1917] 2 Ch. 47.

[3] The following are instances of the misrepresentation being set up by a plaintiff as an answer to a counter-claim or counter-case set up by the defendant: *M'Carthy* v. *Decaix* (1831), 2 Russ. & M. 614; *Mallalieu* v. *Hodgson* (1851), 16 Q.B. 689; *Nelson* v. *Stocker* (1859), 4 De G. & J. 458; *Stewart* v. *Great Western Rail. Co.* (1865), 2 De G.J. & Sm. 319; *Lee* v. *Lancashire and Yorkshire Rail. Co.* (1871), 6 Ch. App. 527; *Hirschfield* v. *London, Brighton and South Coast Rail. Co.* (1876), 2 Q.B.D. 1; *Eyre* v. *Smith* (1877), 2 C.P.D. 435; *Jacobs* v. *Revell, supra*; *Taylor* v. *Oil and Ozokerite Co., supra*; *Lee* v. *Rayson, supra*; *Roberts* v. *Roberts and Temple* (1917), 33 T.L.R. 333; *Paxman* v. *Union Assurance Society, Ltd.* (1923), 39 T.L.R. 424; *Furey* v. *Eagle, Star and British Dominions Insurance Co.* (1922), W.C. & Ins. Rep. 225. In *Reynell* v. *Sprye, Sprye* v. *Reynell, supra*, the defence was successfully pleaded to Sprye's cross-bill (which would now be set up in the form of a counter-claim) for specific performance of the contract which it was the object (attained) of Reynell's original bill to rescind.

[4] This is illustrated by the curious case of *Greenfield* v. *Edwards* (1865), 11 L.T. 663.   There the plaintiff sued for an injunction to restrain the defendant from acting contrary to the terms of a mortgage deed.   The defendant set up and proved misrepresentation by the plaintiff in the recitals and frame of the deed, but it was shown that the defendant was also guilty of misrepresentation in relation to this deed: whereupon STUART V.-C. thought that, in this sense, the defendant's misrepresentation might be set off against the plaintiff's, and neutralised it, and he accordingly granted the injunctions prayed.   The doctrine, however, of *injuria excusat injuriam* seems a somewhat dangerous one.   As applied to a case of one illegal association set up to counteract another, it was emphatically dissented from by the Exchequer Chamber, at p. 77 of *Hilton* v. *Eckersley* (1856), 6 E. & B. 47, Ex. Ch., and, as applied to cross-libels, it was equally condemned by ABBOTT C.J. at p. 126, and LITTLEDALE J. at p. 134 of *May* v. *Brown* (1824), 3 B. & C. 113, and also by BLACKBURN J. at p. 698 of *Kelly* v. *Sherlock* reported in (1866), L.R. 1 Q.B. 686.

insisted on as an answer to applications as well as actions.[1]   It is immaterial whether the representee adds to his defence or answer a counter-
claim for rescission or not.[2]

Extent of applicability of the rules relating to proceedings for rescission

317   With the two exceptions mentioned below,[3] the representee
who relies upon misrepresentation as a defence or answer to proceedings
instituted, or an affirmative case set up, by the representor must allege
and prove precisely the same facts and matters as those which the representee who relies upon misrepresentation as a ground for rescission is
required to allege and prove,[4] and the evidence which is on the one hand
necessary, and on the other sufficient, for the latter purpose is necessary
and sufficient respectively for the former.[5]   Further, all such evidence
as is essential and adequate to sustain any of the recognised affirmative
pleas to proceedings for relief,[6] is equally essential and adequate to support a reply or answer to any case of misrepresentation raised by way of
defence to an action on the contract.[7]

---

[1] As, for instance, by way of answer to a claim in respect of a sale by direction of the court
in the administration of an estate; or to an application to settle the representee's name on the
list of contributories of a company; or to a summons under O.xiv (the number is the same
under the new Rules) as in *Re General Railway Syndicate, Whiteley's Case*, [1900] 1 Ch. 365, C.A.

[2] Such a counter-claim was added in *Andrew v. Aitken* (1883), 31 W.R. 425, *Redgrave v.
Hurd*, *supra*, *Smith v. Land and House Property Corporation* (1884), 28 Ch.D. 7; *Components
Tube Co. v. Naylor* (1900), 2 Ir.R. 1, *Hilo Manufacturing Co. v. Williamson* (1911), 28 T.L.R.
164, C.A., and, though unsuccessfully, in *Re Roberts, Roberts v. Roberts*, [1905] 1 Ch. 704;
Edgar v. Hector, 1912 S.C. 348, and *Shepherd v. Croft*, [1911] 1 Ch. 521.

[3] In paras. 318 and 322 respectively.

[4] As to the *alleganda et probanda* in proceedings for rescission, see Chapter XIII, *ante*.

[5] This proposition is article 46 of the Code.   The authorities are: as to the general identity
of the elements of allegation and proof in the two classes of case, *United Shoe Machinery Co. of
Canada v. Brunet*, [1909] A.C. 330, P.C. (at p. 338); as to particular elements essential in
rescission which have been deemed equally so in a defence, *Nock v. Newman* (1832), 1 L.J.
Ch. 175 (question of who is deemed the representor); *Burnes v. Pennell* (1849), 2 H.L. Cas.
497 (questions of materiality and inducement, *per* Lord CAMPBELL at pp. 522, 523, and Lord
BROUGHAM at pp. 529–533); *Lee v. Lancashire and Yorkshire Rail. Co.* (1871), 6 Ch. App. 527
(question of falsity); *Bentley & Co., Ltd. v. Black* (1893), 9 T.L.R. 580, C.A. (questions of
falsity, and whether alleged representor was so in fact).   On the other hand, the dicta in *Viscount
Clermont v. Tasburgh* (1819), 1 Jac. & W. 112; *Bannerman v. White* (1861), 10 C.B. N.S. 844;
Redgrave v. Hurd (1881), 20 Ch.D. 1, C.A. (*per* JESSEL M.R. at p. 12); *Edgar v. Hector*, 1912
S.C. 348 suggesting that this defence is unaffected by the non-existence or non-proof of fraud
must now be read subject to s. 2 (2) of the Misrepresentation Act 1967.

[6] These affirmative pleas are dealt with in Chapter XIV.

[7] As to affirmation being an answer in both types of case, see *Clough v. London and North
Western Rail. Co.* (1871), L.R. 7 Exch. 26, Ex. Ch. (where it was held that for purposes of an
answer to a defence as well as to a claim of rescission, no affirmation is established in the absence
of proof of complete and exact knowledge on the part of the representee, and where, at pp. 33,
and 35, it was also held, impliedly, that it is not for the representee to prove previous acts
in pais amounting to avoidance, but for the representor to prove previous acts amounting to
affirmation, and that mere delay, as in cases where rescission is sought, see Chapter XIV, paras.

Misrepresentation as an answer to specific performance

318 The first of the abovementioned exceptions applies to those cases only where misrepresentation is set up as an answer to a claim for specific performance. In such cases it is not always necessary to prove as much as would be required if the representee were suing for rescission.

> "The considerations which induce a court to rescind any contract, and the considerations which induce a court of equity to decline to enforce specific performance, are by no means the same".[1]

The reason for this divergence in practice will be apparent from a consideration of the essential distinction between an action for the specific performance of a contract, and an action or proceeding for its enforcement by other means, whether direct (as for the recovery of money due thereunder), or indirect (as where pecuniary damages for the breach thereof are claimed). In the latter class of proceedings, the party is entitled (if his cause of action is established) to the relief he claims *ex debito justitiae*; whence it follows that the other party can invalidate this absolute title only by strict proof of all facts required to negative the validity of the contract itself, in other words, of everything which it would be incumbent on him to establish in an action to rescind the contract; whereas, specific performance being a particular form of equitable remedy which it is within the discretion of the court to grant, or to refuse, either wholly or except upon such terms and conditions as may appear

---

308 *et seq.* is, *per se*, not necessarily of any significance in this regard); *Wakefield and Barnsley Banking Co.* v. *Normanton Local Board* (1881), 44 L.T. 697, C.A. (where the plaintiff representor failed to prove that the defendant representees had knowledge when they were supposed to have affirmed); *Redgrave* v. *Hurd* (1881), 20 Ch.D. 1 (where JESSEL M.R.'s observations, at p. 13, as to the unimportance of delay *in itself*, applied equally to the defence set up by the representee and to his counter-claim for rescission); *Gordon* v. *Street*, [1899] 2 Q.B. 641, C.A. (*per* A. L. SMITH L.J. as to delay, at pp. 650, 651); *Hemmings* v. *Sceptre Life Association*, [1905] 1 Ch. 365 (where the plaintiff representor succeeded in proving the affirmation: *per* KEKEWICH J. at pp. 369, 370); *United Shoe Machinery Co. of Canada* v. *Brunet*, [1909] A.C. 330, P.C. (the like: see p. 339). As to the representor's incapacity to make specific restitution being an answer to an affirmative case of misrepresentation, no less than to a claim for rescission on that ground, see *Harris* v. *Kemble* (1831), 5 Bligh N.S. 730 (where the representee who set up misrepresentation as a plea to an action for the specific performance of an agreement to let a theatre, was met by the allegation that he had been two years in possession of the theatre and had made alterations in it, and in its management; but, whilst recognising that this would have been an answer if it could be shown that thereby the defendant representee had rendered himself unable to restore the subject of the contract substantially as he received it, Lord LYNDHURST L.C. at p. 752, held that it was not so shown in that case); *Urquhart* v. *Macpherson* (1878), 3 App. Cas. 831, P.C. (where it was the plaintiff who set up misrepresentation as a replication to the defendant's affirmative plea of release, and was met by allegation, and in this case, proof, that he—the plaintiff—was unable to make restitution of the property *in specie*).

[1] *Re Banister, Broad* v. *Munton* (1879), 12 Ch.D. 131, C.A., *per* JESSEL M.R. at p. 142.

in the circumstances of the particular case just and convenient, less
evidence of questionable or unfair dealing may induce the court to decline
the exercise of the discretionary jurisdiction thus invoked, and to withhold from the representor a form of remedy which is, in a sense, almost
an indulgence, than will induce it to adjudge and declare, at the instance
of the representee, that the contract is wholly and for all purposes void.
Or, inverting the proposition, more evidence of good faith on the part
of the representor is required to entitle him to the special relief where
misrepresentation is suggested by the representee than where the ordinary remedies only are in question, and, if "upon the evidence, the plaintiff"—in a suit for specific performance—"has been guilty of a degree
of misrepresentation, operating to a certain, though a small, extent, that
misrepresentation disqualifies him from calling for the aid of a court of
equity . . . He must, to entitle him to relief, be liable to *no* imputation
in the transaction," and such a case is to be sharply distinguished from
"a case where the court is called upon to rescind an agreement . . .
which would admit of a different consideration".[1]

> "In all applications to the court involving the exercise of that discretion
> which the court invariably does exercise in ordering or refusing specific
> performance, it is necessary not to confound the principle or rules by which
> contracts are interpreted with the principles or rules which guide the court
> in enforcing or declining to enforce specific performance."[2]

Nor is this rule in the slightest degree unjust to the representor because
he is not being deprived of all his contractual remedies for ever, as he
would be if rescission were decreed against him, but he is still at liberty
to proceed against the representee on the contract by way of alternative
claim for damages,[3] from which claim the representee cannot escape by
proving less than what is essential to prove in proceedings for rescission,
and thus the representee, though his burden of proof may be less, obtains
a correspondingly less complete measure of relief when he has discharged
that burden.

Specific performance granted to representor, but subject to compensation

319   Moreover, it is always open to the court, in a proper case, instead of refusing to grant specific performance on any terms, to refuse it

---

[1] *Cadman* v. *Horner* (1810), 18 Ves. 10, *per* GRANT M.R. at pp. 11, 12.

[2] *Re Terry and White's Contract* (1886), 32 Ch.D. 14, C.A., *per* LINDLEY L.J. at p. 27.

[3] Which is the modern practice: in earlier times, the party was remitted to his remedy at
law.   The court has now complete jurisdiction to grant damages in lieu of, or in addition to,
specific performance: see *Fry, Specific Performance* (6th edn.), para. 1306.   For a misrepresentation case in which both specific performance, and damages, were refused, there being no proof
of damage, see *Holliday* v. *Lockwood*, [1917] 2 Ch. 47 (ASTBURY J. at pp. 56, 57).

only in the event of the representor's declining to make pecuniary compensation by abatement of price, or allowance, specified or to be assessed, or to submit to any other terms which may be deemed equitable.[1] The representor in such cases is given an option of obtaining equity on doing equity, which is the fundamental condition of all discretionary relief. It must not be supposed, however, that, in the absence of a condition to that effect, he has *an absolute right* to specific performance with an abatement or an allowance. Nor, on the other hand, can the representee, in the absence of such a condition, or where there is a condition excluding him from compensation, claim, *as of right*, that abatement shall accompany the order for specific performance, though he might resist the representor's claim to specific performance without such abatement,[2] or obtain rescission.[3] Where it appears to the court that the case is not one for a qualified refusal, or a conditional grant, of relief, specific performance is refused absolutely, or granted absolutely, as the case may be.[4]

The converse case: specific performance at suit of representee

320   *A fortiori*, where it is the representee who sues for and obtains a decree for specific performance of a contract which has been induced by misrepresentation, the representor will not be ordered to pay pecuniary compensation, or to make an allowance against the purchase price, in respect of misrepresentation, in addition to being ordered to perform his contract. For the representee has it in his power to elect to rescind; and if he does so any claim for pecuniary compensation or allowance for

---

[1] Thus specific performance was granted only on the terms of compensation, etc., in the following cases where misrepresentation was established: *Scott* v. *Hanson* (1829), 1 Russ. & M. 128 (by Lord ELDON L.C.); *King* v. *Wilson* (1843), 6 Beav. 124 (*per* Lord LANGDALE M.R. at pp. 128, 129); and *Hughes* v. *Jones* (1861), 3 De G.F. & J. 307 (*per* KNIGHT-BRUCE and TURNER L.JJ., who ordered a reference to ascertain the amount and terms of the compensation). Of course no reference is made in the text to the class of case referred to in Chapter XIV paras. 285 *et seq.*, *ante*, where compensation is a term of the contract.

[2] This was decided in *Cordingley* v. *Cheesebrough* (1862), 3 Giff. 496; *Re Terry and White's Contract* (1886), 32 Ch.D. 14, C.A. (*per* LINDLEY L.J. at pp. 30, 31, citing *Cordingley* v. *Cheesebrough* with approval).

[3] *Re Hare and O'More's Contract*, [1901] 1 Ch. 93.

[4] See *Knatchbull* v. *Grueber* (1817), 3 Mer. 124; *Beaumont* v. *Dukes* (1822), Jac. 422 (*per* PLUMER M.R. at p. 426: "it must stand or fall to the full extent; we cannot cut down the price, and say how much would have been given if this had not been done"); *White* v. *Cuddon* (1842), 8 Cl. & Fin. 766 (at pp. 786, 792–794); *Lord Brooke* v. *Rounthwaite* (1846), 5 Hare 298, *per* WIGRAM V.-C. who, at pp. 303–305, pointed out that it was impossible to estimate the compensation, there being no materials for that purpose before the court, and he accordingly was compelled to dismiss the bill, though the defendant himself was anxious to submit to a decree with compensation. Generally, on this topic, see *Fry, Specific Performance* (6th edn.), paras. 1213–1238, and *Rutherford* v. *Acton-Adams*, [1915] A.C. 866, P.C., at pp. 869, 870.

the loss brought about by the misrepresentation imposed goes with the rescission of the contract which that representation induced. If on the other hand he elects to sue for specific performance, it is submitted that he cannot be heard to say that he has suffered loss through the completion of the contract which he might have rescinded, but did not.[1]

321   It should be noted that, though (having regard to the above rules of practice) it may be justifiable and even prudent in the representee to remain on the defensive where there is a doubt whether the evidence available is sufficient for rescission, it is by no means wise to do so where there is no such doubt; for, generally speaking, a representee who comes promptly to the court to annul a contract procured by misrepresentation before the actual accrual of liability thereunder has a better equity to relief than if he waits to be sued by the representor on such accrual.[2] This observation, of course, does not apply to a case where the contract has been put an end to by the representor, and where, therefore, the representee cannot be blamed for awaiting the enemy's attack[3]; indeed, in such a case, it would seem illogical to apply for rescission of that which *ex hypothesi* does not exist.[4]

Necessity for previous repudiation by a representee

322   The second of the two exceptions referred to in para. 317 above relates to the question of the necessity of a previous repudiation, or at all events non-recognition of the contract by the representee.

---

[1] *Rutherford* v. *Acton-Adams*, [1915] A.C. 866, P.C.; *Gilchester Properties, Ltd.* v. *Gomm*, [1948] 1 All E.R. 493 (ROMER J.). In *New Zealand: Mackenzie* v. *Belcher* (1909), 28 N.Z.L.R. 7; *Rollo* v. *Leineweber* (*No. 2*) (1910), 29 N.Z.L.R. 133; *Schmidt and Bellshaw* v. *Greenwood* (1912), 32 N.Z.L.R. 241, C.A. *Powell* v. *Elliot* (1875), 10 Ch. App. 424 is sometimes cited to the opposite effect; but in *Gilchester Properties, Ltd.* v. *Gomm* (*supra*) ROMER J. records (at p. 497) that counsel had been to the trouble of perusing the original court record of that case, and had been able to report that it turned on a special point, *viz.* that the misrepresentation complained of had been incorporated in the contract as a term, and that the case was therefore one in which the plaintiff could ask for a decree of specific performance subject to an abatement of the contract price called for by defendant's performance with a deficiency of subject matter. In such a case it is well established that he can be compelled to convey what he has, and must reduce the total purchase price proportionately to the deficiency.

[2] *Fenn* v. *Craig* (1838), 3 Y. & C. Ex. 216, *per* ALDERSON B. at p. 222: "it seems to me that, if the allegations in the bill are taken to be true, the contract ought to be rescinded, and that, with reference to that relief, the plaintiffs stand in a better position now than they would have done after the death of the party had occurred".

[3] *Aaron's Reefs, Ltd.* v. *Twiss*, [1896] A.C. 273, H.L., *per* Lord MACNAGHTEN at p. 293. See also the observations of Lord WATSON, at p. 291, who seems to think that, even apart from such special circumstances, a representee who is defendant stands *in all cases* in a somewhat more favourable position, as regards the quantum of proof, than a representee who is suing for rescission. But this view, if it was intended, is clearly not in accordance with principle or authority.

[4] See para. 247, Chapter XIII, *ante*.

Where the representee is suing for rescission, there is no burden on him either of allegation or proof as regards this matter.[1] But it has been held in several cases that, where the representee is defending an action or proceeding on the contract, whatever form that action or proceeding may assume, it is incumbent on him both to allege and prove that, since discovery of the truth, he has repudiated the contract, or is now electing to repudiate it,[2] and has taken no benefit, exercised no right, made no claim, and recognised no interest or liability, under or in respect of it. A plea which contains averments to the above effect is good[3]; a plea which fails to satisfy these requirements is bad,[4] the reason being that merely to assert in a defence that the contract was induced by misrepresentation is to confess, without avoiding.[5] And when the matter is so pleaded, the onus is on the representee to prove the allegations so contained in his plea.[6]

Where defence of rescission available against assignees

323   Where the representee is sued not by the representor himself, but by some person claiming as assignee of the representor, not merely in right of the representor or his estate,[7] and the contract under which he

---

[1] See para. 246, Chapter XIII, *ante*.

[2] *Clough* v. *London and North Western Rail. Co.* (1871), L.R. 7 Exch. 26, Ex. Ch., *per Cur.*, at p. 36: "it seems to us clear on principle that a statement in a plea by the parrty from whom the property passed, that he claims back the property on the ground that he was induced to part with it by fraud, is as unequivocal determination of his election to avoid the transaction as could well be made . . . And no authority was cited in the argument, nor are we aware of any, for saying that this unequivocal determination of his election must be preceded by some act *in pais*". It would seem, therefore, that it is enough to add to the plea a counter-claim for rescission, and, in the case of a contract to take shares in a company, rectification of the register, or where the court has no jurisdiction to order it (e.g. a county court), to allege in a notice of special defence a right to such rectification: *First National Reinsurance Co.* v. *Greenfield*, [1921] 2 K.B. 260, Div. Ct. *Garnac Grain Co. Inc.* v. *H.M.F. Faure and Fairclough, Ltd. and Bunge Corporation*, [1967] 2 All E.R. 353, H.L., is an example of pleadings which do not sufficiently unequivocally express an election. See, too, in Australia, *Nicholas* v. *Thompson*, [1924] V.L.R. 554.

[3] As in *Bwlch-y-Plwm Lead Mining Co.* v. *Baynes* (1867), L.R. 2 Exch. 324.

[4] Mr Spencer Bower cites: *Meldon* v. *Lawless* (1870), 18 W.R. 261; *Anderson* v. *Costello* (1871), 19 W.R. 628; *Dawes* v. *Harness* (1875), L.R. 10 C.P. 166; *Mostyn* v. *West Mostyn Coal and Iron Co., Ltd.* (1876), 1 C.P.D. 145; *Aaron's Reefs, Ltd.* v. *Twiss*, [1896] A.C. 273, H.L. at pp. 277–279 *per* Lord HALSBURY L.C.

[5] See the cases in the last note.

[6] See *Dawes* v. *Harness* (1875), L.R. 10 C.P. 166 (*per* BRETT J. at p. 167, and GROVE J. at p. 168); *United Shoe Machinery Co. of Canada* v. *Brunet*, [1909] A.C. 330, P.C. (at p. 338). In *Aaron's Reefs, Ltd.* v. *Twiss*, *supra*, for the reasons above given, the onus was considered rather to be on the representor company to prove affirmation, than on the representee shareholder, whose shares had been forfeited, to prove a previous repudiation, which would have been an idle and illogical proceeding, and as "there was no evidence, or contention, that the defendant had adhered to the contract" (*per* Lord HALSBURY L.C. *ubi sup.*), his defence succeeded, and the claim failed.

[7] As, for instance, as executor or administrator, trustee in bankruptcy, or guardian *ad litem*.

is being sued would be voidable as against the representor himself because of misrepresentation, the availability of a defence based upon mis-representation will depend upon whether the property assigned is a chose in action, and if so, whether it is negotiable or not, or whether it is a chose in possession.[1]   The general principle applicable alike to all three classes of property is that the assignor transfers what he has acquired and nothing beyond; if he has a limited or defeasible interest, he can transfer only an interest subject to the same limitations, or liable to be defeated by the same events; if he has no title at all, he can confer none; *nemo dat quod non habet*.[2]   The different consequences which result from the application of this governing principle to assignments of the different kinds of property abovementioned have already been dealt with in discussing the right of the representee to recover property from one who has taken an assignment thereof from the representor under a con-tract voidable as against the representor.[3]   The rules there expounded apply *mutatis mutandis*, in most respects, to the case of a representee who is resisting the claim of such an assignee to recover the assigned property as much as to the case of a representee who seeks to recover the assigned property from the assignee.

Plaintiff the assignee of a chose in action

324   Thus, as regards choses in action,[4] the general rule is that the assignee takes subject to all equities which, until the assignment, were and, but for the assignment would continue to be, available against the assignor, and amongst such equities is the equity to avoid the contract for misrepresentation.   Consequently, where a contract has been pro-cured by this means, the representee has as good a defence against an assignee from the representor of a bare right to sue in respect thereof as he had against the representor himself,[5] which right of defence he retains

---

    1 See Article 44 of the Code.
    2 See, for a clear general statement of the principles applicable to the three classes of assign-ment respectively, *Crouch* v. *Credit Foncier of England, Ltd.* (1873), L.R. 8 Q.B. 374 (at pp. 380, 381); *Colonial Bank* v. *Cady and Williams* (1890), 15 App. Cas. 267, H.L. (*per* Lord HERSCHELL at p. 283); *London Joint Stock Bank* v. *Simmons*, [1892] A.C. 201, H.L. (*per* Lord HERSCHELL at p. 215).
    3 In paras. 275 *et seq.*, Chapter XIII *ante*.
    4 As to the meaning of *chose in action* see 4 Halsbury's Laws (3rd edn.) 477 *et seq.*
    5 See *Cory* v. *Gertcken* (1816), 2 Madd. 40 (*per* PLUMER V.-C. at p. 51); *Wakefield and Barnsley Banking Co.* v. *Normanton Local Board* (1881), 44 L.T. 697, C.A. (*per* BRAMWELL L.J. at p. 699); and 4 Halsbury's Laws (3rd edn.) 507 *et seq.*   A mere claim for damages, though liquidated, cannot be set off: *Stoddart* v. *Union Trust, Ltd.*, [1912] 1 K.B. 181, C.A.   *Cf.* para. 276 Chapter XIII, *ante*, and the cases cited in the notes thereto, where the same principle is applied to actions by the representee to rescind the contract as against such an assignee.

after the assignment unless and until he so conducts himself in relation to the assignee as to give him an independent affirmative answer to the plea.[1]

Plaintiff the holder of a negotiable instrument

325 There is, however, a well-established exception to the rule last stated in the case of negotiable instruments, whether made so or recognised as such by statute,[2] as, for instance, the Bills of Exchange Act 1882 and the Bills of Lading Act 1855,[3] or by the custom of merchants.[4] In such cases the assignee is *prima facie* free from all personal equities existing as between his assignor and the representee, and is presumed, until the contrary is shown, to have acquired, and to hold, the instrument "in due course", that is to say, for value, without notice, and in good faith; and the onus is therefore on the representee of showing, not only the misrepresentation of the assignor, but also the fact that the assignee acquired his alleged title to the instrument otherwise than in due course.[5] It is enacted, however, with reference to bills of exchange, that

> "if in an action on a bill it is admitted or proved that the acceptance, issue, or subsequent negotiation of the bill is affected with [*inter alia*] fraud [which would cover fraudulent misrepresentation], the burden of proof is shifted unless and until the holder proves that, subsequent to the alleged fraud . . . value has in good faith been given for the bill",[6]

which means that both value and good faith must be established, and that value without *bona fides* is as inefficacious to discharge the full burden imposed on the holder as *bona fides* without value.[7] The above enactment, which is expressed to relate to bills only, is applied by other sections of the statute to cheques, and, with the necessary modifications, to promissory notes,[8] also. If the instrument comes to the hands of the

---

[1] See the observations of LUSH L.J. at p. 700 of *Wakefield and Barnsley Banking Co.* v. *Normanton Local Board* (*supra*).

[2] See 4 Halsbury's Laws (3rd edn.) 513 *et seq.*

[3] 18 & 19 Vict. c. 111. See *Pease* v. *Gloahec, The Marie Joseph* (1866), L.R. 1 P.C. 219.

[4] There are two marks of an instrument recognised as negotiable by the law merchant: (1) it must pass from hand to hand by delivery, (2) with the intention and effect of conferring a right to sue thereon: see *Crouch* v. *Credit Foncier of England* (1873), L.R. 8 Q.B. 374 (*per* BLACKBURN J. delivering the judgment of the court at pp. 381, 382). As to what documents are comprised within the class of instruments negotiable by mercantile custom, see 3 Halsburys Laws (3rd edn.) 238 *et seq.*; *Earl Sheffield* v. *London Joint Stock Bank* (1888), 13 App. Cas. 333, H.L.; *London Joint Stock Bank* v. *Simmons*, [1892] A.C. 201, H.L.

[5] See, as regards bills of exchange, etc., ss. 29, 30, and 38 (2), of the Bills of Exchange Act, 1882.

[6] Section 30 (2) of the same Act.

[7] *Tatam* v. *Haslar* (1889), 23 Q.B.D. 345, Div. Ct.

[8] See ss. 73, and 89 (1), respectively, of the Act of 1882.

holder when overdue, or after dishonour, or in a form which shows ir-
regularity on its face, the above rules have no application, and the holder
is in the position of any other assignee of a chose in action.[1] Nor have they
any application to a case where the person seeking to enforce the instrument is not an assignee, but an immediate party, though, taken very
literally, the enactment might admit of such a construction.[2]

Plaintiff the assignee of a thing in possession

326 If the thing assigned is a thing in possession, physical or constructive (as, for instance, by receipt of rents and profits), whether the
transaction be a sale of land, or one of chattels, there is no rule that the
assignee takes subject to equities, to assist the representee for the purposes of a defence founded on misrepresentation, any more than there
is for the purposes of a claim so founded when the representee is actively
asserting his right to take the same property out of such assignee's
possession.[3] In the one class of case, as much as in the other, the
representee, having first established such facts as would amount to
a good defence on the ground of misrepresentation against the representor, if such representor were suing, must go on to show, if he can,
one of three things: (i) that he actually avoided the contract before the
assignment[4]; or (ii) that the assignee was a mere donee or volunteer[5];
or (iii) that the assignee acted in bad faith, or with notice of the circumstances rendering the contract voidable.[6] Proof of any one of these three
matters is sufficient, and such as to make it unnecessary to consider the
others.[7] In the first case, the assignee derives his title from that which

---

[1] *Ibid.*, ss. 29, and 36.

[2] *Talbot* v. *Von Boris*, [1911] 1 K.B. 854, C.A. (*per* VAUGHAN WILLIAMS L.J. at pp. 860, 861,
FAREWELL L.J. at pp. 865, 866, and KENNEDY L.J. at pp. 867, 868).

[3] As to which, see paras. 277–280, Chapter XIII, *ante.*

[4] In the following cases there had been no such avoidance, and the representee's defence
failed on that ground: *White* v. *Garden* (1851), 10 C.B. 919; *Pease* v. *Gloahec, The Marie
Joseph* (1866), L.R. 1 P.C. 219 (at p. 229: "so long as the bill of lading remained with the
parties who had fraudulently obtained it, the vendors who had been cheated out of the possession
might have reclaimed and recovered it. But the moment it passed into the hands of Pease & Co.,
to whom it was pledged and indorsed for valuable consideration without notice, the right of
the vendors to follow it was taken away"); and *cf.* para. 277, *ante*, and the cases there cited.

[5] *Cf.* para. 278, *ante*, and the cases cited in the notes thereto.

[6] This was established by the defendants in *Clough* v. *London and North Western Rail. Co.* (1871),
L.R. 7 Exch. 26, Ex. Ch. *Cf.* paras. 279, 280, *ante*, and the cases cited in the notes to those
paragraphs.

[7] Thus in *Clough* v. *London and North Western Rail. Co.*, *supra*, the jury expressly found that
value had been given, but also found that the assignee had given it in bad faith, whereupon the
mere giving of value went for nothing, and so also did the fact that the defendants had not avoided the contract before the assignment, or even before they were sued, on which latter circumstance the plaintiff attempted to found an argument which was effectually disposed of by the

was a nullity at the date of assignment to him; in the second, he has purchased no right to consideration, and, therefore, will suffer no *damnum* which the law can recognise, in handing over that which came to him as a mere gift or windfall; in the third he will suffer a *damnum* but no *injuria*, because he will thereby be properly punished for direct or constructive complicity in the very wrongdoing of which the representee has a right to complain.

But defendant may prove his contract with plaintiff void not voidable

327   The preceding paragraphs discuss the defences available to a representee when sued under a *voidable* contract by the representor's assignee.   But it is to be remembered that in a very limited class of cases the representee will be in a position to contend that the representation which he is setting up as a defence resulted in the contract upon which he is now being sued being not voidable, but void *ab initio*.   This class of cases is discussed in Chapter XIII, paras. 240 *et seq, ante*.   Where this is the case his defence is absolute, and he succeeds, not because of his right to avoid, or to ask the Court to treat as avoided, a contract which was once valid, but because there never was any contract in law at all which required to be avoided.

Exchequer Chamber at p. 33 ("there is a further objection to the plea as a plea at law, that the rescission came after the plaintiff had a vested cause of action against the L. & N.W. Railway Co., and that it could not operate to defeat that vested cause of action by relation", but "it is clear that as a court of equity interferes on the principle of granting relief to the defrauded party, from whom the fraudulent party against conscience seeks to obtain the fruits of his fraud, no such point could arise on a plea pleaded upon equitable grounds", as the plea before the court was, and as every plea now may be).   That burden is on the representee of proving bad faith, where it is relied upon in support of the plea, notwithstanding the somewhat ambiguous language of s. 23 of the Sale of Goods Act 1893 as well as that of establishing any of the other matters referred to in the text, when relied upon for that purpose, is now settled by the decision in *Whitehorn Brothers* v. *Davison*, [1911] 1 K.B. 463, C.A., as to which see note 1 to para. 281, *ante*, and see, generally, on the question of the burden of proof, that paragraph and the notes thereto.

CHAPTER XVI

Statutory Provisions
as to Misrepresentation

Introduction

328 Hitherto, with one notable exception, this commentary has been concerned solely with the general rules and principles governing actions proceedings and pleas based on misrepresentation, as these are laid down in the common law. That exception is furnished by the provisions of general application established by the Misrepresentation Act 1967.[1]

It now becomes necessary to consider certain other statutes in which the legislature has seen fit to declare and adopt special rules in this field of the law. Of these modifying enactments the most important is to be found in that part of the Companies Act which deals with misrepresentations contained in the prospectuses of companies. Then there are the statutory provisions as to the employment of "puffers" at sales of land or goods by auction. Some special reference must also be made to relevant provisions in the Sale of Goods Act. In conclusion a variety of other statutory provisions will be mentioned which declare, or give effect to, or extend the application of, principles of law relating to misrepresentation which had already, before their enactment, been the subject of judicial decision or recognition.

It may be useful to indicate the order in which these subjects are treated in this chapter, which is as follows:

1. Liability for misrepresentations in company prospectuses, imposed by s. 43 of the Companies Act 1948, is dealt with in paras. 329 to 348.

2. The consequences of employing a "puffer" at an auction sale of

---

[1] The Misrepresentation Act 1967, which is to be found reproduced in full in Appendix C, *post*.

land, prescribed by the Sales of Land by Auction Act 1867, are discussed in paras. 349 and 350.

3. s. 58 of the Sale of Goods Act 1893, with parallel provisions as to auctions of goods, forms the subject of para. 351.

4. Para. 352 deals with the provisions of the Auctions (Bidding Agreements) Act 1927.

5. The effect of s. 17 of the Bankruptcy Act 1914, by which a bankrupt remains liable for the payment of a debt in full, notwithstanding bankruptcy, where the debt was incurred by fraud, is discussed in para. 353. Three other sections in the same Act whereby certain releases in bankruptcy proceedings procured by fraud are invalidated are referred to in the same para.

6. In para. 354 s. 41 of the Partnership Act 1890 is discussed.

Misrepresentations in company prospectuses

329 In consequence of the decision of the House of Lords in *Derry* v. *Peek*,[1] which was considered to reveal a defective and undesirable state of the law in relation to the liability of persons issuing prospectuses of companies, and for the purpose of remedying those defects, the Directors' Liability Act 1890 (53 & 54 Vict. c. 64), was, in the year following, put upon the statute book. How far this measure succeeded or failed in attaining even the objects which its framers professed to have in view, is a question which has been made the subject of critical discussion in other places. In this chapter the law is taken as it is to be found laid down in the statute at present in force. By s. 33 of the Companies Act 1907 a slight amendment to the original s. 5 of the Act of 1890 was introduced, and the provision as amended was brought forward into the Companies Acts of 1908 and 1929. The present statutory provision[2] in the main repeats these provisions, but with some amendments of substance which will be noticed in their place.[3] In the main, however, the substance of the Act of 1948 remains much as it was enacted by the

---

[1] (1889), 14 App. Cas. 337.

[2] Companies Act 1948, s. 43. The section is set out in full in Appendix C, *post.*

[3] Some of the principal differences between the text of the Act of 1948 and that of the statutes which preceded it are: (a) the term "offered to the public" has been made the subject of statutory definition, the scope of the Act being widened accordingly; (b) it is now required that an expert whose reports are to be included in a prospectus must give his authority in writing; such experts are consequently caught by the phrase "every person who has authorised the issue of the prospectus", and may be sued directly under the section in respect of the misstatements therein purporting to be made by them, but not otherwise; (c) it is now necessary for a defendant who is sued in respect of an expert's report included in the prospectus to show not only that the report is correctly quoted, but that he himself had reasonable grounds to believe and did believe that the expert was competent to make the report, and that he had authorised its inclusion in the prospectus in writing as required by s. 40.

original provision of 1890, and consequently the cases cited in this chapter, although decided for the most part before 1948, may still be found useful authorities for the interpretation of the provision now governing the matter.

Effect of the statutory provisions summarised

330 The main object and effect of the statutory provisions when they were enacted was to vary the common law rules as to burden of proof in actions for damages for misrepresentations contained in company prospectuses. On the one hand, they relieved the representee of the onus of proving fraud in the first instance, and on the other, they allowed the representor to raise, as a special affirmative defence, which it is for him to establish, that his representation was both innocent and also based on reasonable grounds.[1]   As will be seen, the provision made this alteration in the onus of proof in favour of those members of the public who took up shares and debentures on the faith of prospectuses containing misrepresentations; but besides changing the onus of proof, the statute made certain persons liable to be sued, who might have escaped without being named in the provisions as persons to be liable in the circumstances laid down.   Section 43 (1) of the Act[2] begins by providing that

> "Subject to the provisions of this section, where a prospectus invites persons to subscribe for shares in or debentures of a company, the following persons shall be liable to pay compensation to all persons who subscribe for any shares or debentures on the faith of the prospectus for the loss or damage they may have sustained by reason of any untrue statement included therein, that is to say:
>
> (a) every person who is a director of the company at the time of the issue of the prospectus;
>
> (b) every person who has authorised himself to be named and is named in the prospectus as a director or as having agreed to become a director either immediately or after an interval of time;
>
> (c) every person being a promoter of the company; and
>
> (d) every person who has authorised the issue of the prospectus."

It is expressly provided that where under s. 40 of the Act, the consent of a person is required to the issue of a prospectus, and he has given that consent, he shall not by reason of having given it be liable under s. 43 (1) as a person who has authorised the issue of the prospectus except in respect of an untrue statement purporting to be made by him as an

---

[1] In this regard the statute did little or no more, in prospectus cases as from 1890, than has been done in our own day by the Misrepresentation Act 1967 in all misrepresentation cases. The provisions as to onus of proof, accordingly, no longer require in this edition the elaborate treatment which Mr Spencer Bower gave them at a time when they were unique.

[2] The section is reprinted in full in Appendix C, *post*.

expert.   The section then goes on to provide that no person shall be liable thereunder if he proves one of certain matters there set out in detail, the principal one being *bona fide* belief in the truth of what was represented.   Thus the statutory *privilegium* is conferred by the statute only in respect of a certain class of representation, upon a specific class of representees, and against specific classes of representors.   Special defences are made applicable to the action.   These matters will now be considered in more detail.

To what representations the enactment relates

331   The only representations to which the section applies are "statements" (which must obviously be in writing) contained in a prospectus.   It may be noticed that previous statutes[1] applied the provision to untrue statements made in a prospectus "or in any report or memorandum appearing on the face thereof or by reference incorporated therein, or issued therewith".   The words in inverted commas have been omitted from the section imposing liability in the 1948 Act; but they are to be found in s. 46 of that Act, the result being to leave the effect of the section unchanged.

The prospectus must be a document which, on behalf of the company, offers shares or debentures,[2] as the case may be, to the public for subscription, that is, with a view to allotment.[3]   The words "offer to the public" which form a part of the definition of "prospectus" are the subject of a special section in the 1948 statute,[4] which covers also the expression "invites persons".   The new section extends the provisions of s. 43 to offers or invitations to any section of the public, whether selected as members or debenture holders of the company concerned or as clients of the persons issuing the prospectus or "in any other manner".   But offers or invitations properly to be regarded in all the circumstances as not likely to result in the shares or debentures becoming available for purchase or subscription by persons other than those receiv-

---

[1] e.g. the Act of 1908.

[2] *Drincqbier* v. *Wood*, [1899] 1 Ch. 393, was an instance of a prospectus offering debentures.

[3] In *Booth* v. *New Afrikander Gold Mining Co., Ltd.*, [1903] 1 Ch. 295, C.A., the document there in question was held not to be a prospectus, because, even if an "offer to the public", it certainly was not an offer by the company whose shares were to be applied for (*per* VAUGHAN-WILLIAMS L.J. at p. 312, STIRLING L.J. at p. 314, and COZENS-HARDY L.J. at p. 316).   "For subscription or purchase" is the expression used in the definition in s. 455, but it is clear that, at least in its application to s. 43, "purchase" in the market is intended to be excluded, and that "purchase" must be taken to be a mere synonym of subscription, and "or", to be used in a conjunctive, not a disjunctive sense.

[4] Section 55 of the 1948 Act, the text of which is to be found fully set out in Appendix C, *post*.

ing the invitation are especially excepted. These provisions constitute one respect as to which the cases decided on the earlier statutory provisions have become unreliable.[1]

If, as often happens, there are several prospectuses, or several editions of a prospectus, issued either successively, first as "abridged" and then as complete,[2] or first as "advance", or "subject to revision", and then as final,[3] or simultaneously in different documents, places, or newspapers,[4] each one of these may be a prospectus, though only that one of them upon the faith of which the representee subscribed for shares or debentures is "*the* prospectus" which entitles him to relief.[5] If *that* prospectus contains no untrue statement, or was not issued by the person sought to be made liable, the representee fails, however obnoxious to the statute the other or others of them may be[6]; on the other hand, if *that* prospectus does contain any misrepresentation, it is no answer to point to another which omits it.[7]

---

[1] e.g. some of the cases cited by Mr Spencer Bower in the second edition as holding that the application of the section in this regard was (at the time when he wrote) unduly limited in this regard. Cases cited in the second edition, on this point, are *Booth* v. *New Afrikander Gold Mining Co., Ltd.*, [1903] 1 Ch. 295; *Burrows* v. *Matebele Gold Reefs and Estates Co., Ltd.*, [1901] 2 Ch. 23; *Sherwell* v. *Combined Incandescent Mantles Syndicate, Ltd.* (1907), 23 T.L.R. 482; *Sleigh* v. *Glasgow and Transvaal Options, Ltd.* 1904, 6 F. (Ct. of Sess) 420. More recently, the decision of the Lords in *Nash* v. *Lynde*, [1929] A.C. 158, H.L. may also be thought overruled in this respect by the new statutory provision.

[2] *White* v. *Haymen* (1883), Cab. & El. 101, a case under s. 38 of the Companies Act 1867 where the plaintiff complained of the omission of a material contract from an "abridged prospectus" advertised in a newspaper, and the defendant vainly urged that "constructive notice" was given to the plaintiff by the full prospectus afterwards issued, MATHEW J. holding that, the plaintiff having proved that he took his shares on the faith of the first prospectus, and had no actual notice of the later one, there was no room for the application of the doctrine in question.

[3] *Hoole* v. *Speak*, [1904] 2 Ch. 732.

[4] In *Drincqbier* v. *Wood, supra*, the plaintiff took his debentures on the faith of two documents, a prospectus and a letter, under one cover. Each of them contained untrue statements. BYRNE J. at p. 403, held that each rendered the defendants liable, one as a prospectus, within the meaning of the then more restricted definition contained in s. 3 of the Act of 1890, and the other as a "notice" within the same section. Each of them would now be deemed a prospectus within the more extended definition of that term contained in s. 285 of the Act of 1908. In *Roussell* v. *Burnham*, [1909] 1 Ch. 127, there was a prospectus issued in England, which stated the minimum subscription on which the company might proceed to allotment, as required by s. 81 (1) (d), of the Act of 1908 (the present s. 43), and another advertised in a French newspaper which did not. The plaintiff sued for relief under s. 85 in respect of the French prospectus, on the faith of which he established that he had subscribed for his shares, and PARKER J. held that he was accordingly entitled to the relief prayed.

[5] *Roussell* v. *Burnham, supra, per* PARKER J. at pp. 130–132.

[6] In *Hoole* v. *Speak*, [1904] 2 Ch. 732, the defendants were not shown to have authorised the issue of the advance prospectus, which contained the same misrepresentations as the further and final prospectus which was the subject of *Shepheard* v. *Broome*, [1904] A.C. 342, H.L. The latter *was* shown to have had the authority of the defendants for its issue. Consequently, in the first case the claim failed; in the second, it succeeded.

[7] *White* v. *Haymen* (1883), Cab. & El. 101.

By s. 45 of the Act[1] it is enacted that where a company allots or agrees to allot any shares or debentures with a view to their being offered to the public any document by which the offer for sale to the public is made shall be deemed to be a prospectus. This section, new in the 1948 Act, appears to be intended to extend liability to the case where the company instead of offering shares or debentures to the public directly, allots them instead to some person or persons by whom it is understood that they will be offered to the public by means of some document which, without the new provision, might be held not to be a prospectus.

The persons to whom the action is given

332 The next question to be considered is that of the persons affected by the enactment. To what description of representee is the statutory cause of action given, and against what classes of representors? First, as to the representee: the only person who can take advantage of the *privilegium* is one who is "invited to subscribe" for shares or debentures, in the phraseology of s. 43 (1), by a prospectus of a company, and who in fact takes shares or debentures "on the faith of the prospectus".[2] A company or corporation may be such a person.[3]

The persons liable to be sued

333 Next, as to the persons liable to be sued in the statutory proceedings. These are described in s. 43 (1) as:

(a) every person who is a director of the company at the time of the issue of the prospectus;

(b) every person who has authorised himself to be named and is named in the prospectus as a director or as having agreed to become a director either immediately or after an interval of time;

(c) every person being a promoter of the company; and

(d) every person who has authorised the issue of the prospectus.

Directors

334 The first class of persons who may be sued comprises every person who was a director of the company at the time of the issue of the

---

[1] Section 45 may be found reprinted in full in Appendix C, *post.*

[2] As to what is involved in the expression "on the faith of the prospectus", see para. 342, *post.* As to the meaning of "prospectus" in the section see the definition of "prospectus" in s. 455, and the extended definition in s. 45 referred to in para. 331, *supra.*

[3] Section 19 of the Interpretation Act 1889. The representee who sued under the Act of 1890 in *J. and P. Coats, Ltd.* v. *Crossland* (1904), 20 T.L.R. 800, was a limited company.

prospectus. This is a provision of distinct utility. It includes the not uncommon case of a prospectus issued by co-directors or co-agents or sub-agents of a director, where at common law such director might escape in the absence of proof of express authority,[1] and also the somewhat improbable case of a man who, for some reason, is not named in the prospectus as an existing or prospective director, and who therefore would not be required by s. 41 of the Act of 1948 to sign the filed prospectus (since that enactment only applies to persons so named), but who yet can be shown to have in fact occupied the position of a director at the material date.

Certain affirmative defences are available to directors sought to be made liable under the section, and these are dealt with more particularly in para. 343, below.

Persons authorising their names to appear as directors

335 The second class of persons against whom there is a *prima facie* or defeasible right to proceed under the enactment comprises those who, whether directors in fact or not at the date of the issue of the prospectus were with their authority named therein as such or as having agreed to become so either immediately or after an interval of time. It is clear that the burden is on the plaintiff of proving not only the naming, but the authority, in the first instance. It follows from what has gone before that a false statement in a prospectus that such and such a person is, or has agreed to be or become, a director, gives a cause of action at common law to any one deceived thereby into subscribing for shares against those responsible for the prospectus, but not against the persons so misdescribed; whereas, under the statute, he is in the favourable position of being able to sue thereunder both the named and the actual directors, and also the persons issuing the prospectus; and, if he should fail against the named directors, or if they should succeed in defeating his *prima facie* right by proof of the matters of statutory excuse to be mentioned presently,[2] such failure or proof would be evidence of a further statement on the part of the directors in fact, or those in fact issuing the prospectus, which would entitle him to succeed against them in respect of such misrepresentation, even if he failed to prove any other untrue statement relied upon.

Persons of the class referred to in this paragraph may avail themselves *mutatis mutandis* of the affirmative defences available to directors, referred

---

[1] See para. 150, *ante.*
[2] See paras. 343 *et seq., infra.*

to in the last preceding paragraph. These defences are dealt with in detail in paras. 343 *et seq*, below.

Promoters

336   The third class of persons against whom there is a statutory presumption of liability, in this case irrebuttable, without proof of any actual authorisation of the issue of the prospectus, comprises "every promoter of the company",[1] which is expressed to mean every promoter of the company "who was a party to the preparation of the prospectus, or of the portion thereof containing the untrue statement",[2] so that every promoter of the company, though he was neither a director in fact, nor named with authority as such in the prospectus, and though he may have taken no part in the *issue* of the prospectus, is made amenable to the statutory proceedings if, but only if, he had a hand in the *preparation* of the prospectus, or of so much of it as contained the untrue statement relied upon by the plaintiff as the ground of his complaint. The burden is on the representee of proving each of the above matters; it is not enough to show that the person sought to be brought within the class in question was a promoter, if he did not also take part in the preparation of the prospectus; nor to establish that he was the author, or part-author, of the prospectus, if he was not also *at that time* a promoter of the company. It is desirable to consider separately these two elements in the plaintiff's burden of proof.

First as to promotership. The term "promoter" finds a place in company legislation as early as 1844, when, by the statute of that year,[3] it was expressed to "apply to every person acting by whatever name in the forming and establishing of a company at any period prior to the company obtaining a certificate of registration". The term was not used in the Act of 1862, but reappeared in s. 38 of the Act of 1867. Neither in that statute, however, nor in any later one,—not even in the Act of 1908,— has the legislature attempted any definition of the term. The courts have been equally reluctant, and, with equal wisdom, to make the attempt. Though most willing to indicate in general terms the kind of ideas which the expression may include, judges have abstained from giving any exhaustive enumeration of the acts and proceedings which it excludes, knowing full well that the astute and versatile gentlemen professionally engaged in the genesis of the baser sort of enterprise will make haste to limit their action to just these excluded operations, and to keep on the

[1] Section 43 (1) of the Act of 1948.
[2] Section 43 (5), reproducing s. 3 (2) of the Act of 1890.
[3] Joint Stock Companies Act 1844.

windy side of any cast-iron connotation devised by courts or Parliament. *Quo teneam vultus mutantem Protea nodo*? The *nodus* which is to perform this feat must be as elusive, and as capable of successive transformations, as its intended prisoner. The leaden rule of the Lesbians, which bends itself to the exigencies of the moment, and can be applied to the case of the particular alleged promoter without prejudice to its future application in a different shape to totally different cases of other alleged promoters, is the only apt instrument for this kind of work. It will be found that all the judicial elucidations of promotership are conceived in language no less general, and in most cases even wider, than the term itself. Indeed, not a few of them are as obviously, and (were it not for our appreciation of the excellent object in view) as ludicrously, of the *idem per idem* description as the essays in definition which Shakespeare puts into the mouth of Bardolph,[1] and Lyly into that of Sir Tophas.[2] Thus COCKBURN C.J. characterised a promoter as

> "one who undertakes to form a company with reference to a given project and to set it going, and who takes the necessary steps to accomplish that purpose".[3]

Lord BLACKBURN considered the expression

> "a short and convenient way of designating those who set in motion the machinery by which the Act enables them to create an incorporated company".[4]

In the view of Lord BOWEN (then BOWEN J.),

> "the term 'promoter' is a term not of law, but of business, usefully summing up in a single word a number of business operations familiar to the commercial world by which a company is generally brought into existence".[5]

Lord LINDLEY (then LINDLEY J.), after observing that the word "has no very definite meaning", goes on to speak of it as involving

> "the idea of exertion for the purpose of getting up and starting a company (or what is called floating it), and also the idea of some duty towards the

---

[1] In *King Henry IV, Part II*, Act III, sc. ii: "Accommodated: that is, when a man is, as they say, accommodated; or when a man is, being, whereby he may be thought to be accommodated; which is an excellent thing."

[2] In his *Endymion*, Act I, sc. iii: "Dost thou not know what a poet is? Why, fool, a poet is much as one should say—a poet!"

[3] *Twycross* v. *Grant (No. 1)* (1877), 2 C.P.D. 469, C.A., at p. 541.

[4] At p. 1268 of *Erlanger* v. *New Sombrero Phosphate Co.* (1878), 3 App. Cas. 1218, H.L.

[5] At p. 111 of *Whaley Bridge Calico Printing Co.* v. *Green and Smith* (1880), 5 Q.B.D. 109.

company imposed by or arising out of the position which the so-called promoter assumes towards it'',[1]

a description which, in the earlier part, is a good instance of *obscurum per obscurius*. Four years later, after reviewing the above observations, BACON V.-C. expressed his opinion that "not much assistance is to be derived" from them, and that they are "not satisfactory",[2] which, if regarded as intended definitions, they are not; they were, however, evidently not so intended, but only as general descriptions, in which character they are, for the reasons already given, by no means unsatisfactory. At a later date, COTTON L.J., in one of his judgments, boldly avowed his "dislike" of the term, and after this pronouncement, carefully avoided using it at all.[3]

337   Whether a man was or was not a promoter at all, and if he ever was, whether he began to assume this character, and, having assumed it, continued to hold it, at the material date (which, for the purposes now under discussion, is the date of the issue of the prospectus),—are all questions of fact,[4] the burden of establishing the affirmative of which is on the person seeking to avail himself of the statutory remedy.[5] And, therefore, "it is necessary to see in each case what the so-called promoter really did, before his legal liabilities can be accurately ascertained".[6] It is only in the very rare cases in which all the facts are undisputed that the question of promotership or no promotership can be treated as one of law. In every case in which it has been necessary to prove a defendant's promotership, whether for the purposes of establishing a claim under s. 38 of the Act of 1867, or the fiduciary responsibility of the promoter, as such, to the company which he promoted, or his liability to a liquidator on a misfeasance summons, or his liability under the enactment now under consideration, and the plaintiff has proved such acts and conduct on the

---

[1] At p. 407 of *Emma Silver Mining Co. v. Lewis & Son* (1879), 4 C.P.D. 396. At a later date, as LINDLEY L.J., he characterised the expression as "an ambiguous term", in *Lydney and Wigpool Iron Ore Co. v. Bird* (1886), 33 Ch.D. 85, C.A., at p. 93.

[2] *Re Great Wheal Polgooth Co., Ltd.* (1883), 53 L.J. Ch. 42, at p. 46.

[3] *Ladywell Mining Co. v. Brookes* (1887), 35 Ch.D. 400, C.A., at p. 411.

[4] See *Twycross v. Grant (No. 1)* (1877), 2 C.P.D. 469, C.A., per COCKBURN C.J. at p. 541: "the question as to whether one who in the outset was a promoter of a company continues or ceases to be so, becomes . . . a question of fact". It was so treated by JESSEL M.R. at pp. 925, 941, of *Emma Silver Mining Co. v. Grant* (1879), 11 Ch.D. 918, C.A., and was left specifically to the jury, as such, by DENMAN J. in *Emma Silver Mining Co. v. Lewis & Son* (1879), 4 C.P.D. 396 (see pp. 398, 399).

[5] See the cases cited in the last two, and in the next two, notes.

[6] *Lydney and Wigpool Iron Ore Co. v. Bird* (1886), 33 Ch.D. 85, C.A., per LINDLEY L.J. at p. 93. See generally the cases cited in the next note.

part of the defendant as in the individual circumstances of the case appeared to the tribunal to indicate the existence of promotership at the material date, the plaintiff has succeeded.[1] Whenever, in any such case, he has failed to discharge this burden, that is, whenever he has failed to establish the fact of promotership at any time, or the fact that the defendant was a promoter at the material date, though the defendant may have been a promoter previously, or may have become so afterwards,[2] the plaintiff's claim has failed altogether. It must not be forgotten, however, in considering the question of the date and duration of the promotership, when this is a material question, that, just as a man may be a promoter

---

[1] The following are cases, in which promotership was proved, and which also serve as illustrations of the kind of operations which have been considered by judges and juries as sufficient to establish that fact: *Twycross* v. *Grant (No. 1) supra (per* COCKBURN C.J. at p. 541: "that the defendants were the promoters of the company from the beginning can admit of no doubt. They framed the scheme; they not only provisionally formed the company, but were, in fact, to the end its creators; they found the directors and qualified them; they prepared the prospectus; they paid for printing and advertising, and the expenses incidental to bringing the undertaking before the world"); *Nant-y-Glo and Blaina Ironworks Co.* v. *Grave* (1878), 12 Ch.D. 738 *(per* BACON V.-C. at p. 744); *Emma Silver Mining Co.* v. *Grant* (1879), 11 Ch.D. 918, C.A. *(per* JESSEL M.R. at p. 936: "he himself—whether he actually drafted or whether he settled and approved the memorandum and the articles of association is quite immaterial—was the person who was the author of those instruments, adopted the contract on behalf of the company, and acted from beginning to end for the company, formed it, provided it with directors, made a contract for it, and adopted that contract for it . . . It is not necessary that he should have done all these things to make him a promoter; even some of them would be sufficient"); *Glasier* v. *Rolls* (1889), 42 Ch.D. 436, C.A. *(per* KEKEWICH J. at p. 443: "he is a party to the agreement, he insists upon seeing the prospectus, he was to take a large share of the purchase money, which could only be reached by the successful floating of the company, and I have no doubt whatever that he is properly described as one of the promoters"); *Re Olympia, Ltd.,* [1898] 2 Ch. 153, C.A. *(per* COLLINS L.J. at p. 181, who says of the persons there found to be promoters of the company that "they did every act necessary to give it existence, framed the memorandum and articles, prepared the prospectus, and *generally* dictated the conditions of the company's existence"), and, on further appeal, *sub nom.* *Gluckstein* v. *Barnes*, [1900] A.C. 240, H.L. *(per* Lord ROBERTSON at p. 256: "speculators have found . . . the directors of a company, to be immediately floated for the purpose of buying a property which these same individuals associated to acquire", and "have taken a decisive step in shaping and limiting the company. It may well be asked, if this be not an act of promotion, what is?").

[2] As in *Re Coal Economising Gas Co., Gover's Case* (1875), 1 Ch.D. 182, at p. 187, C.A. (where the alleged promoter was found not to be so at the material time, though he was afterwards); *Re Great Wheal Polgooth Co., Ltd.* (1883), 53 L.J. Ch. 42 at pp. 47–50 (where no promotership at any time was established); *Albion Steel and Wire Co.* v. *Martin* (1875), 1 Ch.D. 580 *(per* JESSEL M.R. at pp. 585, 586); *Ladywell Mining Co.* v. *Brookes* (1887), 35 Ch.D. 400, C.A. *(per* COTTON L.J. at pp. 411–413); *Re Lady Forrest (Murchison) Gold Mine, Ltd.,* [1901] 1 Ch. 582, 589 (where WRIGHT J. found that there was no promotership when the property was acquired, which was in that case the material date). It must also be remembered that a man is not a promoter merely because he is contemplating the possibility of reselling his property to *a company*; he must be shewn to have had in mind *the company* which he is alleged to have promoted: *Erlanger* v. *New Sombrero Phosphate Co.* (1878), 3 App. Cas. 1218 *(per* Lord CAIRNS L.C. at p. 1235, and Lord BLACKBURN at pp. 1267, 1268); *Burland* v. *Earle,* [1902] A.C. 83, P.C. (at pp. 98, 99).

before the company is formed and registered, so also he does not necessarily cease to be such after the incorporation of the company.[1]

"*A party to the preparation of the prospectus*"

338   Although the term "promoter" is not to be found defined in the definitions section (s. 455) of the statute, s. 43 limits the liability which it imposes on promoters so as to impose it only upon a certain sort or class of promoters.   A promoter is liable only if he has been a "party to the preparation of the prospectus, or the portion thereof containing the untrue statement".[2]

Whether the promoter did or did not take part in the preparation of the prospectus is, like the question whether he was a promoter at all, one of fact.[3]   A company or artificial person may be a promoter of the company offering the shares or debentures for subscription,[4] as well as a natural person.

Moreover it is expressly provided by s. 43 (5) that the expression "promoter" is not to include any person simply by reason of his acting in a professional capacity for persons engaged in procuring the formation of the company.

It will be noticed that no such special affirmative defence is given by the statute to the promoter class as is available to the class of directors in fact, or persons named as such with authority in the prospectus.

---

[1] *Twycross* v. *Grant (No. 1)* (1877), 2 C.P.D. 469, C.A., *per* COCKBURN C.J. who, at p. 541, after the passage cited in note 1 on p. 352, goes on to point out that "in all these respects the directors were passive", and that as long as they remained in this state of passivity, and the defendant in a state of corresponding activity, a jury would be justified in finding that he had not lost his character of promoter, nor would he do so until the directors should take the whole direction and management of the concern entirely into their own hands.   So in *Emma Silver Mining Co.* v. *Lewis & Son* (1879), 4 C.P.D. 396, LINDLEY J. at p. 407, remarks that "a person . . . may be a promoter of a company which is already in existence, but the capital of which is not yet taken up, and which is not yet in a position to perform the obligations imposed upon it by creditors".   Cf. *Lydney and Wigpool Iron Ore Co.* v. *Bird* (1886), 33 Ch.D. 85 (*per Cur.*, at pp. 93, 94); *Ladywell Mining Co.* v. *Brookes, supra* (*per* LINDLEY L.J. at p. 414, and LOPES L.J. at p. 415), and the observations of the same two Lords Justices at p. 372 of *Eden* v. *Ridsdale's Railway Lamp and Lighting Co., Ltd.* (1889), 23 Q.B.D. 368, C.A.

[2] Section 43 (5).

[3] *Lydney and Wigpool Iron Ore Co.* v. *Bird* (1886), 33 Ch.D. 85, C.A. (*per* LINDLEY L.J. at p. 93).   In *Greenwood* v. *Leather Shod Wheel Co.*, [1900] 1 Ch. 421, C.A., KEKEWICH J. found, as a fact, that one of the five defendants was a promoter who had been a party to the preparation of the prospectus within the meaning of the corresponding provisions of the Act of 1890.   A useful illustration of the sort of acts which may be held to come within the description of "being a party to the preparation" is to be found in the judgment of KEKEWICH J. in *Glasier* v. *Rolls* (1889), 42 Ch.D. 436, C.A., at p. 442.

[4] In *Re Leeds and Hanley Theatre of Varieties, Ltd.*, [1902] 2 Ch. 809, C.A., the promoter was a company.

Persons who have authorised the issue of the prospectus

339   The fourth class of persons upon whom liability is imposed by
the statute comprises "persons who have authorised the issue of the
prospectus".   Any such person[1] is *prima facie* liable to pay statutory
compensation as a statutory representor, in respect of untrue statements
made in the prospectus, unless he can avail himself of either the *second*
or the *third* of the affirmative defences (setting up withdrawal of consent)
discussed in para. 343, *post*, or the defence of reasonable belief set out in
paras. 344 *et seq*.   Any one of these is an answer.   It is to be observed
that *experts* are not given all these defences[2]; their special position is
noticed in the next paragraph.

Experts

340   Under s. 40 of the 1948 Act it is now mandatory to obtain the
written consent of every expert to the issue of any prospectus containing
a statement by him as such expert.   The consequence of this provision
is that the consent which such an expert is now required to give constitutes him a "person authorising the issue of the prospectus" within
the meaning of s. 43.   The expert may accordingly now be sued directly
by the subscriber for shares, as a person liable under that section, in
respect of untrue statements made by him as an expert appearing in the
prospectus; but the consent which he has given under s. 40 will not
make him liable for other untrue statements in the prospectus.[3]   The
word "expert" has the same meaning in s. 43 as in s. 40.[4]

The expert made liable by the combined effect of ss. 40 and 43 as a
person who has authorised the issue of a prospectus is not given the
same defences as others who have authorised its issue.   The defences
available to the expert are (1) that having given his consent he withdrew
it in writing before registration, or (2) that on becoming aware of the
position he withdrew his consent in writing and gave reasonable public
notice of the withdrawal and the reasons therefor, or (3) that he was
competent in fact to make the statement and reasonably believed it to be
true.

It remains to add that in cases where it proves impossible for any
reason to sue the expert successfully under s. 43, it may now, since the

---

1 "Person" includes "company"—s. 19 of the Interpretation Act 1889—but not the company itself whose prospectus is issued, because s. 84 of the Act of 1908 exhibits abundant
evidence of "a contrary intention", within the meaning of the section of the Act of 1948.

2 Proviso to s. 43 (2).

3 See the proviso to s. 43 (1).

4 Section 40 provides that "expert" includes engineer, valuer, accountant and any other
person whose profession gives authority to a statement made by him.

decision in *Hedley Byrne & Co., Ltd.* v. *Heller & Partners, Ltd.*[1] be possible in some circumstances to claim against him in negligence. But for a consideration of this possibility the reader is referred to Chapter XIX, *post*.

What must be alleged and proved by plaintiff

341 Once the plaintiff has shown that the defendant is one of the persons whom the statute holds presumptively liable, the next thing to be proved is a statement in the prospectus which is *untrue*, or in other words, a misrepresentation.[2] Fraud is not necessary[3] but the "untrue statement" must be something that in law must amount to a "statement",[4] just as at common law the statement made must amount to a "representation". And the "untruth" of the statement must be shown to be substantial,[5] and to have existed down to the date of allotment, which is the date of the representee's alteration of position. Moreover, the statutory "statement" is subject to the same canons of construction, for the purpose of ascertaining its truth or falsity, as is the common law "representation". A "statement" in a prospectus is deemed by the statute to be untrue "if it is misleading in the form and context in which it is included"[6]; this provision must be understood to adopt and to carry forward into the statute law those decisions, antedating its enactment, which interpreted the statute previously in force as conferring a claim in respect of statements which are misleading by virtue of material omis-

---

[1] [1963] 2 All E.R. 575; [1964] A.C. 465, H.L.

[2] *Greenwood* v. *Leather Shod Wheel Co.*, [1900] 1 Ch. 421, C.A. *per* LINDLEY M.R. at p. 434.

[3] Before the passing of the Misrepresentation Act 1967 this was of great importance, for without fraud no action for damages would lie at common law. By the passing of that Act many other representees, outside the field of Company Law, have been placed in substantially the same position as representees under s. 43—i.e. have been given actions for damages for loss suffered by reason of innocent misrepresentations, in the truth of which the representor was left as a defence to prove his belief at the time when they were made. And he who acts upon a false statement in a prospectus, in respect of which he cannot prove fraud, now has, by virtue of the Misrepresentation Act 1967, an action for damages against the *company*, independently altogether of the action given by s. 43 of the Companies Act against its directors, promoters, etc. This action for damages against the company is new; and as is pointed out by the learned editor of *Palmer* (21st edn.) p. 166, one effect of s. 2 of the Misrepresentation Act 1967 may be to substitute actions against the company, under that Act, in practice, for the actions which in the past have been brought against directors or promoters.

[4] Note that a representation is a statement of *fact*; a "statement" is not in terms limited to a statement of fact, and presumably a statement of law, or of opinion, may give rise to an action under s. 43. The test will be whether the statement in its context is such as to mislead the plaintiff—see s. 46.

[5] See Chapter IV, paras. 69 *et seq.*, *ante*. In *Brookes* v. *Hansen*, [1906] 2 Ch. 129, the statement was not "substantially" untrue (pp. 137–138). In *Howell* v. *Dering*, [1915] 1 K.B. 54, C.A., and in *Bird* v. *Standard Oil Co. of Canada* (1915), 85 L.J. K.B. 935, it was.

[6] Companies Act 1948, s. 46 (b). This provision is new.

sions.[1] Where there are several statements they may, in accordance with the rules of construction applicable at common law[2] be read together rather than in isolation. And there must, of course (see in this regard the express words of the statute), be "loss or damage which they may have sustained by reason of any material statement therein". There must be a nexus between the untrue statement and the damage sustained by the representee, or rather, between the statement and the alteration of his position (by subscribing for shares) induced by it. As to materiality and inducement, these topics, upon which the decisions show some differences, are left to the next paragraph below.

Materiality and inducement

342 It is conceived that the rules as to materiality and inducement are the same in claims under the statutory action as they are in fraud. It has been suggested that difficulties may arise from the use of the words "on the faith of the prospectus"; and that it might have been better if the definition had used the word "induce" so that there could be no doubt that no departure from the normal rule was intended.[3]

Affirmative defences

343 The first affirmative defence set up by the statute is one available only to persons sued as *directors*. A director of the company, against whom a *prima facie* cause of action is made out escapes liability if he proves (the onus being upon him) that

> "having consented to become a director of the company he withdrew his consent before the issue of the prospectus and that it was issued without his authority or consent".[4]

Even if he has not withdrawn his consent to act as a director, he may still avail himself of either or both of two other statutory defences which are available to all defendants sued under the section. It is a good defence to any defendant sued under the section if he proves (the onus being upon him) that

> "the prospectus was issued without his knowledge or consent, and that

---

[1] e.g. *Drincqbier* v. *Wood*, [1899] 1 Ch. 393, at p. 407; *Greenwood* v. *Leather Shod Wheel Co.*, [1900] 1 Ch. 421, at p. 434, C.A.; *Broome* v. *Speak*, [1903] 1 Ch. 586, at p. 604, C.A.

[2] *Drincqbier* v. *Wood*, [1899] 1 Ch. 393, at p. 403; *Brookes* v. *Hansen*, [1906] 2 Ch. 129, at p. 137.

[3] See *McConnell* v. *Wright*, [1903] 1 Ch. 546, at p. 550; *Clark* v. *Urquhart*, [1930] A.C. 28, *per* Lord ATKIN at p. 67, *per* Lord TOMLIN at p. 76.

[4] Section 43 (2) (a).

upon becoming aware of its issue he forthwith gave reasonable public notice that it was issued without his knowledge or consent".[1]

A third affirmative defence is given to all defendants; it arises if the defendant

> "after the issue of the prospectus and before allotment thereunder, on becoming aware of any untrue statement therein, (he) withdrew his consent thereto and gave reasonable public notice of the withdrawal *and of the reason therefor*".[2]

Belief that the statement was true

344 It is also a defence to prove that the defendant believed on reasonable grounds that the statement complained of was true.[3] In this regard the statute deals separately with (a) statements contained in experts' reports, (b) statements taken from official sources and (c) other statements. These will now be dealt with one by one.

Statements in experts' reports

345 Persons liable for untrue statements in a prospectus have a special defence available if and in so far as the statement relied upon purports to be a statement made by an expert or to be an extract from an expert's report. It is a good defence that the statement fairly represented the tenor of the report, or was a correct copy of an extract from the report, *and* that up to the time of the issue of the prospectus the defendant had reasonable grounds to believe, and did believe, that the expert was competent to make the statement, and that he had given the consent required by s. 40 to the issue of the prospectus.[4]

This defence is not available, of course, to the expert himself, whose report is in question.[5] It is available only to those other persons made liable by the statute for the inclusion of the expert's report in the prospectus.

"Expert" in this connection has the same meaning as in para. 340, *ante*.

Statements from official sources

346 Defendants on the statutory claim are given another affirmative

---

[1] Section 43 (2) (b).
[2] Section 43 (2) (c).
[3] This is the defence set out at length in s. 43 (2) (d). The whole section is to be found reprinted in full in Appendix C, *post*.
[4] Section 43 (2) (d) (ii).
[5] Section 43 (2) (d) (concluding proviso). For the defences available to the *expert*, see para. 340.

answer in cases where the untrue statement upon which the action is
founded is one purporting originally to have been made by an official
person, or to have been copied or extracted from a public official document. In such a case, though the statement may in fact be untrue, it is a
good defence to prove that the passage in the prospectus is a correct and
fair representation of the statement originally made, or that the extract
from the report is a correct copy.[1]

The words "official person" and "official document" are not defined
by the statute. Presumably "official person" includes any person
holding an appointment under the State, or exercising any office of
public or local administration, or discharging duties to the community
or any section thereof pursuant to statute, charter, letters patent, or
other lawful authority of the like description, as distinguished from
persons owing a merely private duty to individuals in virtue of professional or contractual relations. A statement by such a person would
appear to include an oral statement, if made officially, as (e.g.) a statement by a Minister in Parliament, or by a Judge in court. The "documents" referred to in the section must be both public and official; a
document which is public, without being also official, such as a newspaper, historical work, or dictionary, or encyclopaedia, is not within
the enactment; nor is an official document which is not also "public",
such as a private State paper. A "public official document" includes at
least all such documents as are *publici juris* for the purposes of the law of
evidence. The characteristics, according to Lord BLACKBURN, of any
such document are that it should be "a document that is made for the
purpose of the public making use of it, and being able to refer to it",
and should "be made by a public officer"[2]; and he goes on to point out
that by "the public" is not necessarily meant "the public at large",
and that the expression includes any section of the community.[3] Questions may be thought capable of arising whether a statement made, or
document issued to the public by a public officer of a foreign State, a
member-state of the British Commonwealth, or a British Colony,[4] in
discharge of his duty as such officer, according to the law of the State or
Colony concerned, could be within the true interpretation of the expres-

---

[1] This is the defence set up in s. 43 (2) (d) (iii).
[2] At p. 643 of *Sturla* v. *Freccia* (1880), 5 App. Cas. 623, H.L.
[3] *Ibid.*
[4] Such, for instance, as the report of the Colonial Government Surveyor on which the prospectus in *Re Mount Morgan (West) Gold Mine, Ltd., Ex parte West* (1887), 56 L.T. 622, purported
to be founded, and the various foreign "official" documents which figure so prominently in
prospectuses of companies formed to acquire mines, concessions, or properties abroad.

sions under discussion.   It is submitted that it would not; and that, where a British statute speaks of "official" or "public", it must be taken to contemplate only British officers and officials, and the British public. And it could hardly have been intended that the presumption in favour of the reliability of the utterances of British officials, which was presumably the reason for not permitting a plaintiff to allege or prove that the defendant had no reasonable ground to believe in such an utterance, was to extend to what might be said by the officials of a foreign State.

Reasonable belief

347   There remains the residuary class of untrue statements—the great majority—which are *not* extracted either from the reports of experts or from official sources.   Here a defendant may escape liability if he affirmatively proves that he had reasonable grounds to believe, and did up to the time of the allotment of the shares or debentures, as the case may be, believe, that the statement was true.[1]

Where this defence is affirmatively proved the claim will fail.[2]   But it contains two elements (actual belief, and reasonable grounds for belief) and both must be proved.   Where the defendant fails to show that he actually believed in the truth of the statement, there is no need to embark upon the other branch of the inquiry, or to pronounce upon it; he fails at the first fence, and therefore fails altogether.[3]   Where, having proved, or at least having made out a *prima facie* case of belief in fact, the defendant fails to establish that his belief was based upon reasonable grounds, he equally fails.[4]   What are reasonable grounds is a question of fact.   "Reasonable" means "reasonable in all the circumstances of the case"; it does not necessarily mean "sufficient", or what the tribunal may deem so, nor does it necessarily exclude a reliance upon

---

[1] Section 43 (2) (d) (i).

[2] As in *Stevens* v. *Hoare* (1904), 20 T.L.R. 407 (*per* JOYCE J. at p. 409); *Brookes* v. *Hansen*, [1906] 2 Ch. 129 (*per* JOYCE J. at p. 137); *Howell* v. *Dering*, [1915] 1 K.B. 54, C.A.; *Bird* v. *Standard Oil Co. of Canada* (1915), 85 L.J. K.B. 935, C.A.

[3] The defendant failed to establish actual belief in *Greenwood* v. *Leather Shod Wheel Co.*, [1900] 1 Ch. 421, C.A. (*per* LINDLEY M.R. at pp. 433, 434, and ROMER L.J. at pp. 438, 439); *McConnel* v. *Wright*, [1903] 1 Ch. 546, C.A. (*per* COLLINS M.R. at pp. 551, 552, ROMER L.J. at p. 555, and COZENS-HARDY L.J. at pp. 558, 559); *J. and P. Coats, Ltd.* v. *Crossland* (1904), 20 T.L.R. 800 (*per* SWINFEN EADY J. at p. 806).

[4] The defendant failed in establishing this second element, in the defence (though he established, or was assumed to have established, the first) in the following: *Thomson* v. *Lord Clanmorris*, [1900] 1 Ch. 718, C.A. (at p. 730); *Broome* v. *Speak*, [1903] 1 Ch. 586 (*per* BUCKLEY J. at p. 603, COLLINS M.R. at pp. 619, 620, and ROMER L.J. at p. 627, and in the same case in the H.L., *sub nom. Shepheard* v. *Broome*, [1904] A.C. 342, H.L., *per* Lord JAMES at p. 346, and Lord LINDLEY at p. 347); *Adams* v. *Thrift*, [1915] 2 Ch. 21, C.A.   In *New Zealand*, *Bundle* v. *Davies*, [1932] N.Z.L.R. 1097 (MYERS C.J.).

the judgment or advice of others[1]; but, where reports and communications of third persons are suggested as reasonable grounds, it must be clearly proved that they existed at the time in a shape which would justify the statements,[2] and when the opinion of counsel is put forward as a reasonable ground, it must be shown that the opinion was based on full information, and directed to the very point.[3] The precise nature of the alleged "grounds" must, if the plaintiff requires it, be the subject of particulars.[4] Though the belief itself must be shown to have continued to the date of allotment,[5] the statute appears not to prescribe the like continuance of the reasonable grounds; so that if the defendant in fact believed the representation to be true during the whole of the period mentioned, and at the time of making the statement had reasonable grounds for his belief, he escapes the statutory liability, even if at the date of allotment he had no reasonable grounds, or no grounds at all.

The statutory remedy

348 The enactment provides that the statutory representors "shall be liable to pay compensation for the loss or damage sustained" by the statutory representees.[6] Since "compensation" means neither more nor less than "damages",[7] and "damage" is related to "loss" as genus to species, the intention of the section could have been more simply expressed by saying that the defendants in the statutory action shall be liable in damages.[8] It has already been pointed out that proof of damage, and of its causal connection with the misrepresentation, is just as necessary to establish the statutory, as it is to establish the common law, right

---

[1] *Stevens* v. *Hoare, supra, per* JOYCE J. at p. 409.

[2] *J. and P. Coats, Ltd.* v. *Crossland* (1904), 20 T.L.R. 800, *per* SWINFEN EADY J. at pp. 803, 806.

[3] *Broome* v. *Speak*, [1903] 1 Ch. 586, C.A., *per* COLLINS M.R. at p. 619.

[4] *Alman* v. *Oppert*, [1901] 2 K.B. 576, C.A.; but note the criticism of the dictum of COLLINS L.J. contained in the judgment of Lord DENNING M.R. in *Stapeley* v. *Annetts*, [1969] 3 All E.R. 1541.

[5] In this respect the statute does not depart from the common law rule—see Chapter IV, paras. 73 *et seq., ante.*

[6] Section 43 (1).

[7] *Clark* v. *Urquhart*, [1930] A.C. 28, H.L., *per* Viscount SUMNER at p. 56 ("I cannot hold that compensation here is, either as to the amount recoverable or the mode of measuring it, something different from and even greater than damages"); *per* Lord ATKIN at p. 67 ("In my judgment the effect of the section . . . was merely to eliminate the element of fraud from the cause of action based on misrepresentation in a prospectus, and to give the same remedy in the statutory conditions for an innocent misrepresentation as for a fraudulent misrepresentation"); *per* Lord TOMLIN on p. 76.

[8] Possibly, the word "compensation" was selected merely for the purpose of emphasising the fact that the remedy is a statutory one. And see *per* Viscount SUMNER at p. 56 of *Clark* v. *Urquhart*, [1930] A.C. 28, H.L.

to relief.[1] Further, the rules for computing the quantum of relief, and as to the facts and matters relevant to such assessment, which are applicable in the case of an action of fraud[2] are precisely those which are applicable, and have been judicially applied, in the case of the statutory proceedings.[3]

It has been held, in *New Zealand*, that an election by a shareholder not to repudiate shares for misrepresentation is not a defence to the special cause of action given by the statute.[4]

Sales by auction

349 From the earliest times the secret employment of "puffers" at auction sales, and other tricks and devices of the auction room, were regarded with the utmost disfavour not only by equity, but also by law. Indeed, contrary to the tendency observable in other departments, common law judges, taking their cue from Lord MANSFIELD, as he took his from the Roman law,[5] have been rather more rigorous and unbending in this respect than courts of Chancery. The hiring by a vendor of bidders to force up the price of a property offered for sale, without notification of the fact to the purchasing public, may, no doubt, be regarded as fraudulent concealment of that which it is the duty of the vendor to disclose, or as a breach of an implied contract with the public[6]; but it may be, and has judicially been, considered also as a case of fraudulent, though implied, misrepresentation[7]; and it is in this respect that

---

[1] See para. 341, *ante*.

[2] These rules are stated in Chapter XI, paras. 203 *et seq.*, *ante*.

[3] See, for instance, *Thomson* v. *Lord Clanmorris*, [1900] 1 Ch. 718, C.A.; *Broome* v. *Speak*, [1903] 1 Ch. 586, C.A. (*per* BUCKLEY J. at pp. 604–606, COLLINS M.R. at pp. 622–623 and COZENS-HARDY L.J. at p. 630); same case in the H.L., *sub nom. Shepheard* v. *Broome*, [1904] A.C. 342, H.L. (*per* Lord LINDLEY, at pp. 347, 348), cited in note 2 on p. 233, *ante*. The nature of the "compensation" given by the Act was a matter upon which several members of the House of Lords expressed reservations in *Nash* v. *Lynde*, [1929] A.C. 158, H.L.; but the point was put beyond doubt in the following year in *Clark* v. *Urquhart*, [1930] A.C. 28, H.L., for which see note 7 on previous page.

[4] *Bundle* v. *Davies*, [1932] N.Z.L.R. 1097 (MYERS C.J.).

[5] For the principles of Roman law on this topic stated in their most forcible form by Cicero in a passage at one time familiar in English courts, see Appendix C in the 2nd edition.

[6] *Robinson* v. *Wall* (1847), 2 Ph. 372 (*per* Lord LANGDALE M.R. at pp. 374, 375, who there states the question for the court as being "whether the course pursued by the vendor is, or is not, in violation of the contract which he enters into with the public", though he afterwards goes on to speak of it as a question of "good faith" or "bad faith"); *Warlow* v. *Harrison* (1859), 1 E. & E. 309, Ex. Ch.

[7] Thus, at p. 207 of *Green* v. *Baverstock* (1863), 14 C.B. N.S. 204, WILLES J. observes that "the person so employed is employed for the purpose of *falsely representing* that he is willing to give for the article a price which he never intended to give". So, at p. 15 of *Mortimer* v. *Bell* (1865), 1 Ch. App. 10, Lord CRANWORTH described the transaction proved in that case in the following forcible terms: "When the auctioneer took on himself to make an advance of £100 on Webb's bidding, he must be considered as having *said*, Mr Webb has bid £2500,

the topic, on principles already discussed, falls within the scope of any work on misrepresentation. After a series of decisions which settled the main principles on which any contract of sale by auction tainted by this objectionable practice should be dealt with, but which disclosed a slight divergence between law and equity in the application of such principles to sales of land, the legislature intervened in 1867 for the purpose of removing these doubts and conflicts, and, again, in 1893, for the purpose of declaring (in a codifying statute relating to the sale of goods in general), and giving statutory effect to, the rules which had for a long time prevailed at common law with reference to the sale of goods by auction.

To these statutory provisions, dealt with in earlier editions of this work, must now be added those of the Auctions (Bidding Agreements) Act 1927, dealt with in para. 352, below.

The Sale of Land by Auction Act 1867

350 This statute, still in force, is sometimes referred to as the Puffers Act and is applicable only to sales of land, land being interpreted as including "any interest in land" by s. 3, which also defines "puffer" as "a person appointed to bid on the part of the owner", and "agent" as a "solicitor, steward, or land agent of the seller". Section 4, after reciting that

> "there is at present a conflict between Her Majesty's courts of law and equity, in respect of the validity of sales by auction of land where a puffer has bid, although no right of bidding on behalf of the owner was reserved, the courts of law holding that all such sales are absolutely illegal, and the courts of equity under some circumstances giving effect to them, but even in courts of equity the rule is unsettled",

and that "it is expedient that an end should be put to such conflicting and unsettled opinions", proceeds to enact

> "that, from and after the passing of this Act, whenever a sale by auction of

---

but A.B. has bid £2600, and so on, through all the eleven biddings, up to £3000. The whole proceeding was a *fiction*, calculated, if not intended, to *deceive* persons who thought of becoming purchasers. It was a *false statement* that up to £3600, or at all events up to £3500, there was a real bidder. I can find neither principle nor authority for holding that in such a case a vendor who, *by this misrepresentation, has induced* a third person to bid, can enforce his contract". Again, in *Parfitt* v. *Jepson* (1877), 46 L.J. C.P. 529, GROVE J. at p. 532, points out that "one of the objects of puffing at a sale is to *induce the outsiders to suppose* that a competition for the purchase is going on, and to increase the price which may be obtained for the property by the excitement of such *supposed* competition", and to the same effect LINDLEY J. at p. 533; the meaning of these observations being obviously that, by the proceedings in question, the vendor makes an implied representation to possible purchasers that there is a genuine competition, with real biddings, analogous to the implied representations made by the process of "rigging the market", as to which see para. 58, Chapter III, *ante*.

land would be invalid at law by reason of the employment of a puffer, the same shall be deemed invalid in equity as well as at law''.

Section 5 also has a preamble of its own, to the effect that

''as sales of land by auction are now conducted, many of such sales are illegal, and could not be enforced against an unwilling purchaser, and it is expedient for the safety of both seller and purchaser that such sales should be so conducted as to be binding on both parties'',

and, after this preamble, the section provides that

''the particulars or conditions of sale by auction of any land shall state whether such land will be sold without reserve, or subject to a reserved price, or whether a right to bid is reserved; and, if it is stated that such land will be sold without reserve, or to that effect, then it shall not be lawful for the seller to employ any person to bid at such sale, or for the auctioneer to take knowingly any bidding from such person''.

On the other hand, s. 6 enacts that

''where any sale by auction of land is declared either in the particulars or conditions to be subject to a right for the seller to bid, it shall be lawful for the seller, or any one person on his behalf to bid at such auctions in such manner as he may think proper''.

The two last-cited sections, prohibitory and permissive respectively, do not cohere very well, but it has been decided that the vendor must bring himself strictly within the permissive section, if the sale is to be valid, and that it will not avail him to show merely that he is outside the prohibitive enactment[1]; also that where the ''right for the seller to bid'', to which the sale is declared to be ''subject'', is defined and limited by the particulars or conditions, within the meaning of s. 6, the seller acquires no right under that section to employ a person to bid otherwise than in accordance with the declared limits and qualifications.[2] Section 7 relates to ''the practice of opening the biddings on any sale by auction of land under or by virtue of any order of the High Court of Chancery''

---

[1] *Gilliat* v. *Gilliat* (1869), L.R. 9 Eq. 60, where the sale was stated to be ''subject to a reserved bidding which has been fixed by the judge'', which expression, having regard to the word ''fixed'', clearly meant no more than ''a reserved price'': so that the vendor did not come within the prohibition in s. 5, but, inasmuch as the conditions and particulars of sale nowhere stated that the sale was to be ''subject to a right for the seller to bid'', he did not bring himself within the permissive provisions of s. 6. Accordingly, on proof of an employment of a puffer, Lord ROMILLY M.R. relieved the purchaser of his bargain.

[2] This was the case in *Parfitt* v. *Jepson* (1877), 46 L.J. C.P. 529, where the conditions declared that ''a right was reserved to the vendor *to bid once* by himself or his agent'', and it was proved that he had bid more than once, and therefore was not protected by s. 6, and on this ground, amongst others, his action for damages for breach of the contract of sale was defeated (*per* LINDLEY J. at pp. 533, 534).

(now the Chancery Division of the High Court of Justice), and enacts that such practice

> "shall be discontinued, and the highest *bona fide* bidder at such sale, provided he shall have bid a sum equal to, or higher than, the reserved price (if any), shall be declared and allowed the purchaser, unless the court or a judge shall, on the ground of fraud or improper conduct in the management of the sale—[which latter expression is probably not confined to conduct in the nature of, or bordering upon, fraud[1]]—upon the application of any person interested in the land (such application to be made to the court or judge before the chief clerk's certificate of the result of the sale shall have become binding), either open the biddings, holding such bidder bound by his bidding, or discharge him from being the purchaser, and order the land to be resold upon such terms as to costs and otherwise as the court or judge shall think fit."

The statute is expressed not to extend to Scotland, the reason being that Scottish law has always followed the Roman law as to auction sales, and the Act was consequently unnecessary in that jurisdiction.

The Sale of Goods Act 1893, s. 58

351 There has never been any question about the rules relating to sales of goods by auction where secret "puffing" is resorted to, nor any difference between law and equity in this matter, because equity has not busied itself with auction sales of any property except land and interests in land. Consequently no amending statute or enactment, corresponding to that of 1867 in respect to land, was required with respect to goods. But when the Sale of Goods Act 1893 (56 & 57 Vict. c. 71), for the purpose of codifying the law, both English and Scottish, relating to the sale of goods generally, was passed, it became necessary to state, amongst other rules, the rules relating to this particular form of sale. These are set out in s. 58 (3) and (4), which deal with the "puffer" question as follows:

> "(3) Where a sale by auction is not notified to be subject to a right to bid on behalf of the seller, it shall not be lawful for the seller to bid himself or

---

[1] In *Delves* v. *Delves* (1875), L.R. 20 Eq. 77, MALINS V.-C. dismissed the purchaser's application under s. 7, on the ground that he had proved neither "fraud"—indeed, he had expressly declined even to allege this—nor "improper conduct", in the limited sense which the Vice Chancellor assigned to that term,—*viz.* conduct "bordering upon fraud", but the Irish C.A., in *Re Longvale Brick and Lime Works, Ltd.*, [1917] 1 I.R. 321, distinctly held that a serious, though quite innocent, mis-statement by the court's auctioneer of matters affecting the value of the property sold constituted "improper conduct" within the meaning of the section, and they disagreed with the above dictum of MALINS V.-C. (*per* Lord O'BRIEN L.C. at pp. 326–329, and RONAN L.J. at pp. 330, 331). This decision was referred to, without either approval or disapproval, for it was not necessary to express any opinion on the point, by PETERSON J. at pp. 266, 267, of *Re Joseph Clayton, Ltd., Smith* v. *Joseph Clayton, Ltd.*, [1920] 1 Ch. 257.

to employ any person to bid at such sale, or for the auctioneer knowingly to take any bid from the seller or any such person: Any sale contravening this rule may be treated as fraudulent by the buyer:

(4) A sale by auction may be notified to be subject to a reserved or upset price, and a right to bid may also be reserved expressly by or on behalf of the seller. Where a right to bid is expressly reserved, but not otherwise, the seller, or any one person on his behalf, may bid at the auction".

These rules are expressed with admirable clearness; they represent accurately the judicially declared law on the subject both in England[1] and in Scotland[2]; and, by the simple and succinct provision that the buyer may treat a sale which contravenes the rule as fraudulent,[3] the necessity for cumbrous and detailed enumeration of remedies is avoided. The enactment has raised few serious problems or difficulties for solution by the courts; nor are such problems likely in the future.

The Auctions (Bidding Agreements) Act 1927

352 The provisions considered in the last preceding paragraph were for the protection of *purchasers*. It was for the protection of *vendors* that the Auctions (Bidding Agreements) Act 1927 was enacted. This statute is concerned with agreements between a "dealer" who contemplates bidding at an auction, and other possible bidders by which (for reward) the latter undertake to refrain from bidding by the auction. If any dealer agrees to give any consideration for such an undertaking, or any possible bidder receives or attempts to obtain any such consideration, and such agreement is the subject of the prosecution and conviction of either of them, then any sale at the auction with respect to which such an agreement has been made may be treated by the vendor as a sale induced by fraud.

A "dealer" is defined by the Act as a person who in the normal course of his business attends sale by auction for the purpose of purchasing goods with a view to reselling them.

The statute is patently directed only to sales of goods by auction, and it is submitted that it has no effect as regards sales of land.

---

[1] See *Bexwell* v. *Christie* (1776), 1 Cowp. 395; *Crowder* v. *Austin* (1826), 3 Bing. 368; *Warlow* v. *Harrison* (1859), 1 E. & E. 309; *Green* v. *Baverstock* (1863), 14 C.B.N.S. 204.

[2] Which has always been the same as in England so far as substance is concerned, though the terminology occasionally differs: this is recognised in sub-s. (4) where the Scottish term "upset" is added to the English "reserved", as applied to the price.

[3] Which means that, under this comprehensive formula, the purchaser becomes entitled to all the relief and remedies (whether alternative, or cumulative) to which a representee is entitled in any ordinary case of fraudulent misrepresentation at common law.

The Act excepts from the effect of its provisions the case where a dealer previously to an auction has entered into an agreement with one or more persons to purchase goods at the auction *bona fide* on a joint account, and has before purchase at the auction deposited a copy of the agreement with the auctioneer.

The Bankruptcy Act 1914

353   Some provisions of the Bankruptcy Act 1914 may next be noted, without comment.   By s. 17 it is provided that

> "Notwithstanding the acceptance and approval of a composition or scheme, the composition or scheme shall not be binding on any creditor so far as regards a debt or liability from which, under the provisions of this Act, the debtor would not be released by an order of discharge in bankruptcy, unless the creditor assents to the composition or scheme."

It is clear from a consideration of s. 28 (1) (b) that debts incurred by fraud are within s. 17 and that the fraudulent debtor does not obtain a release from such debts as an incident of a composition, unless the creditor assents to the composition.[1]

Section 28 (1) (b) provides:

> "An order for discharge shall not release the bankrupt . . . (b) from any debt or liability incurred by means of any fraud or fraudulent breach of trust to which he was a party, nor from any debt or liability whereof he has obtained forbearance by any fraud to which he was a party."

Section 93 (3) provides that an order of the Board of Trade releasing a trustee in bankruptcy may be revoked if procured by fraud.

Partnership Act 1890

354–355   Section 41 of the Partnership Act 1890 provides that:

> "where a partnership contract is rescinded on the ground of the fraud or misrepresentation of one of the parties thereto, the party entitled to rescission is, without prejudice to any other right, entitled to a lien on, or right of retention of, the surplus of the partnership assets, after satisfying the partnership liabilities, for any sum of money paid by him for the purchase of a share in the partnership, and for any capital contributed by him, and is to stand in the place of the creditor of the firm for any payments made by him in respect of the partnership liabilities, and to be indemnified by the person guilty of the fraud, or making the misrepresentation, against all the debts and liabilities of the firm".

---

[1] As to what is "assenting otherwise" than as stated, see *Thorp* v. *Dakin* (1885), 52 L.T. 856, Div. Ct.

CHAPTER XVII

Misrepresentation as a Ground of Remedy or Relief at the Instance of Persons other than Representees

Introductory

356 There are a variety of cases of misrepresentation which give rise to civil rights, liabilities, and consequences, though not falling within the definition of actionable misrepresentation adopted for the purposes, and as the foundation, of this Commentary[1] and of the Code which precedes it.[2] These may be divided into two main classes: first, the class of misrepresentation which, though not made to the party entitled to relief, is made in such a way as to injure him, and, secondly, the class of misrepresentation which, though neither made to the party entitled to take advantage of it, nor so as to injure him individually, nevertheless constitutes, not a cause of action, but a defence, which such party may set up to an action of contract or tort, not out of any consideration for him, but purely on grounds of public policy. It seems desirable to devote a chapter to the discussion of these two types of cases, particularly having regard to the fact that the first of them, for a long time in the history of our jurisprudence, was regarded as belonging strictly to the subject of "deceit" in the larger and more fluid interpretation which the word then bore.[3]

In a concluding paragraph there is mentioned, for the sake of completeness, the action for negligence in making a representation, which is

---

[1] See para. 8, *ante*.
[2] See Parts VII, VIII, and IX, of the Code.
[3] See Appendix A, paras. 418 *et seq.*, *post*.

examined in more detail in Chapter XIX, *post*; this action, as will be seen in that chapter, may be available at the suit of persons other than the representee.[1]

Remedies available to a person injured by a representation not made to him

357 Where, by misrepresentation to a public authority, or to the public, any person obtains for himself advantages or privileges, to the prejudice of the proprietary or interests of a third person, whether individually or as a member of the community, that third person, though he is not the representee, and therefore could not sue in an action for misrepresentation in the modern and strict sense, is not left without remedy: on application to the proper court by the proper procedure,[2] and on compliance with all prerequisites as to allegation and proof,[3] he is entitled to a judicial annulment of the instrument by which such advantages or privileges have been obtained, or to have it judicially treated as void, or to relief by way of injunction, *certiorari*, or otherwise in respect of the injury done to him as in this chapter set out. The classes of misrepresentation which it is proposed here to consider comprise the following: (1) fraudulent misrepresentations to an English Court of Justice in the course of proceedings *inter partes*, whereby a judgment or order is obtained in favour of the misrepresentor[4]; (2) the like to a foreign tribunal, with the like result; (3) the like to an arbitrator, with the like result; (4) misrepresentations whereby the Crown or a Department of the State has been induced to grant to the misrepresentor charters, letters patent, licences, certificates, registrations, or other privileges; (5) fraudulent misrepresentations to quasi-judicial tribunals entrusted by statute with the grant of special privileges, licences, etc., as between a number of applicants, whereby the representor's application has been preferred to the exclusion of that of the plaintiff; and (6) misrepresentations to the public of the kind known as "passing off". To the text in which these are considered are added separate paragraphs making mention of two allied topics (7) misrepresentations by which the grant of a patent has been obtained, and (8) misrepresentations made to the Legislature in the course of promoting a private Act of Parliament.

---

[1] See Chapter XIX, para. 515, *post*, and particularly *Ministry of Housing and Local Government* v. *Sharp*, [1970] 2 Q.B. 223; on appeal, *ibid*. at p. 252.

[2] See para. 363, *post*.

[3] See para. 367, *post*.

[4] *MacCarthy* v. *Agard*, [1933] 2 K.B. 417, C.A., *per* GREER and ROMER L.JJ., SCRUTTON L.J. dissenting.

English judgments procured by fraudulent misrepresentation

358   It has been undoubted law, since at least the time of Coke,[1] that "acts of the highest judicial authority", e.g., judgments—though "not to be impeached from within", yet "are impeachable from without", on the ground that they have been procured by fraud; for, "although it is not permitted to show that the court was mistaken, it may be shown that they (sic) were misled.   Fraud is an extrinsic collateral act, which vitiates the most solemn proceedings of courts of justice.   Lord Coke says, it avoids all judicial acts, ecclesiastical or temporal".[2]

> "Fraud is an insidious disease, and if clearly proved to have been used so that it might deceive the court, it spreads to and infects the whole body of the judgment".[3]

Accordingly, either at the suit of the party against whom it was pronounced, or, where both parties have colluded and conspired to deceive the court, at the suit of the Attorney-General or a stranger interested, judgments, orders, decrees, sentences, and other judicial acts of English tribunals, have been set aside or annulled, or treated as void, on proof that they were procured by fraud'[4] or declared, on demurrer or otherwise, to be the proper subject of such proceedings or treatment[5]; and,

---

[1] And *deceptio curiae* was punishable as a contempt of the Crown, and an injury to the party, as early as the time of King John, and was, indeed, the principal, if not the only, subject of the writ of deceit (*breve de deceptione*) in its earliest form: see Appendix A, *post.*

[2] *The Duchess of Kingston's Case* (1776), 2 Sm.L.C. (13th Edition) 644, at p. 651.   In that case the judges were summoned by the House of Lords, and requested to answer two questions: (1) "whether a sentence of the Spiritual Court against a marriage in a suit for jactitation of marriage is conclusive evidence so as to stop the counsel for the Crown from proving the said marriage in an indictment for polygamy: and (2) whether, admitting such evidence to be conclusive upon such indictment, the counsel for the Crown may be admitted *to avoid the effect of such sentence by proving the same to have been obtained by fraud or collusion*".   The judges unanimously answered the first question in the negative, and the second (which alone concerns the present discussion) in the affirmative.

[3] *Per* Lord BUCKMASTER in *Jonesco* v. *Beard*, [1930] A.C. 298, H.L., at p. 301.

[4] As in *Loyd* v. *Mansell* (1722), 2 P.Wms. 73; *Harrison* v. *Southampton Corpn.* (1853), 4 De G.M. & G. 137; *Brooke* v. *Lord Mostyn* (1864), 2 De G.J. & Sm. 373; *Priestman* v. *Thomas* (1884), 9 P.D. 210, C.A.; *Cole* v. *Langford*, [1898] 2 Q.B. 36, Div. Ct.; *Sturrock* v. *Littlejohn* (1898), 68 L.J. Q.B. 165, Div. Ct.; *Nixon* v. *Loundes*, [1909] 2 I.R.1; *White* v. *Ivory* (1910), *Times*, 27th April.   In the nature of the case, the number of successful actions for this purpose must be few, as compared with the number of those which fail, owing to the firm recognition by the courts of the interest of the community *ut sit finis litium*, and the strict burden of proof which is accordingly required of the plaintiff,—proof not merely of the fraudulent misrepresentation, but of the fact that it could not have been discovered and exposed at the trial.   In *Flower* v. *Lloyd*, (No. 2) (1879), 10 Ch.D. 327, C.A., JAMES L.J. at pp. 333, 334, delivers himself of some very strong observations, in which he says that THESIGER L.J. concurs, by way of addendum or appendix to the joint judgment of the court, as to the inconvenience of exercising the jurisdiction.

[5] As, for instance, in the *Duchess of Kingston's Case* (1776), 2 Sm. L.C. (13th ed.) 644; *Davenport* v. *Stafford* (1845), 8 Beav. 503 (*per* Lord LANGDALE M.R. at pp. 522, 523); *Eyre* v. *Smith* (1877), 2 C.P.D. 435, C.A. (unsuccessful demurrer to a reply); *Abouloff* v. *Oppenheimer*

in every one of those cases in which, for one reason or another, the jurisdiction was not exercised, its existence was nevertheless recognised in clear and explicit terms.[1]

359   It does not signify what is the precise nature of the "judicial act" which is sought to be invalidated; whether a judgment, decree, or order of the ordinary kind, pronounced by a court of equity,[2] or by a court of common law,[3] or by an Admiralty court sitting in prize,[4] or an adjudication or order in Bankruptcy,[5] or a judgment of a court of Probate establishing a will,[6] or an order of the Privy Council, following on the advice of the Judicial Committee.[7]   Nor does it signify whether the judgment or order impugned was of a final or an interlocutory character[8]

(1882), 10 Q.B.D. 295, C.A. (*per* BRETT L.J. at p. 308, who there says that the doubts expressed by JAMES and THESIGER L.JJ. as to the jurisdiction—*vid. sup.*—are not well founded); *Wyatt* v. *Palmer*, [1899] 2 Q.B. 106, C.A. (application to strike out statement of claim failed).

1 See *Charter* v. *Trevelyan* (1844), 11 Cl. & Fin. 714 (*per* Lord LYNDHURST L.C.); *Meddowcroft* v. *Huguenin* (1844), 4 Moo. P.C.C. 386; *Perry* v. *Meddowcroft* (1846), 10 Beav. 122 (*per* Lord LANGDALE M.R. at pp. 136, 137); *Dunn* v. *Cox* (1853), 11 Hare, 61; *Patch* v. *Ward* (1867), 3 Ch. App. 203 (*per* Lord CAIRNS L.J. at pp. 206, 207); *Motion* v. *Moojen* (1872), L.R. 14 Eq. 202; *Flower* v. *Lloyd* (*No. 1*) (1877), 6 Ch.D. 297, C.A. (*per* JESSEL M.R. at pp. 299, 300, and JAMES and BAGGALLAY L.JJ. at p. 302); *Same* v. *Same*, (*No. 2*) (1879), 10 Ch.D. 327, C.A. (*per* BAGGALLAY L.J. at p. 334); *Boswell* v. *Coaks* (1894), 6 R. 167, H.L. (*per* Lord SELBORNE at p. 170); *Baker* v. *Wadsworth* (1898), 67 L.J. Q.B. 301, Div. Ct.; *Birch* v. *Birch*, [1902] P. 130, C.A. (*per* COZENS-HARDY L.J. at p. 137).

2 In the following cases judgments, decrees, and orders of a court of equity were the subject of attack: *Loyd* v. *Mansell* (1722), 2 P.Wms. 73; *Patch* v. *Ward, supra*; *Motion* v. *Moojen, supra*; *Flower* v. *Lloyd*, (*No. 1*) *supra*; *Same* v. *Same*, (*No. 2*) *supra*; *Boswell* v. *Coaks, supra*.

3 Judgments of common law courts were sought to be annulled in *Dunn* v. *Cox*, *Baker*, v. *Wadsworth*, *Nixon* v. *Loundes*, and *White* v. *Ivory*, *supra*.

4 *The Alfred Nobel*, [1918] P. 293.

5 *Eyre* v. *Smith* (1877), 2 C.P.D. 435, where it was alleged by the plaintiff in his reply that certain resolutions for the liquidation of the defendant's affairs by arrangement, pleaded as a bar to the action, and the registration of these resolutions, had been procured by fraudulent misrepresentation to the creditors, and to the Bankruptcy Registrar, respectively.

6 *Birch* v. *Birch*, [1902] P. 130.

7 *Ram Narayan Singh* v. *Adhindra Nath Mukerji*, [1917] A.C. 100, P.C.

8 See *Dalglish* v. *Jarvie* (1850), 2 Mac. & G. 231 (*per* ROLFE B. at p. 243); *London Assurance* v. *Mansel* (1879), 11 Ch.D. 363 (*per* JESSEL M.R. at p. 368). The former case was one of an interlocutory injunction in a suit for infringement of copyright in a design, where it was pointed out by Lord CRANWORTH (then ROLFE B. and one of the Commissioners of the Great Seal) that an order for that purpose which has been procured, not only by misrepresentation, but by the withholding of any matter which *uberrima fides* requires to be disclosed, is on that ground subject to dissolution.   In the latter case, which was one of insurance, the former is used as an illustration of the principles of good faith said to be applicable alike to all such transactions.   *Cf.* also *Re S., a Solicitor, etc.* (1910), 55 Sol. Jo. 127, where, on the ground that material facts were withheld from the court, an order to tax, obtained *ex parte* on a petition of course, was discharged; *Toronto Rail Co.* v. *City of Toronto*, [1920] A.C. 426, P.C. (nondisclosure to the Judicial Committee of a certain colonial statute, on a petition for leave to appeal: at pp. 444, 445).

or was pronounced by a court of first instance, or an appellate court,[1] or was made *in invitum*, after a hearing or contest, or merely for the purpose of sanctioning, or giving effect to, a consent of, or compromise between, the parties,[2] or was given by default[3]; nor whether the judgment or order is sought to be set aside *in toto*, or only in part, by the expunging of some entry or recital therein which was procured by the alleged misrepresentation.[4]

Judgments in rem in English courts

360   Judgments *in rem* present certain difficulties peculiar to themselves; for they are effective to create or change the status of persons or things against "all the world", and are not in the first place effective only against the parties to the suit.   Where only the parties are affected by the judgment, it is comparatively simple to rescind a judgment procured through the fraud of one of them—though even this apparently simple solution may become complicated if (say) the fraud of one only of several co-parties has procured the judgment in favour of all.[5]   But the position becomes even more complicated still when the judgment is *in rem*.   What is to be done, for instance, about a grant of probate procured by the perjury or fraudulent evidence of the grantee ?   If this is discovered immediately after the grant, perhaps no complicating factor may yet be present;   but when a debtor to the estate has *bona fide* paid the amount of his debt to the fraudulently appointed executor, is the rescission of the

---

[1] See *Ram Narayan Singh* v. *Adhindra Nath Mukerji*, [1917] A.C. 100 P.C.

[2] Thus in *Davenport* v. *Stafford* (1845), 8 Beav. 503, it was a question whether the party had been induced to consent to the insertion of an entry in the decree or order by misrepresentation: in *Dunn* v. *Cox* (1853), 11 Hare 61, it was alleged that the plaintiff's consent to an order of the Court of Exchequer had been obtained by the like means: *Brooke* v. *Lord Mostyn* (1864), 2 De G.J. & Sm. 373, was a case of a family compromise sanctioned by the court in chambers; *Priestman* v. *Thomas* (1884), 9 P.D. 210, C.A. was a case of a compromise of a testamentary suit, to which the party had been induced by misrepresentation to consent, as well as to a judgment of the Probate Division, in accordance therewith, admitting a certain will to probate; in *Sturrock* v. *Littlejohn* (1898), 68 L.J.Q.B. 165, Div. Ct. the party had been induced by fraud to consent to judgment under O. XIV; in *Wyatt* v. *Palmer*, [1899] 2 Q.B. 106, C.A., a consent to let judgment go by default had been similarly procured; in *Re Pacaya Rubber and Produce Co.*, [1913] 1 Ch. 218, C.A., a consent order for discontinuance had been fraudulently obtained. It will be noted that no reference is made in the text to the class of case in which a compromise or settlement of an action, or a consent judgment or order, is the result of mistake, or as to which there is a question of the extent of the express or implied authority of counsel or solicitor, which fall under another chapter of law altogether.

[3] *Wyatt* v. *Palmer*, [1899] 2 Q.B. 106, C.A.

[4] In *Davenport* v. *Stafford* (1845), 8 Beav. 503, Lord LANGDALE M.R. (at pp. 522, 523) recognised the clear *prima facie* right of a party to be relieved from the consequences of an admission in a decree, the insertion of which, or the consent to the insertion of which, was procured by fraud.

[5] *Boswell* v. *Coaks* (1894), 6 R. 167.

grant of probate to expose him to liability for a second payment? And what of the beneficiaries named in the will which has been propounded? The will must in the words of COZENS-HARDY L.J. be "good or bad against all the world",[1] and this proposition raises problems which the cases do little to resolve with certainty.

Decrees in divorce

361 In earlier editions of this work Mr Spencer Bower included "sentences of an ecclesiastical or matrimonial tribunal in respect of marriages" in the list of judgments, decrees and orders amenable to attack on the ground of fraud.[2] This proposition cannot be accepted in its entirety. It is obvious that decrees in divorce, or at least decrees *absolute* in divorce are not to be governed in all respects by the same rules as apply to judgments given *inter partes* in commercial or financial disputes; for they are decrees *in rem*, and have consequences extending far beyond the parties to the suit from which they spring.[3]

No doubt a *decree nisi* divorcing the parties may be set aside for fraud, on the application of the party against whom it was made, and even upon the intervention of some other person unconnected with the suit, so long as it has not yet been made absolute[4]; but what is the meaning of "decree absolute"? While that term was left undefined in the Matrimonial Causes Act 1965, the consequences, upon the parties, of making a decree *absolute* were clearly enough indicated in that Act, and in those which preceded it.[5] The new Act of 1973, not yet in force as this book

---

[1] *Birch* v. *Birch*, [1902] P. 130 at pp. 137–138. In *Victoria* see *Re Gillard*, [1949] V.L.R. 378.

[2] 2nd edn., p. 359.

[3] *Edwards* v. *Edwards*, [1951] P. 228, at p. 234. For a criticism of the extension, to the field of divorce, of principles based on the practice in commercial courts, see the judgment of Lord DENNING M.R. in *Wiseman* v. *Wiseman*, [1953] P. 79. In *Australia*, see *Brennan* v. *Brennan* (1953), 89 C.L.R. 129 (H. Ct. of Aus.) at pp. 134–145.

[4] And this is expressly recognised by s. 10(1) of the Matrimonial Causes Act 1973, not yet in force as this book goes to press.

[5] Section 8(1) of the Matrimonial Causes Act 1965 provided that "Where a decree of divorce has been made absolute and either (a) there is no right of appeal against the decree absolute; or (b) the time for appealing against the decree absolute has expired without an appeal having been brought; or (c) an appeal against the decree absolute has been dismissed, either party to the marriage may marry again". This provision brought forward the provisions of s. 13(1) of the 1950 Act, which in turn was derived from s. 184 of the Supreme Court of Judicature (Consolidation) Act 1925.

In *McPherson* v. *McPherson*, [1936] A.C. 177, P.C. Lord BLANESBURGH, delivering the advice of the Judicial Committee (in a case admittedly dealing with a Canadian decree, but one as to which the same words were under consideration) said: "But any intervention had to be made before the time for appeal had expired, and before the rights of third parties had intervened. Just as a contract to take shares in a company induced by fraud, and being voidable only, may be set aside before winding up commenced but not later, after the rights of the company's goes to press, has omitted the section which in the former statutes expressly authorised the parties to remarry on the making of the decree absolute; but it is submitted that this omission does not alter the law, and the effect of a decree absolute is still that the parties are free to re-marry. It is for that reason that modern authority has been against the proposition that a decree absolute, once pronounced and sealed, can be impeached for fraud, unless that fraud is one going to jurisdiction, resulting in a failure of natural justice.[1]

Lack of due notice to a respondent at various stages in the proceedings at which notice is necessary has been held to render a decree absolute voidable, or even a nullity[2]; and fraudulent evidence on the question of essential notice, or otherwise, inducing the court to accept jurisdiction when in truth it had none, may have a similar result. There is nothing surprising in the proposition that a decree, though "absolute" in form, may yet be rescinded on such grounds, because, if pronounced by a court with no jurisdiction to pronounce it, it is not a decree absolute at all. There are cases in which the court has gone the full length of rescinding a decree absolute on such grounds, notwithstanding even that the time for appeal has expired and that one or both parties have subsequently gone through a form of marriage.[3] But the fraud has in every such case been fraud bringing about a procedural deficiency, causing a failure of natural justice.[4] And even in such cases, the applica-

---

creditors had intervened, so here, the order absolute cannot be touched after the time for appeal therefrom has passed, and a new status has been acquired . . . . '' For a later criticism of this dictum see note (3) above. *Cf.* in *Australia, Brennan* v. *Brennan* (1953), 89 C.L.R. 129 (H. Ct. of Aus.) at pp. 134–135.

[1] So long ago as *Bater* v. *Bater*, [1906] P. 209 ROMER L.J. said at p. 237: "If a decree absolute for divorce had been obtained in this country at the instance of the wife, and the adultery of the wife had not been disclosed, these courts would not allow that decree to be impeached on any suggestion after the time had elapsed in which the decree had been made absolute". These observations were *obiter*, since *Bater* v. *Bater* was concerned with an application to rescind a New York decree; but the point arose in *Edwards* v. *Edwards*, [1951] P. 228, at p. 234, and that case may be taken as an authority for the proposition that a decree absolute may not be impeached for fraud not going to jurisdiction.

[2] In *McPherson* v. *McPherson* (*supra*) the Judicial Committee held that the privacy which attended the proceedings was such as rendered the decree absolute voidable; but that in the particular circumstances of that case the grant of the decree absolute, after the time for appeal had elapsed, followed by the remarriage of the petitioner, constituted circumstances in which the decree must be allowed to stand, following the general principle that where restoration to the original position has become impossible, rescission will not be ordered. In the later case of *Wiseman* v. *Wiseman*, [1953] P. 79 the analogy from commercial cases was criticised.

[3] *Woolfenden* v. *Woolfenden*, [1947] 2 All E.R. 653; *Everitt* v. *Everitt*, [1948] 2 All E.R. 545 (a case where fraud was not proved); *Wiseman* v. *Wiseman*, [1953] P. 79.

[4] In *McPherson* v. *McPherson*, [1936] A.C. 177, P.C. the defect in procedure consisted of the hearing having taken place behind closed doors. In *Marsh* v. *Marsh*, [1945] A.C. 271 it lay in the decree having been made earlier than the time specified in the notice. No failure of

tion must be that of the respondent, and not that of a mere intervener.[1] And it is submitted that the proper procedure in such a case is by action, and that a decree will not be rescinded on less—e.g. on a motion to rescind.[2]

A decree absolute will not be rescinded, on the other hand, on the ground that it has been procured by the presentation of fraudulent or perjured evidence by the petitioner, if due notice of the proceedings has been given to the respondent at each necessary stage, and if the court has not been deceived into assuming a jurisdiction when in truth it had none.[3]

362 Questions of jurisdiction may arise, depending upon the nature of the "judicial act" impugned. Thus, an application to set aside a bankruptcy order may be made to a judge exercising Bankruptcy jurisdiction[4]; a claim to set aside a judgment establishing a will may be asserted in the Probate Division,[5] and an application to set aside an order of the Privy Council may properly be made to the Judicial Committee.[6] Subject to such questions of exclusive jurisdiction, there seems no reason why the judgment of any court should not be invalidated by proper proceedings by action in either the Queen's Bench, or the Chancery Division of the High Court[7]; and, as will appear in the next paragraph, this course is now generally adopted.

Remedy generally to be sought by action

363 The remedy has in modern times been declared by the House of Lords to be one appropriately to be sought in an action constituted in due

---

natural justice resulted, however, in either case; and the result therefore was that the decree was voidable and not void. For comment on these cases see the judgment of COLLINGWOOD J. in *Edwards* v. *Edwards*, [1951] P. 228.

1 *Kemp-Welch* v. *Kemp-Welch*, [1912] P. 82; *Crosland* v. *Crosland*, [1947] P. 12.

2 *Kemp-Welch* v. *Kemp-Welch supra*. It is difficult to tell from the report which objection was fatal—that the application was that of neither petitioner nor respondent, or that it was not placed before the court by *action*. Perhaps the application would have failed on either ground without the other.

3 *Edwards* v. *Edwards*, [1951] P. 228 per PILCHER J. at p. 238; *per* COLLINGWOOD J. at pp. 244–245.

4 *Motion* v. *Moojen* (1872), L.R. 14 Eq. 202; *Boaler* v. *Power*, [1910] 2 K.B. 229, at p. 232, C.A.

5 *Allen* v. *M'Pherson* (1847), 1 H.L. Cas. 191; *Meluish* v. *Milton* (1876), 3 Ch.D. 27, C.A. (per JAMES L.J. at p. 33); *Priestman* v. *Thomas* (1884), 9 P.D. 210, per HANNEN P. at p. 76 of the report of the case in the court of first instance (1884), 9 P.D. 70. In *Australia*, *In re Gillard*, [1949] V.L.R. 378, in which BARRY J. revoked a grant of Probate obtained by fraud on the court more than 40 years earlier.

6 *Ram Narayan Singh* v. *Adhindra Nath Mukerji*, [1917] A.C. 100, P.C.

7 Thus in *Dunn* v. *Cox* (1853), 11 Hare 61, the bill in Chancery prayed the setting aside of an order made in the Court of Exchequer, and, though the plaintiff failed, because his proof was not sufficient, the jurisdiction was not denied.

form.[1] While in particular cases it may be permissible to use other procedures,[2] the full factual investigation which is possible only in the conduct of a properly constituted action renders this procedure preferable in the absence of exceptional circumstances.[3] The prayer for relief should ask that the judgment impeached be set aside, and may also ask in proper cases for a declaration of the invalidity of the order made.[4]

No leave is necessary before such an action can be commenced,[5] and the plaintiff cannot be put upon terms before being allowed to proceed[6]; but it must appear from the pleadings that the case for the plaintiff will be a strong case, or the claim may be stayed as vexatious.[7]

It is no longer considered good practice to attempt to set up, as an answer in an action founded on a judgment or order, the defence that the judgment or order was in fact procured by fraud.[8] He who alleges this should make a positive allegation in an action brought for the express purpose of having the former judgment declared void for fraud in its procuring.[9] The advantages of this procedure have already been noticed above. But the court of Bankruptcy is in a peculiar position in this respect; it may inquire into the consideration even of a judgment debt, and may go behind a judgment proved to have been obtained by fraud, even though no proceeding has been commenced for its impeachment. But it is by no means bound to do so, and indeed ought not to do so except when a strong *prima facie* case has been made out.[10]

---

[1] *Jonesco* v. *Beard*, [1930] A.C. 298, H.L.; *cf.* the earlier opinion to the same effect expressed by the Judicial Committee in *Hip Foong Hong* v. *H. Neotia & Co.*, [1918] A.C. 888, P.C. at p. 894. In *Australia*, see *McHarg* v. *Woods Radio Pty.*, *Ltd.*, [1948] V.L.R. 496. In *New Zealand*, *Hurlstone* v. *Steadman*, [1937] N.Z.L.R. 708, C.A.

[2] See the special cases referred to in para. 362 above; the application to the Privy Council to recall one of its own judgments on the ground of fraud in *Ram Narayan Singh* v. *Adhindra Nath Mukerji*, [1917] A.C. 100 is an outstanding example. *Cf. Hip Foong Hong* v. *H. Neotia & Co.*, *supra*.

[3] *Jonesco* v. *Beard*, *supra*.

[4] Such relief was prayed in all or almost all of the cases cited in support of the text of paras. 363–365 above.

[5] *Isherwood, Foster and Stacey, Ltd.* v. *Miglio*, [1938] W.N. 189.

[6] *Kennedy* v. *Dandrick*, [1943] 2 All E.R. 606; [1943] Ch. 291.

[7] *Birch* v. *Birch*, [1902] P. 130. The disinclination of the courts to encourage actions without a very strong foundation is well illustrated by the judgments in the Court of Appeal in *Flower* v. *Lloyd*, (No. 2) (1879), 10 Ch.D 327, C.A. For more recent dicta see *Everett* v. *Ribbands* (1946), 175 L.T. 143, C.A. In *Australia*, see *per* HERRING C.J. in *McHarg* v. *Woods Radio Pty.*, *Ltd.*, [1948] V.L.R. 496, at p. 498; *per* GILLARD J. in *Price* v. *Stone*, [1964] V.R. 106.

[8] Mr Spencer Bower notices, in former editions, such cases as the *Duchess of Kingston's Case* (1776), 2 Sm.L.C. (13th edn.) 644; *Perry* v. *Meddowcroft* (1846), 10 Beav. 122 and *Eyre* v. *Smith* (1877), 2 C.P.D. 435, in which the court was asked to remove the obstacles imposed in the way of prosecutions or claims by judgments affecting the parties, on the ground that those judgments had been obtained by fraud.

[9] *Jonesco* v. *Beard* (*supra*); *Stern* v. *Friedmann*, [1953] 2 All E.R. 565.

[10] See *Re Flatau* (1888), 22 Q.B.D. 83, C.A. *per* Lord ESHER M.R. at p. 85, FRY L.J. at p. 86

"Slip rule" not available to remedy fraud

364   When a judgment has been given in favour of the party on the merits entitled to succeed, but by reason of misrepresentation of the other party that judgment has been entered in a form or to an effect different from that which would have followed had the court been correctly informed, the injured party cannot require the court, in the exercise of its inherent powers under the "slip rule", to amend the judgment, in as much as the judgment as it stands represents the true intention of the court, albeit on a wrong view of the facts.   The injured party may in a case of fraud bring an action to set the judgment aside; or, as may in such circumstances appear more convenient, may appeal from the judgment to the Court of Appeal, applying in this regard for an extension of time in which to appeal.[1]

365   The person entitled to maintain the proceedings or set up the defence is the person against whom the decision was pronounced or, where he was not a party to the proceedings, whose status and interests were injuriously affected thereby.[2]   In the former case, the defendant, or person against whom the relief should be sought, is the party who procured the decision; in the latter, the plaintiff must attack both parties to the cause in which it was given, for he can only succeed by establishing the collusion of both in deceiving the court.[3]

Consent judgment may be set aside for innocent misrepresentation

366   While it is necessary, in order to have a judgment set aside which has been given in contested litigation, to show fraud in its procuring, it is possible to set aside a consent judgment on the ground that it has been obtained by innocent misrepresentation to the court, for such a judgment is regarded as of the nature of a contract between the parties.[4]

---

and LOPES L.J. at p. 87; and *Boaler* v. *Power*, [1910] 2 K.B. 229.   In *Australia* see *Cameron* v. *Cole* (1943), 68 C.L.R. 571 (H. Ct. of Aus.).

[1] *MacCarthy* v. *Agard*, [1933] 2 K.B. 417, C.A. *per* GREER L.J. and ROMER L.J., SCRUTTON L.J. dissenting.   This course has obvious advantages in divorce, where a decree absolute is attacked on the ground of lack of notice—see, for instance, *Everitt* v. *Everitt*, [1948] 2 All E.R. 545, C.A. (not a fraud case).

[2] Thus in *Perry* v. *Meddowcroft* (1846), 10 Beav. 122 the plaintiff, who asked the court to treat as a nullity the sentence of the ecclesiastical court pronouncing the marriage of his ancestors void, was, at the time when it was pronounced *en ventre sa mère*.   In *Harrod* v. *Benton* (1828), 8 B. & C. 217 and *Nixon* v. *Loundes*, [1909] 2 I.R. 1 he was an execution creditor.

[3] As in the *Duchess of Kingston's Case* (1776), 2 Sm. L.C. (13 ed.) 644, *Harrod* v. *Benton*, *supra*, *Perry* v. *Meddowcroft*, *supra* and *Nixon* v. *Loundes*, *supra*.

[4] *Ainsworth* v. *Wilding*, [1896] 1 Ch. 673; *Wilding* v. *Sanderson*, [1897] 2 Ch. 534, C.A. at p. 550 *per* LINDLEY L.J.; *Thorne* v. *Smith*, [1947] K.B. 307, C.A. *per* SCOTT L.J. at p. 311.

But it is as necessary in the case of a consent judgment as it is in the case of a contested one, or even more necessary, to take positive action to have the judgment set aside in proceedings constituted for this purpose; for in the case of a consent judgment considerations of estoppel operate to prevent the defence of fraud being set up so long as the judgment relied upon remains upon the record.[1]

What must be alleged and proved

367   The pleadings must allege, and the evidence must prove, more than was before the court in the first proceedings. Fraud must specifically be alleged, and full particulars of it must be given.[2]   The action is much more than merely a rehearing of the earlier one.   It is not open to the court, under the guise of the new action, simply to reinvestigate the same questions of credibility or of proof which exercised the court on the original hearing, and then, on the same or substantially the same evidence, to conclude that the view of the former court was a mistaken one.[3]   The plaintiff must show that the judgment in the first action was procured by the fraud of the party or parties in whose favour judgment was given,[4] except in the case of a judgment as to a will,[5] and in certain other very special cases.[6]   Merely to prove that the judgment was obtained by perjury is in general insufficient.[7]   Fraud in the court itself (not a usual case) will be sufficient to found an action.[8]

---

[1] *Parker* v. *Simpson* (1869), 18 W.R. 204; *Priestman* v. *Thomas* (1884), 9 P.D. 210; *Kinch* v. *Walcott*, [1929] A.C. 482, P.C. at p. 493.

[2] *Jonesco* v. *Beard*, [1930] A.C. 298, H.L. at p. 300. In *Australia*, *Cabassi* v. *Vila* (1940), 64 C.L.R. 130 (H. Ct. of Aus.) *per* WILLIAMS J. at p. 146; *McHarg* v. *Woods Radio Pty.*, *Ltd.*, [1948] V.L.R. 496.

[3] *Everett* v. *Ribbands* (1946), 175 L.T. 143 C.A.

[4] Just as in the ordinary action for misrepresentation, a mere general allegation of fraud will not be sufficient. See *Meddowcroft* v. *Huguenin* (1844), 4 Moo. P.C.C. 386; *Perry* v. *Meddowcroft* (1846), 10 Beav. 122; *Birch* v. *Birch*, [1902] P. 130, C.A. at p. 138. In *Australia* see *Price* v. *Stone*, [1964] V.R. 106, where GILLARD J. pointed out the necessity of proving a deliberate fraud upon the court as a foundation of this relief, and contrasted this with misleading or erroneous evidence falling short of this requirement. In *New Zealand*, *Giffen* v. *Leggatt* (1902), 20 N.Z.L.R. 427. This last point comes in for emphasis in *Jonesco* v. *Beard*, *supra* at the end of the judgment. In *Australia*, see *Ronald* v. *Harper*, [1913] V.L.R. 311 (Full Court of Victoria). In *New Zealand*, *Hurlstone* v. *Steadman*, [1937] N.Z.L.R. 708 C.A.

[5] See *Guardhouse* v. *Blackburn* (1866), L.R. 1 P. & D. 109, *per* Sir J. P. WILDE at p. 116; *Betts* v. *Doughty* (1870), 5 P.D. 26; *Birch* v. *Birch*, *supra*, *per* COZENS-HARDY L.J. at p. 138. And see Chapter XIII of the authors' *Doctrine of Res Judicata* (2nd edn.).

[6] Such as *Ram Narayan Singh* v. *Adhindra Nath Mukerji*, [1917] A.C. 100, P.C.

[7] *Baker* v. *Wadsworth* (1898), 67 L.J. Q.B. 301; *Everett* v. *Ribbands* (1946), 175 L.T. 143 C.A. But there are cases in which, on proof of perjury and little more, the circumstances have been sufficient to persuade the court to grant the relief—see, in *Australia*, *Luxford* v. *Reeves*, [1941] V.L.R. 118; *cf. per* HERRING J. in the later Victorian case of *McHarg* v. *Woods Radio Pty.*, *Ltd.*, [1948] V.L.R. 496 at p. 498; *Price* v. *Stone*, [1964] V.R. 106 (GILLARD J.).

[8] *Cammell* v. *Sewell* (1858), 3 H. & N. 617, 646.

The plaintiff must also establish inducement and materiality,[1] and all the other elements in the burden of proof which would rest upon him in any ordinary action founded on fraudulent misrepresentation,[2] the court being substituted for him as the representee, *quoad* the representation, but not injury, which, of course, he must prove to have been occasioned to himself. This injury in ordinary cases is proved by the judgment itself, but in cases where the aggrieved person was not a party to the suit in which it was pronounced, he must show that his status, title, or rights were necessarily affected by it to his prejudice.[3] He has only to prove the fact of such injury; no question of the amount of damages arises, for the action only lies for annulment, not for compensation. He must always explain why the matters alleged could not have been brought forward at the original trial.[4] The proceedings, when instituted by the person aggrieved, or the defence, when such person relies on the improper procuring of the "judicial act" by way of plea, being alike in the nature of an assertion of the right to have the judgment invalidated or treated as invalid, are both subject to all such affirmative

---

[1] That is to say, he must prove in ordinary cases that the court was induced to give the judgment by the misrepresentation, and that such misrepresentation was of a nature to produce that effect (see Chapter VI, *ante*, as to inducement and materiality). Thus in *Flower* v. *Lloyd*, (*No. 2*) (1879), 10 Ch.D. 327, C.A., one of the grounds on which the plaintiff failed was that he had not established that the misrepresentations to the court were material (see pp. 332, 333); and in *Boswell* v. *Coaks* (1894), 6 R. 167, H.L., the plaintiff failed to show that the disclosure of the whole truth to the court would have had any effect upon its decision (*per* Lord Selborne at pp. 170–174); see also *Hip Foong Hong* v. *H. Neotia & Co.*, [1918] A.C. 888, P.C. Where it is a case of a consent judgment or order, or a compromise sanctioned by the court, the person claiming relief must prove primarily as in ordinary cases, that *he* was deceived by the misrepresentation into consenting, and, incidentally, that the court was also deceived thereby into giving effect to such consent by a duly recorded "judicial act": see *Brooke* v. *Lord Mostyn* (1864), 2 De G.J. & Sm. 373, where Turner and Knight-Bruce L.JJ., reversing Romilly M.R., held that the plaintiff had shown that he was induced by misrepresentation and suppression of material facts and documents to agree to the compromise, and also that it was possible that the Master in Chambers might have been induced thereby to sanction it; *Eyre* v. *Smith* (1877), 2 C.P.D. 435, C.A. (inducement to creditors to consent to resolutions for liquidation by arrangement, and to the registrar to register them); *Sturrock* v. *Littlejohn* (1898), 68 L.J. Q.B. 165, Div. Ct. (consent of party to judgment); *Wyatt* v. *Palmer*, [1899] 2 Q.B. 106, C.A. (where "the defendant induced the plaintiff to allow the defendant to enter judgment"). In *Australia*, see *Ronald* v. *Harper*, [1913] V.L.R. 311 (Full Court of Victoria).

[2] As stated in Chapter XI, para. 185, *ante*.

[3] As in *Perry* v. *Meddowcroft* (1846), 10 Beav. 122.

[4] In *Birch* v. *Birch*, [1902] P. 130, C.A., it was held that there must be a suggestion in the statement of claim, if it is to escape being struck out as frivolous and vexatious, of such facts, only discovered since the trial, as, if proved, would render it reasonably probable that the judgment would be upset, though the facts suggested need not necessarily be such as would have been evidence at the trial (*per* Vaughan Williams L.J. at pp. 136, 137). In *Victoria*, Herring C.J. struck out a statement of claim in *McHarg* v. *Woods Radio Pty., Ltd.*, [1948] V.L.R. 496, where it alleged that the defendant had obtained the judgment by perjured evidence, but there was no allegation of any new discovery or of fresh facts, nor was any such evidence adduced on the hearing of the application to strike out the statement of claim.

answers as would be available to any representor as against a representee asserting the invalidity of a contract in any form of proceeding[1]; such as a plea that the subsequent acts and conduct of the party have been of a nature to render it unjust, either to innocent third parties, or to the guilty party himself, to disturb the "judicial act",[2] or pleas of knowledge, affirmation, and the like.[3]

Foreign judgments procured by fraudulent misrepresentation

368   A foreign judgment, that is to say, a judgment pronounced by any court not within the English jurisdiction, whether a court of a foreign State, or an Irish, Scottish, or Colonial court, or a court of any member-country of the British Commonwealth, is, no less than an English judgment, and on no other principle,[4] treated as void, and ignored by the courts of this country, on proof that it was obtained by the fraud of one or both of the parties,[5] or by that of the court itself[6]; and such proof establishes a defence to an action on the

---

[1] See Chapter XIV, *ante*.

[2] See *Davenport* v. *Stafford* (1845), 8 Beav. 503, *per* Lord LANGDALE M.R. at pp. 522–523.

[3] *Dunn* v. *Cox* (1853), 11 Hare 61, where, though the plaintiff averred that he was ignorant of the true facts at the date of the consent order whereby the defendant was to pay him a certain sum of money, he carefully abstained from suggesting that he did not know of them at the time when he received the agreed sum.   On this, and other, grounds PAGE-WOOD V.-C. allowed the demurrer to the bill.

[4] The principle is that the defendant has entered into an implied contract to pay the amount of the debt declared by the judgment to be payable, and this principle is applicable to English and foreign judgments indifferently: *per* Lord ESHER M.R. at p. 303 of *Grant* v. *Easton* (1883), 13 Q.B.D. 302, C.A.; Lord COLERIDGE C.J. at p. 303 of *Abouloff* v. *Oppenheimer* (1882), 10 Q.B.D. 295, C.A.; LINDLEY L.J. at p. 316 of *Vadala* v. *Lawes* (1890), 25 Q.B.D. 310, C.A. Anything, therefore, which would invalidate any contract, such as fraudulent misrepresentation, would equally invalidate this particular type of implied contract.   "The English court does not seek to assert jurisdiction over the foreign court; it proceeds upon the principle that the person seeking to enforce the judgment is in conscience debarred from doing so", ATKIN L.J. in *Ellerman Lines, Ltd.* v. *Read*, [1928] 2 K.B. 144, C.A. at p. 155.   For a discussion of what is properly meant by a "foreign" court in this context, see the authors' *Doctrine of Res Judicata* (2nd edn.) pp. 65–66.

[5] *Earl of Bandon* v. *Becher* (1835), 3 Cl. & Fin. 479; *Bowles* v. *Orr* (1835), 1 Y & C. Ex. 464, at p. 473; *Bank of Australasia* v. *Nias* (1851), 16 Q.B. 717, *per* Lord CAMPBELL C.J. at p. 735; *Cammell* v. *Sewell* (1858), 3 H. & N. 617, *per* MARTIN B. at p. 646; *Gossain* v. *Gossain* (1860), 8 W.R. 196, P.C. (an Indian judgment); *Ochsenbein* v. *Papelier* (1873), 8 Ch. App. 695 (*per* Lord SELBORNE L.C. at pp. 698–700, and MELLISH L.J. at pp. 700, 701); *Abouloff* v. *Oppenheimer, supra*; *Manger* v. *Cash* (1889), 5 T.L.R. 271, Div. Ct.; *Vadala* v. *Lawes, supra*; *Ellerman Lines, Ltd.* v. *Read, supra*.

[6] See *Price* v. *Dewhurst* (1837), 8 Sim. 279, a case where the foreign tribunal, being interested in the suit, had fraudulently decided in its own favour, and where SHADWELL V.-C. accordingly observes: "it would be idle to say that any regard or attention ought to be paid to such a proceeding as this" (p. 308), and, further, "the court is bound to treat this decision as of no value and no substance.   And my opinion is that I am at liberty to deal with . . . the parties I find upon this record, and with the property, if they have received any by force of the judgment, just in the same manner as if" it had never been given (pp. 308, 309): and he concludes: "I

judgment. It is not necessarily an answer to the plea that the evidence to prove the fraudulent misrepresentation is the very same evidence that was adduced in support of the case set up by the aggrieved party before the court which pronounced the judgment[1]; nor that the court was not ignorant of the truth.[2] But it is an answer to shew that by the practice of the foreign court, evidence of fraud is inadmissible to impeach the agreement or transaction sued upon.[3] The relief available to an aggrieved party against whom a foreign judgment has been obtained by fraud is different from that which the law makes available to one against whom an English judgment has fraudulently been obtained. He against whom a foreign judgment has been obtained by fraud may of course plead and prove the fraud by way of plea or answer to any action or proceedings in this country on the foreign judgment,[4] or wherever, in any action or proceedings in England, the foreign judgment is sought to be made use of in any manner as an obstacle to the success of his claim or defence, as the case may be; and he may ask the English court to treat it as, and for this purpose to declare it to be, a nullity.[5] But obviously he cannot take active proceedings in the courts of England for the purpose of rescinding any decree or order made by a court of a foreign State, or even by a court of any part of Her Majesty's Dominions other than England, on the ground that it was obtained by fraud. Such an order for rescission would be ineffectual, and would in addition constitute a gross breach of international good manners. But it is possible, in cases where such relief would be effective, for the injured party to succeed on an application in

---

am at liberty to declare that this foreign judgment, so far as it has tended to give any interest to Mr Dewhurst, or any of the other defendants, is fraudulent and void" (p. 309). This decision was affirmed (1838), 4 My. & Cr. 76 (*per* Lord COTTENHAM L.C. at pp. 84, 85). *Cf.* the opinion of MARTIN B. at p. 646 of *Cammell* v. *Sewell*, *supra*, who distinctly mentions "fraud in the court itself", as well as fraud practised upon the court by a party, as a ground for impeaching a foreign judgment. In *Abouloff* v. *Oppenheimer*, *infra*, the defence, which was unsuccessfully demurred to, alleged fraudulent misrepresentation to, and concealment from, the High Court of Tiflis in the Caucasus, and also general corruption in that court itself. The last allegation was bad, as not averring any fraud of the court *in hac re*, and, to the (original) author's knowledge, though this incident is not reported, was struck out in chambers.

[1] *Abouloff* v. *Oppenheimer* (1882), 10 Q.B.D. 295, C.A., *per* BRETT L.J. at p. 307; *Vadala* v. *Lawes* (1890), 25 Q.B.D. 310, C.A., *per* LINDLEY L.J. at pp. 316–320.

[2] See the cases cited in notes 5 and 6 above.

[3] *Robinson* v. *Fenner*, [1913] 3 K.B. 835 (*per* CHANNELL J. at pp. 842–843.)

[4] See all cases cited in note 5 on p. 379, except *Gossain* v. *Gossain* (1860), 8 W.R. 196. In *Ochsenbein* v. *Papelier* (1873), 8 Ch. App. 695, the Chancery court refused to entertain a motion to restrain proceedings at law on a foreign judgment said to have been procured by fraud, because proof of such fraud is a complete defence at law.

[5] See *Price* v. *Dewhurst*, cited in note 6 on p. 379; *Gossain* v. *Gossain*, *supra*, where a party, for the purpose of establishing his claim, was forced to rely on an Indian judgment procured by fraud, and in breach of a compromise of previous litigation, and, this judgment being treated as a nullity, his claim fell with it.

this country for an injunction restraining him who has fraudulently obtained a foreign judgment from proceeding to enforce it. So in *Ellerman Lines, Ltd.* v. *Read*[1] where a judgment had been obtained (it was held, by fraud) in Turkey against a British ship, and a British subject, present within the jurisdiction of the English court, was seeking to enforce that judgment in Turkey, the court had no hesitation in issuing a writ of injunction restraining him from doing so.[2]

Where the foreign judgment is registered or is sought to be registered under the Foreign Judgments (Reciprocal Enforcement) Act 1933, the party against whom it has been obtained may apply to have the registration set aside, or may resist registration on the ground that it has been obtained by fraud.

Foreign judgments in rem: foreign decrees in divorce

369   It has been seen in the preceding paragraph that on an action in an English court on a judgment *inter partes* given in a foreign court it is a good defence to show that the foreign judgment was obtained by fraud. Exactly the same considerations do not apply to foreign judgments *in rem*, for a judgment *in rem* takes effect "against all the world" to create or change the status of the persons or things of which it is the subject. *Castrique* v. *Behrens*[3] is an authority of long standing for the proposition that a foreign judgment *in rem* cannot be attacked, on the ground of fraud in procuring it, in an English court, while it remains unreversed in the jurisdiction in which it was pronounced.

This principle is carried into the field of decrees in divorce.[4] When a decree granted in a foreign jurisdiction is made the subject of attack on the ground that it has been procured by fraud, it is necessary to inquire whether the fraud went to jurisdiction, or merely to a decision within jurisdiction. Where the foreign court has been persuaded by fraud to assume jurisdiction which in truth it did not have, the fraud, if proved in an English court, will result in that court's refusal to recognise the

---

1 *Ellerman Lines, Ltd.* v. *Read*, [1928] 2 K.B. 144, C.A.

2 ". . . when the argument against issuing (an injunction) was used (in *Lord Portarlington* v. *Soulby* (1834), 3 My. & K. 104, 107) that this court had no authority to bind a foreign court, the answer was given, that the injunction was not directed to the foreign court, but to the party within the jurisdiction here. A very good answer, it appears to me"—*per* SCRUTTON L.J. at pp. 151–152. The same Lord Justice at pp. 152–153 said "If there is no authority for this it is time that we made one, for I cannot conceive that if an English court finds a British subject taking proceedings in breach of his contract in a foreign court, supporting those proceedings, and obtaining a judgment, by fraudulent lies, it is powerless to interfere to restrain him from seeking to enforce that judgment". So, too, ATKIN L.J. on p. 155, EVE J. on p. 158.

3 (1861), 3 E. & E. 709.

4 A decree in divorce is a judgment *in rem*—*Edwards* v. *Edwards*, [1951] P. 228 at p. 234.

foreign decree—for the court which pronounced it had no jurisdiction to do so.[1] But if the jurisdiction of the foreign court to adjudicate upon the matter is acknowledged, or proved, and the complaint is that the evidence which persuaded the court to its conclusion was perjured or fraudulent, then the decree made by a foreign court within its jurisdiction, will stand as valid in this country until it is set aside in the country of its making.[2]

Setting aside awards

370   The award of an arbitrator rests upon the contract of the disputants to invest such arbitrator with judicial authority as between themselves: and the court will enforce such contracts, and also the awards founded upon them, with certain recognised exceptions; one of which is, where the award was obtained either by fraudulent misrepresentation of a party made to the arbitrator, or by fraudulent collusion between him and the arbitrator, in which case the party aggrieved may apply to the court to set aside the award, and on proof of these facts, the burden of which is on him, he is entitled to the relief prayed,[3] unless there has been an express agreement between the parties, which would appear to be valid,[4] that neither of them should impeach the decision of the arbitrator on any suggestion whatsoever, even of fraud.

In *Victoria*, an award of a capital sum of Workers' Compensation by the Workers' Compensation Board having been obtained by the fraud of the claimant, the defendant was successful in obtaining in the Supreme

---

[1] *Bonaparte* v. *Bonaparte*, [1892] P. 402; *Macalpine* v. *Macalpine*, [1958] P. 35, at p. 42 (SACHS J.); *Middleton* v. *Middleton*, [1967] P. 62, at pp. 69, 76 (CAIRNS J.).

[2] *Bater* v. *Bater*, [1906] P. 209 C.A.   The President, Sir GORELL BARNES, at p. 219 said: "The one form always is to set aside a decree, and not treat it as a nullity because somebody has withheld something. I think these cases differ in their results from cases where there is a decree *inter partes* simply, and upon an action brought on a foreign judgment fraud can be pleaded, . . . there is a defence, and that is because the court will not enforce that foreign judgment. Nothing is done to set it aside, but it is not enforced. That, I do not think, is applicable to cases like this."   He was affirmed on appeal.   At p. 239 on the appeal COZENS-HARDY L.J. said "It (the New York decree) is conclusive there unless and until set aside, and I see no ground for allowing its validity to be impeached in this country. The suppression of evidence does not go to the point of jurisdiction, and it would be dangerous to countenance the idea that a final decree of divorce, changing the status of the parties, can be reopened or questioned in this country when it could not be questioned in the court which granted the divorce." *Macalpine* v. *Macalpine*, [1958] P. 35 (SACHS J.) at p. 42.   In *Middleton* v. *Middleton*, [1967] P. 62 CAIRNS J. said at p. 69 "If a decree of divorce has been obtained in a foreign court by false evidence about the matrimonial offence relied on, it will not on that ground be treated by the English court as invalid provided it has not been set aside in the foreign court: *Bater* v. *Bater*."

[3] For the rules as to setting aside awards, see the authors' *Doctrine of Res Judicata* (2nd edn.) Chapter XIII, para. 374.

[4] *Tullis* v. *Jacson*, [1892] 3 Ch. 440.

Court of Victoria a declaration that the award ought not to be enforced, and an injunction restraining a guilty party from enforcing it—and this notwithstanding that the statute conferring jurisdiction on the Board had provided that no determination or award of the Board should be called in question in any court "on any account whatsoever".[1]

Misrepresentations to the Crown or to public authorities

371 There is a rule of very ancient standing that whenever the Crown, or an officer or department of the State, is induced by misrepresentation of material facts to grant any privilege to a subject, whereby the rights and interests of any other subject, or of the King's other subjects in general, must of necessity be proportionately curtailed, such grant, on the proper proceedings being taken by the proper parties, may be revoked, withdrawn, repealed, or avoided, or, without being so avoided, may be treated as void.[2] This rule has been applied to grants by the Crown of lands and tenements markets,[3] charters of incorporation,[4] privileges and monopolies in respect of inventions,[5] trade marks, or designs, and other exclusive rights and licences.[6]

372 The party entitled to raise the question of the invalidity of the grant by reason of misrepresentation to the Crown, is in the first place, the Attorney-General, as representing the Crown[7]; and, secondly, every fellow-subject of the grantee who is directly or indirectly injured by the

---

[1] *Luxford* v. *Reeves*, [1941] V.L.R. 118 (Full Court of Victoria).

[2] For the general principles applicable when the King is "deceived in his grant", see Com. Dig. Grant, G.8. Similar rules obtained in Roman law with respect to the *fallax petitor* who obtained grants and privileges from the Emperor by misrepresentation.

[3] See the following: *Case of Alton Woods* (1599), 1 Co. Rep. 40b, Ex. Ch.; *R.* v. *Kempe* (1694), 1 Ld. Raym. 49; *Morgan* v. *Seaward* (1837), 2 M. & W. 544 (*per Cur.*, at p. 561); *Gledstanes* v. *Earl of Sandwich* (1842) 4 Man. & G. 995; *Great Eastern Rail. Co.* v. *Goldsmid* (1884), 9 App. Cas. 927, H.L.

[4] See *R.* v. *Boucher* (1842), 3 Q.B. 641; *Eastern Archipelago Co.* v. *R.* (1853), 2 E. & B. 856 (mispaginated 568 in the report), Exch. Ch.; *La Banque d'Hochelaga* v. *Murray* (1889), 15 App. Cas. 414, P.C.

[5] *R.* v. *Wheeler* (1819), 2 B. & Ald. 345; *Hill* v. *Thompson* (1818), 8 Taunt. 375; *Brunton* v. *Hawkes* (1821), 4 B. & Ald. 541; *Morgan* v. *Seaward*, *supra*; *Nickels* v. *Ross* (1849), 8 C.B. 679. Letters patent in respect of inventions are now sealed with the seal of the Patent Office, and not, as previously, with the Great Seal of the United Kingdom,—see Patents and Designs Act 1907 (7 Edw. 7, c. 29), s. 14 (1),—and the procedure to obtain revocation is altered, but the theory on which a patent is revoked in case of misrepresentation, *viz.*, that the State is deceived thereby into granting a privilege that it otherwise would not have granted, remains.

[6] Such as a right to take wreck: *Alcock* v. *Cooke* (1829), 5 Bing. 340; trade marks, it may be noticed, are now the subject of statutory provisions.

[7] *Case of Alton Woods*, *supra*; *R.* v. *Butler* (1685), 3 Lev. 220; *R.* v. *Kempe*, *supra*; *R.* v. *Wheeler*, *supra*; *Eastern Archipelago Co.* v. *R.*, *infra*; *La Banque d'Hochelaga* v. *Murray*, *infra*.

grant,[1] or even one who is not interested, if those interested would be entitled to relief if they chose to apply for it,[2] since the prerogative of the Crown in this respect is the privilege of the subject, and the Crown cannot fetter the exercise and enjoyment of a privilege which is vested in it for the public good, so that, whether directly or indirectly in virtue of his right to call upon the Crown to exercise its powers of revocation, the subject is *ex debito justitiae* entitled to have a franchise procured by misrepresentation forfeited.[3]

373   Effect is given to the opinion of the court that the grant is void on the ground of misrepresentation in one of two ways: either by a repeal— which, ordinarily, must be *in toto*, or not at all[4]—of the charter or patent at the instance of the Attorney-General, whether moving *ex officio*, or on the relation of a subject aggrieved,[5] or by treating the grant as a nullity on the establishment by a party litigant of a right to have it so treated, when it is relied upon by the opposite party as the foundation of his case or a link in his chain of proof.[6]   The procedure to obtain the repeal of a charter, patent, or other grant, is information or action by way of *scire facias*[7] which appears still to be available for this limited purpose.

What must be proved

374   The party claiming to have the grant avoided, or treated as void,

---

[1] See *Alcock* v. *Cooke*, *supra*; *Morgan* v. *Seaward*, *supra* (per PARKE B. delivering the judgment of the Court of Exchequer, at p. 561: "such a grant is void not against the Crown merely, but in a suit against a third person"); *Eastern Archipelago Co.* v. *R.*, *supra*; *La Banque d'Hochelaga* v. *Murray*, *supra* (where the defendants, who were entitled to raise the question of the invalidity of the grant of a charter of incorporation to a certain company as corporators of which they were being sued, fortified their position by procuring the Attorney-General of the Colony to proceed, on their relation, by way of *scire facias* against the company to repeal the charter, such proceeding being consolidated with the action).

[2] *Great Eastern Rail. Co.* v. *Goldsmid*, *supra*, per Lord SELBORNE L.C. at p. 940.

[3] *Eastern Archipelago Co.* v. *R.* (1853), 2 E. & B. 856 (misprinted 568), Exch. Ch., per PLATT B. at p. 884, CRESWELL J. at p. 886, and JERVIS C.J. at p. 914 in the Exchequer Chamber.

[4] *La Banque d'Hochelaga* v. *Murray* (1889), 15 App. Cas. 414, P.C., at pp. 426–428.   *Cf.* Chapter XIII, for the like rule in rescission.   An exception arises in such a case as *Vancouver City* v. *Vancouver Lumber Co.*, [1911] A.C. 711, P.C., at pp. 720, 721.

[5] See the cases cited in note 1 above.

[6] As in *Hill* v. *Thompson*, *Brunton* v. *Hawkes*, *Alcock* v. *Cooke*, *Morgan* v. *Seaward*, *Gledstanes* v. *Earl of Sandwich*, and *Nickels* v. *Ross*, cited in notes 5 and 6 on p. 383.   In *R.* v. *Boucher* (1842), 3 Q.B. 641, where the immediate question for decision was the validity of a rate, which raised incidentally the further question of the validity of the charter of incorporation of the borough making the rate, the court of Q.B., though with great doubt and hesitation, thought it safer not to decide the latter question, but to take the facts as they found them, the rate having been made by a borough which *de facto* existed as such, and none of the inhabitants having taken any steps to get the charter revoked.

[7] And this remedy is in no way curtailed or affected by the mere fact that a new and summary form of relief is provided by the instrument itself: *Eastern Archipelago Co.* v. *R.* *supra* (per TALFOURD J. at pp. 874, 875.).

must prove that a representation, in the proper sense of the word, was made to the Crown.

> "But where the words are the words of the King, and it appears that he has only mistaken the law, then he shall not be said to be deceived, to the avoidance of the grant".[1]

The representation must be shown to have been made either directly, as, for instance, in a petition or memorial,[2] or declaration[3] on which the grant was founded, or presumptively; and such presumption is irrebuttably made when not to make it would necessarily involve an imputation on the honour of the Crown, or, in other words, where the choice is between an inference that the Crown was deceived by the party, and an inference that the Crown itself practised a deceit upon the grantee, as in the case of a grant to two of one and the same estate, or of overlapping estates or interests.[4] But it is impossible to make any such presumption in cases where a grant is only made after a previous inquiry under a writ of *ad quod damnum*,[5] unless clear proof is forthcoming that the inquiry itself was conducted clandestinely and fraudulently.[6] Next, the burden is on the party impeaching the grant of proving that the statements actually or presumptively made, or to be implied from the express statements,[7]

---

[1] *R.* v. *Kempe* (1694), 1 Ld. Raym. 49.

[2] As in *R.* v. *Boucher* (1842), 3 Q.B. 641 (a case of a petition or memorial by a borough praying a charter of incorporation).

[3] As in *La Banque d'Hochelaga* v. *Murray* (1889), 15 App. Cas. 414, P.C. (where the misrepresentation was contained in a declaration verifying a petition for letters patent for the incorporation of a company).

[4] *Alcock* v. *Cooke* (1829), 5 Bing 340, per BEST C.J. delivering the judgment of the Court of Common Pleas, at p. 354. In *Gledstanes* v. *Earl of Sandwich* (1842), 4 Man. & G. 995, TINDAL C.J. delivering the judgment of the same court lays down, at pp. 1028, 1029, that "the cases in which the King's grant has been held to be avoided by reason of any misdescription or mistake therein . . . will be found to fall under one of three classes; first, where the King has by his grant professed to give a greater estate than he had himself in the subject-matter of the grant; . . . secondly, where the King has already granted the same estate, or part of the same estate, to another . . .; thirdly, where the King has been deceived in the consideration expressed in the grant; as when the consideration is untruly stated, or the subject of the grant has been recited to be of less value than it really is, or where . . .the King recites a former grant of an office for life, and then grants the same office to J.S., whereas in truth either the King had not granted the office for life, or the office had not been surrendered; here the grant would be void because there was no such consideration as was recited". In all three classes, the law must presume that the King was deceived by false information or suggestion on the part of the applicant.

[5] *Great Eastern Rail. Co.* v. *Goldsmid* (1884), 9 App. Cas. 927, H.L., per Lord SELBORNE L.C. at pp. 939, 940.

[6] As in *R.* v. *Butler* (1685), 3 Lev. 220, a case noticed, in order to distinguish it from that which was then before the House, by Lord SELBORNE L.C. at p. 942 of *Great Eastern Rail Co.* v. *Goldsmid*, *supra*.

[7] In *R.* v. *Boucher* (1842), 3 Q.B. 641, the petition to the Crown referred to "the condition of the gaol", which was an implied representation that there was a gaol in the borough, and, there being none in fact at the time, an implied misrepresentation.

were false.[1] The misrepresentation proved must be shown to have been material,[2] and to have induced the Crown to issue the charter or letters patent.[3] Though in most of the reported cases the misrepresentation was both false and fraudulent, it does not appear that fraud must necessarily be proved, notwithstanding the constant use of such expressions as "the King is deceived in his grant", which merely import that the Crown has been misled into conferring a privilege upon a subject, to the prejudice of the rest of the community, which prejudice is the real justification for avoiding the grant, and is obviously unaffected by the question of the personal honesty or dishonesty of the grantee.[4]

Principle one of diminishing importance

375 It is thought by the author of this edition that the principles expounded by Mr Spencer Bower in the text of paras. 371–374 inclusive may be found to apply to such a small proportion of modern instances that they can hardly now warrant the detailed attention which he gave them. It is to be noticed that the authorities which the original author cites, though the second edition of this work was published in 1927, contain no case decided since 1889, if *Vancouver City* v. *Vancouver Lumber Co.*[5] be excepted. The evolution of modern administrative law

---

[1] In *Nickels* v. *Ross* (1849), 8 C.B. 679, the Court of C.P. held that WILDE C.J. had misdirected the jury in telling them that the burden was on the patentee of adducing some evidence that his representations to the Crown were true (p. 723).

[2] Illustrations of such material misrepresentations are those referred to in note (4) and 7 on p. 385; also misrepresentations as to the amount of subscriptions to the capital of a company proposed to be incorporated, as in *Eastern Archipelago Co.* v. *R.* (1853), 2 E. & B. 856 (misprinted 568), Ex. Ch., as to the names of the petitioners for such an incorporation, as in *La Banque d'Hochelaga* v. *Murray* (1889), 15 App. Cas. 414, P.C., and as to the applicant for a patent for an invention having been the true and first inventor, as in *R.* v. *Wheeler* (1819), 2 B. & Ald. 345, *Brunton* v. *Hawkes* (1821), 4 B. & Ald. 541, *Morgan* v. *Seaward* (1837), 2 M. & W. 544, and *Nickels* v. *Ross* (1849), 18 C.B. 679.

[3] *Brunton* v. *Hawkes, supra,* per BEST J. at p. 558: "That avoids the patent *in toto*. For the King is deceived; the patentee is represented to have the merit of two things, whereas he has discovered only one; and the Crown might have considered the discovery, as to both, a sufficient ground for granting a patent, when it would not have thought so of the discovery of one alone". And see the form of the third plea set out at pp. 684, 685 of *Nickels* v. *Ross, supra,* which, so far as inducement is concerned, exactly corresponds to the form of an ordinary plea of misrepresentation, substituting the Crown for the defendant as the representee: "that before the granting of the patents, the plaintiff represented to Her Majesty that, in consequence of a communication from abroad, he was in possession of an invention, etc., . . . and that Her Majesty, believing and confiding in the truth of the suggestion so made . . . granted the letters patent . . . such representation was false, whereby the letters patent were null and void."

[4] Neither in *Gledstanes* v. *Earl of Sandwich* (1842), 4 Man. & G. 995, nor in the form of plea in *Nickels* v. *Ross, supra,* nor in *Eastern Archipelago* v. *R., supra* (where the voidability of the grant in cases of misrepresentation is put on the theory of a non-compliance with an implied condition: *per* MARTIN B. at pp. 871, 872), is there any suggestion that active and personal fraud need be alleged or proved.

[5] [1911] A.C. 711.

is one of the most noticeable sociological phenomena of the last half century; certainly during that period the grants of special privileges, charters, licences, indulgences, exceptions, etc. by statutory tribunals invested with special powers has assumed an importance such as Mr Spencer Bower, even at the time of writing the last edition of this work, can hardly have dreamed of. In view of this shift in emphasis, it may be doubted how long the procedure examined in paras. 371–374 will retain any real significance. The true position may however be that the old rules still enure, and that it is merely the area of their applicability that has been diminished.

Grants of licences, privileges, permissions and certificates of exemption by officials or administrative tribunals acting in a quasi-judicial way are in modern times made the subject of elaborate statutory provisions, directed generally to the special subject-matter in question; and the statutes which provide for the procedure by which such privileges may be granted often provide that the decision of the official, or of the tribunal, shall be free from interference by the courts. Such provisions have in recent years been the subject of a constant struggle between the courts and bureaucracy, a determined attempt being made by the latter, on the one hand, to free itself entirely from the threat of revision by the courts, while the courts try to preserve unimpaired the right of the subject, in appropriate cases, to test the final decision by criteria such as natural justice.

Certiorari

376 This effort by the courts to keep in their hands the ultimate control of quasi-judicial tribunals possessing the power to grant special privileges, licences, etc. has manifested itself in a number of cases in which, *inter alia*, it has been held that such grants, if made pursuant to fraudulent misrepresentations made to the tribunal by the grantee or his agent, may be made the subject of a writ of *certiorari* to quash.[1] Where fraud on the part of the grantee or his agent, resulting in the grant, is shown, *certiorari* will certainly go. But the proof of fraud must be clear; the writ will not be granted in a case of doubt, and the question of fraud or no fraud, where this issue is contested, will not be tried by the court.[2] It has been held that the mere fact that perjury has been committed will not be sufficient, if it is not also shown that the successful party was impli-

[1] *Colonial Bank of Australasia v. Willan* (1874), L.R. 5 P.C. 417; *R. v. Recorder of Leicester*, [1947] 1 All E.R. 928; [1947] K.B. 726.
[2] *R. v. Ashford (Kent) Justices, Ex parte Richley*, [1956] 1 Q.B. 167, C.A.

cated[1]; but in a more recent Northern Ireland case it was held that this
was not a rule of universal application.[2]

"*Passing-off*" cases

377 There is a class of misrepresentation made by a trader to the
public in general, or to a section of the community, such as customers or
purchasers, as to goods or articles dealt in by him, which gives a cause of
action not only to any such purchaser or customer, but also to any third
person, usually a rival trader, who is injured thereby. These are known
as "passing off" cases, for the trader "passes off" on the public or palms
off articles of his own manufacture or belonging to his own trade as and
for articles—whether superior or inferior, is irrelevant—manufactured
or dealt in by a rival manufacturer or trader, and which have acquired a
reputation in association with the latter's name or trade. This is a misrepresentation, either express or by acts and conduct, that his goods are
the goods of the competitor. No misrepresentation is made to the competitor himself, but, none the less, that competitor's proprietary rights
and interests are invaded, and on this ground he has a cause of action for
injunction or damages which, though not strictly an action of deceit as
that action is now understood, comprises most of its elements,[3] and was,
indeed, for a very long period in the history of our jurisprudence deemed a
species of that class of action.[4] For this reason it has been thought right

---

[1] *Ibid* at p. 175.

[2] *R.* v. *Tyrone County Court Judge,* [1961] N.I. 167.

[3] As stated in Chapter XI, *ante*. All these elements are common to the ordinary action for
damages for misrepresentation and the action for "passing off", except that in the latter case
fraud need not be established (*Hendriks* v. *Montagu* (1881), 50 L.J. Ch. 456, C.A., *per* COTTON
L.J. at p. 461), and, further, the plaintiff must prove that the public, and not he, was deceived;
otherwise falsity, inducement, and materiality must be proved in the one case as much as in
the other, and no less rigorously. Thus in *London General Omnibus Co., Ltd.* v. *Lavell,* [1901] 1 Ch.
135, C.A., an action for "passing off" a particular type of omnibus on the travelling public,
FARWELL J. thought himself at liberty to adopt a more summary method of determining the
questions of materiality and inducement than would be permissible in an action of misrepresentation of the ordinary kind (see Chapter VI, *ante*), and decided in favour of the plaintiff on a
mere view of the rival vehicles, without evidence, but the C.A. held, reversing him, that this
course was wrong, and that the claim must be established in the usual way by evidence that the
public, or some members of it, had in fact been deceived by the alleged similarity: see also
Hendriks v. *Montagu* (1881), 50 L.J. Ch. 456, C.A., *per* BRETT L.J., at pp. 458, 459. It
should be noted that the remedies also are different in the two cases to this extent that in the
passing off action an injunction is the appropriate remedy, and not damages (except incidentally).

[4] See *Singer Manufacturing Co.* v. *Wilson* (1876), 2 Ch.D. 434, C.A., where MELLISH L.J.
said at pp. 453–454: "All actions of this nature must be founded on false representations.
Originally, I apprehend, the right to bring an action in respect of the improper use of a trade
mark arose out of the common law right to bring an action for a false representation, which of
course must be a false representation made fraudulently. It differs from an ordinary action for
false representation in this respect, that an action for false representation is generally brought
by the person to whom the false representation is made; but in the case of the improper use of

to notice this type of case in the present chapter, but its detailed treatment belongs to another department of law.

Patents

377A   The Patents Act 1949 now provides[1] that the court may revoke a patent on the petition of any person interested, on the ground that the patent was obtained "on a false suggestion or representation". At the time when Mr Spencer Bower wrote, the old procedure, referred to in the preceding paragraphs, was still to be followed; now no fiat from the Attorney-General is necessary, and the matter is dealt with by the court on the simple relation of the objector, who alleges misrepresentation as his ground.

Representations made to the Legislature in the course of promotion of an Act of Parliament

377B   The proposition that a fraud on the Legislature can serve as a foundation on which to challenge the validity of a private Act of Parliament may be thought a bold one; but it is one that has been submitted to the Court of Appeal, and in recent times, without positive rejection.

---

a trade mark, the common law courts noticed that the false representation which is made by putting another man's trade mark, or the trade name of another manufacturer, on the goods which the wrongdoer sells, is calculated to do an injury, not only to the person to whom the false or fraudulent misrepresentation is made, but to the manufacturer whose trade mark is imitated; and therefore the common law courts held that such a manufacturer has a right of action for the improper use of his trade mark". He then notices two extensions of the rules governing this class of action: on the one hand, courts of common law came to consider it immaterial that the original purchaser was not deceived, if subsequent purchasers and sub-purchasers have been, or may probably be, so deceived: on the other, courts of equity deemed it equally immaterial that the wrongdoer was not dishonest, if the other party's property is invaded: and thereupon, he adds: "the courts of equity having taken that step, trade marks began to be considered as property". The above observations are cited and adopted by STIRLING J. at p. 6 of *Tallerman* v. *Dowsing Radiant Heat Co.*, [1900] 1 Ch. 1. It is to be noticed, however, that in *London General Omnibus Co., Ltd.* v. *Lavell*, [1901] 1 Ch. 135, C.A., Lord ALVERSTONE C.J. at p. 138, and VAUGHAN WILLIAMS L.J. at pp. 140, 141, described the action for "passing off" then before them as "an action of deceit", though the latter remarks that such actions "have in course of time come to be treated very much as actions brought against defendants for having trenched upon private rights of the plaintiffs". And, surely, it may be added, this is the correct view. The ground of the plaintiff's complaint in an ordinary action of deceit is that he has been deceived by the defendant: in a passing off action,—that his property has been invaded, not that he has been deceived. Injury to property is the gist and the essence of the "passing off" action. See the valuable observations of Lord PARKER on this point at pp. 449, 450 of *Spalding & Brothers* v. *A. W. Gamage, Ltd.* (1915), 84 L.J. Ch. 449, H.L. So the improper use of the name of an author, or the title of another's work, in literature, is correctly stated by JAMES L.J. at p. 90 of *Dicks* v. *Yates* (1881), 18 Ch.D. 76, C.A., as one of "the three modes" in which "literary property can be invaded".

[1] Section 32 (j).

In *Pickin* v. *British Railways Board*[1] a plaintiff sued the Railways Board for trespass. The defence raised was statutory authority given by a *private*[2] Act. To this the rejoinder was made that this Act had been passed on the representation of its promoters (to the legislature) that it was unopposed by any person having an interest. On the Board's application to strike out the claim the point was argued before the Court of Appeal on the assumption that there had indeed been such a representation; the question was whether, this assumption being accepted, a fraudulent representation to such an effect to Parliament by the promoters of a private bill *might* be ground for contending that the Act was void.

M'Kenzie v. *Stewart*[3] was cited to the court. That was a case decided in 1754 in the House of Lords. The decision was that of a majority, of only seven to six, but it was a majority. There Lord HARDWICKE is reported to have said[4]:

> "The Lord Chancellor, in delivering his opinion, expressed a good deal of indignation, at the fraudulent means of obtaining the act; and said, that he never would have consented to such private acts, had he ever entertained a notion that they could be used to cover fraud".

And in *Blackstone*[5] it is said:

> "A law, thus made, though it binds all parties to the bill, is yet looked upon rather as a private conveyance, than as the solemn act of the legislature. It is not therefore allowed to be a *publick*, but a mere *private* statute; it is not printed or published among the other laws of the session; it hath been relieved against, when obtained upon fraudulent suggestions . . ."

and *M'Kenzie* v. *Stewart* is cited in support.

In *Pickin* v. *British Railways Board* Lord DENNING M.R. in delivering the leading judgment in the Court of Appeal said[6]:

> "I do not think we should pronounce on this point finally or conclusively today. But I must say that there is sufficient material from the eighteenth century for us to allow this plea to remain on the record. It is quite plain that this action has to go to trial on the issue whether or not this branch line was abandoned before 26th July 1968. We should let it go for trial on the further issue whether this Act of Parliament was improperly obtained. That

---

1 [1972] 3 All E.R. 923.
2 "There is an abundance of authority for the proposition that in relation to *public* statutes the court has no alternative but to apply them, and cannot go behind them for investigating the legislative process which preceded their receiving the Royal assent"—*ibid, per* EDMUND DAVIES L.J. at p. 928.
3 (1754), 9 Mor. Dict. 7443.
4 (1754), 9 Mor. Dict. 7445.
5 *Commentaries* 4 ed. 1803 Vol. II p. 346.
6 [1972] 3 All E.R. at p. 928.

is a triable issue. It is deserving of investigation by the court. As I have said in the course of the argument, suppose the court were satisfied that this private Act was improperly obtained, it might well be the duty of the court to report that finding to Parliament, so that Parliament itself could take cognisance of it. Parliament could put the matter right, if it thought fit, by passing another Act. In my opinion it is the function of the court to see that the procedure of Parliament itself is not abused and that undue advantage is not taken of it. In so doing the court is not trespassing on the jurisdiction of Parliament itself. It is acting in aid of Parliament, and, I might add, in aid of justice. If it is proved that Parliament was misled, the court can, and should, draw it to the attention of Parliament.''

Supporting the leading judgment EDMUND DAVIES L.J. said:[1]

''If the matter stopped there I should have found grave difficulty in being persuaded that counsel for the plaintiff was right in his submission here that there was a triable issue. But that is not the position: the cases I have referred to were dealing with public Acts of Parliament but there is ancient authority of the highest court in the land lending some support to the view that a different approach may be properly and indeed possibly ought to be adopted by the court in relation to private Acts of Parliament such as the one we are concerned with, and particularly the case of *M'Kenzie* v. *Stewart*. The curious thing is that the assertion of Lord HARDWICKE L.C. in that case, expressed in the trenchant and powerful words already quoted by Lord DENNING M.R. seems to have disappeared largely from the judicial landscape, for in no case thereafter, as far as we have been apprised, was it even referred to, still less considered. The question that accordingly looms large is, what should this court in the present case now do? Are we to say that Lord HARDWICKE L.C. must be brushed aside, and that learned counsel for the plaintiff is not entitled to claim that on any view there is here a difficult question which ought to be investigated further and which can properly be investigated only by ascertaining all the facts? In *Craies* it is pointed out that in the old cases (*M'Kenzie* v. *Stewart* and *Biddulph* v. *Biddulph*,[2] decided by the House of Lords in 1790) there was no discussion of the proposition there acted on that the court may go behind private statutes and, if satisfied that they were obtained by fraud, decline to act on them. The learned editor then adds 'The question has never been seriously discussed in any modern case'. For my part, I think it is now high time that the matter should be discussed. Furthermore, there are features of this present case which appear to me to make it highly desirable in the public interest that they should be.''

STEPHENSON L.J. in agreeing added *Green* v. *Mortimer* as a further authority. He said[3]:

---

[1] At p. 929.
[2] (1790), 5 Cru. Dig. (4 ed.) 26.
[3] At pp. 929–930.

"I would add *Green* v. *Mortimer*,[1] that the question whether there has been an abuse of the parliamentary procedure which regulates unopposed private bills may be a question for the courts as well as for Parliament in a suit brought by a person who claims that by the alleged abuse he has been deprived of a proprietary right without compensation."

The submission, though perhaps difficult, is therefore not to be rejected as completely unarguable.[2] What remedy would be available, should the court investigate the matter and find fraud, is not made absolutely clear. It is suggested however that such a finding would justify the court in reporting its finding to Parliament, presumably in confidence that at the least such a report would result in some investigation by Parliament itself into the process by which the impugned legislation had been passed.

To the observations of their Lordships the present author adds a note of a case with some parallel implications—*Ontario and Minnesota Power Co.* v. *R.*[3] decided in the Judicial Committee in 1925. There their Lordships held the grantees of a power conferred by an Order in Council estopped by a representation made by them in promoting the authorising legislation, and expressly recorded in the preamble of the authorising Act.

Misrepresentations which operate for the benefit or relief of persons who were neither representees nor injured thereby

378 In the class of cases considered in the preceding paragraphs, the persons entitled to relief, though not representees, have a ground of complaint as persons whose rights are prejudicially affected by the misrepresentation, and who, therefore, on their own merits, as well as on the demerits of the misrepresentors, are entitled to the remedies stated. But there is another class of case, in which the law allows a party who has no merits whatever, and is often, on the contrary, weighted with serious demerits, a way of escape from liability to actions brought against him by a person guilty of fraud upon third persons, not because it desires to do so, but because it cannot accomplish its paramount purpose of making such frauds unprofitable to those who practise them without at the same time incidentally setting unmeritorious persons free. In such cases the

---

1 (1861), 3 L.T. 642.
2 *Cf.*, for a contrary view, perhaps implicit, a century and a half ago, *Cromford and High Peak Rail. Co.* v. *Lacey* (1829), 3 Y. & J. 80.
3 [1925] A.C. 196 P.C. The case is discussed in the authors' *Law of Estoppel by Representation* 2nd edn. at pp. 148–149.

delinquent is deprived of the remedy to which he would otherwise be entitled on those considerations of public policy, morality, and decency, —and on those alone,—which imperatively demand the interposition of the court (whether the party raises the point or not) when the assertion of a claim, or of an affirmative defence, discloses illegality, immorality, or other *turpis causa*.   The result is that the opposite party, who in such cases is generally lacking in merits, and of course has no rights which he can assert in any active proceedings, and who sometimes is even implicated in the very fraud which defeats the claim, derives benefit and relief; but this is inevitable.   In accordance with this principle, whenever in the course of any action or proceeding it is made to appear to the court by evidence or admission that one of the parties has been guilty of acts and conduct in relation to the subjectmatter of the litigation constituting, or necessarily involving, deception of, and injury to, not the opposite party, but third persons, whether specific individuals,[1] or sections of the

---

[1] The following are cases where the third person on whom the fraud had been or was intended to be, practised was a *persona designata* : *Montefiori* v. *Montefiori* (1762), 1 Wm.Bl. 363 (a suit between two brothers, in which it appeared that one of the *par nobile fratrum*, Moses, had given the other, Joseph, a note for a large sum falsely represented to be the balance of an account due on trading, for the purpose of enabling Joseph to delude a lady into marrying him, and Lord MANSFIELD C.J. would not allow Moses to reclaim the note, after the marriage had come off, or to set up "no consideration" as a defence to Joseph's claim under it); *Neville* v. *Wilkinson* (1782), 1 Bro. C.C. 543 (in which Lord THURLOW L.C. cites the last case "from a MS. note of Mr Filmer''); *Jackson* v. *Duchaire* (1790), 3 Term Rep. 551 (a very curious case, in which the defendant, having agreed to buy certain goods from the plaintiff at a valuation, procured one Welch to buy them for her off the plaintiff for £70, the price expressed in the bill of sale granted by the plaintiff to Welch. It appeared, however, that there was a contemporaneous agreement between the plaintiff and the defendant, kept secret from Welch, that the defendant should pay the plaintiff an additional £30 for the same goods, secured by two promissory notes of £15 each, on one of which the plaintiff sued. Lord KENYON C.J. at the trial, without the defendant having raised the point, ruled that the action would not lie, on the ground that the transaction was a fraud upon, not the defendant but Welch, who, but for his belief that £70 was the plaintiff's full price, would not have advanced the money, and this ruling was supported by the K.B. (*per* ASHHURST J. at p. 552, and BULLER J. at p. 553)); *Dalbiac* v. *Dalbiac* (1809), 16 Ves. 116 (*per* GRANT M.R. at p. 125: "it is impossible for the court to recognise and sanction a transaction in which the party has been guilty of an imposition upon it''); *Pidcock* v. *Bishop* (1825), 3 B. & C. 605 (*per* BAYLEY J., at pp. 610, 611: "a contract which is a fraud upon a third person may on that account be void as between the parties to it''); *Sims* v. *Tuffs* (1834), 6 C. & P. 207 (where the plaintiff, fearing an execution, entered into a fraudulent agreement with his landlord, the defendant, whereby the latter was to destroy his receipts for rent, and to make a nominal and sham distraint upon his goods : whereupon the defendant, who was as ready to cheat the plaintiff, as the plaintiff was to cheat the execution creditor, proceeded to distrain upon the goods in real earnest, and the plaintiff sued him for conversion, which he justified as landlord, and the plaintiff set up the agreement in reply.   It was held that this agreement, being a fraud upon the execution creditor, could not stand as an answer to the defendant's affirmative plea, which, therefore, grossly iniquitous as it was, was allowed to prevail); *Howarth* v. *Pioneer Life Assurance Co., Ltd.* (1912), 107 L.T. 155, Div. Ct,

community, such as creditors,[1] customers and purchasers,[2] the reading public,[3] or investors and speculators in public undertakings,[4] and the

---

[1] *Smith* v. *Cuff* (1817), 6 M. & S. 160; *Pidcock* v. *Bishop, supra* (where composition agreements with creditors are referred to by way of illustration); *Howden* v. *Haigh* (1840), 11 Ad. & El. 1033; *Higgins* v. *Pitt* (1849), 4 Exch. 312 (*per Cur.* at p. 324); *Mallalieu* v. *Hodgson* (1851), 16 Q.B. 689, at pp. 712, 714; *Re Gomersall* (1875), 1 Ch.D. 137 (*per* JAMES L.J. at pp. 140, 141, MELLISH L.J. at pp. 143–145, BAGGALLAY L.J. at pp. 146, 147, and BRETT J. at p. 148), which was affirmed, *sub nom. Jones* v. *Gordon* (1877), 2 App. Cas. 616, H.L. The above were all cases where, a composition agreement or arrangement having been made between a debtor and his creditors, the basis of which is an implied representation by each creditor to all the others that he is not stipulating with the debtor for any separate advantage to himself, it has been held that such a stipulation, if secretly made, being a fraudulent misrepresentation to the other creditors (though it may also be put as a case of non-disclosure) cannot be enforced even against the equally fraudulent debtor. See, as to this type of case, regarded as one of non-disclosure, Chapter VII, s. 3, sub-s. (3), of Mr Spencer Bower's *Law of Actionable Non-Disclosure.*

[2] See *Pidding* v. *How* (1837), 8 Sim. 477 (where SHADWELL V.-C. dissolved an *ex parte* injunction restraining the defendants from selling tea under the name of "Howqua's Mixture", by which the plaintiff's tea was known, on the ground that, though the defendant's conduct was pronounced to be most reprehensible, the plaintiffs were proved to have sold their tea by misrepresentations, in their labels and advertisements, to the purchasing public as to the teas of which their "mixture" was composed, and as to the mode of its preparation). Other "passing off" actions and motions defeated under similar circumstances, and on the like grounds of fraudulent misrepresentation (express, or implied from "make up") to purchasers and customers, though as between the parties, the defendants had no merits, are, *Leather Cloth Co.* v. *American Leather Cloth Co.* (1865), 11 H.L. Cas. 523, at p. 543; *Newman* v. *Pinto* (1887), 57 L.T. 31, C.A.; *Lewis's* v. *Goodbody* (1892), 67 L.T. 194: *Bile Bean Manufacturing Co.* v. *Davidson* 1906, 8 F. (Ct. of Sess.) 1181. In *Sen Sen Co.* v. *Britten,* [1899] 1 Ch. 692, STIRLING J. recognised and accepted the principle of the above authorities, but (distinguishing in this respect *Lewis's* v. *Goodbody, supra*) thought that no misrepresentation to the public had been clearly established.

[3] *Wright* v. *Tallis* (1845), 1 C.B. 893 (an action for infringement of copyright in a work entitled "Evening Devotions, etc., from the German of C.C. Sturm"; plea, fraudulent misrepresentation to *the public* by the plaintiff, on the title page and in the preface, that the work was a translation from the German of Dr Sturm, a devotional writer of repute, whereas it was not a translation at all, but the composition of a person in the employ of the plaintiffs, "to the great injury and scandal of Her Majesty's liege subjects", and, as the confessed thief had the unblushing audacity to add, "to the detriment of true religion and public morals". The court was compelled on demurrer to hold this plea good, on public grounds entirely, as TINDAL C.J. delivering its judgment, was careful to explain at p. 907, where he characterised the plaintiff's proceedings as "a serious design to impose on the credulity of each purchaser . . . not merely to conceal the name of the author, and to publish opinions to the world under an innocent disguise . . . The publisher seeks to obtain money by false pretences . . . We think the best protection that the law can afford to the public against such a fraud as that laid open by this plea is to make the practice of it unprofitable to its author"); *Post* v. *Marsh* (1880), 16 Ch.D. 395 (where the plaintiff sued for specific performance of a contract to execute certain literary work on a book, the title page of which falsely ascribed its authorship to one Kenny, whose guide-books had acquired a considerable reputation, and FRY J. gave judgment on two grounds, one of which—p. 406—was that this title page, if allowed to go forth to the world, would be a fraud on the public); *Slingsby* v. *Bradford Patent Truck & Trolley Co.,* [1906] W.N. 51, C.A. (which affirmed the decision of WARRINGTON J. (1905), W.N. 122, that the publisher of an illustrated catalogue of trucks, etc., was not entitled to relief in an action for infringement of copyright, on the ground that the catalogue contained in the headings of its pages, and in its illustrations, a series of misrepresentations to the public.)

[4] *British and American Telegraph Co., Ltd.* v. *Albion Bank, Ltd.* (1872), L.R. 7 Exch. 119 (conspiracy to deceive the Stock Exchange Committee); *Gray* v. *Lewis* (1873), 8 Ch. App.

party so guilty is compelled to rely upon the acts and conduct to support either a claim or an affirmative defence,[1] such claim or defence cannot be enforced or have any effect, even against the opposite party[2]; and for this purpose it does not signify whether the question is raised by the pleadings or not.[3]   But if the fraud on third persons which is proved or admitted relates to other matters than that which form the immediate subject of the action, there is no jurisdiction, on this ground alone, to withhold from the party guilty of the fraud, if a plaintiff, the judgment to which he is entitled on the merits of the dispute, or, if a successful defendant, the costs which could otherwise follow the judgment in his favour.[4]

Misrepresentations giving rise to actions at the suit of persons other than the representee

379   In Chapter XIX there is a discussion of a very modern cause of action—or at least a cause of action which has only in the last few years

---

1035 (the like); *Begbie* v. *Phosphate Sewage Co.* (1875), L.R. 10 Q.B. 491 (where the plaintiffs sued for money had and received by the defendants to their use being money paid for the right to exercise a certain invention in Berlin under a contract the consideration for which, it was alleged, had failed, inasmuch as the defendant had no right to sell.   In fact the defendants had no such right, but it was proved that the plaintiffs were fully aware of this fact, and had issued a prospectus misrepresenting to the prospective shareholders that they were acquiring a right to which they knew they would never be legally entitled: on this ground the Court of Queen's Bench gave judgment for the defendants, reversing the verdict for the plaintiffs in the court below—pp. 499, 500—which decision was affirmed (1876), 1 Q.B.D. 679, C.A.): *Re Great Berlin Steamboat Co.* (1884), 26 Ch.D. 616, C.A. (a case in which it was proved that one Bowden had deposited money with the company for the purpose of enabling it to obtain a delusive credit with bankers and others, and induce them to subscribe to the undertaking, and a claim, in the liquidation of the company, for the repayment of the money on the accomplishment of the purpose for which it was deposited and used was disallowed, on the ground that the design was a fraud upon the subscribers); *Scott* v. *Brown, Doering, McNab & Co.*, [1892] 2 Q.B. 724, 729, 730, 734, C.A. (where the plaintiffs were proved to have conspired with the defendants to "rig the market" in shares of a certain undertaking, and so to have fraudulently misrepresented, by acts and conduct, to the investing and speculating public that the pretended dealings in the shares were genuine, and were accordingly held to have forfeited whatever rights they might otherwise have had even against the equally guilty defendants under contracts with reference to these shares).

6 Thus in *Montefiori* v. *Montefiori* (1762), 1 Wm.Bl. 363, and *Sims* v. *Tuffs* (1834), 6 C. & P. 207, both cited *ante*, the fraud on third persons was the foundation of the affirmative case of the defendant, and of the plaintiff in answer to an affirmative plea, respectively.

7 See, generally, the cases cited in the last six notes, and the observations of VAUGHAN WILLIAMS L.J. at p. 11 of *F. King & Co.* v. *Gillard & Co.*, [1905] 2 Ch. 7, C.A.

8 The point was taken by the court, and not by the parties, in *Jackson* v. *Duchaire* (1790), 3 Term Rep. 551, and in *Scott* v. *Brown, Doering, McNab & Co.*, [1892] 2 Q.B. 724, C.A.   On the other hand, in *Wright* v. *Tallis* (1845), 1 C.B. 893, the point was raised specifically and in detail in the defendant's plea.

9 *F. King & Co.* v. *Gillard & Co.*, *supra*, per VAUGHAN WILLIAMS L.J. at p. 11, and ROMER L.J. at pp. 12, 13.

received adequate recognition—the cause of action *in negligence* which arises from making a negligent misrepresentation in a situation in which a duty of care exists. In some of these situations there will be found to be a duty of care owed by the representor not only to the representee, but also to third parties; and where this is the case such a third party may have a cause of action notwithstanding that he is not the representee, and even in a case where he never had notice of the representation at all.[1] But this cause of action, as will be seen, is not really an action for misrepresentation at all, but one *in negligence* in circumstances in which the negligence consists in making a representation without due care.[2]

---

[1] *Ministry of Housing and Local Government* v. *Sharp*, [1970] 2 Q.B. 223; (on appeal) at p. 252.

[2] See Chapter XIX, and particularly para. 409, *post*.

CHAPTER XVIII

Pleadings and Practice

Introductory

380 To complete this commentary (postponing for the moment a supplementary chapter, added in this edition, on the subject of negligent misrepresentation) it remains only to discuss such rules of pleading and practice as are special to actions in proceedings for misrepresentation. A kindred topic, the standard of proof in actions for fraudulent misrepresentation, has already been the subject of some discussion in Chapter XI, para. 187, *ante*.[1]

Rules of pleadings

381 Whenever fraud (which, of course, includes fraudulent misrepresentation) is intended to be relied upon by either party to any action or proceeding, whether in support of, or by way of answer to, any claim, counter-claim, or affirmative defence, it must be distinctly alleged in that party's pleading, or affidavit.[2] This does not mean that the party need necessarily use the word "fraud", if he sufficiently indicates, by apt and unambiguous language, that he means to rely upon the thing, as, for instance, he does when he alleges acts and conduct which in law amount thereto.[3]

---

[1] Including a reference to cases in which it has been attempted to persuade the Court of Appeal to find fraud where it has not been found in the court of trial.

[2] ". . . the established rule that fraud must be precisely alleged and strictly proved"—*per* Lord WRIGHT in *Bradford Third Equitable Benefit Building Society* v. *Borders*, [1941] 2 All E.R. 205, H.L., at p. 218; *cf. per* Lord RUSSELL OF KILLOWEN in the same case at p. 216—"to make a charge of fraud is a serious thing, and before people make it they should be clear as to the grounds and facts on which they rely". In *L'Estrange* v. *F. Graucob, Ltd.*, [1934] 2 K.B. 394, SCRUTTON L.J. said at p. 403: "There is a further difficulty. Fraud is not mentioned in the pleadings, and I strongly object to deal with allegations of fraud when fraud is not expressly pleaded".

[3] *Myddleton* v. *Lord Kenyon* (1794), 2 Ves. 391 (*per* Lord ELDON L.C. p. 412); *Davy* v. *Garrett* (1878), 7 Ch.D. 473, C.A., *per* THESIGER L.J. at p. 489: "there is another still stronger objection to this statement of claim. The plaintiffs say that fraud is intended to be alleged, yet

382 Whenever fraud or misrepresentation is in fact alleged by a party, whether it was necessary for him to do so or not,[1] and whether the allegation is contained in a statement of claim, counter-claim, or other pleading which asserts a right to active relief,[2] or in a defence, reply, or other pleading by way of answer to any claim,[3] or in any affidavit,[4] full particulars of the alleged fraud or misrepresentation must be given,[5] if the opposite party requires it, but not otherwise; for, though the party

---

it contains no charge of fraud . . . It may not be necessary in all cases to use the word 'fraud'—indeed, in one of the most ordinary cases it is not necessary. The allegation that the defendant made to the plaintiff representations on which he intended the plaintiff to act, which representations were untrue, and known to the defendant to be untrue, is sufficient. The word 'fraud' is not used, but expressions are used pointing at the state of mind of the defendant, that he intended the representations to be acted upon, and that he knew them to be untrue. It appears to me that the plaintiff is bound to show distinctly that he means to allege fraud". See Chapter V, *ante.* And again: "But it is most essential, in the administration of justice in a Court of Equity, that the nature of the case, when it is constituted of fraud, should be most accurately and fully stated in the bill of the plaintiff"—*per* Lord WESTBURY L.C. in *New Brunswick and Canada Railway and Land Co.* v. *Conybeare* (1862), 9 H.L.Cas. 711, H.L., at p. 724.

[1] There is a line of decisions in which *unnecessary* allegations of fraud, in cases where it would have been sufficient to plead innocent misrepresentation, have affected the ultimate award of costs. Mr Spencer Bower mentions, in earlier editions of this work, *Gray* v. *Lewis* (1873), 8 Ch. App. 1035; *Parker* v. *McKenna* (1874), 10 Ch. App. 96; *Thomson* v. *Eastwood* (1877), 2 App. Cas. 215; *Forester* v. *Read* (1870), 6 Ch. App. 40; *Re Consort Deep Level Gold Mines, Ltd., Ex parte Stark*, [1897] 1 Ch. 575, C.A.

[2] *Redgrave* v. *Hurd* (1881), 20 Ch.D. 1 (*per* JESSEL M.R. at p. 12, refusing relief by way of damages on the defendant's counter-claim, on this ground); *Birch* v. *Birch*, [1902] P. 130, C.A. (*per* COZENS-HARDY L.J. at p. 138: "a mere general allegation of fraud, without particulars, cannot avail": the action here was to set aside a judgment on the ground that it had been obtained by fraud).

[3] *Lawrance* v. *Lord Norreys* (1890), 15 App. Cas. 210, H.L., *per* Lord HERSCHELL at p. 219 ("a statement of claim which, if it discloses a concealed fraud within the meaning of the statute, does so in the barest fashion, with much that is most material left vague and undefined, when there ought to have been distinctness and precision"), and Lord WATSON at pp. 221, 222 ("there must be a probable, if not a necessary, connection between the fraud averred and the injurious consequences which the plaintiff attributes to it; and if that connection is not sufficiently apparent from the particulars stated, it cannot be supplied by general averments. Facts and circumstances in that case must be set forth, and in every genuine claim are capable of being stated . . . The amount and kind of explanatory statement required in order to impart relevancy to such charges will necessarily vary according to circumstances"). The action was one in which the plaintiff set up a case of concealed fraud by way of anticipatory answer to the defendant's plea of a statute of limitations. See, also, *Bentley & Co., Ltd.* v. *Black* (1893), 9 T.L.R. 580, C.A.

[4] *Wallingford* v. *Mutual Society* (1880), 5 App. Cas. 685, H.L. (*per* Lord SELBORNE L.C. at p. 697, with reference to an affidavit under O.XIV, setting up fraud as a ground on which the defendant claimed to be allowed to defend: "with regard to fraud, if there be any principle which is perfectly well settled, it is that general allegations, however strong may be the words in which they are stated, are insufficient even to amount to an averment of fraud of which any court ought to take notice").

[5] See O.18, r.12, which expressly mentions "fraud" and "misrepresentation" as among the matters which the party pleading must particularise. The observations of Lord WATSON, cited in note 3, *supra*, as to the amount and kind of details required being dependent upon the circumstances of the individual case, should always be borne in mind.

alleging fraud is rigorously confined at the trial to such particulars as he has given, or has been compelled by his adversary to give,[1] it is too late to object to any insufficiency in this respect at the trial.[2] There would seem to be no reason why, in an ordinary case of misrepresentation, the party alleging it should be excused from giving the required particulars until he has obtained discovery.[3]

383   An amendment of a pleading which raises a charge of fraud which has not appeared in any previous pleading, and where the charge is new in substance, and not merely in form, is not ordinarily allowed.[4] And it is only in the most unusual circumstances, if indeed at all, that such an amendment will be allowed to be made in a Court of Appeal, for if made it must almost necessarily involve the consequence that the party whose honesty is attacked has no real opportunity of giving evidence in his own defence.   He has directed his evidence in the court below to the original charges made.   He is entitled to have his honesty in regard to the new

---

[1] *Cargill* v. *Bower* (1878), 10 Ch.D. 502 (*per* FRY J., after referring to the previous authorities, at p. 516: "above all in cases of fraud the decision of the court must proceed *secundum allegata et probata*").

[2] *Smith* v. *Kay* (1859), 7 H.L. Cas. 750 (*per* Lord CHELMSFORD L.C. at pp. 757, 758, and Lord CRANWORTH at pp. 763–768).

[3] The cases in which discovery has been ordered to precede particulars are non-disclosure cases, where a fiduciary relation exists between the parties, and where, therefore, the party from whom the discovery is required is, in virtue of that relation, under a duty to make the disclosure, for breach of which duty he is being sued, e.g. agent and principal cases, such as *Whyte* v. *Ahrens* (1884), 26 Ch.D. 717, C.A., *Leitch* v. *Abbott* (1886), 31 Ch.D. 374, C.A., *Sachs* v. *Speilman* (1887), 37 Ch.D. 295, and *Edelston* v. *Russell* (1888), 57 L.T. 927; and cases in which the party alleges fraud upon a third person, such as *Waynes Merthyr Co.* v. *D. Radford & Co.*, [1896] 1 Ch. 29 (though, in this case, CHITTY J. on consideration, came to the conclusion that the particulars should come first, and, further, expressed his view that there is no hard-and-fast rule).   It is obvious that, in both the above classes of action, the plaintiff does not, and cannot reasonably be expected to, know the entire facts as to matters which, in the one case, are studiously concealed from him, and, in the other, pass between the defendant and a third person.   But where a misrepresentation to himself is alleged, it is no less obvious that he is in a position to give full particulars without discovery, or, if he is not, he should not have brought his action.   On precisely the same principle, the defamer who pleads justification to an action of defamation is not entitled to discovery from the man he has defamed before he gives particulars of the alleged truth of his imputations: *Zierenberg* v. *Labouchere*, [1893] 2 Q.B. 183, C.A. (*per* KAY L.J. at p. 187, who there carefully distinguishes the non-disclosure type of case above referred to).

[4] *Lawrance* v. *Lord Norreys* (1890), 15 App. Cas. 210, H.L., at p. 213 of which it appears that the plaintiff had been refused leave to amend by setting up concealed fraud, or a more adequate statement thereof, in the Q.B.D.   In *New Zealand* in *Bailey* v. *Munro*, [1953] N.Z.L.R. 577 a plaintiff had sued for damages for breach of contract.   Defendant in his defence alleged accord and satisfaction.   Plaintiff wished at the trial to answer this plea with an allegation that the document purporting to evidence the accord had been obtained by fraud; but he had not filed any pleading giving notice of his intention to make this answer.   It was held that he could not put forward the plea of fraud without adequate notice, and the action was adjourned upon terms in order to give him an opportunity to do so.

particulars specifically challenged, and to have an opportunity in examination or cross-examination, or both, of answering the charge personally.[1]

In a case, however, where an amendment is sought in a court of trial merely for the purpose of putting into better shape, or expanding in greater detail, a case of misrepresentation which has already been sufficiently pleaded in substance, it may be just to give leave to amend.[2] And, in very special circumstances, and on special terms, an amendment raising a case of fraud for the first time, even in the course of the trial, may be allowed.[3] It is too late, after judgment has been given, to apply for an amendment allowing fraud to be put forward, even on evidence appearing in the record, by way of a defence to an action for specific performance, if the allegation has not been raised at the trial; for the opposite party has not been given sufficient opportunity of tendering relevant evidence which might have answered the accusations.[4] Where, on the hearing of a motion for rectification of the register of a company on the ground of fraudulent misrepresentation, there is insufficient evidence of the fraud, or even of the falsity, alleged, an application for an adjournment will usually be refused.[5]

384 Where a fraudulent state of mind (or its equivalent, the *scienter*) is alleged, it is not necessary to particularise the state of mind, any more than in other actions malice is required to be particularised. It is enough to give details of the misrepresentation or acts amounting thereto; any further description of the moral and mental condition of the person responsible is no more than evidence, which is not pleadable. Nor is it incumbent on a representee to put a meaning upon the words alleged to

---

[1] *Bradford Third Equitable Benefit Building Society* v. *Borders*, [1941] 2 All E.R. 205, H.L., where the Lords reversed a finding of fraud in the Court of Appeal on a claim amended in that court. The speech of Lord WRIGHT at pp. 218–219 contains the observations set out in the text above. Viscount MAUGHAM held similarly at p. 207; Lord RUSSELL OF KILLOWEN at p. 217. Lord PORTER elaborated the same point at p. 227.

[2] *Cocksedge* v. *Metropolitan Coal Consumers' Association* (1891), 65 L.T. 432, C.A.

[3] *Riding* v. *Hawkins* (1889), 14 P.D. 56, where, in a probate action, it appeared from admissions made by the defendant in cross-examination at the trial that the plaintiff might have had a possible case of fraud, which he had not pleaded, whereupon BUTT J. gave him leave to amend by adding an allegation, with particulars, that the execution of the will was obtained by the fraud and misrepresentation of the defendant, at the same time offering the defendant a postponement of the trial to enable him to meet the new charges. This course, though a new trial was ordered on another ground, was approved by the Divisional Court, Sir James HANNEN P. and A. L. SMITH J. who said (at p. 59) that, under such circumstances, it was the judge's "duty to allow the plaintiff to amend his pleadings, always taking care that the defendant was exposed to no hardship", which precautions had been taken in the case under appeal.

[4] So it was decided by the High Court of Australia in *Suttor* v. *Gundowa Pty.*, *Ltd* (1950), 81 C.L.R. 418.

[5] *Re British Burmah Lead Co.*, *Ex parte Vickers* (1887), 56 L.T. 815 (*per* KAY L.J.).

have been used by the representor, or to add an innuendo as if the action were one of defamation.[1]

385 Where it is alleged that a fraudulent representation was made by one who had the express or implied authority of another, and that other is sued, it is correct to plead such facts as the fraudulent misrepresentation of the principal.[2]

386 Where misrepresentation is set up as a defence to an action to enforce a contract, it is incumbent on the defendant to allege in his pleading that, from the time when he discovered the truth, he never recognised any liability, or asserted any right, or derived any benefit, under the contract, but did what in him lay to disaffirm it, or that he is now electing to disaffirm it, and, if the action is for a debt under s. 20 (2) of the Companies Act 1948, or any of the old sections which it has replaced, he must add that he has obtained, or is taking steps to obtain, a rectification of the register, or must then and there counter-claim an order for such rectification, or, if the court has no jurisdiction in that behalf, assert his right thereto.[3]

Rules of procedure

387 As to joinder of parties, it will be useful to notice that, where there are several persons claiming to have been deceived by the same misrepresentation, as, for instance, allottees of shares suing in respect of misstatements in a prospectus, each of them can sue separately, or all, or any number of them, can sue together,[4] but each of them must nevertheless in that case prove his separate right to relief[5]; or an order

---

[1] *Barley* v. *Walford* (1846), 9 Q.B. 197, where, at p. 199, there are thirteen lines of innuendo pleaded, in the form used in cases of defamation, or the quasi-defamation constituted by "disparagement of property", and where Lord DENMAN C.J., at p. 209, observes that "the objection that the innuendo is larger than the representation"—an objection appropriate to actions of defamation—"is answered by the remark that no innuendo is required".

[2] *Barwick* v. *English Joint Stock Bank* (1867), L.R. 2 Exch. 259, Exch. Ch., *per Cur.* at pp. 266, 267.

[3] See Chapter XV, para. 322, and the cases cited in note 2 on p. 337.

[4] In *Arnison* v. *Smith* (1888), 41 Ch.D. 348, C.A., fifty-two persons who had taken debenture stock on the faith of the prospectus sued together. In *Drincqbier* v. *Wood*, [1899] 1 Ch. 393, several debenture holders joined as plaintiffs, and were held to have properly done so (*per* BYRNE J. at pp. 396, 397).

[5] *Arnison* v. *Smith*, *supra*, is a good practical illustration of this necessity. Out of the 52 plaintiffs, only 40 appeared at the trial, to prove their individual cases; the other 12 were absent, in the mistaken idea that any judgment in favour of the 40 who did appear would ensure for their benefit also. The consequence was that KEKEWICH J. was compelled to give judgment against them, though the 40, who proved inducement and the other ingredients in the cause of action, succeeded, and the C.A. was unable to say that there was any escape from this result,

may be made for one of several actions to be tried first as a test action[1]; no "representative" proceedings, however, can be instituted in such a case,—that is to say, none of the representees can sue on behalf of himself and all others constituting the class of persons deceived, or for this purpose take advantage of the modern rule relating to "numerous persons"[2]; the reason being that, though questions as to the making of the representation, its falsity or fraud, and its materiality, are common to every member of the so-called "class", every other question, and particularly that of inducement, is special to the individual. A may prove that he read the prospectus, and was induced; B may not be able to prove both these facts; C may not be able to prove either; whilst D may not be able to prove damage, or E his title to rescission, if the action is for that species of relief.[3] If, however, no application is made before the trial to strike out so much of the title of the action as purports to give it a "representative" character, the plaintiff's case cannot be dismissed, but will be heard as if he were suing on his own behalf alone.[4]

388   The usual practice, in such cases, is to resort to the "test action" form of order above referred to. The procedure is as follows. The representees issue separate writs in the first instance, and immediately upon their doing so an application is made in chambers for an order in which one of the actions is selected as a test, and all the others are stayed,

---

however probable it may have been that the absent twelve would have established their case as easily as the others, if they had been there to do so: their appeal, therefore, was dismissed, though "without prejudice to a fresh action" (pp. 374, 375).

[1] See the cases cited in note 1 on p. 403, *post.*

[2] Community of interest or of liability alone justifies a representative suit: *per* SHADWELL V.-C. in *Long* v. *Yonge* (1830), 2 Sim. 369. There is no such community in proceedings for damages or for rescission on the ground of misrepresentation: the case of each representee, *quoad* inducement and other matters, has its own separate equity: *Jones* v. *Garcia del Rio* (1823), 1 T. & Russ. 297; *Croskey* v. *Bank of Wales* (1863), 4 Giff. 314 (*per* STUART V.-C. at p. 330); *Hallows* v. *Fernie* (1868), 3 Ch. App. 467 (*per* Lord CHELMSFORD L.C. at p. 471); *Gray* v. *Lewis* (1873), 8 Ch. App. 1035 (*per* MELLISH L.J. at pp. 1054, 1055). A contrary opinion seems to have been entertained by KINDERSLEY V.-C. in *Beeching* v. *Lloyd* (1855), 3 Drew. 227. This view, though not actively dissented from by all the Lords Justices in *Markt & Co.* v. *Knight S.S. Co.*, [1910] 2 K.B. 1021, C.A., is quite inconsistent with the authorities above cited. The rule relating to representative actions is O.15, r.12.

[3] See *Arnison* v. *Smith* (1888), 41 Ch.D. 348, C.A.; *Churchill* (*Lord*) v. *Whetnall* (1918), 87 L.J. (Ch.) 524 (*per* EVE J. at p. 526). A good illustration of the distinction between an action which is representative, and one which is not, is furnished by *Stroud* v. *Lawson*, [1898] 2 Q.B. 44, C.A., where the plaintiff (1) on his own behalf sued directors of a company for damages for misrepresentation, and (2) in the same action, sued the company, on behalf of himself and the other shareholders of the company, in respect of an alleged improper payment of dividend, and it was held (*per* A. L. SMITH L.J. at pp. 48, 49, and CHITTY L.J. at pp. 51, 52) that the two causes of action were absolutely distinct, and mutually exclusive, since, in the first, the plaintiff could not sue on behalf of the other shareholders, and, in the second, he could not sue otherwise.

[4] This course was adopted in *Hallows* v. *Fernie, supra.*

the parties being bound by the result in the action tried, in so far as the order directs; but room must be left in the order for possible differences in fact between each action stayed, and the action tried, for (e.g.) some of the plaintiffs may not be able to prove inducement, damage, etc., or affirmative defences may be available against some of them which were not available against the plaintiff in the test action. Terms are inserted in the order to protect any of the plaintiffs in the outstanding actions from being prejudiced by any collusive or incompetent conduct of the test action.[1]

389 Another rule that has an important bearing upon actions for misrepresentation is that several plaintiffs may sue, and several defendants may be sued, together in respect of several causes of action, if, in the case of plaintiffs, those causes "arise out of the same transaction, or series of transactions",[2] or if, in the case of either plaintiffs or defendants, evidence in support of the one cause of action would be evidence in support of the other, but not otherwise.[3] Thus, it is not allowable for a representee to sue on his own behalf three directors of a company for fraudulent misrepresentation, and also, on behalf of himself and all other share-

---

[1] See *Twycross v. Grant (No. 1)* (1877), 2 C.P.D. 469, where, without applying to the court, an arrangement was made between the parties to the effect stated in the text (see pp. 473, 474). In *Amos v. Chadwick, (No. 1)* (1877), 4 Ch.D. 869, there were 78 actions for misrepresentation in a prospectus of the Blochairn Iron Co.: on the application of the plaintiffs in all of them to consolidate, MALINS V.-C., declining to make an order for this purpose on the ground that it could only be made at the instance of a defendant, acceded to an alternative application that, on the plaintiffs in two of the actions, *Robinson v. Chadwick*, and *Smith v. Chadwick*, undertaking to prosecute them with due diligence, these two should be taken as test actions, and the time for the delivery of statement of claim in the others enlarged until after the trial of such test actions, imposing the condition that if the plaintiffs therein failed, all the other plaintiffs were to accept the result as conclusive, but that if they succeeded, the defendants were not to be bound, but might call on any of the other plaintiffs to proceed to trial (pp. 872, 873). These terms gave no adequate protection to these other plaintiffs against collusion between the plaintiffs in the test actions and the defendants, as was made apparent in *Robinson v. Chadwick* (1878), 7 Ch.D. 878, when an application was first made by Robinson to MALINS V.-C. to stay proceedings, which was refused on the ground that he was not *dominus litis*, but a trustee for the other plaintiffs, and again to FRY J. at the trial, for postponement or leave to discontinue, which was also refused, and the action dismissed with costs. Thereupon the plaintiffs in the other actions,—see *Amos v. Chadwick (No. 2)* (1878), 9 Ch.D. 459 C.A.—applied successfully to MALINS V.-C. to reinstate *Smith v. Chadwick* as a test action, the other having proved no test, and the C.A. affirmed this decision. To complete the history of this litigation, the plaintiff in the last-named action succeeded, and the judgment was affirmed by the C.A., and ultimately by the H.L., in *Smith v. Chadwick* (1884), 9 App. Cas. 187, H.L. For an elaborate form of order for a test action, see that made by FIELD J. in *Bennett v. Lord Bury* (1880), 5 C.P.D. 339, as set out at p. 340.
[2] O.15, r.4; the words of para. (a) of this Rule are "if some common question of law or fact would arise in all the actions."
[3] *Stroud v. Lawson*, [1898] 2 Q.B. 44, C.A., a case decided under the old Rules, where, on the ground stated in note 3 on p. 402, the statement of claim was ordered to be struck out, unless the plaintiff elected to abandon his claim against either the company or the directors (*per* A. L. SMITH L.J. at pp. 50, 51, CHITTY L.J. at p. 52, and VAUGHAN WILLIAMS L.J. at pp. 54, 55).

holders, sue the company for a declaration that the payment of a certain dividend was illegal and *ultra vires*, and for consequential relief[1]; but a plaintiff may in one action sue several defendants for misrepresentation and non-disclosure in a prospectus, though the remedies sought as against these various defendants are separate and distinct remedies (such as rescission, repayment, and rectification of the register as against the company, and damages for common law and statutory misrepresentation, and for statutory non-disclosure, against the directors), because the act or transaction which furnishes the plaintiff with his ground of complaint is one and the same, *viz.* the issue of the prospectus.[2]

Proceedings commenced by originating summons

390 There has been some difference of opinion whether, where in a proceeding commenced by an originating summons fraud is alleged, an order should be made under O.28, r.8 (1) directing that the matter should proceed as if commenced by writ, or whether the provisions of O.5, r.2, providing that a claim based upon an allegation of fraud must be begun by writ, must result in a stay of proceedings and an actual commencement of a substantial proceeding by action. UNGOED-THOMAS J. has preferred the latter course[3]: STAMP J. the former.[4]

Allegation of fraud not usually referred to arbitration

390A Where in an action, or as a defence to an action, fraud is alleged, the court will, at the instance of the party charged with fraud, refuse a stay of proceedings on the ground of a general agreement by the parties to have their disputes referred to arbitration[5]; for in such a case the party charged ought to be allowed the opportunity of clearing himself from such a charge in open court.[6]

---

[1] *Ibid.*

[2] *Frankenburg* v. *Great Horseless Carriage Co.*, [1900] 1 Q.B. 504, C.A., *per* LINDLEY M.R. at pp. 508, 509 (who distinguished *Gower* v. *Couldridge*, [1898] 1 Q.B. 348, C.A.), and ROMER L.J. at pp. 510–512. This case was followed and applied, though the actions were not for misrepresentation, in the following :—*Compania Sansinena de Carnes Congeladas* v. *Houlder Brothers & Co., Ltd.*, [1910] 2 K.B. 354, C.A.; *Oesterreichische Export A.G.* v. *British Indemnity Insurance Co., Ltd.*, [1914] 2 K.B. 747, C.A. (*per* KENNEDY L.J. at pp. 752, 754, and SWINFEN EADY L.J. at pp. 756, 757); *Re Beck, Attia* v. *Seed* (1918), 87 L.J. Ch. 335, C.A. (*per* SWINFEN EADY L.J. at pp. 338, 339).

[3] *Re 462 Green Lane, Ilford, Gooding* v. *Borland*, [1971] 1 All E.R. 315.

[4] *Re Deadman, Smith* v. *Garland*, [1971] 2 All E.R. 101.

[5] *Radford* v. *Hair*, [1971] 2 All E.R. 1089, [1971] Ch. 758.

[6] *Ibid*; *Minifie* v. *Railway Passengers' Assurance Co.* (1881), 44 L.T. 522; *Charles Osenton & Co.* v. *Johnston*, [1942] A.C. 130, H.L., at p. 137 *per* Viscount SIMON L.C.

CHAPTER XIX

Negligent Misrepresentation: the Hedley Byrne Action

Introduction

391 Between the years 1889, when *Derry* v. *Peek*[1] was decided in the Lords, and 1963, when the House delivered judgment in *Hedley Byrne & Co., Ltd.* v. *Heller & Partners, Ltd.*,[2] it was generally accepted that in the absence of fraud, or of any contractual or fiduciary duty on his part, a representor could not be made liable in damages for negligent misrepresentation.[3] The earlier decision of CHITTY J. in *Cann* v. *Willson*[4] had given ground for the supposition that damages might be recovered for financial loss brought about by negligent misrepresentation; but that decision had been expressly rested upon the judgments in the Court of Appeal in *Peek* v. *Derry*,[5] and when those judgments were reversed in the Lords *Cann* v. *Willson*[4] fell to the ground.

Derry v. Peek

392 *Derry* v. *Peek*[1] was for the next three-quarters of a century—from 1889 to 1963—generally recognised as having decided that an action in

---

[1] (1889), 14 App. Cas. 337, H.L.

[2] [1963] 2 All E.R. 575; [1964] A.C. 465, H.L.

[3] At least in cases in which the misrepresentation had not directly resulted in foreseeable injury to the person or physical damage to property. These have always been in a different category. For example see *Sharp* v. *Avery*, [1938] 4 All E.R. 85; *Clayton* v. *Woodman & Son (Builders), Ltd.*, [1962] 2 Q.B. 533. The present writer suggests for consideration the case of the driver of a motor vehicle approaching a turn in the road, who is signalled to pass by the driver of a slow vehicle ahead; he does so, relying on the signal, and collides with a vehicle coming in the opposite direction. While he could not be absolved from negligence in driving his own car, it is suggested that his claim against the signaller will be one for negligence in making a representation that the road ahead was clear.

[4] (1888), 39 Ch.D. 39.

[5] (1887), 37 Ch.D. 541, C.A.

damages would not lie in respect of a non-fraudulent misrepresentation,[1] unless special circumstances—e.g. contract—imposed a duty of care on the representor.   The facts in that case were that a special Act incorporating a tramway company provided that the carriages might be moved by animal power or, with the consent of the Board of Trade, by steam power. The directors issued a prospectus containing a statement that by the Act the company had the right to use steam power.   On the faith of this statement the plaintiff subscribed for shares.   The Board of Trade subsequently refused its consent to the use of steam power except for parts of the proposed tramway, and in the result the company was wound up. The plaintiff sued the directors for damages for fraud.

In the court of trial STIRLING J. held that the misrepresentation was innocent, the directors believing their statement to be true.   He dismissed the claim for damages.   The Court of Appeal reversed this decision, holding that the directors should have taken care that there were reasonable grounds for their statement.   This was in effect giving damages for a negligent misrepresentation which was not actually fraudulent.   The House of Lords reversed the decision of the Court of Appeal, and restored that of STIRLING J., holding that the action being one for deceit, it was necessary to prove actual fraud.   Fraud, said the judgments, might be proved by showing that the false representation had been made knowingly, or without believing its truth, or recklessly without caring whether it was true or false.   But mere negligence, while it might be evidence which helped to prove fraud, could not of itself constitute fraud.

It is to be noted that in many of the cases which followed, *Derry* v. *Peek*[2] was taken as having expressly decided that *no action in damages* could lie in respect of a false representation unless fraud were proved. But, as will later be emphasised, their Lordships were in *Derry* v. *Peek* dealing only with an action in deceit; they held that negligence was insufficient, without more, to support *such an action*.   It was left for another generation to explore how far in some classes of case a misrepresentation made negligently, but not fraudulently, might not *in the circumstances of that case* support some action for damages other than an action for deceit.   And in the judgment of Lord HERSCHELL there may be found already the first premonition of the modern doctrine.   He said[3]:

"There is another class of actions which I must refer to also for the purpose of putting it aside.   I mean those cases where a person within whose special

---

[1] e.g. it is so cited in 26 Halsbury's Laws (3rd edn.) 857, and in the second edition of this work by Mr Spencer Bower, at pp. 200–201.

[2] (1889) 14 App. Cas. 337, H.L.

[3] At p. 360.

province it lay to know a particular fact, has given an erroneous answer to an inquiry made with regard to it by a person desirous of ascertaining the fact for the purpose of determining his course accordingly, and has been held bound to make good the assurance he has given. *Burrowes* v. *Lock* (1805), 10 Ves. 470 may be cited as an example, where a trustee had been asked by an intended lender, upon the security of a trust fund, whether notice of any prior incumbrance upon the fund had been given to him. In cases like this it has been said that the circumstance that the answer was honestly made in the belief that it was true affords no defence to the action. Lord SELBORNE pointed out in *Brownlie* v. *Campbell* (1880), 5 App. Cas. 925, at p. 935 that these cases were in an altogether different category from actions to recover damages for false representation, such as we are now dealing with.''

These remarks remained almost unnoticed, while the cases which immediately succeeded *Derry* v. *Peek* added support to the proposition that there could be no claim in damages for an innocent misrepresentation.

Angus v. *Clifford*[1]

393   This case, an authority still frequently cited, was a decision of the Court of Appeal in 1890. The directors of a company for purchasing and working a mine issued a prospectus containing a statement that the reports of certain engineers therein mentioned had been ''prepared for the directors''. The reports were appended to the prospectus, and gave a favourable account of the mine. In fact they had been prepared, not for the directors, but for the vendors of the mine, with the view to the formation of the company; but there was no evidence that they were incorrect or exaggerated. The plaintiff took shares on the faith of the prospectus, and, the shares having fallen in value, he brought an action of deceit against the directors claiming damages. The court held, on the evidence, that the directors had had no intention to deceive, and had used the expression ''prepared for the directors'' carelessly, not thinking it important, and without considering the true effect of the words.

It was held (reversing the judgment of ROMER J. in the court below) that the plaintiff could not maintain an action of deceit against the directors for the misrepresentation; and it was queried whether, in the absence of evidence that the reports themselves were incorrect, the falsity of the statement that they were prepared ''for the directors'' was material. The *ratio* of the decision is set out in the headnote as follows:

''If a person who makes a false statement entertains a *bona fide* belief that

---

[1] [1891] 2 Ch. 449, C.A.

the statement is true, an action of deceit cannot be maintained against him on the ground that he formed his belief carelessly or on insufficient reasons. If he had formed no belief whether the statement was true or false, and made it recklessly without caring whether it was true or false, an action of deceit will lie against him. But not so if he carelessly made the statement without appreciating the importance and significance of the words used, unless indifference to their truth is proved.''

Low v. Bouverie

394 *Low* v. *Bouverie*[1] was decided by the Court of Appeal only a year later. This time the court was LINDLEY, BOWEN and KAY L.JJ. A beneficiary in an estate had applied to a moneylender for an advance. The latter wrote to the trustee of the will inquiring what charges (if any) were already secured on the trust fund. The trustee negligently replied, omitting any reference to certain charges of which he had notice, though, as was accepted by the trial judge, he had forgotten about them. As a result the inquirer, having advanced moneys on the faith of the reply, suffered loss. He sued the trustee in damages. Fraud was not alleged; what was averred was that the defendant, having in actual fact had notice of other incumbrances, forgot about them, and so failed in a duty which he owed to the plaintiff to use reasonable care in answering his inquiry. NORTH J. held the defendant liable in damages for misrepresentation "although in fact the representation was made through forgetfulness". This decision was reversed in a reserved judgment of the Court of Appeal.

In holding that judgment must be for the defendant all three Lords Justices relied on *Derry* v. *Peek*.[2] It was plainly the view of LINDLEY L.J. that it had been decided in that case that unless a duty to use care in representation was laid upon the defendant *ex contractu* he could not be liable in damages for a representation made in good faith.[3] KAY L.J. expressed the same opinion.[4] BOWEN L.J. left the door open—perhaps only just open—to the proposition which was to emerge in our own day that there might be cases apart from contract in which the relationship

---

[1] [1891] 3 Ch. 82, C.A.

[2] (1889), 14 App. Cas. 337, H.L.

[3] At p. 100 he said: "I am not aware of any principle or authority which imposes upon him any obligation to do more than give an honest answer to the inquiry—that is to say, to do more than answer to the best of his actual knowledge and belief".

[4] At p. 112 KAY L.J. said: "Where there is no estoppel, an innocent misrepresentation will not support an action *at law* for damages accrued thereby". He had pointed out at p. 111 that there had been from ancient times an equitable jurisdiction to enforce a personal demand against one who made an untrue representation upon which he knew that the person to whom it was made intended to act, if such person did act upon the faith of it and suffered loss by so acting.

of the parties might give rise to a duty to use care, the breach of which could give rise to an action for damages, even though the representation made was an innocent one.   He said:

> "Negligent misrepresentation does not certainly amount to deceit, and negligent misrepresentation can only amount to a cause of action if there exist a duty to be careful—not to give information except after careful inquiry."[1]

Le Lievre v. *Gould*

395   *Le Lievre* v. *Gould*[2] may next be noticed.   Its date is 1893, and it again was a decision of a strong Court of Appeal (Lord ESHER M.R. and BOWEN and A. L. SMITH L.JJ).   A mortgagee of land, having suffered damage by paying out more than was prudent in progress payments to the mortgagor's builder, claimed damages in negligence against the architect on whose certificate the moneys had been paid.   No contract could be shown between the plaintiff and the architect; and the latter, while clearly failing to exercise reasonable care, had equally clearly not acted fraudulently.   Lord ESHER M.R., dismissing *Cann* v. *Willson*[3] as erroneously decided, stated the effect of *Derry* v. *Peek*[4] to be that in the absence of contract an action for damages cannot be maintained where there is no fraud.   With this view A. L. SMITH L.J. expressly agreed.   BOWEN L.J. agreed with the result, but in his judgment there may again be detected the thought that there might be cases even in the absence of contract or fraud in which there might arise a duty—presumably from the relationship of the parties—on the part of the representor to take reasonable care in making his representation.   BOWEN L.J. thought that no such duty arose in the circumstances of the particular case before him.   He said[5]:

> "Now in *Derry* v. *Peek* the House of Lords pointed out that, as common law lawyers had always held, an action of deceit must be based upon fraud, and that negligence is not of itself fraud, although negligence in some cases may be of such a kind as to make it highly probable that there has been fraud. Then *Derry* v. *Peek* decided this further point—*viz.*, that in cases like the present (of which *Derry* v. *Peek* was itself an instance) there is no duty enforceable in law to be careful.   Negligent misrepresentation does not amount to deceit, and negligent misrepresentation can give rise to a cause of action only if a duty lies upon the defendant not to be negligent, and in

---

[1] At p. 105.
[2] [1893] 1 Q.B. 491, C.A.
[3] (1888), 39 Ch.D. 39.
[4] (1889), 14 App. Cas. 337, H.L.
[5] [1893] 1 Q.B. 491, at p. 501.

that class of cases, of which *Derry* v. *Peek* was one, the House of Lords considered that the circumstances raised no such duty. Is there any such duty in the present case, for deceit is out of the question after the finding of the official referee ? If there were no such duty, there can be no breach of duty by negligence.''

Nocton v. Lord Ashburton

396 *Nocton* v. *Lord Ashburton*[1] is the next case to be considered. Nocton, a solicitor, was engaged in a land development scheme in partnership with Lord Ashburton's brother. Lord Ashburton was his client of many years' standing. Nocton and his partner borrowed £65,000 from Lord Ashburton to finance the purchase of the land, securing the loan on a first mortgage of the land purchased. Lord Ashburton found the money by borrowing the same sum from an institution at a lesser rate of interest, giving the lender a submortgage of his mortgage from Nocton and his partner, and also further collateral security to secure the advance. In the course of carrying out the development scheme it became expedient to discharge ''Block A'' from the mortgage, and Nocton obtained the sub-mortgagees' agreement to this, which was given because the sub-mortgagees were adequately secured by the collateral security which Lord Ashburton had given. He then approached Lord Ashburton and represented to him that it would be safe to release Block A from his mortgage. Actually Block A was by far the most valuable part of Lord Ashburton's security, and without it his mortgage did not afford adequate security for the amount which he had advanced. Lord Ashburton allowed his security to be diminished, suffered loss, and sued Nocton for damages, alleging fraud.

NEVILLE J., the trial judge, held that the facts did not show fraud. It was clear from his judgment that he would have held Nocton liable for negligent advice given in breach of his contractual duty as between solicitor and client; but this had not been set up as a cause of action, and NEVILLE J. refused to amend. He consequently gave judgment for the defendant. The Court of Appeal reversed NEVILLE J., holding that on the facts fraud was proved. There was an appeal to the House of Lords. It was not necessary for the Lords to consider the question of liability for breach of contractual duty, for that had not been pleaded; but it appears from the judgment of Lord HALDANE that they were plainly of opinion that negligence had been proved so clearly that if it had been pleaded as a cause of action that action could not have been successfully defended.

---

[1] [1914] A.C. 932, H.L.

The Lords overruled the decision of the Court of Appeal that NEVILLE J. should have found fraud. The necessary intention to deceive was lacking. This was not a case of a representation recklessly made, without belief in its truth. To use the words of Viscount HALDANE L.C. no more was shown than that

> "the solicitor did not consciously intend to defraud his client, but, largely owing to a confused state of mind, believed that he was properly joining with him and guiding him in a good speculation".[1]

The Lords therefore went on to consider whether, notwithstanding *Derry* v. *Peek*, there might not be cases, of which the facts before them constituted one, in which by reason of some special relationship between the parties there was a duty to take care in making a representation, with the consequence that in such cases Equity might order "compensation" to be paid. Their Lordships held this to be such a case. The Lord Chancellor said[2]:

> "My Lords, in *Slim* v. *Croucher*[3] the circumstances were unusual, and it may be that the decision can be supported on the ground that the defendant warranted by implication that he had power to grant a valid lease. It is not, however, necessary to express an opinion on the point. But in the appeal before us I do not think that any question of warranty or estoppel arises, and if moral fraud has not been established the only question which remains is whether there has been such a breach of duty as gives rise to liability. Now such a duty might arise either at law or in equity. And I do not understand Lord HERSCHELL, who mentioned the case of a legal as distinguished from merely a moral duty, to have intended in any way to exclude duty of which only a Court of Equity took cognizance. If among the great common lawyers who decided *Derry* v. *Peek*[4] there had been present some versed in the practice of the Court of Chancery, it may well be that the decision would not have been different, but that more and explicit attention would have been directed to the wide range of the class of cases in which, *on the ground of a fiduciary duty*, Courts of Equity gave a remedy.
>
> My Lords, it is known that in cases of actual fraud the Courts of Chancery and of Common Law exercised a concurrent jurisdiction from the earliest times. For some of these cases the greater freedom which, in early days, the Court of Chancery exercised in admitting the testimony of parties to the proceedings made it a more suitable tribunal. Moreover, its remedies were more elastic. Operating *in personam* as a Court of conscience it could order the defendant, not, indeed, in those days, to pay damages as such, but to make restitution, or to compensate the plaintiff by putting

---

[1] At p. 945.
[2] At p. 951.
[3] (1860), 1 De G.F. & J. 518.
[4] (1889), 14 App. Cas. 337, C.A.

him in as good a position pecuniarily as that in which he was before the injury.

But in addition to this concurrent jurisdiction, the Court of Chancery exercised an exclusive jurisdiction in cases which, although classified in that court as cases of fraud, yet did not necessarily import the element of *dolus malus*. The court took upon itself to prevent a man from acting against the dictates of conscience as defined by the court, and to grant injunctions in anticipation of injury, as well as relief where injury had been done. Common instances of this exclusive jurisdiction are cases arising out of breach of duty by persons standing in a fiduciary relation, such as the solicitor to the client, illustrated by Lord HARDWICKE's judgment in *Earl Chesterfield* v. *Janssen*.[1] I can hardly imagine that those who took part in the decision of *Derry* v. *Peek*[2] imagined that they could be supposed to have cast doubt on the principle of any cases arising under the exclusive jurisdiction of the Court of Chancery. No such case was before the House, which was dealing only with a case of actual fraud as to which the jurisdiction in equity was concurrent.''

There might, said Viscount HALDANE, be cases, of which the one before the House was one, where the conditions and relations of the parties were such as to give rise to duties of particular obligation. Viscount HALDANE went on to say[3]:

''Such a special duty may arise from the circumstances and relations of the parties. These may give rise to an implied contract at law or to a fiduciary obligation in equity. If such a duty can be inferred in a particular case of a person issuing a prospectus, as, for instance, in the case of directors issuing to the shareholders of the company which they direct a prospectus inviting the subscription by them of further capital, I do not find in *Derry* v. *Peek*[2] an authority for the suggestion that an action for damages for misrepresentation without an actual intention to deceive may not lie. What was decided there was that from the facts proved in that case no such special duty to be careful in statement could be inferred, and that mere want of care therefore gave rise to no cause of action. In other words, it was decided that the directors stood in no fiduciary relation and therefore were under no fiduciary duty to the public to whom they had addressed the invitation to subscribe. I have only to add that the special relationship must, whenever it is alleged, be clearly shewn to exist.''

He added that where such a duty arises, and there is a breach of it, an order will go for compensation to the injured party; and that since the Judicature Acts the equitable relief could be ordered in a court of common law.

---

[1] (1750), 2 Ves. Sen. 125.
[2] (1889), 14 App. Cas. 337, H.L.
[3] [1914] A.C. 932, H.L., at p. 955.

Nocton v. *Lord Ashburton*[1] decided at least that where the defendant was in a fiduciary relationship to the plaintiff that relationship might give rise to a duty of care, the breach of which would, notwithstanding the absence of fraud, support an action for compensation, or, since the Judicature Acts, for damages.   But the words of Lord HALDANE, in which such a fiduciary relationship was held to found such an action, were capable of being understood as going further, and as regarding a fiduciary relationship as only one instance of a wider class of special relationships, any of which might support the same kind of cause of action.   This passed in the meantime unnoticed, or almost unnoticed; another half-century was yet to go by before Lord HALDANE's suggestion was to bear fruit.

Robinson v. *National Bank of Scotland*

397   Only two years later *Robinson* v. *National Bank of Scotland*[2] came before the House of Lords.   This was an action for fraudulent misrepresentation in which fraud was held not proved as a fact; the representation was one made by a bank as to the credit of a customer.   It was not argued that the circumstances showed either contract or a fiduciary relationship.   Again it was held that in the absence of some special duty to take care negligence would not support an action for damages for misrepresentation, and that it was necessary to go so far as to prove fraud.[3]   But the case is to be noticed because of the trouble which Viscount HALDANE took to recall what had been said two years before in *Nocton* v. *Lord Ashburton*[4] as to the possibilities in cases in which some special relationship between the parties might be shown to exist.   He said[5]:

> "In saying that I wish emphatically to repeat what I said in advising this House in the case of *Nocton* v. *Lord Ashburton*[4] that it is a great mistake to suppose that, because the principle in *Derry* v. *Peek*[6] clearly covers all cases of the class to which I have referred, therefore the freedom of action of the courts in recognising special duties arising out of other kinds of relationship which they find established by the evidence is in any way affected.   I think, as I said in *Nocton's* case, that an exaggerated view was taken by a good many people of the scope of the decision in *Derry* v. *Peek*.   The whole of the doctrine as to fiduciary relationships, as to the duty of care arising from implied as well as express contracts, as to the duty of care arising from other special relationships which the courts may find to exist in particular

---

[1] [1914] A.C. 932, H.L.

[2] 1916, S.C. (H.L.) 154.

[3] The facts are obscure; see *per* Lord REID in *Hedley Byrne & Co., Ltd.* v. *Heller & Partners, Ltd.*, [1964] A.C. 465, H.L., at p. 491.

[4] [1914] A.C. 932, H.L.

[5] 1916, S.C. (H.L.) 154, at p. 157.

[6] (1889), 14 App. Cas. 337, H.L.

cases, still remains, and I should be very sorry if any word fell from me which should suggest that the courts are in any way hampered in recognising that the duty of care may be established when such cases really occur.''

Candler v. Crane, Christmas & Co.

398 In 1951 *Candler* v. *Crane, Christmas & Co.*[1] was decided by the Court of Appeal. A firm of public accountants had been engaged by a commercial man and a company of which he was the managing director for life to prepare a statement of accounts for the company. It was desirous of increasing its capital resources, and it advertised for persons willing to subscribe for shares. The accountants knew this, and the member of their staff who was preparing the accounts was introduced to the plaintiff, who contemplated taking up shares as advertised. The preparation of the accounts proceeded to the end that they should be shown to the plaintiff to help him to decide whether or not to take up the shares. The statement of accounts was negligently prepared and presented a false picture of the company's assets. The plaintiff took up the shares in reliance on the picture presented by the accounts. The company was wound up. The plaintiff lost his money. He sued the accountants, pleading negligent misrepresentation.

LLOYD-JACOB J. dismissed the action. He held that the staff-accountant who had prepared the accounts and had actually shown them to the plaintiff had done so in the course of his employment, that the accounts were defective and deficient, and that defendants had been ''extremely careless in their preparation'', but he held that the circumstances disclosed no duty of care owed by them to the plaintiff.

This judgment was affirmed by a majority of the Court of Appeal, COHEN and ASQUITH L.JJ., DENNING L.J. dissenting. DENNING L.J. was invited to read the first judgment. In a characteristically vigorous judgment he advocated a review of the law as it was at that moment generally accepted. *Cann* v. *Willson*,[2] he said, might have been rejected in *Le Lievre* v. *Gould*[3]; and if it had been correctly overruled, *George* v. *Skivington*[4] must have gone with it. But in *Donoghue* v. *Stevenson*[5] the Lords had expressly reinstated *George* v. *Skivington*.[4] *Derry* v. *Peek*[6] had been accepted for long as deciding more than it did. The common

---

1 [1951] 2 K.B. 164, C.A.
2 (1888), 39 Ch.D. 39.
3 [1893] 1 Q.B. 491, C.A.
4 (1869), L.R. 5 Exch. 1.
5 [1932] A.C. 562, H.L.
6 (1889), 14 App. Cas. 337, H.L.

tendency to accept it for more than it decided had been exposed in *Nocton* v. *Lord Ashburton*.[1]   The decision of the Lords in *Donoghue* v. *Stevenson*[2] had opened new frontiers, and the Court of Appeal was (he thought) entitled to review its own decision, now three-quarters of a century old, in *Le Lievre* v. *Gould*.[3]   He would have allowed the appeal, holding that the test of proximity foreshadowed in *Heaven* v. *Pender*[4] and adopted in *M'Alister (or Donoghue)* v. *Stevenson*[2] demonstrated in this case a duty between the accountants and him to whom their accounts were shown with their co-operation, notwithstanding that no contract existed between them.   It was in this judgment that DENNING L.J. referred to the "timorous souls" whose lack of resolution in a crisis prevented the law from evolving as changed conditions required.

But DENNING L.J. had ranged himself among the "bold spirits" in vain.   ASQUITH and COHEN L.JJ. could not be persuaded.   ASQUITH L.J. considered with anxious care the submission that *M'Alister (or Donoghue)* v. *Stevenson*[2] had necessarily impliedly overruled *Le Lievre* v. *Gould*.[3]   He found it possible to reconcile the two decisions by limiting the application of the doctrine in *M'Alister (or Donoghue)* v. *Stevenson* to cases where the damage of which the plaintiff complained was "physical".   This boundary, which seemed to some critics to be arbitrarily drawn, was to limit the obligation of *M'Alister (or Donoghue)* v. *Stevenson*[2] for a further thirteen years.[5]   COHEN L.J., reviewing the treatment of negligent mis-statements by the leading textbook writers of the day on that subject, found all of them to agree in principle that an action for damages for negligent, non-fraudulent, misrepresentation would not lie, and for this reason joined ASQUITH L.J. on the conservative side.   The plaintiff's claim was dismissed, and it was not until the Lords gave another plaintiff damages at last in *Hedley Byrne & Co., Ltd.* v. *Heller & Partners, Ltd.*[6] that the doctrine foreshadowed by BOWEN L.J. and actively supported by DENNING L.J. became embodied in a new principle of tortious lia-bility in the textbooks.

Woods v. *Martins Bank, Ltd.*[7]

399   In 1958 SALMON J. had to deal at the Leeds Assizes with a claim

---

[1] [1914] A.C. 932, H.L.

[2] [1932] A.C. 562, H.L.

[3] [1893] 1 Q.B. 491, C.A.

[4] (1882), 9 Q.B.D. 302; reversed (1883), 11 Q.B.D. 503.

[5] It was rejected by the Lords in *Hedley Byrne & Co., Ltd.* v. *Heller & Partners, Ltd.*, [1964] A.C. 465, H.L., 13 years later.   See, in particular, *per* Lord MORRIS at p. 496; *per* Lord HODSON at p. 509; *per* Lord DEVLIN at pp. 517–518, *per* Lord PEARCE at page 538.

[6] [1964] A.C. 465, H.L.

[7] [1958] 3 All E.R. 166; [1959] 1 Q.B. 55.

in negligence brought against a bank for advice as to investments honestly but negligently given to the plaintiff at a time before he had become a customer of the bank (for later he became a customer). SALMON J., in a judgment foreshadowing to a remarkable degree the decision of the Lords five years later in *Hedley Byrne & Co., Ltd.* v. *Heller & Partners, Ltd.*,[1] the next case to be dealt with in this survey, gave judgment in damages for the plaintiff, holding that in the circumstances of the particular case the bank had assumed a fiduciary relationship towards the plaintiff, giving rise to the duty of care of which *Nocton* v. *Lord Ashburton* was the classic example. He said[2]:

> "The plaintiff was a potential customer and one whose custom the defendant Johnson was anxious to acquire and soon did acquire. The plaintiff had asked the defendant Johnson if he would become his financial adviser, to which the defendant Johnson had replied that the defendant bank would be glad to take charge of his financial affairs. In my judgment, a fiduciary relationship existed between the plaintiff and the defendants. No doubt the defendant Johnson could have refused to advise the plaintiff, but, as he chose to advise him, the law in these circumstances imposes an obligation on him to advise with reasonable care and skill. This seems to me to be an even stronger case from the point of view of the plaintiff than cases of gratuitous deposit, such as *Giblin* v. *McMullen*,[3] or gratuitous services, such as *Whitehead* v. *Greetham*,[4] where it has been held that an obligation to use due care and skill may arise."

Hedley Byrne & Co., Ltd. v. *Heller & Partners, Ltd.*

400 So the law stood until 1963, in which year *Hedley Byrne & Co., Ltd.* v. *Heller & Partners, Ltd.*[5] came before the Lords. In this case again it was a firm of bankers which was the defendant. The representation complained of was again one as to the creditworthiness of a third party. Plaintiffs, a firm of advertising agents, in the course of dealing with television corporations and newspaper companies on behalf of their clients, found that they might become personally liable for their clients' engagements. Before going further they deemed it prudent to make inquiries as to the financial standing of one of these, E Ltd. They asked their own bankers for a report. Those bankers, in accordance with

---

[1] [1964] A.C. 465, H.L. Lord HODSON referred to the decision in *Woods* v. *Martins Bank, Ltd.* with approval at p. 510; Lord DEVLIN at pp. 528–529; and Lord PEARCE at p. 539.

[2] [1959] 1 Q.B. 55, at p. 72. It may be noted, as a matter of interest, that the sentence "In my judgment a fiduciary relationship existed between the plaintiff and the defendants" did not appear in the judgment as reported in [1958] 3 All E.R. 166, at p. 174.

[3] (1868), L.R. 2 P.C. 317.

[4] (1825), M'Cle. & Yo. 205.

[5] [1964] A.C. 465, H.L.

current banking practice, made an inquiry from E Ltd.'s banker. The referee made a written report favourable to E Ltd. It was headed: "Confidential. For your private use and without responsibility on the part of the bank or its officials". Plaintiffs suffered loss, and sued in damages for negligent misrepresentation.

The Lords affirmed the judgment of the Court of Appeal, and of the trial judge, dismissing the claim. They did not decide the question of fact, in so far as it was a question of fact, whether the report was made negligently, for they held (as the Court of Appeal had done) that whether defendants had been careful or careless they had answered the inquiry made to them on the definite understanding that in doing so they should incur no legal responsibility. For that reason the claim failed.

But their Lordships did not stop there. This was one of the rare occasions when they were not to be inhibited by a strict consideration of the actual requirements of the case before them. They went on to deal, *obiter*, with the argument, urged upon them for plaintiff-appellant, that *Candler* v. *Crane, Christmas & Co.*[1] had been wrongly decided. All the members of the House agreed in accepting this submission, even though on the facts of the particular case the appeal was dismissed. In the result the propositions foreshadowed in *Nocton* v. *Lord Ashburton*[2] and *Robinson* v. *National Bank of Scotland*[3] were accepted as correct in principle, and for the future the law was to recognise that there may be a relationship between representor and representee, apart from contract, and not amounting to fiduciary relationship, sufficient to impose a duty of care in making a representation; and that the breach of this duty may found an action in damages. Their Lordships held, moreover, that the facts in the case before them gave rise to just such a relationship; and that in that case plaintiffs failed only because the liability which would otherwise have arisen had been expressly excluded by the terms of the representation itself. *Le Lievre* v. *Gould*[4] was overruled, Lord DENNING's dissenting view in *Candler* v. *Crane, Christmas & Co.*[5] was vindicated, and notice was given that henceforth parties might stand in such a relationship, one to the other, as to give rise to an action in damages for negligence in making a misrepresentation, even though not bound to each other either by contract or by a fiduciary relationship. One may pause for a moment's com-

[1] [1951] 1 All E.R. 426; [1951] 2 K.B. 164, C.A.
[2] [1914] A.C. 932, H.L.
[3] 1916, S.C. (H.L.) 154.
[4] [1893] 1 Q.B. 491, C.A.
[5] [1951] 1 All E.R. 426; [1951] 2 K.B. 164, C.A.

miseration with the unsuccessful plaintiff in *Candler* v. *Crane, Christmas &*
Co.,[1] to whom it could have been little consolation to realise that the
law had at last caught up with his case.

The test of "special relationship" as indicated by Hedley Byrne

401   It has always been accepted that a relationship between representor and representee such as will give rise to a duty of care, the breach
of which will support an action in damages, may arise *ex contractu*.   This
was implicit in all the judgments in *Hedley Byrne & Co., Ltd.* v. *Heller &*
Partners, Ltd.,[2] and was expressly stated by some of their Lordships.   And
at least since *Nocton* v. *Lord Ashburton*[3] it has been apparent that there may
be other cases—e.g. where a fiduciary relationship exists between representor and representee—which will lead to the same result.   In *Hedley*
Byrne the question plainly arose, what were the criteria by which it could
be determined whether in a given case such a relationship would arise?
A persual of their Lordships' judgments does not indicate any plainly
apparent test by which the question may be decided.   Some of their
Lordships thought that the duty must arise out of a voluntary assumption
of responsibility on the part of the representor.[4]   Others thought that it
arose through the representor being known to possess, or having held
himself out as possessing, some special skill or competence, or access to
special information, upon which the plaintiff had to his knowledge relied.[5]
This special skill, competence, or knowledge, it was said by some, should

---

[1] [1951] 1 All E.R. 426; [1951] 2 K.B. 164, C.A.

[2] [1964] A.C. 465, H.L.

[3] [1914] A.C. 932, H.L.

[4] *Per* Lord REID at p. 483—"The most natural requirement would be that expressly or by
implication from the circumstances the speaker or writer has *undertaken some responsibility*";
and again at p. 486: "I can see no logical stopping place short of all those relationships where
it is plain that the party seeking information or advice was trusting the other to exercise such a
degree of care as the circumstances required, where it was reasonable for him to do that, and
where the other gave the information or advice when he knew or ought to have known that the
inquirer was relying on him.   At p. 503 Lord MORRIS speaks of the representor "taking it
upon himself to give information . . .".   The same phrase was repeated by Lord HODSON
at p. 514.   Though Lord DEVLIN at pp. 529–530 expressly disclaimed any attempt at definition,
his judgment at p. 531 and again at p. 533 appears to insist on this element of the voluntary
assumption of responsibility.   It has become clear since *Hedley Byrne* that the requirement of
voluntary assumption of responsibility cannot be a universal one, applicable in all cases—see
Ministry of Housing and Local Government v. *Sharp*, [1970] 1 All. E.R. 1009, considered in para. 404
post.   But it seems to be necessary in a case where the situation is essentially similar to that in
Hedley Byrne.   This test is apparently the one on which the hypothetical cartographer is generally
agreed to be immune—see para. 412, *post*.

[5] *Per* Lord MORRIS at p. 502: "If someone possessed of a special skill undertakes, quite
irrespective of contract, to apply that skill for the assistance of another person who relies upon
such skill, a duty of care will arise".   For further discussion on this test see paras. 412–413,
post.

or might be that of a professional man, who by the practice of his profession must be deemed to hold himself out as possessing or exercising it whenever he gave advice.[1] In two of the judgments the test was proposed as whether, in circumstances

> "in which a person is so placed that others would reasonably rely upon his judgment or his skill or upon his ability to make careful inquiry, he takes it upon himself to give information or advice to . . . another person whom . . . he knows will place reliance upon it".[2]

Lord PEARCE preferred to inquire simply whether the representation or advice was given in connection with a business or professional transaction whose nature made clear the gravity of the inquiry and the importance and influence attached to the answer.[3] All their Lordships were emphatic that the duty was not a general one, imposed by the law on all who chose to make representations, or offer advice, of whatever kind and in whatever circumstances.[4] And representations of fact, or advice, offered without thought of legal responsibility on e.g. social occasions, cannot, said their Lordships, support an action.[5]

But while all these tests were put forward by one or other of their Lordships as determinative of liability, it has been remarked by critics of *Hedley Byrne* that no test was proposed which received the approval of a majority of those giving judgment as final in all cases, or even in the normal run of cases. It was agreed that the tests must be different in different classes of case, and it was left to later cases to attempt to apply, to different sets of facts, the various tests set out above, and any others which might later be suggested as appropriate.[6] Some of these have in

---

[1] *Per* Lord MORRIS at p. 494, and again at pp. 502–503; *per* Lord PEARCE at p. 539—"To impart such a duty the representation must normally, I think, concern a business or professional transaction whose nature makes clear the gravity of the inquiry and the importance and influence attributed to the answer". And *cf.* the dissenting judgment of DENNING L.J. in *Candler* v. *Crane, Christmas & Co.*, [1951] 2 K.B. 164, C.A., at pp. 179 and 180—"Herein lies the difference between these professional men and other persons who have been held under no duty to use care . . ." This test is further discussed in paras. 412–413, *post.*

[2] *Per* Lord MORRIS at p. 503; *per* Lord HODSON at p. 514.

[3] At p. 539. This was very like the test proposed by the minority in *Mutual Life and Citizens Assurance Co., Ltd.* v. *Evatt*, [1971] A.C. 793, P.C. at p. 811; but the majority judgment narrowed the test to make special skill or means of knowledge essential.

[4] *Per* Lord REID at p. 483: "So it seems to me that there is a great good sense behind our present law that in general an innocent but negligent misrepresentation gives no cause of action". Lord PEARCE at p. 539 said. "The true rule is that innocent misrepresentation *per se* gives no right to damages". In *Australia*, see *per* MENZIES J. in *Mutual Life and Citizens Assurance Co., Ltd.* v. *Evatt* (1968), 42 A.L.J.R. 316, at p. 334.

[5] *Per* Lord REID at pp. 482–483; *per* Lord MORRIS at p. 494; *per* Lord PEARCE at p. 539. *Cf. per* DENNING L.J. in his dissenting judgment in *Candler* v. *Crane, Christmas & Co.*, [1951] 2 K.B. 164, C.A., at p. 180.

[6] See the judgment of Lord REID at p. 482; of Lord DIPLOCK at pp. 529–530.

the subsequent decisions received a greater degree of acceptance than others; and now, after ten years,[1] it is possible to suggest a list of cases in which it may be thought tolerably certain that the courts will find a duty of care, to compare with others in which the opposite result has been indicated. An attempt to list these is made at the end of this chapter.[2]

402 *Hedley Byrne & Co., Ltd.* v. *Heller & Partners, Ltd.*[3] must be acknowledged to be one of the great cases of our time. It opened the gate into a new field of tortious liability—liability for negligence consisting of *saying something*, at the suit of persons to whom the speaker (or writer) was not bound in contract, nor yet by any fiduciary relationship imposing on him a duty in respect of his utterance. And not only did it recognise a cause of action for negligence in making a *representation*, in the sense accepted in this work, of a statement of existing fact; it was clear that negligence *in giving advice* was covered by the new principle.[4] It is interesting to note that this extension of liability for negligence, like the almost equally important extension of liability in estoppel introduced by *Central London Property Trust, Ltd.* v. *High Trees House, Ltd.*,[5] owed much of its inspiration to Lord DENNING, who, as DENNING L.J., had unsuccessfully sponsored the new development in his vigorous dissenting judgment in *Candler* v. *Crane, Christmas & Co.*[6] The parallel is not without its points of interest. The new estoppel in *High Trees* had been founded on *dicta* plainly *obiter*, the doctrine being laid down by DENNING J. as one available to support a claim by plaintiffs in a case where the plaintiff had in the event failed; but this inauspicious beginning did not prevent *High Trees* from holding its own against attacks by orthodox critics, and ultimately establishing itself soundly as a new principle in the law of the twentieth century. History repeated itself in *Hedley Byrne*. Again, the new doctrine was unashamedly put forward as *obiter dicta*. The Lords, in a case in which it was necessary to say no more than that any possible liability on the part of the bank had been stifled at birth by the disclaimer of liability which it had included in the very text

---

[1] Written in 1973.
[2] See paras. 412 and 413, *post*.
[3] [1964] A.C. 465, H.L.
[4] Lord REID at p. 486; Lord MORRIS at p. 503; Lord HODSON at p. 514 specifically used the word "advice", and the point is clear beyond words in all the judgments.
[5] [1947] K.B. 130.
[6] [1951] 2 K.B. 164, C.A.

of its representation, went out of their way to lay down the law as it would have been applicable had it not been for that disclaimer. Again time has shown that the fact that the new doctrine was founded on *obiter dicta* was not to be any disadvantage; it has survived the same kind of attack as was made upon *High Trees*, made by the same critics. In this country the point was expressly taken before CAIRNS J. in *W. B. Anderson & Sons* v. *Rhodes (Liverpool), Ltd.*[1]; he firmly rejected it, saying:

> "When five members of the House of Lords have all said, after close examination of the authorities, that a certain type of tort exists, I think that a Judge of first instance should proceed on the basis that it does exist without pausing to embark on an investigation of whether what was said was necessary to the ultimate decision."

And much the same was said in other cases in other jurisdictions. A similar attitude was subsequently taken in higher courts; in *Ministry of Housing and Local Government* v. *Sharp*[2] and *Mutual Life and Citizens Assurance Co., Ltd.* v. *Evatt*,[3] the Court of Appeal, and the Judicial Committee respectively accepted the authority of *Hedley Byrne*. Any controversy has been not as to the existence of the new liability, but as to its limits. It will be convenient now to notice in a little detail some of the more important decisions in which these limits have been explored by the courts.

Anderson & Sons v. *Rhodes (Liverpool), Ltd.*

403 Though the principle enunciated in *Hedley Byrne & Co., Ltd.* v. *Heller & Partners, Ltd.*[4] was soon accepted in other Commonwealth jurisdictions,[5] and was almost immediately applied in litigation in this country, the first significant addition to the doctrine did not appear in the Reports till 1967. In *W. B. Anderson & Sons* v. *Rhodes (Liverpool), Ltd.*,[6] CAIRNS J. had to consider a series of representations as to creditworthiness made by one company to a number of persons contemplating trading with another, in circumstances in which the representor was a commission agent, having itself a financial interest in the trading opera-

---

[1] [1967] 2 All E.R. 850. The case is considered in some detail in para. 403, below.
[2] [1970] 2 Q.B. 252, C.A.
[3] [1971] A.C. 793, P.C.
[4] [1964] A.C. 465, H.L.
[5] e.g. in *New Zealand*, in *Smith* v. *Auckland Hospital Board*, [1965] N.Z.L.R. 191, C.A.; in *N.S.W.*, *Dominion Freeholders, Ltd.* v. *Aird*, [1966] 2 N.S.W. S.R. 293.
[6] [1967] 2 All E.R. 850.

tions contemplated. It knew of the unsatisfactory state of the accounts existing between it and the company about which the inquiries were made; but negligently represented it as worthy of credit. CAIRNS J. applied *Hedley Byrne*, and, in the claims before him in which he was able to find that representations as to credit had actually been made (for the facts differed as between different plaintiffs) he awarded damages.

The case is significant in two respects. The first of these is the acceptance by CAIRNS J. of the new principle as one which does not recognise an action for damages for misrepresentation, but rather allows an action for damages for negligence, in which the duty to take care consists of a duty to take care in making a representation. This distinction was essential in *W. B. Anderson & Sons* v. *Rhodes (Liverpool), Ltd.*[1]; for the defendant pleaded Lord Tenterden's Act,[2] which provides that no action for damages will lie "upon a representation" as to credit unless in writing signed by the representor. CAIRNS J. held that the defence given by the Act was unavailable in a *Hedley Byrne* claim, saying that

> "The action in respect of a negligent misrepresentation *is not an action on the representation*, and is an action for breach of duty of care".[3]

This distinction was to become more clearly apparent in later cases, in which claims were to be allowed which were presented not by representees at all, but by persons to whose notice the representation never came, but who were nevertheless damaged by the negligence of the representor in making it.[4]

The second significant point in *W. B. Anderson & Sons* v. *Rhodes (Liverpool), Ltd.*[5] lies in the kind of relationship which CAIRNS J. held in that case sufficient to give rise to the duty of care. This was *not* a case like *Candler* v. *Crane, Christmas & Co.*,[6] or *Hedley Byrne*[7] itself, in which the

---

[1] [1967] 2 All E.R. 850.
[2] Statute of Frauds Amendment Act 1828 (9 Geo. 4, c. 14). The same reasoning as appealed to CAIRNS J. was accepted in Australia in *Mutual Life and Citizens Assurance Co., Ltd.* v. *Evatt* (1968), 42 A.L.J.R. 316 *per* BARWICK C.J. at pp. 325–326. An appeal to the Judicial Committee succeeded; but their Lordships did not allude to this point.
[3] At p. 865. He recalled the speech of Lord WRENBURY in *Banbury* v. *Bank of Montreal*, [1918] A.C. 626, H.L. 713: "An innocent misrepresentation constitutes no cause of action. If there existed a duty, an action lies for negligence and breach of duty, and in that action the fact that there was misrepresentation, though innocent, is material. But an action cannot be brought upon an innocent misrepresentation *simpliciter*. It is maintained upon the breach of duty."
[4] e.g., *Ministry of Housing and Local Government* v. *Sharp*, [1970] 2 Q.B. 252, C.A., for a note on which see para. 404, below.
[5] [1967] 2 All E.R. 850.
[6] [1951] 1 All E.R. 426; [1951] 2 K.B. 164, C.A.
[7] [1964] A.C. 465, H.L.

representor was a banker or a professional adviser. Defendant company made no claims to any special professional skill or judgment. It was held, however, that in the circumstances of the case the special information to which the representor, but not the plaintiffs, had access, considered in conjunction with the fact that the inquiry was made in a business context, the gravity of the inquiry, and the importance which the plaintiffs attached to the answers, brought the case within at least the tests proposed by Lord REID and Lord PEARCE in *Hedley Byrne*. And though in the crucial passage in his judgment CAIRNS J. did not rely upon the point, it cannot be overlooked that he was dealing with a case in which the defendant had a financial interest in the continuance of the course of dealing between the plaintiffs and the third party as to whom the inquiries were made. This circumstance was one which was thought worthy of mention by the Judicial Committee when in a later case they gave their tacit approval to this decision.[1]

Ministry of Housing and Local Government v. *Sharp*

404 The next case to be noticed, *Ministry of Housing and Local Government* v. *Sharp*,[2] was one in which the "representation" which founded the action was never brought to the attention of the plaintiff, nor was it intended that it should reach him. The claim was brought by the Minister of Housing, who in 1960 paid to the then owner of certain land statutory compensation under the Town and Country Planning Act in respect of certain land for which planning provision had been refused. The Minister duly registered with the local land registry a charge upon the land in question. This step had the effect of entitling the Minister to recover the money paid as compensation from any future developer of the land, should provision to develop later be granted. In 1962 the owner of the land obtained permission to develop it, and a prospective purchaser caused a search to be made of the Register. This search was made in the usual way by a clerk in the employ of the local authority; he searched negligently,[3] and his search omitted to include the charge registered by the Minister. As a result the Registrar issued a clear certificate to the purchaser, who completed his purchase on the footing disclosed by the certificate. When the matter was noticed the purchaser declined to repay the compensation to the Minister. The Minister there-

---

1 *Mutual Life and Citizens' Assurance Co., Ltd.* v. *Evatt*, [1971] A.C. 793, P.C., at p. 809. The case is considered in paras 407 *et seq.*, *post*.

2 [1970] 2 Q.B. at p. 252, C.A.

3 i.e. using less than proper care, if those words can be thought to mean anything when the question is begged as to whether he owed any duty of care to anyone.

upon sued (a) the Registrar and (b) the local authority by whose servant the search had been made. It was conceded for the Minister, at the hearing, that the certificate of the searching clerk was conclusive, and that it left the Minister with no claim against the purchaser to recover the compensation moneys such as he would have had against the vendor had the vendor himself developed the land.

FISHER J., who tried the action,[1] held that its conduct had been misconceived, and that the Minister had been in error in conceding, as he did, that he was precluded in the circumstances from recovering the compensation moneys from the purchaser. He held that they would have been recoverable from the purchaser of the land, had he been sued. He held further that the Registrar was under a statutory duty to possible purchasers to keep the register in order, and that the purchasers, if held liable to make the refund to the Minister, would have had an action in damages against the Registrar for breach of his statutory duty. As for the local authority, he held that it was liable for the negligence of its servant who was "under a duty of care towards the encumbrancer" and "liable to him if he is in breach of it and foreseeable damage results". On this basis, therefore, the local authority would have been liable to the Minister for whatever damage he could prove; but as, according to the judge, he could show no damage, his claim failed.

The Minister appealed, and the appeal was successful.[2] The Court of Appeal reversed FISHER J.'s decision as to the liability of the purchasers to refund the compensation to the Minister. They held that the purchaser was protected by a specific section in the statute. This decision left the Minister out of pocket; but the Court of Appeal had no difficulty in agreeing with FISHER J. that the local authority, once the Minister had suffered damage, was liable for the negligent search of its servant which had been at the bottom of the transaction. They exonerated the Registrar on the claim against him, holding that he was not in breach of any statutory duty.

It is, of course, that part of the decision of the Court of Appeal which held the local authority liable for the search of its clerk that is the point of interest in this chapter. The three judgments of the members of the Court of Appeal (Lord DENNING M.R., SALMON and CROSS L.JJ.) while they to some extent elucidated the principles governing liability for

---

[1] FISHER J.'s judgment is reported in [1970] 2 Q.B. 223.
[2] [1970] 2 Q.B. at p. 252, C.A.

negligent misrepresentation, also raise other questions of difficulty which must again require resolution in later cases. Lord DENNING said[1] :

> "I have no doubt that the clerk is liable. He was under a duty at common law to use due care. That was a duty which he owed to any person— incumbrancer or purchaser—who, he knew or ought to have known, might be injured if he made a mistake. The case comes four square within the principles which are stated in *Candler* v. *Crane, Christmas & Co.*,[2] and which were approved by the House of Lords in *Hedley Byrne & Co., Ltd.* v. *Heller & Partners, Ltd.*[3] . . . In my opinion the duty to use due care in a statement arises, not from any voluntary assumption of responsibility, but from the fact that the person making it knows, or ought to know, that others, being his neighbours in this regard, would act on the faith of the statement being accurate. That is enough to bring the duty into being. It is owed, of course, to the person to whom the certificate is issued and who he knows is going to act on it, see the judgment of CARDOZO J. in *Glanzer* v. *Sheppard*.[4] But it also is owed to any person who he knows or ought to know, will be injuriously affected by a mistake, such as the incumbrancer here."

405 It will be seen that the doctrine conceived in the dissenting judgment of DENNING L.J. in *Candler* v. *Crane, Christmas & Co.* has already undergone a remarkable development. In that case the cause of action had been plainly put by the plaintiff as *misrepresentation*; it was a misrepresentation by a representor, who was sought to be made liable to a representee to whom the representation had actually been made, when the clerk to the accountants handed him the balance sheets of the company's affairs which he had prepared. But in *Ministry of Housing and Local Government* v. *Sharp*[5] it was the Minister who was the plaintiff, and on no possible view of the matter could it be said that any misrepresentation had been made *to him*. The search which the clerk made was not made for him, but for the purchaser of the land; it was communicated to the purchaser, not to the Minister. It never came to the Minister's notice, nor was it ever contemplated by the searcher that it should. The Minister did not act in any way upon it. It is therefore a little difficult to see how it could have been said with any exactitude that the case "came four-square within the principles stated in *Candler* v. *Crane, Christmas & Co.*" It might have been more precise to say that the case came within the ultimate development of those principles if they were extended to their full logical limits. This view of the matter was per-

---

[1] At p. 268.
[2] [1951] 2 K.B. 164, C.A.
[3] [1964] A.C. 465, H.L.
[4] (1922), 233 N.Y. 236.
[5] [1970] 2 Q.B. at p. 252, C.A.

haps more clearly set out in the judgment of SALMON L.J., who in agreeing with the Master of the Rolls as to the result of the appeal, said[1]:

> "The present case does not precisely fit into any category of negligence yet
> considered by the courts. The Ministry has not been misled by any careless
> statement made to it by the defendants or made by the defendants to some-
> one else who the defendants knew would be likely to pass it onto a third
> party such as the Ministry, in circumstances in which the third party might
> reasonably be expected to rely on it, see for example, DENNING L.J.'s
> dissenting judgment in *Candler* v. *Crane, Christmas & Co.* which was adopted
> and approved by the House of Lords in *Hedley Byrne & Co., Ltd.* v. *Heller &*
> *Partners, Ltd.* I am not, however, troubled by the fact that the present
> case is, in many respects, unique. I rely on the celebrated dictum of Lord
> MACMILLAN that 'the categories of negligence are never closed'."

Effect of the decision

406 In *Ministry of Housing and Local Government* v. *Sharp*[2] the cause of
action which inauspiciously made its earlier appearances as a claim by
representor against representee for negligent misrepresentation in *Le
Lievre* v. *Gould*,[3] now appears ultimately transformed into a claim in
negligence presented against a representor, it is true, but by a person
who on no view of the matter can be thought of as a representee. The
representation which was the foundation of the action never came to the
notice of the plaintiff, nor was it intended or contemplated by the representor that it might do so. The plaintiff suffered damage not by acting
upon the representation himself, but because others acted upon it. It is
now a claim in negligence pure and simple, and the relationship between
plaintiff and defendant is no longer the relationship of representee and
representor but is that of Atkinian neighbours. And the cause of action
has undertaken such a degree of evolution and mutation that it may now
properly be said, not that an action for damages will lie in some circumstances for an innocent misrepresentation but rather that so long as
between plaintiff and defendant there can in the circumstances of the
case be discerned a duty of care, then the breach of that duty will give
rise to an action for damages notwithstanding that it consisted of a misrepresentation or even of unsound advice.[4]

Mutual Life and Citizens Assurance Co., Ltd. v. *Evatt*

407 The most recent case at the time of writing is *Mutual Life and*

---

[1] At p. 278.
[2] [1970] 1 All E.R. 1009, C.A.
[3] [1893] 1 Q.B. 491, C.A.
[4] See para. 410, *post*.

Citizens Assurance Co., Ltd. v. *Evatt*,[1] a decision of the Privy Council on appeal from the High Court of Australia. The representation was again as to the financial standing of a third party, and for the purposes of the decision, which was given on a plea of demurrer, it was assumed that the advice given was given without that careful consideration which would, if accorded to the inquiry, have led to different advice. Respondent was a policy-holder of appellant (M Ltd.). He was contemplating investing moneys in P Ltd. That company and appellant company were both subsidiary companies of M Ltd., and it might therefore be supposed that appellant company had access to information, as to the financial standing of P Ltd., which respondent had himself no means of obtaining.

In the High Court of Australia[2] it was held by a majority (Sir Garfield BARWICK C.J. and KITTO and MENZIES JJ., TAYLOR and OWEN JJ. dissenting) that although appellant company did not have or hold itself out as having any special skill such as (for instance) is ordinarily possessed by solicitors, bankers, etc., yet the facts were sufficient to demonstrate a "special relationship" such as would support a *Hedley Byrne* claim.

Sir Garfield BARWICK C.J., addressing himself to the criteria of such a special relationship, thought that three tests should be cumulatively complied with. First, that the circumstances should be such as to have caused the representor to realise that it was being trusted by the representee to give information or advice to which it had access or as to which it had opportunity to exercise judgment[3]; second, that it must realise that the representee intended to act upon the information or advice "in connection with some matter of business or serious consequence"[4]; and third, it must be reasonable in the circumstances for the representee to rely upon the utterance.[5] MENZIES J., agreeing with the result, himself set out the tests as (1) a position of special advantage on the part of the representor, (2) an election on his part to give the advice, and the giving of it without disclaimer of responsibility and (3) knowledge that the representee relied upon the advice.[6] Both judges expressed the opinion that special skill or facilities for obtaining information were not essential to the necessary relationship.[7] KITTO J. agreed with the result;

---

[1] [1971] A.C. 793, P.C.

[2] At the time of writing the case had not been reported in the Commonwealth Law Reports; the references are to (1968), 42 A.L.J.R. 316.

[3] At pp. 321–322: "I should think", he said, "that in general this element will arise out of an unequal position of the parties which the recipient reasonably infers to exist."

[4] At p. 322.

[5] At p. 322.

[6] At p. 340.

[7] BARWICK C.J. at p. 323; MENZIES J. at p. 340.

he thought that special facilities for obtaining information were sufficiently alleged in the pleadings.[1]   For these rather different reasons all three judges thought that respondent had made out his case on the pleadings.

TAYLOR and OWEN JJ. dissented.   Their reasons were simple. TAYLOR J. said:

> "Where a person is simply asked for his *opinion* concerning the financial standing or reputation of another person or company he will not, in expressing his opinion, be subject to a duty of care unless it sufficiently appears that the advice was sought because of his skill and judgment in the field of the inquiry and that the inquirer proposes to rely upon such skill and judgment and that this was, or should reasonably have been, known to him".[2]

OWEN J. was content with the proposition that failing proof of "special relationship" the duty owed by representor to representee is no more than honesty,[3] and that the relationship proved in the case before the court was no more than that which existed between representor and representee in *Derry* v. *Peek*,[4] *Low* v. *Bouverie*,[5] and *Robinson* v. *National Bank of Scotland*.[6]   In the High Court of Australia, then, the plea of demurrer failed, and the plaintiffs pleadings were held to disclose a cause of action.

The Privy Council[7] reversed the decision of the High Court of Australia —again by a majority of three to two.   In this crucial conflict as to the scope of *Hedley Byrne* & *Co.*, *Ltd.* v. *Heller* & *Partners*, *Ltd.*,[8] five of the most eminent living judges of the British Commonwealth were on either side.   The champions of the liberal view, holding the gate open, were Lords REID and MORRIS, Sir Garfield BARWICK C.J. and KITTO and MENZIES JJ.—a formidable team indeed.   The conservative view, which in the event prevailed, was advanced by Lords HODSON, GUEST, and DIPLOCK in the Privy Council and by TAYLOR and OWEN JJ. in the High Court.   This was an interesting division of opinion indeed, in which it may be observed that the senior judges in each jurisdiction supported the liberal, the less senior the conservative attitude.

Lord DIPLOCK, delivering the advice of the majority in the Privy Council, came down for restricting the special relationship, in the kind of case before the court, to two classes of case, not very different from each

---

[1] At p. 329.
[2] At p. 334.
[3] At p. 344.
[4] (1889), 14 App. Cas. 337, H.L.
[5] [1891] 3 Ch. 82, C.A.
[6] 1916 S.C. (H.L.) 154.
[7] Reported in [1971] A.C. 793, P.C.
[8] [1964] A.C. 465, H.L.

other; first, the case where, by carrying on a business or profession which involves the giving of advice calling for special skill and competence the defendant has let it be known that he claims or possesses and is prepared to exercise the skill and competence used by persons who give such advice in the ordinary course of their business. Second, the case where, though the defendant does not carry on any such business, he has let it be known in some other way that he claims to possess skill and competence in the subject matter of the particular inquiry comparable with that of persons who do carry on the business of advising on that subject matter, and is prepared to exercise that skill and competence on the occasion in question. The judgment of the majority observed that in their view there could be no half-way house between these as minimum requirements and other cases in which, no special skill being pretended to, or represented, a representor, as shown by such cases as *Low* v. *Bouverie*,[1] owed no duty more than to be honest in what he said.

Lord REID and Lord MORRIS dissented. As original participants in the *Hedley Byrne* judgment, they could perhaps feel some sense of injury when they heard their own speeches in that case "interpreted" by Lord DIPLOCK to support the narrower view. They protested that the door which they had helped to open in the earlier case should not now be closed again, at least to the extent which the judgment of the majority must contemplate. The minority judgment puts this point of view succinctly[2]:

> "In our judgment when an inquirer consults a business man in the course of his business and makes it plain to him that he is seeking considered advice and intends to act on it in a particular way, any reasonable business man would realise that, if he chooses to give advice without any warning or qualification, he is putting himself under a moral obligation to take some care. It appears to us to be well within the principles established by the *Hedley Byrne* case to regard his action in giving such advice as creating a special relationship between him and the inquirer and to translate his moral obligation into a legal obligation to take such care as is reasonable in the whole circumstances."

As at the time of writing the matter stands thus: in cases showing the kind of facts proved in *Robinson* v. *National Bank of Scotland*,[3] *Candler* v. *Crane, Christmas & Co.*,[4] *Hedley Byrne & Co., Ltd.* v. *Heller & Partners, Ltd.*[5]

---

[1] [1891] 3 Ch. 82, C.A.
[2] [1971] A.C. 793, P.C., at p. 812.
[3] 1916 S.C. (H.L.) 154.
[4] [1951] 2 K.B. 164, C.A.
[5] [1964] A.C. 465, H.L.

or *Mutual Life and Citizens Assurance Co., Ltd.* v. *Evatt*,[1] it is necessary for the plaintiff to show that the advice on which he relied was given in the course of business by a person holding himself out as one having a special skill or special access to information which he is prepared to use in giving the advice. But the extent of the ambit of *Hedley Byrne & Co.* v. *Heller & Partners, Ltd.* can hardly as yet be said to be finally decided beyond any future dispute. With a majority of three to two in the Privy Council, with five eminent judges on each side in *Evatt*'s case when all are counted, and with Lord REID and Lord MORRIS still to reckon with in any future appeal to the Lords, who shall say what the result of a further argument in the House of Lords on this subject may be? It is possible that the personnel of the court may decide the day.

Principles emerging

408 From the cases decided up to the time of writing, certain principles seem to have emerged which are worth recording, though it is not suggested that any of them is yet so thoroughly established that it may not undergo further modification before the law on this subject finally settles down into a state of stability. These principles will be stated, with such elaboration as is possible as matters now stand, in the next succeeding paragraphs.

The action is one in negligence and not in misrepresentation

409 In *Hedley Byrne & Co., Ltd.* v. *Heller & Partners, Ltd.* the judgments pose the crucial question as being whether an innocent but negligent misrepresentation can give the representee a cause of action[2]; the principal argument in that case centred around the contention for the plaintiff, which had been rejected by the Court of Appeal in *Candler* v. *Crane, Christmas & Co.*,[3] that a non-fraudulent misrepresentation could support an action for damages, notwithstanding that it was innocently made, if the representor made it negligently, *viz.* in breach of a duty to use care owed by the representor to the representee, using that word so as to include all to whom it should have been contemplated that the representation would come. Such a duty, it had always been understood, could arise *ex contractu*, or by virtue of a fiduciary relationship between representor and representee; the special point of *Hedley Byrne & Co.*,

---

[1] [1971] A.C. 793, P.C.
[2] [1964] A.C. 465, H.L. See for instance the judgment of Lord REID at p. 483.
[3] [1951] 2 K.B. 164, C.A.

Ltd. v. *Heller & Partners, Ltd.* was that it held that such a duty would arise out of "special relationships" other than these, the tests for which it did not precisely define—and that indeed that the facts in that case were such as would give rise to a "special relationship".

The cases subsequently decided place much more emphasis upon the fact that the *Hedley Byrne* action is not an action for misrepresentation at all; that it is an action for damages for negligence, the negligence consisting (as always) of the breach of a duty to take care—here in making a representation or giving advice—owed by one person to another.[1]   In a *Hedley Byrne* action it is the representor who owes a duty to some other person, and the duty is to take care in making the representation. *But the duty is not always owed exclusively to the representee.* If the representation is made negligently—i.e. in breach of a duty to make it carefully—and if someone is damaged by reason of it being made, in circumstances in which that damage, and the person suffering it, were or should have been in the contemplation of the representor when he made the representation, then that person will have a *Hedley Byrne* claim against the representor, and this notwithstanding that the representation was never communicated to him at all.   Whether there is any duty to make a representation carefully, however, will depend upon whether such a "special relationship" exists between the representor and the claimant as is referred to in *Hedley Byrne & Co., Ltd.* v. *Heller & Partners, Ltd.*

Advice will support the action

410   Not only is it unnecessary that a plaintiff should have been a representee; the "representation" which will support a *Hedley Byrne* action *need not be a representation of fact at all.* For this reason, then, independently of what has been said earlier in the text, a *Hedley Byrne* action cannot be regarded properly as an action for misrepresentation. Advice, in which no factual element is present, is quite sufficient to support the action.   This is clear from a consideration of the judgments in *Nocton* v. *Lord Ashburton*,[2] though perhaps this was not at once universally recognised;   and all the judgments in *Hedley Byrne* include advice negligently given as sufficient to found an action.[3]   It is submitted,

---

[1] This was not new, but in the post-*Hedley Byrne* cases it becomes more and more important. For an early recognition of the true basis of the action see the judgment of Lord WRENBURY in *Banbury* v. *Bank of Montreal*, [1918] A.C. 626, H.L. at p. 713 noted in note 3 on p. 422, *ante.*

[2] [1914] A.C. 932.

[3] See, too, BARWICK C.J. at p. 322 and MENZIES J. at p. 326 of *Mutual Life and Citizens Assurance Co., Ltd.* v. *Evatt* (1968), A.L.J.R. 316.

though no case has yet gone so far, that principle will not preclude an action based on a negligent prediction of a future event.

Limits of the duty to take care

411 The duty to take care is one which arises out of the *relative situations* of plaintiff and representor.   To this extent, at least, *Hedley Byrne* can be seen as another step in the series of cases, of which *M'Alister (or Donoghue)* v. *Stevenson*[1] is so conspicuous an example, which illustrate the reversal, in the development of the common law in recent years, of that tendency of progressive societies noticed more than a hundred years ago by Sir Henry Maine, to proceed from status to contract.[2]   Liability in respect of misrepresentation, for long thought necessarily to derive from contract, and without contract impossible to sustain, is now seen to be dependent upon status, although in special cases that status may itself derive from contract.

Situations in which there is no duty

412 It seems that the relationship which will give rise to a *Hedley Byrne* action is not one to be recognised by any single criterion—or at least, not by one so far clearly defined.   The cases so far decided say that certain situations, or relative situations, will give rise to a legal duty of care, and that others will not.   But the categories are by no means closed, and different criteria may be applicable to different kinds of situation.

> "Their Lordships would emphasise" (said Lord DIPLOCK, delivering the advice of the majority of the Judicial Committee in *Mutual Life and Citizens Assurance Co., Ltd.* v. *Evatt*[3]), "that the missing characteristic of the relationship which they consider to be essential to give rise to a duty of care in a situation of the kind in which Mr Evatt and the company found themselves when he sought their advice, is not necessarily essential in other situations— such as, perhaps, where the adviser has a financial interest in the transaction upon which he gives his advice (*cf. W.B. Anderson & Sons, Ltd.* v. *Rhodes (Liverpool) Ltd.*[4] *American Re-statement of the Law of Torts 3rd Tentative Re-*

---

[1] [1932] A.C. 562, H.L.
[2] *Ancient Law* (4th edn. 1870) 170.
[3] [1971] A.C. 793, P.C., at p. 809.
[4] [1967] 2 All E.R. 850, H.L.   It may be noticed as a matter of interest (from the judgment of Lord REID at pp. 481–482) that in *Hedley Byrne* the defendant had a financial interest in the continuing commercial operations of the company about which inquiry was made, very similar indeed to that which appeared in *Anderson* v. *Rhodes*; but McNAIR J., the trial judge, expressly rejected this as a proper basis for a special relationship of which liability might be founded. This factor seems to have been completely ignored by all the Lords in their enumeration in *Hedley Byrne* of the tests relevant to the existence of a special relationship.

draft).   On this, as on any other metes and bounds of the doctrine of *Hedley Byrne* their Lordships are expressing no opinion.   The categories of negligence are never closed, and their Lordships' opinion in the instant appeal, like all judicial reasoning, must be understood *secundum subjectam materiam.*''

It is possible, however, to enumerate certain types of situation in which the duty has been held to exist, or not to exist, as the case may be. Thus it is clear that observations, statements, or advice given on a social or informal occasion will not support a *Hedley Byrne* claim.[1]   This is plainly because of the absence of the element pronounced in the *Mutual Life and Citizens Assurance Co., Ltd.* v. *Evatt*[2] to be essential—*viz.* that the advice was given in the way of business.

Nor will advice or representations made, even by a professional man possessed of special skill, support a *Hedley Byrne* action even if given in a business context, if it is given in circumstances which ought to have led a reasonable inquirer to understand that he was not prepared to exercise, in relation to the particular inquiry made, that degree of diligence which he would exercise in giving such advice for reward in the course of his business or profession.[3]   It is clear from *Hedley Byrne* itself that liability may, even in a case which otherwise might appear to be a classic instance of a duty of care, be excluded by a formal disclaimer of responsibility, sufficiently unequivocal, made contemporaneously with the representation.[4]

Advice given or representations made by counsel, at least if made or given in the course of the conduct of litigation, will not found a *Hedley Byrne* action even if negligent, for public policy requires the immunity which alone can ensure the independent status of the Bar and justify the rule that counsel must accept any brief offered to him with the appropriate fee, without being free to pick and choose.[5]

---

[1] See note 5 on p. 419, *ante.*   So, too, the judgment of the majority in *Mutual Life and Citizens Assurance Co., Ltd.* v. *Evatt* (*supra*) observes at p. 806: ''Casual advice given by a professional man upon a social or formal occasion is the typical example (leading to no liability) of which *Fish* v. *Kelly* (1864), 17 C.B.N.S. 194 provides an illustration among the decided cases''.

[2] [1971] A.C. 793, P.C., at pp. 803, 805.

[3] *Mutual Life & Citizens Assurance Co., Ltd.* v. *Evatt* (*supra*) at p. 806.

[4] This was the reason for the failure of the claim in *Hedley Byrne & Co., Ltd.* v. *Heller & Partners, Ltd.*, [1964] A.C. 465, H.L.   Those from whom advice is frequently sought on financial matters (e.g. bankers) will no doubt consider the desirability of giving such advice only on letterheads on which appears in large print a carefully-worded disclaimer of liability.   Their position may be thought not very different from that of the novelist who prefixes to his story the notification, fondly thought to exclude liability of the kind exemplified by *Hulton & Co.* v. *Jones*, that his characters are fictitious, and that no reference to any living person is intended.

[5] *Rondel* v. *Worsley*, [1969] 1 A.C. 191, H.L.   Though a barrister is undoubtedly immune from any *Hedley Byrne* liability for any act done in the course of litigation, the decision of the Lords leaves more open the position of counsel when advising otherwise than in the course of

Mutual Life and Citizens Assurance Co., Ltd. v. *Evatt*[1] restricts still further the class of situations in which an action will lie. In that case the advice was given by a commercial corporation to an inquirer who wanted the information for business purposes—as indeed was the case in *Low* v. *Bouverie*,[2] where the inquirer was a moneylender. In both these cases the business context of the inquiry and answer was insufficient to support liability. It was held in *Evatt*'s case essential that the representor should be one who was known to possess, or who held himself as possessing, special means of knowledge or skill or competence in judgment which he was prepared to exercise in giving his advice or making his representation.

There may be some difficulty in justifying on purely logical grounds the exclusion of liability in the "cartographer" cases. The hypothetical cartographer makes his appearance in the course of argument, or in *obiter dicta*, in a number of the decisions.[3] He is assumed to have published a cheap map, through relying upon which some yachtsman—or even the captain of a commercial vessel—has run his ship aground on a shoal negligently omitted from the published chart—if, indeed *Hay or Bourhill* v. *Young*[4] will permit of the use of the word "negligently" where there is no duty of care in law. All the cases since *Hedley Byrne* agree that there can be no claim against the cartographer; but why? DENNING L.J. is content to say that is was because "he publishes his work simply for the purpose of giving information and not with any particular transaction in mind", and differentiates the case from that in which a scientific expert gives an opinion "for the very purpose of a particular transaction".[5] But is this reasoning completely satisfying? The reader may say that common sense gives the answer—but should it not be easy, if this is really so, to express in simple language the exact reason for this result? It is submitted that this is not easy to do; and this may indicate

---

litigation—e.g. when settling the terms of a deed. It was formerly supposed that he would be immune by reason of his services being notionally gratuitous; but it was generally accepted by all the Lords in *Rondel* v. *Worsley* that this basis of immunity disappeared with the emergence of the *Hedley Byrne* doctrine, if indeed it was ever sound—see the judgments of Lords MORRIS and UPJOHN.

[1] [1971] A.C. 793, P.C.
[2] [1891] 3 Ch. 82, C.A.
[3] He probably owes his origin to Professor Winfield. DENNING L.J. spent some time considering his case in *Candler* v. *Crane, Christmas & Co*., [1951] 2 K.B. 164, C.A., at p. 183 (see text above); and ASQUITH L.J., following on, was assailed at p. 194 by the same doubts as are expressed in the text above. CROSS L.J. again alludes to him in *Ministry of Housing and Local Government* v. *Sharp*, [1970] 1 All E.R. 1009 at pp. 1037–1038—but most of the authorities are in agreement that an action against him must fail.
[4] [1943] A.C. 92, H.L.
[5] [1951] 2 K.B. 164, at p. 183.

that here there remains a logical difficulty in the *Hedley Byrne* doctrine which has not yet been completely resolved.

Situations where liability exists

413 It is clear that the *Hedley Byrne* liability may arise *ex contractu*; and also by reason of a fiduciary relationship between the parties.[1] It will arise where a representation is made, or advice given, by a person (or corporation) who by reason of his profession, calling, or business is known to have, or holds himself out as having, special skill or competence or special information which he is prepared to use in making his representation or giving his advice.[2] Such cases may involve an inquiry as to whether the representor "voluntarily assumed" the responsibility of a duty of care[3]; but a consideration of other situations soon demonstrates that this is not essential in all cases. A duty may for instance be cast upon the representor by statute, by virtue of which he is left with no choice but to make his representation or give his advice. It will then be necessary only to ascertain whether the statute casts upon him a duty to use care. It is not necessary to consider, in his case, whether he is, or holds himself out as having special skill or competence—the statute imposes the duty upon him. Other factors, different from those enumerated, may result in a duty of care in cases where some of the criteria reviewed above are absent. So in *W. B. Anderson & Sons, Ltd.* v. *Rhodes (Liverpool), Ltd.*[4] although the advice was given by a company which did not have, or hold itself out as having, any special skill or competence, the fact that it chose to advise in a matter in which it had itself a financial interest seems to have been regarded as sufficient to turn the scale. The tests for the liability are still in the course of formulation, and the matter at present stands as was said by the majority in the Judicial Committee in *Mutual Life and Citizens Assurance Co., Ltd.* v. *Evatt*[5]:

> "As with any other important case in the development of the common law *Hedley Byrne* should not be regarded as intended to lay down the metes and bounds of the new field of negligence of which the gate is now opened. Those will fall to be ascertained step by step as the facts of particular cases which come before the courts make it necessary to determine them. The instant appeal is an example: but . . . the categories of negligence are never closed."

---

[1] *Nocton* v. *Lord Ashburton*, [1914] A.C. 932, H.L.

[2] *Mutual Life & Citizens Assurance Co., Ltd.* v. *Evatt*, [1971] A.C. 793, P.C.

[3] *Hedley Byrne & Co., Ltd.* v. *Heller & Partners, Ltd.*, [1964] A.C. 465, H.L.; the passages are more particularly referred to in note 4 on p. 418 (*supra*).

[4] [1967] 2 All E.R. 850.

[5] [1971] A.C. 793, P.C., at p. 809.

The ultimate question

414   It must seem to the legal philosopher less than satisfactory that the criteria of liability are left so ill-defined.   *Hedley Byrne* is one of a series of cases in which in our own time the Lords have legislated to extend the boundaries of some legal doctrine, without finding themselves able to define where the next boundary should be drawn.[1]   *M'Alister (or Donoghue)* v. *Stevenson*[2] was another of these.   In extending the area of tortious responsibility, as it should henceforth be delineated, the Lords adopted Luke X, 25–37 as stating the new principle—but only with the addition of a modern gloss upon the simple admonition there recorded.   For it had of course to be acknowledged at once that the duty to one's neighbour so clearly stated in the parable is not recognised by the common law as extending to *all* cases.   But the Lords did not attempt to say, to what cases it did apply; and the courts are still involved in defining the classes of case to which they must be deemed to have intended the duty of an Atkinian neighbour to be limited.   *Indyka* v. *Indyka*[3] was another of these cases in a very different field.   There, the validity of foreign decrees in divorce was "liberalised"—but without anybody being able to say with any certainty, after the decision, whether his particular case was within or outside the liberalised rule.   Again, the effect of the decision in the Lords was a crop of cases tried in lower courts.   Now *Hedley Byrne* has said that in certain relationships there will be liability—but it has left it to further litigation to determine what those relationships are.

It is inevitable, in these circumstances, that there should ensue a struggle between those who wish to hold the gate wide open and those who are glad to see it held only ajar.   This struggle came to a head, with regard to liability for negligent misrepresentation, in *Mutual Life and Citizens Assurance Co., Ltd.* v. *Evatt*,[4] which has been discussed in an earlier paragraph.   A majority of their Lordships in the Judicial Committee limited the class of cases in which a plaintiff could succeed, in the kind of circumstances disclosed in that case, to cases in which, in a business context, the representor had held himself out as possessing special skill.

But Lord REID and Lord MORRIS thought otherwise.   They were unwilling that the gate should be closed, which they had with so many

---

[1] See *per* Lord REID at p. 482;   Lord DEVLIN at pp. 529–530.
[2] [1932] A.C. 562, H.L.
[3] [1969] 1 A.C. 33, H.L.
[4] [1971] A.C. 793, P.C.

pains opened.   And it must be remembered that they had both participated in the *Hedley Byrne* decision, and that Lord HODSON, now ranged
with the majority, had in his judgment expressly agreed with the test of
special relationship proposed by Lord MORRIS.   Their feelings may be
imagined when in *Evatt*'s case Lord DIPLOCK, speaking for the majority
of the Judicial Committee, analysed the words of their judgments and
proceeded to say what the effect of those words must be, in setting limits
to the new liability.

What of the future?

415   But the limits set by *Mutual Life & Citizens Assurance Co., Ltd.* v.
Evatt[1] may prove in the long run to possess greater elasticity than at
present appears.   In the first place, it is evident that even on the question
there decided there are two schools of thought, very evenly divided[2];
and this question has not yet been decided in the House of Lords.   Then
it is very plain that the majority judgment in the Privy Council did not
intend to lay down a principle applicable to all *Hedley Byrne* actions.
The majority were careful to say that while the test which they adopted
must govern the situations of the kind which were pleaded in the case
before them, other cases might be decided on a different test.[3]   The same
view runs through all the judgments on both sides;   and indeed it is
inherent in the speeches in *Hedley Byrne* itself.   Whether the theoreticians
like it or not it is certain that the limits of *Hedley Byrne* will not be worked
out for a long time, and that when they are, they will be the result of
much backing and filling, and of reasoning from case to case on the facts
of each.   When all this is remembered, those who hoped for more from
Mutual Life and Citizens Assurance Co., Ltd. v. *Evatt*[1] may—if they live long
enough—yet see that the gate is left wider open than at first appeared.

---

[1] [1971] A.C. 793, P.C.

[2] It will be remembered that Lords HODSON, GUEST and DIPLOCK, on the Judicial Committee, and TAYLOR and OWEN JJ. in the High Court of Australia were ranged on one side,
and Lords REID and MORRIS, and Sir Garfield BARWICK C.J. and KITTO and MENZIES JJ. on the
other.

[3] See p. 35—"As with any other important case in the development of the common law,
Hedley Byrne should not be regarded as intended to lay down the metes and bounds of the new
field of negligence of which the gate is now opened.   These will fall to be ascertained step by
step as the facts of particular cases which come before the courts make it necessary to determine them."

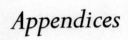

Appendices

History of the Place and Treatment of Deceit and Fraud in English Jurisprudence

(Note by the editor of the third edition. The following eleven paragraphs, reprinted exactly from Mr Spencer Bower's text in earlier editions of this work, find their place in this edition, published sixty-two years after they were first written, as a historical summary of some of the processes by which the law of fraudulent misrepresentation has evolved. The excursus of Mr Spencer Bower proceeds, in earlier editions, to canvass a number of terminological and philosophical considerations which, for considerations of space, have had to be omitted from this volume.)

History of the common law action of deceit

416 It is unfortunate that the term "action for fraudulent misrepresentation" is so frequently described as synonymous with "action of deceit," which implies that actions of deceit have always assumed the same form. This, however, is very far from being the fact, as a cursory reference to the history of forms of action will at once demonstrate.

Earliest form of the writ of deceit

417 The earliest traceable form of the writ of deceit was the *breve de deceptione* existing in the time of King John.[1] The relief given by this writ was of an extremely limited character. The only deceit against which it was directed was *deceptio curiæ*, a form of wrong which (see Chapter XVII, para. 358, *ante*) is not now considered as technically coming within the conception of misrepresentation at all. No other kind of fraud was the subject of any writ or special remedy in those times, when it was deemed much more vital to preserve the King's peace from

---

[1] Pollock and Maitland's *History of English Law*, vol. ii, p. 533.

turbulence and violence than the individual subject's private property from invasion. And even the deception in question was regarded rather as an offence against the King than as a private injury to the party.[1]   The person guilty of thus obtaining a judgment from the King's Court was liable to imprisonment in the first place, though he might also be sentenced to amerce the party; he was summoned *ad respondendum tam regi quam parti*.[2]   At a later date we are told by Fitzherbert that "this writ lieth properly when one man doth anything *in the name of another*, by which the other person is damnified and deceived; then he who is so damnified shall have his writ," which looks as if personation of any kind was then the proper subject of the action, but on reference to the form of the writ which Fitzherbert sets out, and the illustrations which he there gives of the matters in respect of which it was usually issued, it becomes apparent that in his time the remedy was still limited to cases of a party procuring a judgment by personation, or a sheriff making false returns, or an officer of the Crown conspiring with a party to commit any improper act in his office, or collusive recoveries, and the like.[3]

The action of deceit in its second stage

418   After the lapse of two centuries or so from the period above referred to, the action of deceit had entered upon the second stage of its history: that is to say, its limits had begun to be extended so as to comprise other species of tort, and this process of expansion continued until by the date at which Sir John Comyns published his Digest, the term "deceit" included not only several of the acts now considered to belong to the province of misrepresentation, but also a miscellaneous collection of wrongs which are undoubtedly outside it, whilst at the same time excluding at least one important head of misrepresentation as now understood.

419   Thus, in the time of Henry VI, we find what would in these days be considered an action of negligence, if such action were still deemed to lie at all (which it is not[4]), described as an action of deceit:

" Si jeo retaine luy d'estre de mon counsel al Guildhall en Londres, al

---

[1] *Ibid.*, pp. 534, 535.

[2] Com. Dig. Action on the Case for a Deceipt, F. 1.

[3] Fitzherbert, *De Naturâ Brevium*, pp. 95–100.   The form of writ there given summons the delinquent "as well as to answer Us as the aforesaid A., wherefore he fraudulently and maliciously in our Court of Chancery obtained our certain writ in the name of the aforesaid A., who was wholly ignorant of this, in deceit of our Court to the great damage of the said A."

[4] Now to be read subject to Chapter XIX, *ante*.

certes jour, sil ne vient al jour, per que mon cause perish, action de disceit gist vers luy''.[1]

Much later, in the time of James I, the case[2] which is famous for having evoked, or being supposed to have evoked, the proposition of CROKE J. that "fraud without damage, and damage without fraud, gives no cause of action",[3] and which is entitled in the report "a special action upon the case for a deceit," turns out, on examination of the facts, to be nothing but an action of either negligence or breach of contract, as it would now be understood, the ground of complaint being that the plaintiff contracted with the defendant to supply a team of horses to carry a load of a stated weight, and the defendant "superonerated" the team with a much larger weight, whereby the horses were compelled *ita vehementer laborare et trahere*, that seven of them *ratione inde peribant*, to the plaintiff's great damage and loss.[4] Again, when COKE lays down that

> "if the client would have the attorney to plead a false plea he ought not to do it, for he may plead *quod non erat veraciter informatus, et ideo nullum responsum*, and this shall be entered into the rolls to save him from damages in an action of deceit,"

he clearly regards as coming within that description what is now a very familiar type of action for negligence.[5]

420 The number of wrongs included under the head of "deceit" had, by the time of Comyns' Digest received enormous increment. The term then seems to have been as vague and comprehensive as "malice" in the earlier stages of our law,[6] or *fraus* in Roman law,[7] or "fraud" in such

---

[1] 20 H. 6 24, pl. 1, cited in Rolle's Abridgm. p. 91.

[2] *Baily* v. *Merrell* (1615), 3 Bulstr. 94; Cro. Jac. 386; 1 Rolle Rep. 278. The principle on which an action of this description was thought to lie is stated succinctly and unqualifiedly at p.275 of Rolle's report: "si jeo loane un chivall a carrier bois, et il superonerate le chivall, per que jeo luy perde, jeo avera action vers luy pur le deceit et damage."

[3] See para. 186 in Chapter XI, *ante*.

[4] The three reports are at variance as regards figures and details in the narrative of the facts, but the substance is as stated in the text, and in note 2, *supra*. The court was inclined to think that the plaintiff had not brought the facts within the principle enunciated and "directed this matter to stay till the plaintiff moved the same again, and no judgment pronounced one way or other; but the plaintiff, perceiving the opinion of the court to be against him, never moved the court again herein," 3 Bulstr. 96.

[5] Coke, 2 Inst. 215.

[6] Particularly in the law of defamation (as shewn in App. II of Mr Spencer Bower's *Code of the Law of Actionable Defamation*), and in the law relating to conspiracy and procurement of breaches of contract by a third person, as to which Lord MACNAGHTEN, at pp. 144 of *Allen* v. *Flood*, [1898] A.C. 1, H.L., confessed: "sometimes, indeed, I rather doubt whether I understand that unhappy expression myself." The form cited in note 3 on p. 442 couples "fraudulently" and "maliciously," using the terms as practically synonymous.

[7] As distinguished from *dolus*, though the latter expression is also extremely comprehensive.

expressions (still current) as "in fraud of his contract," or "in fraud of his promise," meaning thereby no more than a breach of the contract or promise.[1] It was apparently made to indicate almost every kind of tort other than assault or defamation. Comyns included amongst his illustrations of "deceit" such miscellaneous matters as the following: tricks and cheating "in play"[2]; forgery[3]; personation[4]; breach of duty as trustee[5]; the like in an official position[6]; "other falsity," by which he means dishonesty[7]; "false affirmation on other occasions," the examples given being mainly cases of false pretences[8]; and "passing off" cases.[9] The above may, in each case, cover acts of express or implied misrepresentation, though they may also include acts which could not be so described. But he adds to the list other wrongs which no one at the present day would term "deceit," such as negligence, whether assuming the form of want of care, or want of skill in one who *spondet peritiam artis*,[10] vexatious proceedings in litigation, oppression,[11] and that which is now regarded as the very antithesis of misrepresentation, *viz.* "false warranty",[12] whilst he expressly excludes the "falsity without warranty",[13] which, according to the modern view, if actionable at all, is pure misrepresentation.

421 The assimilation of actions for breach of warranty, or later (when *assumpsit* came to be substituted for *warrantizando vendidit* in pleadings) of actions for breach of promise, to actions of deceit, may be traced as a survival in declarations down to at least 1842, until which date it was quite usual to append to the averments of warranty, undertaking, promise, and breach, allegations of deceit, fraud, subtlety, and craft, as well as falsity, on the one side, and trust, confidence, reliance, and in-

---

[1] Though the expression "in fraud of a person's rights," when used in a statute, has been construed strictly; see, for instance, *Ex parte Watson* (1888), 21 Q.B.D. 301, 309; *Re Avery's Patent* (1887), 36 Ch.D. 307; *Re Ralston's Patent* (1909), 100 L.T. 386.

[2] Com. Dig. Action on the Case for a Deceipt, A. 1.

[3] *Ibid.*, A. 2.

[4] *Ibid.*, A. 3.

[5] *Ibid.*, A. 5.

[6] *Ibid.*, A. 6.

[7] *Ibid.*, A. 8.

[8] *Ibid.*, A. 10.

[9] *Ibid.*, A. 9.

[10] *Ibid.*, A. 7, described as deceit "in a man's trade," and the illustrations given are the negligence, or incompetence, of a furrier, surgeon, tailor, etc.

[11] *Ibid.*, A. 4.

[12] *Ibid.*, A. 11.

[13] *Ibid.*, E. 4.

ducement on the other.[1] Indeed Lord ABINGER C.B. as late as the year 1840, expressed the bold and comprehensive view that "every action for breach of promise, or of warranty," as well as "of misrepresentation, in equity comes within the legal definition of fraud".[2]

422 From the earliest times, if the *Gloucestershire Clothier's Case*[3] is to be treated as a "passing off" case,[4] the action of deceit was deemed to

---

[1] See, for instance, *Stuart* v. *Wilkins* (1778), 1 Doug. K.B. 18 (a case in which *assumpsit* was pleaded instead of *warrantizando vendidit*, according to a practice which ASHHURST and BULLER JJ. said was then well settled, and where an averment that the defendant "undertook and then and there faithfully promised that the said mare was sound" is followed by an allegation of the plaintiff's "confiding," etc., and of the defendant's contriving and fraudulently intending," etc., and of his having "craftily and subtilly deceived the said David," etc.); *Parkinson* v. *Lee* (1802), 2 East 314 (a sale of hops by sample, in which the defendant "did not regard his said promise, but thereby deceived and defrauded the plaintiff"); *Williamson* v. *Allison* (1802), 2 East 446 ("falsely and fraudulently warranted," and "falsely, fraudulently, and deceitfully sold the said claret"); *Pickering* v. *Dowson* (1813), 4 Taunt. 779 ("false and fraudulent warranty" of a ship pleaded in the first count of the declaration and fraudulent misrepresentation in the others); *Jones* v. *Bright* (1829), 5 Bing. 533 (a case of breach of warranty, pure and simple, if there ever was one, but labelled in the headnote as "an action in the nature of deceit," in which it was alleged, with much pomp and circumstance, that "the defendant falsely and fraudulently deceived the plaintiff . . . by then and there falsely and fraudulently warranting the said sheets of copper to be," etc.); *Bywater* v. *Richardson* (1834), 1 Ad. & El. 508; *Brown* v. *Edgington* (1841), 2 Man. & G. 279; *Moens* v. *Heyworth* (1842), 10 M. & W. 147 (where there were three counts, the first alleging that the defendants had "falsely and fraudulently warranted," and the others that he had "falsely and fraudulently represented," the copper to be . . . etc.).

[2] At p. 377 of *Cornfoot* v. *Fowke* (1840), 6 M. & W. 358.

[3] This is an anonymous case, which it is convenient to cite by the title given it in the text. It is not the subject of any report, but is referred to in a summary fashion by DODERIDGE J. at p. 471 of *Southern* v. *How* (1617), Cro. Jac. 468, at p. 144 of the same case as reported in Poph. 143, and at p. 28 of the same case as reported in 2 Rolle Rep. 26. The accounts of the case are meagre, and vary materially in one important point, *viz.* as to whether the vendee or the rival trader was the plaintiff, and also as to the date of the decision, which is given as 33 Eliz. by Croke, as 22 Eliz. by Popham, and as 23 Eliz. by Rolle. The importance of identifying the character in which the plaintiff is supposed to have sued is manifest: if he sued as vendee, the case is one of ordinary misrepresentation by acts and conduct: if he was the competing trader, it is one of the earliest, if not the earliest, reported instance of a "passing off" action.

[4] As it probably is. It is true that, in Croke's report, *supra*, we read that "Doderidge cited a case to be adjudged 33 Eliz. in the Common Pleas. A clothier of Gloucestershire made very good cloth, so that in London if they saw any cloth of his mark, they would buy it without searching thereof; and another who made ill cloth put his mark upon it without his privity; and an action upon the case was *brought by him who bought the cloth*, for this deceit; and adjudged maintainable." Rolle reports the case substantially as above, except that he concludes "mes Mr Justice Dodridge ne dit pur qual d'eux ceo gist, lou pur le Cloathier que primierement avait le dit marke, on pur le vendee, mes semble que gist pur le vendee," whereas Croke reports that DODERIDGE J. did say who was the plaintiff, *viz.*, the vendee, at whose instance Rolle thought that it ought to lie. Popham, on the other hand, distinctly reports DODERIDGE J. as giving the cause of action to the clothier: "Doderidge saith that 22 Eliz. an action upon the case was brought in the Common Pleas by a clothier that, whereas he had gained great reputation for his making of his cloth, by reason whereof he had great utterance to his great benefit and profit, and that he used to set his mark to his cloth, whereby it should be known to be his cloth; and another clothier perceiving it, used the same mark to his ill-made cloth, *on purpose to deceive him*, and it was resolved that the action did well lie." It seems, on the whole quite clear that the action was brought by the clothier who made the good cloth, otherwise there was

include an action by a trader against a competitor for misrepresenting to the public goods of his own make as goods of the plaintiff's make, to the prejudice of the plaintiff's proprietary rights and interests. This class of case, however, if not technically an action of deceit, as it is even now considered to be by some high authorities,[1] undoubtedly approaches it very nearly, and has many features in common with it, and for that reason has already been dealt with in the chapter devoted to forms of action which are on the border line of misrepresentation proper.[2]

The action of deceit in its present form

423 Early in the nineteenth century, the action of deceit gradually began to be understood in its present limited sense, as an action for damages for fraudulent misrepresentation made by the defendant to the plaintiff inducing him to alter his position to his damage. And, once having learnt to apply the term "deceit" to that which alone is "deceit," as a separate and distinct cause of action, the law becomes as prudishly strict in maintaining the assigned boundaries as, in the immediately preceding stage, it had been lavish and lax in extending them. Particularly is this tendency noticeable in the extreme reluctance which several of the common law judges evinced, from 1789 to at least 1818, to apply the principles of the law of deceit to the case of misrepresentation of a third person's credit, imbued, as they were, with the idea that the so-called application was really an extension of that law, and a dangerous one; the grounds assigned being that for the first time representations which were not part of a contract were made as much the subject of liability as those which were; further, that statements made with the object of helping a third person, and not with that of injuring the representee or benefiting the representor, ought not to be treated as fraudulent; and, lastly, that the innovation tended, if not to repeal, to give a way of escape from the

---

no point in the elaborate introductory references in all three reports to the excellence of his manufacture, and his success and reputation in trade. And the case has so been regarded by Lord HARDWICKE L.C. in *Blanchard* v. *Hill* (1742), 2 Atk. 484, 485 (who speaks of the defendant having acted "with a fraudulent design to *put off bad clothes by this means, or to draw away customers* from the other clothier"), and by PAGE-WOOD V.-C. at pp. 427, 428 of *Collins Co.* v. *Brown* (1857), 3 K. & J. 423 (another "passing off" case, in which the above passage from Lord HARDWICKE's judgment is cited). Further, in note (*b*) to p. 386 of the judgment of CRESSWELL J. who cites the case from Popham's report, in *Crawshay* v. *Thompson* (1842), 4 Man. & G. 357, Serj. Manning, a most accomplished jurist, remarks that its citation in *Southern* v. *How*, *supra*, would not have had much point or relevancy if the action is supposed to have been brought by the vendee. And, in his note to 61 R.R. 555, Sir Frederick Pollock seems to take the same view.

[1] See note 4 on p. 388, *ante.*
[2] See Chapter XVII, para. 377, *ante.*

salutary provisions of the Statute of Frauds.[1]   This criticism, and the opposition founded upon it, was quite irrational,[2] but, initiated by GROSE J.[3] it was persisted in by LAWRENCE J., LE BLANC J.,[4] Lord ELLENBOROUGH C.J.,[5] DALLAS J.,[6] PARK J.[7] and ERLE C.J.,[8] though discountenanced by Lord KENYON C.J.,[9] Lord MANSFIELD C.J.[10] and, ultimately, by Lord ELDON L.C.[11] who, however, admitted that "it was long before he was reconciled" to the doctrine which was the subject of the criticism.[12]   It should be added, however, that this hostile attitude,

---

[1] See the references in the next six notes.

[2] As regards evasion of the Statute of Frauds, the criticism seems to have been particularly irrational, as pointed out by Lord KENYON C.J. at p. 103 of *Haycraft* v. *Creasy* (1801), 2 East 92.   The fears expressed were that, by pleading an oral guarantee as an oral representation, the party could "evade" the statute, which requires guarantees to be in writing.   But pleading cannot evade anything.   Only proof of the allegations pleaded can bring the case outside a statute.   If, on the evidence the alleged representation is shown to have been a contract, it is amenable to the Statute of Frauds, however skilfully it may have been pleaded as a representation.   If there is no evidence of the statement being other than a contract, the judge so rules: if there is evidence both ways, the issue is one for the Court, as in the case of any other issue of fact in a case of this description.   The mere declaring upon a misrepresentation will not make the action one of misrepresentation, if the facts disclose a cause of action on contract only; just as, conversely, the mere declaring on a contract will not make the cause of action one of contract, if on the evidence it appears that there was only a misrepresentation: *Thompson* v. *Bond* (1807), 1 Camp. 4; *Read* v. *Hutchinson* (1813), 3 Camp. 352.   There could have been no difficulty in properly directing a jury on these points so as to avert the supposed dangers, and Lord ELDON, when sitting in the Common Pleas, does not seem to have found any: see note 11, *post.*

[3] The dissentient judge in *Pasley* v. *Freeman* (1789), 3 Term Rep. 51.   See his judgment at pp. 52–56, which proceeds mainly on the grounds that the defendant was not party to the contract between the plaintiff and Falck, and had no interest in it, and was not colluding with him, and that the representation was no part of such contract; some one or more of which facts he considered to be, according to all the previous authorities, essential elements in the cause of action.   To this opinion GROSE J. adhered at pp. 105, 106 of *Haycraft* v. *Creasy* (1801), 2 East 92, though he was of course bound to recognize *Pasley* v. *Freeman, supra,* as having overruled it.

[4] LAWRENCE J. at pp. 106, 107, and LE BLANC J. at pp. 108, 109, of *Haycraft* v. *Creasy, supra,* stated their agreement with the views of GROSE J. but, as in his case, could not deny that *Pasley* v. *Freeman, supra,* was binding on them.

[5] In *De Graves* v. *Smith* (1810), 2 Camp. 532, where he seems to have deliberately disregarded *Pasley* v. *Freeman, supra,* and to have decided according to his own personal views, remarking that, if he were to rule otherwise, he would be "repealing the Statute of Frauds."

[6] In *Ames* v. *Milward* (1818), 8 Taunt. 637, at p. 642 ("these actions ought not to be encouraged").

[7] In *Ames* v. *Milward, supra,* at p. 642 ("in *Pasley* v. *Freeman* great objections were made to the action the novelty of which is within all our recollections.   Justice LE BLANC's opinion in *Haycraft* v. *Creasy* gave universal satisfaction").

[8] In *Wright* v. *Leonard* (1861), 11 C.B. N.S. 258, at p. 269: "liability for false representations which are unconnected with contract was first affirmed in *Pasley* v. *Freeman.*   The motive for the judgment of the majority of the judges in that case is the desire to suppress fraud: but by that desire they created an indefinite liability, of which parties have availed themselves for fraudulent purposes; so that the effect of the decision has been the reverse of what was intended."

[9] In his dissentient judgment in *Haycraft* v. *Creasy, supra.*

[10] See *Hamar* v. *Alexander* (1806), 2 Bos. & P. N.R. 241, at p. 244.

[11] At p. 186 of *Evans* v. *Bicknell* (1801), 6 Ves. 174.

[12] At p. 110 of *Ex parte Carr* (1814), 3 Ves. & B., 108.

though not justified in so far as it was intended for an attack on the judicial exposition of the law originating in *Pasley* v. *Freeman*,[1] was by no means without justification in so far as it disclosed a legislative oversight, and a *casus omissus* in the Statute of Frauds.[2]   Nor, in this latter aspect was it without practical utility, for it bore fruit, though rather late fruit, in the passing of the Statute of Frauds Amendment Act 1828 under the auspices of Lord TENTERDEN C.J. a measure which, together with the decisions interpreting it, has already been commented upon.[3]

The conception and treatment of fraud as applied to misrepresentation at common law

424   "Fraud," in the action for damages for fraudulent misrepresentation, has since about the middle of the last century[4] been understood in the common law courts in the sense in which it is now understood.[5] But it must not be supposed that this result was achieved *uno saltu*, or that, as has been said or assumed by certain authorities whose opinion is entitled to the highest respect,[6] that the modern definition of a fraudulent misrepresentation issued complete in all its members from the *gremium judicis*, like Athene, in full panoply, from the forehead of Zeus. On the contrary, the process was one of slow stages, and it was some time before the common law disposition was habituated to treat as fraudulent a misrepresentation which was not known to be false, though not known or believed to be true, or one which was not actuated by any intention to injure the representee, or to benefit the representor, or to injure or benefit anybody.

The conception and treatment of "fraud" as applied to misrepresentation in equity

425   "Fraud" has always been treated by Chancery Judges as a

---

[1] (1789), 3 Term. Rep. 51.

[2] In *Tapp* v. *Lee* (1803), 3 Bos. & P. 367, Lord ALVANEY C.J. at p. 370, invites legislation on the subject, pointing out forcibly the existing anomaly: "if a man say, 'if you trust A, I will pay you,' he is not liable upon the credit which he has obtained for A; yet, if he say that A is a good man, he is held liable for the credit which by that assertion he obtained for A."

[3] See Chapter XI, paras. 197 *et seq.*, *ante*, and the cases cited in the notes thereto, particularly *Lyde* v. *Barnard* (1836), 1 M. & W. 101, where the history of the common law which led up to the passing of the statute is discussed, and the judges of the Court of Exchequer (*per* Lord ABINGER C.B. at pp. 117–119, GURNEY B. at pp. 103, 104, ALDERSON B. at p. 107, and PARKE B. at pp. 114, 115) give a parting kick to *Pasley* v. *Freeman*, and remark how justified by the event was GROSE J.'s forecast of the crop of litigation to spring from that decision.

[4] *Taylor* v. *Ashton* (1843), 11 M. & W. 401, may, perhaps, be said to mark the point at which the modern doctrine had fully matured, and before which it was *in fieri*.

[5] See Chapter V, paras. 96 *et seq.*

[6] See the dicta of BOWEN L.J. in *Angus* v. *Clifford*, [1891] 2 Ch. 449 and *Le Lievre* v. *Gould*, [1893] 1 Q.B. 491.

nomen generalissimum.　This generic term, in equity, has from the earliest times[1] been used to connote no more than a transgression of equitable rules, and to denote no less than every species of act or omission which can reasonably answer to that description, such as non-disclosure, unaccompanied by misrepresentation, in contracts and relations *uberrimæ fidei*,[2] abuse of the influence arising from a dominant position on the one side, and incapacity or distress or necessity on the other, unconscionableness, oppression, and the like, though nothing is more certain than that actual dishonesty, or "fraud" in the common law sense, is not required to render such acts or omissions actionable.　A great master of equity jurisprudence includes within his description of "constructive fraud" all

> "such acts and contracts as, although not originating in any actual evil design . . . are yet, by their tendency to deceive or mislead other persons . . . deemed equally reprehensible with positive fraud, and therefore are prohibited by law, as within the same reason and mischief as acts and contracts done *malo animo*".[3]

This high authority admits that these doctrines "may seem to be of an artificial, if not of an arbitrary, character; yet," he contends, "on closer observation they will be perceived to be founded on an anxious desire of the law to apply the principle of preventive justice".[4]　The apology, however, should have been made, not for the doctrines, which are admirable, but for the nomenclature, which is vile.　There is nothing "artificial" or "arbitrary" in applying the principles of public policy and "preventive justice" to acts of which the tendency is mischievous, whatever the intention may have been.　The "arbitrariness" is in describing these acts by a name in popular use to which they do not answer, —with the inevitable consequence that those who affix the epithet and stigma are forced to explain that they do not attach to it the meaning which the rest of the world does,—instead of simply laying down that certain acts and omissions are prohibited, irrespective of fraud or honesty, on the ground of the tendency and temptation to evil which would otherwise result.

---

[1] See 14 Halsbury's Laws (3rd edn.) 473–481.

[2] *Pearson* v. *Morgan* (1788), 2 Bro. C.C. 388 (*per* BULLER J. sitting in Chancery, at p. 389; "fraud is a question of law, and of fact.　In cases where it is a question of fact, it is always considered a constructive fraud when the party knows the truth and conceals it"); *Traill* v. *Baring* (1864), 4 De G.J. & Sm. 318; *Brooke* v. *Lord Mostyn* (1864), 2 De G.J. & Sm. 373.

[3] Story's *Equity Jurisprudence*, vol. i, ch. vii, para. 258.　So, at pp. 946–955 of *Nocton* v. *Lord Ashburton*, [1914] A.C. 932, H.L., Lord HALDANE L.C. elaborates the distinction between "moral fraud in the ordinary sense," and "constructive fraud," which is "a breach of the sort of obligation which was enforced by a Court that from the beginning regarded itself as a Court of Conscience."

[4] Story's *Equity Jurisprudence*, vol. i, ch. vii, para. 258.

426 Being prepared to take liberties with the principles of sound terminology, to the extent of stigmatising as fraudulent that which is not misrepresentation at all, it is not surprising to find that many equity lawyers have taken the same liberties with the word "fraud" as applied to misrepresentation in proceedings for rescission. Instead of merely stating that for the avoidance of a contract proof of a misrepresentation inducing it is sufficient, whether it was fraudulent or innocent, many equity judges have gone out of their way to say that the misrepresentation must be fraudulent, but that "in the eye of a court of equity"—a very favourite phrase—"fraudulent" means anything which misleads, whether fraudulent or not[1]; and in one case it has even been suggested, as a possible justification for the use of the word in this connection, that any one who insists on the observance of a contract induced by a misrepresentation which was innocent when made, but which, after it had been acted upon by the representee, he discovered to have been untrue, is a fraudulent representor *ipso facto*, or, rather *ex post facto*[2]—a theory which would not only put subsequent discovery of falsity on the same plane as that contemporaneous knowledge which is admittedly essential to establish fraud, but would also turn every obstinate persistence in a hopeless claim or defence of any kind into a fraudulent act.[3]

---

[1] *Rawlins* v. *Wickham* (1858), 3 De G. & J. 304 (*per* TURNER L.J. at pp. 316–318); *New Brunswick and Canada Railway and Land Co.* v. *Conybeare* (1862), 9 H.L. Cas. 711; *A.-G.* v. *Ray* (1874), 9 Ch. App. 397 (*per* HALL V.-C. at p. 405, who described the innocent misrepresentation which is enough for rescission as "what Lord ELDON would have considered as fraud, not in its offensive sense, but what the court considers as fraud," and treats "as if actual fraud"); *Mathias* v. *Yetts* (1882), 46 L.T. 497 (*per* JESSEL M.R. at p. 502).

[2] JESSEL M.R. at pp. 12, 13 of *Redgrave* v. *Hurd* (1881), 20 Ch.D. 1, C.A., is responsible for this laborious and strained explanation. He there says that the theory on which innocent misrepresentation, as it would be called by ordinary people, renders the representor liable in rescission proceedings may be put in two ways: "a man is not to be allowed to get a benefit from a statement which he now admits to be false"—which is a sound and intelligible proposition—and "the other way of putting it was this: even assuming that fraud must be shown in order to set aside a contract you have it when a man, having obtained a beneficial contract by a statement which he now knows to be false, insists upon keeping that contract. To do so is a moral delinquency," which, latter view, it is submitted, involves a gross *petitio principii*.

[3] This strange doctrine, however, finds a place in Roman jurisprudence.

Tenth Report
of the
Law Reform Committee
(Innocent Misrepresentation)

(Under the Chairmanship of Lord Jenkins and presented to Parliament by the Lord High Chancellor by Command of Her Majesty July 1962.)[1]

We were invited by your Lordship in January, 1959, to consider whether any alterations are necessary or desirable in the law relating to innocent misrepresentation and the remedies available for such misrepresentation. In our examination of this problem we have given careful consideration to suggestions for changes in the law made by The Law Society, the Society of Labour Lawyers and members of The Institute (a body representative of conveyancers at the Bar), and we have derived much valuable information from memoranda submitted to us by the Standing Joint Committee of the motoring organisations (Royal Automobile Club, the Automobile Association and the Royal Scottish Automobile Club), the Society of Motor Manufacturers and Traders and the Retail Trading Standards Association.

2. We have been impressed by the fact that there is extensive criticism of three aspects of the existing law. First, in the majority of the memoranda we have received the restrictions on the right to rescind a contract on account of misrepresentation are attacked as being too stringent, although opinions differ as to the extent to which rescission should be made easier; secondly, there is an almost unanimous demand

---

[1] H.M.S.O., London, Cmnd. 1782.

for a remedy in damages, either in addition to, or in lieu of, rescission; thirdly, it is said by those speaking from practical experience of sales and other commercial transactions that there ought to be some curtailment of the freedom to exclude liability for misrepresentation by a provision in the contract in cases where the parties are nor bargaining as equals.   To these criticisms must be added others of a more technical character, such as the artificiality of the present distinction between damages which cannot, and an indemnity which can, be granted in the course of rescission; and the fact that some anomalies and much uncertainty result from the distinction between the legal consequences of a misrepresentation and of a breach of a term in the contract.   We have examined these criticisms in turn in order to see how far the present law is capable of producing injustice and to canvass the possible remedies.

Right to rescission under the existing law

3. As a starting point it may be convenient to consider the scope of the right to rescission as a remedy for an innocent misrepresentation.   A person who has been induced to enter into a contract by such a misrepresentation can, if he discovers the true facts before the contract has been executed, refuse to carry out his undertakings, resist any claim for specific performance and, if necessary, obtain rescission.   It is generally accepted (although, as we shall show later, the authorities are by no means clear outside the narrow field of real property law) that after execution of the contract he can no longer rescind.   The evidence we have received leaves us in little doubt that there are cases where the inability to rescind a contract after it has been executed can work serious injustice.

4. The recent decision in *Long* v. *Lloyd*, [1958] 2 All E.R. 402, serves as an illustration of a purchaser being left without a remedy in a case in which there was little merit on the vendor's side.   The plaintiff, who bought a lorry on the strength of representations that it was a first-class vehicle with a low petrol consumption, had little opportunity to discover its very extensive defects until after he had taken delivery.   By that time he had, as the law now stands, probably lost his remedy (although his subsequent conduct in continuing to use the lorry for some days provided the specific grounds for the court's decision).   We are told by the Standing Joint Committee of the motoring organisations that the accuracy of a representation about the quality and construction of a motor vehicle is seldom apparent from an inspection by a person who is not an expert, or even from a short trial run.   No doubt similar difficulties occur on the sale of other articles of a mechanical or technical

nature, where defects are unlikely to come to the notice of the uninitiated until some time after the sale is completed. These considerations are particularly relevant to the common practice (to which the Retail Trading Standards Association has drawn our attention) of selling articles in sealed containers or packages. The buyer of such an article has no opportunity of examining it until after he has taken delivery by which time the sale has been completed and any right to rescind for misrepresentation has been lost.

5. Most of the examples we have been given of hardship resulting from the absence of a remedy by way of rescission relate to contracts for the sale of goods, but some of the memoranda we have received suggest that a change in the law is also needed in the case of certain transactions affecting land. While we agree that here too the present bar on rescission after completion may be too rigid, it seems to us that different considerations apply to contracts relating to interests in land from those which apply to other contracts, and we therefore propose to examine the two classes separately.

Rescission in case of contracts affecting land

6. The rule that there can be no rescission for an innocent misrepresentation after completion of a contract for the sale or other disposition of an interest in land is generally attributed to the decision in *Wilde* v. *Gibson* (1848), 1 H.L. Cas. 605, and is now firmly established. *Wilde* v. *Gibson* was concerned with a conveyance, but subsequent cases have established that the rule also applies to leases: *Angel* v. *Jay*, [1911] 1 K.B. 666; *Edler* v. *Auerbach*, [1950] 1 K.B. 359. The exact origins of the rule are obscure, but it seems probable that it derives from the fact that every purchaser has an opportunity to examine the title to the land he is buying between the time of the contract and the conveyance. Once the property has been conveyed, it would be intolerable if a purchaser who has had a full opportunity of investigation were able to raise objections to the title by reason of a defect which he could have discovered before. It is arguable that the same opportunities for examination do not exist in the case of defects not relating to title—for example, structural flaws or disrepair and decay in parts of a building—and it may be that at the present time, when housing accommodation is still scarce, a prospective purchaser is often unable to examine a house as thoroughly as he would like. Nevertheless, we think that in the case of sales of land finality should be the predominant consideration. The vendor will often have

spent the proceeds of sale on the purchase of another house and so be unable to repay them. The purchase of a house is commonly linked with the raising of a mortgage and perhaps a sequence of other transactions. Rescission of one sale may thus start a chain reaction. The purchaser who buys a house in reliance on the vendor's representations and without an adequate survey, like one who buys without fully investigating the title, must know that he is taking a risk.

7. The same considerations do not necessarily apply to all leases and tenancies. A lease for 999 or even 99 years is very different from a yearly or a weekly tenancy, both in substance and in the practice followed in negotiating the lease. The grant of a long lease is in many respects closely akin to a conveyance, and we think that it should be subject to the same rules in regard to innocent misrepresentations. On the other hand, in some respects the grant of a short tenancy more nearly resembles a contract than a conveyance of land. The tenant is less likely to be professionally advised and consequently more prone to be deceived by a misrepresentation, and short tenancies are less frequently linked with other transactions so that there is not usually the same difficulty in restoring the parties to their original position. The difficulty has been to decide where the line is to be drawn between long and short leases. In the end we have come to the conclusion that s. 54 (2) of the Law of Property Act 1925 provides the most convenient dividing line, and that to employ a well-known provision such as this would be more satisfactory than to devise some new classification. Section 54 (2) contains an exception to the rule requiring interests in land to be created in writing. The exception relates to leases taking effect in possession for a term not exceeding three years (whether or not the lessee is given power to extend the term) at the best rent which can reasonably be obtained without taking a fine. We recommend that in such cases execution of the lease or tenancy agreement should not be a bar to rescission, but that the lessee should have the same right to have the lease or agreement set aside as a party to a contract not relating to an interest in land.

Rescission after execution in other cases

8. Although it is generally accepted that a contract not relating to land, like one for the sale or other disposition of an interest in land, cannot be rescinded after execution, the legal basis for the rule is slender. The decision in *Seddon* v. *North Eastern Salt Co.*, *Ltd.*, [1905] 1 Ch. 326, which is generally cited as authority for the rule, was a case at first instance concerning a contract for the sale of shares which had been completed by

transfer. The judgment, insofar as it seeks to lay down that there can be no rescission following execution of a contract, appears to be mainly based on precedents from real property law. As well appears from Cheshire and Fifoot's *Law of Contract* (5th Edition, page 237), the correct reason for the decision appears to have been the plaintiff's failure to seek rescission until he had carried on the business of the company whose shares he had acquired for over three months after he had discovered the true facts: by implication his conduct had affirmed the contract. Other cases are sometimes cited as authority for the rule (*e.g. Rawlins* v. *Wickham* (1858), 3 De G. & J. 304; *A.-G.* v. *Ray* (1874), 9 Ch. App. 397; *Redgrave* v. *Hurd* (1881), 20 Ch.D. 1; *Newbigging* v. *Adam* (1886), 34 Ch.D. 582) but they all seem to us to be capable of explanation on other grounds. It is well known that the rule in *Seddon's* case has been frequently criticised in subsequent decisions. In *Armstrong* v. *Jackson*, [1917] 2 K.B. 822, MCCARDIE J. acknowledged the existence of the rule with regret and avoided its application to the case before him by reason of the fiduciary relationship between the parties; in *Lever Brothers, Ltd.* v. *Bell* [1931] 1 K.B. 557 at p. 588, SCRUTTON L.J. doubted its correctness; and in *Solle* v. *Butcher*, [1950] 1 K.B. 671, *Leaf* v. *International Galleries*, [1950] 2 K.B. 86, and *Curtis* v. *Chemical Cleaning and Dyeing Co.*, [1951] 1 K.B. 805, DENNING L.J. expressed the view that the operation of the rule is limited to misrepresentations as to title made on a sale of land. The other judges in the last-mentioned cases did not go as far as DENNING L.J. in disowning the rule, but they too avoided applying it to the facts before them, and expressed some doubts as to its application outside the law of real property. It seems to us, therefore, that the authority for the rule still rests on the judgment of JOYCE J. in *Seddon's* case, which could be said to apply only to the special circumstances of a sale of shares completed by formal transfer; indeed, as was pointed out in Dr Hammelmann's article "*Seddon* v. *North Eastern Salt Co.*" (1939, 55 L.Q.R. 90) the judge's statement of the law concerning misrepresentation can be treated as *obiter*, having regard to his final observation ([1905] 1 Ch. at p. 335) that he was not satisfied that the representation had the effect of causing the plaintiff to enter into the contract or that it had any effect upon him at all.

9. However, whatever its merits in law, the rule in *Seddon's* case is to-day generally accepted and acted upon. Even if, as we think, it is not impossible that the rule may yet be held by the Court of Appeal or the House of Lords to be without foundation, it cannot be right to leave a matter of such everyday importance to be settled by the accidents of litigation. In our view, it should be provided by statute that (except in the case of those contracts for the sale or other disposition of an interest in

land to which we have already referred) the fact that a contract has been executed should not of itself be a bar to proceedings for rescission.

10. We appreciate that our recommendation is open to certain objections, the most serious being lack of finality. It is important that the rights of the parties to a contract should crystallise within a reasonable time without risk of the transaction being reopened. But since we do not suggest any relaxation of the other restrictions on the exercise of the right to rescission, there will in our view be no serious risk of prolonged uncertainty. Delay in seeking rescission (either by itself or because it raises an implication that the contract has been affirmed) will continue to operate as a bar, and so will any change of circumstances making *restitutio in integrum* impossible, such as the intervention of rights of third parties. In addition, the normal periods of limitation will apply. Even at the present time there are many contracts of a continuing nature, like partnership, agency or service agreements, which in a sense always remain executory and therefore open to rescission. In practice, the impossibility of restoring the parties to their original position operates after a short time to prevent rescission and we are not aware of the lack of finality having given rise to complaint.

Damages as an alternative to rescission

11. A more fundamental objection which may be advanced against our recommendation concerns the drastic character of the remedy to which the plaintiff would be entitled. Unless the court's power to grant rescission is made more elastic than it is at present, the court will not be able to take account of the relative importance or unimportance of the facts which have been misrepresented. A car might be returned to the vendor because of a misrepresentation about the mileage done since the engine was last overhauled, or a transfer of shares rescinded on account of an incorrect statement about the right to receive the current dividend. In some cases the result could be as harsh on the representor as the absence of a right to rescind under the present law can be on the representee. Moreover, the conflict between the remedies for misrepresentation and those for breach of contract would be aggravated. There is already the anomaly that a statement embodied in the contract and constituting a minor term of it is treated as a warranty, the breach of which gives only a right to damages, whereas the same statement as a representation inducing the contract enables the latter to be rescinded. Before the contract is executed and at a time when the parties can be relatively easily restored to their original positions, this anomaly may not matter

very much, but the position would be very different if the court had no option but to order rescission after the contract had been executed.

12. To meet these objections we recommend that wherever the court has power to order rescission it should, as an alternative, have a discretionary power to award damages if it is satisfied that these would afford adequate compensation to the plaintiff, having regard to the nature of the representation and the fact that the injury suffered by the plaintiff is small compared with what rescission would involve. The courts were given power to award damages in addition to or in substitution for an injunction or a decree of specific performance by s. 2 of Lord Cairns' Act (the Chancery Amendment Act 1858), and since the decision of the House of Lords in *Leeds Industrial Co-operative Society, Ltd.* v. *Slack*, [1924] A.C. 851, this power has been exercised on principles similar to those we have just mentioned.

13. We think that the discretionary power to award damages which we recommend as an alternative to rescission should, like rescission itself, be available before as well as after the contract is executed. Although there may not be many occasions on which damages would be appropiate before execution, it would be wrong not to give the courts power to do substantial justice by an award of damages wherever the consequences of rescission would be out of all proportion to the injury suffered by the plaintiff.

Repercussions on contracts for sale of goods

14. Any alteration of the law relating to rescission for an innocent misrepresentation will make it necessary to re-examine the statutory provisions governing the sale of goods, for under our proposals a party who has been induced by a misrepresentation to enter into a contract of sale will be able to rescind his bargain even after the purchase has been completed. Only when the contract has been affirmed or restitution has become impossible will the remedy be barred. But where an identical misstatement is a term of a contract of sale, the Sale of Goods Act 1893 in many cases makes rejection impossible immediately the purchase is completed. Section 11 (1) (c) of that Act provides that where the contract is not severable and the buyer has accepted the goods or where the contract is for specific goods the property in which has passed to the buyer, a breach of condition can be treated only as a breach of warranty (which under s. 53 gives only a right to damages) and not as a ground for rejecting the goods. So far as acceptance is concerned, s. 35 provides that goods are deemed to be accepted when, *inter alia*, the buyer intimates his

acceptance to the seller or does any act in relation to the goods which is inconsistent with the seller's continued ownership.[1] So far as the passing of property in specific goods is concerned, the rules laid down in s. 18 provide that the property passes either when the contract is made or when the buyer has received notice that the goods are ready for delivery. Consequently, in some cases as soon as the goods have (in this highly technical sense) been accepted, and in others as soon as the contract is made or the goods are ready for delivery, the buyer's remedy for breach of a term of the contract will be less satisfactory than his remedy for an identical misrepresentation inducing the contract.

15. Although consideration of the Sale of Goods Act 1893 is outside our terms of reference, we think that the provisions to which we have drawn attention are already far from satisfactory and ought to be re-examined: in future, if effect is given to our recommendations about the power to grant rescission, they will produce a serious anomaly. Where there has been a genuine acceptance of goods by a buyer who has been able to form an opinion of their quality, it is not unreasonable that he should have no right to reject them, just as the right to rescind for misrepresentation is lost if the buyer affirms the contract with full knowledge of the facts. But in many cases the Sale of Goods Act appears to deprive the buyer of any right to reject defective goods before he has had an opportunity of examining them. This is plainly unsatisfactory. We accordingly suggest, first, that it should be made clear that acts which would amount to acceptance within the meaning of s. 35 should not be held to do so until the buyer has had a reasonable opportunity of examining the goods as contemplated by s. 34; secondly, that in the case of specific goods the right to reject for breach of condition should depend not on the passing of the property (which is the test under s. 11 (1) (c)) but, as it does in the case of other goods, on acceptance by the buyer. The evidence we have received indicates that this is of particular importance in connection with the practice of selling goods in sealed containers, where acceptance ought not to be a bar to rescission until the buyer has had an opportunity of examining the goods.

Misrepresentation subsequently incorporated in contract

16. Another minor anomaly, which will be accentuated if rescission becomes available as a remedy for misrepresentation after the contract

---

[1] In *Hardy & Co.* v. *Hillerns and Fowler*, [1923] 2 K.B. 490 it was held that s. 35 overrides s. 34, which provides that a buyer is not deemed to have accepted the goods until he has had a reasonable opportunity of examining them in order to ascertain whether they are in conformity with the contract.

has been executed, relates to representations first made independently and later incorporated in the contract. Where this happens the victim may actually be worse off, because there is some authority for saying that the remedy for a misrepresentation which has attained the status of a contractual term is not the equitable one of rescission but the common law one of damages; see *Pennsylvania Shipping Co.* v. *Compagnie Nationale de Navigation,* [1936] 2 All E.R. 1167 at p. 1171; *Leaf* v. *International Galleries,* [1950] 2 K.B. 86. In our view it is clearly desirable that the same remedies should be available to a purchaser whether or not the false statement is incorporated in the contract. We suggest therefore (although the point is not strictly within our terms of reference) that there should be a right to rescission for breach of a contractual term whenever under our recommendations the original independent misrepresentation would be a ground for rescission. The court should of course have the same power to award damages as an alternative to rescission that we have recommended in paragraph 12.

Damages for negligent misrepresentation

17. We now turn to the second of the criticisms made against the present law, namely that it does not give a right to damages to compensate for loss resulting from an innocent misrepresentation. The recommendations we have made earlier in this Report meet this criticism only to a limited extent, for under those proposals damages could be awarded only where the court has power to grant rescission, and even then the plaintiff would be in the hands of the court. It has been suggested to us that a person who has entered into a contract in reliance on a representation which has proved to be false should be able to bring an action for damages independently of any right he may have to rescind the contract. The need for this has been emphasised by the Standing Joint Committee of the motoring organisations, who have drawn our attention to the fact that although there may in many cases be every indication of deliberate misrepresentation and concealment of the truth there is rarely enough evidence to establish fraud, which is notoriously difficult to prove. We agree that the present law does not provide an adequate remedy but we do not think it would be right to give every victim of an innocent misrepresentation the right to claim damages, as The Law Society have suggested. If neither party has culpably misled the other, there is everything to be said for holding the parties to their bargain when the deal can no longer be undone. In such a case the loss should rest where it falls. On the other hand, we think that where one

of the parties was at fault in making the representation, the other ought to be entitled to damages as of right. We also think that the onus should be on the representor to satisfy the court that he was not at fault. He will normally be in a better position to know the true facts than the other party. For instance, a vendor should know the likely defects in the articles he sells from his specialised knowledge of the trade. If he was truly innocent of any desire to mislead, he will suffer little hardship by being put to the proof of his innocence but, if he cannot stablish this, the loss should fall on him rather than on the other party. We see no reason why this should not apply to all contracts, including those relating to land. The objections to allowing rescission in the case of an executed contract for the sale or other disposition of an interest in land which we have described in paragraph 6 do not in our view apply to a claim for damages.

18. There is a precedent for legislation on these lines in s. 43 of the Companies Act 1948. That section makes those responsible for the issue of a prospectus inviting persons to subscribe for shares or debentures in a company liable for any untrue statement in the prospectus unless they can show that they had reasonable ground to believe, and did up to the time of the allotment believe, that the statement was true. We think a similar rule should apply where any contract has been induced by a representation which is untrue. We accordingly recommend that any person who has, either by himself or his agent, induced another to enter into a contract with him by an untrue representation made for the purpose of inducing the contract should be liable in damages for any loss suffered in consequence of the representation. But the defendant should not be liable if he proves that up to the time the contract was made he (or his agent, if the representation was made by him) believed the representation to be true and had reasonable grounds for his belief.

Hire-Purchase Contracts

19. We think it is appropriate for us to refer at this stage to the special case of hire-purchase contracts. It is the common practice in these cases for the hirer to do business with a trader, or "dealer" as he is generally known, who is not himself in a position to give the credit required by the hirer. Accordingly, after arranging the transaction with the hirer, the dealer sells the goods to a finance house which then enters into the hire-purchase contract with the hirer and allows the dealer commission. Where the contract has been induced by a misrepresentation made by the dealer the position of the hirer is, as matters now stand, most unsatis-

factory; for the dealer, who is not a party to the hire-purchase contract, is not liable for anything short of fraud and the finance company expressly excludes, by the terms of its contract, all liability for warranties and other representations made by the dealer. We recognise that there is a limited statutory protection which at present applies to goods up to the value of £300, but even in these cases no provision is made for the problem of misrepresentation by the dealer.

20. We think it is only right, and in accordance with the realities of the situation, that the dealer should be treated as the agent of the finance company for the purpose of doing business with the hirer. The business of the dealer is to induce the hirer to make a written offer to the finance company on a printed form supplied to the dealer by the company and to forward the offer to the company for acceptance. The deposit is paid by the hirer to the dealer and while it is true that he does not transmit it to the finance company (which deducts the amount of the deposit from the cash price it subsequently pays the dealer for the goods) the company nevertheless in its written contract with the hirer treats the deposit as having been paid to the company by the hirer as part of the hire-purchase price. When the dealer delivers the goods to the hirer he takes from him a delivery receipt addressed to the finance company in a form supplied by the company irrespective of whether the property in the goods has by that time passed to the company from the dealer. In inducing the hirer to make an offer to the finance company the dealer in substance acts, as has been explained, as agent of the company and does so for reward. We think, therefore, that it should be made clear in any legislation on this subject that where negotiations for a hire-purchase contract are in fact conducted by a dealer he shall, notwithstanding any agreement to the contrary, be deemed to be the agent of the finance company[1] for the purpose of any representations in respect of the goods which are the subject-matter of the contract.

Remedy for negligent misrepresentation not to depend on right to rescission

21. The right to claim damages which we have recommended above should be independent of and without prejudice to any right the injured party may otherwise have to claim rescission of the contract. We do not think the present limitations on the right to rescission have any relevance

---

[1] We use the expression "finance company" in a general sense as indicating any third party who enters into a hire-purchase agreement with a person who has in fact obtained delivery of the goods in question from another person who has been responsible for negotiating the agreement.

to the independent claim for damages for a negligent misrepresentation. It may be unjust to order rescission where the parties cannot be restored to their original position, but that is no reason for refusing damages for any loss that may have been suffered as a result of the representor's carelessness. Some guidance may be derived here from the way in which the courts have developed the power to award damages in lieu of specific performance or an injunction. This power was conferred by s. 2 of the Chancery Amendment Act 1858 and was at first confined to cases in which the equitable remedy was available (see *Ferguson* v. *Wilson* (1866), 2 Ch. App. 77). It was however extended by the Supreme Court of Judicature Act 1873 (since re-enacted in s. 43 of the Supreme Court of Judicature (Consolidation) Act 1925), and can now be invoked in a much wider range of cases. In Australia and New Zealand the courts have taken the view that it is possible to award damages when the alternative equitable remedy has become barred: see *McKenna* v. *Richey*, [1950] V.L.R. 360; *Dell* v. *Beasley*, [1959] N.Z.L.R. 89. We see no reason why the same should not be done in cases in which rescission has hitherto been the only remedy.

22. We appreciate that the independent remedy in damages which we have recommended will be available in any case in which, under the present law, fraud has to be proved. The damages obtainable for misrepresentation will be no less extensive and the plaintiff's burden of proof very much lighter. It may be therefore that, so far as misrepresentations, inducing a contract are concerned, actions for fraud will fall into disuse and be replaced by our proposed remedy. We see no harm in that. The fact that a person has been led to enter into a contract on the strength of a statement which is untrue ought by itself to entitle him to compensation unless the representor can establish his innocence. If the statement has in fact been fraudulent, no doubt the victim's right to be compensated is even clearer, but it is not in general the function of the civil law to grade the damages which an injured person may recover in accordance with the moral guilt of the defendant. The tort of deceit will still be needed for those cases where a fraudulent statement has induced a person to act to his detriment otherwise than by entering into a contract. There may also be some cases where the victim, for special reasons of his own, wishes publicly to brand the defendant as dishonest and therefore voluntarily takes upon himself the heavy burden of proof needed to establish fraud.

Limitation to power to exclude liability

23. We turn now to the third of the major criticisms which have been

made of the existing law.   Our recommendations will be of little practical value unless there is some curtailment of the present freedom to exclude liability by a provision in the contract to that effect.   The decision in the House of Lords in *Boyd & Forrest* v. *Glasgow Railway* 1915 S.C. (H.L.) 20, leaves little doubt that the parties are at present free to contract out of liability for misrepresentation unless it can be shown to have been fraudulent, in which case the agreement will be disregarded as being contrary to public policy.   Many transactions today are governed by standard forms of contract which the party to whom the form is presented is required to sign, very often without any clear appreciation of the rights which he may be renouncing.   It is not uncommon to find such forms excluding all liability for misrepresentation.   We are naturally chary of interfering with freedom of contract in normal business transactions, but we think that there is a case for doing so where one party is in a much weaker position than the other, either through lack of expert knowledge or absence of professional advice, or because he is presented with a standard form of contract to which no alteration is permitted.   The justification for such interference is of course much stronger where (as in the case of the new remedy in damages which we have recommended in paragraph 18) the defendant will be under no liability if he can show that he was not at fault.   In cases of this kind the need for a provision excluding liability can only arise where the defendant either did not believe the representation to be true or had no reasonable grounds for believing it.

24.   We accordingly recommend that it should not be possible to rely on a provision purporting to exclude liability for any misrepresentation made with the intention of inducing a contract unless the representor can show that up to the time the contract was made he had reasonable grounds for believing the representation to be true.   We think that this should apply not only to our proposed new remedy in damages for a negligent misrepresentation but also to the right to claim rescission of the contract.   Any hardship to which this might otherwise lead will be tempered by the court's power to award damages in lieu of rescission in appropriate cases.   It follows from what we have said in paragraph 20 about hire-purchase contracts that it should not be possible for a finance company, by seeking to disclaim the authority of a dealer to make representations on the company's behalf, to exclude liability for a negligent misrepresentation made by the dealer for the purpose of inducing a prospective hirer to enter into a contract with the company.

Effect of recommendations

25. We believe that if our recommendations are accepted they will go far towards removing the uncertainties and anomalies which surround the law relating to innocent misrepresentation. The most serious of these at present is the difference between the remedies available for breach of a term in a contract and those in respect of an independent misrepresentation which has induced the contract. The significance of the distinction between the independent misrepresentation (which sometimes enables the contract to be rescinded) and breach of an identical term in the contract itself (which gives only a right to damages) will largely disappear. So, too, will the anomaly that after execution of a contract breach of a term embodied in it will confer a right to damages or (if the term was a fundamental one) to rescission, whereas for an identical statement not incorporated in the contract there is no redress at all. The dividing line between a contractual warranty and an independent representation is a narrow one and at present it is far from easy to advise with confidence whether a particular statement is one or the other. The task of the legal adviser is further complicated by those cases (of which *Brown* v. *Sheen and Richmond Car Sales, Ltd.*, [1950] 1 All E.R. 1102, and *Andrews* v. *Hopkinson*, [1957] 1 Q.B. 229, are examples) in which the courts have treated a representation preceding a contract as a preliminary or collateral contract, the consideration for which is found in the making of the subsequent contract. The fact that the courts can sometimes be persuaded to treat a representation as a contractual term or as part of a preliminary or collateral contract may be satisfactory to the successful plaintiff, but it leaves the law in a state of uncertainty and the fact that a good deal of ingenuity is often needed in order to achieve the desired result is in itself an indication that the present law is felt to be unjust. We believe that, if effect is given to our recommendations, it will no longer be necessary for the plaintiff who is claiming redress for the consequences of an innocent misrepresentation to assert in the alternative, as is often done now, that the representation formed an oral part of a written contract, or an implied or collateral warranty, or that it amounted to a collateral or preliminary contract.

26. It is true that an independent misrepresentation on a matter which does not go to the root of the contract will continue to give a right to rescission, whereas a corresponding statement incorporated in the contract will be a warranty for breach of which damages alone can be awarded. But as the court will have a discretion (if our recommendation is adopted) to award damages instead of rescission, we believe that what

may appear to be an anomaly will be of small importance in practice. Finally, our recommendations will leave little room for the narrow and ill-defined distinction drawn in such cases as *Newbigging* v. *Adam* (1886), 34 Ch. D. 582, and *Whittington* v. *Seale-Hayne* (1900), 82 L.T. 49, between damages for breach of contract and an indemnity awarded in the course of rescinding a contract for innocent misrepresentation.   The court will in every case have power to award damages instead of rescission, and where the defendant has been at fault both rescission and damages will be available.   Only in the rare case where, in addition to rescission, the plaintiff seeks to recover an indemnity from a wholly innocent defendant will it still be necessary to apply the subtle distinction between damage necessarily and inevitably resulting from the position which a party has assumed upon entering into the contract and any other loss he may have suffered.

Summary of recommendations

27. Our recommendations may be summarised as follows:—

(1) Contracts for the sale or other disposition of an interest in land should not be capable of being rescinded after execution (paragraph 6).   An exception should, however, be made for leases to which section 54 (2) of the Law of Property Act, 1925, applies, viz. those taking effect in possession for a term not exceeding three years, and these should be treated in the same way as contracts not affecting land (paragraph 7)

(2) All other contracts should be capable of being rescinded after execution (paragraph 9) but the other bars to rescission should remain as at present (paragraph 10).

(3) Where the court has power to order rescission (whether before or after the execution of the contract) it should have a discretion to award damages instead of rescission if it is satisfied that damages would adequately compensate the plaintiff, having regard to the nature of the representation and the fact that the injury is small compared with what rescission would involve (paragraph 12).

(4) Where a misrepresentation is made independently and is later incorporated in the contract the plaintiff should have the same right to rescission (or to damages in lieu of rescission) as he would have had in respect of the original misrepresentation (paragraph 16).

(5) Where a person has, either by himself or his agent, induced another to enter into a contract with him (including a contract relating to land) by an untrue representation made for the purpose of inducing

the contract he should be liable in damages for any loss suffered in consequence of the representation unless he proves that up to the time the contract was made he (or his agent, if the representation was made by him) believed the representation to be true and had reasonable grounds for his belief (paragraph 18).

(6) In the case of any hire-purchase agreement to which a finance company is a party, where negotiations for the agreement are conducted by a dealer he should, notwithstanding any agreement to the contrary, be deemed to be the agent of the finance company for the purpose of any representations in respect of the goods which are the subject-matter of the agreement (paragraph 20).

(7) It should not be possible to exclude liability to damages or rescission for any misrepresentation made with the intention of inducing a contract unless the representor can show that up to the time the contract was made he had reasonable grounds for believing the representation to be true (paragraph 24).

(8) It is suggested that some of the remedies available under the Sale of Goods Act, 1893, are unsatisfactory and will become still more so if the foregoing recommendations are adopted; and it might therefore usefully be considered whether—

(i) acts amounting to acceptance within the meaning of section 35 of the Act of 1893 should not be held to do so until the buyer has had an opportunity of examining the goods as contemplated by section 34;

(ii) the right to reject specific goods for breach of condition should depend not on the passing of the property in the goods to the buyer but on his acceptance of the goods (paragraph 15).[1]

---

[1] The signatories to the Report were:

The Rt. Hon. Lord Jenkins (*chairman*), The Rt. Hon. Lord Pearce, The Rt. Hon. Lord Justice Donovan, The Rt. Hon. Lord Justice Diplock, The Hon. Mr. Justice Ashworth, R. J. F. Burrows, Esq., J. G. Foster, Esq., Q.C., M.P., Gerald Gardiner, Esq., Q.C., Professor A. L. Goodhart, K.B.E., Q.C., D.C.L., LL.D., R. E. Megarry, Esq., Q.C., G. W. R. Morley, Esq., O.B.E., T.D., R. J. Parker, Esq., Q.C., Professor Sir David Hughes Parry, Q.C., Professor E. C. S. Wade, Q.C., LL.D., and R. H. Walton, Esq.

The Text of Certain Statutory Provisions Referred to in this Treatise

Below is reproduced the full text of a number of the more important statutory provisions referred to in this treatise. The provisions here reproduced are:

(1) The Misrepresentation Act 1967 (the whole Act). These provisions are referred to in the text *passim*, but are particularly discussed in Chapter XII.

(2) The Companies Act 1948, ss. 40, 43–46, and 55, which provide for the liability of persons concerned or deemed to be concerned in the preparation of a misleading prospectus; see Chapter XVI, paras. 329–348.

(3) Lord Tenterden's Act (ss. 6 and 9 of the Statute of Frauds Amendment Act 1828). See Chapters VIII, para. 161, XI, paras. 197 *et seq.*, and XIX *passim*.

(4) Sections 3 and 4 of the Sale of Land by Auction Act 1867. See Chapter XVI, paras. 349–350.

(5) Section 58 of the Sale of Goods Act 1893. See Chapter XVI, para. 351.

(6) Sections 1 and 2 of the Auctions (Bidding Agreements) Act 1927. See Chapter XVI, para. 352.

(7) Section 41 of the Partnership Act 1890. See Chapter XVI, para. 354.

(8) Parts of ss. 1 and 4 of the Law Reform (Contributory Negligence) Act 1945. See Chapter XI, para. 192, note 10a.

MISREPRESENTATION ACT 1967

An Act to amend the law relating to innocent misrepresentations and to amend sections 11 and 35 of the Sale of Goods Act 1893

(22nd March 1967)

1   *Removal of certain bars to rescission for innocent misrepresentation.* Where a person has entered into a contract after a misrepresentation has been made to him, and—

   (*a*) the misrepresentation has become a term of the contract; or

   (*b*) the contract has been performed;

or both, then, if otherwise he would be entitled to rescind the contract without alleging fraud, he shall be so entitled, subject to the provisions of this Act, notwithstanding the matters mentioned in paragraphs (*a*) and (*b*) of this section.

2   *Damages for misrepresentation.*—(1) Where a person has entered into a contract after a misrepresentation has been made to him by another party thereto and as a result thereof he has suffered loss, then, if the person making the misrepresentation would be liable to damages in respect thereof had the misrepresentation been made fraudulently, that person shall be so liable notwithstanding that the misrepresentation was not made fraudulently, unless he proves that he had reasonable ground to believe and did believe up to the time the contract was made that the facts represented were true.

(2) Where a person has entered into a contract after a misrepresentation has been made to him otherwise than fraudulently, and he would be entitled, by reason of the misrepresentation, to rescind the contract, then, if it is claimed, in any proceedings arising out of the contract, that the contract ought to be or has been rescinded, the court or arbitrator may declare the contract subsisting and award damages in lieu of rescission, if of opinion that it would be equitable to do so, having regard to the nature of the misrepresentation and the loss that would be caused by it if the contract were upheld, as well as to the loss that rescission would cause to the other party.

(3) Damages may be awarded against a person under subsection (2) of this section whether or not he is liable to damages under subsection (1) thereof, but where he is so liable any award under the said subsection (2) shall be taken into account in assessing his liability under the said subsection (1).

3 *Avoidance of certain provisions excluding liability for misrepresentation.* If any agreement (whether made before or after the commencement of this Act) contains a provision which would exclude or restrict—

(*a*) any liability to which a party to a contract may be subject by reason of any misrepresentation made by him before the contract was made; or

(*b*) any remedy available to another party to the contract by reason of such a misrepresentation;

that provision shall be of no effect except to the extent (if any) that, in any proceedings arising out of the contract, the court or arbitrator may allow reliance on it as being fair and reasonable in the circumstances of the case.

4 *Amendments of Sale of Goods Act 1893.*—(1) In paragraph (*c*) of section 11 (1) of the Sale of Goods Act 1893 (condition to be treated as warranty where the buyer has accepted the goods or where the property in specific goods has passed) the words "or where the contract is for specific goods, the property in which has passed to the buyer" shall be omitted.

(2) In section 35 of that Act (acceptance) before the words "when the goods have been delivered to him, and he does any act in relation to them which is inconsistent with the ownership of the seller" there shall be inserted the words "(except where section 34 of this Act otherwise provides)".

5 *Saving for past transactions.* Nothing in this Act shall apply in relation to any misrepresentation or contract of sale which is made before the commencement of this Act.

6 *Short title, commencement and extent.*—(1) This Act may be cited as the Misrepresentation Act 1967.

(2) This Act shall come into operation at the expiration of the period of one month beginning with the date on which it is passed.

(3) This Act, except section 4 (2), does not extend to Scotland.

(4) This Act does not extend to Northern Ireland.

COMPANIES ACT 1948
(11 & 12 Geo. 6 c. 38)

40 *Expert's consent to issue of prospectus containing statement by him.*—
(1) A prospectus inviting persons to subscribe for shares in or debentures of a company and including a statement purporting to be made by an expert shall not be issued unless—

(a) he has given and has not, before delivery of a copy of the prospectus for registration, withdrawn his written consent to the issue thereof with the statement included in the form and context in which it is included; and

(b) a statement that he has given and has not withdrawn his consent as aforesaid appears in the prospectus.

(2) If any prospectus is issued in contravention of this section the company and every person who is knowingly a party to the issue thereof shall be liable to a fine not exceeding five hundred pounds.

(3) In this section the expression "expert" includes engineer, valuer, accountant and any other person whose profession gives authority to a statement made by him.

*   *   *

43 *Civil liability for mis-statements in prospectus.*—(1) Subject to the provisions of this section, where a prospectus invites persons to subscribe for shares in or debentures of a company, the following persons shall be liable to pay compensation to all persons who subscribe for any shares or debentures on the faith of the prospectus for the loss or damage they may have sustained by reason of any untrue statement included therein, that is to say:—

(a) every person who is a director of the company at the time of the issue of the prospectus;

(b) every person who has authorised himself to be named and is named in the prospectus as a director or as having agreed to become a director either immediately or after an interval of time;

(c) every person being a promoter of the company; and

(d) every person who has authorised the issue of the prospectus:

Provided that where, under section forty of this Act, the consent of a person is required to the issue of a prospectus and he has given that consent, he shall not by reason of his having given it be liable under this subsection as a person who has authorised the issue of the prospectus except in respect of an untrue statement purporting to be made by him as an expert.

(2) No person shall be liable under subsection (1) of this section if he proves—

(*a*) that, having consented to become a director of the company, he withdrew his consent before the issue of the prospectus, and that it was issued without his authority or consent; or

(*b*) that the prospectus was issued without his knowledge or consent, and that on becoming aware of its issue he forthwith gave reasonable public notice that it was issued without his knowledge or consent; or

(*c*) that, after the issue of the prospectus and before allotment thereunder, he, on becoming aware of any untrue statement therein, withdrew his consent thereto and gave reasonable public notice of the withdrawal and of the reason therefor; or

(*d*) that—

(i) as regards every untrue statement not purporting to be made on the authority of an expert or of a public official document or statement, he had reasonable ground to believe, and did up to the time of the allotment of the shares or debentures, as the case may be, believe, that the statement was true; and

(ii) as regards every untrue statement purporting to be a statement by an expert or contained in what purports to be a copy of or extract from a report or valuation of an expert, it fairly represented the statement, or was a correct and fair copy of or extract from the report or valuation, and he had reasonable ground to believe and did up to the time of the issue of the prospectus believe that the person making the statement was competent to make it and that person had given the consent required by section forty of this Act to the issue of the prospectus and had not withdrawn that consent before delivery of a copy of the prospectus for registration or, to the defendant's knowledge, before allotment thereunder; and

(iii) as regards every untrue statement purporting to be a statement made by an official person or contained in what purports to be a copy of or extract from a public official document, it was a correct and fair representation of the statement or copy of or extract from the document. :

Provided that this subsection shall not apply in the case of a person liable by reason of his having given a consent required of him by the said section forty, as a person who has authorised the issue of the prospectus in respect of an untrue statement purporting to be made by him as an expert.

(3) A person who, apart from this subsection would under subsection (1) of this section be liable, by reason of his having given a consent required of him by section forty of this Act, as a person who has authorised the issue of a prospectus in respect of an untrue statement purporting to be made by him as an expert shall not be so liable if he proves—

    (*a*) that, having given his consent under the said section forty to the issue of the prospectus, he withdrew it in writing before delivery of a copy of the prospectus for registration; or

    (*b*) that, after delivery of a copy of the prospectus for registration and before allotment thereunder, he, on becoming aware of the untrue statement, withdrew his consent in writing and gave reasonable public notice of the withdrawal, and of the reasons therefor; or

    (*c*) that he was competent to make the statement and that he had reasonable ground to believe and did up to the time of the allotment of the shares or debentures, as the case may be, believe that the statement was true.

(4) Where—

    (*a*) the prospectus contains the name of a person as a director of the company, or as having agreed to become a director thereof, and he has not consented to become a director, or has withdrawn his consent before the issue of the prospectus, and has not authorised or consented to the issue thereof; or

    (*b*) the consent of a person is required under section forty of this Act to the issue of the prospectus and he either has not given that consent or has withdrawn it before the issue of the prospectus;

the directors of the company, except any without whose knowledge or consent the prospectus was issued, and any other person who authorised the issue thereof shall be liable to indemnify the person named as aforesaid or whose consent was required as aforesaid, as the case may be, against all damages, costs and expenses to which he may be made liable by reason of his name having been inserted in the prospectus or of the inclusion therein of a statement purporting to be made by him as an expert, as the case may be, or in defending himself against any action or legal proceeding brought against him in respect thereof:

Provided that a person shall not be deemed for the purposes of this subsection to have authorised the issue of a prospectus by reason only of his having given the consent required by section forty of this Act to the inclusion therein of a statement purporting to be made by him as an expert.

(5) For the purposes of this section—

    (*a*) the expression "promoter" means a promoter who was a party to the preparation of the prospectus, or of the portion thereof containing the untrue statement, but does not include any person by reason of his acting in a professional capacity for persons engaged in procuring the formation of the company; and

    (*b*) the expression "expert" has the same meaning as in section forty of this Act.

44   *Criminal liability for mis-statements in prospectus.*—(1) Where a prospectus issued after the commencement of this Act includes any untrue statement, any person who authorised the issue of the prospectus shall be liable—

    (*a*) on conviction on indictment, to imprisonment for a term not exceeding two years, or a fine not exceeding five hundred pounds, or both;

    (*b*) on summary conviction, to imprisonment for a term not exceeding three months, or a fine not exceeding one hundred pounds, or both; or

unless he proves either that the statement was immaterial or that he had reasonable grounds to believe and did, up to the time of the issue of the prospectus, believe that the statement was true.

(2) A person shall not be deemed for the purposes of this section to have authorised the issue of a prospectus by reason only of his having given the consent required by section forty of this Act to the inclusion therein of a statement purporting to be made by him as an expert.

45   *Document containing offer of shares or debentures for sale to be deemed prospectus.*—(1) Where a company allots or agrees to allot any shares in or debentures of the company with a view to all or any of those shares or debentures being offered for sale to the public, any document by which the offer for sale to the public is made shall for all purposes be deemed to be a prospectus issued by the company, and all enactments and rules of law as to the contents of prospectuses and to liability in respect of statements in and omissions from prospectuses, or otherwise relating to prospectuses, shall apply and have effect accordingly; as if the shares or debentures had been offered to the public for subscription and as if persons accepting the offer in respect of any shares or debentures were subscribers for those shares or debentures, but without prejudice to the liability, if any, of the persons by whom the offer is made, in respect of mis-statements contained in the document or otherwise in respect thereof.

474 Actionable Misrepresentation

(2) For the purposes of this Act, it shall, unless the contrary is proved, be evidence that an allotment of, or an agreement to allot, shares or debentures was made with a view to the shares or debentures being offered for sale to the public if it is shown—

(a) that an offer of the shares or debentures or of any of them for sale to the public was made within six months after the allotment or agreement to allot; or

(b) that at the date when the offer was made the whole consideration to be received by the company in respect of the shares or debentures had not been so received.

(3) Section thirty-eight of this Act as applied by this section shall have effect as if it required a prospectus to state in addition to the matters required by that section to be stated in a prospectus—

(a) the net amount of the consideration received or to be received by the company in respect of the shares or debentures to which the offer relates; and

(b) the place and time at which the contract under which the said shares or debentures have been or are to be allotted may be inspected;

and section forty-one of this Act as applied by this section shall have effect as though the persons making the offer were persons named in a prospectus as directors of a company.

(4) Where a person making an offer to which this section relates is a company or a firm, it shall be sufficient if the document aforesaid is signed on behalf of the company or firm by two directors of the company or not less than half of the partners, as the case may be, and any such director or partner may sign by his agent authorised in writing.

46 *Interpretation of provisions relating to prospectuses.*—For the purposes of the foregoing provisions of this Part of this Act—

(a) a statement included in a prospectus shall be deemed to be untrue if it is misleading in the form and context in which it is included; and

(b) a statement shall be deemed to be included in a prospectus if it is contained therein or in any report or memorandum appearing on the face thereof or by reference incorporated therein or issued therewith.

55 *Construction of references to offering shares or debentures to the public.*—
(1) Any reference in this Act to offering shares or debentures to the public shall, subject to any provision to the contrary contained therein, be construed as including a reference to offering them to any section of the public, whether selected as members or debenture holders of the company concerned or as clients of the person issuing the prospectus or in any other manner, and references in this Act or in a company's articles to invitations to the public to subscribe for shares or debentures shall, subject as aforesaid, be similarly construed.

(2) The foregoing subsection shall not be taken as requiring any offer or invitation to be treated as made to the public if it can properly be regarded, in all the circumstances, as not being calculated to result, directly or indirectly, in the shares or debentures becoming available for subscription or purchase by persons other than those receiving the offer or invitation, or otherwise as being a domestic concern of the persons making and receiving it, and in particular—

(*a*) a provision in a company's articles prohibiting invitations to the public to subscribe for shares or debentures shall not be taken as prohibiting the making to members or debenture holders of an invitation which can properly be regarded as aforesaid; and

(*b*) the provisions of this Act relating to private companies shall be construed accordingly.

LORD TENTERDEN'S ACT
(Statute of Frauds Amendment Act 1828 (9 Geo. 4 c. 14).)

6 *Action not maintainable on representations of character, etc., unless they be in writing signed by the party chargeable.*—No action shall be brought whereby to charge any person upon or by reason of any representation or assurance made or given concerning or relating to the character, conduct, credit, ability, trade or dealings of any other person, to the intent or purpose that such other person may obtain credit, money, or goods upon, unless such representation or assurance be made in writing, signed by the party to be charged therewith.

*   *   *

9 *Act not to extend to Scotland.*—Nothing in this Act contained shall extend to Scotland.

SALE OF LAND BY AUCTION ACT 1867
(30 & 31 Vict. c. 48)

3 *Interpretation of terms.*—"Auctioneer" shall mean any person selling by public auction any land, whether in lots or otherwise:

"Land" shall mean any interest in any messuages, lands, tenements, or hereditaments, of whatever tenure:

"Agent" shall mean the solicitor, steward, or land agent of the seller:

"Puffer" shall mean a person appointed to bid on the part of the owner.

4 *Sales of land invalid in law from employment of a puffer to be also invalid in equity.*—And whereas there is at present a conflict between Her Majesty's courts of law and equity in respect of the validity of sales by auction of land where a puffer has bid, although no right of bidding on behalf of the owner was reserved, the courts of law holding that all such sales are absolutely illegal, and the courts of equity under some circumstances giving effect to them but even in courts of equity the rule is unsettled: And whereas it is expedient that an end should be put to such conflicting and unsettled opinions: Be it therefore enacted, that from and after the passing of this Act whenever a sale by auction of land would be invalid at law by reason of the employment of a puffer, the same shall be deemed invalid in equity as well as at law.

SALE OF GOODS ACT 1893
(56 & 57 Vict. c. 71)

58 *Auction sales.*—In the case of a sale by auction:

(1) Where goods are put up for sale by auction in lots, each lot is prima facie deemed to be the subject of a separate contract of sale:

(2) A sale by auction is complete when the auctioneer announces its completion by the fall of the hammer, or in other customary manner. Until such announcement is made any bidder may retract his bid:

(3) Where a sale by auction is not notified to be subject to a right to bid on behalf of the seller, it shall not be lawful for the seller to bid himself or to employ any person to bid at such sale, or for the auctioneer knowingly to take any bid from the seller or any such

person: Any sale contravening this rule may be treated as fraudulent by the buyer:

(4) A sale by auction may be notified to be subject to a reserved or upset price, and a right to bid may also be reserved expressly by or on behalf of the seller.

Where a right to bid is expressly reserved, but not otherwise, the seller, or any one person on his behalf, may bid at the auction.

AUCTIONS (BIDDING AGREEMENTS) ACT 1927
(17 & 18 Geo. 5 c. 12)

1   *Certain bidding agreements to be illegal.*—(1) If any dealer agrees to give, or gives, or offers any gift or consideration to any other person as an inducement or reward for abstaining, or for having abstained, from bidding at a sale by auction either generally or for any particular lot, or if any person agrees to accept, or accepts, or attempts to obtain from any dealer any such gift or consideration as aforesaid, he shall be guilty of an offence under this Act, and shall be liable on summary conviction to a fine not exceeding one hundred pounds, or to a term of imprisonment for any period not exceeding six months, or to both such fine and such imprisonment:

Provided that, where it is proved that a dealer has previously to an auction entered into an agreement in writing with one or more persons to purchase goods at the auction *bona fide* on a joint account and has before the goods were purchased at the auction deposited a copy of the agreement with the auctioneer, such an agreement shall not be treated as an agreement made in contravention of this section.

(2) For the purposes of this section the expression "dealer" means a person who in the normal course of his business attends sales by auction for the purpose of purchasing goods with a view to reselling them.

(3) In England and Wales a prosecution for an offence under this section shall not be constituted without the consent of the Attorney-General or the Solicitor-General.

2   *Right of vendors to treat certain sales as fraudulent.*—Any sale at an auction, with respect to which any such agreement or transaction as aforesaid has been made or effected, and which has been the subject of a prosecution and conviction, may, as against a purchaser who has been a party to such agreement or transaction, be treated by the vendor as a sale induced by fraud:

Provided that a notice or intimation by the vendor to the auctioneer that he intends to exercise such power in relation to any sale at the auction shall not affect the obligations of the auctioneer to deliver the goods to the purchaser.

*   *   *

4 *Short title, commencement and extent.*—(1) This Act may be cited as the Auctions (Bidding Agreements) Act 1927 . . .

(2) This Act shall not extend to Northern Ireland.

PARTNERSHIP ACT 1890
(53 & 54 Vict. c. 39)

41 *Rights where partnership dissolved for fraud or misrepresentation.*— Where a partnership contract is rescinded on the ground of the fraud or misrepresentation of one of the parties thereto, the party entitled to rescind is, without prejudice to any other right, entitled—

(*a*) to a lien on, or right of retention of, the surplus of the partnership assets, after satisfying the partnership liabilities, for any sum of money paid by him for the purchase of a share in the partnership and for any capital contributed by him, and is

(*b*) to stand in the place of the creditors of the firm for any payments made by him in respect of the partnership liabilities, and

(*c*) to be indemnified by the person guilty of the fraud or making the representation against all the debts and liabilities of the firm.

LAW REFORM (CONTRIBUTORY NEGLIGENCE) ACT 1945
(8 & 9 Geo. 6 c. 28)

1 *Apportionment of liability in case of contributory negligence.*—(1) Where any person suffers damage as the result partly of his own fault and partly of the fault of any other person or persons, a claim in respect of that damage shall not be defeated by reason of the fault of the person suffering the damage, but the damages recoverable in respect thereof shall be reduced to such extent as the court thinks just and equitable having regard to the claimant's share in the responsibility for the damage :

Provided that—

(*a*) this subsection shall not operate to defeat any defence arising under a contract :

(*b*) where any contract or enactment providing for the limitation of liability is applicable to the claim, the amount of damages recoverable by the claimant by virtue of this subsection shall not exceed the maximum limit so applicable . . .

*   *   *

4 *Interpretation.*—. . . "fault" means negligence, breach of statuory duty or other act or omission which gives rise to a liability in tort or would, apart from this Act give rise to the defence of contributory negligence.

Index

A

ACT OF PARLIAMENT,
procured by misrepresentation, 368
  private Act, possible remedy at suit of
  person injured, 389 *et seq.*
"ACTIONABLE",
defined, 199
what representations are actionable, 201
kinds of proceedings, 201–202
compensation in specific performance cases,
  203
misrepresentations of authority, 203
at suit of persons other than representees,
  Chs. XVII, XIX
AFFIRMATIVE DEFENCES,
to actions for damages, 212, 244
to actions for rescission, 299 *et seq.*
to actions on company prospectuses, 356
  et seq.
AGENT,
co-agents and sub-agents, 171, 172
company, of, 170, 171
divided responsibility of, 173–176
estoppel, implied, 183
forgery by, 181
fraudulent, continuing liability of, 177,
  178
fraudulent misrepresentation, liability for,
  172, 173
implied authority of, 179, 180
innocent misrepresentation, liability for,
  178, 179
negligent misrepresentation of, principal's
  liability, 179
personal liability of, 172, 177
principal and, as parties to representation,
  169, 170
ratification of contracts of, 181–183
ALTERATION OF POSITION,
defined, 158–160
essential to cause of action, 158 *et seq.*
AMBIGUITY,
designed by representation, 92–94
examples of, 90–92
innuendo, whether necessary to plead, 89,
  90
representation, in, generally, 89–94

AMENDMENT,
pleadings, of, 399, 400
ARBITRATION,
allegations of fraud not usually referred to
  404
award obtained by fraudulent misrepresentation, setting aside of, 382, 383
AUCTION,
bidding agreements, 365, 366
"puffers", 361
sale of goods, 364, 365
  land, 362–364
sales by, generally, 361, 362
statutory provisions, 475–478
AUTHORITY,
misrepresentation of, 203–205
AWARD. *See* ARBITRATION

B

BANKRUPTCY,
fraudulent debtors, 366
BELIEF,
statements of—
  generally, 48
  representor's own belief, 48–51
  third person's belief, 51

C

CERTIORARI,
quashing of grants by tribunals by writ of,
  387, 388
CHOSE IN POSSESSION,
aasignee of, 340, 341
COMPANY,
agent of, 170, 171
directors, 347, 348
  persons authorising names to
  appear as, 348, 349
liquidation of, where contract to take
  shares, 314 *et seq.*
not yet formed, representation to pro-
  motor of, 188
promoters, 349–353